D1341451

KEY TEXT

REFERENCE

What is a Nation?

Europe 1789–1914

Edited by
TIMOTHY BAYCROFT
and
MARK HEWITSON

OXFORD
UNIVERSITY PRESS

OXFORD
UNIVERSITY PRESS

Great Clarendon Street, Oxford OX2 6DP

Oxford University Press is a department of the University of Oxford.
It furthers the University's objective of excellence in research, scholarship,
and education by publishing worldwide in

Oxford New York

Auckland Cape Town Dar es Salaam Hong Kong Karachi
Kuala Lumpur Madrid Melbourne Mexico City Nairobi
New Delhi Shanghai Taipei Toronto

With offices in

Argentina Austria Brazil Chile Czech Republic France Greece
Guatemala Hungary Italy Japan Poland Portugal Singapore
South Korea Switzerland Thailand Turkey Ukraine Vietnam

Oxford is a registered trade mark of Oxford University Press
in the UK and in certain other countries

Published in the United States
by Oxford University Press Inc., New York

British Library Cataloguing in Publication Data

Data available

Library of Congress Cataloging in Publication Data

Data available

Typeset by Newgen Imaging Systems (P) Ltd., Chennai, India
Printed in Great Britain
on acid-free paper by
CPI Antony Rowe, Chippenham, Wiltshire

ISBN 978–0–19–929575–3(Hbk)
ISBN 978–0–19–956250–3(Pbk)

1 3 5 7 9 10 8 6 4 2

Acknowledgements

The fact that this is a commissioned volume rather than a collection of conference papers has not prevented the editors accumulating a long list of debts. The authors were able to hear each other's contribution at a conference kindly hosted by the German Historical Institute in London. Hagen Schulze, the Director of the Institute, was instrumental in helping to initiate the project and made very much appreciated suggestions throughout.

For a comparative topic of this scale, we required—and found—a large number of sponsors. In addition to the German Historical Institute, we are indebted to the British Academy, the German History Society, the Association for the Study of Modern Italy, Sheffield University's Centre for Nineteenth-Century Studies, and UCL's Centre for European Studies for their financial and logistical support.

We are also very grateful to Peter Alter, John Breuilly, Miles Taylor, and Martin Brown for acting as chairs of panels and for stimulating discussion of various questions, as well as sharing their expertise on the subject of nationalism more generally. Together with intellectual stimuli provided by the contributors themselves, their interventions made possible—we hope—a coherent volume on a bewilderingly broad and unwieldy topic. At a later stage, we also received welcome suggestions and support from Oxford University Press's editorial staff and anonymous referees. Any remaining errors in the volume, which are of course difficult to excise completely from a book of this type, are very much our own.

Mark Hewitson, University College London
Timothy Baycroft, University of Sheffield
March 2006

Contents

Notes on Contributors

TIMOTHY BAYCROFT is a Senior Lecturer in Modern French History at the University of Sheffield. He works on questions of identity and borders in France and Europe. His publications include *Culture, Identity and Nationalism: French Flanders in the Nineteenth and Twentieth Centuries* (Woodbridge, 2004) and *Nationalism in Europe 1789–1945* (Cambridge, 1998). He is currently completing a book on the construction of the French nation entitled *France: Inventing the Nation* to appear in the Arnold Inventing the Nation series.

STEFAN BERGER is Professor of Modern German and Comparative European History at the University of Manchester. He is working on issues of nationalism and national identity, as well as on historical theory and historiography and on comparative labour history. Currently he is directing a five-year European Science Foundation programme on the writing of national histories in nineteenth- and twentieth-century Europe. Among his recent publications in the area of nationalism are *Germany: Inventing the Nation* (London, 2004) and *The Search for Normality: National Identity and Historical Consciousness in Germany since 1800* (Oxford, second edn., 2003).

MARK CORNWALL is Professor of Modern European History at the University of Southampton. He specializes in the dissolution of the Habsburg Empire and nationalist conflict in the Czech and Yugoslav regions of East-Central Europe. His publications include a monograph about nationalist propaganda in the First World War: *The Undermining of Austria-Hungary* (Basingstoke, 2000); and an edited volume of essays: *The Last Years of Austria-Hungary* (Exeter, 2002). He has also written extensively on the Czech-German relationship in Bohemia, and is currently completing a book about *Youth, War and National Regeneration in Bohemia 1900–1940*.

MARK HEWITSON is a Senior Lecturer in German Politics and History at University College London. His publications include *National Identity and Political Thought in Germany: Wilhelmine Depictions of the French Third Republic, 1890–1914* (Oxford, 2000) and *Germany and the Causes of the First World War* (Oxford, 2004). He has written various articles on German foreign policy, the construction of national identities, and aspects of economic, military, and constitutional history. He is currently working on a study of the politics of nationalism in Germany in the period from the 1840s to the 1930s.

MARY HILSON is a Lecturer in Contemporary Scandinavian History at University College London. She has published on Swedish and British social history, and has recently finished a book entitled *Political Change and the Rise of Labour in Comparative Perspective: Britain and Sweden, c.1890–1920* (Lund, forthcoming).

CONSTANTIN IORDACHI, is a Junior Research Fellow at the Pasts, Inc. Center for Historical Studies, and is Assistant Professor of History at the Central European University, Budapest. His publications include: *Charisma, Politics and Violence: The Legion of the 'Archangel Michael' in Inter-war Romania* (Trondheim, 2004); *Citizenship, Nation- and*

State-Building: The Integration of Northern Dobrogea in Romania, 1878–1913 (Carl Back Papers in Russian and East European Studies, University of Pittsburgh, 2002); and his book *The Making of Nation-State Citizenship in Southeastern Europe during the Long Nineteenth Century: The Case of Romania* is forthcoming with the CEU Press, Budapest. He is also the co-editor of *Nationalism and Contested Identities: Romanian and Hungarian Case Studies* (Budapest/Iaşi, 2001).

STEPHEN JACOBSON is a Lecturer in European Studies at King's College London. His major publications on nationalism include: ' "The Head and Heart of Spain": New Perspectives on Nationalism and Nationhood', *Social History*, 29/3 (2004), 393–407; and 'Law and Nationalism in Nineteenth-Century Europe: The Case of Catalonia in Comparative Context', *Law and History Review*, 20/2 (2002), 307–47. He is currently writing a book on Barcelona lawyers during the eighteenth and nineteenth centuries.

MICHAEL JEISMANN lectures at the University of Basel and works for the *Frankfurter Allgemeine Zeitung*. His publications include *Das Vaterland der Feinde: Studien zum nationalen Feindbegriff und Selbstverständnis in Deutschland und Frankreich 1792–1918* (Stuttgart, 1992) and *Auf Wiedersehen Gestern: Die deutsche Vergangenheit und die Politik von Morgen* (Frankfurt a. M., 2001).

DAVID LAVEN is a Lecturer in Italian History at the University of Reading. His research focuses on the impact of Napoleonic rule and Habsburg domination in the Italian peninsula. He is the joint editor of *Napoleon's Legacy* (Oxford, 2000) and is completing a monograph entitled *The Habsburg Administration of Venetia 1814–35*.

JÖRN LEONHARD is the Friedrich Schiller Reader in West European History at the Historical Institute of the University of Jena. His publications include a study of Liberalism, and he has jointly edited *Nationalismen in Europa: West- und Osteuropa im Vergleich* (Göttingen, 2001).

CARL STRIKWERDA is the Dean of Arts and Sciences at the College of William and Mary in Virginia. He is the author of numerous works on the Low Countries, including *A House Divided: Catholics, Socialists, and Flemish Nationalists in Nineteenth-Century Belgium* (Lanham, Md., 1997). He has also edited works on labour activism and migration and the consumer cooperative movement, and is currently working on a book on globalization and the First World War.

VERA TOLZ is a Professor of Russian Studies at the University of Manchester. She has published widely on various aspects of Russian nationalism and the relationship between intellectuals and the state under the communist regime. Her books include (co-editor) *Gender and Nation in Contemporary Europe* (Manchester, 2005); *Russia: Inventing the Nation* (London, 2001); (co-editor) *European Democratization since 1800* (Basingstoke, 2000); and *Russian Academicians and the Revolution: Combining Professionalism and Politics* (New York, 1997).

MAIKEN UMBACH is a Senior Lecturer in Modern European History at the University of Manchester, and an Honorary Senior Research Fellow at University College London. In the past few years, she has also held visiting appointments at the Australian National University, Harvard, and the Universitat Pompeu Fabra in Barcelona. She is author of *Federalism and Enlightenment in Germany, 1740–1806* (London, 2000), editor of *German Federalism: Past, Present and Future* (Basingstoke, 2002) and, with Bernd Hüppauf, *Vernacular*

Modernism: Heimat, Globalization and the Built Environment (Stanford, Calif., 2005), as well as numerous articles on the cultural politics of European 'second cities' and regionalism. Umbach is currently completing a book-length study on *German Cities and the Genesis of Modernism, 1890–1930*.

BRIAN VICK is Lecturer in Modern European History at the University of Sheffield. In addition to two articles on nineteenth-century German nationalism, he is author of the book *Defining Germany: The 1848 Frankfurt Parliamentarians and National Identity* (Cambridge, Mass., 2002). Currently he is working on a new project that takes a fresh look at the Vienna Congress of 1814–15 within the context of European political culture, in which the Congress is explored as an event in intellectual and cultural as well as political and diplomatic history.

CHRIS WILLIAMS is Professor of Welsh History at the University of Wales Swansea. He has published on many areas of modern Welsh and British history, nationalism, and identity. He is the editor of *A Companion to Nineteenth-Century Britain* (Oxford, 2004), and is currently working on a book on collective identities in Newport, Monmouthshire, as well as jointly editing a volume on Wales at War and Peace.

OLIVER ZIMMER is a Lecturer in History at the University of Oxford. His research focuses upon German-speaking Europe 1760–1914, with particular reference to the development of nations and nationalism. He is the author of *A Contested Nation: History, Memory and Nationalism in Switzerland, 1761–1891* (Cambridge, 2003), *Nationalism in Europe, 1890–1940* (Basingstoke, 2003), and is the co-editor of *Power and the Nation in European History* (Cambridge, 2005).

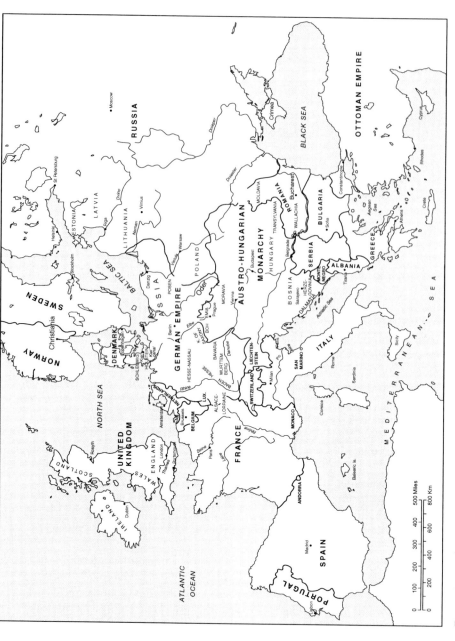

Europe in 1914

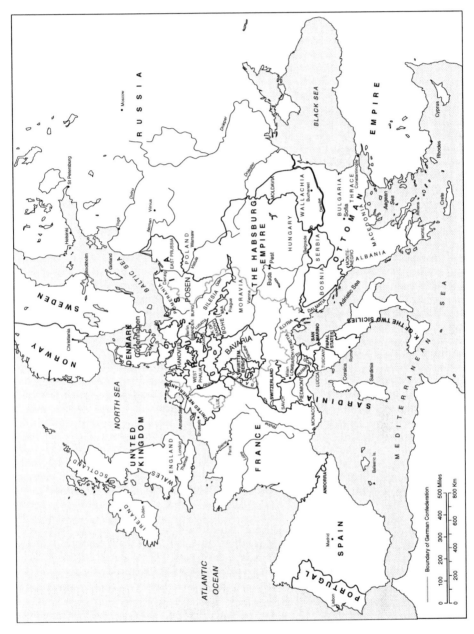

Europe in 1815

Introduction

What was a Nation in Nineteenth-Century Europe?

Timothy Baycroft and Mark Hewitson

A nation is therefore the expression of a great solidarity, constituted by a feeling for the common sacrifices that have been made and for those one is prepared to make again. It presupposes a past; however, it is epitomised in the present by a tangible fact: consent, the clearly expressed desire that the common life should continue. The existence of a nation is (excuse the metaphor) a daily plebiscite, just as the existence of the individual is a perpetual affirmation of life. . . . In the order of ideas I am placing before you, a nation has no more right than a king to say to a province: 'You belong to me, therefore I am taking you.' A province, for us, is its inhabitants, and if anyone has the right to be consulted in this matter, it is the inhabitant. A nation never has a genuine interest in annexing or retaining a country against its will. The desire of nations to be together is the only real criterion that must always be taken into account. . . .

Human desires change; but what does not change on this earth? Nations are not something eternal. They have begun, they will end. They will be replaced, in all probability, by a European confederation. But such is not the law of the century in which we live. At the present time the existence of nations happens to be good, even necessary.

Ernest Renan, *Qu'est-ce qu'une nation?* (1882)[1]

The question 'what is a nation?', posed over a century ago by the French historian Ernest Renan, still awaits a satisfactory answer. During the last three decades, as Western European nation-states appeared to be breaking up under the impact of European integration and globalization, and as the boundaries of the post-war order began to be challenged after the fall of the Iron Curtain, scholars have helped to make the 'national question' one of the most pressing problems of contemporary historical and political debate. There is a danger, however, that much of the general literature which such

[1] Cited in T. Baycroft, *Nationalism in Europe, 1789–1945* (Cambridge, 1998), 32.

scholars have produced overlooks the conditions and causes of nationalism's genesis and diffusion. In particular, commentators have ignored Renan's acknowledgement that 'ethnic' mythology and history—'the sentiment of sacrifices which one has made'—frequently existed alongside the 'civic' and political voluntarism of a daily plebiscite'. This study re-examines such nineteenth-century 'contradictions' in order to place historical European forms of nationalism in a more appropriate context and to understand contemporary nationalism more fully.

Few political forces have had greater impact in the modern world than nationalism. At the root of wars, revolutions, social and cultural movements, inspiring works of art and forming the basis of extensive political ideologies, nationalism has had global repercussions throughout the modern period, yet its tremendous diversity renders it difficult to analyse. Europe in the period from the French Revolution of 1789 up to the outbreak of the First World War was central to the development of nationalism. Boundaries shifted, a system of nation-states came to cover the map of Europe, much of the world was divided up into nation-states' empires, waves of social and political unrest erupted throughout the continent, and new political languages of nationalism were developed. In order to understand nationalism, its nature and impact on the contemporary world it is necessary to examine the place where it emerged in its modern forms: Europe in the long nineteenth century.

The study of the growth of nationalism in nineteenth-century Europe has been the object of countless works, ranging from case studies of individual countries or regions, through comparative analysis to overarching explanatory frameworks drawing on the theory and methodology of numerous disciplines. Debates about chronology, causality, the essence of nationalism, and whether it is 'natural' have engaged scholars for several decades.[2] Nationalism itself can be understood in a variety of ways, as 'an ideology or political religion, a political movement seeking state power, a cultural formation allowing industrial societies to function, a modern cognitive framework, a movement of cultural and historical revival, or a combination of these factors'.[3] This volume analyses and compares these different forms of nationalism, many of which emerged for the first time between 1789 and 1914, across a range of European countries and regions. It aims to put detailed studies of nationalist politics and thought, which have proliferated over the last ten years or so, into a wider European context. Furthermore, it questions the theoretical framework of specific 'types' of nationalism as an explanatory mechanism, through both case studies and comparative analysis. To begin with, an understanding of the existing theories and the debates nationalism has generated is essential.

---

[2] For excellent coverage of the historiography of nationalism, see P. Lawrence, *Nationalism: History and Theory* (Harlow, 2005).

[3] O. Zimmer, *Nationalism in Europe 1890–1940* (Basingstoke, 2003), 5.

THE HISTORIOGRAPHY OF MODERN NATIONALISM

The main explanatory theory in the general literature on nationalism still concerns the existence of distinct civic and ethnic types, with the former supposedly preponderant in Northern and Western Europe, and the latter in Southern, Central, and Eastern Europe. According to this explanation, civic nations are those characterized by an emphasis on citizenship, individual rights, and obligations within a political community, and which have been observed in countries with the early development of a unified state, a long and shared political history, and strong and adaptable political elites within a defined territorial and legal framework. Countries where the emergence of nationalism is held to have followed a civic form include Britain, France, and the Netherlands. Ethnic nations, on the other hand, have the emphasis placed upon shared myths of ancestry and historical memories, as well as common culture, and have been observed in places with threatened elites, and early democratization or late modernization. The repressive presence of polyglot empires or the defenceless fragmentation of small states are seen to have underpinned the growth of more unstable forms of ethnic nationalism in Germany, Italy, Russia, and the Austro-Hungarian and Ottoman Empires. Underlying the model is the idea that the growth and nature of nationalism, as well as the kinds of effects it has in the long-term development of individual nation-states can to a great extent be explained by the type of nationalism—civic or ethnic—which is found there.[4]

The origins of this model can be found in Hans Kohn's distinction between 'western' and 'eastern' types of European nationalism, and was arguably already implicit in Friedrich Meinecke's analytical separation of French and British 'state-nations' from German and Italian 'cultural nations', which was first made in 1907.[5] Their work continues to resonate in contemporary accounts of nineteenth-century nation-building, nationalist politics, and the invention of national ideas, symbols, and rituals. The numerous influential works by Ernest Gellner sustain and refine the distinction between the two types of nationalism, linking the development of political nationalist movements with cultural definitions of the nation. While he does attempt to create a more complicated model, the basic dual distinction remains.[6] The same dichotomy can be detected in analyses of civic, liberal, and democratic traditions, such as Rogers Brubaker's comparison between French and German forms of citizenship, Jack Snyder's recent thesis about the

---

[4] For a critical discussion of the strengths and weaknesses of the ethnic/civic framework of analysing nations see D. Schnapper, 'Beyond the Opposition: "Civic" Nation versus "Ethnic" Nation', *ASEN Bulletin*, 12 (1996/7), 4–8, and A. D. Smith, 'Civic and Ethnic Nationalism Revisited: Analysis and Ideology', *ASEN Bulletin*, 12 (1996/7), 9–11.

[5] H. Kohn, *The Idea of Nationalism: A Study in its Origin and Background* (New York, 1944).

[6] E. Gellner, *Nations and Nationalism* (Oxford, 1983), 97–101.

radicalizing effects of rapid democratization, or Michel Winock's distinction between 'open' nationalism, filled with the rhetoric of the civilizing mission and expressing solidarity with other would-be nations, and 'closed' nationalism, which arises in times of crisis (especially economic) and focuses on internal purity and rivalry with the 'enemies' who are ostensibly responsible for the crisis.[7] It can also easily be discerned in investigations of ethnic and national mythologies, such as Liah Greenfeld's typology of modern nationalism.[8] While refining the model through the addition of an individualistic-libertarian versus collectivistic-authoritarian dichotomy to the civic and ethnic categories, her five individual case studies are nevertheless based on long-established 'dual' traditions in the historiography of Germany, Russia, and elsewhere.[9]

Distinctions which have subsequently been made between reformist, unificatory, and secessionist types, between revolutionary and counter-revolutionary forms, and between successive liberal and conservative variants of nationalism in Europe tend to overlay rather than undermine the dichotomy between civic and ethnic traditions. This volume aims to reassess the fundamental premises of the civic-ethnic model, as well as the much less visible framework of assumptions which underpins many specialized investigations of the national question in specific countries. It also attempts to unite two largely separate literatures; namely, historical accounts of nationalism as a form of politics, tracing the establishment of movements, parties, and institutions, on the one hand, and historical analyses of national identities as sets of competing ideas and images, representations and perceptions, on the other.

The most influential theoretical study within the first of these literatures is John Breuilly's *Nationalism and the State*, where he argues that the modern state is the most important feature of the political context in which a nationalist movement can arise.[10] Without implying that nationalism is a direct product of the modern state, his position is that within the context of power struggles to control such a state, nationalism has much greater potential as a political force able to mobilize, coordinate, and legitimate certain claims for power. For him, nationalist thinking only has serious consequences when it is actively adopted by a political movement. In such an interpretation, the character and specific composition of any particular nationalist ideology will be determined by the structure of the state to which it is opposed and 'closely related to the institutional framework within which the conflict took place'.[11] Eric Hobsbawm offers another interpretation of nationalism as an essentially political phenomenon, as a tool for elites to use to further their own interests. In his opinion, nationalist ideology served as a means

[7] R. Brubaker, *Citizenship and Nationhood in France and Germany* (Cambridge, Mass., 1992), J. Snyder, *From Voting to Violence: Democratisation and Nationalist Conflict* (New York, 2000), and M. Winock, *Nationalisme, antisémitisme et fascisme en France* (Paris, 1990), 37–8.

[8] L. Greenfeld, *Nationalism: Five Roads to Modernity* (Cambridge, Mass., 1992).

[9] See also E. J. Hobsbawm, *Nations and Nationalism since 1780: Programme, Myth, Reality* (Cambridge, 1990), and A. D. Smith, *National Identity* (London, 1991), 99–142.

[10] J. Breuilly, *Nationalism and the State* (Manchester, 1982), x.   [11] Ibid. 44, 61, 115.

to obtain and then to preserve power at a time in which European nations were giving increasing influence to the masses through the extension of the franchise.[12] Neither of these positions contradicts the basic premisses of a civic-ethnic dichotomy. Rather, both scholars are primarily interested in identifying and analysing the political causes behind different types of nationalism in order to debunk the idea that communities of descent are real or ancient (Hobsbawm) and that cultures or ethnies are politically significant (Breuilly).[13] It could be contended that the very terms of Hobsbawm's and Breuilly's arguments are framed against the backdrop of a dispute between 'modernists', who have stressed the civic, political, and constructed aspects of nationalism, and 'primordialists' or 'perennialists', who have paid more attention to supposedly common ethnicities and cultures.[14]

An alternative view of nationalism holds that it was not merely an ideology developed to support a political movement seeking power within the context of a modern state, but rather a cultural and ideological movement in its own right, which had political applications, and which can best be understood through an analysis of ideas, images, and perceptions of the nation. A good example is Ernest Gellner's claim that the basic characteristic of nations and of nationalism is the development of a literate, standardized high culture, and its extension to an entire population through education and communication.[15] Nationalism developed in the modern period with the growth of industrial society because communication was easier and because such societies functioned more efficiently in the context of linguistic and cultural homogeneity which resulted from nationalism. As mentioned above, this position preserves the distinction between different types of nationalism along the lines of the civic-ethnic model, distinguishing 'Habsburg', unificatory (Germany and Italy) and diaspora 'varieties' in accordance with the relationship between political power, education, and high culture. The 'identity or diversity' of the latter is, he asserted, 'most crucial from the viewpoint of nationalism'.[16] Nations are also essentially cultural constructions for Benedict Anderson, who defined them as 'imagined political communities'.[17] 'Imagined' because they are too large for all of the members to know each other, nations are special sorts of communities because they are imagined as both limited and sovereign. Furthermore, the attachment of members to their nations can be extremely powerful, to the extent that it can be compared to that of a religion, yet the philosophical or theoretical position underlying it is far from coherent.[18]

---

[12] See E. J. Hobsbawm, 'Introduction: Inventing Traditions', in E. J. Hobsbawm and T. Ranger (eds.), *The Invention of Tradition* (Cambridge, 1983).

[13] J. Breuilly, 'The State and Nationalism', in M. Guibernau and J. Hutchinson (eds.), *Understanding Nationalism* (Cambridge, 2001), 33–4, 49–51; id., *Nationalism and the State*, 2nd edn. (Manchester, 1992), 1–15, 404–6. Hobsbawm, *Nations and Nationalism*, 5–13.

[14] On this debate from the 'other' side, see A. D. Smith, 'Nations and History', in Guibernau and Hutchinson (eds.), *Understanding Nationalism*, 9–31.

[15] Gellner, *Nations and Nationalism*, 35–8.   [16] Ibid. 92.

[17] B. Anderson, *Imagined Communities*, 2nd edn. (London: 1991), 6–7.   [18] Ibid. 5.

Although not analysing nations specifically in categories, Anderson's extensive case studies are perfectly compatible with the civic-ethnic model. They are based on the premise that the disappearance of an all-embracing religious realm and the concomitant transformation of political ideas and public spheres created the cultural and intellectual conditions necessary for the emergence of nationalism, first in Western Europe, then—with the national model formulated during the French Revolution—in other parts of the continent and the rest of the world.[19] Arguably, both Gellner and Anderson assume that nationalism in Western Europe appeared earlier and was less problematic than in Eastern and Southern Europe.

Whether stressing cultural and ideological content or political context, each of the significant theoretical explanations of nationalism discussed so far is in agreement that nationalism is a modern phenomenon, for which the long nineteenth century was a key period of its development in Europe. This position is not universal, however, and a body of scholarship exists which challenges the notion that the development of nationalism was directly linked to the arrival of modernity, and asserts that examples can be found in the pre-modern period.[20] Belonging to either the 'perennialist' or 'primordialist' schools, their arguments tend either to centre on exceptions to the general 'modernist' chronology, or rely upon less rigid definitions of nationalism than those used by the modernists, in particular leaving out the element of self-determination with its assertions of national sovereignty and political legitimacy.[21] Without this dimension, nationalism essentially becomes reduced to national sentiment or identity, which even those in the modernist school would agree existed in the pre-modern period. Some of the perennialists themselves would also concede that nationalism and its role in European society underwent a change with the advent of modernity, making their distinction from the modernists more semantic than substantial.[22] In neither of the positions is the civic-ethnic model seriously questioned, and often lies at the heart of individual works. The position in this work is that even if there are exceptions to the rule, nationalism is an essentially modern phenomenon, since claims for the political legitimacy of national sovereignty which were developed and promoted intensely from the time of the French Revolution onward are central to an understanding of nationalism in Europe.

The past ten years have seen a wealth of case studies of individual nations and regions which have demonstrated that the complexity of each case makes any

---

[19] B. Anderson, *Communities*, 2nd edn. (London: 1991), 9–36, 67–82.

[20] See for example J. A. Armstrong, *Nations before Nationalism* (Chapel Hill, NC, 1982), and A. Hastings, *The Construction of Nationhood: Ethnicity, Religion and Nationalism* (Cambridge, 1997).

[21] See Zimmer, *Nationalism*, 15–18.

[22] On the debate between the two interpretations, see L. Johnson, 'Imagining Communities: Medieval and Modern', and A. D. Smith, 'National Identities: Modern and Medieval?', both in S. Forde, L. Johnson, and A. V. Murray (eds.), *Concepts of National Identity in the Middle Ages* (Leeds, 1995), 1–19 and 21–46; E. Gellner, *Encounters with Nationalism* (Oxford, 1994), 182–200; and especially A. D. Smith *Nationalism and Modernism: A Critical Survey of Recent Theories of Nations and Nationalism* (London, 1998), who provides a very thorough analysis of the debate.

understanding of nationalism based on a simple typology at best a place to start, and rarely a satisfactory explanatory mechanism. Taken together, they suggest that the civic-ethnic model, which has not been seriously challenged—if, also, not positively defended—by all of the main theoretical works within the literature on nationalism, needs to be re-examined. A new typology or set of historically grounded concepts is required, which takes account, for instance, of the uncontroversial nature of race in many nineteenth-century contexts or of diverse kinds of political or civic involvement across the entire continent. This work aims, therefore, not only to challenge existing theories of the nation, but also to suggest novel ways of comparing, categorizing, and explaining the development of nationalist politics and the construction of national identities in what was arguably the most critical period and locus for the genesis of modern and contemporary nationalism.

BEYOND CIVIC AND ETHNIC TRADITIONS

All authors in this volume agree that the dichotomy between civic and ethnic forms of nationalism corresponds, at most, to an ideal type. In most cases, it fails to describe the diversity and contradictoriness, and to explain the evolution—and discontinuities—of nationalism in modern Europe. This inadequacy, which is the subject of Part I, is particularly apparent in the two classic points of reference in academic studies of nationalism: France and Germany. Michael Jeismann, whose chapter relies on a comparison of the two countries, demonstrates how any scheme based on functionalist theories of modernization, such as that implied in the divergence of voluntary, civic forms of nationalism and organic types of cultural and ethnic belonging, necessarily neglects the emotional and irrational mechanisms of national antipathy and political identification. The delineation of internal and external enemies, as well as other kinds of religious belief and cultural affiliation, was common to most European nation-states in the nineteenth century, leading to long-standing national rivalries and short-term explosive national conflicts. As the experiences of France and Germany showed, it proved difficult to predict the outcome of different instances of political identification. Civic and ethnic components were usually combined.

The majority of authors concur that other ways of explaining the scope and significance of nationalism in nineteenth-century Europe are necessary, in addition to—or instead of—a typology based on ethnic and civic traditions.[23] In France, as Timothy Baycroft points out in Chapter 2, there were significant and largely unquestioned ethnic and cultural components in republican ideology

---

[23] See Jörn Leonhard's and Ulrike von Hirschhausen's excellent Introduction to U. v. Hirschhausen and J. Leonhard (eds.), *Nationalismen in Europa: West- und Osteuropa im Vergleich* (Göttingen, 2001), 11–48.

and policy-making, from insistence on a common French language to a broad championing of French imperialism. The 'reactionary nation' in France, partly because it drew on popular criticism of state corruption or widespread opposition to national enemies such as Germany, overlapped in important respects with the 'revolutionary nation'. Similarly, in the German lands, liberal and conservative strands of nationalism were difficult to disentangle. Stefan Berger shows in Chapter 3 how liberal ideas such as 'national education' and civic associations, which carried the national movement for much of the nineteenth century, respectively implied the existence of an exclusive national culture and a close relationship with the state, not least because of the central role of civil servants and academics in associational and party politics. Although radical nationalist organizations became more prominent after 1871, their claim to monopolize national debate continued to be challenged by the left-liberal, social-democratic, and Catholic Centre parties, and by associations such as the Jewish League for the Defence against Anti-Semitism. The fact that 'many nationalists used both civic and ethnic definitions of the nation depending on what specific goal they wanted to achieve' means that Germany, like France, cannot serve as an ideal-typical pole in a geographical typology of nationalism.[24]

National movements and national-minded policy-making were characterized, above all, by their diversity and discontinuity. In the Conclusion, it is contended that the nature, strength, and significance of nationalist sentiment and politics can better be explained through an examination of the context in which they arose, rather than relying on the civic-ethnic dichotomy or on developmental theories of 'modernization'. Nineteenth-century European manifestations of nationalism, in the form of a body of ideas or a series of actions, developed within a framework of different types of conflict, five potential sources of which are explored: economic dislocation, democratization, tension between different cultural groups, increasing state intervention, and foreign rivalries and wars. Depending upon the source of the conflict and the degree of radicalization in each case, nationalism took different courses across Europe. For the purposes of this volume, these five explanatory types have been grouped in three sections: those relating to conflicts caused by democratization and economic distribution (*demos*); those resulting from cultural and historical conflicts in areas of mixed settlement (*Kultur*); and those involving state intervention at home and abroad, including the waging of wars (*état*). Each section opens with a comparative thematic chapter, followed by three specific examples in which the main sources of conflict against which nationalism developed were similar.

Part II examines cases in which political struggles over power and resources were especially salient. Sometimes, as Jack Snyder has pointed out, rapid democratization and economic change led to violent conflicts and a radicalization of nationalism. At other times, however, such conflicts were defused or averted by the plurality of

---

[24] For example, see S. Berger, *Inventing the Nation: Germany* (London, 2004).

politics in the nineteenth century. In particular, as Maiken Umbach rightly proposes in Chapter 4, many of those areas of political activity later associated with individuals' experience of state power tended to be exercised primarily by regions. These regions and towns, which were strongest in areas of 'early-modern sub-state-building' such as Italy, Germany, and the Low Countries, provided a locus for patriotism, political discussion, and policy-making. Long-established political practices, economic growth, or constitutional guarantees within federal structures allowed cities such as Turin, Venice, Munich, Hamburg, and Barcelona to protect their civic cultures and, by insisting on the complementarity of region-alism and nationalism, to counteract the radicalization of politics at the centre. Of course, such municipal and regional traditions and centres of power did not override the claims of the central state nor prevent separatism, as the twentieth century has demonstrated, but they did encourage the trading of interests within moderate and composite, rather than unitary and exclusive, political systems.

One area with particularly pronounced local civic traditions was that encompassed by Belgium and the Netherlands. Yet Carl Strikwerda outlines in Chapter 5 how unusual the conditions permitting such traditions were in the nineteenth century. They included—in addition to local and regional affiliations—international neutrality, only possible in small states; the necessity of free trade, given the economic weight of mercantile interests; and the strength of Flemish and Catholic opposition parties, which were able to use the machinery of a representative system of government. What was more, civic nationalism in the Low Countries rested on 'pillarization' (*verzuiling*), or the formation of vertically integrated subcultures—Catholic, conservative Protestant, Liberal, and Socialist in the Netherlands, weaker Liberal, Catholic, and Socialist subcultures in Belgium—which militated against individualism and many of the tenets of liberalism.

In some respects, Switzerland's position was similar to that of the Low Countries, with powerful local and cantonal traditions both underwriting civic voluntarism and reinforcing inward-looking, communal, or exclusive attitudes to the outside world, both within and beyond the nation-state. Like its Dutch counterpart, the Swiss case revealed the paradoxes, contradictions, and limitations of civic or liberal nationalism, above all in respect of citizenship, which had become an unusually pressing political question partly because it seemed to challenge the constitutional rights of the *Gemeinden* and cantons within the federal system. Thus, as Oliver Zimmer shows in Chapter 6, Switzerland's poor record of naturalization and its refusal to introduce *jus soli* resulted to a considerable extent from the unwillingness of rural municipalities, which retained ultimate control over the granting of citizenship, to take on burdens such as additional poor relief. However, although—like Belgians—Swiss officials and politicians were obliged to tie such debates to a broader voluntarist understanding of national identity, given the polyglot and polyethnic nature of their country, they also tended to bolster these arguments, not least in opposition to Pan-Germans who contended that Switzerland was not a real nation, by referring to the historical and natural integrity of a Swiss national 'character'. Even liberals regularly treated 'foreigners'—the very large numbers of whom (14.7 per cent in 1910) accounted for the visibility of citizenship as a political issue—as cultural outsiders, threatening an organic indigenous population with 'inundation' or 'Überfremdung'. At best, foreigners were to be assimilated; at worst, they were to be excluded.

In the Swiss case, political debates within civic institutions could, partly under the impact of democratization and disputes over resources, lead to unexpected national outcomes. The same was true within the Ottoman Empire, which aggravated a series of nationalist struggles by introducing imperial forms of citizenship from 1839 onwards. As in Switzerland, debates about citizenship were significant, but for different reasons. Here, Constantin Iordachi explains in Chapter 7, the central state imposed Ottoman citizenship from above, although in accordance with inclusive and liberal criteria, including the right of all foreigners' children born in the empire to claim citizenship at the age of majority and the opportunity for immigrants to apply for naturalization after five years of residence. Such measures were introduced as part of 'a process of socio-political transformation and economic modernisation that included strategies of modernisation and a change in the rhetoric of state legitimisation'.[25] In effect, debates about citizenship took place against a background of struggles for independence and great power intervention, which in turn occasioned fundamental political restructuring, as newly independent states such as Romania and Bulgaria sought to integrate their disparate populations and the Ottoman Empire attempted to stem the flow of its citizens from diaspora to these new states. In such circumstances, as elites tried to defend or extend their powers and states struggled for survival and pre-eminence in an unstable region, political conflicts—including those concerning citizenship rights to property, voting, and office—were closely connected to the emergence of nationalism. Even then, notwithstanding the possibility of extremism, international monitoring and the need for both 'old' and 'new' states to integrate their disparate populations militated against a uniform or incremental radicalization of national politics in the Balkans.[26]

Political conflicts often derived in part from cultural differences. Part III of the volume examines cases in which such cultural differences played an important role, usually in conjunction with other historical processes. Thus, in the Habsburg Monarchy, which is examined by Mark Cornwall in Chapter 9, the existence of distinct vernacular cultures frequently gave the impression—or were used as proof—of separate communities of descent. Partly as a consequence, both Hungary and Bohemia experienced an ethnicization of politics in the latter part of the nineteenth century. Yet ethnic myths and oppositions remained one element, albeit a very significant one, in broader economic and political struggles involving

---

[25] See below, Chapter 7, p. 129.
[26] This did not rule out anti-Semitism and xenophobia, of course, for example when Romania used laws of religious exclusion inherited from the Ottoman era to deny state citizenship and political rights to Jews.

local notables and the imperial state, as the latter refashioned itself in order to try to meet domestic criticism and external challenges. Even many nationalist intellectuals continued to pursue claims based on 'historical rights' and resistance to 'centralism' rather than what the Hungarian liberal József Eötvös called a 'fashionable' linguistic and ethnic interpretation of nationality, which he believed had come from France. In contrasting ways, Hungarian leaders, who insisted on the observance of constitutional and historical procedures in their dealings with the other parts of the Habsburg lands, and their Czech counterparts, who continued to prefer a reformed monarchy to secession, went on balancing cultural claims and recognition of 'ethnic' differences against other political goals. Despite the significance of cultural politics in areas of mixed settlement, limits were placed on antagonism between Czechs and Germans in Bohemia and on policies of Magyarization in Hungary.

The close and complex relationship between cultural conflict and politics could be observed in other areas of Europe. In Scandinavia, for instance, Romantic folk traditions remained influential. They were reinforced by conflicts between nationalities, such as that between Germans and Danes in Slesvig. Yet in Denmark, Norway, and Sweden, peasants, who were the main object of folk myths, were also citizens and political actors, forming the backbone of rural democracies or, at least, representative institutions. Accordingly, legends of common descent, cultural particularity, historical rights, constitutional guarantees, and political praxis were, as Mary Hilson evinces in Chapter 10, frequently combined. This contiguity and overlap between politics and culture could also be seen in Spain, where antagonism between different cultural identities (*pueblo, región, patria, nación*) and territories (Catalonia, Castille, the Basque lands) have been the focus of one of two main schools of thought on the subject of Spanish nationalism. The other school, however, has concentrated on the political, economic, and cultural consequences of a weak, or 'invertebrate', state. In addition, in Chapter 11, Stephen Jacobson points to other political discourses, many of which had been imported from France, and to religious traditions such as 'National Catholicism', which had both political and cultural implications, and which cut across the boundaries of Spain's various nationalities and regions. *Ipso facto*, the existence and consolidation of cultural differences do not explain the divergent paths taken by Basque nationalists, who emphasized race and descent, and Catalan nationalists, who championed constitutional and civic causes such as the legislation of a separate Civil Code.

The consequences of cultural difference, although often essential to the genesis and perpetuation of nationalist conflicts, were difficult to predict in a nineteenth-century setting. Even policies concerning language, which counted—as Brian Vick makes clear in Chapter 8—'as one of the most important markers of the difference between peoples', could not be understood in terms of a dichotomy between voluntarism and liberalism in the West, and determinism and authoritarianism in the East. Instead, policies of assimilation were pursued most vigorously by republicans in France, although always with a degree of toleration and accommodation. For much of the nineteenth century, the less liberal German states and the Habsburg Monarchy acknowledged and underwrote the use of 'minority' languages at a local and, in the latter case, at a national level, even if such provisions were partially overturned from the 1880s onwards. Vick concludes that toleration, assimilation, forced assimilation, and total exclusion were possibilities that could emerge from almost any type of nationalism in different times and places. The national implications of culture certainly became less ambiguous during the course of the nineteenth century, but they were only occasionally sufficient in themselves to explain an intensification of nationalist conflict.

Such conflict was more commonly provoked by state intervention, either at home or abroad. The cases presented in Part IV, however, show that the relationship between nationalism and the state was neither linear nor exclusive. Official nationalism was regularly ineffectual or counter-productive. In Italy, for example, statesmen and politicians used national propaganda in a failed attempt to conceal the inactivity of a weak state. In the absence of other foundation myths, leaders relied unsuccessfully on the lustre of the Risorgimento and the unification of the Italian state itself to mobilize and unite the population. As David Laven contends in Chapter 13, an appeal to the material interests of ordinary Italians was necessary to attach citizens to a united state but, among those who set up the new political order, neither radical romantics like Mazzini nor the pro-Piedmontese moderates were prepared to introduce the sort of sweeping reforms necessary to accomplish this.

Other states were more successful in harnessing the national sentiments of at least some sections of their populations. The United Kingdom succeeded in winning over the majority of the political nation in Scotland and Wales, because of its constitutional flexibility, a series of successful wars, and its expanding and apparently lucrative imperial mission. Yet, even here, there were many sources of resistance and opposition to official nationalism, as Chris Williams demonstrates in Chapter 14: Catholic Ireland never fitted into a Protestant 'Britain', established through wars against Spain and France; the unifying effects of war were only felt on a large scale during the 1810s and 1850s, and those of empire only from the late nineteenth century onwards; and both the idea of 'England' and that of the state were only vaguely defined. In Russia, a state tradition was long established, to the extent that Vera Tolz—in Chapter 15—characterizes Russian nationalism as 'state framed'.[27] Nationalists, however, abetted by the late conversion of Russian governments to national-minded policy-making, failed to realize that the state had outstripped the nation, so that Russians did not have a state within the borders of which nation-building could take place. Furthermore, the gap between intellectuals, officials, and the peasantry was too wide to allow national unity. In some respects, in spite of its belated efforts to 'nationalize' the peasantry, the tsarist state had unintentionally foiled attempts to build a viable Russian nation.

---

[27] This is in line with Rogers Brubaker's definition, below Chapter 15, p. 293.

One of the most effective means of nation-building, which was squandered by the Russian state in the Crimea in 1856 and in Manchuria in 1905, was a victorious war. The consequences of armed conflict, however, were difficult to foresee, as Jörn Leonhard indicates. Thus, although 'war nationalism' in France was founded on the notion of the *levée en masse*, with its democratic and civic implications, it also enshrined common historical and cultural memories in popular consciousness, particularly those involving suffering. As wars became more 'absolute' in Carl von Clausewitz's phrase, the same combination of citizen-soldiers and an ethnic community of fate was present in Germany, despite Helmuth von Moltke's resistance to the democratic ramifications of mass conscription. Even Britain, which avoided conscription, witnessed the transformation of its army from an amateurish, aristocratic institution into a professional imperial force symbolizing the British Empire and Britishness. Here, under the impact of colonial small wars and repeated war scares, ethnic and racial identities had been consolidated, notwithstanding the absence of a 'cult of a nation in arms'.

In Britain, as elsewhere, civic and ethnic components combined in unpredictable ways, variously reinforcing and contradicting each other. Such unpredictability militated against a more or less linear process of radicalization, which occurred during the interwar period in many areas of the continent. Before 1914, nationalism was a changing compound of different elements. It was sometimes obtrusive, at other times unnoticed. It is not comprehensible as a series of relatively straight-forward and closely intertwined 'roads to modernity'. Instead, the paths taken by nationalism were uneven, varied, and occasionally led nowhere, depending upon the nature of the conflict in which they arose, and the particular context in which they developed.[28] This volume studies such paths during the critical period of nationalism's genesis in Europe over the course of the long nineteenth century.

[28] Greenfeld, *Nationalism: Five Roads to Modernity*.

PART I

CIVIS *AND* ETHNIE

1

Nation, Identity, and Enmity

Towards a Theory of Political Identification

Michael Jeismann

The hopes of the short People's Spring of 1989/90 were gradually eroded by a global process of fermentation which, fuelled by enmity, seems to be constantly producing new kinds of animosity: animosity between cultures or civilizations, enmity between religions and enmity between social strata. We are, in theory, ill-equipped to predict whether and under what conditions the potential for national aggression could develop again. Certainly, we have some historical points of departure for analysis. These can basically be divided up into two types, both of which derive from nineteenth-century Europe and which cut across the dichotomy between civic and ethnic forms of nationalism.

The first explanatory model, which is focused primarily on foreign policy, considers national aggression an additional element in the perpetual rivalry between European states, a rivalry which became uncontrollable when it became a mass phenomenon. It was an additional, and also a new, element, the effect and impact of which, however, remained bound to the constellation of long-term foreign interests and conflicts. National aggression and images of the enemy therefore posed a challenge to the art of diplomacy insofar as powerful states had to take them into account when making their political moves.[1]

---

[1] M. Jeismann, *Das Vaterland der Feinde: Studien zum nationalen Feindbegriff und Selbstverständnis in Deutschland und Frankreich 1792–1918* (Stuttgart 1992); M. Kennedy, *The Rise of the Anglo-German Antagonism, 1860–1914* (London, 1980); H.-J. Schröder (ed.), *Confrontation and Cooperation: Germany and the United States in the Era of World War I* (Oxford, 1993); F. Fischer, 'Das Bild Frankreichs in Deutschland in den Jahren vor dem Ersten Weltkrieg', *Revue d'Allemagne*, 4 (1972), 505–19; Milza and R. Poidevin (eds.), *La Puissance française à la belle époque* (Brussels, 1992); N. Hampson, *The Perfidy of Albion: French Perceptions of England in the French Revolution* (London, 1998); J.-J. Becker and S. Audoin-Rouzeau (eds.), *La France, la nation, la guerre, 1850–1920* (Paris, 1995); B. Joly, 'La France et la Revanche, 1871–1914', *Revue d'histoire moderne et contemporaine*, 46 (1999), 325–47; H. D. Schmidt, 'The Idea and Slogan of Perfidious Albion', *Journal of Historical Ideas*, 14 (1953), 604–16; I. F. Clarke, *Voices Prophesying War, 1763–1984* (Oxford, 1966); J. H. Grainger, *Patriotisms: Britain, 1900–1939* (London, 1986).

The other explanation is of a domestic nature and is known by the phrase 'negative integration'.[2] According to this, national enmities were fuelled and exploited by ruling elites in order to safeguard their own power. Unpleasant political and social demands and conflicts at home were transferred onto an external enemy. But then we have to ask from where the masses, manipulated in such a way, derived their will. Not only historical research into propaganda but also the propagandists themselves knew that indoctrination merely reinforced and sharpened already existing value judgements and views and could not engender these itself. Images of the enemy were not simply created by the state from 'above'. In the end, only those who want to be persuaded can be persuaded. If this predisposition does not exist, all propaganda is ineffective. In this sense there is an extensive blindspot within the theory of 'negative integration', for the self-image of contemporaries is only perceived in its political-functional aspect.[3]

Both explanatory models consequently only throw light on the state apparatus's functionalization of nationalism. They do not identify the cause of national aggression. This deficiency is also due to the fact that in general it is presumed that nationalism in its early stages is revolutionary or liberal but eventually becomes integral and aggressive. Here we must, however, stop and reflect further. It cannot be denied that the early German nationalist movement at the time of the 'wars of liberation' did fashion the image of its own German nation out of its hostility towards Napoleon, the French nation, and the French. Arndt's 'feasting on the French' was actually not a lapse, as Treitschke thought, it was in fact necessary and constitutive. However, this movement did not just take place in Germany: it was not a coincidence that the claim to sovereignty made by the revolutionary French people's campaign in 1792 went hand in hand with the declaration of war on Austria.

More recent research into nationalism rightly emphasizes that the 'nation' was a draft, an artefact which was based on the will for collective action and commonality. Out of this came emphatic national self-discovery in the form of a common national history, language, and culture,[4] as well as the need for demarcation. It is therefore not a relapse into an idealistic history of ideas to claim that the 'nation' is grounded primarily in a fundamental concept of the 'national', to which all later functionalizations remained attached. The distinguishing of voluntary, civic forms of political identification, linked to processes of modernization, as opposed

---

[2] This notion has been put forward above all by adherents of the 'Hamburg' and 'Bielefeld schools' in Germany: F. Fischer, *Krieg der Illusionen: Die deutsche Politik 1911–1914* (Düsseldorf, 1969), translated into English in 1975; H.-U. Wehler, *Das Deutsche Kaiserreich 1871–1918* (Göttingen, 1973), translated in 1985. Similar works have been written on France: G. Krumeich, *Armaments and Politics in France on the Eve of the First World War* (Oxford, 1984).

[3] For a good overview of older international literature of different disciplines see: H. A. Winkler (ed.), *Nationalismus* (Königstein, 1985) as well as O. Dann (ed.), *Nationalismus und sozialer Wandel* (Hamburg, 1978).

[4] B. Anderson, *Die Erfindung der Nation: Zur Karriere eines erfolgreichen Konzepts* (Frankfurt am Main 1993), translated from the English edition of 1983.

to organic, ethnic types of belonging, can be understood as one example of such functionalization. A more compelling concept of the nation can be seen to have developed out of an oscillation between two poles: national self-definition, on the one hand, and the image and idea of the enemy, on the other.[5] The concept of nationalism is just as inadequate for an analysis of this interrelation as an interpretation of the national merely in terms of political and socio-economic interests.

Without being able to go into the details of reciprocal national concepts, it is at least important to raise the question of where the intensity of such national demarcation comes from, and why at all times a fundamental enmity is inherent in supposed difference. The reason for this is to be found in a specific self-definition, the characteristics of which, irrespective of different peculiarities, are identifiable in most European nations.[6] This self-definition comes from the idea of being the 'chosen people': every nation believed that it embodied the greatest attributes of 'humanity', values which it was its duty to protect. Whether this national mission was understood as expansionist and universalist, as in France, or Christian, moral and self-reflexive, as in Germany and a few other Central European nations, had ramifications right through to the organizational level of nation-state politics. This did not, however, alter the structural analogy of a national 'calling'. Where the interests of the nation were identified with 'humanity', where consequently non-transmissible claims clashed, the boundary between political opposition, on the one hand, and existential enmity, on the other, was quickly transgressed. On the other side of this boundary diplomacy and traditional 'statecraft' had to fail to the point where even the securing of one's own political interests became redundant. Paradoxically, these developments are evident precisely within that impassioned discourse of 'national interests' in the nineteenth and early twentieth centuries, in which competition was activated not by level-headed political calculations but by a spiral of emotionally charged claims. The difficult peace deal at the end of the Franco-German war in 1870/1 is as much an example of this as is the outbreak of the First World War.[7]

This basic requirement of 'old' nationalism is a good indicator when identifying 'new' forms of nationalism today. Where neither a sense of mission nor a discourse of the 'chosen people' can be identified, the category of 'nationalism' is probably misleading. In this the role of the nation's real or merely desired unified

[5] See Jeismann, *Das Vaterland der Feinde*, 11–23. Also, H. A. Winkler, 'Der Nationalismus und seine Funktionen', in id., *Nationalismus* (Königstein, 1985), 5–48.

[6] For more on this and related themes, see M. Jeismann, 'Was bedeuten Stereotypen für nationale Identität und politisches Handeln?', in J. Link and W. Wülfing (eds.), *Nationale Mythen und Symbole in der zweiten Hälfte des 19. Jahrhunderts* (Stuttgart, 1991), 84–93.

[7] Jeismann, *Das Vaterland der Feinde*, 161–373; R. Poidevin and J. Bariéty (eds.), *Les Relations franco-allemandes, 1815–1975* (Paris, 1977), 75–122; D. Pick, *War Machine: The Rationalisation of Slaughter in the Modern Age* (New Haven, 1993), 88–114, 136–164; J. Joll, 'The Mood of 1914', in id., *The Origins of the First World War*, 2nd edn. (London, 1992), 199–233; R. N. Stromberg, *Redemption by War: The Intellectuals and 1914* (Lawrence, 1982); M. Stibbe, *German Anglophobia and the Great War, 1914–1918* (Cambridge, 2001).

action—what it was and what it can be—becomes clear: it is a point of anchorage for highly dissimilar world-views, offering an apparently solid ground of collective existence. The definition of this commonality can be of a political, religious, cultural, or even biological nature. It is linked to the state, but not merely a product of state action. It can be ethnic or political. Nationalism consequently consists of a symbiotic relationship in which the 'national' as a foundation represents the value of collectivity, characterized by relatively unchangeable attributes, grounded in dualistic and polarized friend-foe models which then had to be furnished with specific colourings. Out of the alliance between this foundation—a foundation which in the form of the modern nation-state in the nineteenth and early twentieth centuries was more sustained and more durable than any other political agency had been—and specific political or other views, there arose those inseparable layers of loyalties and identifications which together constituted nationalism. None of these layers in themselves—whether political or cultural, civic or ethnic—could have offered this binding potential. How significant the 'national' element actually was for common ground can be seen in the way it could build up quiet reserves of emotional and political energies even after specific components of its substance had been detached. But nationalism was only activated by the state- and culture-based binding potential described above. So political classification is inadequate because it has a one-sided perspective of this multi-layered process of constitution.[8] Typologies such as the civic-ethnic one largely overlook the causes of emotional identification and enmity, which can be recent, civic, and political as well as primordial, cultural, or ethnic in nature. In this sense it bypasses the essence of what makes nationalism so attractive.

NATIONALISM AND RELIGION

The attractions of nationalism can be understood by looking at the continually resurfacing connection between nation and religion. The relation between nationalism and religion is palpable but simultaneously elusive and contradictory. The conflicts in the former Yugoslavia, like those in the Balkans in the nineteenth century, show this all too clearly.[9] If this relation is termed 'political religion', what is meant initially is a kind of political aesthetics. Myths, symbols, metaphors, and the 'liturgy of the national' emerge only as tokens transferred from the religious to the political world. This transfer is invisible because on its completion receiver and sender cannot be distinguished anymore. It marks, first of all, formal

---

[8] See M. Jeismann (ed.), *Obsessionen: Beherrschende Gedanken im wissenschaftlichen Zeitalter* (Frankfurt am Main, 1994).

[9] M. Mazower, *The Balkans* (London, 2000), 86–151; B. Jelavich, *History of the Balkans*, 2 vols. (Cambridge, 1983); Sugar, *East European Nationalism, Politics and Religion* (Aldershot, 1999); N. Malcolm, *Bosnia: A Short History* (London, 1994) and id., *Kosovo: A Short History* (London, 1998); B. Anzulovic, *Heavenly Serbia: From Myth to Genocide* (London, 1999).

borrowings which are of course only possible and effective because they correspond to an undetermined symbiosis between nation and religion. The altar of the church and the 'altar of the fatherland' do not just stand side by side; rather the one can replace the other. Religions can be quasi-nationalized and nations can be furnished with religious signs. Here we have the cause of the enormous, affective, unifying power of the nation, the irrational moments, the testimonies of a national faith or a national 'calling'. However, it cannot be taken for granted that this political emotionality, for which research into nationalism still today struggles to find an explanation, is, so to speak, the dowry of religion. The term 'political religion' raises, but does not answer, the question of how the oscillation between love of God and love for the fatherland became possible in the first place. In short, it helps us out of a difficulty we would do better to confront. Since the work of Gerhard Kaiser and Hasko Zimmer we have known that precisely identifiable motifs and rituals from philosophy and from collective faith were transferred from religion onto the nation.[10] Only with the aid of this transfer could the nation become the subject of a salvation history which was expressed not only in historical and worldly terms but also in terms of religion and transcendence.

One of the most important motifs of this salvation history was that of the 'chosen people' whose history has been traced by Conor Cruise O'Brien in a splendid, but in academic circles often overlooked, essay entitled *God Land*.[11] O'Brien makes a distinction at the beginning of his essay which allows him to trace the interdependence of nationalism and religion from the Old Testament onwards. As a doctrine or ideology nationalism seems to be a phenomenon which at the end of the twentieth century no longer plays an important role anywhere in the world. However, a second type of nationalism, which can only imperfectly be described as emotional nationalism, represents a very old and still very effective phenomenon. The concept he forms here clearly does not work and invites counter-arguments: in the course of the essay, however, it becomes clear that by 'emotional nationalism' O'Brien means nothing other than the need of different peoples to distinguish themselves from each other, to be able to feel that they are of a higher status—and this is where the concept of the chosen people comes into play. This essay therefore complements Arno Borst's monumental work *The Building of the Tower of Babel* in which he explores 'views on the origin and variety of peoples'.[12]

The question which dominates O'Brien's essay is: how do worldly, political actions take on a religious quality? From the Jewish religion through early Christianity, from the Christian faith as the Roman state religion through to

---

[10] G. Kaiser, *Pietismus und Patriotismus im literarischen Deutschland: Ein Beitrag zur Säkularisation* (Wiesbaden, 1961); H. Zimmer, *Auf dem Altar des Vaterlandes: Religion und Patriotismus in der deutschen Kriegslyrik des 19. Jahrhunderts* (Frankfurt am Main, 1971).

[11] C. Cruise O'Brien, *God Land: Reflections on Religion and Nationalism* (Cambridge, Mass., 1988).

[12] A. Borst, *Der Turmbau zu Babel: Meinungen über Ursprung und Vielfalt der Völker*, 4 vols., (Stuttgart 1957).

Rousseau's philosophy of nature and the function of Marxism in national and other political movements, this question allows us to see proportions and super-impositions. There are three distinct kinds of combination of nation and religion, although admittedly these are ideal types.

First of all, the primarily religious concept of the 'chosen people' which not only owes God humility and submission but is also punished by this God, and indeed may be dropped by Him in favour of another people. A strict religious code, a law standing over the 'chosen people', limits the temptation to behave in an autocratic and high-handed manner towards other peoples. This does not exclude 'national' pride but keeps it, as it were, in check. The religious idea raises up a people and disciplines them at the same time.

Secondly, the status of 'chosenness' is permanent. The 'holy nation', as this type can be called, still understands itself to be subject to God's will and law. The supposed permanent privilege of this 'holy nation' can of course, according to O'Brien, lead to its members feeling that they are called to rule over other peoples. They still feel subject to God but on earth the 'holy nation' has the right, indeed the duty, to subjugate others.

Thirdly, the 'deified nation' does not perceive itself as subject to any kind of law or authority. The nation itself, its interests and needs, are the law which legitimates its actions. To the extent that this nation idolizes itself, it negates other nations' right to existence. What would be the precondition for the nation's detachment from religion, smoothly developing from one type to another? Early Christianity had de-territorialized the concept of the 'promised people', moving away from the Old Testament; God's kingdom was not of this world. If as a result the idolization of political action was initially destabilized, the elevation of the Christian faith to a state religion under Constantine and Theodosius meant a consequent break with early Christian tradition. For now it was not a just worldly state and religion which were connected to one another; emperors and kings could stand between God and the faithful, entitled to represent God's dominion on earth. But if the worldly ruler was consecrated in his function then the means to secure this rulership were also, so to speak, divinely sanctioned. The secularization of the Christian martyr-death during the crusades lay exactly within this identification of the political and the religious. With the advent of modern European states the precondition was set, furthermore, for competing, analogous claims with reference to Christianity. In this way 'national' enemies were at the same time the 'enemies of God'. State and religion had become intertwined.[13]

When in the American and French Revolutions the 'people' replaced the king, religious factors entered the concept of the 'sovereignty of the people'. However, these were above all social-utopian motives of equality and happiness for those

[13] A. Hastings, *The Construction of Nationhood: Ethnicity, Religion and Nationalism* (Cambridge, 1997).

who attributed a considerable amount of legitimacy to the nation.[14] It was also these factors which contributed substantially to the attractiveness of the 'national'. In the concept of the national, social barriers were ideologically lifted, for not membership of a class but membership of a nation was supposed to be the primary mark of identity. 'The idol of the anti-popular party has been defeated', declared the President of the electoral assembly of the Department of Seine-et-Marne in 1792: 'a pen of fire would barely suffice to trace in a worthy manner the energetic courage and heroic devotion of the patriots fighting for liberty and equality against despotism'.[15] Although this basic structure underlies all modern concepts of nationality, the political consequences in their detail turned out very differently, as shown in the comparison between the French and American Revolutions. *Inter alia*, this depended on the nature of existing political traditions and on the character and scope of the state.

As Heinz Gollwitzer has convincingly proved in his essay on the dialectic between ideologies of identity and expansion in German history, the ideology of the national mission which inspired the French revolutionaries could not be taken on by Germany.[16] The reason for this was that the early German national movement had, in contrast to Napoleonic France, elevated the national-particular, namely the 'German', as the mark of true quality. 'I want this hatred against the French', proclaimed Ernst Moritz Arndt: 'This hatred glows as the religion of the German people, as a holy madness in every heart and maintains us forever in our loyalty, honesty and bravery.'[17] This particular national quality was supposed to represent a universal humanity but at the same time it excluded attempts at expansion, for only Germans could be German. In addition to this the connection between dynastic and religious, ecclesiastical legitimation was by no means given up on in the course of the nineteenth century. That led in fact, on the one hand, to a momentous political identification above all of the Protestant church with 'king and fatherland'; on the other hand, however, these traditional formulae for the legitimation of the ruler could, if not prevent, then make it more difficult for a nation to elevate itself to the position of law-giver.[18] Here, religion, state, and nation stood in an ambiguous and potentially contradictory relationship to each other in the nineteenth century, complicated further by the proclivity of most states to expand during an age of imperialism. All attempts on the German side in the era of imperialism to break through this self-reflexivity were doomed to fail ideologically and in terms of propaganda. Only with the help of constructions of

[14] A. Forrest, *The French Revolution* (Oxford, 1995), 78–91; M. Vovelle, *The Revolt against the Church: From Reason to the Supreme Being* (Cambridge, 1991).

[15] Cited in Jeismann, *Das Vaterland der Feinde*, 138.

[16] H. Gollwitzer, ' "Für welchen Weltgedanken kämpfen wir?" Bemerkungen zur Dialektik zwischen Identitäts- und Expansionideologien in der deutschen Geschichte', in K. Hildebrandt and R. Pommerin (eds.), *Deutsche Frage und europäisches Gleichgewicht* (Vienna, 1985), 83–109.

[17] E. M. Arndt, *Über Volkshass und über den Gebrauch einer fremden Sprache* (Leipzig, 1813), 9.

[18] H. Walser Smith, *German Nationalism and Religious Conflict: Culture, Ideology, Politics, 1870–1914* (Princeton, 1995).

biological race could these reservations about expansionist politics be completely dispelled.[19]

The interconnection of nation and religion, the replacement of one by the other, also involved an extensive adoption of function: the nation endowed not just the collective but also the individual with meaning. It made possible a world-view as well as a stabilization of subjectivity. The precondition for this was a pronounced 'culture' of nationalism which extended deep into daily life.[20]

CULTURES OF THE NATION

How was it possible to identify national similarities which did not present themselves directly? How did affective relationships and identifications develop? It was after all not a given that the nation in the nineteenth century would become the primary unit of identity. There were strong traditional relationships of a local and regional kind, and the church and clergy continued to be undisputed authorities.[21] In opposition to this, socialism in the second half of the nineteenth century offered possibilities of identification within, as it were, an integrated world-view which was effective to the same extent within the collective and the individual mode.[22] The same could be said of liberalism and anti-Semitism.[23] Each of these ideological and political identifications could appeal to 'scientific rigour', but none of them was able to distance itself from the concept of the national before the First World War, despite the fact that it employed no binding theory. How can this superiority of the 'nation' be explained? What promise was so attractive and so close that all others faded in its light?

The great promise of nationalism, which came—very gradually—to underpin a number of nineteenth-century states, was equality in unity. Whilst most ideological-political programmes regarded unity or 'harmony' as just a means to an end or all in all did not pay much attention to it, nationalism elevated unity to this very end. Equality in unity needed no social or political reforms or revolutions; its single indispensable precondition was the faith that all members of a nation could feel equal to one another independently of their social status

---

[19] See, for example, W. D. Smith, *The Ideological Origins of Nazi Imperialism* (Oxford, 1986).

[20] For the German case, see D. Langewiesche, *Nation, Nationalismus, Nationalität in Deutschland und Europa* (Munich, 2000), 82–171; S. Berger, *Inventing the Nation: Germany* (London, 2004), 13–110. For France, see R. Tombs (ed.), *Nationhood and Nationalism in France from Boulangism to the Great War, 1889–1918* (London, 1991).

[21] J. McManners, *Church and State in France, 1870–1914* (Oxford, 1872); D. Blackbourn, *The Marpingen Visions: Rationalism, Religion and the Rise of Modern Germany* (Oxford, 1993); J. Sperber, *Popular Catholicism in Nineteenth-Century Germany* (Princeton, 1984).

[22] V. L. Lidtke, *The Alternative Culture* (Oxford, 1985); R. Magraw, *A History of the French Working Class*, 2 vols. (London, 1992).

[23] J. Leonhard, *Liberalismus: Zur historischen Semantik eines europäischen Deutungsmusters* (Munich, 2001) covers France, Germany, Italy, and Britain. On anti-Semitism, see above all L. Poliakov, *The History of Antisemitism* (Philadelphia, 2003), vols. iii–iv.

and precisely in the quality of being German, French, Italian, or Spanish. Both unity and equality therefore were based primarily on the same 'national' feelings. It should be remembered in this context that even the idea of the 'citizen' included not only political participation but also emotional identification. The revaluation of the position of the soldier which took place in the nineteenth century in all European nations is clear evidence of this.[24] As one revolutionary observer noted at the very start of the long nineteenth century, 'It is in the name of its own injuries [in war] that the Republic claimed and obtained the Terror.'[25] Whilst the modern pre-national state was based precisely on the separation of individual or group-specific faiths and world-views from politics, these came together again in the concept of the 'nation' and the 'nation-state'.

This unity was at the same time also the most rapid form of a democratization which was to be realized, to a large extent, independently of the existing socio-political system. Of course this unity and equality were open to be filled by very different kinds of politics: missionary-humanist during the French Revolution, religious and self-reflexive in the Germany of the wars of liberation or in Poland, imperial during the last third of the nineteenth century. Racial-biological ideas could also take national unity as their starting point.[26] The political openness of national unity explains how it could be adopted by the very different ideologies mentioned above. Another factor was involved: nationalism was more capable of tradition than all the other political views.

It was capable of tradition and in this it surpassed even conservatism, for it could to a greater extent make traditions dynamic, avoiding the label of 'reactionary'. This propensity for adoption, dynamization, and transformation was to prove durable in the area of institutional administration, but most of all in the area of culture. A few examples may prove this. The national fitted into traditional social forms and cultures. The patriotic choir societies, the celebrating of historical commemoration days, or the erecting of memorials to the 'great men' or the war-dead fell back in particular on elements of religiosity amongst the people and in general on older mechanisms of socialization.[27] The reference to the nation gradually re-centred social communication and covertly changed it. The same is true of the composition of the state: particularisms, dynasties, and regionalisms in many other European countries did not necessarily have a dangerous counterpart in nationalism. Rather they could mutually

---

[24] For Germany and France, see J. Vogel, *Nationen im Gleichschritt: Der Kult der Nation im Waffen in Deutschland und Frankreich 1871–1914* (Göttingen, 1997) and M. Ingenlath, *Mentale Aufrüstung: Militarisierungstendenzen in Frankreich und Deutschland vor dem Ersten Weltkrieg* (Frankfurt a. M., 1998).

[25] Cited in A. de Baecque, 'Le Corps meurti de la Révolution: le discours politique et les blessures des martyrs 1792–1794', *Annales historiques de la Révolution française*, 59 (1987), 40.

[26] See the section on 'The Ubiquity of Ethnicity' in the Conclusion of this volume.

[27] R. Koselleck and M. Jeismann (eds.), *Der politische Totenkult: Kriegerdenkmäler in der Moderne* (Munich, 1994). Also, U. Schie, *Die Nation erinnert sich: Die Denkmäler der Deutschen* (Munich, 2002); M. Ozouf, *Festivals and the French Revolution* (Cambridge, Mass., 1988); R. Gildea, *The Past in French History* (New Haven, 1994).

enhance each other, symbiotically, or in a kind of hierarchically graded identification.[28]

The process of national transformation was accelerated once again in the second half of the nineteenth century. The nation-state had, in school and the military, two instruments with which it could steer society, and it was able in this way to promote widespread acceptance of certain national dispositions.[29] Of course the state was not the only and perhaps not even the most important authority for the 'nationalisation of the masses'.[30] The masses nationalized themselves through the adoption and production of a publicity which, regardless of diverse political opinions, basically consisted of national ideas of selfhood. Besides this the arts and culture industry did its best to strengthen such dispositions. A not inconsiderable number of today's federal museums in Germany are a result of the efforts of particularist states to secure their original place in the nation. In France the famous Salon, the exhibition of the plastic arts, originated in an event of royal patronage in association with the Académie.[31] The calculated giving of medals to artists, the special attention the French nation-state—of all the regimes from the Revolution to the Third Republic—paid to the Salon, as well as the eventual, explicit invitation to artists to glorify France's history and genius, all make clear how important cultural self-portrayal was to the nation-state. In fact there was no area of art or science which was excluded from the centralization of the nation, quite the opposite, for a number of modern sciences—like German or 'national economics'—only came about because they were anchored in the nation.

In the last decades of the nineteenth century sport eventually came to play an important part in the widespread mediation of the national. International mass events especially, like the Olympics (first held in 1896), in which in place of war there was athletic competition between nations, contributed to national identification and promoted, in the eyes of the ruling military, stamina, nerve, and military virtues. Besides this, there was a proliferation of national consumer goods: games for children, card-games as well as bread baskets bearing the portrait of Bismarck or Hindenburg, and many other objects for everyday use, including cigarette brands. Overall, it is likely that such forms of cultural identification served to consolidate the link between state, polity, and people, but rarely in a straightforward way.

---

[28] See Chapter 4. Also, see C. Applegate, *A Nation of Provincials: The German Idea of* Heimat (Oxford, 1990); A. Confino, *The Nation as a Local Metaphor* (Chapel Hill, NC, 1997); A. Green, *Fatherlands: State-Building and Nationhood in Nineteenth-Century Germany* (Cambridge, 2001); C. Ford, *Creating the Nation in Provincial France: Religion and Political Identity in Brittany* (Princeton, 1993).

[29] E. Hobsbawm and T. Ranger (eds.), *The Invention of Tradition* (Cambridge, 1983).

[30] G. L. Mosse, *The Nationalisation of the Masses: Political Symbolism and Mass Movements from the Napoleonic War through to the Third Reich*, new edn. (Ithaca, NY, 1991).

[31] A. Sfeir-Semler, *Die Maler am Pariser Salon 1791–1880* (Frankfurt a. M., 1992).

CONCLUSION

There has been no unified historical research on such cultural and national phenomena either in European countries or in the United States. With a few exceptions such as Pierre Nora's collection *Les Lieux de mémoire* it has been limited to positivist interpretation.[32] With regard to the development of a 'new' nationalism out of the 'old nationalism' of the nineteenth century, and taking into account the non-European reception of national ideas, a theory of national identification and integration such as the sociologist Eugen Lemberg has already tried to develop would be desirable. Moreover nationalism's chameleon-like propensity for a, so to speak, detailed and slow-motion metamorphosis would have to be investigated. This would not only make it possible to gain insight into the mechanisms of political identification but also to find evidence of constant factors which are essential to the definition of nationalism, if the term is not to become a cheap, convenient label. Regarding a theory of political identification, the question arises as to whether nationalism, as it were, can proceed from one political agency to the next. Will a united Europe take on precisely those nationalistic motifs which previously shaped the relationship between individual European nations? It seems that this cannot be ruled out, and in fact it is perhaps more probable than the presumption that individual nations will regain that status in collective political perception which they had in the nineteenth century. As is apparent from the case of France and Germany in the nineteenth century, the emotional and irrational quality of nationalism rendered it protean and, as is evident from a reading of nineteenth-century history, pushes it beyond a dichotomy of (largely rational) civic and (substantively irrational) ethnic types. Nationalism was not merely orchestrated by states and elites. Rather, the emotional and irrational mechanisms of national identification and alienation were related to long-established cultural and religious sources, but could also be activated by short-term enmities and conflicts, which themselves were a product—at least in part—of particular political interests. Such emotional and irrational mechanisms or sources have still not been explored in sufficient detail. What does seem certain is that research into nationalism must begin anew;[33] the question of the 'old' nationalism will not, though, lose its significance or topicality, even if the 'new' nationalism has long since had a different name.

---

[32] Nora, *Les Lieux de mémoire*, 7 vols. (Paris, 1984–92).

[33] See F. Gschnitzer, R. Koselleck, B. Schönemann, and K.-F. Werner, 'Volk, Nation, Nationalismus, Masse', in O. Brunner, W. Conze, R. Koselleck (eds.), *Geschichtliche Grundbegriffe: Historisches Lexikon zur politisch-sozialen Sprache in Deutschland* (Stuttgart, 1992), 141–431. This is a pioneering piece of work which contains the most important literature. For recent work, see also D. Langewiesche, 'Nationalismus im 19. und 20. Jahrhundert: zwischen Partizipation und Aggression,' in D. Dover (ed)., *Gesprächskreis Geschichte* (Bonn, 1994).

2

France

Ethnicity and the Revolutionary Tradition

Timothy Baycroft

> France was made by France, and the fatal element of race seems to me to be completely secondary. She is the daughter of her freedom.[1]
>
> Michelet, preface to the *Histoire de France*, 1869.

France is often given as the archetypal model of the 'civic' nation-state, based upon a liberal, inclusive, voluntarist social contract of free citizens which arose out of the political thought of the Enlightenment. France was the country which gave birth to the Declaration of the Rights of Man, and which, after a prolonged struggle, later proclaimed democratic, 'revolutionary', and egalitarian principles as the foundation of the republican institutions which represented the essence of the modern French nation. To belong to the French nation, individuals did not need to be born French, but could be assimilated into it through an acceptance of the principles of the Republic encapsulated in the revolutionary slogan 'liberty, equality, fraternity'. Such an interpretation can be found in the discourse of later nineteenth-century republican nation-builders, such as Ernest Renan, who proclaimed in 1882 that 'it is France's glory to have proclaimed through the French Revolution that a nation exists by itself'.[2] Nineteenth-century republican politicians hoped to secure support for their anti-monarchist position by associating themselves with this vision of the revolutionary heritage, which has also appeared in the work of later historians as indicating the fundamentally 'civic' character of French nationalism which grew

Research that informs this account was generously supported by the Arts and Humanities Research Board (AHRB).

[1] 'La France a fait la France, et l'élément fatal de race m'y semble secondaire. Elle est fille de sa liberté.'

[2] Ernest Renan, 'Qu'est-ce qu'une nation?' 'What is a nation?' in *Qu'est-ce qu'une nation? Et autres essais politiques* (Paris, 1992).

out of the revolutionary tradition.[3] While not denying the existence of a second tradition of reactionary or right-wing nationalism which is not fundamentally civic, republicans considered the contribution of such thinking to mainstream French nationalism peripheral, compared with the civic, republican, and revolutionary visions of the nation. This chapter will examine both traditions, first to see whether the 'opposition' nationalism of the right was as successfully marginalized as has occasionally been supposed, and secondly to examine the revolutionary republican tradition itself, looking for the ethnocultural components within it, to come to a final assessment about the appropriateness of the civic model for understanding French nationalism during the long nineteenth century.

THE REVOLUTIONARY NATION

The origins of the civic vision of the French nation go back to the Revolution itself. Inspired by the ideas of Enlightenment thinkers such as Rousseau, the revolutionary political and intellectual elite sought to put into practice new political theories which would destroy the *ancien régime*'s 'natural' (or God-ordained) political order based on a hierarchical society, replacing it with a new 'social contract' between all the equal citizens of the French nation. One of the first organized political groups to defend these ideas was the 'patriots' of the Estates General, led by Talleyrand, fighting for equality among each of the three orders that were supposed to represent France (clergy, nobility, and commoners). Since sovereignty and legitimacy ought to be derived from the nation as a whole, they argued, a single representative body would be more appropriate. Writers such as the Abbé Sieyès rebaptized the Third Estate the 'National Assembly', and went so far as to exclude the nobility and the clergy from his conception of the French nation, in which there could only be equal citizens.[4] The Revolutionaries of 1789 were not fighting against a 'foreign' tyrannical ruler, but against what they considered to be an unfair political system. They did not understand the oppressed French nation seeking reforms via revolution as an ethnic or cultural entity, nor (as Marxists would later do) in terms of social class. For them it was first and foremost a legal and philosophical entity, that principle from which sovereignty should be derived, as defined in The Declaration of the Rights of Man and the Citizen.[5] This position was not incompatible with beliefs in common descent or ancestry, but such ethnic or racial thinking was simply taken for granted, and therefore neither stressed nor often even mentioned in revolutionary

[3] See for example M. Agulhon, *The French Republic 1789–1992*, trans. Antonia Nevill (Oxford, 1990), 4–6.

[4] E. J. Sieyès, *Qu'est-ce que le Tiers État?* ('What is the Third Estate?') (Paris, 1982). Originally published January 1789.

[5] See article III of The Declaration of the Rights of Man and the Citizen, August 1789.

writings. It is only to later thinkers projecting backwards that the two types of nation might have appeared incompatible.

Due to repeated shifts of power internally, as well as the destabilizing external pressure of a war with several major European powers at once, these revolutionary ideals of the legal nation of citizens were only partly achieved during the years immediately following 1789. Universal suffrage, for example, would not be put into practice for men until 1848, and for women until 1944. Numerous short-lived Revolutionary governments tried to consolidate the political system, falling one after the other, and giving way completely after a few troubled years, first to the empire created following Napoleon Bonaparte's *coup d'état*, and finally to the restoration of the monarchy following French military defeats in 1814 and 1815. Nevertheless, several of the principles behind the Revolution which endured, such as the abolition of privileges by birth and the recognition of individual equality before the law, enshrined in the Napoleonic Civil Code, went on to become symbols of the republican vision of the French nation, heralded as victories of the revolutionary years. A further legacy of the revolutionary and Napoleonic wars, with their radicalizing effect upon French domestic politics, was the increased 'national' sentiment among the population, engendered after years of the masses being called upon to fight in defence of the nation.[6]

Once the Revolution had been defeated, the republicans were forced into opposition, and the remainder of the nineteenth century saw innumerable conflicts, both peaceful and violent, in which republicans sought to cultivate nationalist sentiment in order to further their political aims.[7] Republican politicians like the young Adolphe Thiers or Gambetta, hero of the National Defence in the winter of 1870–1, continually sought to depict the French nation as the free association of willing citizens in an inclusive national body, and the history of the Revolution in terms of its emphasis on individual liberty and equality.[8] This was clearly a part of their political agenda: in seeking to secure a lasting republican constitution for the country, they depicted a decided link between civic republicanism and the universal and eternal French nation and character, in this way hoping to discredit any monarchical or imperial regime as in some way or another opposed to the nation they ostensibly ruled.

The earliest historians of the French nation were also among the early nation builders, contributing to this representation of the republican national tradition, presenting French history in such a way as to highlight the voluntarist character of France's identity. Reference to the ideals and conflicts of the French Revolution

---

[6] For more on the impact of war on the growth of national sentiment during the Revolutionary years see Michael Jeismann, Chapter 1 and Jörn Leonhard, Chapter 12 in this volume.

[7] For a good history of the political struggles in nineteenth-century France, see R. Tombs, *France 1814–1914* (London, 1996).

[8] See P. Pilbeam, 'Revolution, Restoration(s) and Beyond: Changes, Continuities and the Enduring Legacies of 1789', in M. S. Alexander (ed.), *French History since Napoleon* (London, 1999), 31–58.

was almost unavoidable for the proponents of the republican cause in France. More than one historian (Michelet), politician (Thiers), or literary figure (Lamartine, Victor Hugo) associated with the republican cause wrote his History of the Revolution seeking to find in it the justification of his vision of the French nation, its nature, and its mission.[9] Michelet, Ernest Renan, and numerous others also wrote more general histories of France which themselves contributed to the notion that France was what we now term a 'civic' nation. Renan claimed that the consent of the people in the formation of a nation should be true for all nations, that the principle of nationality was markedly different from the principle of race.[10] The fact that these early historians were not only republicans themselves, but clearly believed in their political mission as historians to contribute to the republican cause through their presentation of France and French history, at the very least leads to questions regarding their conclusions about the fundamental nature of the French nation.

When the Second Empire of Napoleon III collapsed in military defeat and the Third Republic was founded out of the wreckage in 1870, the subsequent republican leadership was able to use the power of the state to solidify the republican vision of a French nation characterized primarily by its civic heritage. Using François Furet's metaphor it could be said that 'the French Revolution was coming into port'.[11] The historical vision of France presented by those discussed above was used as a basis for the primary school curriculum which was at the heart of the republican school project of Jules Ferry in the early 1880s. Overtly designed to integrate the masses into the national life of the Republic through education, the programme included the promotion of the republican vision of an inclusive French nation based upon citizenship, equality, and the principles of the French Revolution. Historical analysis of the period has described this process as the transformation of 'Peasants into Frenchmen'.[12] According to this interpretation the bulk of the masses, the uneducated population of France, was assimilated into French national culture and gained a sense of national identity through the modernization of the communications network throughout France, the teaching of French language and history in the republican primary schools which became compulsory, secular, and free in the early 1880s, and through compulsory military service which mixed the population from the different regions together, forging a collective identity as well as increasing patriotic feeling. Although much of the original theory has been criticized or nuanced, the image has remained central to the notion that individuals from different backgrounds could be assimilated into

[9] Jules Michelet, *Histoire de la Révolution française* (1847–53); Adolphe Thiers, *Histoire de la Révolution* (1840); Alphonse de Lamartine, *Histoire de Girondins* (1847); Victor Hugo, *Quatre-vingt treize* (1874).   [10] See Renan, 'Qu'est-ce qu'une nation?'
[11] F. Furet, *La Révolution française*, vol. iv of *Histoire de France* (Paris, 1988), 517. Furet is another example of a historian whose work supports the notion of a 'civic' French nation.
[12] E. Weber, *Peasants into Frenchmen: The Modernisation of Rural France 1870–1914* (Stanford, Calif., 1976).

the French nation if they freely chose to do so.[13] Thus the idea that the French nation was characterized by the free association of individual citizens, and therefore fundamentally civic in character, was perpetuated by successive republican governments in the latter decades of the nineteenth century, as well as by mainstream historical analysis of the whole of the nineteenth century, from the revolutionary years through to the Third Republic.

A crucial dimension in the ability of the republicans to have their vision of the nation more widely adopted was the agency of the highly centralized state. Already relatively centralized during the *ancien régime*, significant institutional reform during the revolutionary and Napoleonic years had bequeathed to France a highly centralized bureaucracy so that whatever the constitutional arrangement, few powers were left outside the control of the central state. Domestic conflicts were therefore encouraged to grow and develop at the national level between alternative political visions for the entire nation, rather than between regional and national elites or institutions, or around questions of decentralization. In the latter part of the century, the republican state used the ever increasing means at its disposal to further the development of its vision of the nation, and extend nationalist sentiment in the way discussed above.

THE REACTIONARY NATION

Opposed to the official republican 'civic' nationalism, one can also find traces in the nineteenth century of a second nationalist tradition, which could be called reactionary. Surfacing at different times in slightly different guises, it was more directly linked to the monarchy, to the Catholic church, and to traditional culture as the key elements of the French nation in a way which more resembles the ethnic or cultural model of nationalism. Conceiving France primarily in terms of the 'eldest daughter of the church' left little space for non-Catholics within this embodiment of the French nation. The associated traditional, rural (often local) culture, and folk-type traditions are also not of the sort which encourage penetration from outside, or the kinds of voluntaristic, cosmopolitan symbolism normally associated with civic nationalism. Because of the perpetual political struggles during the nineteenth century between republicanism, monarchism (in its two forms of legitimism and Orleanism), and Bonapartism, and the fact that it was the republicans who 'won' in the sense that from 1870 onwards France

---

[13] For more recent analyses of the process, see for example C. Ford, *Creating the Nation in Provincial France: Religion and Political Identity in Brittany* (Princeton, 1993); B. Singer, *Village Notables in Nineteenth-Century France: Priests, Mayors, Schoolmasters* (Albany, 1983); J. R. Lehning, *Peasant and French: Cultural Contact in Rural France During the Nineteenth Century* (Cambridge, 1995); T. Baycroft, 'Changing Identities in the Franco-Belgian Borderland in the Nineteenth and Twentieth Centuries', *French History*, 13 (1999), 417–38; and P. Sahlins, *Boundaries: The Making of France and Spain in the Pyrenees* (Berkeley, 1989).

had a republican constitution, such an exclusivist vision of the French nation was as often as not on the margins of the political culture.[14]

Although such a vision of the French nation was held by those peripheral to the domination of politics, this did not mean that it did not have a great deal of impact within wider French society, nor that the republicans themselves were not influenced by the kind of nationalism that was used as a weapon by their political opponents. The popular success of the press led by, for example, Charles Maurras in the 1890s shows the actual presence of such thinking among the wider public. A movement created in 1898 by Maurice Pujo, 'l'Action Française', was first supported by the radical left which had refused Dreyfusism and went on to become royalist after Maurras joined in 1899. His vision scorned the inclusivist dimensions of the revolutionary republican tradition, focusing much more instead on local people and their long-established village cultures as the link between the different parts of the French nation, and criticized 'the four confederate states' (Jews, Protestants, Freemasons, and foreigners) who controlled the Republic and destroyed the spirit of the nation.[15] Likewise, the success of Maurice Barrès's novel *Les Déracinés*, depicting a group of 'uprooted' provincial young men spiritually destroyed by the 'rootless' Kantian (and hence foreign) philosophy taught in the Parisian 'grandes écoles' controlled by the republicans, went far beyond reactionary circles.[16]

More generally, the appeal of anti-rationalist, anti-liberal nationalist thinking grew rapidly towards the end of the nineteenth century.[17] The itinerary of the socialist poet and journalist Charles Péguy is a good illustration of this phenomenon, the potential overlap between the two visions of the French nation. He started his political life as a Dreyfusard, praising the glory of the primary schoolteachers, the 'black hussars of the Republic', symbols of the republican assimilationist school project, and went on to die a fervent warmonger in 1914, a hero of the nationalist right, claiming 'blessed are those who died for their little corner of land'.[18] François Mitterrand, the first socialist president of the Fifth Republic, had been an avid reader of Barrès in his youth, demonstrating how his vision of the French nation had been deeply influenced by both of France's nationalist traditions. These examples show the potential proximity between these two nationalisms and suggests that the radical opposition presented in much of the literature may partly be a later reconstruction,

[14] For a more specific distinction between two types of reactionary nationalism, in the early and late nineteenth century, see J. McMillan, 'Introduction: Republic and Nation in the *belle époque*', in J. McMillan (ed.), *Modern France 1880–2002* (Oxford, 2003).

[15] For more on the Action Française and Maurras, see R. Gildea, *The Past in French History* (New Haven, 1994), 309–11.   [16] Maurice Barrès, *Les Déracinés* (1897).

[17] See for example R. Tombs, 'Culture and the Intellectuals', in McMillan (ed.), *Modern France*, 181. This trend was pronounced in France, but was Europe-wide.

[18] 'Heureux ceux qui sont morts pour quatre coins de terre'. Charles Péguy, 'Eve', *Quatorzième cahier de la quinzième série* (28 December 1913) in *Œuvres poétiques complètes* (Paris, 1957), 1028.

and that the boundaries between the two French nationalist traditions should not be seen as so clear cut. It is certain that the republican national tradition partly included an overt distancing of 'their France' from these ideas of the far right, presenting them as, if not anti-French, at least as marginal to the true essence of the (republican) French nation. However, the impact of both types of thinking was quite widespread, and an examination of several key elements of French identity will show just how far ethno-cultural elements of what has been labelled reactionary nationalism influenced even traditional republican nationalism.

ATTRIBUTES OF THE FRENCH NATION

Although not stressed by the republican nation-builders or historians themselves and thus picked up by their adversaries in the political arena, it was not only this reactionary type of nationalism which contained elements identifiable as a part of the ethno-cultural type of nationalism. During the debates and texts dealing with citizenship during the revolutionary years the concept of *jus sanguinis*—nationality passing automatically to a child from its parents—was already present as a means of determining nationality. While there were other parallel ways to become a French citizen, from birth in France to naturalization, in the Napoleonic Civil Code of 1803, the primary definition was ethnic: a Frenchman was anyone 'born of a French father'.[19] Indeed, much of the ethnic definition of nationality throughout Western Europe in the nineteenth century actually had its origin in this French legal text, carried throughout the continent on the backs of the Napoleonic armies.[20]

A more well-known case of ethno-cultural nationalism in France is the great emphasis placed upon the French language from within the revolutionary republican tradition. From the report of the Abbé Gregoire during the Revolution calling for uniformity of language throughout France through to the republican schools of Jules Ferry during the Third Republic, all of the French elites agreed that it was imperative for the members of the nation to become fluent in French, the language of the Enlightenment. While on the one hand the model of teaching the national language to the people in order for them to participate fully in national life can be seen as a part of the open, civic model whereby individuals can choose (or not) to be integrated, on the other hand the centrality of such a cultural characteristic in the national mythos corresponds far more closely to the ethno-cultural model of the nation. The destruction of local languages by the French state-sponsored schoolteachers, although it has certainly been exaggerated

---

[19] For a full discussion, see P. Weil, *Qu'est-ce qu'un Français? Histoire de la nationalité française depuis la Révolution* (Paris, 2002).

[20] For more on the legal definition of citizenship, see the Conclusion to this volume, and for an example of the concept's spread through Europe, see David Laven's chapter on Italy.

in its efficiency, has nevertheless been at least as drastic as any other such programmes in so-called ethno-centric nations or imperiums.[21]

Even in its most civic representation, a personal identification with the main thrusts of French history by every citizen was central to the republican concept of the French nation. As discussed briefly above, the republican schools of the late nineteenth century also set out to teach this national history to the masses. While much of it concentrated on the republican tradition of Enlightenment and citizenship, references were also made to an ethnic tradition. The history textbooks used in the schools of the Third Republic which later came to be credited with the spread of French national identity throughout the countryside often began with the famous phrase 'Our ancestors the Gauls' in an attempt to link France with the pre-Roman tribe which inhabited the same territory.[22] Many of the pre-revolutionary symbols of the French nation often associated with reactionary nationalism, such as Joan of Arc or the monarchy itself, were also incorporated positively into republican national histories, insofar as they increased the longevity, prestige, and greatness of the French nation.[23] In this way, although highlighting the civic, republican tradition, the republican history curriculum nevertheless made use of ethnic and religious symbols of France in its classic representation. This ethno-cultural component of French history necessarily posed limits upon the civic openness and ability to integrate the nation via identification with its history.

In addition to elements of history and language, other cultural characteristics can be found within the republican tradition. Indeed, the presence of local cultures (with the exception of patois or regional languages) was very much a part of the republican model and not at all the unique preserve of the marginal right. The same school textbooks teaching national history were full of the value of localities and local cultures. Such examples as *La Tour de France par deux enfants* praised the diversity of the different regions of France, and children were encouraged to love their nation in the same way that they loved their village, for indeed the two were one and the same.[24] This idealization of local culture as a part of the national included local costume, culinary traditions, folklore, and rural patterns of work and settlement, and conforms to the cultural model of nationalism. Much of the

[21] See Brian Vick's Chapter 8 for more comparative elements of language use and education between France and other European nations.

[22] On the mythical place of the Gauls within French national history see the conference proceedings *Nos ancêtres les Gaulois* (Clermand-Ferrand, 1982). The phrase remained in use in French schoolbooks well beyond the Second World War.

[23] Joan of Arc inspired works by republican historians, see for example Jules Michelet, *Jeanne d'Arc* (Paris, 1853) reprinted in *Jeanne d'Arc et autres textes* (Paris, 1974); Henri Martin, *Jeanne Darc* [*sic*] *et le conseil de Charles VII* (Paris, 1856); Charles Péguy, *Le Mystère de la charité de Jeanne d'arc* (1904); or Anatole France, *La Vie de Jeanne d'Arc* (Paris, 1908). Even Léon Gambetta declared himself to be devoted to Joan of Arc. See also M. Winock, 'Jeanne d'Arc', in P. Nora (ed.), *Les Lieux de mémoiré*, 3 vols., vol. iii (Paris, 1997), 4427–73.

[24] See A-M. Thiesse, *Ils apprenaient la France: l'exaltation des régions dans le discours patriotique* (Paris, 1997).

work which has been done on national collective memory in France has been devoted to the study of such national symbols. One of the best examples is the large collection edited by Pierre Nora entitled *The Realms of Memory (Les Lieux de mémoire)*, which contains 132 essays on the cultural construction of French nationalism, each examining a particular national image and its history. The conclusion is to suggest that their place in the development of French identity has been great, and very much of the cultural sort described in the classic works on ethno-cultural nations. Another example is the work of Stéphane Gerson, which suggests that the cult of local memories demonstrates the willingness of the French republican left to use the symbolism of local cultures, which was an area of appeal across the political spectrum.[25] As mentioned above, regionalism, insofar as it existed in France, was solely in the cultural domain and the preserve of local antiquarian societies and the like, rather than associated with historical regional institutions, representative or otherwise, such as were of great importance in the development of nationalism elsewhere in Europe, as demonstrated by Maiken Umbach in Chapter 4. Thus nation-builders sought to embrace regional cultural traditions as evidence of a quality of diversity within the nation, perfectly compatible with French nationalism, but were not burdened with negotiations with regional institutions which had already been swept away during the revolutionary years.[26]

Turning more directly to the question of ethnicity or race, it is true that within the revolutionary republican tradition there are relatively few direct and overt references to 'the French race'. The term which is more likely to be used is 'the French people', often referring to that part of the population which was not noble. At the time of the Revolution, some French nationalists subscribed to the view that all nations were kin, especially insofar as the struggle was perceived to be against absolutism. This did not entirely prevent the use of ethnic symbolism even at the time, as for example in verse three of the 'Marseillaise', the fear is expressed that 'hoards of foreigners' would come and dictate the law in the French 'homeland'.[27] By the mid-nineteenth century, and certainly after the founding of the Third Republic in 1870, the conception of the French people defined against others, while not often employing the terminology of 'race', was nevertheless couched in terms which correspond to the ethnic model of nationalism. Particularly following the defeat in the Franco-Prussian War (1870–1), images of Germany as the enemy, and the German people against the French people were common.

---

[25] S. Gerson, *The Pride of Place: Local Memories and Political Culture in Nineteenth-Century France* (Ithaca, NY, 2003), 277–8.

[26] For more on the mechanics of this process, see T. Baycroft, *Culture, Identity and Nationalism: French Flanders in the Nineteenth and Twentieth Centuries*, Royal Historical Society New Studies in History series (London, 2004). See also Michael Jeismann's chapter for more on the way in which both culture and politics can take on religious qualities through radicalization.

[27] The text is 'Quoi des cohortes étrangères, Feraient la loi dans nos foyers,' and refers at least in part also to the fact that it was foreign monarchs and troops which were waging war against France in order to re-establish the monarchy.

An ethnic conception of the French nation comes even more clearly to the fore when one examines French colonial expansion and the rhetoric of the French Empire. Such republicans as Jules Ferry advocated colonial expansion for 'humanitarian' reasons, to help to spread Enlightened French thinking through-out the world.[28] On the one hand, Ferry and the other members of what became known as the 'colonial party', a cross-party grouping of those who favoured greater colonial expansion, used a language of inclusion and assimilation similar to that which was applied to the various regional subcultures within France. On the other hand, what they were assimilating in the colonies was not elements of the 'French people' but 'foreign races', as distinguished from the French race.[29] Based on the scientific concepts of race which became more widespread in the second half of the nineteenth century, the concept of distinct peoples remained present in republican attitudes, and lay at the base of much colonial legislation. The overall political, legal, and administrative structure, according to much of mainstream republican thinking, was theoretically supposed to make no distinc-tion between the motherland and the colonies; all would form a part of the single French nation once French culture and political values had been sufficiently accepted in the colonized territory. This may have been true in the rhetoric, although in practice colonies and their populations were treated quite differently from regions of metropolitan France. The first difference was the semantic dis-tinction between French nationality and French citizenship in the colonies. The 'indigenous people' in the colonies were French subjects, had French nationality, but were not entitled to French citizenship, by which was meant the rights, privileges, and duties inscribed in the Civil Code.[30] So, for example in French Algeria, even when it was divided into three departments as an approximation of the administrative substructure of metropolitan France, the majority of the Muslim population remained excluded from the main benefits of French citizen-ship. Naturalization, or the acquisition of the full rights of citizenship, was difficult to obtain, and even those who were considered 'foreign' but still European, such as Italians, had an easier time obtaining it. To reflect this situation and preserve the ethno-cultural distinction in legal terms, specific laws often had to be drafted especially for the colonies with that in mind, with the word race even occasionally making an appearance in French legal texts.[31] The repeated exclusion of the indigenous peoples of the French colonies from citizenship is the most

[28] Jules Ferry, speech to the Chamber of Deputies, 28 July 1885, reproduced in G. Pervillé, *De l'Empire Français à la décolonization* (Paris, 1991), 47–8. See also J. Ganiage, *L'Expansion coloniale de la France sous la Troisième République 1871–1914* (Paris, 1968), 47.

[29] See for example Alfred Rambaud, *La France coloniale* (1886), quoted in C.-R. Ageron, *France coloniale ou parti coloniale?* (Paris, 1978), 194.

[30] L. Blévis, 'Droit colonial algérien de la citoyenneté: conciliation illusoire entre des principes républicains et une logique d'occupation coloniale (1865–1947)', in *La Guerre d'Algérie au miroir des décolonisations françaises, Actes du colloque international* (Saint-Denis, 2000), 87–103.

[31] See E. Saada, 'Citoyens et sujets de l'Empire Français: les usages du droit en situation coloniale', *Genèses*, 53 (2003), 4–24.

striking example of the ethno-cultural model of nationalism in nineteenth-century France.

'THE OTHER'

The character and nature of the French nation and its ethnic or civic components can also be approached through an examination of the status of 'the other' in France during the nineteenth century. It is often as revealing to analyse who is excluded from the nation and for what reasons, as to come up with a positive definition of national membership. The most obvious examples are those other nations, particularly those which can be seen as enemies, such as Germany after 1870, but such enmities or outsiders are common to all nations, and reveal little about the character of a given nation. 'Others' are not restricted to those outside of the nation, however, and it is those within but who are nevertheless excluded from the nation who will reveal more about the civic character of a given nation. In addition to the indigenous populations of the French colonies referred to above, which remained excluded from French citizenship (but not nationality) throughout the nineteenth century, two further case studies need to be examined here: first the way in which immigrants were treated and assimilated (or not), and secondly the presence of anti-Semitism in French society and the position of Jews within the French nation.

The capacity of France to integrate or assimilate individuals, including immigrants, into the national body was a point of honour and pride for the French establishment. French society had the highest proportion of immigrants of any European nation throughout the nineteenth century, with the exception of Switzerland, and republicans claimed that France was the country which, rather than scorning its immigrants and excluding them from the national community, was able to integrate them.[32] Indeed, many individuals were able to assimilate into French national culture, especially among the educated after a second generation, but several limits can be found to this utopian vision of a civic nation. In border regions it is clear that the French regarded those across the border, to say nothing of those from further afield, as distinctly 'other'.[33] Within working-class communities, friction and occasionally violence broke out periodically between 'French' workers and 'foreign' workers, with the number of incidents increasing throughout the nineteenth century.[34] In some cases, groups of immigrants remained isolated for several generations, remaining 'other' for the French workers. This may, of course, have been a purely cultural distinction in certain cases, but could

[32] Tombs, *France 1814–1914*, 324.

[33] See for example P. Lawrence, T. Baycroft, and C. Grohmann, ' "Degrees of Foreignness" and the Construction of Identity in French Border Regions during the Interwar Period', *Contemporary European History*, 10 (2001), 51–71.

[34] See G. Noiriel, 'Français et étrangers', in Nora (ed.), *Les Lieux de mémoire*, ii. 2440–3.

also be ethnic or racial, fed by the regular arrival of new immigrants to the separate community. Difficulties in complete integration were particularly experienced by non-white immigrants, who, although relatively limited during the nineteenth century (compared with the twentieth), were nevertheless unable to gain the same degree of assimilation into mainstream French society and culture as others could. The fate of French soldiers from the colonial empire and the use of racial rhetoric during the First World War are good illustrations.[35]

France's record with respect to the inclusion of its Jewish community within ideas of the nation during the long nineteenth century is mixed. On the one hand it is true that within the secular republican tradition a place was made for Jews among the elite of the French nation which would have been unlikely, if not unimaginable in other European nations. The republican elite sought on many occasions to defend freedom of religion, and with it the complementary idea that different religious backgrounds should not be grounds for exclusion. This was not mere rhetoric, for Jews did penetrate elite circles in nineteenth-century France, and from as early as the citizenship laws of 1790–1, Jews had recognized legal rights within the French nation.

The fact that a significant segment of the republican elite sought to defend Alfred Dreyfus in the late 1890s is a further illustration of the extent to which the principle of inclusion was central to the republican position. A few years after Dreyfus, a Jewish army officer, had been convicted of treason in 1894, it was brought to the attention of some members of the Chamber of Deputies and the Senate that there were grounds to reopen the case, as his guilt was far from clear. The resulting political pressure put upon the government and the army to reopen the case blew up into a huge national scandal, with the army resenting interference, and the popular press siding primarily against 'the Jewish traitor'. Those defending Dreyfus were a minority among the elite, but they refused to give up and ended up victorious, claiming the whole as a victory for justice and the law.

Such examples from among the elite do not belie the fact that a significant popular anti-Semitism underlay this republican gloss on the French nation, nor that anti-Semitism could be found within the republican elite. The popular republican historian Michelet was among those who considered that Jews were not a part of the French nation, because 'their fatherland was the London stock exchange'.[36] In spite of clear evidence of his innocence, the majority of the population remained critical of Dreyfus, and the anti-Semitic press grew dramatically in the decades leading up to the First World War, fuelled by the affair. Thus in spite of the rhetoric to the contrary, France was not simply a nation which could include anyone who wished to join, as ethno-cultural concepts of France went far

---

[35] See L. Dornel, 'Les Usages du racialisme, le cas de la main d'œuvre coloniale en France pendant la Première Guerre Mondiale', *Genèses*, 20 (1995), 48–72, and A. Becker, *Oubliés de la Grande Guerre* (Paris, 1998), 317–25.   [36] Michelet, quoted in Tombs, *France 1814–1914*, 313.

deeper than the opposition reactionary right, but could be found within the republican conception of the nation, as well as within the mainstream population.

CONCLUSION

It is clear from this analysis that any understanding of French nationalism throughout the long nineteenth century primarily as an archetype of the 'civic' model must be either extremely oversimplified or derived in a large part from republican rhetoric emerging from their conflicts with their political opponents. In spite of the historic links between nationalism and a republicanism which wanted to be seen as founded upon liberty and equality through citizenship, French nationalist rhetoric included much that can only be understood as conforming to the ethno-cultural model of nationalism. In part originating in the right-wing anti-republican tradition, and far more influential than it is often given credit for at the level of popular opinion, elements of ethno-cultural exclusivity and xenophobia can be found even at the heart of the republican national project, coming to the surface whenever the republican elites were confronted with the concrete political realities of the nineteenth century such as war, immigration, or colonialism. While it was possible in some circumstances to integrate the French nation from the outside, obvious and real limits can be found to this openness. It was also the case that one could be born French, and adhesion to republican principles associated with citizenship was never a necessity to integrate the nation. By the outbreak of the First World War, the republican regime was more secure in itself, and foreign enemies seemed the greater threat. Far from diminishing, representations of the French nation in terms of ethnicity and common cultural heritage were extremely widespread at that time. No wonder then that Romain Roland, exiled from his country at the time, exclaimed bitterly in 1915 'The idol of race or of civilization or of Latinity . . . which the intellectuals so greatly abuse, does not satisfy me.'[37]

French nationalism was born out of the French Revolution, and the numerous conflicts which followed throughout the nineteenth century over what form the revolutionary legacy—institutional, political, or representational—would take. Such conflicts involved numerous further revolutions and regime changes, external wars and colonial expansion as a diversion, as well as significant intellectual and political campaigning over different visions of the French nation, all against the backdrop of an extremely centralized and increasingly powerful state institutional structure. Within these conflicts, the eventually dominant republicans clearly sought to present the French nation as essentially 'civic'. This was a part of their political campaign throughout the nineteenth century, a collective construction of a civic national past overtly designed to further the ends of the republican

---

[37] Romain Roland, *Au dessus de la mêlée* (Neuchâtel, 1915).

political community.[38] So the foundation for the civic vision of the French nation had already been laid in the nineteenth century, as the way the republicans wanted the French nation to be seen and thought of, and a rhetorical tool to sell republicanism to the wider public within the broader context of internal conflict over regime and state control. It was by no means incompatible with a variety of ethnic discourses of the nation which formed a subtext to French nationalism of all varieties throughout the century.[39]

[38] See Gildea, *The Past in French History*, 10–12 for an excellent explanation of the theory and history of this kind of collective memory at the service of political communities.

[39] See the Conclusion to this volume for more on the emergence of nationalism from within a structure of conflict.

3

Germany

Ethnic Nationalism par excellence?

Stefan Berger

INTRODUCTION

In existing typologies of European nationalism Germany tends to figure as a key example where the nation was defined predominantly in ethno-cultural terms.[1] Following Hans Kohn's influential book on *Nationalism, its Meaning and History* (1955), many scholars have argued that nationalism changed its meaning significantly when it travelled from West to East in the course of the nineteenth century. The Western idea of the nation was perceived as predominantly voluntarist, culturally inclusive, and founded on liberal political principles. Eastern Europe, by contrast, was haunted by ethnic nationalisms, culturally exclusive, and politically authoritarian. Germany, geographically situated in the middle of Europe, occupied a middling position with regard to its national self-images. Most commentators, however, tended to emphasize that it was already tainted by the Eastern European nationalist virus. From Helmuth Plessner's book on *The Belated Nation* (1935) to Liah Greenfeld's *Nationalism: Five Roads to Modernity* (1992) German nationalism has been described as primarily rooted in factors such as blood, common traditions, language, and religion rather than politics. In this chapter I will question any neat delineation between a good liberal, cosmopolitan, civic, and political nationalism and a bad antiliberal, xenophobic, ethnic, and cultural nationalism. Instead, I will underline the fluidity, plurality, and contestedness of German nationalism in the long nineteenth century.

Having traced the emergence of liberal nationalism in the eighteenth century, I will briefly analyse the deep impact of the French Revolution of 1789 on the historical-cultural turn of the national imagination in the early nineteenth century. As the revolution of 1848 remains a major watershed in the history of

---

[1] For an overview of research traditions, agendas, and lacunae see U. v. Hirschhausen and J. Leonhard (eds.), *Nationalismen in Europa: West- und Osteuropa im Vergleich* (Göttingen, 2001).

liberal nationalism, its impact on constructions of the nation will also have to be discussed at some length. Subsequently I will comment on the importance of national 'others' for definitions of Germanness. Both internal and external 'enemies of the nation' played a crucial role in self-definitions of Germany. The Imperial German nation, which emerged in 1871, was in many respects quite different from the one imagined by the revolutionaries of 1848, and we will discuss the diverse attempts to 'make Germans' in the Kaiserreich. We shall pay particular attention to the gendering of the national discourse, the increasing ethnicization and militarization of citizenship, and the importance of federal constructions of the nation. Finally we will comment on the rise of *völkisch* nationalism before 1914.

Discursive constructions of the nation are much older than the nineteenth century. Key ideas and tropes can be traced back to the humanists' concern with the nation in the sixteenth century.[2] From the sixteenth right through to the eighteenth century ethnic and civic elements could already be found side by side. An allegedly liberal and tolerant Enlightenment discourse of the nation did not exist. Rather it was already infused with considerable doses of xenophobia and aggressive notions of cultural superiority.[3] Much of this chapter will be concerned with the question whether we can claim the reverse for the nineteenth century. Did many of the more cosmopolitan and liberal elements of eighteenth-century nationalism survive into the nineteenth?

LIBERAL NATIONALISM AND THE STATE: POLITICAL AND CULTURAL DEFINITIONS OF THE NATION

As early as the 1720s a strong indigenous liberal-democratic national tradition existed in the German lands. Especially in the south-western states an intense reception of British constitutional thought led to a strong social movement. It incorporated as many as 10 per cent of the total population, demanding freedom of the press, the rule of law, constitutional government, and greater political participation in the affairs of the state.[4] Liberal and democratic nationalists supported the American War of Independence and greeted the French Revolution as the beginning of the long-awaited age of freedom. The vast majority of liberals were soon disillusioned by the way in which the revolutionaries drowned that freedom in blood. However, they rescued their core liberal-national beliefs from the fiasco of the French Revolution by turning to history and culture. Germanic freedoms, they argued, were not rooted in the abstract universal ideals of the French Revolution.

---

[2] J. Helmrath, U. Muhlack, and G. Walther (eds.), *Diffusion des Humanismus: Studien zur nationalen Geschichtsschreibung europäischer Humanisten* (Göttingen, 2002).

[3] H.-M. Blitz, *Aus Liebe zum Vaterland: Die deutsche Nation im 18. Jahrhundert* (Hamburg, 2000).

[4] J. Riethmüller, *Die Anfänge des demokratischen Denkens in Deutschland* (Neuried, 2001).

They were anchored in the past of the Germanic tribes roaming Germanic forests and defending their Germanic freedom against Roman invaders.[5] Reference to history and culture legitimized demands for greater political participation in the imagined national community.

Those who did the imagining came, by and large, from a new social class of state employees—judges, civil servants, professors, and teachers. They did not fit the traditional estates-based social order. It was among such 'marginal men' (Elie Kedourie) that nationalism found its early standard bearers. A highly educated public in a highly literate society ensured a high market value of the national topic. At a time of great socio-economic and political upheaval after 1793 nationalism provided orientation and new perspectives. More specifically, it allowed nationalists to demand a greater say in the affairs of the state. The 'marginal men' were staking out their claim to become more central. The key apologists for the nation in the late eighteenth and early nineteenth century, such as Johann Gottfried Herder and Johann Gottlieb Fichte, relied heavily on culture, language, literature, history, geography, climate, customs, and religion to construct national characters of Germans and others. Germans, they argued, had to be taught the nation. The idea of a national education was popular throughout the nineteenth century as were attempts to standardize and codify the German languages.[6] If a specific national culture was inherent in the national character and in need of development, then national feeling could easily be constructed as something that could not be acquired but something that one was already born with. It was a priori to any form of political choice. Herder, Fichte, and most other ideologues of the national idea in the late eighteenth and early nineteenth century did not define the nation ethnically, but their emphasis on culture lent itself to later ethnic constructions of the nation.

Eighteenth- and nineteenth-century nationalists, like Fichte, Arndt, and Jahn, bemoaned the absence of state-driven processes of nationalization. Hence they sought to create a stronger (nation-) state. In the Holy Roman Empire the state had not been entirely absent from nationalization processes,[7] but given the weakness of central government in the Altes Reich, any attempts at nationalization had to be significantly less effective than in the more centralized nation-states of France and England. In the territorial states of the German Confederation after 1815 state-building became a prime task, but these efforts were made at state and not at national level. Right up to 1871 terms such as 'nation' and 'patriot' referred either to the Reich/Bund or the territorial states or even city-states, such as Hamburg.

[5] J. Echternkamp, *Der Aufstieg des deutschen Nationalismus 1770–1840* (Frankfurt am Main, 1998), 149–62.

[6] On the relationship between languages and national identity politics in Europe see also Brian Vick's chapter.

[7] G. Schmidt, *Geschichte des Alten Reiches: Staat und Nation in der frühen Neuzeit 1495–1806* (Munich, 1999).

Before the establishment of the nation-state, the national idea, whichever territorial shape it took, was not primarily propagated by state initiatives, but through a dense network of civic associations, where the new middle classes practised a new kind of sociability. Gymnasts, choral societies, historical societies, shooting clubs, citizens' guards, town guards, self-help associations, and student fraternities (*Burschenschaften*) mobilized precisely those social strata which saw in the national principle a powerful means to demand a greater say in the affairs of the state. In their voluntary associations they already practised the kind of participatory democratic processes that they wished to introduce at state level as well. Members of these associations, regardless of their social status, tended to address each other with the familiar 'Du' rather than the more formal 'Sie'. It was the most direct expression of a strong social levelling that was characteristic of these voluntary associations. Everyone was equal within the boundaries of the association, just as everyone was imagined equal within the boundaries of the future nation-state. Especially armed civil organizations, which began to appear in the late eighteenth century and aimed at the maintenance of public order in towns and cities, often followed a model of a levelled middle-class society which wanted to protect itself against repression from above and revolution from below. The people had to be armed in order to protect their freedom. These associations were particularly strong between 1806 and 1820, around 1830 and then again between 1847 and 1850. All members of civil guard type organizations were formally and by law equal. It is hard to overestimate their importance for early liberalism, city republican traditions, and the formation of other bourgeois societies.[8] Of course, liberal egalitarianism had its limits: members of these civic associations were male, propertied, and highly educated. Jews were not always welcome. Inclusion was paired with exclusion. Social levelling went hand in hand with the creation of new social hierarchies.

A strong civil society soon dominated public opinion formation. Repressive legislation aimed at undermining the liberal national associationalism after 1819 (the Karlsbad decrees) could not prevent the spread of liberal nationalism. The 'marginal men' were slowly but surely moving to the centre. But a strong civil society did not necessarily produce tolerant and cosmopolitan images of the nation.[9] National festivals, such as the Wartburg one of 1817 or the Hambach one of 1832 combined aggressive anti-French feelings with demands for greater participation. Cultural and ethnic definitions of the nation continued to overlap with political and civic ones. The development of a strong civil society went hand in hand with statism. Many liberal nationalists were civil servants and as such close to the state. They abhorred any idea of conflict between state and civil society.

---

[8] R. Pröve, *Stadtgemeindlicher Republikanismus und die 'Macht des Volkes': Civile Ordnungsformationen und kommunale Leitbilder politischer Partizipation in den deutschen Staaten vom Ende des 18. Jahrhunderts bis zur Mitte des 19. Jahrhunderts* (Göttingen, 2001).

[9] F. Trentmann (ed.), *Paradoxes of Civil Society: New Perspectives on Modern German and British History* (Oxford, 2000).

The state was seen as the great impartial arbiter banishing partisan conflict and restraining the egotisms of civil society. Characteristically the German term for 'citizen'—*Staatsbürger*—included a more passive, subject-like element which was absent from the English but also from the French term—*citoyen*.[10] Civil society was imagined as working in harmony with and alongside the state. The potential interest fragmentation and pluralism of civil society frightened many liberals who saw in the state the only guarantor of a harmonious, classless, levelled middle-class society. The utopianism of the language of *Gemeinschaft* merged with a militarized authoritarianism and informed the discourse about the nation well before 1871.[11]

THE IMPACT OF 1848

The high point of German liberal nationalism during the first half of the nineteenth century came with the revolution of 1848. The constitutional debates in the Paulskirche testified to the strength of civic nationalism—with its commitment to a generous male suffrage, to the rule of law, and constitutional government. Democratic republicanism split the national movement. Most liberals shied away from questioning dynastic legitimacy and monarchical rule. But nationalism moved from the cultural sphere back to the political. Laws and freedoms were meant to constitute Germandom, not ethnicity, nor even culture. At the same time, however, the 'spring of the nations' revealed the cracks in the tolerant cosmopolitanism of German nationalism. After centuries of alleged national humiliation and weakness, many liberals were obsessed with creating a strong and powerful Germany. The Frankfurt parliamentarians justified German expansionism using both civic and ethnic notions of the nation, depending on situation and context.[12] Certainly many nationalists in 1848 used notions of a hegemonic medieval Reich to legitimate territorial demands in the present: the Netherlands, the Flemish part of Belgium, Alsace and Lorraine, the Balkans, Bohemia, Moravia, the Polish-speaking Prussian province of Posen, Trieste, and southern Tyrol were now all declared part and parcel of the German nation, even if only a minority of their population was German-speaking. A Romantic Reich ideology justified superpower dreams and extended the borders of Germany as far as possible. Tensions with many other nationalisms in Europe followed as a result.

The defeat of the 1848 revolution was only partial. Even the Prussian constitution of 1850 had considerable potential as a basis for more liberal constitutional

---

[10] J. Keane, 'Despotism and Democracy: The Origins and Development of the Distinction between Civil Society and the State', in id. (ed.), *Civil Society and the State: New European Perspectives* (New York, 1988), 63.

[11] D. Klenke, 'Nationalkriegerisches Gemeinschaftsideal als politische Religion: Zum Vereinsnationalismus der Sänger, Schützen und Turner am Vorabend der Einigungskriege', *Historische Zeitschrift*, 260 (1995), 395–448.

[12] B. Vick, *Defining Germany: The 1848 Frankfurt Parliamentarians and the National Question* (Cambridge, Mass., 2002).

government.[13] It allowed, after all, for the creation of state-wide political organizations and parties focused on parliament. The long-term democratization of the monarchical principle continued after 1848. Liberal nationalism forced the German monarchies to change and seek legitimization from the people.[14] Monarchy and nationalism had to be brought into one. Monarchism became a national ideology to placate the nationalist movement and provide an alternative anti-democratic legitimization of the nation.[15] The post-revolutionary governments across the German lands recognized that public opinion could not be repressed and concentrated on attempts to direct it instead. In particular the official press became an important means with which governments attempted to influence public opinion. The German Confederation was reconstituted but a multitude of plans were afoot to reform the Confederation. Liberals wanted it to develop from a federation of sovereign princes to a federation of the German people, or at least its male, educated, and propertied parts.

The Paulskirchen left did not simply disappear after 1849. Its members often continued to work as journalists or political activists, but they tended to become adherents of *Realpolitik*,[16] which meant, above all, the acceptance of power politics. This made them look towards the one state which was militarily powerful and capable of uniting Germany: Prussia. As the 'humiliation of Olmütz' had demonstrated, Austria was still capable of bullying Prussia into accepting its political predominance in the German Confederation. But Austria was losing ground to Prussia economically. Although its growth rates were respectable by European standards, it could not hope to compete with the extraordinary dynamism of Prussia's economic development around the middle of the nineteenth century. Furthermore Austria was caught in a national dilemma which surfaced fully for the first time during the revolution. Austria's multinational empire could not be squared with the national principle. Every move towards culturally homogeneous nation-states threatened its existence. Hence 'greater German' sentiments tended to be anti-Prussian sentiments. The more constructive suggestions for German unity came from the 'small-German' camp. The only problem for 'small-German' liberals was how to make Prussia less authoritarian and more liberal. But liberals were optimists: time, they were convinced, was on their side. Their opponents were fighting, after all, against progress.

The debates between 'greater German' and 'small-German' advocates was one which ran parallel to the question of ethnic versus civic nationalism. Both forms

[13] R. Paetau, 'Die regierenden Altliberalen und der "Ausbau" der Verfassung Preußens in der Neuen Ära (1858–1862): Reformpotential—Handlungsspielraum—Blockade', in B. Holtz and H. Spenkuch (eds.), *Preußens Weg in die politische Moderne: Verfassung—Verwaltung—politische Kultur zwischen Reform und Reformblockade* (Berlin, 2001), 169–92.

[14] A. Green, *Fatherlands: State-Building and Nationhood in Nineteenth-Century Germany* (Cambridge, 2001), 62–96.

[15] P. Burg, 'Monarchism as a National Ideology', in H. Lehmann and H. Wellenreuther (eds.), *German and American Nationalism: A Comparative Perspective* (Oxford, 1999), 71–96.

[16] C. Jansen, *Einheit, Macht und Freiheit: Die Paulskirchenlinke und die deutsche Politik in der nachrevolutionären Epoche 1849–1867* (Düsseldorf, 2000).

could be found in different mixtures in both camps. One of the most important outcomes of 1848 was one which also cannot be described in terms of civic versus ethnic nationalism. Disappointment about the limited success of the political construction of the nation led to attempts to imagine the nation in economic terms.[17] It was only after 1848 that Friedrich List's idea of the Customs Union (established in 1834) as a stepping stone on the road to national unity rose to prominence. The phenomenal rise of the national school of economics is testimony to the fact that economic acumen was now increasingly linked to notions of a German national character. 'Made in Germany' became the most influential slogan encapsulating German pride in German economic achievements.

TOWARDS THE IMPERIAL GERMAN NATION

With the beginning of the New Era in Prussia in 1858 'small-German' liberal nationalism thrived and eventually found an associational form in the National Association. At its zenith, in 1862/3, it had 20,000–25,000 members.[18] It was well supported by a dense network of liberal newspapers across Germany, but it was by no means speaking with one voice. Some of its supporters imagined Germany to be created by a popular movement from below along the lines of 1848. Many still regarded the 1849 democratic constitution of the Paulskirche as the ideal. Others abhorred the mobilization of a mass movement and argued for closer cooperation with the Prussian government in a common endeavour to unite Germany. Many liberals had come to fear the masses. Their elitist stance was reflected in the setting of very high membership dues for the National Association which excluded poorer artisans and workers. Civic, cultural, and ethnic forms of nationalism could all be found side by side in the National Association. Its optimism turned to despair in the conflict over military reform after 1862 when Bismarck simply ignored parliament and ruled unconstitutionally for the best part of four years. When, following victory in the Austro-German 'civil war',[19] Bismarck offered a compromise to liberal nationalists, most accepted it in the hope that they might be able to shape the development of the new nation-state which was now on the horizon. When, after yet another war with France, this nation-state became a reality, liberal national politicians had already begun the work of pushing through parliament a considerable amount of unifying legislation. Arguably, on the eve of German unification in 1871 the national imagination was already more unified than was the case, for example, in Italy. But it was one in which ethnic and civic elements were to be found side by side.

---

[17] H. James, *A German Identity 1770–1990*, rev. edn (London, 1990).

[18] A. Biefang, *Politisches Bürgertum in Deutschland 1857–1868: Nationale Organisationen und Eliten* (Düsseldorf, 1994).

[19] J. J. Sheehan, *German History 1770–1866* (Oxford, 1989), 899–911.

German nation-builders after 1871 were still confronted with the enormous task of forging a national identity which remained elusive in large parts of rural Germany and highly contested in the urban centres. Even large sections of the national camp had been shocked by the way in which Prussia had ruthlessly pushed Austria out of Germany in 1866 and destroyed the 'greater German' option. After the Austrian-Prussian war much of southern Germany (which had been allied to Austria) was occupied by Prussia. The occupiers were not popular. Power politics and economics were on their side, but popular sentiment was against them.[20] The German Confederation was destroyed, but it seemed unclear what precisely was going to replace it. A state-driven nationalization process kicked in only after 1871. It relied on monarchical and ethno-cultural constructions of the nation and downplayed civic and political national traditions. It was of symbolic significance that at the time when the new nation-state was declared in the Hall of Mirrors at Versailles, no representative of the German people was in attendance. The famous painting by Anton von Werner depicted the German princes and Bismarck. The new nation derived its legitimacy through its dynasties not through its people. The constitutional law in Imperial Germany regarded the people primarily as an object of power, not as subject. Party politics and the Reichstag were frequently denounced as dividing and not uniting the German nation, as parties represented partisan interest and not the state. A strong statist streak of Imperial Germany gave some credence to the claim that the Prussian state had acquired a nation in 1871. But the ensuing history of Imperial Germany showed clearly that the nation-state could not be built without strong popular and civic elements. Within the hybrid constitutional framework of Imperial Germany a dynamic political culture developed. The political elites found it increasingly difficult to ignore public opinion which was effectively mobilized through party politics, mass political organizations, interest groups, and elections. A democratizing mass political culture could not be suppressed by the political elites and the Imperial governments.[21]

NATIONAL 'OTHERS'

Imperial Germany did not lack a strong civil society. Quite the contrary: the German man (and increasingly woman) continued to be a *Vereinsmensch*. But Germany's civil society was a deeply divided one and these divisions were reflected in strongly contested notions of the German nation. The divisions were exacerbated by

---

[20] The best short summary is J. Breuilly, *The Formation of the First German Nation State, 1800–1871* (London, 1996).

[21] M. L. Anderson, *Practising Democracy: Elections and Political Culture in Imperial Germany* (Princeton, 2000); B. Fairbairn, *Democracy in the Undemocratic State: The Reichstag Elections of 1898 and 1903* (Toronto, 1997); J. Sperber, *The Kaiser's Voters: Electors and Elections in Imperial Germany* (Cambridge, 1997).

Bismarck's policy of creating 'internal enemies' of the nation. Catholics and Socialists respectively faced prolonged periods of repression and persecution in the 1860s and 1880s which alienated them from the official nationalism propagated by the Imperial German state. Bismarckian claims about their apparent disregard for the nation, their antinationalism even, were clearly not borne out by any closer look at the positioning of Catholics and Socialists vis-à-vis the national question. The vast majority of Catholics followed Ignaz Döllinger's belief that Catholicism should in fact be viewed as the essence of German nationality. It could, after all, lay claim to a centuries-old tradition. Yet in the *Kulturkampf* of the 1860s the Protestant nation was portrayed as struggling for unity in the face of the alleged transnationalism of the Catholic church. Confessional affiliation became the biggest single factor in dividing German national identity in the Kaiserreich.[22]

The anti-French and anti-Catholic symbolism of the Hermann monument indicated the importance of both external and internal 'national enemies' for the construction of the nation in Imperial Germany.[23] Hermann, previously better known by his Roman name Arminius, had been an integral part of thinking about Germany since the humanists of the sixteenth century. The memorial depicted a 26-metre high Germanic warrior figure on top of a dome. The raised sword in his right hand carried the inscription: 'Germany's unity is my strength, my strength is Germany's power.' The shield in his left also carried an inscription: 'steadfast in loyalty' (*treufest*). The Germanic warrior who had defeated the Romans in AD 9 prefigured the struggles against France in 1813/14 and again in 1870/1. The battle in the Teutoburg forest created the illusion of a foundational act of the German nation allowing the nationalists to create a teleology of German national development which culminated in 1871. Furthermore Hermann's sword was directed against Rome, and at the height of the *Kuturkampf* this was widely interpreted as the nation struggling for unity in the face of the alleged transnationalism of the Catholic church.

From the first organizational efforts in the 1848 revolution onwards German Socialists insisted on the necessity of the democratic and unified nation-state as the precondition for social reform. The SPD was among the strongest critics of official nationalism in Imperial Germany. Its members perceived themselves as heirs to the democratic revolutionaries of 1848 and they paid allegiance to the ideals of the Paris Commune. The Imperial German 'garrison state' and the militarization of civilian life, as witnessed in the Protestant Sedan celebrations in the Kaiserreich, were anathema to their understanding of the German nation. Yet even on the left civic nationalism was shot through with ethnic elements. Many followed Lassalle

---

[22] H. Walser Smith, *German Nationalism and Religious Conflict: Culture, Ideology, Politics, 1870–1914* (Princeton, 1995).

[23] C. Tacke, *Denkmal im sozialen Raum: Nationale Symbole in Deutschland und Frankreich im 19. Jahrhundert* (Göttingen, 1995).

in his belief in the cultural superiority of the German nation over Slav 'barbarity'. The revered leader of German Social Democracy was, after all, adamant in his belief that Poland did not deserve to be a nation.[24]

The creation of internal enemies increased the heterogeneity of the national imagination in Germany. On the right, opponents of Catholicism and Socialism attempted to ethnicize these groups of German citizens by referring to them as 'inner France'. National minorities were, as we have seen, the favourite objects of hatred among the nationalist right in Imperial Germany. And the nationalist discourse remained infected with anti-Semitic sentiments.[25] The construction of the Jew as inner enemy had a variety of socio-economic, political, and cultural reasons and resulted in a series of nasty pogroms in the first half of the nineteenth century. But in the second half of the nineteenth century the position of Jews in German society improved immeasurably. Legal emancipation was a long-drawn-out process, but it was complete at the point of the foundation of the German Empire in 1871. Powerful defence organizations, the Central Union of German Citizens of Jewish Faith and the Jewish League for the Defence Against Anti-Semitism, fought known cases of continued discrimination and promoted the continued integration of Jews into German society. The German-Jewish middle classes saw in Moses Mendelssohn the key symbol of what they came to describe as 'German-Jewish symbiosis'. Mendelssohn, a key member of the eighteenth-century Berlin Enlightenment and a friend of Lessing, seemed to represent perfectly the belonging of the Jews to the German nation. Culturally the vast majority of German Jews felt German and believed in the possibility of a dual identity. The Jewish tribe may have been ethnically different, but culturally it belonged firmly to Germany. Zionist calls for a Jewish homeland were far stronger in states where anti-Semitism was more vociferous such as Austria-Hungary and particularly Russia.

The national community was one which could at times be deeply solidaristic with other nations—especially where they were suppressed or in the process of liberating themselves from their oppressors. The Greek and Polish associations of the 1820s and 1830s were grounded in the cosmopolitan belief in national self-determination. The identification with Italian nationalism in 1859 led directly to the formation of the National Association which, in turn, gave a major boost to liberal nationalism. But the very same national community also depended heavily on the construction of external enemies.[26] Russia, for example, was already declared a part of Asia and hence 'un-European' in the early modern national discourse.[27] France had been a favourite target for attacks ever since the humanist discourse of

---

[24] S. Berger, 'British and German Socialists between Class and National Solidarity', in S. Berger and A. Smith (eds.), *Nationalism, Labour and Ethnicity 1870–1939* (Manchester, 1999), 31–63.

[25] O. Heilbronner, 'From Antisemitic Peripheries to Antisemitic Centres: The Place of Antisemitism in Modern German History', *Journal of Contemporary History*, 35 (2000), 559–76.

[26] See also Michael Jeismann's chapter in this volume.

[27] E. Klug, 'Das "asiatische" Rußland: Über die Entstehung eines europäischen Vorurteils', *Historische Zeitschrift* 245 (1987), 265–89.

the sixteenth century. The wars under Louis XIV as well as the wars of liberty in the early nineteenth century and the Rhine crisis of 1840 embedded that enmity and after the Franco-Prussian war the idea of France as the 'hereditary enemy' was firmly established in the German imagination.[28] At the same time, however, the Rheinbund nationalism of the early nineteenth century demonstrated that ideas of Germandom could go hand in hand with pro-French sentiments. Many liberal nationalists celebrated the French 1830 constitution as a model of its kind. The Rhine crisis of 1840 not only produced anti-French pamphlets. It also raised a major debate whether German freedoms, allegedly defended against France at the German Rhine, would not have to be won against the oppressive regime of the German princes first. And bourgeois society throughout the entire nineteenth century defined good taste through what was à la mode in France. Even in its upbeat assessments of Imperial Germany's economic performance, the Wilhelmine public contrasted their own performance with the more sluggish one of France.[29]

Similarly Anglo-German rivalry before 1914 produced images of the 'perfidious Albion' which culminated in the First World War in Werner Sombart's famous distinction between tradesmen (*Händler*) and heroes (*Helden*). Heinrich von Treitschke celebrated the idea of Germanic inner freedom and contrasted it with the allegedly more shallow idea of Western (i.e. British and French) political freedom. At the same time Britain was a model industrially and politically. Throughout the nineteenth century Anglo-Saxonism provided the foil for a vigorous mutual exchange of ideas.[30] The dialogue contained ethnic, cultural, religious, and constitutional elements. The British constitution was heralded as having been born in the Teutonic forests of the Germanic tribes. Britons and Germans were connected by blood ties which justified not only German Rhodes scholarships to Oxford but also the idea of the superiority of the Germanic races in Europe and the wider world.[31]

The rivalry with Polish nationalism in the Eastern provinces in Prussia was equally rooted in the Germanic past, more precisely in the assumption of a Germanic civilizing mission in Slav Eastern Europe. As early as the 1830s Prussia implemented harsh Germanization policies in the province of Posen. The Frankfurt parliament in its debates about the shape of the future German nation-state sought to extend its boundaries as far eastwards as possible. And in Imperial Germany the attempt to enforce a German national identity on national

---

[28] M. Jeismann, *Das Vaterland der Feinde: Studien zum nationalen Feindbegriff und Selbstverständnis in Deutschland und Frankreich, 1792–1918* (Stuttgart, 1992).

[29] M. Hewitson, 'German Public Opinion and the Question of Industrial Modernity: Wilhelmine Depictions of the French Economy', *European Review of History*, 7 (2000), 45–62; see generally on Wilhelmine perceptions of France id., *National Identity and Political Thought in Germany: Wilhelmine Depictions of the French Third Republic 1890–1914* (Oxford, 2000).

[30] M. Oergel, 'The Redeeming Teuton: Nineteenth-Century Notions of the "Germanic" in England and Germany', in G. Cubitt (ed.), *Imagining Nations* (Manchester, 1998).

[31] S. Berger, P. Lambert, and P. Schumann (eds.), *Historikerdialoge: Geschichte, Mythos und Gedächtnis im deutsch-britischen kulturellen Austausch* (Göttingen, 2003).

minorities was counter-productive. In particular the millions of Polish-speaking German citizens reacted by reinforcing their Polish identities and joining the Polish national movement and a strong Polish-speaking milieu.[32]

GENDER, CITIZENSHIP, THE MILITARY, AND *HEIMAT* AS INTEGRAL ELEMENTS OF THE NATIONAL DISCOURSE

Members of different races and generally all perceived enemies of the nation were continuously feminized by nationalist discourse. In a patriarchal society, their inferiority was demonstrated by showing them to be the female 'other'.[33] At the same time, however, the nation was widely imagined as family. In the family women clearly had an important part to play, and the bourgeois women's movement argued persistently that women fulfilled vital services to the nation. They bore the future generations of warrior soldiers and reared them in the national sense. They cared for the soldiers in times of war and fulfilled a wide range of charitable and social roles in society. Yet the path to citizenship remained blocked to women before 1914. Right-wing nationalist women's associations, such as the women's wing of the Ostmarkenverein, championed racialized, ethnic discourses of the nation, whereas more progressive bourgeois and social democratic women's associations spoke the language of human rights and citizenship. Once again we encounter ethnic as well as civic patterns of argument within the women's movement's discourse about the nation.

The Kaiserreich found it hard to accept ethno-cultural differences among those who were German citizens, and it defined German citizenship by using predominantly ethnic criteria. Rogers Brubaker's dichotomous construction of a German citizenship law tied to the idea of blood (*jus sanguines*) and a French citizenship law informed by ideas of territory (*jus soli*) has been relativized by important studies by Andreas Fahrmeier and Dieter Gosewinkel.[34] Throughout the first half of the nineteenth century citizenship laws in the German lands relied heavily on notions of a *jus domiciles*. Residency, not ethnicity, was the most important means of determining citizenship. Starting with the Prussian citizenship law of 1842 ethnic elements became more and more important. In 1842 the Prussian state wanted to determine clearly who belonged to the Prussian state and who did

[32] W. Hagen, *Germans, Poles and Jews: The Nationality Conflict in the Prussian East, 1772–1914* (Chicago, 1980).

[33] For a good survey of the close relationship between gender and nationalism see I. Bloom, K. Hagemann, and C. Hall (eds.), *Gendered Nations: Nationalisms and Gender Order in the Long Nineteenth Century* (Oxford, 2000).

[34] R. Brubaker, *Citizenship and Nationhood in France and Germany* (Cambridge, Mass., 1992); D. Gosewinkel, *Einbürgern und Ausschließen: Die Nationalisierung der Staatsangehörikeit vom Deutschen Bund bis zur Bundesrepublik Deutschland* (Göttingen, 2001); A. Fahrmeier, *Citizens and Aliens: Foreigners and the Law in Britain and the German States, 1789–1870* (Oxford, 2000).

not. Despite a wide range of exceptions the basic answer was clear: those who had been born to Prussian parents, or more precisely, to Prussian fathers. Such clarity allowed Prussia to deal with the increasing migration between the German lands and send back those immigrants that it did not want. This move towards an ethni-cization of citizenship culminated in the reform of the citizenship law in 1913. The new law underlined the increasingly exclusionary and xenophobic tendencies of the German imagination which were fuelled by fears of waves of Eastern European (especially Jewish) immigrants. Social Darwinist fears of the degenera-tion of the 'racial stock' contributed to this ethnicization of the citizenship law, but other reasons were also important: fears of increasing the country's social problems and national political considerations foremost among them. As ethnic homogeneity was made a priority the acquisition of dual nationality was becom-ing ever more difficult. The naturalization of foreigners was rare—in particular where they were Poles, Jews, or Socialists. Instead an increasing concern about keeping the Germans living abroad German led to the inclusion of the *Auslandsdeutsche* in the national census after 1900. However, the patriarchal defi-nition of citizenship retained priority over ethnic definitions even in 1913: despite attempts of *völkisch* groups to exclude children of mixed marriages between German fathers and native mothers in German colonies, the law ruled that citizenship would continue to go with the father.

From the early nineteenth century onwards citizenship in the German lands was increasingly tied to military service.[35] Initially liberal nationalists were sceptical of the states' conscription laws. The educated middle classes were distrustful of an institution which they understood as the very opposite of the cultured and civilized ideas they wanted their offspring to represent. When they finally came round to accepting conscription they did so under the condition that it was tied firmly to citizenship. Jewish groups in particular defended their right to serve in the army, because it gave them access to citizenship rights and prevented them from being excluded from the state on ethnic grounds. Military service was the duty of the citizen who in turn could demand a greater say in the government of the state. Such reasoning, of course, excluded women from citizenship. It also marked the line of conflict between a monarch who had an interest in strong professional standing armies and liberal nationalists who preferred citizens' guards which, they hoped, could not so easily be used by the government to repress internal opposition. It was only under the impact of the wars of unification that militarism became a marked feature of German society. The army was celebrated as school of the nation, but that school remained under the firm control of the emperor, not of the people's representatives in parliament. The cult of the army did not eclipse civic versions of nationalism; it merged them with monarchical constructions of the nation. The link between active citizenship and military

---

[35] U. Frevert, *A Nation in Barracks: Modern Germany, Military Conscription and Civil Society* (Oxford, 2004).

service was increasingly lost, and the militarization of civilian life was supported by a vibrant civic culture. The *Kriegervereine* came to dominate national festivities in a way which marginalized notions of the soldier citizen and instead emphasized the virtues of loyal subjects.[36]

Throughout the nineteenth century citizenship was a matter for the territorial states. Even in Imperial Germany national citizenship came with belonging to one of the territorial states making up the new Germany. Such a federal definition of citizenship is a timely reminder that federalism in Germany added considerably to the fluidity of the national discourse.[37] Federalism had characterized the constitutional framework of Germany since the Holy Roman Empire.[38] Germany was imagined quite differently in the diverse territories making up the whole. Notably the South-West German states, Baden, Württemberg, and Bavaria, but also a northern city-state such as Hamburg had far stronger civic and liberal traditions than was the case in Prussia or Saxony.

The widespread federal construction of Germany gave rise to attempts to unify Germany through the notion of *Heimat*.[39] *Heimat* effectively mediated between the local and the national. As it was far easier to identify with constructs of what was knowable and had been experienced, i.e. the local, the linking of *Heimat* discourses with the national idea was ideally suited to generate the much sought-after greater degree of national cohesion. The language of *Heimat* was infused with ethnic, cultural, and historical references to national belonging, but it could also contain, especially in the south-west of Germany, considerable civic elements. Its strong links with the early environmental movement produced a marked anti-urbanism and anti-modernism which glorified the authenticity of peasant life and decried the depravity of urban existence. There were links between such celebrations of an exclusively rural *Heimat* and the blood-and-soil ideology of *völkisch* groups. The older idea of the cosmopolitan, urbane bourgeois as arch-representative of German national ambitions was supplemented by notions of the peasantry as the real foundation of Germanness. The idealization of peasant lifestyles can be traced back to the works of the brothers Grimm on folk culture and fairy tales and to Georg Barthold Niebuhr's *Roman History*. The iconography of German nationalism was moving between images of middle-class urbanity and rural peasant idylls. The prominent *Heimat* discourse did not have to be anti-modern. It could equally seek to harmonize the advances of such modernity with the preservation of the traditional land- and mindscape of the *Heimat*. The

---

[36] T. Rohkrämer, *Der Militarismus der 'kleinen Leute': Die Kriegervereine im deutschen Kaiserreich 1871–1914* (Munich, 1990).

[37] On the impact of federalism on European constructions of national identity see also Maiken Umbach's Chapter 4.

[38] M. Umbach (ed.), *German Federalism: Past, Present, Future* (Houndmills, 2002); D. Langewiesche and G. Schmidt (eds.), *Föderative Nation: Deutschlandkonzepte von der Reformation bis zum ersten Weltkrieg* (Munich, 2000).

[39] A. Confino, *The Nation as Local Metaphor: Württemberg, Imperial Germany and National Memory 1871–1918* (Chappel Hill, NC, 1997); C. Applegate, *A Nation of Provincials: The German Idea of Heimat* (Berkeley, 1990).

critique of civilization and the various naturist movements, which were so popular around the turn of the century, were often seeking a 'different modernity' rather than advocating straightforward anti-modern world-views.[40]

The popular construction of a federal Germany as a community of different tribes tended to emphasize an ethnic element in German nationalism—with its obvious links to descent, culture, and language. The equally popular body metaphor worked in the same direction. Imagining the nation as a body naturalized the nation and emphasized 'objective' ethnic over subjective civic elements. As parts of the body had no option of choosing to belong or not, so the citizen did not have to perform a 'daily plebiscite' (Ernest Renan). Furthermore body metaphors emphasized harmony over interest fragmentation. Different parts of the body functioned as one; they supplemented each other and did not work against each other. Imagining the nation as one body was an inherently anti-pluralist device which tended to negate differences of interest and supported the harmonious and state-oriented ideas of German liberalism.

VÖLKISCH NATIONALISM

In line with the shift towards more ethnic definitions of Germanness, variants of an explicitly *völkisch* nationalism began to appear in the 1890s. Throughout the Kaiserreich, however, they remained weak and divided.[41] What is more, *völkisch* agitators were often regarded by more mainstream German public opinion as cranks who could not be taken seriously. If organized *völkisch* groups and anti-Semitic parties were weak, elements of *völkisch* thought were undeniably popular in Imperial Germany. Felix Dahn's three-volume novel *Struggle for Rome* (1876) was a clear example of such growing acceptance of a primarily ethnic construction of the nation. It went through thirty editions between 1876 and 1900 and sold approximately 600,000 copies. No lending library in Germany was complete without one. Its topic was basically the struggle of the Goths against the Roman Empire in classical times. At the highpoint of the *Kulturkampf* it could be read as confirmation of the importance of the struggle against the Catholic church. But the Goths in Dahn's novel are not religious. They have substituted a belief in the *Volk* for a belief in God. The historical Goths had actually converted to Christianity, but in the novel they are described as heathens critical of the Christian religion. They are also depicted as a people of courageous, loyal, and honest peasants led by the nobility. The family is described as the basis of their society—with a clear separation of spheres: women are mothers and carers, men are warriors. The urban middle classes, for

[40] T. Rohkrämer, *Eine andere Moderne? Zivilisationskritik, Natur und Technik in Deutschland 1880–1933* (Paderborn, 1999).

[41] U. Puschner, *Die völkische Bewegung im wilhelminischen Kaiserreich: Sprache—Rasse—Religion* (Darmstadt, 2001).

so long the standard bearers of the national idea in the nineteenth century, were completely absent from the novel.

Dahn's vision of the national community linked up with the idealization of peasant life which was also a hallmark of the propagandistic efforts of agricultural pressure groups such as the Association of Farmers (Bund der Landwirte), founded in 1893. Hans Grimm and Adolf Bartels belonged to the most popular blood and soil ideologues praising peasant life and contrasting it positively with the degenerate city life of urban tradesmen. In 1902 public support for the Boers in the Boer War was frequently connected to ideas of an organic peasant people of Germanic origin being suppressed by the cunning of a hypocritical trades people, the English. *Völkisch* monuments, such as the Völkerschlacht monument in Leipzig (1913), began to replace older monarchical and liberal-national forms of commemorating the nation in stone.[42] They celebrated the ethno-cultural community of the nation. The final volume of Dahn's novel deals with the demise of the Goths who are surrounded by envious and devious enemies planning their downfall. It was read widely as an analogy of the young and dynamic Germany which also was allegedly surrounded by envious enemies scheming to prevent the German nation from occupying its proper leading place in the world.

Völkisch elements penetrated liberal national and conservative thinking about the nation alike and further contributed to a pluralization of the national discourse in Imperial Germany. Conservative anti-national civic associations had already been stronger than their liberal national counterparts in early nineteenth-century Prussia.[43] In the course of the nineteenth century conservatives moved from anti-nationalism to developing their own variants of nationalism. Conservative ideologues such as Friedrich Julius Stahl and Wilhelm Heinrich Riehl did not link the nation with notions of greater participation of the people and more freedom. Instead they emphasized monarchism, Christianity, ethnicity, culture, and language as the essence of national identity. Nationalism was effectively depoliticized. Older national liberal and younger conservative ideas about the nation both found expression in the hundreds of Bismarck and Wilhelm memorials, built largely in Wilhelmine Germany. They testified to the strength of popular nationalism, as the vast majority of them were not paid for by the state but by voluntary civic associations.

German colonialism and the pursuit of *Weltpolitik*, especially after 1890, fostered an ethno-cultural understanding of the nation. Long before the advent of a colonial policy, racial theories about the 'natural inferiority' of colonized peoples legitimized colonial exploitation. Anthropological essentialism was criticized by many of those whose inclinations were for a more liberal and cosmopolitan nationalism, but those who, from early on, espoused a racialized version of Germandom, such as the Göttingen-based professor of philosophy Christoph

---

[42] U. Schlie, *Die Nation erinnert sich: Die Denkmäler der Deutschen* (Munich, 2002), 66–8.

[43] E. Trox, *Militärischer Konservatismus: Kriegervereine und 'Militärpartei' in Preußen zwischen 1815 und 1848/49* (Stuttgart, 1990).

Meiners (1747–1810), remained respected members of the world of middle-class associationalism.[44] A century after Meiners, propagandists of xenophobic mass nationalist organizations, such as the Naval League, the Pan-Germans, or the Colonial Association, popularized the modern race dogma that he had pioneered. Following Charles Darwin's *The Origin of Species*, published in 1859, biology was widely regarded as the most modern of sciences. Many authors wrote about cultural diversity and national identity being rooted in racial character. Anthropology took up Social Darwinist discourses from the 1860s and discussed the evolution of Germanic tribes in terms of a 'struggle of the fittest for survival'.

But radical nationalist mass organizations, powerful as they were, did not speak for a majority of Germans in the Kaiserreich. The 'banal nationalism' of the everyday remained far more important.[45] National rituals and ceremonies, books and newspapers, symbols and stories, maps and postcards, tourist travel and exhibitions all had successfully anchored diverse and often contradictory notions of Germanness in the hearts and minds of Imperial German citizens. Many of these ideas were focused on culture and national character. Notions of German cultural superiority also justified ideas of the German domination of Europe. Germans had a mission not only in the wider world but also in Europe to bring culture and civilization to those of inferior racial stock.

CONCLUSION

This review of the German national imagination in the nineteenth century has demonstrated how difficult it is to delineate neatly civic from ethnic elements. Seeking to define nationalism according to whether it adhered to more ethnic or more civic forms seems a cul-de-sac. The *Heimat* movement in Imperial Germany, the revolution of 1848, religious and cultural identities, as well as gendered images of the nation and federal constructions of national identity always contained both elements in different mixtures. Many nationalists used both civic and ethnic definitions of the nation depending on what specific goal they wanted to achieve. What we can say with some conviction is that the national movement, when it was still an oppositional one in the German lands in the first half of the nineteenth century, contained many civic elements—something which has often been under-estimated in the older literature on German nationalism. A strong associational culture demanded a greater role for its members in the decision-making processes

---

[44] S. Zantop, 'The Beautiful, the Ugly, and the German: Race, Gender and Nationality in Eighteenth-Century Anthropological Discourse', in P. Herminghouse and M. Mueller (eds.), *Gender and Germanness: Cultural Productions of Nation* (Oxford, 1997), 21–35.

[45] M. Hewitson, '*Nation* and *Nationalismus*: Representation and National Identity in Imperial Germany', in M. Fulbrook and M. Swales (eds.), *Representing the German Nation: History and Identity in Twentieth Century Germany* (Manchester, 2000), 19–62; for the concept of 'banal nationalism' see M. Billig, *Banal Nationalism* (London, 1995).

in the state, i.e. more constitutional government, freedom of the press, and the rule of law. But even then the idea of the nation as a future society of equal citizens under the rule of law was accompanied by backwards-oriented projections of the Germanic past. Calls for freedom and emancipation mingled with aggressive xenophobia. And egalitarianism was matched by notions of a strictly hierarchical community of warriors. Nationalism promised both emancipation and repression, inclusion as well as exclusion. It was this openness of the discursive construction of nationhood which made it so adaptable and flexible. It could be used in different contexts with different intentions by different social players.

A strong civil society developed in nineteenth-century Germany, but it was one which was highly divided and in which definitions of the nation were strongly contested. The rise of nationalism from the late eighteenth century was closely linked to liberal political ideas of freedom and participation of the propertied, educated, and male sections of the population in the affairs of the state. As a reaction to the French revolution many liberals ditched the universalism of Enlightenment ideas of liberty and instead sought to anchor their demands in specifically German history and culture. The 1848 revolution did not succeed in creating a unified liberal nation-state, but it contributed to the constitutionaliza-tion of the monarchical principle throughout the German lands. After 1848 even conservatives increasingly spoke the language of the nation and adapted it to their own concerns for stabilizing an existing social order. It was, after all, an arch-conservative, Bismarck, who, together with Prussian liberals, shaped the outlook of the first German nation-state to a considerable extent. Imperial Germany sought to build a nation by constructing external and internal enemies of the nation—France, Britain, the Slavs, Catholics, Socialists, and Jews—and adopting a strongly statist and antipluralist understanding of the nation. Against those 'others' Germanness could develop a sharper profile. But the 'other' could be construed as enemy or as model. Xenophobia stood next to expressions of national solidarity with oppressed nations in Europe.

In Imperial Germany the impact of Social Darwinist ideas under conditions of accelerated economic and industrial growth brought an ethnicization of historical-cultural definitions of Germanness. However, racial definitions of Germanness remained the preserve of a *völkisch* fringe which was not taken seriously by mainstream bourgeois society. The irony was that the increasing ethnicization of the predominantly cultural imagination of Germany was carried out on the back of a very strong but equally intolerant civil society which vigor-ously debated the issue of national identity. Notions of a homogeneous national identity appealed to those who were intent on creating a Germany as great and powerful as possible and on overcoming the manifold divisions within Imperial Germany. Many among the Protestant middle classes wanted to unify Germany around ideas of Protestantism, militarism, *Weltpolitik*, and the ethno-cultural superiority of the German nation. But many others did not. Catholics, for a start, resented the strong links between Protestantism and the national idea. Left liberals and socialists upheld visions of a different, more democratic Germany, although their own nationalism was shot through with ethno-cultural assumptions about Germandom. And, of course, the greater inclination of conservatives to appeal to ethno-cultural forms of national identity still had to mobilize the masses. It needed to appeal, in the age of mass politics and male suffrage, to their fellow compatriots as citizens. It was not so much the case that an earlier civic and liberal oppositional nationalism was replaced by an ethnic and conservative state nationalism in the last third of the nineteenth century. Rather, what we can observe is a vibrant debate on the precise contents of national identity in Imperial Germany. It indicated, above all, the widespread acceptance of the Imperial German nation-state among the population at large. Its shape and outlook, however, continued to be strongly contested.

PART II

DEMOS

4

Nation and Region

Regionalism in Modern European Nation-States

Maiken Umbach

The debate which has sprung up around the dichotomy between 'ethnic' and 'civic' nationalisms in nineteenth-century Europe, although long established, remains problematic. Ideal types rarely apply to complex historical realities. Moreover, the ethnic-civic divide has often been linked to a dubious geographical determinism, contrasting progressive 'Western' with reactionary 'Eastern' patterns—and a German *Sonderweg* in the middle. The contributors to this volume strive to avoid such stereotypes, and present a more nuanced account of developments within many of the countries on which this debate has focused. Many non-geographical factors distinguished different nationalisms in nineteenth-century Europe, including social milieu, confession, and, last but not least, chronology. Some of these movements resembled analogous nationalisms in other countries more than those championed by compatriots from a different background. Thus, to take just one example, the nationalism of educated, wealthy liberal elites in Northern Italian cities during the Risorgimento in many ways had more in common with the nationalism of German liberals during the pre-March era than with that of the Neapolitan peasant armies mobilized in 1848.[1]

Further differentiation does not imply that the categories of ethnic and civic are entirely meaningless. The flaws of the older historiography that are being critiqued in this volume stem from the fact that analytical categories were solidified

For their invaluable criticisms, I am grateful to the editors of this volume, as well as Jo Whaley, Stephen Jacobson, colleagues at the Center for European Studies at Harvard, and the participants of the *Nationalism in Europe* conference at the German Historical Institute in London. Research that informs this account was generously supported by the Arts and Humanities Research Board (AHRB), the Leverhulme Trust, and the Universitat Pompeu Fabra, Barcelona.

[1] On Italian liberal nationalism in this era, see M. Clark, *The Italian Risorgimento* (London, 1998); and F. Della Peruta, *L'Italia del Risorgimento: problemi, momenti e figure* (Milan, 1997). On the German equivalent, D. Langewiesche, *Liberalism in Germany*, trans. Christiane Banerji (Basingstoke, 2000); Wolfgang Schieder (ed.), *Liberalismus in der Gesellschaft des deutschen Vormärz* (Göttingen, 1983); and R. Schöttle, *Politische Theorien des süddeutschen Liberalismus im Vormärz: Studien zu Rotteck, Welcker, Pfizer, Murhard* (Baden-Baden, 1994).

into national 'essences'. This does not preclude their use as heuristic devices. Most nineteenth-century nationalisms did indeed oscillate between more ethnic and more civic components, even if these were not their only defining features. The problem with the older literature is less that it classified *per se*, but rather, that it equated these categories with particular nations. In reality, ethnic and civic elements were to be found within most nationalisms, and even within a national-ist discourse championed by a single political milieu or party. Take another example. From the time of the Greek War of Independence, liberals throughout Europe championed the notion that the right to national self-determination applied to members of all national communities. Supporting these inalienable rights was every upstanding liberal's civic duty. To express their solidarity, liberals in Germany and England founded pro-Greek associations during the 1820s, and condemned the repressive policies of the Ottomans. In the 1840s, pro-Polish associations sprang up based on the same principle.[2] Yet in 1848, the same German liberals serving in Frankfurt's provisional parliament came out in favour of a Prussian-led anti-Polish campaign, quashing the dream of Polish independ-ence. Delegates invoked all manner of ethnic stereotypes to justify their decision to put 'German interests first'.[3] This example not only shows that boundaries between civic and ethnic are hard to draw, it also shows that Kohn's classification of ethnic nationalism as conservative, and civic nationalism as progressive and democratic, is misleading. Few in the Frankfurt parliament used ethnic idioms more blatantly than the left-liberals; at the same time, the conservative Prussian government treated the same campaign simply as a matter of strategic interest. There is another, more general sense in which this classification does not hold. The view of the nation or the *Volk*, which Fichte articulated so powerfully in his famous *Addresses to the German Nation*,[4] was informed by Romantic notions of a national community of culture and fate that was far removed from the idea of voluntary and conscious citizenship. Yet ever since the time of the so-called Wars of Liberation, this same vision was also used to critique the anti-democratic nature of the German states, and contained a powerful participatory promise to the masses. By comparison, the civic discourse of liberal nationalists was typically based on a socially much more exclusive conception of citizenship. Whether or not a particular strand of nationalism is best classified as primarily ethnic or primarily civic thus tells us little about the presence or otherwise of exclusion

---

[2] E. François (ed.), *Sociabilité et société bourgeoise en France, en Allemagne et en Suisse, 1750–1850* (Paris, 1986); O. Dann (ed.), *Vereinswesen und bürgerliche Gesellschaft in Deutschland* (Munich, 1984); and H. Best (ed.), *Vereine in Deutschland: Vom Geheimbund zur freien gesellschaftlichen Organisation* (Bonn, 1993).

[3] J. Sperber, *The European Revolutions, 1848–1851* (Cambridge, 1994); D. Dowe, H.-G. Haupt, D. Langewiesche (eds.), *Europa 1848: Revolution und Reform* (Bonn, 1998). A useful collection of primary sources is in H. Schulze, *The Course of German Nationalism from Frederick the Great to Bismarck, 1763–1867*, trans. by Sarah Hanbury-Tenison (Cambridge, 1991).

[4] Johann Gottlieb Fichte, *Addresses to the German Nation*, ed. by George Armstrong Kelly (New York, 1968).

mechanisms—it merely denotes which categories such exclusions were based on: broadly speaking, on class or culture.

REGIONALISM IN EUROPEAN HISTORY

One factor that is rarely considered in conjunction with the ethnic-civic typology is the issue of regionalism. Regions—of many different shapes and sizes—were the territorial sub-units out of which most nineteenth-century European nation-states were formed. For a long time, historians regarded the importance of regions both as administrative units and as markers of collective identity as a pre-modern phenomenon, to be tackled under the heading of 'particularism', or, in German historiography, even more devastatingly: *Kleinstaaterei*. Recent historiography has been more sensitive to the continued importance of regions in the modern period, pointing out that they were rarely entirely dissolved in the larger national whole.[5] More typically, regions continued to play an important role within the new and typically far-from-unitary nation-states. Indeed, many of those areas of political activity which we today consider most indicative for the citizens' experience of state power in the nineteenth century tended to be exercised primarily by regions, while the nation-state concentrated its resources on foreign politics. Many European regions had their own political institutions, their own electoral processes, raised their own taxes, and, collectively, controlled more of the national budget than the 'national' governments.

Small wonder, then, that regions also served as the matrix through which political identities were imagined. This was not, as was long assumed, an alternative to identification with the nation.[6] During the heyday of European nationalism, in the decades around 1900, regional and national identities coexisted, and were mutually reinforcing. This also means that civic and ethnic identity constructions intermingled. Abigail Green's study *Fatherlands*, for example, shows that the same individuals who wrote about their *national* selves in terms of myths of common ancestry and culture may well have written about themselves as Württembergers or Saxons by invoking civic qualities.[7] In the cases examined by Green, liberal patriots praised their regional fatherland for traditions of political reform, technological success, and achievements in public education. To this list one could add a range of other civic elements, of which the law—that is, pride in autonomous legal and constitutional traditions—is perhaps the most significant. To this point we shall return later.

[5] C. Applegate, 'A Europe of Regions: Reflections on the Historiography of Sub-National Places in Modern Times', *American Historical Review*, 104 (1999), 1157–82. A remarkable selection of pioneering case studies is Philipp Ther and Holm Sundhaussen (eds.), *Regionale Bewegungen und Regionalismen in europäischen Zwischenräumen seit der Mitte des 19. Jahrhunderts* (Marburg, 2003).

[6] H.-J. Pohle (ed.), special issue on regionalism, *Geschichte und Gesellschaft*, 20 (1994), 321–401.

[7] A. Green, *Fatherlands: State-Building and Nationhood in Nineteenth-Century Germany* (Cambridge, 2001).

On the basis of such observations, a more general hypothesis can be formulated. The assumption of a civic-ethnic divide with geographical coordinates is based on a systematic failure to take the civic discourse of regionalism into account when considering countries with allegedly ethnic nationalisms. In states with a relatively long-standing history of political centralization, such as France and England, civic values tended to be associated with the national centre. By contrast, in much of Central and Southern Europe, the discourse of civic virtue—no less pronounced than elsewhere—tended to be associated primarily with local and regional government. Why, in 1871, would a well-to-do, educated city dweller from Florence look to the new government in Rome as the guardian of civic virtue, when his own town practically invented the concept? It would be absurd to conclude that Italian society had weaker civic values simply because its nationalism seems less civic. Thus, the question about geographical patterns needs to be posed in a different manner. At its heart are the different paths along which the relationship between region and nation unfolded. Practically all nineteenth-century European nation-states had regional foundations, yet only in some was this regional civic tradition fully transferred to the national level in the course of the nineteenth century. The question why this transfer occurred more completely in some countries and not in others may be the real question behind the chimera of the civic-ethnic dichotomy.

This was partly a function of the length of time during which concerted state-building occurred prior to the age of nationalism. Certainly, the power of early modern states was much more limited than that of modern nation-states.[8] Nevertheless, the emergence during the seventeenth century of single, non-peripatetic administrative centres, staffed by bureaucrats with increasingly professional training (the latter being principally a development of the later, 'enlightened' phase of absolutism during the eighteenth century) set an important precedent.[9] It encouraged administrative rationalization, and, in terms of symbolic politics, fostered an image of the state as a 'natural force' deeply wedded to its political territory.[10] The long-term legacy of so-called absolutist regimes therefore lay not in the status of the king, but in this pattern of concerted state-building, which finds analogies in parts of Europe that were not, in the legal sense, absolutist. Britain is a prime example, as Linda Colley's work has shown.[11] Both France and Britain are therefore examples of states where civic values were transferred to a national centre at an early stage. Consequently, modern historiography has come to regard their 'regions' as agrarian backwaters, wedded

---

[8] N. Henshall, *The Myth of Absolutism: Change and Continuity in Early Modern European Monarchy* (London, 1992).

[9] H. M. Scott (ed.), *Enlightened Absolutism: Reform and Reformers in later Eighteenth-Century Europe* (Basingstoke, 1990).

[10] This image assumed a concrete physical shape in projects by military engineers to create networks of canals and geographical boundaries. C. Mukerji, *Territorial Ambitions and the Gardens of Versailles* (Cambridge, 1997).

[11] L. Colley, *Britons: Forging the Nation, 1707–1837* (New Haven, 1992).

to folklore, tradition, and religion, but doomed to fail in any effort to resist modern state-building.[12]

Regions in nation-states that emerged from early modern composite states had very different traditions to mobilize.[13] In Italy and Germany, political institutions and civic culture developed in regional cities and autonomous city-states long before capital cities emerged in the later nineteenth century. As Adrian Lyttleton observed about the Italian case: 'The territorial states of the sixteenth to the eighteenth centuries each had their distinctive style of government and political personality.'[14] Recent historiography has emphasized the relevance of this early modern sub-state-building, which undercuts the assumption of a simple North–South divide, the prime organizing principle of Italian history for thinkers like Gramsci. The so-called 'new southern history' argues that this bipartite division needs to be broken down into much smaller units, where individual regions contain their own North–South divide in micro-form.[15] Michael Broers has recently deconstructed the analogous idea of a coherent Northern or Padanian Italy.[16] Broers also challenged received wisdom on the impact of the Napoleonic occupation. Most histories of modern nationalism in Europe suggest that nationalism in Europe emerged as a direct response to the Napoleonic Empire. Thomas Nipperdey famously started his history of modern Germany with the sentence: 'In the beginning, there was Napoleon.'[17] Broers argues against the idea that the common experience of Napoleonic occupation generated a feeling of solidarity that transcended the boundaries of the autonomous *ancien régime* states. This was not because French rule in the *départements réunis* was weaker than assumed. On the contrary, French imperialism was so effective that it functioned without the cooperation of local elites. As a result, after 1814, traditional units re-emerged largely unchanged, and continued to dominate Northern Italian life after 1859. Hence, as John Davis put it, the northern regions provide 'endless examples of the survival of forms of private power and influence that remained almost untouched by the presence or realities of the state until 1900 or beyond'.[18]

By comparison, the autonomy of early modern German territories in the Holy Roman Empire had been much more limited. Since the Middle Ages, they belonged to a single constitutional system. Even if its ties loosened after 1648,

---

[12] E. Weber, *Peasants into Frenchmen: The Modernization of Rural France, 1870–1914* (London, 1979).

[13] J. H. Elliott, 'A Europe of Composite Monarchies', *Past and Present*, 137 (1992), 48–71.

[14] A. Lyttleton, 'Shifting Identities: Nation, Region and City', in C. Levy (ed.), *Italian Regionalism: History, Identity and Politics* (Oxford, 1996), 33–52, quotation 33.

[15] For this view, see J. Schneider (ed.), *Italy's Southern Question: Orientalism in One Country* (Oxford, 1998); and J. Dickie, *Darkest Italy: The Nation and Stereotypes of the Mezzogiorno, 1860–1900* (London, 1999).

[16] M. Broers, 'The Myth and Reality of Modern Italian Regionalism: A Historical Geography of Napoleonic Italy, 1801–1814', *American Historical Review*, 108 (2003), online citation, paras. 1–41.

[17] T. Nipperdey, *Germany from Napoleon to Bismarck 1800–1866*, trans. D. Nolan (Dublin, 1996).

[18] J. A. Davis, 'Casting off the Southern Problem, or: The Peculiarities of the South Reconsidered', in Schneider, *Italy's Southern Question*, 205–24, quotation 217.

the Empire as an 'order for the maintenance of law and peace' survived until the arrival of Napoleon. As the disappearance of the majority of Italian city-states during the age of absolutism powerfully demonstrated,[19] in a highly competitive international order, belonging to a larger umbrella organization like the empire was advantageous for small territories.[20] The Swiss Confederation was the purest example of such a voluntary union. This created the foundation for the later liberal idea of the nation-state as a confederate *Rechtsstaat*. It also set a precedent for a mutually reinforcing coexistence of *Kleinstaat* and *Gesamtstaat*, that found its modern equivalent in the federal state.[21]

The comparison between Italian and German nation-state formation is a staple of the historiography of European nationalism. Here was a parallel plot of two classical composite states being transformed into nation-states at about the same time, which features in numerous survey accounts and textbooks.[22] Post-unification developments do, however, present a paradox. Given their earlier histories, one might have expected a relatively greater degree of centralization in Germany, and a more extreme form of devolution in Italy. In fact, the opposite occurred: the Italian nation-state became more centralized than the German Reich. Different explanations suggest themselves. Daniel Ziblatt argues that the German Reich's decision to devolve authority after 1871 was a sign of strength, whereas the Italian state, a much more fragile entity, had to cling to all power it could centralize.[23] Broers makes a similar point when he argues that the Italian regions, once excluded from modern state-building under Napoleon, became reactionary, and thus had to be regarded as politically hostile by the progressive liberal state.[24] Generally, then, the Italo-German comparison should teach us not to assume that modern regionalism was a direct continuity of early modern particularism. History mattered—but it did not determine outcomes. Rather, history provided an arsenal of arguments and precedents that could be invoked

---

[19] R. MacKenney, *The City State, 1500–1700: Republican Liberty in an Age of Princely Power* (Basingstoke, 1989).

[20] J. Whaley, 'Federal Habits: The Holy Roman Empire and the Continuity of German Federalism', in M. Umbach (ed.), *German Federalism, Past, Present, Future* (Basingstoke, 2002); G. Schmidt, *Der Dreissigjährige Krieg* (Munich 1995), esp. 7–8, 94–8; and C. Dipper, *Deutsche Geschichte 1648–1789* (Frankfurt a. M., 1991), esp. 252–62.

[21] For the early modern period, Schmidt coined the phrase of the 'Doppelstaatlichkeit des Reiches' to describe this phenomenon. G. Schmidt, *Geschichte des Alten Reiches: Staat und Nation in der frühen Neuzeit, 1495–1806* (Munich, 1999). On the transition from early modern polycentric government to modern federalism, see M. Umbach, *Federalism and Enlightenment in Germany, 1740–1806*; and D. Langewiesche and G. Schmidt (eds.), *Föderative Nation: Deutschlandkonzepte von der Reformation bis zum Ersten Weltkrieg* (Munich, 2000).

[22] For example W. G. Shreeves, *Nationmaking in Nineteenth-Century Europe: The National Unification of Italy and Germany 1815–1914* (Walton-on-Thames, 1984). A critical overview is F. J. Bauer, 'Nation und Moderne im geeinten Italien, 1861–1915', *Geschichte in Wissenschaft und Unterricht*, 46 (1995), 16–31.

[23] D. Ziblatt, 'Constructing a Federal State: Political Development, Path Dependence, and the Origins of Federalism in Modern Europe, 1815–1871', Ph.D. dissertation (Berkeley, 2002).

[24] Broers, 'The Myth and Reality', para. 17.

by modern regionalists if and when it suited their purpose. To explain the evolution of modern regionalism, and the relative attribution of civic and ethnic discourses of belonging to the region or the nation, we therefore need to examine the developments during the nineteenth century in more detail. For this was a period during which political structures—nations, regions, even localities— came to be charged with an unprecedented ideological significance. Specifically modern discourses about collective identities were grafted onto different political traditions. As a result, a political language that sounded deceptively similar throughout Europe could have very different implications in different national settings. The discourse of *Heimat* is a case in point. The celebration of *Heimat*, i.e. the idealized image of a locality, typically portrayed as a home town largely unaffected by the forces of modernization, was long regarded as a German peculiarity. During the Nazi regime, *Heimat* was aligned with the blood-and-soil ideology of Aryan descent and juxtaposed to the 'decadence' of city life.[25] The late nineteenth century, when the *Heimat* discourse first took shape, was long seen as a precursor to these trends.[26] Neither the teleology nor the national peculiarity inherent in such arguments have withstood the text of recent historical scholarship.[27] *Heimat*, according to the new consensus, was an integral feature of modern European nationalism: the locality became a metaphor that made the abstraction of the 'nation' imaginable for ordinary people.[28] During the First World War, propaganda images extolling the virtues of an idyllic locality as representative of the nation that needed defending were produced in France and in England just as much as they were in Germany.[29] Indeed, recent research has shown that this *Heimat* iconography was accepted by ordinary soldiers much more readily than any other forms of war propaganda,

[25] N. Bormann, *Paul Schultze Naumburg, 1869–1949: Maler, Publizist, Architekt, vom Kulturreformer der Jahrhundertwende zum Kulturpolitiker im Dritten Reich* (Essen, 1989); D. von Reeken, *Heimatbewegung, Kulturpolitik und Nationalsozialismus: Die Geschichte der 'Ostfriesischen Landschaft' 1918–1949* (Aurich, 1995).

[26] J. A. Williams, 'The Chords of the German Soul are Tuned to Nature: The Movement to Preserve the Natural Heimat from Kaiserreich to the Third Reich', *Central European History*, 29 (1996), 339–84; D. Kramer, 'Die politische und ökonomische Funktionalisierung von Heimat im deutschen Imperialismus und Faschismus', *Diskurs*, 6–7 (1973), 3–22.

[27] W. R. Rollins, *A Greener Vision of Home: Cultural Politics and Environmental Reform in the German Heimatschutz Movement, 1904–1918* (Ann Arbor, 1997); and D. Midgley, 'Los von Berlin! Anti-Urbanism as Counter-Culture in Early Twentieth-Century Germany', in S. Giles and M. Oergel (eds.), *Counter-Cultures in Germany and Central Europe: From Sturm und Drang to Baader-Meinhof* (Oxford, 2003), 121–36.

[28] C. Applegate, *A Nation of Provincials: The German Idea of Heimat* (Berkeley, 1990); A. Confino, *The Nation as a Local Metaphor: Württemburg, Imperial Germany and National Memory 1871–1918* (Chapel Hill, NC, 1997).

[29] On the French imagery of the local, see the works by Stéphane Audoin-Rouzeau, for example his *Men at War, 1914–1918: National Sentiment and Trench Journalism in France during the First World War*, trans. H. McPhail (Oxford, 1992); S. Baker, 'Describing Images of the National Self: Popular Accounts of the Construction of Pictorial Identity in the First World War Poster', *Oxford Art Journal*, 13 (1990), 24–30.

and readily absorbed into a popular discourse of belonging throughout Europe.[30]

The discourse of *Heimat* thus occurred in many different countries. But it meshed with political structures in quite different ways, and it is at this intersection of culture and politics that distinct national patterns emerge. French and English regions had comparatively weak institutional, legal, and political infrastructures (quite unlike 'British' regions, namely Scotland and Wales). In France and England, regional identities were primarily culturally (at times linguistically) based, and modern regionalism was more about creating a momentum towards devolution than preserving already existing civic frameworks.[31] It was not only the conceptual framework of modernization theory which led Eugen Weber to talk of French regions as primarily agrarian and often traditionalist units that were forcefully modernized by a centralizing nation-state.[32] In states such as Germany and Italy, however, localist and regionalist sentiment could be mobilized to support the political autonomy of the subnational units. One characteristic of such units was that they then tended to have a prominent urban core. Some regional cities had emerged as capitals of independent principalities, such as Turin or Munich.[33] Others had been independent city-states, such as Hamburg, though in some cases, as in Venice, these had conquered a substantial hinterland, the *terra ferma*.[34] Due to their political power and economic weight, these urban regional centres were less easily subdued by the central state than agrarian provinces. Centuries of commercial prosperity and political self-determination had given rise to a strong sense of civic patriotism. In the nineteenth century, industrialization added a further twist to the tale. Several regional cities turned economic expansion to their advantage. Barcelona's textile manufactures were crucial in starting Spanish industrialization, the cities of the Italian northern 'industrial triangle' (and not Rome) were engines of economic development, and in Germany, Hamburg became the launch pad for the nation's conquest of new overseas' markets. For such cities, the relationship with the newly formed nation-state took the form not of subjection, but of negotiation between mutually dependent partners. In such contexts, the imagery of *Heimat* could be combined with allusions to this civic tradition to provide its advocates with powerful cultural

---

[30] Compare Confino, *The Nation as a Local Metaphor*; J. Verhey, *The Spirit of 1914: Militarism, Myth and Mobilization in Germany* (Cambridge, 2000); B. Ziemann, *Front und Heimat: Ländliche Kriegserfahrungen im südlichen Bayern 1914–1923* (Essen, 1997); A. Reimann, *Der große Krieg der Sprachen: Untersuchungen zur historischen Semantik in Deutschland und England zur Zeit des Ersten Weltkriegs* (Essen, 2000).

[31] N. J. G. Wright, 'Jean Charles-Brun and the Birth of Regionalism in France, 1890–1914', unpublished D.Phil thesis (Oxford, 2001).   [32] Weber, *Peasants into Frenchmen*.

[33] For a stimulating comparative discussion of some such cities, see H. Meller, *European Cities 1890–1930: History, Culture and the Built Environment* (Chichester, 2001).

[34] This was not a clear-cut division. Milan, for example, was a regional capital, yet for much of its history, its relationship with other Lombard cities had been that of partner rather than ruler. G. Rumi, 'La vocazione politica de Milano', in C. Mozzarelli and R. Pavoni (eds.), *Milano fin de siècle e il caso Bagatti Valsecchi: memoria e progetto per la metropoli italiana* (Milan, 1991), 17–22.

idioms in the defence of autonomy vis-à-vis the nation-state. That is not to say that most regions in formerly composite states championed separatist agendas. Typically, region and nation were not defined in opposition to one another, but reconciled in a single political framework best described as federal. Similar patterns of civic-national cooperation can be observed even where, as in Italy, there was no formal federalism.[35] Within this balancing act, regional cities often represent the civic dimension of national discourse—thus leaving historians who focus only on the national level of politics alone to conclude that civic culture was absent in such countries.

CITY-STATE TRADITIONS, CIVIC CULTURE, AND EMPIRE

Germany, long classified as an ethnically defined nation, provides the best example for this type of misinterpretation. Berlin, the Prussian capital and military head-quarters, which attracted a larger immigrant population of workers during industrialization, had few civic themes to bring to the symbolic politics of nation-alism.[36] By contrast, Hamburg, the former city-state, preserved its independent status in the German Confederation, and after 1871 maintained at least nominal economic autonomy outside the German customs union. Yet as the principal gateway for German (and indeed European) transatlantic trade, it was also vital to national economic development. In their negotiations with Berlin, Hamburg's elites used this position of strength, which was presented as a discourse of civic virtue and tradition. References to the glory days of the city-state under the old imperial constitution, and the heyday of its trading organization, the Hanseatic League, abounded, and the cityscape was transformed to include more and more three-dimensional representations of these claims.[37] One striking example was the new Town Hall, erected between 1885 and 1897, which, according to Alfred Lichtwark, director of the Hamburg art museum at the time, did 'not serve as the site of municipal administration—rather, it represents the government of an independent state'. The design took the Renaissance Empire as its iconographic reference point, resourcefully combining regional and imperial imagery.[38] The

---

[35] The urban development of later nineteenth-century Milan synthesized traditional civic themes with national and pan-European symbols. S. Della Torre, 'La nuova Milano monumentale', in Mozzarelli and Pavoni, *Milano*, 69–84.

[36] K. Zelljadt, 'History as Past-time: Antiquarians and Old Berlin, 1870–1914', unpublished Ph.D. dissertation, Harvard University, 2005.

[37] H. Hipp, *Freie und Hansestadt Hamburg: Geschichte, Kultur und Stadtbaukunst an Elbe und Alster* (Cologne, 1989).

[38] J. Grolle (ed.), *Das Rathaus der Freien und Hansestadt Hamburg* (Hamburg, 1997). This was no isolated incidence in Wilhelmine Germany. In the later 1880s and 1890s, a large number of German cities began erecting new town halls that followed the pattern established in Hamburg. See M. Damus, *Das Rathaus: Architektur- und Sozialgeschichte von der Gründerzeit zur Postmoderne*

structure of the Town Hall was designed to reflect the city republic's traditional constitution. The space was divided between the senate in one wing, the city parliament in the other. The first floor contained the 'Hall of the Republics', with wall paintings representing the city republics of Athens, Rome, Venice, and Amsterdam. The façade of the building featured twenty life-size statues of emperors of the Holy Roman Empire. This demonstration of imperial power was matched by a series of keystones showing the crests of the members of the Hamburg senate of 1892 and figures carrying the attributes of local crafts and trades. Additionally, there were statues of the patron saints of Hamburg's seven medieval parishes, and allegories of virtue. The spire, the expressed emblem of bourgeois liberty, was adorned by the coat of arms of the City of Hamburg, but above it towered the imperial eagle. One member of the Hamburg architect team commented: 'As long as the great views of our Imperial Chancellor of the importance of small, vigorous and independent states within the German federal states are respected, so long is our project safe.'[39]

Together, such emblems not only invoked a spirit of autonomy and city republicanism. They also suggested that these virtues could usefully contribute an element of civic patriotism to the larger whole of the nation. Of course, this civic discourse was neither democratic nor particularly charitable in nature. Hamburg's liberals looked with a certain condescension at the monarchical pomp and circumstance associated with the culture of the capital city Berlin. Yet, as Richard Evans's study of the cholera epidemic in Hamburg has shown, if their economic privileges were brought into question, the political and civil elites of this regional society could treat the lower classes just as harshly as the likes of Bismarck.[40] Moreover, civic patriotism had its own political exclusion mechanisms. In 1910, 53.5 per cent of those who lived and worked in Hamburg had migrated into the city, the vast majority being unskilled workers, who had no connection with the particularist traditions of the old imperial city.[41] Hamburg became the principal centre of the German working-class movement. The workers' politics were national, their thinking was shaped by the ideal of a modern, uniform nation-state. The trade unionists, as representatives of labour immigrants, challenged the notion of political legitimacy based on ownership and wealth, and rejected any allusion to Hanseatic traditions as the basis of legitimate power. They regarded the symbolism of the Hamburg Town Hall with open hostility, and, in 1900, commissioned an anti-building, the Trade Union Hall, which employed a deliberately national, anti-regionalist

---

(Berlin, 1988); and G. U. Großmann, 'Die Renaissance der Renaissance-Baukunst', in Großmann and P. Krutisch (eds.), *Renaissance der Renaissance: Ein bürgerlicher Kunststil im 19. Jahrhundert*, vol. i (Munich, 1992), 201–19.

[39] Wilhelm Hauers, 1885, quoted from H. Hipp, 'Das Rathaus der Freien und Hansestadt Hamburg', in Grolle, *Das Rathaus*, 15–35, quotation 24.

[40] R. J. Evans, *Death in Hamburg: Society and Politics in the Cholera-Years, 1830–1910* (Oxford, 1987).   [41] I. Möller, *Hamburg* (Stuttgart, 1985), 71.

rhetoric, and was accompanied by a guidebook which extolled its national spirit.[42]

Faced with such challenges, civic patriotism appropriated the idiom of *Heimat*. The Town Hall itself marks this transition. In keeping with the historicist iconography of the building, the main chamber walls were supposed to be decorated with allegorical figures culminating in the apotheosis of the city goddess Hammonia. Before the scheme was completed, however, it was decided to adopt a more realistic mode of representation: in 1908, Hugo Vogel created four large wall paintings that depicted Hamburg's historical development from glacial valleys to modern seaport and steamboats. This new modernist realism was in keeping with the spirit of another civic project: the evolution of Hamburg's Art Museum under Alfred Lichtwark's directorship. Lichtwark, the subject of a recent study by Jennifer Jenkins,[43] sought to widen the appeal of Hamburg's civic patriotism by appealing to themes that transcended the boundaries of a political history defined by the patrician elites. On the one hand, Lichtwark looked to religion, specifically to altarpieces, which he recovered from Hamburg's churches and exhibited in the Art Museum, to discover a style and sentiment specific to the city. On the other hand, he encouraged young painters like Max Liebermann to use the style of the 'modern' French impressionists to create images that captured the essence of Hamburg's cityscape and the surrounding countryside. Both collections still form the backbone of the museum's exhibits today. A similar ambition inspired the activities of Fritz Schumacher, Hamburg's building director from 1911 to 1933. By promoting the exemplary use of the archetypal vernacular material red brick, and by fostering an aesthetic idiom that stayed clear both of literal historicism and the abstractions of the International Style, Schumacher reconfigured the city as a place with a strong local 'character', that invited emotional identification. Thus, the civic ideals of the patrician city republic were redefined so as to appeal to a wider public, notably the vast (and mostly working-class) immigrant population in the industrializing city. The idiom of *Heimat* presented an opportunity to recast civic particularism as a localism that spoke to modern subjectivity without presupposing privileged political status.[44]

[42] E. Domansky, 'Das Hamburger Gewerkschaftshaus', in A. Herzig, D. Langewiesche, and A. Sywottek (eds.), *Arbeiter in Hamburg* (Hamburg, 1983), 373–84. Much of the building's programme was explained in the contemporary guidebook produced by the trade union, *Das Hamburger Gewerkschaftshaus: Ein Führer durch das Hamburger Gewerkschaftshaus* (Hamburg, 1914). Compare also M. Umbach, 'History and Federalism in the Age of Nation-State Formation', in id., *German Federalism*, 42–69.

[43] J. Jenkins, *Provincial Modernity: Local Culture and Liberal Politics in Fin-de-Siècle Hamburg* (Ithaca, NY, 2003). It was characteristic of Lichtwark's eminently bourgeois outlook that well into the 1900s, he saw impressionism as the pinnacle of modernist culture, and ignored all subsequent developments. The somewhat antiquated 'enlightened' rhetoric of Lichtwark's writings are discussed in the H-NET review of J. Jenkins, *Provincial Modernity*, by Katherine B. Aaslestad, published by h-german@h-net.msu.edu, July 2003.

[44] On Schumacher, see chapter 8 of Jenkins, *Provincial Modernity*; *Zur Aktualität der Ideen von Fritz Schumacher: Fritz-Schumacher-Colloquium 1990* (Hamburg, 1992); and H. Frank (ed.), *Fritz Schumacher: Reformkultur und Moderne* (Stuttgart, 1994).

To be sure, civic patriotism and the new popular nationalism could find alternative common denominators that were less benign. Imperialism was one such issue. For Germany, the decades around 1900 were a time of intense, though largely informal, empire-building. The creation of HAPAG's merchant fleet was as widely celebrated as the construction of Tirpitz's famous navy.[45] For an otherwise land-locked empire, Hamburg's Hanseatic past provided the only precedent of the new Reich's 'sea-going' ambitions—a point that was not lost on Wilhelmine imperial propagandists.[46] When the city was granted the privilege of becoming Germany's only free harbour in the 1880s, the construction of the new warehouse district was appropriately executed in the north-German red-brick gothic style characteristic of the glory days of the Hanseatic League. When it was inaugurated in 1888, Emperor William II gave a speech suggesting that Hanseatic particularism provided a precedent for Germany reaching out to the world at large: 'You are the ones who connect our fatherland with invisible ties to distant parts of the globe, trade with our products, and more than that: you are the ones who transmit our ideas and values to the wider world, and for this the fatherland owes you a debt of special gratitude'.[47] Thus, imperialism could be invoked to reconcile Hamburg's regional interests with the official rhetoric of Wilhelmine nationalism.

MODERN CITIES, ETHNIC REGIONALISMS, AND THE LAW

A final case to be considered in this brief sketch of European regionalisms is that of Spain. It presents us with a particular paradox, for the usual attribution of the labels civic and ethnic seems to be reversed here. Most recent studies regard the nineteenth-century Spanish state as the brainchild of a 'liberal revolution'.[48] Conversely, the Basque and Catalan counter-movements that responded to the 'failure' of this liberal vision during the later nineteenth century are typically classified as 'ethnic', and have been likened to the German idea of *Volksgeist*.[49] One important distinguishing factor from the examples considered so far is that

---

[45] L. Cecil, *Albert Ballin: Business and Politics in Imperial Germany, 1888–1918* (Princeton, 1967); A. Quaas, 'Der Schiffbau', in V. Plagemann (ed.), *Übersee: Seefahrt und Seemacht im deutschen Kaiserreich* (Munich, 1988), 126–34; H. H. Herwig, *Luxury Fleet: The Imperial German Navy, 1888–1918*, rev. edn. (London, 1987). HAPAG = Hamburg-Amerikanische Packetfahrt-Actien-Gesellschaft.

[46] V. Plagemann, 'Kultur, Wissenschaft, Ideologie', in Plagemann, *Übersee*, 299–308.

[47] Quoted from K. Maak, 'Die Freihäfen', ibid. 107–10, quotation 110.

[48] The constitutional convention of Cádiz, held from 1810 to 1813, is central to this argument, which is explored in Stephen Jacobson's contribution to this volume.

[49] D. Conversi, *The Basques, the Catalans, and Spain* (London, 1997), classifies Basque and Catalan nationalisms as ethnic responses to the bureaucratic state nationalism of Spain. A similar view is offered by A. Balcells, *Catalan Nationalism: Past and Present* (New York, 1996). On the German influence on Catalan nationalism, see J. Llobera, 'La formació de la ideologia nacionalista catalana: la idea de Volksgeist com a element definidor', *L'Avenç*, 63 (1983), 24–35. On Basque nationalism, see S. Payne, *Basque Nationalism* (Reno, 1975); and A. Elorza, *Un pueblo escogido: genesis, definición y desarollo del nacionalismo vasco* (Barcelona, 2001).

these regionalisms were influenced by the Basque and Catalan countryside and their respective peasant populations. When intellectuals pursuing autonomy for these regions appealed to a spiritual locus in the landscape, language, and heritage, so this argument runs, they rejected the civic traditions of the city in favour of folklore and the *Volk*. Such claims require careful deconstructing. To be sure, the fact that Basque and Catalan are languages in their own right, rather than just dialects, set these movements apart from regionalisms in Germany and Italy.[50] Yet linguistic differences did not determine political outcomes. After all, Frisian, too, is a language, but not one that gave rise to a nationalist movement in the nineteenth century. Similarly, the relationship with the countryside can be read in different ways. This is especially true in the Catalan case. Nineteenth-century Catalanism inspired the *excursionisme* movement, which reconnected city dwellers with the rural *Catalunya profunda*—or their fantasy of it. The same movement reached back to a past that had few civic attributes, namely the early Middle Ages: Romanesque churches in the Catalan countryside became iconic for the heyday of Catalan independence before the onset of absolutist state-building, and were widely regarded as the spiritual locus of the nation's cultural identity. Yet none of this necessitated an anti-civic discourse. Rather, like the *Heimat*-idiom in Hamburg, this imagery could be grafted onto a political way of thinking that was eminently urban. This remained true even after the official rhetoric of Catalanism, still overwhelmingly 'regionalist' in the nineteenth century, had changed to nationalism in the early twentieth century. One of the leading figures of Catalanism was architect-cum-politician Puig i Cadafalch (1867–1956), president of the Catalan Lliga Regionalista from 1901, and thereafter president of the Mancomunitat de Catalunya. Puig was one of the instigators of the movement to restore Catalan Romanesque churches, which he regarded as central to Catalan identity.[51] At the same time, his own architectural oeuvre offers a fascinating insight into the modernity of this movement. His houses in the new model district of Barcelona, the Eixample, emancipated themselves not only from the historical 'authenticity' of the Catalan Romanesque, but also more generally from the grammar of historicist architecture. Instead of the lexicographic reference system of historicism, in which standardized architectural tropes invoked academically defined historical precedents, Puig's architecture was fantastic in the true sense of the word. Allusions to 'memory', a vital constituent of the sense of

[50] J.-L. Marfany, *La llengua maltractada: el Castellà i el català a Catalunya del segle XVI al segle XIX* (Barcelona, 2001). See also J. M. Fradera, *Cultura nacional en una societat dividida: patriotism i cultura a Catalunya, 1838–68* (Barcelona, 1992).

[51] Puig himself conducted restorations of several Catalan monasteries. A. Mesecke, *Josep Puig i Cadafalch, 1867–1956: Katalanisches Selbstverständnis und Internationalität in der Architektur* (Frankfurt a. M., 1995); Jordi Romeu Costa, *Josep Puig i Cadafalch: obres i projectes des del 1911* (Barcelona 1989); L. Permanyer and L. Casals, *Josep Puig i Cadafalch* (Barcelona, 2001); and J. Rohrer, I. de Solà-Morales, X. Barral, J. Termes, *Josep Puig i Cadafalch: l'arquitectura entre la casa i la ciutat. Architecture between the House and the City*, exhibition catalogue, Centre Cultural de la Fundació Caixa de Pensions (Barcelona, 1989).

place, abounded, yet these were highly idiosyncratic, subjectivized, and inter-mingled with the consciously fictitious imagery of fairy tales. Methodologically, Puig's architectural narratives find an analogue in literary devices like the 'stream of consciousness' and the memory-associations explored by Proust, Bergson, and Warburg.[52] Puig never abandoned the concrete commitment to the agenda of political regionalism. But he placed this agenda on a new intellectual footing. For him, the region was not an organic unit determined by its history. Rather, it was a space located in the collective imagination, in which modern political identities could be grounded.

The social basis of this intellectual modernism lay in the fact that, economically speaking, the Catalans—and later the Basques—spearheaded industrialization when Spain at large was still overwhelmingly agrarian. In the later nineteenth-century, Barcelona's textile industry provided the backbone for the politics of regional autonomy.[53] Payne convincingly argues that a major incentive for the development of Catalan regionalism (or, in Payne's terminology: micro-nationalism) was the sluggishness of economic modernization in Spain at large.[54] In this project, the law, that ultimate building-block of civic culture and bourgeois hegemony, played a defining role. This was no Catalan peculiarity. Typically, regions in former composite states produced not only sophisticated political infrastructures, but also legal systems that were geared to the requirements of these commercially based mini-states. For Italy, this is a well-documented fact.[55] Even in the German lands, where individual-state autonomy was traditionally more limited, the right to legal and constitutional 'home rule' was a long-standing method of emancipating a region from central authority. The key lay in the creation of territorial courts of appeal;[56] a goal that was harder to accomplish for city-states than for more expansive principalities.[57] The nineteenth century was a time when, throughout Europe, national codifications of the law were achieved. In Germany, this process began in 1867, still under the auspices of the North-German Confederation, and culminated in the drafting of the national civil code of 1896, the Bürgerliches Gesetzbach, which came into force in 1900. The Hanseatic cities, led by the largest and wealthiest, Hamburg, took steps to

---

[52] A political interpretation of Puig's 'fantastic' architecture is the theme of my current research.

[53] C. Ehrlich, 'The Lliga Regionalista and the Catalan Industrial Bourgeoisie', *Journal of Contemporary History*, 33 (1998), 399–417.

[54] Stanley G. Payne, 'Nationalism, Regionalism and Micronationalism in Spain', *Journal of Contemporary History*, 26 (1991), 179–91.

[55] On the legal dimension of Milanese autonomy, see G. Santini, *Lo stato estense tra riforme e revoluzione* (Milan, 1987).

[56] H. Duchhardt, *Deutsche Verfassungsgeschichte, 1495–1806* (Stuttgart, 1991); H. Gross, 'The Holy Roman Empire in Modern Times: Constitutional Reality and Legal Theory', in J. A. Vann and S. W. Rowan (eds.), *The Old Reich: Essays on German Political Institutions*, 1495–1806, 3–29.

[57] Even together, Hamburg, Bremen, and Lübeck only counted 170,000 inhabitants, while the constitution of the Confederation required 300,000 for a court of appeal. When Frankfurt was included as the fourth free German city-state, a joint court of appeal could be set up in 1820. C. Rothenberger (ed.), *Das Hanseatische Oberlandesgericht: Gedenkschrift zu seinem 60jährigen Bestehen* (Hamburg, 1939), 16–111, is biased against 'particularism' for obvious reasons.

limit this erosion of their sovereign rights, and together with Lübeck and Bremen, set up the Hanseatic High Court of Appeal (Hanseatisches Oberlandesgericht) in 1879. This court became an important instrument for championing Hanseatic interests on the national level, for example in the national debates over *Wechselfähigkeit*, the right of drawing private bills of exchange.[58] The first president of the Hanseatic High Court, Ernst Friedrich Sieveking (1836–1909), was a specialist in international maritime law, which proved crucial to the new global orientation of Hanseatic policy. This ambition to maintain control over areas of the law that were vital to Hamburg's special trading economy found a visual expression in the cityscape with the construction of the gigantic Forum of Justice, culminating in the erection of a monumental Hanseatic High Court of Appeal.[59]

In Barcelona, resistance to national codification assumed an even greater importance, and became an important goal of the Lliga Regionalista.[60] Catalonia had lost its political independence much earlier than the territories of Germany or Italy. As a result, Catalan law came to be seen as the only surviving manifestation of regional autonomy.[61] In 1859, the draft national code threatened the special character of Catalan 'foral' law, which was centred around the nuclear family and partible inheritance.[62] Catalan defenders of this peculiarity cited two reasons for its superiority—one backward-looking, the other distinctly modern. Conservatives felt that foral law allowed for the ideal of the traditional patriarchal Catalan family to be projected onto the new industrial economy. Modernists suggested that testamentary liberty was integral to Catalonia's status as Spain's most industrialized region, resembling the English rather than the French legal system, which had allowed the Industrial Revolution to unfold.[63] As in Hamburg, such arguments achieved a visual manifestation in the cityscape, which was transformed into a three-dimensional manifestation of this type of legal-civic patriotism. The city's Palau de Justicia was an eminently symbolic building.[64] Built during the years of legal codification, it provides an example of the way in

[58] A. Engel, 'Die rechtsgutachtliche Tätigkeit des Hanseatischen Oberlandesgerichts', in Rothenberger, 128–41.

[59] K. Wiedemann, *Von der Gerichtslaube zum Sievekingsplatz: Gerichtsgebäude in Hamburg* (Hamburg, 1992).

[60] S. Harty, 'Lawyers, Codifications, and the Origins of Catalan Nationalism, 1881–1901', *Law and History Review*, 20 (2002), 349–84. See also A. Balcells, *Catalan* Nationalism.

[61] S. Jacobson, 'Law and Nationalism in Nineteenth-Century Europe: The Case of Catalonia in Comparative Perspective', *Law and History Review*, 20 (2002), 307–47; Joseph Pella y Forgas, *Llibertats y antich govern de Catalunya* (Barcelona, 1905).

[62] While Catalan public law had been abolished by the Bourbons in 1716, civil or 'foral' law remained autonomous, even though it could no longer be amended. S. Sobreques i Vidal, *Historia de la produccio del dret catala fins al decret Nova Planta* (Girona, 1978). On the Catalan response to national codification, see Jacobson, 'Law and Nationalism', 326–8.

[63] B. Clavero, 'Formacion doctrinal contemporanea del derecho catalan de sucesiones: la primogenitura de la libertad', in *La reforma de la Complicion: el sistema successori* (Barcelona, 1984), 10–37.

[64] Juan Miró y Murtó, *El Palacio de Justicia y la ciudad de Barcelona* (Barcelona, 1883), and, for a modern description, J. M. Mas i Solench, *El Palau des Justicia de Barcelona* (Barcelona, 1990). On its architect, see S. Barjau, *Enric Sagnier* (Barcelona, 1992).

which regional civic traditions were reconciled with a Spanish national discourse, rather than posited in opposition to it. Every detail of Sagnier's building combined Catalan and Spanish motifs. The Palau's surprisingly delicate entrance arch was reminiscent of the slim naves of the famous monasteries of the Catalan Romanesque, yet crowned by the Spanish-language inscription 'Palacio de Justicia' and a Spanish coat of arms. Above it towered a statue of Moses, the lawgiver, flanked by two allegorical female figures representing Spanish Law and the Law and Privileges of the Regions. Forty-eight large statues at first-floor level represented legal scholars and rulers from different centuries, with an exact 50 : 50 quota of Catalan and non-Catalan figures.[65] This was no empty rhetoric. When the Palau was completed in 1908, legal codification was a *fait accompli*—but so was the special status that Catalonia enjoyed within the new national framework. The Spanish Civil Code of 1889 was only applied as a supplement in Catalonia, and granted unprecedented degrees of autonomy to other regions, too.[66]

CONCLUSION

To conclude, regionalism in the nineteenth century should be thought of not as a rival to nationalism, but a complementary phenomenon. Regions offered the nation-state a mode of collaboration which left autonomous traditions intact, but which involved them in national decision-making. It was only when this balancing act failed, as it did in fascist Germany, Italy, and Spain, and in several of the rather artificial nation-states of the Soviet Eastern bloc, that regional identities came to be framed as alternatives to national identities—a process strikingly evident in the periods following the collapse of totalitarian regimes and their centralist ambitions.[67] But such confrontational scenarios were the exception. More typically, regionalists did not reject membership in the wider nation. To them, the nation was no mythical collective in which all smaller affiliations—be they individual, local, or regional—would be dissolved for the benefit of the whole. Their view of the nation-state was not charismatic, but pragmatic; they expected not salvation,

[65] The statues received much attention in the contemporary press and several official guidebooks. Descriptions appeared in the *Diari de Barcelona* on 13 December 1894, 14314; by the architects themselves, as 'Palacio de Justicia', *Annuario para 1899*, ed. the Associación de Arquitectos de Cataluña, 201–19; and again in *Arquitectura y Construcción: Revista mensual illustrada*, 12 (1908), ed. D. Manuel Vega y March, 176–83. The selection process for the statues is documented in the 'Actas de la Junta creada para erigir un Palacio de Justicia en Barcelona. Expediente número 27 relativo a la ejecucion de las cuarenta y ocho estátuas del piso 3° del Palacio de la Justicia', Arxiu Administratiu, Barcelona, Q140 (Palau de Justícia), 2-E-7, Boxes 8–9.

[66] J. Baro Pazos, *La codificaion del derecho civil en Espana, 1808–1889* (Santander, 1992).

[67] On the repression and resurgence of regionalism in Germany, see Umbach (ed.), *German Federalism*, especially Jeremy Noakes, 'Federalism in the Nazi State', 113–45. On regionalism in post-Soviet Eastern Europe, Ther and Sundhaussen (eds.), *Regionale Bewegungen*, especially Section Three, 'Die Renaissance der Regionen', 161–260. On the pattern of forceful centralization and centrifugal backlashes in twentieth-century politics, P. Waldmann et al. (eds.), *Die geheime Dynamik autoritärer Diktaturen* (Munich, 1982).

but political balance; not intervention, but a constitutional framework for autonomy. They also did not regard the nation as the ultimate and exclusive source of collective identity. By emphasizing that localism, regionalism, and nationalism coexisted, regional politics undermined what some historians have defined as the very essence of nationalism itself, at least nationalism of the ethnic variety: its claim to exclusivity, which turned it into the only legitimate focus of its citizens' loyalty.[68] In this way, regional self-interest itself became a vehicle for promoting a political vision which was inherently pluralist, and one that added to the national discourse of this period a primarily civic dimension. This is not to claim that regions were guardians of political idealism, as some scholars are quick to point out whenever they fear antinationalist political correctness at work.[69] Regional politics were driven by interests. Yet these interests, especially in former composite states, were those of elites that had evolved in and through civic culture and institutions. Their 'regional egotism' was therefore inexorably linked to the civic idiom, and they stood to lose out if the charismatic politics of ethnic nationalism were to sideline the institutional compromises between region and the centre that had been hammered out over decades and centuries. Modernization changed the balance, but did not always favour the nation-state, as classical modernization theory assumed.[70] Often, regional elites were at the forefront of economic progress. In such advanced regions, the strategies adopted to safeguard economic development against the 'conservatism' of the national centre could vary from free trade to protectionism, depending on whether the region's wealth was based on trade or industry.[71] Neither, however, was anti-modern. Another implication of modernization was the widening scope of political participation—only grudgingly granted by those who enjoyed privileged political status. This affected region and nation-state alike, but there is no reason to assume that as a consequence, civic culture was doomed. Schumacher's appropriation of *Heimat* for the city of Hamburg, or Puig's elaborate Catalan 'fantasy' architecture can serve as exemplars of the reconciliation of the civic idiom with modernity, namely an appeal to emotion, the imagination, and modern subjectivity.

In current debates about devolution, it is important to remember that, 'civic' as the legacy of European regionalism was, it provided no safeguard against totalitarian

[68] D. Langewiesche, 'Nation, Nationalismus, Nationalstaat in der europäischen Geschichte seit dem Mittelalter: Versuch einer Bilanz', in id. and G. Schmidt (eds.), *Föderative Nation*, 9–30.

[69] A. Green, 'The Federal Alternative: A New View of Modern German History?', *Historical Journal*, 3 (2002).

[70] W. W. Rostow, *The Stages of Economic Growth: A Non-Communist Manifesto* (Cambridge, 1960); P. Abrams, *Historical Sociology* (Ithaca, NY, 1982), especially 108–46. Excellent surveys of modernization and nation-building are G. Eley and R. G. Suny (eds.), *Becoming National: A Reader* (New York, 1996); and H.-U. Wehler, *Modernisierungstheorie und Geschichte* (Göttingen, 1975).

[71] Hamburg's commercial classes were free traders, whose stance became progressively more oppositional, the further German imperial politics, driven by the interests of agrarian *Junkers* and heavy industrialists in the Ruhr, moved towards protectionism. By contrast, Barcelona's burghers were textile manufacturers, who stood to lose a lot more than their Spanish neighbours if the national and colonial market were to be opened to cheaper English imports.

Maiken Umbach

and fascist brands of nationalism. In Germany, Italy, and Spain, regional autonomy
was one of the first victims of the centralizing policies of twentieth-century fascist
regimes. Regionalism is not identical with democracy and pluralism; indeed, it is
best thought of not as a political force, but as a political idiom.[72] Regionalism did
not 'cause' anything. It was a discourse that could be mobilized if and when it
suited the particular individuals and groups who did so. It provided a repository
of political arguments with a *longue durée*: easily cast aside by dictators, submerged, but never wholly absent from the political imagination of Europeans.
It is instructive that the national search for identity after the end of the dictator-
ships in Germany and, much more recently, in Spain, has in both cases led to a
significant resurgence of political and cultural regionalism. Regionalism is
certainly no substitute for a genuinely democratic political impulse. But it can be
a helpful political ingredient in building and rebuilding a civil society. Either way,
regionalism was an integral part of European nation-building, in the nineteenth
century as much as it is today.

[72] The term is borrowed from American sociologist T. Skocpol, *Social Revolutions in the Modern
World* (Cambridge, 1994).

5

The Low Countries

Between the City and the *Volk*

Carl Strikwerda

INTRODUCTION: THE PROBLEM OF LIBERAL NATIONALISM

Nationalism in nineteenth-century Belgium and the Netherlands, two small neighbouring states often referred to together as the Low Countries, was typically inclusive or civic in nature, rather than exclusionary or ethnic. Neither Belgian nor Dutch nationalism experienced the 'sharp shift to the political right of nation and flag . . . in the last decades of the nineteenth century' which historians such as Hobsbawm describe as typical for most of European nationalism.[1] Yet like other European countries, Belgium and the Netherlands experienced industrialization, church–state struggles, Socialism, and imperialism. What accounts for the nationalism in these societies being generally able to align itself with liberal or civic values as opposed to ethnicity? To answer this question, one must look first at their history before the nineteenth century that allowed them to develop a tradition of local liberties. Looking at the two countries' history in the nineteenth century reveals the complexities of civic nationalism, the power of civic nationalism in spite of its flaws, and why civic nationalism was harder to replicate elsewhere.

To understand how a kind of civic nationalism could grow up in the Low Countries in the nineteenth century, it is important to see that their history up to 1815 made it more possible, in some ways, for civic nationalism to develop over ethnic definitions of nationalism.[2] A strong sense of ethnic nationalism was more

---

[1] E. J. Hobsbawm, *Nations and Nationalism since 1780* (Cambridge, 1990), 12. For alternative views, D. Langewiesche, *Nationalismus im 19. und 20. Jahrhundert: Zwischen Partizipation und Aggression* (Bonn, 1994); C. Strikwerda, 'Nationalism, Ethnicity, and Social Movements', *Brood en Rozen: Tijdschrift voor Geschiedenis van Sociale Bewegingen*, 1 (1997), 11–20.

[2] For useful overviews, P. Bolk et al. (eds.), *Algemene Geschiedenis der Nederlanden*, vol. xiii (Harlem, 1978); E. H. Kossmann, *The Low Countries, 1780–1940* (Oxford, 1978); Jean Stengers, *Les Racines de la Belgique*, i: *Histoire du sentiment national en Belgique des origines* à 1918 (Brussels, 2000).

difficult to develop later because neither Dutch nor French, the two languages spoken in the two countries, coincided with political boundaries. Dutch was spoken in both countries, while the large portion of the Belgian population who spoke French shared cultural ties with the wider French-speaking world. Both countries had been part of the Holy Roman Empire that was never centralized into absolute monarchies. Instead of absolute monarchy, they shared a history of strong local communal or city governments. Ghent, Bruges, and Antwerp, in the southern Netherlands, and, to some degree, Amsterdam, Leiden, and Utrecht, in the north, regardless of which monarch ruled them in the late Middle Ages to the sixteenth century, were more city-states ruled by oligarchies than they were provinces or parts of a kingdom.

The two countries both owed their identity to political factors, more than long historical or ethnic continuities. The whole region in which the modern day countries of Belgium and the Netherlands were later to arise was ruled in the late Middle Ages by the counts of Burgundy. The region came under Spanish rule in the 1500s, as part of the Burgundian inheritance, first, of Charles V and then Philip II of Spain. In the 1570s, the whole region revolted against the Spanish, with the southern Netherlands initially more Protestant and more rebellious than the northern Netherlands. By 1589, however, only the northern Netherlands, the core of what would be the modern day Dutch state, had successfully revolted against the Spanish.[3] The southern Netherlands remained under Spain until 1715, when it passed by the verdict of the great powers to Austria.

There was also an elastic sense of identity in the region that eventually became the two states. The whole region from northern France to north-eastern Germany was sometimes known as 'Belgiae'. Even in what later became the northern Netherlands or Dutch kingdom, people could think of themselves as 'Belgic'. The 'Belgic Confession', for example, was one of the major doctrinal statements of the Calvinist Reformation in the Netherlands. In French, 'Pays-Bas' is low country, and only in the nineteenth century did it clearly become synonymous with the Dutch kingdom of the Netherlands. Before then, 'Pays-Bas Autrichienne' meant the southern Netherlands, just as the English referred to 'southern Low Countries' to designate the part of the Low Countries that was ruled by, first, Spain, then after 1715 Austria, and which, in 1830, became Belgium. Complicating the situation of the southern Netherlands still more was the independent prince-bishopric of Liège, which contained a large minority of the population, and one of the region's largest cities, Liège, but which was never under Spanish or Austrian rule. The northern provinces which broke away successfully from Spain in the late 1500s were, and sometimes inaccurately still are, referred to as 'Holland', which is really just the name of the largest province. After 1579, with the Union of Utrecht, the 'United Provinces of the Netherlands' gradually came to mean the Dutch Republic, but it was really not a nation-state in either an ethnic or political sense.

---

[3] G. Parker, *The Dutch Revolt*, rev. edn. (London, 1985).

Neither the southern Netherlands nor the northern Netherlands—that is, the Dutch Republic—were ethnically or religiously homogeneous. The Dutch Republic was about two-thirds Protestant and one-third Catholic, Catholics being almost 80 per cent concentrated in the southern region of the Republic, what is now the two modern provinces of Noord-Brabant and Limburg. (Revealingly, there are two Belgian provinces with the same names, Brabant, in which lies the capital of Brussels, and Limburg.) The Calvinist Dutch Reformed church was the established Protestant church of the Republic, but there were always substantial dissenters, mostly Mennonites and pietists. Taking into account the small Jewish population, the Catholics, and Protestant sects as being outside the Reformed church, the Calvinist established Reformed church represented only a little over half of the population.

Belgium, after the Spanish reconquest around 1600, became and remained, at least nominally, almost 100 per cent Catholic. Linguistically, and one could say ethnically, it has always been divided. The Flemish in the northern part of the southern Netherlands or modern-day Belgium speak Dutch or dialects of Dutch. Although observers often speak of the language of Flanders as '*Vlaams*', '*Flamande*', or 'Flemish', in linguistic terms, it is the same language as Dutch, the language of the northern Netherlands. Because French remained the language of business, the church, and government in Flanders for so long, the dialects spoken in Flanders remained stronger much longer than one would expect, but they have never been any more distinct from Dutch than their equivalents, say, in Italy or Germany. The Flemish or Dutch-speakers in the southern Netherlands or Belgium have always represented half to 60 per cent of the population, with French-speakers in the south and in the capital of Brussels together about 40 per cent.

The success of the Dutch revolt against Spain not only created the Dutch state in the early modern period, but it formed the bedrock of Dutch identity. The Netherlands' golden age of the 1600s, when the Dutch thrived briefly as a great power, served later, in the nineteenth century, as the touchstone of what Dutch people saw as their national greatness. To be Dutch was to be economically advanced, urban, and tolerant of diversity. The Dutch Republic probably was the first urban society in the world, certainly in Europe, with newspapers, stock exchange, central bank, the microscope, and art market, and one of the most open and most tolerant states in the world. Jews from Spain and Portugal and Protestants from France fled to the northern Netherlands in the 1600s. Books that the Bourbon French monarchy banned were printed in Amsterdam.

Yet, as modern as the United Provinces were, they did not create civic nationalism in the nineteenth-century sense. Power was held by a group of great urban families in the cities in the provinces of Holland and Zeeland. In a world of monarchies, the Dutch Republic was exceptional, but it was still ruled by an oligarchy. The House of Orange, which traditionally provided the executive or *stadthouder* of the Estates of Holland and almost all the other provinces, was never a 'royal' house. The most powerful of the urban patriciate were those chosen as Regents of the province of Holland. While not an aristocracy, they ruled as an elite, elected by a tiny electorate of the patriciate. Furthermore, their rule, and that of the other provincial oligarchies, rested on the specific privileges of the provinces. There was no common Dutch citizenship. Citizens of one province did not necessarily enjoy the same rights in another province. Holland, Gelderland, and Groningen acted, on the provincial level, as separate states, with different laws, weights and measures, and taxation. Religious toleration was far in advance of the rest of Europe of the early modern period. But Catholics, Protestant groups outside the established Dutch Reformed Church such as Mennonites, and even dissenters within the Reformed or Calvinist community suffered legal disabilities. As 'liberal' as the Dutch Republic was by the standards of the seventeenth century, it was no surprise that in the age of democratic revolution, the Netherlands experienced its own revolution, the so-called 'Patriot Revolt' in 1786–7, which was crushed by Prussian troops.[4] Thus, in the nineteenth century, the Dutch had a strong heritage of local liberties and sense of identity, but they had not yet created modern nationalism.

The southern Netherlands under Spanish and Austrian rule from 1600 to the French Revolution was viewed, in the nineteenth century by Belgian historians, as a country ruled by foreigners.[5] In fact, the oligarchies who ruled the cities and provinces in the southern Netherlands in the seventeenth and eighteenth centuries saw themselves at the time as enjoying a great many 'liberties'.[6] The region was never integrated into the Habsburg realm of Spain or the Habsburg lands of Austria. It paid fairly high taxes, but it was also wealthier than most of the rest of the monarchs' domains. When Joseph II of Austria tried to create more uniformity between the southern Netherlands and the rest of the Austrian lands, the region rose in revolt, in the so-called 'Brabaconne Revolution' of 1788–9.[7] But only its historic liberties formed a basis of identity among the 'Belgian' provinces. Otherwise, there was little to define the southern Netherlands as any kind of 'nation' from its neighbours. French culture spanned the border between France itself and the southern Netherlands. Despite over half the population speaking Dutch, French culture was almost everywhere in the southern Netherlands the dominant culture. The language of administration, even in relations with Vienna, was French, as was the language of most of commerce and the church. The independent prince-bishopric of Liège, which cut through the southern Netherlands, was a stronghold of French culture as well, even though the peasantry and middle

---

[4] S. Schama, *Patriots and Liberators: Revolution in the Netherlands, 1780–1813* (New York, 1977), 120–32.

[5] J. Stengers, 'Le Mythe des dominations étrangères dans l'historiographie belge', *Revue belge de philologie et d'histoire*, 59 (1981), 382–401.

[6] J. Roegiers, 'Belgian Liberties and Loyalty to the House of Austria', in K. Deprez and L. Vos (eds.), *Nationalism in Belgium: Shifting Identities, 1780–1995* (London, 1998).

[7] J. Craeybeckx, 'The Brabant Revolution: A Conservative Revolution in a Backward Country?' *Acta Historica Neerlandica*, 4 (1970), 40–73.

class in the northern part of the bishopric were Dutch-speaking. In the eastern and south-eastern parts of the southern Netherlands, some of which became the duchy of Luxemburg, the population spoke dialects of German, although here, too, the language of the elite was French.

Before the creation of the modern Belgian and Dutch states in the early nineteenth century, some fundamental traits had emerged that would have a profound effect on the possibilities for civic nationalism. After their brief glory as a military power in the seventeenth century, the Dutch rejected great power status. Their last fling at having an independent foreign policy amidst the great powers was in the War of American Independence, or the Fourth Anglo-Dutch War, 1780–6. The successful British attacks on Dutch shipping during the War devastated the Dutch economy. The Dutch hesitated to be tempted again, and until the present have earnestly eschewed militarism, except for a brief period in opposing Belgian independence in the 1830s. The Dutch also maintained a deep tradition as a merchant and financial capitalist power and as a transit route. This meant that they leaned toward free trade. Maintenance of free trade and the vested interest in finance and shipping reinforced the distaste for a large military establishment. The religious division meant diversity was part of the Dutch identity. To be Dutch was, in part, to have a real sense of pride in the heritage of toleration.

In contrast to the Dutch, who emerged from the early modern period with a sense of national identity, the 'Belgians' of the southern Netherlands had a strong sense of local identity in their towns and provinces, but little sense of being a distinct people. The Belgians developed some manufacturing, but given the small size of the country, this meant, too, that they had to promote trade and good relations with their neighbours to be able to export. However, with little shipping or capital of their own, they were dependent often on the English, Dutch, or Germans for their foreign economic connections.[8] The almost uniform Catholicism divided them from the Dutch and was a possible basis for exclusivity, but Catholicism, particularly for the Belgian church, was international in uniting them with Catholics in France and western Germany. Even the impact of the French Revolution and Napoleon did not turn the church into a political force. As Kossmann explains the situation by 1815: 'The Belgian clergy was counter-revolutionary, anti-Gallican, and ultramontane; it was not anti-French. It did not, and never wanted to, represent a national idea.'[9] Because the economic elite, provincial and municipal government, and the Church all used French, the linguistic diversity of the country was not recognized. But, at the same time, the overwhelming presence of French culture so close by meant that it was unlikely that a francophone Belgian ethnic identity would ever be successful in being imposed on the country. To be Belgian in the early and mid-nineteenth

[8] J. Mokyr, *Industrialization in the Low Countries, 1795–1850* (New Haven, 1976), 8–25.
[9] Kossmann, *Low Countries*, 81.

century meant to use French. But this was a political and cultural identity, not an ethnic one. It is not surprising that most 'Belgians' in 1810, at the height of Napoleon's empire, probably felt that they were French.

THE SUCCESS OF CIVIC NATIONALISM

The tradition of local liberties and the lack of emphasis on an exclusive ethnic or religious identity made the transition to constitutional monarchies and civic nationalism in both countries in the early nineteenth century more possible. The two countries were joined as one state, briefly from 1815 to 1830, in a United Kingdom of the Netherlands, after the great powers at the Congress of Vienna decided to build a strong state to block possible French aggression northward. But the Dutch King William I, the descendant of the traditional *stadhouder* family, the House of Orange, alienated the Belgians with authoritarian policies to check the power of the Catholic church and limit the use of French. The Belgians revolted in 1830, but were only able to become independent because of the support of Britain and France.[10] The direct result of Belgian independence was constitutional monarchy in both of the successor states, although it took longer for the Dutch to wrest confirmation of this from King William I. By his mishandling of Belgian grievances in the 1820s, the king had involved the Dutch in a costly war, nearly wrecked relations with the great powers—Britain, France, and Prussia—and diverted energy from the liberal programme. When he abdicated in 1840, however, it was clear that parliament was the real seat of power in the state. Most Dutch were not sorry to see the separation from Belgium. After the costly wars of the eighteenth century and the upheaval of the Napoleonic wars, they had little taste for the role of an 'almost great power' that the Congress of Vienna had envisaged for the United Kingdom of the Netherlands. The separation from Belgium meant, too, that those who advocated a colonial policy, that is, exploiting the small hold that the Dutch had in the East Indies, could now do so without having to balance manufacturing interests in Belgium with the financial and trading priorities in the Netherlands.

While the blessing of the great powers allowed an independent Belgium to survive, the alliance of liberals and Catholics that supported the Belgian Revolution of 1830 against the Dutch was a remarkable achievement of civic nationalism. Almost all liberals were themselves nominally Catholic, and many were practising as well, but they all opposed an established state church and wanted to limit the subsidies and support for the Catholic church to the minimum level that would win Catholic support for proponents of an independent Belgium and a constitutional state. In contrast to their co-religionists elsewhere in Europe in the 1830s,

---

[10] J. S. Fishman, *Diplomacy and Revolution: The London Conference of 1830 and the Belgian Revolt* (Amsterdam, 1988).

and in defiance of the pope, Belgian Catholics accepted constitutional freedom of worship in order to win liberal support to oppose the policies of the Protestant Dutch king, William I. This unusual coalition of liberals and Catholics, known as 'Unionism', ruled Belgium, with only a few interruptions until the 1860s. The Catholic church found that it was able to use the liberal rights of association given by the constitution to win back its losses from the French and Dutch periods and greatly expand its hold on education and social welfare.[11]

This 'Unionist' coalition founded Belgium as an independent kingdom that was, for its time, justifiably known as a 'crowned republic'.[12] It boasted a free press, a responsible parliament, the right of assembly, and, for its time, a reasonably extended suffrage. About 10 per cent of males voted. Despite pressure from other powers, Belgium generally defended the right of asylum.[13] Victor Hugo and Karl Marx were two of the famous exiles who lived for a time in Brussels. Belgium was, in many ways, a creation of Britain, which decided that if the Netherlands could not make a united state in the Low Countries work, then an independent Belgium was the next best way to prevent France from absorbing the southern Netherlands. The first Belgian King, Leopold I, was Queen Victoria's uncle. Liberal and conservative Belgian politicians in the Parliament in the mid-nineteenth century looked to Britain for a model and even took to calling themselves 'Whigs' and 'Tories' to emphasize that Belgium was not French. Similarly, social and political movements in mid-nineteenth-century Belgium were deeply impressed with the Anti-Corn Law League and Chartism. They could employ a 'British-ism' to describe their activities. One could be described in French as a *'meetinguiste'*, i.e. one who organized 'meetings'. One of the most important Belgian political movements of the period of the 1860s was, in fact, the 'Meeting Partij' in Antwerp that championed Flemish grievances and local autonomy.[14]

In both countries, governments avoided revolution in 1848 by making small changes that placated enough liberals to preserve stability. The Belgian liberals managed to expand the suffrage and provide greater freedoms to the press. The changes in the Netherlands had a more profound impact in marking the end of the influence of the old urban patriciate that had governed during the Republic. Despite vigorous opposition from these conservative urban elites, the demands for a genuinely liberal constitution in the Netherlands led King William II to allow for a new constitution providing for direct elections and full cabinet responsibility for government. In the midst of the controversy, the king died and his son, William III, succeeded him. After months of political infighting, the new Dutch King William III in November 1849 named as prime minister the great liberal of

[11] A. Simon, *L'Église catholique et les debuts de la Belgique indépendante* (Wetteren, 1949).

[12] L. Dhont, 'De Conservatieve Brabantse Omwenteling van 1789 en het Proces van Revolutie en Contrarevolutie in de Zuidelijke Nederlanden tussen 1780 en 1830', *Tijdschrift voor Geschiedenis*, 102 (1989), 448.

[13] N. Coupain, 'L'Expulsion des étrangers en Belgique (1830–1914)', *Revue belge d'histoire contemporaine*, 32/1–2 (2003), 5–48.   [14] Kossmann, *Low Countries*, 245–55.

nineteenth century Netherlands, J. R. Thorbecke (1798–1872).[15] The reforms of 1848–9 were most important, in retrospect, in creating a genuine 'public sphere' in the Netherlands. An ongoing debate over issues through the press, the formation of modern political parties, and electoral campaigns all began to emerge in the years after 1848.[16]

The other great success of liberal politics in the mid-nineteenth century in both countries was the strengthening of market economies. Liberals in the governments managed to end the *octroi*, the local taxes around the cities that had hampered trade.[17] They built railroads and improved harbours so that Antwerp in Belgium and later Rotterdam in the Netherlands have ever since vied for being two of the five largest ports in Europe. Charles Rogier (1800–85), Belgian prime minister twice in the 1850s and 1860s, saw railroads in a Saint-Simonian sense as liberating society from the past and ensuring that Belgium would be integral to both the European economy and culture. Karl Marx sarcastically described Belgium as the 'Paradise of the landlord, the capitalist, and the priest'.[18] Neither state invested in the well-being of the workers or rural populations until the end of the nineteenth century, although the Netherlands was about at the level of France, Britain, and Prussia in most respects, and Belgium was still ahead of Italy, Spain, and Austria-Hungary.

THE COMPLEXITIES OF CIVIC NATIONALISM: ELITISM AND IMPERIALISM

Beneath this picture of relatively successful liberal states that enjoyed many aspects of civic nationalism, the two countries reveal the complexities of liberal nationalism as well. In particular, the liberalism that was part of civic nationalism was subverted by its very proponents because of their elitism and support for imperialism.

Liberal elites delayed sharing political power as long as possible with groups they perceived as anti-liberal—Catholics, Calvinist dissenters, Socialists, or Flemish rights activists. Only in 1887 did the Dutch revise the constitution of 1848 in order to extend the suffrage to all independent male property owners over the age of 23. The suffrage was extended from about 6.4 per cent of

---

[15] J. C. Boogman, *Rondom 1848: De Politieke Ontwikkeling van Nederland 1840–1858* (Amsterdam, 1978), 85–9.

[16] I. De Hann and H. te Velde, 'Vormen van Politiek: Veranderingen van de Openbaarheid in Nederland, 1848–1900', *Bijdragen en Medelingen Betreffende de Geschiedenis der Nederlanden*, 111 (1996), 167–200.

[17] Y. Segers, 'Een omstreden verbruiksbelasting: de stedelijke octrooien in Belgie (1799–1860)', *Belgisch Tijdschrift voor Nieuwste Geschiedenis*, 30/3–4 (2000), 325–69.

[18] 'The Belgian Massacres', reprinted in J. Dhondt (ed.), *Geschiedenis van de Socialistische Arbeidersbeweging in Belgie* (Antwerp, 1960), 282. This broadside was published by the International League of Workingmen, but almost certainly written by Marx.

adults to 13.9 per cent, or from a little over a tenth of the adult males to about a quarter. Only in 1917 did the conservative Catholic, Protestants, and liberal parties agree to universal male suffrage, but it was extended to women, too, in 1920. In Belgium, conservative Catholics only granted universal suffrage in 1893, after a massive general strike led by Socialists.[19] Even then, they only granted it because they feared that Liberals would ally with Socialists out of frustration from being out of power, and that democratic Catholics might also ally with Liberals and Socialists out of frustration with their lack of influence in the Catholic government. Universal suffrage even then was watered down by plural votes, with up to three total votes given to those who paid more taxes. This granting of universal male suffrage kept democratic Catholics within the Catholic party ranks, but it severely diluted workers' votes. After universal suffrage came in 1918, the first elections revealed that the conservative Catholics and Liberals had been artificially strengthened by the plural vote system. All the so-called 'emancipation' movements of the nineteenth century—Socialists in both countries, Catholics in the Netherlands, democratic Catholics and Flemish activists in Belgium—were tempted to turn against liberalism because of the hypocrisy of the system.

The elitism of the liberal elites in both countries was all the more risky because Liberals pushed a strong anticlerical policy that angered Catholics and, in the Netherlands, conservative Protestants as well. State-sponsored, neutral schools were always a centrepiece of liberal policy. In practice, up to the 1870s, most government-supported schools on the local level incorporated religious instruction, or, they were so poorly supported that independent or 'free' religious schools were as successful in attracting students. However, in 1878, in the Netherlands, and 1879, in Belgium, Liberals introduced education bills that sought to secularize education by greatly expanding the government school. For J. Kappeyne van de Coppelo, Thorbecke's successor in the Netherlands, and W. Frere-Orban, Rogier's in Belgium, secular, state-supported and state-regulated schools would not only free the population from the ignorance of the past and equip the lower classes for a modern, progressive future, but they would also create a national spirit.[20] This newly invigorated nationalism was to be patriotic and unifying, but clearly secular.

In both cases, anticlerical educational policies provoked a backlash and divided the countries almost to the present day. In Belgium, the 1879 education law provoked a groundswell of popular protest by lower- and middle-class Catholics who pushed aside many of the more traditional Catholic leaders who had tried to compromise with the liberals. To the Catholic masses, the new educational law was the 'law of evil'. New religious schools were built, new Catholic newspapers and organizations created, and the re-energized Catholic party displaced the

[19] C. Strikwerda, *A House Divided: Catholics, Socialists, and Flemish Nationalists in Nineteenth Century Belgium* (Lanham, Md., 1997), 119–20.
[20] V. Mallinson, *Power and Politics in Belgian Education 1815–1961* (London, 1963).

liberals in power in the elections of 1884.[21] They were to hold power alone until a coalition government formed during the First World War. The new, more militant Catholics in the party's ranks eventually led to Christian Democratic elements making the Catholic party into a mass political party with a wider network of farmers' leagues, clubs, labour unions, and mutual insurance societies grouped around it.

In the Netherlands, the reaction against liberal anticlericalism was not as dramatic but just as profound in its consequences. Before the 1860s, many Catholic leaders in the Netherlands collaborated with liberal leaders in order to weaken the power of the traditional Protestant establishment that had held Catholics down. In 1853, a Catholic-liberal alliance in Thorbecke's government allowed, for the first time since the 1500s, Catholic bishoprics to be established in the Netherlands and their incumbents to be named directly by the pope, in this case, the conservative Pius IX. (The new bishoprics sparked a wave of protest, known as 'the April movement' by anticlerical Liberals and conservative Protestants.) The Liberals' education bill of 1878 ended the Liberal–Catholic alliance once and for all, but the lead in mobilizing against the Liberals came from the conservative Protestants. Under the charismatic leadership of Abraham Kuyper (1837–1920), who was to be prime minister 1901–5, conservative Protestants organized the Anti-Revolutionary Party, as well as their own denomination, religious schools, newspapers, and associations.[22] The education law was weakened, but the state still retained more control over education in the Netherlands than in Belgium, until a system of religious pluralism was enacted definitively in 1917. The Catholics in the Netherlands followed the conservative Protestant lead in organizing their own party, newspapers, and clubs, but with more circumspection in order to avoid provoking anti-Catholicism.

As weakened as liberal or civic nationalism was by these deep divisions over religion, ethnic nationalism was not an option for the Catholics or conservative Protestants fighting the secular Liberals. The crucial elements—nobles, small farmers, and lower middle class—that supported ethnic or conservative nationalism in Imperial Germany, France, Austria-Hungary, and other countries created a nationalist programme by claiming to redress economic grievances through high tariffs, imperialism, and militarism. These same social groups were much weaker in the Netherlands and Belgium or they aligned with political movements that until 1914 accepted civic nationalism. The Netherlands had traditionally had an urban patriciate as an elite; the nobility or *ridderschap* was poorer than the urban elite and even in the landward provinces had lost power to merchants in the cities. Belgium lacked a real nobility at all: a few families claimed noble status from

[21] J. Lory, 'La Resistance des catholiques belges a la "loi de malheur", 1879–1884', *Revue du Nord* 7266 (1985), 729–47; E. Witte and Jan Craeybeckx, *Politieke Geschiedenis van Belgie sinds 1830* (Antwerp, 1983), 92–9.
[22] J. Bratt, 'Abraham Kuyper: Puritan, Victorian, Modern', in C. van der Kooi and J. de Bruijn (eds.), *Kuyper Reconsidered: Aspects of his Life and Work* (Amsterdam, 1999).

Austrian or Napoleonic times, but otherwise, the only legal nobles were those created on the basis of wealth or status by the new Belgian state. Small farmers in the Low Countries suffered like their counterparts across Europe with the fall of grain prices in the late nineteenth century. Some emigrated—the Dutch to the United States, the Belgians, mostly Flemish, to France.[23] Politically, they were not strong enough to alter the support for free trade provided by the mercantile and manufacturing sectors. Like the lower middle class, they supported Catholic or, in the Netherlands, conservative Protestant parties. While making populist appeals, these parties chose to aid the farmers and the lower middle class through subsidies, education, and support to create associations. As described below, imperialism was important for both countries. But the political leaders who supported it did so largely on economic grounds alone, not as part of a programme of militarism and ethnic nationalism.

The challengers to liberalism, in one sense, strengthened civic nationalism by expanding it to include themselves. The conservative Protestants organized around Kuyper in the Anti-Revolutionary Party in many ways were not conservative at all in a political sense. They were 'conservative' in a theological sense in that they upheld an orthodox interpretation of Scripture and disapproved of a wide range of modern cultural changes such as feminism and secularism. But in their techniques of organization and their ambition to influence Dutch society, they were thoroughly modern. They looked back to the Golden Age of the Dutch Republic in a sense of patriotic and religious pride, but they did not call for a return to the rule of the Regents. Kuyper wanted a democratic state, based in popular sovereignty that would also follow Christian morality. His ideals may have been unrealistic, but they ignited his followers into a populist, institution-building frenzy that thrust the previously passive conservative Protestants into the mainstream of Dutch life. Using liberal laws on association, the conservative Protestants built schools and a university, started labour unions and newspapers, and created a kind of Calvinist subculture in all aspects of life. Kuyper even claimed to have a Christian stance on foreign policy issues that helped justify his claim to the position of prime minister.[24]

This reaction against liberalism which led to the political integration of outsiders was particularly striking in the case of the Dutch Catholics. As a marginalized and economically poor minority, they had never had much sense of being Dutch. Under the Republic, they had been 'foreigners in their own land'. The territory in which around 80 per cent of the Catholics in the Republic lived, what is now the southern provinces of Noord Brabant and Limburg, was never allowed self-government like the self-governing provinces ruled by the Regents. The two

[23] R. Swierenga (ed.), *The Dutch in America* (New Brunswick, NJ, 1985); C. Strikwerda, 'France and the Belgian Immigration of the Nineteenth Century', in C. Guerin-Gonzales and Strikwerda (eds.), *The Politics of Immigrant Workers* (New York, 1998).

[24] R. Kuiper, 'Orthodox Protestantism, Nationalism, and Foreign Affairs', in A. Galema et al. (eds.), *Images of the Nation: Different Meanings of Dutchness, 1870–1940* (Amsterdam, 1993).

provinces were also overwhelmingly agricultural and benefited only marginally from the capitalist development of the cities near the coast. In 1814, Dutch Catholics celebrated the return of the pope to Rome, not the return of William of the House of Orange to become king of the new United Kingdom of the Netherlands.[25] Following the lead of Kuyper's Anti-Revolutionary party, however, the Catholics in the late nineteenth century created a similar subculture of school leagues, farmers' associations, labour unions, newspapers, and political clubs. In the process of fighting those aspects of Dutch society that threatened them, secular state schools, in particular, they learned how to participate in politics. In this process, they became Dutch.

It was crucial in both the Netherlands and Belgium that challengers to liberalism could claim certain pieces of the national heritage as justifications for their opposition. Kuyper often appealed to the historic role of Calvinism in making the Netherlands great in the past, and in guaranteeing God's favour for the present and future. But one of the major leaders of the conservative Protestant movement was Isaac Da Costa (1798–1860), a converted Jew who symbolized the deep tradition of diversity and toleration that had accompanied Dutch identity since the 1600s.

In Belgium, the Catholics who fought the liberals' secular school law called their organizations 'Constitutional Clubs'. It was, in their interpretation, the Belgian Constitution of 1831 that had allowed for religious instruction in the schools. In creating a mass movement and appealing to the masses, the Catholics were defending, so they wished to say, tradition, even if it was the failed tradition of 'Unionism' that had brought liberals and Catholics together to oppose Dutch rule in 1830 and found the Belgian state. In the sense that Liberals had wanted a constitutional system resting on popular sovereignty, it was the upsurge of Catholic electoral organizing against the Liberals that made Belgian politics genuinely constitutional. As late as 1878, parliament was effectively run by an oligarchy: over half the seats were not even contested in elections. Even before universal suffrage was enacted in 1893, the Catholics, in opposition to liberal anticlericalism, had brought more of the masses into the political system by organizing their middle- and lower-class supporters and contesting every parliamentary seat that they could. The proportion of seats uncontested in elections, for example, dropped in 1880 to only 18 per cent.[26] Ironically, those initially outside the liberal tradition helped broaden the basis of civic nationalism.

Just as complicated a part of civic nationalism as the battle over anticlericalism was the drive to conquer non-Western territories for the national state. Both states developed large empires based on theories of European racial supremacy over

[25] P. Raedts, 'Tussen Rome en Den Haag: De Integratie van de Nederlandse Katholieken in Kerk en Staat', in H. te Velde and H. Verhage (eds.), *De Eenheid en De Delen: Zuilvorming, Onderwijs, en Natievorming in Nederland, 1850–1900* (Amsterdam, 1996), 32.
[26] H. De Smaele, '*Omdat We Uwe Vriendin Zijn': Religie en Partij-Identificatie, 1884–1914* (Leuven, 2000), 75–79.

Africans or Asians. Imperialism abroad coexisted with civic nationalism at home. After the loss of Belgium, the Netherlands especially pushed to expand its control over all of the East Indies, present-day Indonesia. The so-called 'culture system' forced Javanese peasants to produce staple crops that could be sold to the Dutch colonial government to meet its demands for taxes and allowed a monopoly, the Nederlandsche Handel-Maatschappij, or Dutch Trading Company, to control exports. Until the system was dismantled, it meant an influx of wealth into the Netherlands and the impoverishment of Java. It was surprising how little criticized the exploitation of the culture system was in Dutch politics, although the greatest Dutch novel, *Max Havelaar* by 'Multatuli' (Edward Douwes Dekker) owes its origin to the author's attack on Dutch colonialism.[27] Although the 'culture system' produced important profits for monopoly traders and the Dutch government, eventually pressure from liberal free-traders and excluded business firms, as well as trading partners such as the British, led the Dutch government to abolish it in 1870.[28]

The Belgian experience with colonialism is, tragically, much grimmer still. Leopold II, who ruled from 1865 to 1909, desired to remake Belgium into an influential power, if not a great military power, and to free his dynasty from the hold of the constitution by creating a huge and lucrative empire in the Congo. For several decades, in the name of the great powers, he ruled the 'Congo Free State' as his personal realm. Although, to please other powers, he allowed free trade, in fact, his companies controlled the economy. They wreaked a horrible reign of terror on the Congolese population. Congolese suffered mutilation and execution if they did not produce enough ivory or rubber to meet the companies' exactions. The horror of imperialism described in Joseph Conrad's *Heart of Darkness* is based on the atrocities committed in the Congo under Leopold's rule. Finally, one of the first successful international human rights campaigns, led by British journalist E. D. Morel, and political pressure by other countries forced the Belgian government to make the Congo a government possession and end the Congo Free State. Again, what is striking is that imperialism was hardly a factor in Belgian politics. Many Liberals, Catholics, and Socialists alike opposed it, but this meant not taking any responsibility for the king's misrule until they were forced to by foreign governments. When they did take over the Congo as a Belgian possession in 1908, they resolutely avoided making it the centrepiece of a programme for nationalist policies.[29]

Imperialism, however, as dreadful as its consequences were for the Congolese and Indonesians, never created an interest-group in Dutch or Belgian society that was committed to militarism and a strong, ethnic, or exclusivist state. Certainly, the very vulnerability of the two small states made a militarist ideology a risky prospect. This

---

[27] Multatuli [Edward Douwes Dekker], *Max Havelaar, or the Coffee Sales of the Netherlands Trading Company* [Amsterdam, 1860] (London, 1927).

[28] C. Geertz, *Agricultural Involution: The Processes of Ecological Change in Indonesia* (Berkeley, 1963); M. Wintle, *An Economic and Social History of the Netherlands 1880–1920* (Cambridge, 2000), 217–23.

[29] N. Ascherson, *The King Incorporated: Leopold II in the Age of Trusts* (New York, 1984).

was especially true after the dramatic reordering of the balance of power in the Franco-Prussian War of 1870–1. With France's defeat, and the creation of a new Imperial Germany, the Low Countries were much more exposed to pressures to take sides. The Grand Duchy of Luxemburg had survived, even after Belgium's creation in 1830–1, to be tied to the Netherlands as a separate possession of the House of Orange, although it had been garrisoned for a time by Prussian troops. In the wake of the Franco-Prussian War, when both France and Prussia had contemplated annexing Luxemburg, the great powers agreed that, at the end of William III's reign, Luxemburg would be completely independent. This was a potent symbol of how small states could have their fates dictated by the great powers.

Belgium and the Netherlands nonetheless insisted on their neutrality, and did very little to build up their military commitments. This rejection of militarism was one of the clearest signs of the power of civic over ethnic nationalism. Late nineteenth-century conservative or ethnic nationalism, according to Michael Howard, 'was almost invariably characterized by militarism'.[30] By contrast, the Dutch imperial venture was maintained almost as a separate activity from the rest of Dutch political life.[31] There was a movement in the 1880s calling for a 'stronger nationalism' among the Dutch. Among other goals, it would create Dutch solidarity with the Boers or Afrikaners, the white South Africans of Dutch descent who opposed British imperial expansion. The conservative Protestants under Kuyper supported this, and a small strand of liberals, who were generally pro-British, flirted with it as well. But it largely failed, and the Boer War showed its limits. The Netherlands as a whole was strongly opposed to British conquest of the Boer republics, but the Dutch could do nothing to stop it.[32] The Belgian Catholics, in power continually from 1884 to 1914, were only very reluctantly supportive of improving Belgium's defences in order to maintain the country's neutrality. In 1906, Christian Democrats, Socialists, and a small group of Progressive Liberals nearly defeated the conservative Catholic government, supported by mainstream Liberals, over expanding the forts protecting Antwerp.[33] Instead, there was a limited, but still prophetic interest in both the Netherlands and Belgium before 1914 in an internationalism that would save the two countries' neutrality. The international peace congresses in the Hague in 1899 and 1907 were the most striking symbols of this interest. Agitation for an alliance in favour of peace—an 'Entente Cordiale des Petits États' of the Low Countries—was another manifestation.[34] Belgium, like Switzerland, was a centre for internationalism before 1914.[35]

[30] M. Howard, *The Causes of War* (London, 1983), 26.

[31] H. J. Wesseling, 'Bestond er een Nederlands Imperialisme?', *Tijdscrift voor Geschiedenis*, 99 (1986), 214–25.

[32] H. te Velde, *Gemeenschapzin en Plichtsbesef: Liberalisme en Nationalisme in Nederland, 1870–1918* ('s Gravenhage, 1992), 63–8.

[33] T. Luykx, *Politieke Geschiedenis van Belgie van 1789 tot Heden* (Brussels, 1964), 236–7.

[34] E. Delfoort, 'Het Belgische Nationalisme voor de erste Wereldoorlog', *Tijdschrift vor Geschiedenis* (1972), 524–42.

[35] A. Iriye, *Global Community: The Role of International Organizations in the Making of the Contemporary World* (Berkeley, 2002), 17.

THE FAILURE OF CIVIC NATIONALISM AND THE DEVELOPMENT OF ETHNIC NATIONALISM

Where civic nationalism failed most vividly, in the case of the Flemish, ethnic nationalism emerged. How this ethnic consciousness arose is a long, complicated story. It was not a product of nostalgia for Dutch rule, nor was it ever fostered by the Dutch. In the 1830s, there was little sense of loss among the Dutch over the separation from Belgium. Ethnic solidarity between the Dutch in the northern Netherlands and the Dutch-speaking Flemish was not a strong sentiment. Literary and academic figures kept up a modest effort at cultural ties. Beginning in 1871, a Language and Literature Congress began regular meetings to try to standardize the language on both sides of the border and bring Dutch and Flemish scholars and writers into contact with each other. When Dutch Catholics became a strong force in politics in the Netherlands in the late nineteenth century, they spread a limited sympathy for Flemish grievances. But this was as much based on religious solidarity as ethnic, and it did not affect Dutch politics as a whole.

Flemish consciousness arose independently from the influence of the northern Netherlands. There was, however, a good deal more Orangist, that is, pro-Dutch sentiment among the Flemish in Belgium than was recognized in the nineteenth century. Contemporaries were aware that some aristocrats and manufacturers in Belgium, almost all of whom were French-speaking, were Orangist. Even after the initial defeat of the Dutch in 1831, they wanted administrative unity with the Netherlands. They feared that a small Belgian state could not survive in a world of great powers, and they feared the loss of the Dutch colonial markets. By the late 1830s, these groups reconciled themselves to Belgian independence. But Orangism persisted longer among the lower classes in Flanders. The liberal elites of nineteenth-century Belgium were francophone but also did nothing about social problems in Flanders. Well into the 1840s and 1850s, crowds in industrial cities such as Ghent continued to shout Orangist slogans at public gatherings in honour of the Belgian state. Orangism was a kind of protest against the failures of the liberal and francophone Belgian state.[36] While the Dutch, and certainly the Dutch king, would not have been likely to do anything about social problems had their rule continued, Orangism demonstrates that Belgian national identity was never deeply rooted in Flanders, that is, Dutch-speaking Belgium.

Over the mid to late nineteenth century, a Dutch-speaking middle class arose in Flanders, and lower-class emancipation movements, that is, the Socialists and democratic Catholics, emerged in Flanders as well. The Dutch-speaking leaders of the middle class and the Socialist and democratic Catholic movements

---

[36] P. De Witte, *Alles Is Omkegeerd: Hoe De Werklieden Vroeger Leefden 1848–1918* (Leuven, 1986), 71.

increasingly resented the hold of the French language over Flanders. Once the suffrage was expanded in 1893, the only way to mobilize the lower-class and middle-class voters in Flanders was through Dutch. By the First World War, a loose coalition of democratic Catholic and Socialist parliamentary deputies had wrested linguistic rights for Dutch in education and social welfare in Flanders from the francophone national government. No one in pre-1914 Flanders called for Flemish independence. Calls for Flanders to become a unilingual Dutch-speaking region were even rarer. The most nationalist or aggrieved Flemish were able to develop a dual identity, Flemish in language and everyday culture, and deeply opposed to French culture, while at the same time, Belgian in political identity.[37] The Flemish activists generally avoided flirting with Pan-German appeals before 1914. It was only under German occupation in the First World War that a branch of the Flemish movement espoused a more radical anti-Belgian programme. Most Flemish Belgians rejected this stance, as they did again in the Second World War.[38]

WHY CIVIC NATIONALISM WAS LESS SUCCESSFUL OUTSIDE THE LOW COUNTRIES

Belgium and the Netherlands may suggest why civic or liberal nationalism proved less hardy elsewhere. Only by clinging to neutrality and free trade could governments in the Low Countries weaken the rise of large military or conservative economic interests. In trying to suppress the Belgians, King William I made an attempt at great power status. The Dutch as an imperial power were certainly willing to use military power—often using German troops—in the East Indies. But the coercion of 1830–1 failed, and the use of the military in the East Indies never militarized Dutch politics at home. Similarly, Belgium avoided creating an aristocratic or militarist element in politics because it was a neutral country. Even the war scare before 1914 did not change the weakness of a militarist element in Belgian politics. Some Catholics saw anti-militarism and neutralism as Catholic policies. At the same time, the pressure from Catholics for low taxes was also important in weakening support for a stronger military. Thus, there was no basis for a Pan-German or Action Française element in either Belgian or Dutch politics.

Similarly, there was no element pushing seriously for protectionist tariffs in the name of strengthening the nation against outsiders. There was an aggressive lobby for agricultural tariffs in Belgium in the late nineteenth century, but a few small increases took away this element's aggressiveness. On balance, Belgian tariffs remained low, on both agricultural and industrial imports, as did the Dutch.

---

[37] H. Van Velthoven, *De Vlaamse Kwestie, 1830–1914: Macht en Onmacht van de Vlaamsgezindheden* (Kortrijk, 1982).

[38] W. Dolderer, *Deutscher Imperialismus und belgischer Nationalitenkonflikt* (Kassel, 1989).

In both countries, there was a strong realization, on the part of all classes, that the country's economy depended on international markets. Antwerp and Rotterdam were two of the biggest ports in the world. They only thrived by allowing goods from Britain, the United States, Germany, and the rest of the world to flow through, relatively untaxed. In fact, 'Antwerp f.o.b.'—'Antwerp, free on board'— that is, the price of a good when it was to be shipped out of Antwerp after fees and taxes had been paid, was the standard world price for many commodities. Other countries of similar size to the Low Countries may not have had the luxury of neutrality without the protection of Britain or other great powers, or the generally expansive international economy of the nineteenth century. In other words, as exemplary as the Dutch and Belgian cases of civic nationalism may be, they also benefited from certain circumstances that might not have been likely to occur elsewhere.

THE POWER OF CIVIC NATIONALISM, IN SPITE OF ITS FLAWS

Ironically, the complexities of civic nationalism could also demonstrate the very power of civic nationalism. The elitism, the incipient militarism of imperialism, and the failure to deal with linguistic grievances all undermined civic nationalism. But, except in the case of the Flemish, and then only weakly so before 1914, ethnic nationalism did not emerge as a real threat to civic nationalism. Civic nationalism survived the challenges of the nineteenth century in both countries in part because it was an elastic enough creed that it could be used by challengers of the liberal elites. The Low Countries thus reveal some of the power of the liberal qualities of civic nationalism. Even as liberal elites lost power, new political groups largely accepted the liberal 'rules of the game'. They appealed to civic nationalism to enter, not break down the system. Workers and peasants, too, deserved *les droits de la cité*, the rights to the city. Even for the Flemish nationalists, until the rise of fascism, to be *volksgezind*, popular-minded, was to be democratic, not reactionary.[39]

The means by which civic nationalism in the Low Countries acted as an inclusive force, however, challenges the liberal tradition in an important way. The Netherlands by the early twentieth century had developed as a society with separate subcultures—Catholic, conservative Protestant, Socialist, and Liberal, with the latter two sometimes overlapping in a conjoined 'neutral', that is, non-religious set of organizations. Each subculture—if the Liberals and Socialists are treated as one—had its own labour unions, political parties, farmers' leagues, mutual insurance societies, newspapers, and even its own schools. In other words, the crucial divisions were largely vertical and, except for the confrontation

---

[39] *Zesde Vlaamsche Sociale Week, 1913* (Ghent, 1914), 146; 'Guide Gezelle en 't Ontwakken van Vlaanderen', *De Metaalarbeider*, 5 June 1914, 43.

between Socialists and Liberals within the neutral camp, cut through class lines. The Dutch term *verzuiling*, usually translated as 'pillarization', captures this process of vertical division. By 1900, the Catholic, conservative Protestant, and the Socialist/liberal 'pillars' provided the first identity of the vast majority of Dutch people. One was Dutch to the outside world beyond the Netherlands, but within the circle of 'Dutchness' the Catholic, or conservative Protestant, or Socialist/ Liberal identity was the most salient.

It is crucial to see that *verzuiling*, in its origins, was a product of the dissolution of the liberal system. Liberals broke the hold of the patriciate over Dutch politics, but then were unable to carry out their vision of an individualist society. The liberal opposition, in part, mobilized many of the marginalized groups of Dutch society. The landward provinces, much of whose population were conservative Protestant, and Catholics, many of whom were concentrated in the south, had had little access to power held by the urban elites in Holland.[40] There are real parallels here to the situation in Britain and Prussia, except that in Britain, of course, the disenfranchised—the Welsh, Scots, dissenters, and Catholics—stuck with the Liberals much longer. As in Prussia and early Imperial Germany, in the Netherlands the Liberals gradually lost the support of the formerly disenfranchised groups to populist or class-conscious leaders who could appeal to the lower classes more directly, groups such as the conservative Protestants, Catholics, and Socialists.

Thorbecke and the Liberals, however, made a crucial contribution to Dutch nationalism. Unlike the German Liberals, they succeeded in propagating their notion of the Netherlands as a society and a state dependent on inclusivity. As N. C. F. van Sas puts it, for the mid-nineteenth-century Liberals, 'National pride and liberal reform were to be bound up in the closest possible way.'[41] Even as the Liberals lost power to conservative Protestants and Catholics, their ideal of a strong national identity bound up with a diversity of groups lived on. One could even say that it took on a fuller meaning than the Liberals themselves had intended. By the early twentieth century, some Liberals were able to come to grips with the new reality of confessional and ideological politics coexisting with a sense of national unity. Cornelis Van Vollenhoven, an internationally known scholar and, appropriately, a proponent of vigorous international law policies, argued for a new 'Unity of the Land' (*Eendracht van het Land*). As Henk te Velde puts it, 'For Vollenhoven, the nation was the community of all social groups.'[42]

In Belgium, the Catholics who had once allied with the Liberals in creating a constitutional state helped create a similar, though weaker sense of pluralism. The Catholic 'pillar' in late nineteenth-century Belgium was so politically dominant

---

[40] T. van Tin, 'The Party Structure of Holland and the Outer Provinces in the Nineteenth Century', in J. S. Bromley and E. Mataalarbeider (eds.), *Britain and the Netherlands*, vol. iv (The Hague, 1971), 179–85.

[41] N. C. F. van Sas, 'Van Anti-Kraten en Burgerheren', *Tijdschrift voor Geschiedenis*, 107 (1994), 55–6.　　　　　　　　　　　　　　　　　　　[42] Te Velde, *Gemeenschapzin*, 233.

that it was within the Catholic camp that the model for pluralism developed. It was in the tough-minded negotiations between conservative Catholics and Christian democrats, between Catholic unionists and employers, and between the francophone elite and Flemish militants that a politics of accommodation was forged. The success of the Catholic brand of pluralism could be seen in the cross-cutting and complicated set of voting patterns in Parliament. In 1907, when the conservative Catholic government tried to bury proposed mining regulations in committee, the motion was voted down 63 to 53. The 63 votes came from 30 Socialists, 20 Christian Democrats, and 13 Progressive Liberals with conservative Catholics and mainstream Liberals in favour.[43] The power of civic nationalism was revealed in that the three parties—Liberals, Catholics, and Socialists—contested for power in elections while still managing to ally in diverse ways on certain issues.

Civic nationalism, in other words, survived by allowing the 'nation' to become a set of power-sharing arrangements between tightly organized groups. Rather than ethnic unity or a truly individualist civil society, politics in the Low Countries by the twentieth century evolved into a system of competing groups, what Arendt Lijpardt called 'consociational democracy'.[44] Perhaps a more guarded assessment of the Belgian version of well-organized groups coexisting within a single state is captured by Luc Huyse's term, a *gewapende vrede*, an armed peace.[45]

[43] Luykx, *Politieke Geschiedenis*, 239–40.
[44] A. Lijpardt, *The Politics of Accommodation: Pluralism and Democracy in the Netherlands* (Berkeley, 1981).   [45] L. Huyse, *De Gewapende Vrede* (Antwerp, 1980).

6

Switzerland

Circumscribing Community in Constructions of Swiss Nationhood

Oliver Zimmer

Scholars of nationalism, partly because there was little empirical evidence that suggested otherwise, often agreed that ethno-cultural homogeneity was a significant factor for the long-term survival of modern nation-states. Thus Switzerland, according to this logic, constitutes an anomaly. If Switzerland has repeatedly attracted the curiosity rather than the systematic attention of scholars of nationalism, this is indeed because its very existence seems to defy the nationalist doctrine that nations are essentially language communities. Those who have attempted to solve the Swiss puzzle have usually singled out one aspect, be it the cross-cutting of cultural cleavages,[1] efficient communication,[2] or the alleged absence of nationalism before 1900.[3] But the most influential explanation of Switzerland's nineteenth-century *Sonderweg* has insisted on the civic and territorial nature of Swiss nationalism. Switzerland emerged against the odds of modern nationalism, so we are told, because its dominant elite fostered an ideology centred on liberal values and institutions—a voluntaristic patriotism rather than an organic nationalism—that would come to define the country's political culture.[4]

In this chapter I wish to challenge this view. I shall argue that Switzerland, though frequently cited as an example of civic exceptionalism, is particularly well suited to bringing out the limitations of this perspective. In fact, the Swiss case suggests that the traditional approach of looking at nations and nationalism in terms of civic and ethnic 'traditions' or 'mentalities' rests on a holistic view of

---

[1] A. Lijphart, *Democracy in Plural Societies: A Comparative Exploration* (New Haven, 1994), 156; André Siegfried, *Switzerland* (London, 1950), 123–41.

[2] K. W. Deutsch, *Die Schweiz als paradigmatischer Fall politischer Integration* (Bern, 1976).

[3] B. Anderson, *Imagined Communities: Reflections on the Origin and Spread of Nationalism*, 2nd edn. (London, 1991), 139.

[4] See in particular H. Kohn, *Nationalism and Liberty: The Swiss Example* (London, 1956).

nationhood that tends to obscure more than it illuminates. The limitations of the classical model have become particularly obvious to historians and social scientists studying national movements and political ideologues in their specific historical context rather than focusing on a handful of selected thinkers and intellectuals or taking a broadly comparative approach.[5] Rooted in the ethno-nationalist discourse that has been with us ever since the nineteenth century, it fails to do justice to the dynamic and contested nature of nationhood in the nineteenth century.

This is not to deny that nationalism had shaped nineteenth-century Switzerland in vital ways. The first Swiss nation-state, the Helvetic Republic (1798–1803), was committed to the concept of the one and indivisible nation first elaborated by the French revolutionaries. Yet the fact that this nationalist vision was out of touch with Switzerland's confederalist political culture, along with the Republic's total dependency on France's strategic interests, was largely responsible for its downfall. It was not until the 1840s that the language of modern nationalism gained currency among wider sections of the Swiss population. Democrats and radicals in particular employed nationalist arguments to justify their constitutional programmes and to win popular support for their political demands. The defeat of the conservative Sonderbund cantons in the short and relatively bloodless Civil War of November 1847 paved the way for transforming the existing Staatenbund into a liberal Bundesstaat. Rather than marking the end of nationalism as a political force, however, the nation-state of 1848 transformed its nature along with the role it would play within a rapidly modernizing society. The decades leading up to the First World War thus witnessed a series of nation-building initiatives which engaged ever wider sections of the Swiss population with the ideology and reality of modern nationhood.[6]

In terms of its formal ideological structure, however, Swiss nationalism was almost by necessity a blend of two visions of community—the 'voluntarist' (where the nation appears as constructed by its members) and the 'organic' (where the nation is seen as determined by particular cultural, political, historical, or geographical forces)—in accordance with its proponents' twofold aim of creating a new political community while at the same time circumscribing its cultural boundaries. What the Swiss case brings into sharp relief, therefore, is that particular definitions of national identity rise to prominence in particular historical situations where they serve to address specific political and cultural problems. While the conspicuous prominence of the voluntarist vision in the public debate about Swiss nationhood remains undisputed—the propagation of an ethnic understanding of nationhood would have called into question

[5] For an intellectual history approach to national identity, see M. Viroli, *For Love of Country: An Essay on Patriotism and Nationalism* (Oxford, 1995).

[6] These political and cultural initiatives are discussed in greater detail in O. Zimmer, *A Contested Nation: History, Memory and Nationalism in Switzerland, 1761–1891* (Cambridge, 2003), ch. 5.

Switzerland's territorial integrity as a multilingual state-nation—organic definitions of national identity were anything but marginal.[7] This chapter focuses on two main loci of organic nationalism: internationalist competition and citizenship legislation.[8]

INTERNATIONALIST COMPETITION AND THE LIMITS OF CIVIC EXCEPTIONALISM

Once nationalism had established itself as the dominant political ideology in nineteenth-century Europe, it was bound to stir up competition among different conceptions of nationality and to serve as a major catalyst for national self-assertion. In Switzerland, the significance of internationalist competition was particularly marked throughout most of the long nineteenth century. Unlike their counterparts in countries such as Germany, France, or England, Swiss would-be nation-builders could not refer to shared ethnicity, in the sense of common ethnic descent or linguistic affiliation, to bolster their claims. That Swiss nationhood flew in the face of nationalism's normative parameters did indeed present a major predicament for successive generations of Swiss public intellectuals, politicians, and members of civic associations. Yet it simultaneously provided a major incentive for fostering a national identity from the rich arsenal of available ideological resources—particularly history, geography, political institutions, and culture—that was both distinctive and in accordance with nationalism's norm of cultural authenticity. The ability to display such an identity was a sine qua non for legitimate statehood in a Europe in which the national principle held sway.

As early as 1841 the Swiss poet and political radical, Gottfried Keller, fiercely criticized the view promoted by the editors of several German and Italian newspapers which reduced nationality to a matter of linguistic affiliation and ethnic descent. Keller responded to such views by stressing the voluntarist nature of Swiss nationhood. What held Switzerland together, he asserted, was the explicit commitment of its citizens to a set of political values and institutions, a distinctive way of life, and what he called a 'love of a small yet beautiful fatherland'. Foreign nationals who shared this appreciation for Swiss political institutions ('schweizerische Staatseinrichtungen') and who voluntarily adopted Swiss customs ('unsere Sitten und Gebräuche') were to be considered Swiss. In fact,

---

[7] Unlike the terms 'civic' and 'ethnic', which carry strong normative connotations, the distinction between 'voluntarist' and 'organic' mechanisms of identity construction remains analytically useful in my view. On this topic, see my essay 'Boundary Mechanisms and Symbolic Resources: Towards a Process-Oriented Approach to National Identity', *Nations and Nationalism*, 9 (2003), 173–93.

[8] In focusing on the reconstruction of national identity over time, I do not wish to advocate a radical constructivism which assumes that nationhood is purely contingent. For a critique of such a perspective, see my essay 'Competing Memories of the Nation: Liberal Historians and the Reconstruction of the Swiss Past', *Past and Present*, 168 (2000), 194–226.

Keller went so far as to argue that those native Swiss who preferred foreign values, institutions, and ways of life to those they found in Switzerland—a position which he considered entirely legitimate—had ceased to be members of the Swiss nation.[9]

Keller's voluntaristic nationalism undoubtedly enjoyed wide currency, particularly in liberal and radical circles. Yet if we consider the nineteenth century as a whole, then a somewhat different picture emerges. Switzerland, so many argued, was both a *Willensnation* and a *Wesensgemeinschaft*. While this construction may have been at odds with rigorous standards of logical consistency, it was effective as a multi-layered response to a complex ideological challenge. The coalition that contributed most to fostering this ideological pattern was remarkably broad, with liberal and democratic associations, parties, and newspapers constituting the core.[10]

It was perhaps during the political turmoil of 1848 that the public significance of this complex pattern of identity construction was revealed for the first time. During the March revolutions of 1848, the campaign against German republicans soon turned against those states that had offered them asylum. It was in this context that Switzerland, where in November 1847 the liberal-democratic coalition had been victorious in the Sonderbund war, became a prime target. From April 1848 German newspapers launched a sustained campaign against the Swiss authorities, accusing them of lending support to leading German revolutionaries. An official note by the Imperial Ministry reiterated these accusations in October, and shortly afterwards it emerged that 40,000 German troops were stationed near Switzerland's northern border. The Ministry's demand to expel all German refugees met with broad condemnation. The Swiss government declared that there had been no armed raids from Swiss territory into Germany, nor had they found evidence that the refugees had established depots of weapons. Liberals and democrats, meanwhile, insisted that Switzerland knew the freedom of association, a right from which refugees could not be excluded. The democratic *Landbote* asked sarcastically if Prussia expected the Swiss cantons to 'create a special police unit to control the German refugees' every single step'.[11]

Yet in practice, German pressure led to a more restrictive policy towards political refugees. Several cantons, on the advice of the federal authorities, suspended the residence permits of those actively involved in the revolutionary uprisings in Baden.[12] This was accompanied, from the autumn of 1848, by a shift in public perception. In the post-civil-war climate and with a national constitution to defend, the official rhetoric of *raison d'état* and political neutrality became increasingly pervasive. This political stance was now seen as a precondition for

---

[9] Gottfried Keller, 'Vermischte Gedanken über die Schweiz', in W. Morgenthaler et al. (eds.), *Gottfried Keller: Sämtliche Werke. Historisch-Kritische Ausgabe*, vol. xvi/1. (Zurich, 2001).

[10] See Zimmer, *Contested Nation*, ch. 4.   [11] *Der Landbote*, No. 41 (12 Oct. 1848).

[12] The Diet's declaration to the cantons was published in the *Neue Zürcher Zeitung*, No. 63 (3 Mar. 1848).

Switzerland's survival as a democratic state and her international recognition as 'Europe's only genuine republic'.[13] From the beginning of 1849 onwards, newspaper editorials began to present a less favourable image of political refugees than had been the case during the 1830s and much of the 1840s. Against a few, increasingly isolated, voices who demanded that Switzerland join the European struggle against despotism in the name of the 'springtime of the peoples', the majority insisted that political liberation could only come from the people themselves.[14]

This preoccupation with 'significant others'—the reactionary powers, German authorities and political movements, the political refugees—was only matched by a compulsive inclination towards national self-introspection; and the two trends mutually reinforced one another. 'Despite sympathies for the cause of liberty', a group of democrats declared in April 1848, 'we must not forget that we are Swiss first and foremost and that our interest dictates that we remain neutral in the face of a new war.'[15] At a more basic level, the confrontation with states and national-ities served the construction and fortification of a distinctive national identity, culminating in a quasi-ethnographic discourse about national character. Among the main character traits identified as distinctively Swiss was the appreciation of a contract-based social order. 'There can no longer be any doubt', a liberal editorial declared in January 1850, 'that what Germany lacks is a common belief in, or an appreciation for, constitutional life, and that in this respect democrats and aristo-crats show little difference.'[16]

In the last third of the nineteenth century, the significance of international developments for Swiss national identity became even more obvious. In this respect, the rise of 'ethno-linguistic nationalism' (Hobsbawm) in much of Europe had particularly strong repercussions. The challenge posed by Italian irredentism, which had been in evidence since the 1850s, was conducive to the emergence of an official counter-nationalism. Yet the prime point of reference in this regard was Germany. Although the first German nation-state rested on a state-centred rather than an ethnic conception of nationhood, significant voices within Germany regarded smaller Germany as an incomplete nation-state. For the Pan-German League and other nationalist pressure groups Switzerland did not constitute a 'nation' but was a conglomerate of different nationalities.

On the one hand, Italian and German irredentism favoured the emergence of a discourse of civic exceptionalism in the decades between 1870 and the First World War. In its late-nineteenth-century application, the notion of civic exceptionalism went beyond the claim to represent Europe's republican *Sonderfall*. Specifically, it combined the traditional narrative of political republicanism with a reinforced emphasis on voluntarism and polyethnicity. What set Switzerland apart from its neighbours, so its central premiss ran, was the voluntary commitment to a set of values and institutions, which in turn secured Switzerland's existence as a

---

[13] *Landbote*, No. 34 (23 Aug. 1849).   [14] *Neue Zürcher Zeitung*, No. 51 (20 Feb. 1849).
[15] *Landbote*, No. 14 (6 Apr. 1848).
[16] *Neue Zürcher Zeitung*, No. 29 (29 Jan. 1850); see also *Der Landbote*, No. 46 (15 Nov. 1849).

polyethnic nation-state. This argument perhaps received its clearest expression in the work of Carl Hilty. An academic and influential public intellectual, Hilty maintained in 1875 that Switzerland's secular mission was to uphold a truly political conception of nationality in a Europe in which the ethno-cultural ideal was rapidly becoming the norm. In Hilty's words: 'What holds Switzerland together vis-à-vis its neighbours is an ideal, namely the consciousness of being part of a state that in many ways represents a more civilized community; of constituting a nationality which stands head and shoulders above mere affiliations of blood or language.'[17]

Yet the champions of civil exceptionalism were on the whole not internationalist advocates of the inclusive nation-state. Although underpinned by a voluntarist conception of nationality, their claim to Switzerland's special status often went hand in hand with a conservative rhetoric of communal self-preservation. Most adherents of civic exceptionalism argued that the essence of Swiss nationality—its ethnic pluralism—was under threat. From this they concluded that a certain degree of national self-centredness, even isolation from the outside world, was a prerequisite for national survival. This exclusive patriotism—political in nature yet preoccupied with polyethnic self-preservation—took on the quality of common sense among supporters of the nationalizing state. It was again Carl Hilty who expressed most cogently what in fact was a widely held view. In 1888 he pointed out that 'the increasingly precarious state of European peace' had inevitably resulted in 'sharper emphasis being placed upon one's own [national] individuality'.[18] To secure Switzerland's national mission 'to represent the idea of a sharply distinctive historical-political nationality' a certain degree of isolation from the outside world was necessary. As Hilty concluded: 'Even abroad the attitude begins to take root that the Swiss must remain a distinct people with a particular...character...We must retain this character at any price; we must remain an independent, peculiar state that exists in isolation from the outside world. Therein consists our first duty.'[19] This view was not confined to German-speaking Switzerland. In a speech held at the national festival in Schwyz in 1891, Henri Secrétan, a minister from Lausanne, asserted that while Switzerland had to remain open to developments abroad, 'nous devons avant tout rester nous-mêmes'.[20]

There are clear indications, however, that the discourse of civic exceptionalism—even its more fortified and self-centred versions—was still felt to be somewhat deficient as a response to ethno-linguistic nationalism. To be sure, it was useful insofar as it placed the stress on what was distinct about Switzerland. Yet nationalism, as an international ideological movement, also exerts pressure on societies to conform to its constitutive premises. As the historian Karl Dändliker lamented in 1884: 'The Swiss people do not enjoy the advantage of their neighbours: being a

---

[17] Carl Hilty, 'Die schweizerische Nationalität', in Carl Hilty, *Vorlesungen über die Politik der Eidgenossenschaft* (Bern, 1875), 29.   [18] *Politisches Jahrbuch der Schweiz* (1889), 473.
[19] Ibid. 474.
[20] Cited after T. Widmer, *Die Schweiz in der Wachstumskrise der 1880er Jahre* (Zurich, 1992), 619.

nation in the true and literal sense of the word, that is to say, being a uniform entity in terms of linguistic and ethnic composition.'[21]

Faced with the centrifugal pull of Italian and (particularly) German nationalism, a good portion of Switzerland's political and cultural elite began to embark on efforts at fortifying Swiss national identity. Yet given that claims to shared ethnic descent would have made little sense in view of Swiss polyethnic reality, 'history'—along with 'nature'—came to dominate the national discourse. During the national festival of 1891, for example, held in celebration of Switzerland's 600th anniversary, continuity was singled out as the main feature of Swiss history and as an asset to be preserved. The claim to a venerable and long historical pedigree seemed to offer proof that Switzerland was as authentic a nation as those of its counterparts able to claim shared ethnicity. An editorial in the *Neue Zürcher Zeitung* had it that in terms of old age, historical continuity, and faithfulness to the republican ideal Switzerland had few if any rivals.[22] The Catholic-conservative *Vaterland*, too, identified historical continuity as one of the distinctive features of Swiss nationhood: 'Of all the European republics that in the medieval period could rightly claim a glorious history, only one remained: The Swiss Confederation.'[23]

Along with historicism went an increased interest in the natural environment and its presumed impact on the historical evolution of 'national character'. What was new about this geographic discourse was the particular ways in which (alpine) nature was put to use. Ever since nature had become a prominent tool in the definition of national identities in the late eighteenth century, two conceptualizations of the relationship between nation and alpine landscape competed for hegemony. The first was metaphorical. That is to say, popular historical myths, memories, and supposed national virtues were projected into a significant landscape in an attempt to lend more continuity and distinctiveness to Swiss national identity. The Alps in particular were conceived of as reflecting national characteristics. As Gottfried Keller put it in 1854: 'With the thoughtlessness of youth and childish age, I believed that the natural beauty of Switzerland was a reflection of historical and political merit and of the patriotism of the Swiss people: an equivalent of freedom itself.'[24] The second conceptualization of the relationship between nature and nationhood was deterministic rather than metaphorical. Here the Alps did not just represent national virtues or form an organic link between past and present. Instead, they were seen as acting as a unifying device, even as a force capable of creating a national character that superimposed itself on existing linguistic and religious differences. Thus in a context in which Swiss nationhood

---

[21] Karl Dändliker, *Geschichte der Schweiz mit besonderer Rücksicht auf die Entwicklung des Verfassungs- und Kulturlebens von den ältesten Zeiten bis zur Gegenwart*, 3 vols. (Zurich, 1884–7), i.14.
[22] *Neue Zürcher Zeitung* (2 Aug. 1891).   [23] *Vaterland* (1 Aug. 1891).
[24] Cited after H.-U. Jost, 'Nation, Politics, and Art', in Swiss Institute for Art Research on behalf of the Coordinating Commission for the Presence of Switzerland abroad (ed.), *From Liotard to Corbusier: 200 Years of Swiss Painting* (Zurich, 1988), 18–19.

was increasingly perceived as underdetermined vis-à-vis the ideal type of the ethnically homogeneous nation, alpine nature became a stock item in national discourse.[25] The tripartite construction of Swiss national identity—with its three core narratives of civic exceptionalism, historicist continuationism, and geographical determinism—found its most elaborate expression in the historical play that formed the centrepiece of the 600-year anniversary of 1891.[26]

TOWARDS THE NATIONAL CITIZEN: CREATING AN INSTITUTION

Let me now turn from the international and ideological to the more domestic and institutional level, and more specifically to the evolution of national citizenship. In the long nineteenth century, citizenship emerged as the central institutional device by which state authorities separated members from non-members. It is therefore hardly surprising that students of nationalism have shown a particular interest in this phenomenon.[27]

In Switzerland as in many other European societies, however, the discourse over nationhood preceded the creation of national citizenship by several decades. Already in the late eighteenth century Swiss patriots invoked the national idea to lend moral weight to a programme of reform whose central political demand was the drawing back of regional and local patriotism, which many saw as a roadblock to the formation of a national consciousness. As a member of the Helvetische Gesellschaft put it in 1774: 'Love your own fatherland; but love even more the

---

[25] For a more detailed discussion of this phenomenon, see O. Zimmer, 'In Search of Natural Identity: Alpine Landscape and the Reconstruction of the Swiss Nation', *Comparative Studies in Society and History*, 40 (1998), 637–65.

[26] *Festspiel für die Eidgenössische Bundesfeier in Schwyz vom 1. und 2. August 1891* (Schwyz, 1891), 60–1. For a fuller analysis of these different patterns of national discourse, see Zimmer, *Contested Nation*, 201–7.

[27] Limitations of space prohibit even an outline of the debate in this field. See especially R. Brubaker, *Citizenship and Nationhood in France and Germany* (Cambridge, Mass., 1992). For recent criticisms of Brubaker's conclusions on the nature of German citizenship, see A. K. Fahrmeir, *Citizens and Aliens: Foreigners and the Law in Britain and the German states, 1789–1870* (London, 2000); D. Gosewinkel, *Einbürgern und Ausschliessen: Die Nationalisierung der Staatsangehörigkeit vom Deutschen Bund bis zur Bundesrepublik Deutschland* (Göttingen, 2001). Regrettably, the state of research on Swiss citizenship in the long nineteenth century is rather poor. As an outline of the legislative development over the nineteenth century, E. Huber, *Die Naturalisation in der Schweiz nach Bundes- und Vertragsrecht* (Zurich, 1912), is still eminently useful. On the late nineteenth century, see especially R. Schlaepfer, *Die Ausländerfrage in der Schweiz vor dem Ersten Weltkrieg* (Zurich, 1969); G. Romano, 'Zeit der Krise—Krise der Zeit: Identität und verschlüsselte Zeitstrukturen', in A. Ernst and E. Wigger (eds.), *Die neue Schweiz? Eine Gesellschaft zwischen Integration und Polarisierung (1910–1930)* (Zurich, 1996). For an overly descriptive overview that focuses overwhelmingly on the post-war period, see G. Kreis and P. Kury, *Die schweizerischen Einbürgerungsnormen im Wandel der Zeiten* (Bern, 1996). New insights into the genesis of Swiss national citizenship in the nineteenth century can be expected from the forthcoming monograph by Regula Argast, 'Staatsbürgerschaft und Nation: Ausschliessungs- und Integrationsprozesse in der Schweiz 1848–1928', Diss. Phil. I., University of Zurich (2005).

wider, more extended fatherland, for it was for the latter that our forebears went to war and sacrificed their blood and fortune.'[28] Such demands often went hand in hand with calls to cultivate 'national character' and with complaints about the subversive influence of cosmopolitan culture. But in terms of their concrete political objectives, the eighteenth-century patriots remained remarkably vague. The question of citizenship legislation, for example, was not just peripheral to their discussions. It was not addressed at all.[29]

The creation of the Helvetic Republic with the aid of French troops in March 1798 would change all this. Article 1 of the Helvetic Constitution of April 1798 abolished cantonal boundaries, and Article 19 literally invented Swiss national citizenship. Those who held citizenship rights in a commune, as well as those who possessed the right of residence and were born in Switzerland (*Hintersassen*), were declared Swiss citizens. In the eyes of the new authorities, the creation of a single citizenship status was the hallmark of the one and indivisible republic. In the new republic, every citizen was to be 'at home everywhere in his fatherland'.[30] Article 20 decreed that *Fremde* (aliens) who had resided in Switzerland for a minimum of twenty years could become Swiss citizens, provided they had no criminal record and subject to satisfactory references. Dual national citizenship was prohibited, and the naturalized foreigners had to take an oath on the constitution.[31]

The fall of the Helvetic Republic in 1803 did not lead immediately to the abolition of national citizenship. In fact, both national citizenship and freedom of residence were explicitly preserved by Napoleon's *Acte de Médiation* of 19 February 1803.[32] Only when the latter was removed in 1813 was national citizenship nominally abolished.[33] What followed was a period of thirty-five years in which the authority of granting citizenship lay solely with the cantons and the *Gemeinden*. The liberal nation-state of 1848 reintroduced the institution of national citizenship, along with the freedom of residence for Swiss citizens of Christian confession.[34] Yet in significant contrast to the centralist Helvetic

---

[28] *Verhandlungen der Helvetischen Gesellschaft* (1775), 39.

[29] See Zimmer, *Contested Nation*, 65–79.

[30] 'Erklärung der helvetischen Konstitution in Fragen und Antworten. Lerne sie kennen, um dich zu beruhigen. Zweyte Auflage gedruckt bey Balthasar und Meyer auf dem Kornmarkt (1798)'.

[31] On the Helvetic Constitution, see Carl Hilty, *Oeffentliche Vorlesungen über die Helvetik* (Bern, 1878), 731–3.

[32] See Wilhelm Oechsli, *Quellenbuch zur Schweizergeschichte* (Zürich, 1886), 474–6.

[33] *Aufhebung der Mediationsakte in der Eidgenossenschaft und Stiftung eines neuen Bundes.* Zürich, 29 Dec. 1813. Printed in Wilhelm Oechsli, *Quellenbuch zur Schweizergeschichte*, 2nd edn. (Zürich, 1901), 561–652.

[34] The restriction of the freedom of residence to Swiss citizens of Christian denomination in Article 41 of the 1848 constitution caused a heated debate in the diet. The delegate of Aargau—the canton where before 1874 most Swiss Jews lived in the two Jewish corporations of Endingen and Lengnau—recommended that the religious qualification be dropped, a proposition supported by Geneva, Neuchâtel, Vaud, and Bern. The Catholic delegates, along with liberal politicians from several Protestant cantons, including Zurich and Thurgau, opposed it. All attempts to revise Article 41 failed in sixteen successive ballots. Jews would remain excluded from this essential element of

Constitution, Article 42 of the Constitution of 1848 defined Swiss citizenship as derived from cantonal citizenship: 'Everyone who possesses the citizenship of a canton is also a Swiss citizen.'[35]

However, in the last third of the nineteenth century numerous contemporaries lamented that Swiss citizenship legislation was out of touch with the needs of a modern society. Two problems were particularly pressing. On the one hand, the Franco-German antagonism had demonstrated the significance of national citizenship in the context of European military conflict. On the other, the expansion of industrial production and the growth of transport and communication (and particularly the construction of new railway lines through mountainous terrain) had created an unprecedented demand for foreign labourers and thus dramatically increased the percentage of the foreign population. Between 1870 and 1910 the proportion of Switzerland's foreign population had risen from 5.7 to 14.7 per cent. In some cantons, such as Zurich, Schaffhausen, and Ticino, it had reached over 20 per cent, while in Basel and Geneva it was close to the 40 per cent mark. In some towns—Geneva, Arbon, and Lugano—it was even higher. Of the total foreign population living in Switzerland in 1910, 39.8 per cent were German, 36.7 Italian, 11.5 French, and 7.5 per cent were from Austria-Hungary.[36] By 1910, more than 50 per cent of all resident foreigners had been either born in Switzerland or been legally resident there for more than ten years.[37]

These developments put pressure on the federal authorities to initiate reforms. The *Bürgerrechtsgesetz* of 1876 was an early attempt to address the problems that had arisen due to the military antagonism between France and Germany. A government report singled out the case of German and French nationals whose main motive for applying for Swiss citizenship was to avoid the draft. The report criticized the fact that several Swiss cantons had granted citizenship to such candidates in the past, mainly out of financial considerations. Quite apart from undermining the 'dignity of Swiss citizenship', this practice was condemned because it had frequently led to diplomatic tensions with neighbouring states.[38] The chief objective of the 1876 law was thus to improve the central state's control over the pool of applicants, and specifically to prevent those who still held citizenship

national citizenship until the partial constitutional reform of 1866. See *Teilrevision der Bundesverfassung vom 22. Februar 1866*. Printed in Kaiser/Strickler, *Geschichte und Texte der Bundesverfassungen der schweizerischen Eidgenossenschaft von der helvetischen Staatsumwälzung bis zur Gegenwart* (Bern, 1901), 303–4.

[35] See *Offizielle Sammlung der das schweizerische Staatsrecht betreffenden Aktenstücke, Bundesgesetze, Verträge und Verordnungen seit der Einführung der neuen Bundesverfassung vom 12. September 1848 bis 8. Mai 1850*, 2nd edn. (Bern, 1850), 3–5.

[36] 'Botschaft des Bundesrates and die Bundesversammlung vom 9. November 1920 betreffend Revision des Art. 44. Der Bundesverfassung', *Bundesblatt*, 48 (1920), v. 1–7.

[37] Schlaepfer, *Die Ausländerfrage in der Schweiz*, 9–11, 99. For detailed statistical material, see *Die Einbürgerung in den Kantonen der Schweiz 1889–1908*, ed. Eidgenössisch Statistisches Bureau (Bern, 1911).

[38] See 'Botschaft des Bundesrates and die Bundesversammlung vom 9. November 1920', 27.

in another country from acquiring Swiss citizenship.[39] The law determined that every applicant for Swiss citizenship had to apply for permission from the federal authorities in the first instance, an option open to all those who had been legally resident in Switzerland for at least one year. Only those applicants that had been granted permission were entitled to proceed to the next step: apply for citizenship in a particular canton or *Gemeinde*. Yet while the 1876 law undoubtedly improved the Swiss authorities' ability to exercise control over the pool of applicants for Swiss citizenship, it did not enable them to take measures to reduce Switzerland's foreign population. The real power in this sphere still resided in the cantons and *Gemeinden*. As Article 4 of the 1876 law stipulated: 'A candidate only effectively acquires Swiss citizenship when federal permission has been supplemented by the acquisition of citizenship status in both a commune and a canton in accordance with cantonal legislation.'[40]

But the pressure on reforming the existing regime was growing steadily. From the 1880s onwards, liberal groups, deeply concerned about the low naturalization rate in the face of increasing labour immigration from southern Europe, began to press for the introduction of *jus soli*; and on 28 March 1899, the Federal Council sent a circular to all cantonal governments inquiring about their views on the introduction of this new principle. Of twenty-five cantons only eight (Zurich, Basel Town, St Gall, Aargau, Thurgau, Ticino, Vaud, and Geneva) expressed their support for a change of legislation. The *Bürgerrechtsgesetz* of 1903 went one step further by encouraging cantons to make unconditional *jus soli* the basis of their citizenship laws. Now cantons were entitled to grant Swiss citizenship to children of foreign residents born in a Swiss canton, provided either the mother was Swiss or both parents had been resident in the same canton for at least five years without interruption at the time of the child's birth. Not a single canton was to introduce the unconditional *jus soli* that the federal law of 1903 encouraged the cantons to adopt.[41]

The public debate over citizenship and naturalization intensified again in the decade before the First World War. The *Bürgerrechtsgesetz* of 1903 was a mere recommendation, and as such it had proved largely ineffective in preventing

---

[39] See 'Botschaft des Bundesrates an die hohe Bundesversammlung zum Gesetzesentwurf, betreffend den Erwerb des Schweizerbürgerrechts und den Verzicht auf dasselbe (2. Juni 1876)' and 'Entwurf Bundesgesetz betreffend die Ertheilung des Schweizerbürgerrechtes und den Verzicht auf dasselbe'. Published in *Bundesblatt*, 26 (1876), ii. 897–904.

[40] *Bundesblatt*, 26 (1876), ii. 906.

[41] In 1905 and 1907 respectively, Geneva and Ticino made territoriality the basis of their citizenship legislation. However, both cantons introduced the conditional *jus soli* practised in France, Denmark, and Sweden, where candidates would acquire citizenship voluntarily at the age of majority, rather than the unconditional one proposed in the federal legislation. This led the Federal Council to declare their legislation invalid. By 1912, most cantonal authorities had begun to adopt a more favourable view. Now all, except Glarus, Zug, Appenzell Innerrhoden, and the Vaud, expressed support for *jus soli*. See 'Bundesgesetz betreffend die Erwerbund des Schweizerbürgerrechtes und den Verzicht auf dasselbe (Vom 25. Juni 1903)'. Published in *Bundesblatt*, 26 (1903), iii. 718–24. More generally, see Schlaepfer, *Die Ausländerfrage in der Schweiz*, 70.

the steady increase in Switzerland's foreign population. Several initiatives, both inside and outside parliament, were launched to tackle the problem. Liberal-minded organizations and politicians in particular argued that the principle of *jus soli*—and most Swiss liberals advocated the automatic acquisition of Swiss citizenship at birth without the right to opt for another citizenship at the age of majority, a right that existed in France and other countries—reflected the fact that birth in the territory was the best guarantee to accelerate assimilation via schooling, upbringing, and military service. At its annual congress in 1910, the Schweizerischer Juristenverein adopted a resolution which identified the 'assimilation of aliens' and their 'ability to acquire citizenship' as a top priority. Only one year later, the Schweizerischer Städteverband justified its call for a new legislation with similar arguments. The 'nationalization of those foreigners that are intimately linked to Switzerland by birth and long residence', so a common declaration put it, was a question of 'national self-preservation and social justice'. Most conservatives fiercely opposed the radical version of *jus soli* favoured by liberals, describing it as *Zwangseinbürgerung* that would undermine the dignity of national citizenship. In a controversial debate on this issue in the National Council in 1902, for example, the Conservative Councillor von Planta argued that citizenship should only be granted to those who expressed an explicit wish to exercise Swiss civil liberties and rights. In 1912, the Liberal C. A. Schmid condemned these reservations in an article that appeared in the *Neue Zürcher Zeitung*: 'All this talk of *Musschweizer* and *Papierschweizer* is far-fetched and exaggerated. Ultimately, these views reveal a chauvinism that reflects our peculiar conceit and arrogance; as if no place on earth was as beautiful, or as prosperous, as [Switzerland].'[42]

With the publication of the national census of 1910 the situation regarding Switzerland's foreign population was put into sharp relief. In May 1914, a report of the Swiss Ministry of the Interior described the existing legislation as grossly inadequate in dealing with the 'threat of *Überfremdung*'. Another government report expressed concern at the formation of 'colonies of foreigners', particularly in more industrialized and urban regions.[43] The only solution to the problem, so the report concluded, was the encouragement of assimilation through the introduction of *jus soli*. Allied to this was the recommendation that foreign nationals who wished to assimilate were to be offered the possibility of acquiring citizenship more easily and more quickly. At the same time, the state was to provide clear incentives for assimilation. The group of experts spearheading the movement for a change in citizenship legislation, the so-called Neunerkommission, convinced

---

[42] Cited after Schlaepfer, *Ausländerfrage*, 169. As W. Burckhardt, 'Die Einbürgerung der Ausländer', *Politisches Jahrbuch der Schweizerischen Eidgenossenschaft*, 27 (1913), 13, put it: 'There is something profoundly wrong with a situation where large sections of our society, in spite of making a substantial contribution to its proper functioning, do not form part of the *Staatskörper* where civic rights are concerned.'

[43] 'Botschaft des Bundesrates und die Bundesversammlung vom 9. November 1920 . . .', 12.

the government and the liberal public that there was no alternative to automatic naturalization at birth as this was increasingly perceived as a precondition for successful assimilation.[44] Yet in the face of widespread opposition, in 1920 the government proposed a slightly altered version of *jus soli*: unconditionally where either both parents were born in Switzerland or the mother was Swiss; conditionally (i.e. the candidate must explicitly demand national citizenship at the age of majority) where neither of the parents was born in Switzerland. Had the proposed law been adopted, half of all foreign residents born in Switzerland would have acquired Swiss citizenship automatically.[45]

But this was not the case. This leads to the inevitable conclusion that Swiss citizenship law, at least at the federal level, has been based solely on *jus sanguinis* from the moment the conception of a national citizenship was first introduced in 1798 by the authorities of the Helvetic Republic. While there have been various attempts since the late nineteenth century to introduce legislation by which foreign citizens born on Swiss territory would acquire national citizenship either automatically or voluntarily at the age of majority, they all ultimately failed.[46] Although Switzerland introduced dual nationality after the Second World War, it made no special provision for conferring citizenship on second-generation immigrants. Does this mean that Switzerland, as a society, has historically been preoccupied with 'blood and soil'? Did the introduction of *jus soli* fail because of a widespread belief in the principles of ethnicity and ethnic descent?

Blunt questions often ask for relatively complex answers. On the one hand, there can be no doubt that a significant part of the debate over Swiss citizenship was couched in the language of organic nationalism, a language that defines the national community via the erection of boundaries that are hard to overcome. Assimilation, from this point of view, may still be regarded as possible, but it tends to be conceived in terms of a long-drawn-out process whose completion takes decades, even generations. Everyone reasonably familiar with government and parliamentary records as well as the stream of reports, speeches, and pamphlets that appeared between 1870 and the outbreak of the First World War will be aware of these exclusionary tendencies. This applies in particular to the decade before the First World War, when the public discussion surrounding citizenship and naturalization became integrated, and sometimes submerged, in a wider discourse of *Überfremdung*. As an ideological device, the term *Überfremdung*

---

[44] See 'Petition der "Neunerkommission" betreffend Massnahmen gegen die Überfremdung der Schweiz. Ende November 1912'; *Bundesblatt*, 47 (1922), iii. 665; Burckhardt, 'Die Einbürgerung der Ausländer', 1–114.

[45] 'Botschaft des Bundesrates an die Bundesversammlung vom 9. November 1920', especially 44–6.

[46] The revision of Article 44 of the Federal Constitution that found the support of the Swiss voters in 1927 still favoured *jus soli*; but as with previous federal and constitutional reforms in this area, it merely outlined the direction for a future reform. It did not formulate rules that the cantons and communes would have to follow, nor did it turn the acquisition of Swiss citizenship into a legal entitlement under certain conditions. See *Bundesblatt*, 41 (1927), ii. 269–70.

presumed the existence of an organic national community whose character ('Eigenart') had come under threat through foreign immigration.

The means proposed to preserve this community were sometimes more than a little dubious. A liberal and supporter of *jus soli* like Walter Burckhardt, for example, argued that the 'preservation of one's own *Volksstamm*' could only be accomplished through the exclusion of certain 'foreign races', including Poles, Russians, and Jews.[47] Even the influential Neunerkommission spoke of an 'imminent threat of *Überfremdung*'.[48] What remains decisive, however, is that for the large majority of Switzerland's political class *Überfremdung* was to be fought not through large-scale exclusion but through large-scale naturalization. There was simply no alternative, in the opinion of the federal government and liberal pressure groups, to unconditional *jus soli*. The prospect of acquiring Swiss citizenship swiftly and without undue financial sacrifice was seen as the best guarantee, a precondition even, for successful assimilation and thus for the preservation of Swiss national character. There was a functional nexus, it seemed, between the preservation of an organic national community and the automatic acquisition of Swiss citizenship through birth in the territory.

IMAGINING THE NATION AS A *GEMEINDE* WRIT LARGE

The main opposition to *jus soli* emanated not from liberals who for whatever reason employed the rhetoric of organic nationalism, but from the municipalities (*Bürgergemeinden*), which in Switzerland formed legal corporations. Yet the absence of a binding federal legislation on national citizenship led to great regional variety in the practice of granting citizenship rather than to the uniform adoption of *jus sanguinis*. Between 1908 and 1913, 72 per cent of Switzerland's *Gemeinden* did not naturalize a single foreign resident, while twenty—mostly larger towns—were responsible for 63 per cent of all naturalizations. Broadly speaking, the larger and more industrialized cantons and municipalities such as Basel, Geneva, and Zurich showed a more liberal attitude to naturalization while many of their rural counterparts were much less accommodating.[49] Thus if liberal

---

[47] See Burckhardt, 'Die Einbürgerung der Ausländer', 21; W. Ehrenzeller, 'Die geistige Ueberfremdung der Schweiz: Eine Untersuchung zum schweizerischen Geistesleben unserer Zeit' (Zürich, 1917).

[48] Whether proponents of *jus soli* used the term *Überfremdung* out of strategic reasons (i.e. to increase the moral weight of their campaign) or out of genuine belief remains difficult to ascertain and may differ from case to case. See 'Petition der "Neunerkommission" betreffend Massnahmen gegen die Überfremdung der Schweiz' (no place or publisher, November 1912).

[49] In Schlaepfer, *Ausländerfrage*, 9–11. But even in the three cantons with the largest populations of foreign residents and the most accommodating approach, the figures are humbling. The canton with the most progressive attitude, Basel-Town, naturalized 10,066 foreign nationals between 1889 and 1910 while its total foreign population rose from 25,210 in 1888 to 52,025 in 1910. In Geneva, where the foreign population grew from 39,910 to 63,866 during the same period, the number of

attempts to integrate foreign residents through swift naturalization largely failed despite the pressures created by rapid industrialization and rising labour immigration, this was because the federal authorities did not possess the legal authority to turn foreigners into nationals. At the same time, pragmatism dictated that the Swiss government took account of widespread support for local self-determination. Thus when, in 1909, a commission of the National Council recommended that national citizenship be completely detached from communal citizenship, the Swiss government expressed reservations, predicting that the proposed solution was likely to provoke 'hostile reactions' among large sections of the Swiss population.[50]

What these observations suggest is that the history of Swiss citizenship in the nineteenth century needs to be conceived as a contentious process rather than in terms of its 'outcome' before the First World War. A process, moreover, in which different levels of society—federal state, cantons, and *Gemeinden*—were engaged and which stood in a dynamic relation to different forms of communal identity (regional and, above all, local). In strictly political terms, the history of citizenship represents a struggle over who was entitled to exercise authority in this area: federal state, canton, or *Gemeinde*? Looking at national citizenship in this way—as a contentious process with various participants rather than as a state-driven project that eventually failed—also enables us to explore the more cultural aspects of collective membership. How did ordinary Swiss appropriate the idea of nationhood in the course of the long nineteenth century, and how did they link national and subnational forms of identification? Given the near total lack of studies addressing these issues, the answer which I will present is bound to take the form of a working hypothesis for future research rather than a thoroughly substantiated argument. It is that, first, for many people, the nation appeared as a *Gemeinde* writ large; and that, secondly and consequently, the sources of organic (rather than ethnic) understandings of the nation need to be located in a locally embedded pattern of national imagining that is rooted in powerful institutions.

Let me illustrate my argument by offering a few examples of conflicts over citizenship. I have already alluded to the introduction of new citizenship

---

naturalized foreigners was 10,099. Finally, Zurich, which experienced the most dramatic rise in its foreign population of all Swiss cantons (from 33,389 in 1889 to 102,904 in 1910) naturalized only 10,366 foreign nationals during these two decades. See *Die Einbürgerungen in den Kantonen der Schweiz 1889–1908*, ed. Eidg. Statistisches Bureau (Bern, 1911).

[50] The other case where municipalities had a significant influence on the genesis of national citizenship is Germany. See in particular Andreas Fahrmeier, 'Nineteenth-Century German Citizenship: A Reconsideration', *Historical Journal*, 40 (1997), 739. Yet unlike in Switzerland, in Germany national citizenship got detached from communal citizenship in the last third of the nineteenth century. Gosewinkel (*Einbürgern und Ausschliessen*, 127, 234) observes a process of 'decommunalization of citizenship' that manifested itself in the Gothaer Konvention of 1851 and the federal law of 1870. See also W. Cahn, *Das Reichsgesetz über die Erwerbung und den Verlust der Reichs- und Staatsangehörigkeit vom 1. Juni 1870 erläutert mit Benutzung amtlicher Quellen und unter vergleichender Berücksichtigung der ausländischen Gesetzgebung*, 2nd edn. (Berlin, 1896).

legislation by the authorities of the Helvetic Republic in 1798. This was part and parcel of a broader attempt to increase the mobility of the Swiss population through a concentrated assault on the thick tapestry of economic and political privilege that was the legacy of the *ancien régime*. Yet the ensuing conflicts over the new citizenship law show that many communes were determined to defend the traditional practice. Numerous popular petitions from the hinterland of Luzern, for example, expressed profound irritation at the new legislation; and when the Helvetic Minister of the Interior asked all cantonal governors to produce reports on the 'state of the Republic' the governor of Basel put the issue of citizenship on top of his list of concerns. 'The true and heartfelt love for the fatherland', he insisted, could only exist 'where one is proud of being a citizen, and where this right is only very sparsely granted to foreigners.'[51] A memorandum of the Helvetic parliament points to the close interaction of socio-economic, political, and cultural motives behind efforts to defend communal citizenship: 'The traditional presumption and practice almost everywhere in Switzerland was that each *Gemeinde* take care of its poor. This made the acceptance of a non-citizen as full citizen of the *Gemeinde* an extremely arduous affair, since each *Gemeinde* used to be its own state, as it were, which regarded all other *Gemeinden* as foreign.'[52] In the end, the Helvetic authorities felt unable to resist the concentrated opposition of the municipalities. The new laws of 13 and 15 February 1799 explicitly preserved the political autonomy of the *Bürgergemeinde*, a measure that clearly contradicted the spirit of the Helvetic Constitution with its credo of the one and indivisible nation.[53]

As shown previously, the creation of a Swiss nation-state in 1848 to some extent altered the institutional reality and practice of citizenship in Switzerland. Above all, the new constitution reinstated national citizenship, and the *Bürgerrechtsgesetz* of 1876 to some extent strengthened the federal government's position vis-à-vis the cantons and *Gemeinden*. All future applicants for national citizenship would have to apply for permission from the federal authorities before they could proceed. Even so, the ultimate legislative and practical authority in the field of citizenship remained with the municipalities and cantons. To the great dismay of exponents of industrial and urban interests, every applicant still had to take not only one but three hurdles. Receiving the permission from the federal authorities was relatively straightforward. Meeting the cantonal requirements was equally attainable in most cases. What for many applicants turned out to be a stumbling block, however, were the municipalities or *Gemeinden*. As the government's 1911 statistical report concluded: 'As several cantonal authorities have told us over

[51] Reply of 23 Nov. 1798. *Aktensammlung aus der Ziet der Helvetischen Republik* (ASHR), iii. 274.
[52] *ASHR* vi. 942.
[53] For the debate on these issues in the Helvetic parliament, see ASHR III, 1190–93, 1208. See also A. Fankhauser, ' "... da viele sich einbilden, es seie nun unter dem Titel Freiheit alles zu tun erlaubt": Der Kanton Bern unter der Trikolore 1798–1803', *Berner Zeitschrift für Geschichte und Heimatkunde*, 60 (1998), 126–8.

the years, there are still *Gemeinden* which don't even consider granting communal citizenship to foreigners while others set the naturalization tax at a level that prevents even the relatively well-to-do, who may have lived in a particular community all or at least a substantial part of their lives, from applying.'[54]

The fact that many Swiss municipalities were hardly more welcoming towards Swiss citizens wishing to become *Gemeindebürger* than towards foreign nationals pursuing the same aim shows that viewing citizenship and naturalization solely in terms of ethnicity is highly flawed as it often results from an ignorance of complex historical traditions and socio-political structures. Some Swiss municipalities even attempted to extend their power vis-à-vis the cantons. Thus in 1880, the government of the small municipality of Bülach launched a popular initiative which called for restrictions of the rights of Swiss citizens who had recently taken up residence in the canton of Zurich. The initiative demanded that new residents had to wait for at least three months before they could vote in communal and cantonal elections. This was justified by the unfamiliarity of new residents with the local political affairs. In addition, and much more boldly, the supporters of the initiative sought to prevent Swiss citizens from acquiring the *Gemeindebürgerrecht* automatically and free of charge after ten years of residence—a provision that Zurich had introduced along with several other liberal cantons in the 1860s. This provision was challenged on two grounds. First, because it was viewed as an undue infringement on the political autonomy of the *Gemeinde*; and secondly, because it represented a potential threat to the financial integrity of Zurich's municipalities. In the text of the initiative, the existing law was condemned as an unjustified 'coercion' of the *Gemeinde* 'into accepting the undesirable elements of all other cantons'.[55]

These conflicts over citizenship rights provide information that is vital for an understanding of how wide sections of the Swiss public defined their collective identities when confronted with the demands of the nineteenth-century nation-state. The autonomy of the communes in the political, economic, and social realm, which was considerable in many Swiss regions, was based on a notion of belonging that centred upon the *Gemeinde*. It was a consequence of what we might call the failure of attempts at absolutist-style control in the seventeenth and

---

[54] *Die Einbürgerungen in den Kantonen der Schweiz 1889–1908*, 25. For a similar line of argument, see A. Estopey, 'Die Einbürgerung der Ausländer in der Schweiz: Referat am freisinnig-demokratischen Parteitag in Lausanne', *Neue Zürcher Zeitung*, 141 (21 May 1912).

[55] The initiative was opposed by both the parliament and government of the canton of Zurich. When put before the voters, 25,252 opposed and 16,518 supported it. Staatsarchiv des Kantons Zürich MM 30.1 (7). 'Initiative betreffend Stimmrecht in kantonalen und Gemeindeangelegenheiten für Schweizerbürger und Eintritt in das Gemeindebürgerrecht vom 14. February 1880'. On the complexities of communal citizenship in the canton of Zurich, see Ernst Albert Kündig, *Die zürcherischen Civilgemeinden*, Ph.D. dissertation at the University of Zurich (1917). For a particularly instructive examination of the impact of industrialization on communal citizenship, see Ruldolf Braun, *Sozialer und Kultureller Wandel in einem ländlichen Industriegebiet (Zürcher Oberland) unter Einwirkung des Maschinen- und Fabrikwesens im 19. und 20. Jahrhundert* (Zurich, 1965), 272–8.

eighteenth centuries.[56] In fact, the autonomy of the *Gemeinde* and its direct-democratic institutions had produced a political culture that was markedly at odds with a modern notion of nationhood that was voluntary rather than organic, abstract rather than concrete.[57]

Yet however prominent the rhetoric of local autonomy may have been in the Swiss case, regions and localities did not exist in isolation from the wider political and cultural sphere in whose creation and successive expansion nationalism and the nation-state had played such an instrumental part. The creation of the liberal Bundesstaat in 1848 undoubtedly represents a watershed in this respect. Partly because national loyalty had assumed such a central role in the moral economy of the modern nation-state, the regions and localities had little alternative but to engage with national institutions and state-led political and cultural initiatives. The talk of the multiplicity of identities, which has become a stock item in the scholarly literature, or the emphasis on opposition to state centralization, tends to obscure this vital fact. It was only by engaging with national institutions and policies that subnational communities could hope to defend their traditional status and to receive recognition for their contribution to the life of the 'wider fatherland'.[58]

From this interaction between nation-state and regions/localities emerged a particular pattern of identity construction. Men and women, so my admittedly sparse evidence suggests, began to imagine the nation as a concrete *Gemeinschaft* rather than an abstract *Gesellschaft*. Locally based people began to imagine the nation with the aid of a projection through which locality and nation coalesced into a single imagined community. They conceived of the nation as an extended family, village, or canton—as a social unit, that is, which, though considerably larger than these communities, was essentially of the same basic structure. It was this pattern of imagining the nation through the cognitive prism of a highly institutionalized locality—rather than an obsession with ethnicity and ethnic descent—which explains why a polyethnic society like Switzerland could evolve a rather exclusionary national self-image. In more general terms, we can thus argue that (in the Swiss case at least) it was the linking of national terrain and locality which provided the source of much organic nationalism in the nineteenth century; and not, as is so often claimed, an alleged mentality as manifested in a concept like *Kulturnation* or an ethnic understanding of nationhood.

---

[56] Rudolf Braun has pointed to the frequency with which small communities in the countryside managed to prevail over the towns' bailiffs in legal conflicts in the seventeenth and eighteenth centuries, thus creating a legacy of communal self-determination. See his book, *Das ausgehende Ancien Régime in der Schweiz: Aufriss zu einer Sozial- und Wirtschaftsgeschichte des 18. Jahrhunderts* (Göttingen, 1986), 239–44.

[57] On Germany, see D. Langewiesche, '"Staat" und "Kommune": Zum Wandel der Staatsaufgaben im Deutschland im 19. Jahrhundert', *Historische Zeitschrift*, 248 (1989), 621–35.

[58] A point I try to develop in *Contested Nation*, esp. Chapter 5.

CONCLUSION

This chapter has highlighted two processes that shaped Swiss nationhood in the long nineteenth century in critical ways. The first concerns the competition between different nation-states and the nationalist visions they represented. This competition was clearly visible from the French Revolution onwards, when French expansionism and the various reactions it provoked across the European continent began to challenge, and ultimately transform, the traditional European state system. In Switzerland, the significance of internationalist competition became even more conspicuous after the creation of the liberal state in 1848. The scores of official speeches, the staging of public festivals and commemorations, the passing of new legislation to promote national art, and the provision of extra funding to promote the scholarly study of the national past provide an impressive testimony to this increasingly ostentatious project of national self-assertion. In a Europe dominated by the norm of the culturally and ethnically homogeneous nation, the Swiss authorities, public intellectuals, and various political representatives were desperate to display an image of national authenticity to the outside world. On the one hand, they sought to demonstrate that Switzerland was a distinct nation. This led to a discourse of civic exceptionalism which gave prominence to political institutions and to Switzerland's polyethnic composition. In this discourse, Switzerland's history, culture, and political institutions were defined as the product of human will rather than of natural forces. On the other hand, they endeavoured to prove that Switzerland was as authentic as the linguistically uniform societies around it. This resulted in an organic discourse of nationhood in which these elements were portrayed in evolutionary terms—as externally determined rather than as products of deliberate human action.

The second process considered in this chapter concerns citizenship, conceived not only as a social and legal institution, but also as a cognitive prism through which ordinary men and women defined their membership in the national community. What was particularly striking in the Swiss case—more striking even than in other confederalist polities such as Germany—is the federal state's failure to acquire the power that would have enabled it to determine the rate at which foreigners could be turned into Swiss nationals. In spite of successive recommendations to adopt *jus soli* in their constitutions, the cantonal authorities, partly because they expected the *Gemeinden* to be hostile to such a measure, resisted any significant change in this area. As a consequence, the authority in granting national citizenship to foreign nationals (including children of foreign residents who had been born in Switzerland) remained firmly in the hands of the cantons and localities. More crucially, it meant that the *Gemeinde* provided the institutional and cognitive frame through which nationhood was primarily experienced, imagined, and defined.

That Switzerland represents a particularly strong case of confederalist political organization should not prevent us from recognizing that here is a potentially fertile area of research—what one might call the social history of nationalism and nation-building—that is still largely unexplored. The path-breaking accounts of Alon Confino, Celia Applegate, Abigail Green, and others notwithstanding, we still know rather little about how ordinary men and women experienced the nation-state in the long nineteenth century. The study of nation formation could therefore benefit, I think, from accounts that compare highly institutionalized local communities: *Gemeinden* and small towns that represent different socio-cultural and socio-economic contexts—not just the cultural abstractions we call 'regions'. This would also allow us to interrelate the two most important conceptual debates informing the study of nations and nationalism in recent years—that concerning regionalism and locality on the one hand, and that relating to the distinction between voluntarist and organic (or 'civic' and 'ethnic', if one prefers) forms of nationhood on the other. At the moment they largely exist as separate discussions.[59]

[59] See especially A. Confino, *The Nation as a Local Metaphor: Württemberg, Imperial Germany and National Memory, 1871–1918* (Chapel Hill, NC, 1997); C. Applegate, *A Nation of Provincials: The German Idea of Heimat* (Berkeley, 1990); A. Green, *Fatherlands: State-Building and Nationhood in Nineteenth-Century Germany* (Cambridge, 2001); C. Ford, *Creating the Nation in Provincial France: Religion and Political Identity in Brittany* (Princeton, 1993). For a recent examination of nationalism and regionalism that adopts a state-centred approach, see S. Weichlein, *Nation und Region: Integrationsprozesse im Bismarckreich* (Düsseldorf, 2004).

7

The Ottoman Empire

Syncretic Nationalism and Citizenship in the Balkans

Constantin Iordachi

The aim of this chapter is to refute the idea of a clear-cut dichotomy between a 'Western type' of civic nationalism and an 'Eastern type' of ethno-cultural nationalism and to question the explanatory power of these generic labels for describing the concrete historical experience of entire countries or regions. The chapter takes as a relevant case study the history of the Balkans—or 'Turkey in Europe' as it was named at the time—a region that is generally regarded as the realm of ethnic nationalism *par excellence*. The chapter adds a new analytic dimension, that of citizenship, to the role of language, ideas, politics, and identity in delineating civic versus ethnic types of nationalism, explored by other chapters in the current volume. It is argued that the analysis of the making of citizenship in the Balkans can modify our view on the existence of distinct civic and ethnic types of nationalism. Instead of following 'classical' typologies that contrast a normative and unified 'West' with an equally homogeneous but illiberal and backward 'East', the chapter highlights the syncretic nature of national ideologies and citizenship legislation, encompassing—in a peculiar symbiosis—civic as well as ethnic elements. Exposing the prevailing 'obsession' with labelling and classifying historical case studies, the chapter invites theoretically minded empirical research on processes of state-building in various non-Western contexts as a precondition for engaging in informed and elaborated regional and global comparisons.

To date, scholarly works on the Balkans have mainly concentrated on the history of nationalism and national ideologies. One can identify four main approaches to the process of nation- and state-building in the region. A first one, promoted primarily by Ottomanist scholars, regards the Ottoman Empire as a 'golden age' of religious tolerance and multi-ethnic coexistence. These scholars contrast the Ottoman inclusive and pluralistic societal order with the inter-ethnic violence, exclusion, and forced migrations that accompanied the establishment and consolidation of nation-states in the region in the modern period. They also credit external factors with a decisive role in the collapse of the Ottoman Empire, and emphasize the responsibility of narrow circles of local intellectuals in instigating national movements of secession in the Ottoman Balkans. Such an argument is developed by Kemal H. Karpat, who states that the Balkan nation-states carved out of the Ottoman territory were legitimized exclusively by 'historical nationalism', 'built on false premises and nourished by myth'.[1] In his view, the new states were ad hoc and illegitimate constructions, 'created by Britain, France, Russia, and Austria through the mechanism of the Berlin Treaty of 1878'.[2] Therefore, 'none of these states was a true "nation" at the time when official sanction was made; but the small group of intellectuals in each of them took possession of the state apparatus and sought to build a nation in fact out of the patchwork of ethnic religious groups within its assigned territory.'[3]

Second, in opposition to this approach, which stems from the official discourse put forward by the Ottoman ruling elite during its last phase of existence, national historiographies in the Balkans have traditionally focused on their historical rights to territorial statehood, commonly traced back to pre-Ottoman principalities, claiming their legitimate right to national self-determination. Their different perspective also has theoretical and methodological implications. While Ottomanist scholars generally adhere to a 'modernist' view of nationalism in order to emphasize the 'invented' nature of nationalist movements in the Balkans, local scholars employ a 'primordialist' view, asserting the 'ethnic basis' of modern nations and the historical roots of national statehood.[4] Moreover, in order to legitimize strategies of modernization and catching up with the West adopted by political elites in the newly-born Balkan states, local historians portray the Ottoman Empire as an illegitimate occupier of the Balkans and a ruthless oppressor of Christian populations, unilaterally blaming it for the economic backwardness of the region, and arguing for the removal of the material or demographic 'traces' of the Ottoman legacy.

A third discourse on the Balkans is external. A majority of foreign (mainly Western) works on the Balkans have argued that the region is the primary site of 'ethnic' forms of nationalism, in view of the secessionist nationalist movements that developed in the region under late Ottoman rule and the recurrent patterns of *irredenta* wars that followed the collapse of the empire, culminating with the Balkan wars (1912–13). In these works, the ethnic violence that accompanied state-building in the region has been almost exclusively explained in terms of the

---

[1] K. H. Karpat, 'The Balkan National States and Nationalism: Image and Reality', *Islamic Studies*, 36 (1997), 329–59. [2] Ibid. 329.

[3] Ibid. 356.

[4] For an example of scholarly polemics on contested issues such as national rights, demographic statistics, and policies of forced conversion and ethnic assimilation, see K. H. Karpat, 'By Way of Introducing this Issue: Bulgaria's Methods of Nation Building—the Annihilation of Minorities', *International Journal of Turkish Studies*, 4/2 (1989), 1–22; K. H. Karpat, 'The Situation of the Christians in the Ottoman Empire: Bulgaria's View', *International Journal of Turkish Studies*, 4 (1989), 259–66; and I. Sardamov, 'The Turks of Bulgaria: Karpat's Excursion into Nationalist Propaganda', *Nationalities Papers*, 24 (1996), 743–5.

'primitive mentality' of the Balkan inhabitants, and the 'backward' Ottoman imperial state-structure and 'incomplete modernization', while Balkan nationalism has been stigmatized as a form of 'tribalism' and contrasted with a tolerant Western version of 'civic nationalism'.[5]

The first comprehensive typology contrasting Eastern and Western forms of nationalism was put forward by Hans Kohn. Building on Frederich Meinecke's distinction between *Staatsnation* and *Kulturnation*, Kohn argued that in Western Europe and the United States nationalism developed either before or concomitant with the formation of homogeneous nation-states, while 'in Central and Eastern Europe and in Asia, nationalism arose not only later, but also generally at a more backward stage of political and social development'.[6] To exemplify this distinction, Kohn contrasted the case studies of France, regarded as representative for the Western type of civic nationalism, and that of Germany, which in his view best epitomized the Eastern type of ethnic nationalism.[7] Building on Kohn's perspective, Peter F. Sugar further explores the main features of the Eastern European type of nationalism. He argues that—similarly to nationalism in Western Europe— Eastern European nationalism was 'a revolutionary force', sharing with it an 'anticlerical, constitutional, and egalitarian orientation'. At the same time, it differed in important respects from its Western counterpart. In Western Europe nationalism developed organically and 'corresponded to changing social, economic, and political realities', while in Eastern Europe nationalism spread 'long before a corresponding social and economic transformation' could develop.[8] Therefore, 'Western nationalism was based on reality, Eastern nationalism on myths and dreams.'[9] Western nationalism was inclusive, Eastern nationalism 'tending toward exclusiveness'.

Sugar also argues that, although sharing common main features, Eastern European nationalisms differed from one another in important respects.[10] Rejecting the differentiation between 'historic' and 'non-historic' Eastern European nations as too simplistic—since it was solely based on the political role various groups played in their states—Sugar builds a new typology in view of other criteria such as 'religious and laic institutions, constitutions and other political documents, the aversion to foreign rule, class privileges and economic change, the various forms of xenophobia, belief in a special mission, real or imaginary historical interpretations of the past, and western ideas.' Although all these elements were 'adding up to

---

[5] For a comprehensive analysis of the Western discourse on the Balkans, see Maria Todorova, *Imagining the Balkans* (New York, 1997).

[6] Hans Kohn, *The Idea of Nationalism: A Study in its Origins and Background* (New York, 1944), 457.

[7] See H. Kohn, *Prelude to Nation-States: The French and German Experience, 1789–1815* (Princeton, 1967). For a recent conceptualization of a 'German versus French' dichotomy of political ideologies, see Liah Greenfeld, *Nationalism: Five Roads to Modernity* (Cambridge, 1992), 278, 358.

[8] Kohn, *The Idea of Nationalism*, 457.

[9] P. F. Sugar, 'External and Domestic Roots of Eastern European Nationalism', in Peter F. Sugar and Ivo J. Lederer (eds.), *Nationalism in Eastern Europe* (Seattle, 1969), 10.　　　[10] Ibid. 46.

Eastern European nationalism,' they produced different 'variants of the basic picture' out of 'the same basic puzzle pieces'.[11] Sugar classified Eastern European nationalisms 'into four main groups,' namely bourgeois, aristocratic, popular, and bureaucratic.[12] Bourgeois nationalism resembled most closely Western nationalism, and was developed by Czechs. The aristocratic version of nationalism was developed by Poles and Hungarians and 'produced the least constructive results'. Popular nationalism (also called 'egalitarian nationalism') was developed by Serbs and Bulgarians. Bureaucratic nationalism developed in Romania, Greece, and Turkey, and had 'much in common' with that developed in emerging countries in contemporary Africa and Asia.

The comparison between Eastern European nationalism and Asian and African nationalisms was also employed by John Plamenatz, although he did not elaborate on it, but focused on the case study of nationalism of the Slavs living within the Habsburg Empire.[13] Plamenatz defined nationalism as 'a reaction of people who feel culturally at a disadvantage', especially during the social revolution brought about by modernity.[14] He contrasts Western nationalism, exemplified by the case study of Italy and Germany, with the Eastern one, best represented by the Habsburg Empire. In his view, Italians and Germans were well equipped culturally to deal with modern social revolution. Therefore, 'Nationalism in the West, though it was not entirely liberal, was so more often than not.'[15] In contrast, nationalism in the East originated 'in a world where social mobility and trade and a cosmopolitan culture are growing fast, where much the same standards, much the same ambitions are taking root everywhere, or at least over large areas, and yet some people are culturally better equipped than others are to live well by those standards and to achieve those ambitions.' It was therefore 'disturbed and ambivalent', 'imitative and competitive', 'hostile to the models it imitated', and 'illiberal, not invariably but often'.[16] Eastern nationalism was based on a double rejection: 'rejection of the alien intruder and dominator who is nevertheless to be imitated and surpassed by his own standards, and rejection of ancestral ways which are seen as obstacles to progress and yet also cherished as marks of identity.'[17]

Although these typologies of nationalism are very diverse and often divergent in their definition of 'East' and 'West', in their evaluation of the position of German nationalism, and in the main features they attribute to 'civic' as opposed to 'ethnic' nationalism, they all converge in contrasting 'Western' nationalism with a unified 'Eastern' nationalism (specific to Central, South-Eastern, and Eastern Europe), the former being portrayed mainly in positive terms, the latter in negative ones.

[11] Ibid. 44–5. [12] Ibid. 46.

[13] J. Plamenatz, 'The Two Types of Nationalism', in E. Kamena (ed.), *Nationalism: The Nature and Evolution of an Idea* (London, 1976), 22–36. [14] Ibid. 27.

[15] In order to account for the rise of Italian fascism, German national-socialism, and the French right, Plamenatz asserts that Western nationalism became illiberal only in the twentieth century, and even then was 'the nationalism of peoples already united politically and humiliated or disregarded in spite of this unity'. Ibid. 29. [16] Ibid. 33, 35.

[17] Ibid. 34.

More recently, as part of a new wave of historiographical interest in the region, local and foreign historians react against the essentialization of the historical experience of the Balkans. Instead, they propose a 'realistic' approach to the history of the region, regarding nation-states in the Balkans not as 'mutant' phenomena, but as viable, legitimate, and relatively successful political structures, modelled on Western patterns.[18] This chapter builds on the latter historiographical discourse, but approaches the process of nation- and state-building from a novel perspective. It argues that the making of nation-states in the Balkans cannot be understood without focusing on the emergence and evolution of the institution of state citizenship as a new type of legal frontier demarcating membership in national collectivities. The unilateral concentration on the history of nationalism and national-ideologies has neglected an essential aspect in the making of nation-states in the region: national communities are not exclusively cultural creations, but also legal-institutional constructions. They have been forged not only by dominant cultural discourses about the nation, dispersed through state-sponsored educational systems, but also by processes of formal delimitation of the border between citizens and aliens, legal codification and classification of the inhabitants, practices of ascribing citizenship and of naturalization, and ethnic and national policies for protecting kin-minorities abroad.

To date, the importance of the institution of citizenship for the process of nation-building has been either entirely neglected, or approached in view of 'classical' typologies opposing civic to ethnic forms of nationalism. In a path-breaking analysis of citizenship in France and Germany, Rogers W. Brubaker linked the contrasting understandings of nationhood in the two countries with the dominant legal techniques employed for ascribing state citizenship, *jus sanguinis* in the case of Germany, and a combination of *jus sanguinis* and *jus soli* in the case of France. He argued that the political outcome of these techniques is significantly different: the principle of *jus soli* fosters 'a territorial community', while the principle of *jus sanguinis* creates 'a community of descent'.[19] On this basis, Brubaker identified two opposing models of citizenship: the French one, which is liberal, 'state-centered', 'secular', and 'assimilationist', and the German one, which is Romantic, '*Volk*-centered' and 'differentialist'.[20] Their features were shaped by the different political

---

[18] For the process of nation- and state-building, see D. Mishkova, 'Modernization and Political Elites in the Balkans before the First World War', *East European Politics and Societies*, 9 (1995), 63–89; for a seminal deconstruction of the Western discourse on the Balkans, see Todorova, *Imagining the Balkans*; on the Western perception of ethnic violence in the Balkans, see Mark Mazower, *The Balkans: A Short History* (New York, 2001); on recent works on the Ottoman Empire in its last phase of existence, rejecting both the idealization and the stigmatization of its political order, see Selim Deringil, *The Well-Protected Domains: Ideology and the Legitimization of Power in the Ottoman Empire, 1876–1909* (London, 1998).

[19] Rogers Brubaker, *Citizenship and Nationhood in France and Germany* (Cambridge, Mass., 1992), 85–114, 123.

[20] See Rogers W. Brubaker, 'Immigration, Citizenship, and the Nation State in France and Germany: A Comparative Historical Analysis', *International Sociology*, 5/4 (1990), 379–407; and *Citizenship and Nationhood*, mostly 1–17. More recent works on citizenship have relativized the

traditions and geopolitical position of the two countries: in France, the confidence in the power of assimilation of the French people led to the acceptance of the *jus soli* principle as a complementary criterion in ascribing citizenship, while in Germany—where scepticism toward assimilation prevailed—an exclusive *jus sanguinis* citizenship legislation was adopted, mainly as a protection against 'unwanted' immigrants.

In a similar vein, equating legal policies of citizenship and naturalization with 'fixed' and 'internally unified' traditions of nationhood, prominent scholars specializing in East European studies reinforced the dichotomy between civic and ethnic nations, by associating them with the opposition of 'formal' versus 'substantial', 'thick' versus 'thin' or 'primordial' versus 'learned' definitions of citizenship.[21] For example, arguing for the necessity of a 'high culture' as a precondition for nation-building, Ernest Gellner put forward a typology of four distinct time zones in the making of citizenship and nation-states in Europe. The first one, composed of regions along the Atlantic coast in the early modern process of national building, was based mainly on 'forgetting' rather than on reawakening ethnic identities. The second time zone, corresponding to the territories of the former Holy Roman Empire, was characterized by the existence of viable high cultures, a feature that favoured the political unification of Germany and Italy at the end of nineteenth century. In the third time zone, that of East-Central Europe, the locus of 'classical Habsburg-and-east-and-south type of nationalism',[22] both political units and dominant high cultures were missing. Instead, 'a patchwork of folk cultures and cultural diversities separating social strata' and 'adjoining territories' transformed the inter-war national nation-building process into a more 'arduous' and 'brutal' process. The fourth time zone of Europe was contained within the imperial borderlands of the enduring Tsarist/Soviet Empire, which considerably delayed the nation-building process of many peoples.[23] Gellner found the specificity of citizenship in East-Central Europe in the distinction between *Bürgerschaft* or substantial citizenship, and *Staatsangehörerigkeit*, or formal citizenship. In the West, substantial citizenship was used as a form of social integration, while in East-Central Europe it was rather formal citizenship that prevailed. While very speculative, these typologies lacked a strong empirical basis, founded on the evolution of citizenship in the Balkans. Given the paucity of

dichotomy between the French and German citizenship legislation. According to Andreas K. Fahrmeir, prior to the 1913 Citizenship Act, German citizenship legislation included a strong *jus soli* component. The adoption of *jus sanguinis* as the exclusive principle in ascribing citizenship in the Wilhelmine Empire thus appears as 'a new departure rather than a traditional German concept of nationality'. See Fahrmeir, 'Nineteenth-Century German Citizenship: A Reconsideration', *Historical Journal*, 10 (1997), 721–52, 721. On the same point, see also Dieter Gosewinkel, *Einbürgern und Ausschließen: Die Nationalisierung der Staatsangehörigkeit vom Deutschen Bund bis zur Bundesrepublik Deutschland* (Göttingen, 2001).

21 On 'primordial' versus 'learned' and 'thick' versus 'thin' definitions of citizenship, see Charles Tilly, 'Citizenship, Identity, and Social History', in Tilly (ed.), *Citizenship, Identity and Social History* (Cambridge, 1996), 1–17. 22 E. Gellner, *Nations and Nationalism* (Oxford, 1988), 99.
23 E. Gellner, *The Condition of Liberty: Civil Society and its Rivals* (New York, 1994), 115–17.

elaborated case studies on the topic, the Balkans served as a testing ground for 'grand' and 'ahistorical' theories of social change, which tended to reify geographical boundaries into analytical ones.

Addressing this insufficiency, the current chapter proposes a first historically grounded comparative analysis of the main features of the institution of nation-state citizenship in the Balkans during 'the long nineteenth century', from the emergence of the first movements of liberation to the end of the Balkan Wars. The analysis makes reference to six states: the Ottoman Empire, Greece, the principalities of Moldova and Wallachia (which united in 1859 to constitute Romania), Bulgaria, Greece, and Serbia. It focuses mainly on mechanisms of state formation and legal codification in the region, differentiating between 'new' versus 'old' principalities, and between *jus soli* and *jus sanguinis* citizenship legislation. Without belittling other aspects of nationalism or denying the multi-dimensional nature of the subject, the chapter underscored the role of citizenship as a privileged angle through which to analyse patterns of nation- and state-building, highlighting transient definitions of the boundaries of the nation.

The analysis of citizenship legislation and practices in the Balkans in the modern period is a particularly difficult undertaking, given the great complexity of peoples and lands, their different social and religious compositions, and the great variation in their historical experiences and paths to modernization. To the complex history of citizenship, one has to add more general theoretical and methodological challenges posed by citizenship studies, such as the need to construct a valid definition of citizenship, to unite into a comprehensive methodological model the formal legal aspect of citizenship with issues of demographic and social-political change, and to apply creatively Western analytical concepts to the study of citizenship in the Balkans without either sacrificing local specificity or falling into the trap of essentializing the differences in the historical experience of the two regions. In coping with these challenges, I first distinguish between the intellectual history of citizenship as a socio-political concept; and the history of citizenship as an institution. In regard to the latter, I make an additional differentiation between two institutional dimensions of citizenship: the legal category of nationality defining membership in a state understood as a territorial and national organization; and citizenship as rights and duties stemming from membership in a political community. The first dimension encompasses the construction of legal and political borders between state citizens and aliens. The second dimension refers to civil, political, and social entitlements of citizenship.[24]

The chapter is organized in four parts. The first part focuses on the socio-political background of the Ottoman Empire and its impact on the construction of an Ottoman citizenship, an issue largely neglected in the academic literature.

---

[24] On this distinction, see Theodor Marshall, *Citizenship and Social Class* (Cambridge, 1950).

The second part examines the emergence of nation-state citizenship in the Balkan states that were carved out of the European territory of the Ottoman Empire. After highlighting the main legal techniques used by Balkan states in order to forge homogeneous ethnic communities, it focuses mainly on the case studies of Moldova, Wallachia, and Bulgaria. The third section examines demographic changes generated by the emergence and consolidation of homogeneous nation-states in the region. The conclusion reviews the main peculiar features of the construction of nation-state citizenship in the Balkans, and evaluates its impact on the 'classical' typologies contrasting civic and ethnic forms of nationalism.

THE OTTOMAN EMPIRE AND THE EMERGENCE OF AN IMPERIAL CITIZENSHIP

The Ottoman Empire was a heterogeneous conglomerate of lands and peoples, a mosaic of ethnic and religious groups governed by a Muslim elite, dominating the army and the administration. Until the Tanzimat period starting in 1839, the empire did not employ a concept of citizenship codified in terms of rights and obligations, modelled on the Western pattern. It was organized as a theocratic state based on the Qu'rān and the religious law named the *Shari'a*, which concomitantly served as a civil, ritual, and religious code.

The *Shari'a* divided the world into two main spheres, the *Dar-al Islam* (the House of Peace), and the *Dar-al Harb* (the House of War). The inhabitants of the *Dar-al-' ahd* (the House of Peace)—the realm of the empire itself—were divided into three main categories. First, there were the Muslims, equally placed under the authority of the Sultan, and having access to state positions and the bureaucratic apparatus. Second, there were non-Muslim subjects living under Ottoman jurisdiction, generically called *raya*. In return for their exemption from military service, non-Muslims were granted a covenant of protection, the *dhimma*, being regarded as protected people, the *dhimmis*, in exchange for which they had to pay a special tax called the *cizye*. Third, there were foreigners living temporarily in Ottoman territory, named *Harbis*. Although they belonged normally to the *Dar-al Harb*, the abode of war, in the Ottoman territory *Harbis* were issued an *Aman* protecting their property and the practice of their religion. In cases where an alien was living for more than one year in Ottoman territory, he was considered an Ottoman subject, *dhimmi*, and automatically subjected to the payment of *cizye*.

Motivated by economic incentives, the Ottoman Empire also employed an inclusive population policy, providing shelter for fugitive and rebels and encouraging immigration. A foreigner could become an Ottoman subject either by voluntary conversion to Islam, in which case he was granted all rights available to other Muslims, or by settling in the country, becoming *raya* and obliging itself to pay the *cizye*.

A special category of foreigners were the subjects of Great Christian Powers, whose status was regulated on the basis of Capitulation Treaties signed with the Sublime Porte, starting in the sixteenth century.[25] Capitulations granted important personal rights and privileges to foreign citizens in the Ottoman territory, namely freedom of travel, religious liberty, and the right to practise trade, as well as tax exemption and a privileged regime of border taxation. Subjects of great European states living in Ottoman territory could also totally escape the authority of the Ottoman law and administration, since they enjoyed the inviolability of their domicile, and—in the case of juridical contentions—they were judged according to the laws of their country of origin, by a representative of their own government appointed in the Ottoman Empire, called a consul (from here the name of consular jurisdiction). However, if such an alien lived more than ten years in Ottoman territory, he was automatically assimilated to the status of an Ottoman subject, and obliged to pay the *cizye*.

Among the *raya*, non-Muslim religious communities possessing a written 'holy book' formed a special legal category. The three leading non-Muslim religious communities 'of the book'—the Jews, the Greek Orthodox Church, and the Armenian Church—were established as recognized *dhimmi* communities, known as *millets* (meaning in Turkish 'nation' or 'people'), and led by their appropriate religious dignitary: the chief rabbi, as the head of the *millet-i Yahudi*, the Armenian patriarch, the head of the *millet-i Ermeni*, and the Orthodox patriarch. Within each *millet*, communities were responsible for the allocation and collection of their taxes, their educational arrangements, and internal legal matters pertaining especially to issues of personal status such as marriage and inheritance. The origins of the institution of the *millet* and the terminology employed by the Ottoman administration to designate it have been a matter of deep controversy in the recent scholarship on the Ottoman Empire. While the traditional view asserted that the institution of *millet* was established ever since the conquest of Constantinople, new historical evidence suggests that both the institution and the term *millet* first appeared in the seventeenth century, and became prevalent only in the nineteenth century. In the sixteenth and seventeenth centuries the Ottoman administration used the term *Kefere* (infidels) to designate the Orthodox Christians.[26]

Neither was the patriarch of Constantinople the head of a unified Orthodox community, but exercised partial authority over numerous segregated Orthodox groups or *tevâ'if* (so-called *Tâ'ife*). The unification of the Orthodox community

---

[25] The first capitulation was granted to Francis I of France in 1535, followed later by England in 1675, and by commercial agreements with the Habsburg Empire in 1718, with Prussia in 1761, with Russia in 1783, and with Sardinia in 1823. For a comprehensive presentation of these capitulations, see Francis Rey, *La Protection diplomatique et consulaire dans les échelles du Levant et de Barbarie* (Paris, 1899).

[26] B. Braude, 'Foundation Myths of the Millet System', in B. Braude and B. Lewis (eds.), *Christians and Jews in the Ottoman Empire: The Functioning of a Plural Society*, 2 vols. (New York, 1982), i. 70–5.

under the authority of the patriarch occurred only gradually during the eighteenth century, facilitated by the steady decline of the Ottoman administration, the growing influence of the Phanariot Greeks, and their efforts to gain new juridical and economic privileges for the Orthodox church. Through the extension of the authority of the patriarch over independent autocephalous archbishoprics, the patriarch became the head of a unified community, subsequently called the *Milletbaşi* of the *Rum-milleti or millet-i Rum* and encompassing all the Orthodox believers under the sultan's authority.[27] Notwithstanding these debates, a majority of scholars agree that in the eighteenth and nineteenth centuries the institution of *millet* was an important component of the socio-political organization of the Ottoman Empire, greatly contributing to shaping identity along religious lines.

In sum, the Ottoman political and administrative structure was based on a formal inequality between Muslims and non-Muslims. Although one cannot point to a fully-fledged system of 'organized discrimination' in every sphere of life, non-Muslim inhabitants were tolerated as long as they lacked public visibility. While many individual Christians and Jews reached positions of power, non-Muslims did not enjoy full equality as groups. This hierarchical structure was challenged in the second quarter of the nineteenth century, when there was a process of legal codification, delimitation of the body of Ottoman subjects, and a move toward formal individual equality before the civil law.

Between Ottomanism and Pan-Islamism: Dilemmas of Ottoman Citizenship

Starting in the second quarter of the nineteenth century, the Ottoman Empire embarked on a process of socio-political transformation and economic modernization that entailed strategies of modernization and change in the rhetoric of state legitimization. This process, regarded by Benedict Anderson as part of a more general tendency toward 'the nationalization of the dynasties', led to the development of an 'official nationalism', defined as 'an anticipatory strategy adopted by dominant groups which are threatened with marginalization or exclusion from an emerging nationally-imagined community.'[28] The main components of official nationalism were 'compulsory state-controlled primary education, state-organized propaganda, official rewriting of history, militarism [...] and endless affirmation of the identity of dynasty and nation'.[29] While in the Habsburg Empire official nationalism was based on Germanification, and in Russia on Russification, in the Ottoman Empire the ethnic component was weak. Although incorporating

---

[27] See Paraskevas Konortas, 'From Tâ'ife to Millet: Ottoman Terms for the Ottoman Greek Orthodox Community', in Dimitri Gondicas and Charles Issawi (eds.), *Ottoman Greeks in the Age of Nationalism: Politics, Economy, and Society in the Nineteenth Century* (Princeton, 1999), 169–79.

[28] B. Anderson, *Imagined Communities: Reflections on the Origin and Spread of Nationalism* (London, 1994), 101.   [29] Ibid.

elements of the Turkish ethnic identity (such as Ottoman language, an uneven combination of Turkish, Arabic, and Persian, written in the Arabic script) and combined with Islamism, Ottoman 'official nationalism' can be regarded as predominantly a type of civic nationalism, emphasizing equality among various ethnic groups living in the empire. It encouraged their Ottoman patriotism and loyalty to the sultan, offering in exchange equality, modernization, and social mobility. This strategy was nevertheless weakened by internal contradictions and political hesitations of Ottoman elite factions, by the spread of secessionist nationalism among the Balkan people, and by Western military and political intervention into the internal organization of the empire.

   The creation of an Ottoman citizenship was mainly the result of the reform programme initiated in 1839 by the Sultan Abd al-Madjid (1839–61) known as the *Tanzimat* ('reorganization'). It began with a proclamation of the sultan issued on 3 November 1839, called the *Khatt-i Humāyūn* or *Khatt-i Sherīf* of *Gülkhāne*, promising personal security, comprehensive administrative reforms, fiscal reorganization, and the abolition of farm-tax. The proclamation instituted a formal equality between subjects irrespective of religion. It was meant to discourage national separatism and to promote the development of Ottoman patriotism, contained by the doctrine of *Ottomanism*. The Ottoman administration also developed a system of permanent registration of the population for facilitating the census, taxation, and military services, and issued passports for travel abroad starting in 1844. In 1856, in response to strong Western diplomatic pressure following the Crimean war, a second reform edict continued the *Tanzimat* process, by reconfirming formal individual equality between Muslims and non-Muslims. In addition, there occurred a process of civil codification of the *Shari'a*, together with the adoption of penal and commercial codes inspired by the French model.[30]

   Although stimulated by a combination of domestic challenges and external pressures, the gradual process of building an all-encompassing Ottoman citizenship was considerably slowed down by internal tensions between the religious and the secular dimensions of the legal system, and by political hesitations of the Ottoman elites. Consequently, the first law regulating citizenship in Turkey was adopted as late as 19 January 1869, at a time when autonomous Balkan principalities had already passed their nationality laws. Motivated by a combination of political and demographic concerns, the law codified the heterogeneous body of Ottoman subjects in terms of rights and duties of a generic Ottoman citizenship. The law set clear rules for the acquisition, loss, and renunciation of Ottoman nationality, combining Western patterns.[31] It conferred Ottoman citizenship *jure sanguinis* to a child born of an Ottoman man. In line with traditional inclusive Ottoman demographic policy, the law also encompassed a strong inclusive *jus soli* component, by conferring

---

[30] For the codification of civil law in Turkey, see Dora Glidewell Nadolski, 'Ottoman and Secular Civil Law', *International Journal of Middle East Studies*, 8 (1977), 517–43.

[31] See the text of the law in Demétrius Nicolaides, *Législation ottomane ou recueil des lois, règlements, ordonnances, traités et capitulations et autres documents officiel de l'Empire Ottoman* (Constantinople, 1873).

on all individuals born on Ottoman territory of foreign parents the right to Ottoman citizenship, provided they demanded it during the first three years following their adulthood. The conditions for the naturalization of aliens were equally liberal: foreigners who resided five consecutive years in the Ottoman Empire could be naturalized, upon request, by the Ministry of Foreign Affairs.

The main aim of the law was to delimit clearly the Ottoman citizenry, to formally assure the loyalty of Ottoman subjects, and to strictly control their emigration. This concern was in direct relation to the overlapping citizenship policy of the newly established Balkan states, such as Greece, which unilaterally granted state citizenship to numerous Greek-speaking Orthodox inhabitants of the Ottoman Empire. In order to counter this policy, the Ottoman law unequivocally stipulated that all inhabitants of the Ottoman territory were considered Ottoman subjects, unless expressly proven otherwise. Moreover, Ottoman nationality could be lost only with the express authorization of the Ottoman government. Any naturalization abroad made without Ottoman consent was to be considered null, and the respective person was still to be considered an Ottoman subject. In addition, the government reserved its right to withdraw the Ottoman citizenship of its subjects naturalized abroad or enrolled in the service of a foreign government without imperial permission, and to impose certain interdictions upon them. In view of these stipulations, the Ottoman citizenship law can be characterized not only as inclusive but also as *reactive* to nationality laws passed by neighbouring Christian states, a feature highlighted by the delegation of citizenship matters to the Ministry of Foreign Affairs.

On 11–13 December 1876, the first Ottoman constitution issued by the Grad Vezir Midhat Pasha took further steps toward the developing of an all-encompassing Ottoman citizenship, based on political equality between Muslims and non-Muslims. The constitution reduced the autocratic powers of the sultan and introduced a parliament elected through a restricted franchise and a system of electoral colleges. It declared the territory of the Ottoman Empire as indivisible, and placed it under the suzerainty of the sultan, in his dual quality as the *Kalif* and protector of Holy Places, and as the *Padishar* of all the Ottomans. It also regarded all subjects of the empire as *Ottomans*, irrespective of their religion, and granted them individual liberty. Most importantly, Article 17 read that all Ottomans were equal before the law. It granted them the same rights and duties, and promised their individual liberty. Articles 18 and 19 opened public office to all Ottomans as a function of their capacity and merit. However, while stipulating the 'free exercise' of all 'recognized religions' and preserving their legal privileges, the Constitution declared 'Islamism' 'the religion of the state' in the Ottoman Empire, and made public office conditional on knowledge of the Ottoman language. In regard to admission and loss of state citizenship, the constitution reconfirmed the stipulations of the 1869 law.

By the end of the *Tanzimat* period (1876), the Ottoman legal and political system made decisive steps toward building an all-inclusive imperial citizenship. The constitutional experiment was nevertheless short-lived (December 1876–February 1878). On a political level, there were no organized parties and unified opposition to take full benefit of the elections held in 1876 and 1877.[32] To the lack of parliamentary experience, one has to add the hesitations of the ruling elites to open up the system of political representation. After a short experiment in constitutional rule, the Sultan Abdülhamid II (1876–1909) suspended interme-diary organs of powers, opting for the centralization of state attributes in his own hands.[33] Moreover, adopted during the dramatic unfolding of 'the Eastern Crises', the 1876 constitution could not prevent the secession of the autonomous Balkan principalities. The Treaty of Berlin (June 1878), following the 1877–8 Russian-Turkish War, consecrated the independence of Romania, Serbia, and Montenegro, and recognized the internal autonomy of Bulgaria, paving the way toward the total dissolution of the Balkan component of the empire.

The loss of the Balkan Christian principalities increased the religious homogeneity of the empire. Grasping the importance of Islam as a cohesive factor among heterogeneous ethnic groups, such as Arabs, Turks, and Kurds, Abdülhamid II based his political legitimacy on calls for religious unity, capitalizing on the idea of the universal Caliphate. His cultural policies promoted an officially endorsed version of Islam, while new 'invented' civic traditions, such as public symbols, celebrations', and a state-sponsored educational system, aimed at increasing social cohesion and loyalty to the sultan.[34] Despite the strong emphasis on religion, the legal-institutional dimension of Ottoman state citizenship pervaded religious solidarity: in 1889, Algerian Muslims seeking refuge in the Ottoman Empire were accepted only on the condition of their immediate renunciation of French citizenship.[35]

On a political level, the autocracy of the sultan, treating Ottoman inhabitants as subjects, contradicted the rhetoric of egalitarian citizenship introduced by the *Tanzimat* reforms. The growing internal opposition finally led to the demise of the sultan's rule. In 1909, the Ottoman state embarked on a long constitutional period (1908–1918), marking the transition from the multinational empire to a Turkish national state. Political life was dominated by the Young Turks, a group which was previously in political opposition and exile (1878–1908). Once in power, they were by and large divided between two tendencies, a liberal one arguing for decentralization and cooperation with all ethnic groups living in the empire, and a nationalist one, pleading for a strong central authority based on the political domination of ethnic Turks. In order to inspire new political loyalties and to forge a unified and homogeneous community, Young Turks had to dismantle the Ottoman communal traditions centred on the *millets* and based on communal

[32] See Robert Devereux, *The First Ottoman Constitutional Period: A Study of the Midhat Constitution and Parliament* (Baltimore, 1963).

[33] See Selim Deringil, 'Legitimacy Structure in the Ottoman State: The Reign of Abdulhamid II (1876–1909)', *International Journal of Middle East Studies*, 23 (1991), 345–59.   [34] Ibid.

[35] Selim Deringil, 'Some Aspects of Muslim Immigration into the Ottoman Empire in the Late 19th Century', *Al-Abhath*, 38 (1990), 37–41; Selim Deringil, 'The Invention of Tradition as Public Image in the late Ottoman Empire, 1808 to 1908', *Comparative Studies in Society and History*, 35/1 (1993), 24–5.

rights and privileges. The doctrine of Ottomanism thus encountered a dual form of political resistance, from the part of the leadership of the ethnic groups living in the empire, such as the Greeks, who did not want to renounce their communal privileges, on the one hand, and from Turkish nationalism, which fought for political domination, on the other hand. Until the advent of the First World War, the Ottoman state organization was thus dominated by the contradiction between the emergence of a generic Ottoman citizenship based on the legal equality of all its inhabitants, irrespective of their religion or ethnicity, and calls for an Islamic based Ottoman nationality, supported by a legal order that would favour the political and socio-economic interests of the Muslims. The tension between the egalitarian doctrine of Ottomanism and appeals to pan-Islamism and pan-Turkism generated recurrent political crises. The conflict was ultimately resolved under the impact of external shocks. The military collapse of the empire following the First World War removed the Arab component of the empire, while the 1918–23 Greek-Turkish war catalysed the idea of a secular Turkish nation-state.

Notwithstanding its internal contradictions, Ottoman citizenship can thus be characterized as a civic type of citizenship based on moderate nationalism, inclusion, and modernization. Why did this offer of modernization and political equality not appeal to Balkan peoples? The failure of Ottomanism is to be found in the timing and content of the reforming process. The Ottoman offer of formal legal equality between Christians and Muslims came too late, at a time when Balkan populations had already developed comprehensive nationalist movements of secession. Its implementation was hampered by the trauma of Turkish rule, exacerbated by nationalist rhetoric and hostile propaganda. Moreover, although certain European provinces of the empire, such as Rumelia, were regarded as pilot-projects of the Ottoman programme of modernization and benefited from substantial central investment, the promise of material progress and social mobility associated with the imperial world economy were perceived as inferior to similar processes that had taken place in Western Europe, which captured the attention of local Christian elites. Although they were largely the product of the Ottoman modernization process, Christian elites found it more appealing to establish independent principalities in order to gain full control over the process of change, rather than to renegotiate their position within the imperial hierarchy. The Ottoman Empire thus fell victim to its own strategy of modernization and equality. The organization of communities along ethno-religious lines made possible the preservation of cultural identities, facilitating the birth of nationalist movements. The decentralization of the decision-making process and of granting political equality weakened central control over local elites, while the Western diplomatic and military involvement in the internal affairs of the empire discouraged the suppression of secessionist movements by military means. In the following section, I turn to the development of independent citizenship in the Balkan principalities under Ottoman suzerainty.

'NEW' VERSUS 'ANCIENT PRINCIPALITIES':
CITIZENSHIP LEGISLATION IN THE BALKANS

As compared to other historic regions, the making of nation-state citizenship in the Balkans exhibited several particularities, shaped by the Ottoman imperial legacy. The first major impact of Ottoman rule in the Balkans was demographic. The Balkans were traditionally an area of intense migration, serving as a boulevard of transit from the demographic reservoir of Eurasia and the northern steppes of the Black Sea to the Mediterranean basin and Asia Minor. The Ottoman occupation added to the legacy of population movements. The most notable populational change associated with Ottoman rule was the massive infiltration of Muslims into traditional Christian areas. Their migration was largely the result of state-sponsored military colonization, and involved primarily ethnic Turks from Anatolia and Asia Minor. Turkish settlers were particularly numerous in the territory of Bulgaria, mainly in the region between the Balkan Mountains and Dobrudj, the Maritsa valley toward Plovdid, and the area between the Danube and Vidin.[36] In addition, in the sixteenth and seventeenth centuries, numerous conversions to Islam occurred among Albanians and Bosnians, as well as among Greeks, Vlahs, and Serbs.[37] These demographic changes transformed certain Balkan provinces into Islamic or partially Islamic areas, such as Albania, southern Serbia, northern Montenegro, parts of Bosnia and Herzegovina, Dobrudja, as well as certain regions of Greece. Ethnic diversity in the Balkans was further aggravated by the recurrent series of Austrian-Russian-Ottoman wars (1768–1878), resulting in significant Ottoman territorial losses, anarchy in the administration and great fluctuations in population, mainly on the frontier belt between the empires that served as a battleground, ranging from the Caucasus to southern Bessarabia, Dobrudj, and the Balkan military border. After the Crimean war (1854–6), fears of Russian persecution triggered a massive emigration of Tartars from Crimea and Circassians from Kuban and the Caucasus to Ottoman territory. The Ottoman economic system also favoured demographic changes, encouraging the economic specialization of certain ethnic groups, such as Jews, Armenians, and Greeks, who acted as urban elites. Ottoman rule in the Balkans thus resulted in the relative deterritorialization of ethnic groups, which gradually lost their compact territorial distribution, and dispersed according to the role they performed in the Ottoman economic system.

Second, the construction of state citizenship in the Balkan principalities began under the regime of Ottoman suzerainty. Prior to the achievement of their state independence, the autonomous provinces of Greece (1821–32), Serbia (1828–78), Moldova and Wallachia (1821–78), and Bulgaria (1878–1908) had

---

[36] 'Turks', in *Encyclopedia of Islam*, ed. Henry A. R. Gibb et al. (Leiden, 1986–2002), 698.
[37] Ibid.

already developed most of the attributes of a distinct state citizenship, such as internal autonomy, administrative separation, citizenship legislation delimiting their citizenry from aliens, and legal systems of identification and control of demographic movements. This situation resulted in a multi-tier citizenship resembling dual nationality: one at principality level, and another one at the upper imperial level. The relationship between these two levels of citizenship was rather ambiguous. In their domestic affairs, Balkan principalities largely ignored the imperial authority. Outside their territory, until they obtained international recognition of their statehood, their inhabitants were nevertheless compelled to use Ottoman passports and to appeal to the protection of Ottoman diplomacy.

Third, on an international level, the making of citizenship in the Balkans was shaped by the gradual and 'monitored' demise of the Ottoman Empire. Ever since the emergence of the 'Eastern Question', Western powers took an active part in the conflict, transforming the reorganization of the Ottoman Empire into a major European diplomatic issue. Since autonomous Balkan principalities lacked sufficient military capabilities to defect from the empire, they had to rely on the foreign intervention of great powers, being in exchange forced to make certain political or territorial concessions to Western interests. The involvement of great powers in the region evolved from the regime of consular jurisdiction over their subjects living in Ottoman territory to an international regime for protecting ethno-religious minorities. Inaugurated in its incipient form by the Conference of Constantinople (1855) and the Congress of Paris (1856), the regime of minority protection evolved during the Congress of Berlin (1878), to be fully articulated under the Minority Convention of the 1919 Versailles Treaty System.

Besides these common features, Balkan principalities exhibited numerous variations, as a function of their different administrative status within the Ottoman Empire, their different degrees of ethnic mixing, and the relation between their national ideology and territory. In regard to citizenship legislation, one can differentiate between 'new principalities', such as Serbia, Bulgaria, and Greece, which, lacking a statehood continuity, had to create their own citizenship *ex nihilo*, and generally conferred rights on all permanent residents on a territorial basis; and 'ancient principalities', such as Moldova and Wallachia, which could retain their administrative structure under Ottoman rule and relied on previous administrative practices in building their common national citizenry. The distinction had important legal consequences, most evident in the interplay between the principles of *jus soli* and *jus sanguinis* in ascribing citizenship in the Balkans. In their effort to create their own citizenship, the new principalities used in a first phase an inclusive combination of *jus soli* and *jus sanguinis* principles in ascribing citizenship. This inclusive legislation was amended only in a second period, when the institutionalization of the citizenship body allowed a more selective policy of naturalization, in accordance with newly defined national goals. In contrast, 'ancient principalities' had a body of defined subjects that could serve as an administrative basis. In codifying their citizenship rights, they could therefore favour the legal principle of *jus sanguinis*, accompanied by a selective policy of *jus soli* naturalization. While delineating the two types, my analysis focuses on the case studies of Moldova and Wallachia, and Bulgaria.

Citizenship Legislation in Moldova and Wallachia

Citizenship legislation in Moldavia and Wallachia was shaped by their peculiar diplomatic status. In the fifteenth century, the two principalities were placed under the suzerainty of the Ottoman Empire, on the basis of treaties signed between the sultan and native princes, called *ahdnames* or *sulhnames* (agreement-acts). According to these treaties, Moldavia and Wallachia were considered by the Ottoman ideology as *ahd* or 'tribute-paying states', and were placed in the *Dar al-'ahd* ('The House of the Pact'), an intermediary realm between the *Dar-al Islam* (the House of Islam), and the *Dar-al Harb* (the House of War).[38] Under the terms of the *ahdnames*, the principalities had to pay to the High Porte an annual tribute, and to renounce attributes of formal sovereignty, such as the right to conduct an independent foreign policy. In exchange, they were entitled to Ottoman military protection in case of foreign aggression, were allowed to choose their own native princes—conditioned also by the confirmation of the sultan—and enjoyed almost complete autonomy in their internal legislative, administrative, and religious organization.

The diplomatic status of the two principalities had a direct impact on their citizenship practices, among which the most important were a lack of formal attributes of state suzerainty, external intrusion into their domestic affairs, the inferior legal status of non-Christian inhabitants, and consular jurisdiction over the subjects of great European powers living on their territory. The following analysis delineates several legal models of community membership which competed for political dominance in the first three-quarters of the nineteenth century: an inclusive one, called the Byzantine model (and having as a subtype the 'Phanariot model' that functioned in the principalities in the period 1711/1716–1821), a more restrictive and xenophobic one, called the 'nobility estate model' implemented in the period 1831–58, the 1848 'revolutionary model', the 'state-national model' (1858–66) and the 'constitutional nationalism model' (1866–1918). Each of them put forward different systems of legal classification of the inhabitants, attitudes toward immigration, and the configuration of the political space.[39]

---

[38] See K. Hitchins, *The Romanians, 1774–1866* (Oxford, 1996), 5–6; and M. Maxim, 'The Romanian Principalities and the Ottoman Empire', in D. C. Giurescu and S. Fischer-Galați (eds.), *Romania: A Historic Perspective* (Boulder, Colo., 1998), 105–32, 112. See also M. Maxim, *Țările Române și Inalta Poartă: Cadrul Juridic al relațiilor româno-otomane în evul mediu* (Bucharest, 1993), especially ch. 3; and Ș. Gorovei, 'Moldova în "Casa Păcii." Pe marginea izvoarelor privind primul secol de relații moldo-turce', *Anuarul Institutului de Istorie si Arheologie 'A. D. Xenopol'*, 17 (1980), 629–77.

[39] On the Romanian citizenship, see Constantin Iordachi, *From the 'Right of the Natives' to 'Constitutional Nationalism': The Making of the Romanian Citizenship, 1817–1918*, Manuscript, CEU Library, Budapest. The dissertation is forthcoming with the CEU Press, within the series 'Studies of Pasts'. See also Constantin Iordachi, 'Citizenship and National Identity in Romania: A Historical Overview', *Regio Yearbook 2003*, 2–34.

The first legal model in the principalities emulated the Byzantine political tradition, based on the autocratic power of the prince, interdependence between state and church, and an inclusive population policy. The tradition was adapted to local social conditions and legal mores, and combined with Ottoman and Central European institutional influences. This complex syncretism resulted in a heterogeneous socio-political organization of Byzantine inspiration that functioned in the principalities during two distinct periods, in the fifteenth and sixteenth centuries, and was revived, in a peculiar configuration, in the eighteenth century. The seventeenth century, the interval in-between the two periods, was marked by a confrontation between the autocracy of the prince and the oligarchic tendency of the local nobility, called boyars (boieri).

The revival of the Byzantine political model occurred during the so-called Phanariot regime (1711/1716–1821), when the princes of the two principalities were recruited predominantly among the Greek clientele living in the district of Phanar, in Istanbul. Phanariot princes bought their throne directly from the High Porte, and came into the country accompanied by a numerous clientele, rewarding them with leading positions in the state apparatus. Facing a dramatic increase in their material obligations to the Porte, Phanariot princes implemented numerous reforms meant to achieve fiscal stability, since their political survival depended upon their ability to raise taxes. Motivated by financial needs, they also promoted an inclusive population policy, encouraging foreign rural and urban colonization. Although on a small scale, rural and urban colonization resulted in a multi-ethnic and multi-religious population, with ethnic and religious minorities making up one-tenth of the population in both principalities. The legal order of the regime was indifferent to ethnicity. For tax purposes, it classified inhabitants according to their religion, profession, and aristocratic status.

Politically, Phanariot princes initiated a campaign of centralization of the administration, which led them into conflict with the local nobility. On the one hand, this conflict was fuelled by two opposing views on the form of government for the principalities, namely enlightened absolutism based on the centralizing power of the prince versus a 'nobiliary state'. On the other hand, the conflict was exacerbated by the clash of interests between the entourage of the prince, recruited mainly from Greek Ottoman subjects and assigned posts of high influence in the administration, and local boyars. The conflict between the 'nobility of blood' claimed by local boyars and the emerging Greek 'nobility of office', stimulated the development of citizenship legislation. Local nobles demanded measures against the unchecked penetration of foreigners, and tried to reduce the political and economic dependence on the Ottoman Empire, which facilitated foreign penetration. This dual tension resulted in embryonic citizenship legislation, framed by a process of enlightenment codification, and encompassing selective forms of closure, based on the local legal practice named *drit de pământean* (the right of the native).

The first citizenship regulations were contained by the first modern codes adopted in the principalities, the Moldavian *Codul Calimach* (1817) and the

Wallachian *Legiuirea Caragea* (1818). The two codes put forward a heterogeneous synthesis between Byzantine collections of laws, customary law, and influences from contemporary Western legal codes, most notably the 1804 French *Code Civil* and the 1811 Austrian *Gesetzbuch*. They adopted the *jus sanguinis* principle in ascribing citizenship, and employed for the first time the word 'foreigners' (*străini*), defined as a separate legal category. Despite the lobbying of the local boyars, the two codes did not contain rules of naturalization, but preserved the inclusive naturalization practice of customary law, which facilitated the access of Ottoman Greeks to landed property and noble status. Naturalization could be obtained through ennoblement, marriage to a local noble woman, or, in the case of the peasants, merchants, and artisans, simply by settlement in the country.

Codul Calimach and *Legiuirea Caragea* contributed to the unification and harmonization of the legal system, setting the legal foundations of the modern type of state citizenship. They classified the inhabitants according to gender, nobility status, religion, and citizenship, and strictly regulated their rights and duties. One can identify several autonomous legal spheres in the socio-political organization of the principalities. First, there was the sphere of the Orthodox church, an institution which enjoyed numerous privileges and became a 'state-within-a-state'. Second, non-Orthodox ethno-religious communities in the principalities—most notably the Jews and the Armenians—were organized on a corporate basis, similarly to the Ottoman *millets*. They enjoyed religious liberty, internal autonomy, and a special taxation regime, but worked under certain civil disabilities. The principalities thus had a theocratic political order based on Byzantine Orthodox canon law, which regulated civil relations among Orthodox inhabitants, and promoted an attitude of 'hostile tolerance' toward other religious communities.

The end of the Phanariot regime in 1821 and the return to the rule of local princes marked the final demise of the cosmopolitan Byzantine political model in the principalities, opening the way for the establishment of a regime of estates assemblies resembling the Hungarian and Polish patterns. In both principalities, there existed great assemblies composed of the nobility, court dignitaries, the army, and the clergy, while the cities were feebly and irregularly represented. Assemblies were convoked in exceptional situations, such as the election of new princes, or during grave events, and assisted princes in reaching major decisions concerning foreign or domestic policy. In the post-1821 period, the political importance of the assemblies increased, developing as a counter-power to that of the prince. Internally, assemblies were dominated by the confrontation between great nobles who wanted an exclusive monopoly over political life, and lower strata of the nobility who attempted to share these monopolistic political priv-ileges. The main principles of the new regime were embedded in the stipulations of the *Organic Statutes* (1831/2), which crystallized citizenship legislation in the principalities.

The *Statutes* consolidated the autonomous state citizenship of the two principalities, by delimiting the body of citizens from foreigners, stipulating formal naturalization rules, forbidding dual citizenship, taking measures against illegal immigration, and establishing a system of statistical evidence of the inhabitants. They also introduced for the first time political rights and electoral processes. The *Statutes* nevertheless endorsed the political monopoly of the nobility, by granting political rights only to Orthodox boyars in Moldova and to Christian boyars in Wallachia, differentiated according to their ranks. These political changes reflected the interests of the great nobles, who imposed their view on the new organization of the principalities.

The *Statutes* instituted a multi-tier citizenship. On a lower level, that of 'narrow naturalization', they consecrated the 'rights of the natives', granted to all inhabitants, including the Jews and the Armenians, and encompassing civil and residential rights. On a higher level, that of 'broad naturalization', they distinguished the quality of being a native from full citizenship rights, which were granted only to boyars. Advancement from one citizenship level to another was possible only by the ennoblement of native inhabitants, or by naturalization of Orthodox foreigners. Non-Orthodox foreigners in Moldova and non-Christians in Wallachia were denied access to broad naturalization, being thus excluded from exercising political rights.

This multi-tier citizenship was challenged by a third model of citizenship emerging in the principalities in the first half of the nineteenth century, namely revolutionary citizenship, put forward mostly in political programmes, pamphlets, and manifestos during the 1848 revolution. While in Moldova the revolutionary movement was defeated at an incipient stage, the political programme of the Wallachian liberals is representative of the revolutionary citizenship model. It was based on a heterogeneous combination of French republicanism and Christian socialism, and adapted to local socio-political realities. It demanded a republican political order, composed of an elected prince and a representative assembly. It did not envision universal suffrage based on individual representation, but demanded a democratic representation of all social estates, including the peasantry. This corporate organization was seen as a return to the medieval system of social estates, pervaded by the abuses of the great *boieri*.

Wallachian liberals strengthened the national dimension of citizenship. They demanded the union of the principalities, and granted ethnic Romanians living in neighbouring countries rights to preferential naturalization. Their model of civic nationalism thus encompassed a weak ethnic component. Largely, however, they defined the citizenship body as a community of political values, proclaiming the emancipation of Jews and Gypsies. While the multi-tier citizenship of the *Statutes* dissociated between the residential 'rights of the natives' and political rights, the revolutionary model of citizenship granted full citizenship status to all permanent inhabitants. This programme was implemented during the short rule of the revolutionary government (July–September 1848).

The defeat of the revolution by the joint Russian and Ottoman military intervention opened the way for the restoration of the *ancien régime*, against strong internal opposition. After a decade of political turmoil (1848–58), the arduous confrontation between the oligarchic regime of the nobility and revolutionary citizenship in the principalities was ultimately decided by the external intervention of the great powers. Following the Crimean war (1854–6), the 1856 Congress of Paris reconfirmed the suzerainty of the Ottoman Empire over the principalities, but also placed them under the collective protectorate of the European great powers. In addition, it instituted a forum of consultation of the inhabitants of Moldavia and Wallachia—called the *Ad-Hoc Divans*—concerning the prospective union of the two countries, and their future political organization. Based mainly on the deliberations of the *Divans*, in August 1858, the great powers granted a common constitution to the principalities, entitled the Convention of Paris, marking a formal legal border between the *ancien régime* and the nation-state. It abolished aristocratic titles and privileges, instituting civil equality before the law. It also set the basis of a modern political system, but endowed with political rights only a small oligarchy of large landowners. The Convention emancipated all Christian ethno-religious communities, granting them full civil and political rights, and including a promise for the future citizenship emancipation of Jews, who were granted civil rights but were 'temporarily' excluded from political rights.

The Convention also addressed the desire for union expressed by the *Ad-Hoc Divans*. Instead of endorsing a full unification between the two countries, it permitted only a formal political union, under the name of the 'United principalities of Moldavia and Wallachia', in which each principality was to preserve its separate prince, administrative system, and political institutions. Nevertheless, in early 1859 Romanian political elites went far beyond the stipulations of the 1858 Convention: on 5 and 24 January, the Moldavian and Wallachian Assemblies elected Alexandru I Cuza as a *dual prince* of Moldavia and Wallachia. The new prince started a process of legal and administrative unification of the two countries that resulted in a common capital, government, and legislative body. On December 1861 Prince Cuza was able to proclaim that 'the Union is achieved and the Romanian nationality is established'.

The rule of Alexandru Ioan Cuza (1859–1866) set the basis of a unified Romanian national citizenship, by emulating the French legal and political model, with its inclusive, secular, and homogenizing features. Internally, the main battle over political power was fought between the prince and oligarchic political elites. Acting as an enlightened despot, the prince introduced from above a 'learned' definition of citizenship based on civic nationalism, promoting the emancipation of the peasants and their integration into the political body through landownership, conscription, education, and political participation, and favouring the emancipation of Romanian Jews. Implemented in 1865, the new Romanian Civil Code automatically ascribed Romanian citizenship to a child born from the marriage of a Romanian man, following the *jus sanguinis* principle. The rule of *jus soli* had no bearing on ascribing Romanian citizenship at birth, but—under the direct influence of the Napoleonic Code—was employed as a criterion of naturalization of Christian residents born in the country, at the time of their adulthood. Most importantly, the Code also admitted the naturalization of non-Christian inhabitants—mainly Jews—providing they lived in Romania for at least ten years, and that their requests for naturalization met with the approval of the prince and of the parliament. Cuza's reforms, as well as his autocratic tendencies, provoked the resistance of the oligarchy, who forced his abdication in 1866.

The establishment of constitutional monarchy in 1866, through the enthrone-ment of Carol-Ludovic of Hohenzollern-Sigmaringen and the adoption of a new constitution, brought significant changes to Romanian citizenship. The content of the new constitution had a composite nature, due to the complex bargaining among various social actors. It combined a system of civic rights and liberties inspired by the 1831 Belgian constitution with a restrictive electoral system based on property and education, and a bourgeois civil code that followed closely the Code Napoléon. In regard to state citizenship, the 1866 constitution amended the 'state-national' model in significant aspects, by introducing numerous amend-ments inspired by lower and middle strata of the former nobility, who played an important political role after the fall of Cuza, and managed to revive practices of citizenship closure characteristic of the former regime of estates. The constitution preserved the *jus sanguinis* principle in ascribing citizenship and the instant *jus soli* naturalization of second generation Christian immigrants. In addition, it inaugu-rated an active ethnic policy, by granting ethnic Romanians from abroad access to a privileged procedure of naturalization by the parliament, without a naturaliza-tion stage. While preserving the stipulations regarding the naturalization of foreigners, the constitution annulled certain stipulations of the Civil Code, per-petually excluding from access to citizenship *non-Christian* permanent residents or immigrants, such as the Romanian Jews, making them *heimatlos*.

These changes led to profound mutations in the system of political represent-ation of the country, bringing to the surface new criteria of legal classification. The cosmopolitan community of native inhabitants was redefined as a national community. The parliamentary assembly was not conceived as a corporate representation of social estates, as under the *ancien régime*, but as representative of the *Romanian nation*. This marked a complete dissociation of the 'rights of the natives', granted to all inhabitants of the country, and nation-state citizenship. The new constitutional order differentiated between native inhabitants and citizens, the former being classified according to such criteria as ethnicity and religion.

The evolution of the legal status of the Gypsies, Jews, and Armenians is suggest-ive of the patterns of continuity and discontinuity between the *ancien régime* and the nation-state. Under the 1817–18 civil codes and the 1831–32 *Organic Statutes*, Gypsies were in a state of slavery. Gypsies were gradually emancipated between 1844 and 1856, and ceased to be a separate legal category. Jews and Armenians were regarded as native inhabitants in both principalities (*pământeni*), but were classified as distinct legal corporations. In Moldova, they were denied political rights and certain civil rights, which were reserved for Orthodox inhabitants. Wallachian laws did not discriminate against non-Orthodox Christians, but kept the Jews from the exercise of certain civic and political rights. The 1858 Convention of Paris emancipated Moldavian Armenians, granting them full civil and political rights. The principle of citizenship equality did not apply to Jews, who were denied political rights. Moreover, with the consolidation of Romanian national citizenship, indigenous Jews gradually lost their state citizenship and their rights to participate in local institutions which were granted to them under the *ancien régime*. While in 1865 they were transformed into foreigners, in 1866 they were denied access to naturalization as Romanian citizens, on the grounds that they were not Christians.[40]

The exclusion of Jews from citizenship was triggered by a process of 'securitization' of the Jewish question, at the time of a rising tide of Romanian ethnic nationalism. The Jews—those born in the country as well as those immigrating from neighbouring Austrian Galicia and Polish Russia—were portrayed as a 'danger' to the new national political order, accused of being 'socially inassimilable' and of lacking national loyalty. From a juridical point of view, the citizenship exclusion of non-Christians represents an inventive but illiberal utilization of a local juridical practice, inserted into a Westernized legal framework. This practice was based on the tradition of the medieval capitulations granted by the Ottoman Empire, which forbade the settlement of Muslims on the territory of the principalities. However, while the old capitulations were directed against Muslims, in the modern period Romanian politicians modified both their content and their range of application, by directing their stipulations against the Jews. Gradually, they expanded the scope of civil discrimination against non-Christians, developing it into a comprehensive legal doctrine of a 'Christian state' emulating similar concepts developed at the time in certain German states.

Due to external diplomatic pressure of the great powers, in 1879 the Romanian parliament removed the practice of Christianity as a condition for naturalization. In order to avoid an instant naturalization of Romanian Jews, it nevertheless shifted to a more exclusive naturalization practice, by replacing the simple *jus soli* naturalization of *second generation* immigrants by local authorities with a conditional and 'delayed' *jus soli* naturalization of *third generation* immigrants by the parliament, through an individual law for each case of naturalization. Moreover, while practically excluding non-Christian permanent residents from

---

[40] For the legal status of non-citizens in Romania, with an emphasis on the case studies of the Jews, women, and the inhabitants of the former Ottoman province of northern Dobrudja, annexed to Romania in 1878, see Constantin Iordachi, 'The Unyielding Boundaries of Citizenship: The Emancipation of "Non-Citizens" in Romania, 1866–1918', *European Review of History*, 8 (2001), 157–86.

full citizenship status, Romanian political elites established a direct relationship between citizenship and the exercise of certain civil rights and economic activities. Possession of land, access to various liberal professions, jobs in the state apparatus, state-sponsored education, and membership in public institutions and organizations were declared exclusive 'privileges' of Romanian citizens. One can thus identify the formation of a Romanian citizenship doctrine in the period 1859–79 that functioned, with several modifications, until 1918. It had the following main features: (1) admission to citizenship was placed under the control of the parliament; (2) conditions of naturalization, as well as citizenship rights and duties, were inscribed in the Constitution; (3) landownership and access to certain liberal professions and economic activities were defined as citizenship rights, opened only to Romanian citizens; and (4) Romanian laws refused to recognize the legal category of indigenous Jews, who as a consequence were stripped of citizenship rights. This 'thick' definition of citizenship accounts for the great importance of the debates over citizenship in the socio-political life of the country, prompting a new intervention of the international community, which materialized in the 1919 Minority Convention.

A New Principality: The Making of Bulgarian Citizenship

Compared to Moldova and Wallachia, Serbia, Greece, and Bulgaria exhibit state discontinuity. Following the Ottoman occupation, their statehood was abolished, their territory occupied, and their aristocracy largely eliminated. The three principalities nevertheless experienced certain variations in their transition to nation-states. Bulgaria was the last state among the four to restore its statehood in 1878, and had to wait until 1908 to see Ottoman suzerainty formally abolished. However, the newly-born principality built up a quasi-national citizenry from its very inception, having most of the attributes of formal statehood, analysed in the following section.

During the first half of the nineteenth century, a Bulgarian national movement made significant progress, moving from the phase of nationalist agitation to that of a mass movement. The main carrier of the nationalist movement was the autonomous Bulgarian church, reorganized in 1870 under the form of the Bulgarian exarchate. However, while the process of nation-building was under way, the country was missing an administrative and territorial nucleus of its own, the Bulgarian lands being an integral part of the Ottoman Empire.

In a first stage, the administrative nucleus of the new state was established by the Preliminary Treaty of Peace between Russia and Turkey signed at San Stefano on 9 February/3 March 1878. Article VI of the treaty recognized Bulgaria as an autonomous tributary principality, led by a Christian government and entitled to its own administrative organization and national militia. Although it contained all the elements of an independent state citizenship, the newly established Bulgarian nationality was nevertheless dependent on the relationship of vassalage to the

Ottoman Empire. By Article VII of the San Stefano Treaty, the basis of the internal organization of the new principality was to be devised by 'an Assembly of Bulgarian Notables' which was to issue a written constitution. Since the constitutional assembly was to be elected on a large and representative basis, it equalled an act of national sovereignty. The assembly was, however, to work 'under the superintendence of an Imperial Russian Commissioner, and in the presence of an Ottoman Commissioner', and to be in line with certain rules enacted by the treaty.

In carving a citizenry for the new state out of the body of the Ottoman *raya*, the Treaty of Berlin paid attention to the status of non-ethnic Bulgarians. It guaranteed the property rights of Muslim inhabitants on the territory of the new principality. According to Article XII, 'Mussulman proprietors or others who may take up their abode outside the Principality may continue to hold there their property, by farming it out, or having it administered by third parties.' It also specifically demanded that in multi-ethnic localities, 'proper account is to be taken of the rights and interests of' Turks, Greeks, and Wallachians (Koutzo-Vlachs) in the election of the Assembly and during the preparation of the Organic Law.' The sovereignty of the new principality was also limited by the stipulation of Article VIII of the Berlin Treaty, which read that 'The immunities and privileges of foreigners, as well as the rights of Consular jurisdiction and protection as established by the Capitulations and usage, shall remain in full force so long as they shall not have been modified with the consent of the parties concerned.'

The main stipulations regulating Bulgarian citizenship were contained in Chapter XII, Articles 54–6 of the constitution of Tyrnovo, adopted on 16 April 1879. In line with the spirit of the Treaty of Berlin, the constitution put forward an inclusive definition of citizenship, based concomitantly on the *jus soli* and *jus sanguinis* principles. Thus, Article 54 ascribed Bulgarian citizenship to all inhabitants born in the province who did not acquire a foreign nationality, as well as to all those born abroad from Bulgarian parents. At the same time, the constitution instituted a sharp control over the granting and renunciation of citizenship status. According to Article 55, naturalization to Bulgarian citizenship could be granted only by the *Sobrànie*. Finally, Article 56 stipulated that renunciation of Bulgarian citizenship was possible only after fulfilling military service and other basic citizenship duties toward the Bulgarian state.

The concrete details on the acquisition and loss of Bulgarian citizenship were soon spelled out by a special law adopted by the *Sobranie* in December 1880. This law was necessitated by the demographic changes enacted by the war, but also by the need to reinterpret the Berlin Treaty in accordance with the national aims of the new Bulgarian state. The 1880 law was soon replaced by a princely decree regulating Bulgarian citizenship, granted on 26 February 1883. The new law was adopted following a *coup d'état* conducted by Prince Alexander I that resulted in the suspension of the 1879 constitution. It contradicted in many respects the spirit of the former 1880 law. The most important change was that it transferred the right to decide over granting naturalization from the *Sobranie* to the prince, by a princely decree. This change reflected the political confrontation between the prince and the assembly over the control of access to citizenship

The Bulgarian legislation on citizenship changed yet again in 1895. The new law granted citizenship to all 'Turkish subjects' born or domiciled in Bulgaria at the time of the 1878–9 war (Art. 2). Article 4 extended these rights to all inhabitants born in the interval 1879–83. It also stated that all individuals living in Bulgaria 'are considered Bulgarians until proven contrary'. The law inaugurated an active ethnic policy in Bulgaria. Article 11 gave ethnic Bulgarians instant access to Bulgarian citizenship, upon their renunciation of their former state affiliation and settlement in Bulgaria with the manifest intention to remain there. Last but not least, the law also conferred access to naturalization to foreigners born in Bulgaria from parents born in the country, thus applying the *jus soli* principle for the naturalization of the second generation immigrants. The only formal condition was their renunciation of their father's citizenship.

Another particularity of the process of building a unitary national citizenship in Bulgaria was the ambiguous legal relationship with the newly created province of Eastern Rumelia. Considered originally by the Treaty of San Stefano as an integral part of the principality of Bulgaria, Eastern Rumelia was carved out by Article XIII of the subsequent Treaty of Berlin as a semi-autonomous administrative unit under Ottoman jurisdiction. By Article XV of the same treaty, the province was entitled to a native gendarmerie and a local militia, and was to be led by a governor-general nominated by the sultan, with the assent of the powers, for a five-year term. The future financial, juridical, and administrative organization of the province was to be regulated by an 'Organic Statute', drafted by a European Commission specially established to this end under the Treaty.

The 'Organic Statute' of Eastern Rumelia was adopted on 26 April 1879 by the European Commission assembled at Philippopoli. In regulating the legal status of the inhabitants of the province, it established a distinct Rumelian *indigenat*, granted—according to article 23—to all Ottoman subjects born in the province or residing there as of 1 January 1877. Since Rumelians were nominally Ottoman citizens, the *indigenat* was also granted to those Ottoman subjects who established their domicile in the province and resided there for one year. Any alien who wished to acquire the Rumelian *indigenat* had to first be naturalized as an Ottoman citizen, according to the 1869 Ottoman citizenship law. Although de facto incorporated into Bulgaria, from a legal point of view, until 1908, Rumelians were still Ottoman citizens, and were governed by different laws.

Another conflict of interest was the inclusive citizenship policy of Greece, which granted its citizenship to all ethnic Greeks living abroad, even without them travelling to Greece, provided they took an oath of allegiance to the consul. This generated a conflict with the Bulgarian authorities, mostly since the Bulgarian law forbade naturalization without the consent of the Bulgarian state. The issue was settled in two interstate agreements in 1885 and 1893, in accordance with Greek interests, creating a category of privileged Bulgarian subjects. The new Law on Bulgarian citizenship of 1903 strengthened the *jus soli* component of citizenship in response to the Greek policy of naturalizing Bulgarian subjects.

The Bulgarian doctrine of nationality was thus substantially modified in 1903. Directly inspired by the French citizenship legislation, namely the *Code Civil* and the 1889 nationality law, the new law reintroduced the *jus soli* principle in ascribing Bulgarian citizenship, removed by the 1880 and 1883 laws. First, in line with previous legislation, the law reconfirmed the Bulgarian citizenship of all *inhabitants* who had been residing in the country at the time of the creation of the principality (Art. 2) or were naturalized at a later date (Art. 3). Second, Bulgarian citizenship could be subsequently obtained by birth, naturalization, and marriage, combining the *jus sanguinis* and *jus soli* principles in ascribing citizenship. It also granted citizenship *jure sanguinis* to descendents of present or *former* Bulgarian citizens even if they were born abroad and did not reside in Bulgaria (Art. 7). The law also granted access to Bulgarian citizenship *jure soli* to persons born on Bulgarian soil of foreign parents, regardless of their subsequent place of residence.

Bulgarian citizenship legislation is illustrative of the 'new principalities' carved out of the Ottoman territory. The evolution of the Bulgarian citizenship legislation can be summarized as follows: in 1878, Bulgarian citizenship was granted to all inhabitants of the country, according to the principle of *jus soli*. In 1880, this inclusive policy was amended in several respects. The principle of *jus soli* was replaced by a policy of *jus sanguinis* in the transmission of citizenship; the principle of *jus soli* in the naturalization policy was transferred from the first to the second generation of immigrants; and the Bulgarian state adopted an active ethnic policy for absorbing ethnic Bulgarians living abroad. In this way, while the Bulgarian citizenship legislation remained remarkably inclusive, it nevertheless encompassed an ethnic component. In 1903, following the French example, Bulgarian citizenship legislation returned to an inclusive combination of *jus soli* and *jus sanguinis* principles in ascribing citizenship, while preserving a permissive policy of naturalization of resident aliens. These changes, as well as the conditions set for naturalization, reflected the utilitarian character of the legislation, aiming at attracting under Bulgarian law as many people as possible while instituting an effective control over the cultural identity and loyalty of new immigrants.

Judged from the perspective of ethnic vs. civic typologies of nationalism, Bulgarian citizenship can be characterized as eclectic: on the one hand, it was liberal and inclusive, since it granted state citizenship and full civic and political rights to all inhabitants, regardless of their ethnic or religious affiliation. On the other hand, it built institutional ties with ethnic Bulgarians living abroad, emphasizing the national character of the new state and thus adding to it an ethnic component. Institutionally, Bulgarian citizenship legislation set a strong emphasis on citizenship *duties* and placed the process of naturalization under a strict parliamentary control.

CITIZENSHIP, ANNEXATION, AND BUREAUCRATIC ETHNIC CLEANSING IN THE BALKANS

A major challenge to citizenship legislation in the Balkans was the integration of newly annexed territories. The recurrent pattern of *irredenta* 'wars of succession' for the former Ottoman territory resulted in frequent changes of territories occurring in several major waves, from the general territorial reorganization of the Balkans implemented by the 1878 Congress of Berlin, the Greek-Turkish convention on Thessaly and parts of Epirus, to the 1885 unification of Bulgaria and Eastern Rumelia and the ensuing Serbian-Bulgarian war. Another stage was represented by the arduous 1912–13 Balkan Wars, and the radical territorial reorganization following the First World War and the prolonged Greek-Turkish military conflict (1919–23).

As a consequence of military operations, supplemented by a complicated web of political alliances, diplomatic bargaining and international mediation, Balkan states expanded their territory, in a first phase at the expense of the Ottoman Empire and, in a second phase, also of each other. The integration of the new provinces posed numerous economic, administrative, and political problems. Unlike the mainland provinces that experienced decades of state-building and cultural homogenization, the newly annexed provinces still bore the imprint of Ottoman rule. Some of them, such as Dobrudj and Macedonia, were genuine mosaics of ethno-religious communities. In these provinces, to the cleavage between Muslims and Christians, one had to add the great diversity of the Christian population. Facing the arduous task of political integration, cultural homogenization, and economic reorganization in newly annexed provinces, Balkan states often resorted to practices of denaturalization of alien groups as an effective instrument of ethnic homogenization and land nationalization. These practices transformed citizenship conflicts in the region into a European diplomatic problem.

From a legal point of view, the situation was further complicated by the lack of clear codes of conduct in international law concerning the annexation of new territories. Widely accepted practice stipulated that the inhabitants of a territory changed their citizenship status together with the land they inhabited. But it was a matter of controversy whether only citizens of the former state who were residing in that particular area at the moment of the annexation were to be considered inhabitants, or all persons born in the respective province, regardless of their residency at the time of the annexation. Another generally accepted principle was the right of the inhabitants of an annexed territory to opt for preserving their original citizenship. In such cases, the status of their property remained a matter of international debate, especially in cases when the legislation of the annexing state forbade foreigners to own real estates.

Until the Congress of Berlin, annexations of territories resulted mainly in the emigration of Muslims. They had to sell their property within a certain period of time, varying between one and three years. The Treaty of San Stefano concluded between Russia and Turkey on 3 March 1878, stipulated in its Article 21 that the inhabitants of the new provinces ceded to Russia had a right to immigrate, but were obliged to sell their properties within three years.

The subsequent Treaty of Berlin reversed this stipulation. Its Articles 12, 30, and 39 granted Muslims emigrating from the former Ottoman territories ceded to Bulgaria, Serbia, and Montenegro the right to preserve their property in the annexed provinces, and to administer them by intermediaries. Nevertheless, this stipulation applied only to Muslims—generally assumed to be the losers of the new territorial arrangements—not to Christian immigration or to non-Christians following the Ottoman authorities, such as Jews. The protection of property rights of the inhabitants became an international practice, being reconfirmed and enlarged by the Convention of Constantinople signed on 24 May 1881 between the great powers and Turkey concerning the rectification of the Greek-Turkish frontier. The convention granted the inhabitants of Thessalia the right to opt for Ottoman citizenship, while preserving at the same time their properties in Greece.

A second problem was the citizenship status of the inhabitants of the newly annexed provinces. Legal practices varied between granting citizenship only to citizens of the former state, to all the inhabitants of the annexed province regardless of their former citizenship status, or to every person born in that province regardless of their place of residence at the time of the annexation. In multi-ethnic areas, Balkan states were tempted to apply an ethnic principle, by granting citizenship only to kin population, with the exclusion of alien groups. M. Perich, a professor at the University of Belgrade and a reputed expert in Serbian and international law, pleaded for such a solution, defending the right of Serbia to implement a policy of selective naturalization.[41]

An additional challenge posed by territorial changes in the Balkans was the great ethno-religious diversity of the newly established states. This problem became imperative with the massive territorial and populational transfer caused by the First Balkan War, necessitating a regional diplomatic arrangement. The preliminaries of the peace treaty between Turkey and the allied Balkan states stipulated the need for a future international convention regulating the citizenship and property status of the inhabitants of the annexed provinces. Given the outbreak of the Second Balkan War, this convention was never signed, so that new states regulated the issue according to their own legal tradition and in accord with their specific interests. Moreover, in order to attract their co-ethnics living in neighbouring countries for colonizing annexed territories, Balkan states granted them the possibility of fast naturalization, without a residential stage. How could one prove one's ethnicity? Generally, immigrants had to provide certificates of

---

[41] J. Péritch, 'De la nationalité suivant la législation serbe', *Journal du droit international privé et de la jurisprudence comparée* (1899), 940–61.

nationality issued by the Ottoman, Russian, or Austro-Hungarian authorities. However, since in practice immigrants were missing identity papers, authorities had to take into account other 'markers' of ethnicity, such as knowledge of the language of the country, or affiliation to Eastern Orthodox Christian religion. These practices of privileged naturalization illuminate legal mechanisms of constructing ethnicity.

One final problem raised by the annexation of territories was the collection of rights and duties granted to the inhabitants of the newly inhabited territories. The case of Dobruja's integration into Romania is emblematic in this respect. By the Treaty of Berlin, Romania lost southern Bessarabia to Russia, and received in exchange the province of northern Dobrudja, while southern Dobrudja was granted to Bulgaria. In the ensuing period, Dobrudja became the object of an acute Romanian-Bulgarian territorial conflict: both states engaged in assiduous and competing processes of national expansion and border-making in the province. The paths chosen to integrate the two provinces were nevertheless different. In order to legitimize its *irredenta* policy toward Romania's northern Dobrudja, Bulgaria adopted an inclusive citizenship policy. Instead, fearing the multi-ethnic composition of the province could disrupt its ethnic homogeneity, Romanian political elites implemented in northern Dobrudja a separate administrative regime under which Dobrudjans were granted only a local type of citizenship, which denied them the right to political participation and to acquire properties outside the province (1878–1913).[42] It was only after 35 years of gradual and successful assimilation that Romania granted full citizenship rights to Dobrudjans.

CONCLUSION

This chapter has pleaded for a refocusing of scholarly attention on the making of nation-state citizenship in the Balkans and on the legal and demographic mechanisms that this process entailed. It has been argued that the emergence of citizenship in the Balkans was framed by the peculiar Ottoman imperial legacy. The occupation of the Balkan peninsula in the fourteenth century and its integration into the Ottoman system had profound and long-lasting consequences for the development of the peoples in the region, most evident in the multi-ethnic composition of the empire, its peculiar socio-political organization, and the gradual decline of imperial rule in the region. Political elites in the Balkans claimed that the achievement of their countries' independence was a restoration of their statehood and historical rights that had existed prior to the Ottoman

---

[42] Constantin Iordachi, *Citizenship, Nation and State-Building: The Integration of Northern Dobrogea in Romania, 1878–1913*, Carl Back Papers in Russian and East European Studies No. 1607 (Pittsburgh, 2002).

occupation. Despite this claim, the making of nation-states in the Balkans was shaped by an underlying conflict between political visions of homogeneous national 'imagined communities', and the complex ethnic reality on the ground. In order to carve their national space out of the Ottoman inter-ethnic mosaic, Balkan nation-states engaged in a complex military, demographic, and legal warfare. The unmixing of the Ottoman jigsaw was particularly strenuous in contested multi-ethnic borderlands in the Balkans, such as Dobrudja, Macedonia, and Bosnia-Herzegovina. The implementation of sharp boundaries of territory and population radically changed the function of state frontiers in the region. Previous forms of permissive boundaries were discontinued, being replaced by rigid state demarcations of citizenries.

The making of nation-state citizenship in the Balkans exposes the hybrid nature of nationalism in the region. Balkan nationalisms originated as revolutionary movements opposed to the hierarchical and unequal legal and political structure of the Ottoman Empire, claiming civic and religious equality. With the gradual decentralization of the empire, the fight against discrimination developed into secessionist national movements, based on ethno-religious claims. The creation of autonomous 'embryos' of nation-states in the region brought forward claims for national unification, similar to Risorgimento nationalism. With the consolidation of independent nation-states states in the region, Balkan nationalism took the form of *irredenta* wars among successor states of the Ottoman Empire.

It is tempting to describe this evolution as a transition from civic forms of nationalism in the pre-independence period to ethnic forms in the post-independence period. Nevertheless, Balkan nationalism never became purely 'exclusive', but exhibited in fact peculiar patterns of inclusion and exclusion. Most Balkan states were remarkably open to immigration, being genuine melting pots of ethnic and even religious differences. At the same time, they implemented practices of selective closure against 'unwanted' foreigners, mostly Muslims and Jews, who were perceived as endangering the consolidation of their nationhood.

While rejecting a unilateral reading of citizenship practices in the Balkans, I argue that the emergence of nation-state citizenship in the region was a complex historical outcome of several variables: (1) local mores and administrative practices, surviving mostly at the level of customary law or in legal practices inspired by Byzantine jurisprudence; (2) regional variations of political cultures and citizenship rights, and differences in patterns of elite formation in various principalities; (3) the peculiar international status of the autonomous Balkan principalities, stemming mostly from their vassalage to the Ottoman Empire, the collective protection of great European powers over them and European diplomatic intervention in favour of the political emancipation of non-Christians (1878); (4) the emergence of nationalism, with its primordialist view of collective identity; and (5) 'Western' citizenship rules of residence and political participation that found their most paradigmatic expression in the French model of the nation-state. Since these factors stood at times in manifest contradiction, nation-state citizenship in the Balkans appears as a complex syncretism between local and universal trends that refutes clear-cut generalizations based on only one of its components. The comparative analysis of citizenship in the Balkans highlights institutional, legal, and intellectual transfers over temporal and geographical borders, in an area characterized by multiple layers of historical legacies, most notably the Byzantine, the Ottoman, and various waves of Western-patterned modernization.

The eclectic and composite nature of Balkan nationalism suggests that there are no 'pure' civic as opposed to ethnic types of nationalism, or 'cultural' as opposed to 'political' ones. As Brian C. J. Singer pertinently points out, civil and cultural nations are ideal-type models used for methodological purposes. In historical reality 'almost all nations appear formed of a promiscuous blend of civic and cultural elements'.[43] Neither are there fixed 'codes of nationality' or traditional understandings of nationhood based on static practices of ascribing citizenship or naturalization. In fact, citizenship is an essentially contested legal category, whose meaning is never stable but is continuously recreated as a function of wider socio-political phenomena in society. On a more general level, this case study of the citizenship in the Balkans points out the need to abandon 'teleological' typologies of nationalism based on 'normative' ideological premises, and to look for alternative analytical criteria, such as mechanisms of state-building and homogenization employed in highly ethnically mixed areas, different practices of ascribing citizenship in 'new' or 'old' principalities, the timing of nation and state-building, and the impact of foreign intervention in the region.

[43] B. C. J. Singer, 'Cultural versus Contractual Nations: Rethinking their Opposition', *History and Theory*, 35 (1996), 316.

PART III

KULTUR

8

Language and Nation

National Identity and the Civic-Ethnic Typology

Brian Vick

At least since biblical times language has counted as one of the most important markers of difference between peoples; whether language also constitutes a main criterion of national identity in the modern age of nationalism, however, is a different question, particularly where this involves the distribution of civil rights. Since the earlier part of the twentieth century, the standard position has been that there are in fact two types of nationalism—civic-voluntarist and ethnic-cultural—having corresponding forms of national identity, in the latter of which language does indeed play a central role while in the former it need not.

Along with this difference in the attribution of nationality, the civic-ethnic typology also assigns differences in the definition of civil rights and in attitudes towards ethnic diversity in the national state. Nations imbued with a civic form of nationalism are typically said to respect the rights of individuals in good natural law tradition, while nations defined according to ethnic criteria allegedly follow a more romantic line and subordinate the rights of the individual to those of the collectivity. Similarly, nations with an ethnocultural approach to nationalism are said typically to disapprove of ethnic and linguistic diversity and to discriminate against minorities either through their exclusion and subordination or through their wholesale cultural assimilation. Political nations, on the other hand, are supposed to adopt a much more open and welcoming stance, in which representatives of non-dominant groups are to be assimilated into the nation on presumably more equitable and culturally neutral terms.

It is also significant for the present discussion of language rights that the civic versus ethnic typology has often been cast in terms of a distinction between nationalisms in Eastern and Western Europe, with western nations such as France and Britain seen as harbouring political forms of identity and liberal political frameworks, while the lands of the east adopted romantic, illiberal, ethnocultural forms of identity. Differing levels of modernity have often been seen as playing a role here too. In the typology's early formulation by historian of ideas Hans Kohn, the dangerous turn of eastern, ethnic nationalism was already linked to the delayed socio-economic and political modernization of Central and Eastern Europe compared to the western lands, a connection highlighted even more strongly by more recent sociologically oriented historians of 'nation-building' influenced by modernization theory.

The following comparative chapter will examine these issues of linguistic diversity for countries on both sides of the putative geographic and typological divide, in each of three periods of European history during the long nineteenth century, roughly those from 1789–1840, 1840–70, and 1870–1914. Attention will be paid above all to the situation in France and the German and Habsburg lands of Central and Eastern Europe as the prototype cases of the civic-ethnic categories. As should become clear, the political versus cultural typology of nationalisms frequently fails to provide much analytical guidance to the intricate landscape of linguistic politics and national identity. At the very least, in partaking of both civic and ethnic components of identity, nationalisms across Europe often broke with the East–West typology. This is certainly true for the French and German cases explored here, and even in Britain the non-dominant language groups experienced pressure to assimilate to English language and identity—the Swiss example of multilingual equality within a civic federalism remained unique. It is also possible, however, that the examples discussed below point to more fundamental problems with the civic-ethnic typology itself. Even more than with other aspects of nationhood, after all, language and minority language policy implicated both the public realm of political culture and the realm of national culture per se, and at least in this respect cut across and blurred the discursive boundaries between those typological categories.

LANGUAGE AND REVOLUTIONARY
POLITICS AND CULTURE, 1789–1840

While debate continues about how far it is permissible to speak of nations and nationalism before 1789, even those wary of overemphasizing nationalism's modernity acknowledge the pivotal role of France and the French Revolution in the development of modern nationhood. In terms of the role of language, observers in France (or for that matter in other European lands) were certainly aware of linguistic diversity before 1789, but for most it did not matter much one way or the other, neither as a problem nor as a benefit. After the French Revolution, however, it did begin to matter to some in the political and cultural elites, and perhaps nowhere more so than in France itself.

As already noted, French nationalism has generally served as a prototype case of the civic or political form, with assimilation into the nation admittedly expected, but with the process seen as an opportunity offered by a generous polity rather than a sacrifice demanded by a chauvinistic ethnic nation. It has also often been observed that the upsurge in French nationalism during the revolution was accompanied by a heated debate about linguistic diversity in France that resulted in the adoption of a rather strict set of policies aiming at linguistic uniformity. This fact would itself seem problematic for the supposedly civic nature of French nationalism; at the least it should cause us to step back and rethink what we mean when we use the term, insofar as it suggests that assimilation was not meant to occur solely at the level of political culture (adherence to a certain canon of political values and rules of behaviour) but also at that of culture more generally in the form of language.

Attitudes and policies towards other languages in France were actually somewhat less clear-cut than expressions such as 'linguistic terrorism' might lead one to believe. It was indeed during the period of the Terror in 1793 and 1794 that the harshest legislation was adopted by the National Assembly, but this occurred after a phase during the first years of the revolution when linguistic diversity was treated more tolerantly. Previously, for example, the National Assembly had agreed to the translation of its laws into regional languages or dialects, something it now forbade. Moreover, as David Bell has shown, publishing in regional languages at first burgeoned after 1789 as both proponents and opponents of the revolution tried to influence public opinion, but this early bloom wilted after 1792 as the regime began to discourage publication in anything but standard French.[1]

Previous scholars of the revolution's language policies have sometimes avoided the problem of such a strongly cultural component to a civic identity by suggesting that the drive for uniformity either derived from the rationalist enlightenment programme of modernizing social reform or constituted part of the democratic impulse toward homogeneous equality. Bell for his part has also pointed to the religious dimension of language struggles, as the anticlerical revolutionaries at first attempted to compete with the Catholic church's vernacular missionary efforts before ultimately deciding that the mere existence of the other languages already played too much into the hands of reactionary forces. In all these accounts the struggle against French dialects or 'patois' has tended to be conflated with or to overshadow the attacks on non-French idioms, with the Abbé Grégoire figuring as the key player and source of evidence. Bell notes the potential distinction between attitudes towards dialects and those towards languages such as Breton and Basque but on the whole still treats the case of the patois as central.

It may be, however, that one should make more of that distinction and grant more importance to the fact that such intransigent opponents of linguistic diversity as Louis Saint-Just and Bertrand Barère singled out precisely the peripheral,

---

[1] D. A. Bell, *The Cult of the Nation in France: Inventing Nationalism, 1680–1800* (Cambridge, Mass., 2001), 169–97; also see M. McDonald, *'We are not French!': Language, Culture and Identity in Brittany* (London, 1989), 29–34.

non-French languages for attack: Breton, Basque, Italian, and particularly German. As Saint-Just declaimed in 1793, it was no longer possible to be 'German in language and patriotic in heart'.[2] As enshrined in the legislation of 1794, the efforts of the revolutionary commissars and schoolmasters were to be directed first and foremost at these literally marginal groups. Such emphasis on the distinction between French and other languages (as opposed to French dialects) seems to point to a decidedly ethnic dimension of a radically civic nationalism. At the very least the revolutionary nationalists thought that knowledge of French as the national language would be necessary to national cohesion now that patriotic popular involvement in the political life of the nation became so crucial. Even more, however, many of them seem to have believed that the existence of other languages posed a threat to the nation and should be combated accordingly.

After the Terror, attention shifted away from the drive for uniformity through education, as France's young men were more needed on the battlefields than in the classroom, but the revolutionary language legislation remained on the books and influenced approaches to pedagogy and administration. In the German territories acquired by the victorious French armies in the course of the 1790s, for example, subsequent revolutionary regimes attempted to make French the language of courts and bureaucracy. In France itself there was sporadic discussion all the way through the 1830s and 1840s about whether the regional languages would retain an auxiliary role in schools (which was allowed by the second law on languages of November 1794) or whether they would yield to standard French entirely, but the ultimate aim of making sure that all Frenchmen and Frenchwomen knew French was still the order of the day.[3] The means to realize this goal, however, had to await the later nineteenth century and the Third Republic.

In the German lands, governments in the decades from the late eighteenth century to the 1830s had a rather mixed record regarding the treatment of linguistic minorities. The most famous attempt at linguistic uniformity was that of the Austrian Emperor Joseph II in the 1780s. The standard interpretation of Joseph's efforts to make German the language of administration throughout his domains stresses that this should not be seen as inspired by nationalism at all. As

---

[2] Bell, *Cult of the Nation*, 182–97; P. L.-R. Higonnet, 'The Politics of Linguistic Terrorism and Grammatical Hegemony during the French Revolution', *Social History*, 5 (1980), 41–69, Saint-Just quoted at 54; M. Lyons, 'Regionalism and Linguistic Conformity in the French Revolution', in A. Forrest and P. Jones (eds.), *Reshaping France: Town, Country and Region during the French Revolution* (Manchester, 1991), 179–92; and M. de Certeau, D. Julia, and J. Revel, *Une politique de la langue: la Révolution française et les patois. L'Enquête de Grégoire* (Paris, 1975), 11 and 291–9 for Barère.

[3] McDonald, *We are not French*, 29, 34, 36–38, 44–47 for the Breton case. For Alsace, R. McCoy emphasizes the ability of local authorities to pursue their own bilingual policies under the royal administrations after 1815: 'Alsatians into Frenchmen: The Construction of National Identities at Sainte-Marie-aux-Mines, 1815–1851', *French History*, 12 (1998), 429–51. For the German Rhineland, see A. Grilli, 'Sprache und Recht in den französischen Rheinlanden: Die Einführung des Französischen als Gerichtssprache im Saardepartement 1798', *Rheinische Vierteljahrsblätter*, 57 (1993), 227–52. The present claim goes against the standard view that the end to the Terror in 1794 saw a return to the old toleration, as Certeau et al., *Une politique*, 11.

an 'enlightened despot' Joseph was according to this line of thinking simply engaging in the rational reform of his empire, where homogenization of the language of government business was merely a measure of efficiency and expediency.[4] Seen from this perspective it would be useless to ask whether Joseph's policy reflected a more 'civic' or 'ethnic' conception of nationhood, insofar as conceptions of nationhood were precisely what was not behind it. If nothing else, however, comparison with the French example at least suggests similarities in the assumptions about the necessity of linguistic uniformity in insuring political cohesion. On the whole it is true that Joseph was not an ethnic nationalist in the sense of being a patriotic proponent of German cultural supremacy, nor was he even a political nationalist insofar as he was not trying to call the citizens to patriotic participation in the life of the nation in the manner of the French revolutionaries. Yet in replacing Latin with the more prestigious German rather than with the empire's other vernaculars, Joseph at least shared with German patriots certain unflattering stereotypes about the various language groups, even as he underscored the connection between modernizing reform and the creation of a standardized monolingual realm of print culture which is usually seen as a core component of modern nationalism. Moreover, if Joseph's move was not inspired by nationalism, it did inspire it, as certain non-German groups successfully resisted the policy, thus leaving Latin as the language of administration in the Hungarian half of the empire.

Elsewhere in Germany the period's most interesting developments occurred in Prussia, which had vastly increased its Polish-speaking population in the late eighteenth-century partitions of Poland. Language policy in these new Prussian territories fluctuated over the years between regimes of relative toleration and of Germanization (or at least 'Prussianization'). Frederick the Great, for instance, hoped to encourage the settlement of German peasants and schoolmasters as a means of promoting the enlightenment and assimilation of his new Polish subjects. As in the case of his fellow enlightened despot Joseph II, Frederick too has typically been seen as motivated by desires for modernization rather than by nationalism, which is again largely true, though it is still worth noting the compatibility between Frederick's assumptions and those of would-be chauvinist ethnic nationalists. Frederick's immediate successor still pressed for limited Prussianization in Prussian Poland, again with the presupposition that the adoption of a civic Prussian identity also required at least some linguistic accommodation (learning German if not giving up Polish)—assimilation implied a certain measure of acculturation in this case as well.[5]

At the close of the Napoleonic wars, recognition of the rights and legitimacy of nationalities had reached the stage where figures such as Prussian King Frederick William III and even the arch-conservative Austrian chief minister Prince

---

[4] T. C. W. Blanning, *Joseph II and Enlightened Despotism* (London, 1970), 48.

[5] W. W. Hagen, *Germans, Poles, and Jews: The Nationality Conflict in the Prussian East, 1772–1914* (Chicago, 1980), 44 on Frederick II, 59–61 on Frederick William II.

Metternich guaranteed Poles their linguistic and cultural rights if not their national sovereignty in the 1815 Vienna settlements. Prussian Minister of Culture Baron Altenstein promoted such policies even more wholeheartedly, observing in a memo of 1822 that 'Religion and mother tongue are the most sacred possessions of a nation,' and that it was much more politic to win the hearts of subjects by respecting their nationality than by suppressing it. Under these conditions Polish saw some use in administration and in secondary education, while primary education was conducted in the mother tongue.[6] After the revolutions of 1830, the Prussian government changed course and tried to end the threat posed by Polish nationalism through a Germanizing policy of undermining Polish national identity. When the new king Frederick William IV ascended to the Prussian throne in 1840, however, policy changed yet again, with a more liberal regime established in Polish areas.

The year 1815 also saw Prussia acquire a new linguistic minority in the form of the Sorbs of Lusatia, part of its new Saxon territories. Here the onset of Germanization occurred sooner, by the early 1820s. What is interesting in the present context is the fact that it was provincial and local officials who (in the end successfully) opposed the bilingualist line of Altenstein's Ministry of Culture and pressed for restrictions on the use of Sorb, as during the dispute over the introduction of a Sorb textbook in the 1820s.[7] An oft-heard critique of much recent literature on nationalism is that it has neglected the peculiarities and particularities of individual national experiences in favour of transnational theorizing, and to this extent the example of Sorb language policy in Prussia rather tellingly points up the need for careful attention to finer-scale historical context even within individual national histories. Global generalizations about East and West and about civic and ethnic nationalisms begin to lose some of their conceptual clarity when applied to smaller geopolitical scales.

TENSIONS BETWEEN THE CIVIC AND ETHNIC CONCEPTIONS: THE CASE OF CENTRAL EUROPE IN THE ERA OF THE 1848 REVOLUTION

During the 1840s and above all during the 1848 revolution the most revealing developments relating to language policy and minority rights occurred in the German and Habsburg lands. For the ostensibly civic but clearly problematic French case, the situation during this period remained in the state of administrative limbo that had held since the days of the Terror. Politically French was the national language, while in educational policy pressure was exerted against other

---

[6] W. W. Hagen, *Germans, Poles, and Jews: The Nationality Conflict in the Prussian East*, 76–82, Altenstein quote at 82.

[7] E. Hartstock and P. Kunze (eds.), *Die Lausitz im Prozeß der bürgerlichen Umgestaltung 1815–1847* (Bautzen, n.d.), 19–20, and documents at 160–4, 181–92.

languages without wholly excluding them. Bureaucratic punctilio meant that other tongues could still fill an auxiliary role in the teaching of French and of other subjects in French, a status quo that continued even during the French Second Republic and Second Empire under the Falloux Law of 1850.[8]

Insofar as German nationalism has tended to serve as the prototype of an intolerantly ethnocultural form of national identity, it is certainly noteworthy that at the Frankfurt Parliament of 1848–9 delegates voted to guarantee the rights of linguistic minorities in the constitution for a newly united Germany with whose drafting they had been entrusted. For some scholars this toleration has been taken at face value and simply shows that nationalism in its 'liberation' phase during the first half of the nineteenth century truly was liberal in this as in other matters, or even that German nationalism may have been more civic in orientation at this stage. For other commentators the Frankfurt Parliament's vote for minority rights was merely a cynical and opportunistic ploy to entice certain non-Germans—above all in the Habsburg realm—into a new German Reich that would be as large as possible in population and territorial extent. From this perspective the ethnic basis of an intolerant nationalism remains intact; chauvinistic German nationalists were simply willing to tolerate the existence of minorities as a means of maximizing overall German power.

While several historians have dealt briefly with language rights in their accounts of German nationalism or of the 1848 revolution, with some highlighting the role of Austrian deputies in promoting a liberal nationality policy, there has been surprisingly little further investigation of the Frankfurt decision and its background. Deeper analysis of the debates about language rights in fact reveals that attitudes towards minority groups were more complex and ambiguous than either of the above perspectives would have it. The toleration was more genuine than often believed, but there were restrictions on that toleration that were soft-peddled at the time and that have gone unnoticed since. Crucially for the present discussion, this mixture of toleration and limitation of linguistic diversity suggests that German nationalism was neither civic nor ethnic in orientation but rather at a fundamental level some fusion of the two.[9]

The Frankfurt Parliament made its initial declaration of minority rights within two weeks of opening proceedings, at the end of May 1848, but this decision was in many ways just a revival of proclamations already given in April by its precursor body the Frankfurt Committee of Fifty. While most historians have stressed the ease and near unanimity with which these decisions were reached, it is important to note that in each case there was actually considerable debate about the topic, and much the same limits were placed on the rights guaranteed. None of the deputies called for forced Germanization, and in fact they explicitly rejected it.

---

[8] McDonald, *We are not French*, 37–8.

[9] For fuller treatment of 1848 and nationality rights, see Brian Vick, *Defining Germany: The 1848 Frankfurt Parliament and National Identity* (Cambridge, Mass., 2002), ch. 4, and the literature cited there.

Just as much as with the decrees of political rights that granted citizenship in the new German state regardless of language, there was near-universal support for the use of other languages in local administration and schooling.

Delegates at each body did, however, introduce into the guarantee a key clause regarding territorial extent which subtly emphasized that it was only in the local affairs of non-German speaking groups that these rights would hold. The addition meant that in areas without a strong minority presence German would be the sole language of administration, but the words also bore the less obvious implication that German would be the only language spoken in the new Germany's national parliament. Objecting to the absence of the crucial phrase in certain proposed amendments to the constitutional draft when it came up for its second reading in February of 1849, the Constitutional Committee rapporteur Georg Beseler made this extra restriction plain enough when he exclaimed: 'What is it supposed to mean when it is proposed to omit the clause "so far as their territories extend." Do you want to let all the non-German peoples who have equal rights with Germans speak in the National Assembly in their own dialects? None of you want that, and yet this right would be given if we intended to extend equal rights in Germany so far.' Beseler's remarks underscore two things. First, German conceptions of national identity were flexible enough to allow a multilingual or multinational nation, in part because they adopted a notion of citizenship that did not depend on language, that was in some sense civic in orientation. At the same time, however, there was still a sense in which even this civic German state had to satisfy certain cultural criteria of Germanness, at least at the symbolically paramount level of the national parliament.

Insistence on parliamentary monolingualism was not in fact the invention of the Frankfurt Parliament or even of the Committee of Fifty. Rather, it had already become an issue during the late 1830s and early 1840s in the mixed-language Duchy of Schleswig, a majority-German province of the Kingdom of Denmark. German nationalists there—including such future Frankfurt deputies as the brothers Beseler—were willing to concede Danish language rights at the local level, but more reluctantly than in 1848, as they were more concerned to maintain the German 'national character' of the duchy's legal superstructure, upon which were based their claims to a certain political autonomy within the Danish monarchy. Above all they wanted to preserve German as the official language of the diet. At first they were willing to let Danish delegates from North Schleswig speak Danish if they were truly incapable of speaking German (an exception that could still prove the rule of German), but later on the Beseler party decided that when added to the already-granted use of Danish in local administration even this concession was too much, and that in future diets the Danes would simply have to send deputies who did know German.[10]

[10] Brian Vick, *Defining Germany*, 131–2, and see esp. W. Carr, *Schleswig-Holstein 1815–1848: A Study in National Conflict* (Manchester, 1963), 154–6, 166–79, and J. Rohweder, *Sprache und Nationalität: Nordschleswig und die Anfänge der dänischen Sprachpolitik in der ersten Hälfte des 19. Jahrhunderts* (Glückstadt, 1976), 166, 247–51.

Given developments in Schleswig during the 1840s, German nationalists in 1848 thus had a ready-made position on language rights. This was even more true when one remembers how close the connections between the Schleswig movement and the broader German national movement became in the course of the 1840s. The stakes were clearly much higher for a German minority in Denmark than for a German majority in a German national state, and one might have thought that German nationalists could have been even more generous in the latter case. In this sense it is interesting to think about the role of contingency in history, as German national identity and nationalism were shaped in one political and ideological context and were slow to change even in very different circumstances later on. The biggest lesson for the present investigation, however, is to bear in mind the fact that the civic versus ethnic typology of nationalisms really does not take us very far in understanding German attitudes towards linguistic and ethnic diversity. This is true above all if the point of departure is thinking of German nationalism as inflexibly and chauvinistically ethnocultural in character, but the conclusion even holds if one tries to go the other way and conclude that German national identity must have been tolerantly civic after all. The realms of politics and culture in the public sphere intersected at too many points for them to be kept neatly separate, or for toleration and equality to be other than relative.

The role of German nationalists from Austria during the 1848 revolution is also important to consider in the present context. Austrian delegates at the Frankfurt Parliament did indeed play an active part in promoting guarantees of linguistic rights, but in Vienna the German-speaking nationalists occasionally adopted a somewhat more restrictive line. There was considerable debate, for example, about whether the Austrian Reichstag should provide translations of the measures on which it was to vote for the benefit of those deputies who did not know German, of whom there were more than a few. Deputies were clearly still allowed to speak in other languages, but there was pressure to maintain German as the language of business. On the whole the German nationalists of Austria probably had more tolerance for linguistic diversity than their North German counterparts—after all, if the Habsburg realm was to have any kind of constitutional future it would have to be one of multinational cooperation. This pragmatic sanction of multilingualism notwithstanding, German Austrians also felt that much more defensive about maintaining their privileges in face of the greater demands for political and cultural autonomy made by the various national groups of the Habsburg lands.[11]

Some comparisons with the case of the French Revolution of 1789–94 are in order here. At the most obvious level, the ostensibly ethnic nationalism ended up

---

[11] Vick, *Defining Germany*, 129–31, and see Roman Rosdolsky, *Die Bauernabgeordneten im konstituierenden österreichischen Reichstag 1848–1849* (Vienna, 1976), 195–202. P. D. Judson emphasizes the ethnically neutral aspect of Austrian liberal national identity: *Exclusive Revolutionaries: Liberal Politics, Social Experience, and National Identity in the Austrian Empire, 1848–1914* (Ann Arbor, 1996), 58–62, 85.

being more open to linguistic diversity than the allegedly civic example. Even more than with the French case, however, the German one serves to reveal some of the shortcomings of the cultural-political model of nationalism. Among other issues, notions of assimilation once again prove problematic. German nationalists did not intend to enforce assimilation in the way the French did, particularly not at the level of language; participation in a locally multilingual but nationally German public sphere and polity would have sufficed. On the other hand, German nationalists did still hold out hopes for continued Germanization as a longer-term historical outcome, voluntarily and gradually, as the result of living and participating in a powerful German national state. Schleswigers thought this would continue to happen in Schleswig, and German and Austrian nationalists thought the same of Central and Eastern Europe more generally. Assimilation would thus take place partly in the political, partly in the cultural arenas. Through living within the institutional framework of the liberal public sphere, citizens of France or Germany would have to exhibit a national identity that was a composite of civic and cultural elements, with more or less (but never complete) toleration of linguistic diversity within the nation state.

THE CLASSIC AGE OF NATIONALISM: FRANCE, GERMANY, AND THE HABSBURG REALM, 1870–1914

If there had been some variability in attitudes towards linguistic diversity in the first half of the long nineteenth century, both in France and in Central Europe, the second half of that period saw a ratcheting up of the pressure on minority languages in most parts of the continent. In both the French Third Republic and the German Kaiserreich, successive governments led a drive towards Frenchification or Germanization of their linguistically heterogeneous provinces, while in the Habsburg Empire the government swayed in the winds of popular nationalism as competing ethnic groups attempted to influence policy in their own interests in this land without a majority nationality. The increasing tensions regarding the position of minorities in each case played out against the backdrop of socio-economic modernization and a new mass politics that together changed the nature of European political culture.

In the French Third Republic, the new regime was by the 1870s and 1880s already pushing forward with its 'civilizing mission' in the French provinces, an effort designed to instil a good republican education in the minds of those peasants and provincials who during the reigns of both Napoleons had proven themselves all-too-susceptible to anti-republican appeals. As at the time of the Terror, anticlerical republicans were above all concerned to combat the supposedly pernicious influence of the Catholic church in such regions, but then as previously language played an important role as well. Along with bringing enlightenment to the superstitious, the army of black-frocked republican educators inculcated—if slowly—the pure strains of standard French into their young pupils' minds. In this sense knowledge of French was once again a clear prerequisite of commitment to France-as-republican-nation, and for some of the same reasons seen decades before. The historian Eugen Weber has described this whole process in his classic work *Peasants into Frenchmen*, and as with other students of nationalism in the 1970s and 1980s he stressed the connection of this linguistic and educational standardization—and national identity itself—with the more general process of modernization, a modernization that came to France later and more slowly than often thought, at about the same time as to the lands to the east.[12]

For historian of national identity Caroline Ford, however, it was only in the late 1890s or even after 1900 that the republican regime began to prioritize the role of language in national identity to the extent of putting pressure on other languages. She admits the drive to teach French in provincial schools in preceding decades but points out that as often before this was combined with a continued auxiliary role for local languages. It was only with decrees such as that in 1902 forbidding clerics from preaching in Breton that the local languages began to be actively discriminated against, not least in education. In terms of the civic-ethnic duality, Ford has interpreted this change in policy to indicate that a fundamental shift had occurred in the nature of French republican national identity, from the civic to the ethnic form. As with many recent scholars of nationalism Ford posits national identity as a plastic construct rather than a cultural given. Nationhood becomes in this way a concept contested among various cultural and political groups, and hence Ford argues here that the change in republican values took place in reaction to the rise of right-wing nationalism around the time of the Dreyfus affair. Ironically enough, this nationalism itself was cast in ethnocultural form, and for all that its proponents were imbued with ethnic and racialist thinking of the 'blood and soil' sort, they actually defended the use of regional languages as a means of counteracting insidious, denatured republican centralization.[13] In terms of the present argument, however, this give-and-take between republican and right-wing nationalists seems to show not the utility of the civic-ethnic typology in describing changes in national identity but rather the lack of any firm correlation between allegedly cultural or political conceptions of nationality on the one hand and attitudes towards linguistic pluralism and multi-ethnic states on the other.

In Central Europe, Germany had finally taken unified geopolitical shape in the form of the Prussian-led Habsburg-less 'Little Germany' in the wars of unification

---

[12] E. Weber, *Peasants into Frenchmen: The Modernization of Rural France, 1870–1914* (Stanford, Calif., 1976); on Brittany in particular, see McDonald, *We are not French*, 38–43.

[13] C. Ford, *Creating the Nation in Provincial France: Religion and National Identity in Brittany* (Princeton, 1993), 10–28 for the general argument, 159–67 on the 1902 decrees and their aftermath. For the Franco-Belgian frontier, Timothy Baycroft also emphasizes both the anticlerical motivation behind republican language policy and its relatively late adoption and even later success, after 1900 and the Second World War: 'Changing Identities in the Franco-Belgian Borderland in the Nineteenth and Twentieth Centuries', *French History*, 13 (1999), 417–38, esp. 426, 429.

from 1864 to 1871, but the borders were not the only things to have changed in the landscape of German political culture during these years. Whereas governments in the German states had previously looked with suspicion at a national movement that seemed too liberal and anti-establishment, after Bismarck's successful unification conservative elites were much more willing to engage with liberal forces and even to take advantage of the new democratic political structures in order to buttress their regime, with German nationalism the trump card in this high-stakes political gamble to modernize conservative rule. Moreover, the forms of national identity had themselves begun to change after unification. Perhaps paradoxically, perhaps not, a Little German Kaiserreich that harboured a relatively much smaller population of non-Germans than had the old German Confederation in 1848 now saw the growth of a national identity much less tolerant of allegedly foreign elements and much more firmly predicated on a sense of cultural Germanness as the root of national belonging. The most famous of the German government's campaigns against the 'enemies of the Reich' was the anti-Catholic *Kulturkampf,* but Danes, Poles, and Alsace-Lorrainers were also singled out for nationalistic abuse. Poles in particular as both Catholic and non-German came doubly under fire.

In these circumstances it comes as no surprise to hear of the administration's efforts to Germanize the new Germany's Polish provinces. Moreover, such initiatives were not just government led. Above all in the 1890s and the years running up to the First World War, various right-wing popular pressure groups emerged as increasingly significant elements on the political scene, and they too often pushed for Germanization, indeed in some cases for more radical measures than the government's. Already in the 1870s Bismarck had placed severe restrictions on the use of Polish in administration and education, while the 1880s saw yet further reductions. By the early 1900s Polish was debarred even from elementary religious instruction, previously its strongest institutional bastion. Finally, in 1908 under Chancellor Bülow the culmination of Germanization policy was reached with the reform of the law of associations to enforce the exclusive use of German at almost all public gatherings.

Language policy was somewhat more moderate in Schleswig and considerably more so in Alsace-Lorraine, but the ultimate goal of Germanization was the same—if anything the government's more flexible approach netted greater rewards in those regions in the decades leading up to 1914. Among the Poles Germanization decisively backfired, as the grass-roots self-help and 'organic work' projects of organized Polish nationalists always kept a good step or two ahead of the government's own best efforts, with the result that there was an ever-greater number of Polish-speakers and self-defining Poles throughout the period.[14] It is important to understand that both German and Polish nationalists engaged in a contest

---

[14] On Prussian Poland see Hagen, *Germans, Poles, and Jews,* 127–30, 135–6, 170, 182, 191; on Schleswig and Alsace-Lorraine, see C. Baechler, 'Le Reich allemand et les minorités nationales 1871–1918', *Revue d'Allemagne,* 28 (1996), 31–48, esp. 39–42 and 42–6. On Prussian Poland, Alsace-Lorraine, and the 1908 law, see also E. Rimmele, *Sprachenpolitik im Deutschen Kaiserreich vor 1914* (Munich, 1996).

of what one might call competitive assimilation, in which from a perspective of supposedly primordialist ethnic nationalism both sides recognized that nationality was not innate but was rather a plastic identity to be fought for in the civic realm of the public sphere. In this competition over language and identity too, then, civic and ethnic components of nationhood intermingled in significant ways.

In the Habsburg realm as well language came to seem much more central to the national identity of all the empire's minority populations, from the Germans to the Czechs to smaller groups such as the Slovenes. The growth of nationalism and mass politics went hand in hand in Austria-Hungary as elsewhere, and the age of both franchise extensions and the linguistic or 'nationality' census had arrived. Although the most important effects of these changes were probably to be seen at the national level, where the future of the empire as a viable multinational parliamentary monarchy seemed increasingly in doubt from the 1880s onwards, local life was altered in a no less radical way. Local issues of schooling and administration could be used to mobilize political-national movements that now depended on grass-roots support, all the more so as the influence of each minority group increasingly hung on the results of the all-important linguistic census, which depended in turn on how the languages were deployed locally and how they were taught in the schools. Rural populations and common folk came to identify themselves as members of national groups in ways they had not before, and language was the key or at least a key to that identity.[15] The spoken vernacular in particular took pride of place in national movements and national identity in a way that it had not in the years before the 1848 revolutions, when—romanticism notwithstanding—the print culture of the urban elites was much more the medium and the locus of national identity.

Precisely because there was not a single large, dominant majority nationality, government policy was never fully directed to any programme of assimilation. Rather it wavered depending on circumstances and local conditions. In Habsburg Hungary 1868 saw the promulgation of a quite tolerant-sounding Nationalities Law that while maintaining Magyar as the official language of state still guaranteed the use of other languages in schools and local administration. In the event, however, the law was interpreted in such a way as to promote rather far-reaching and not unsuccessful policies of Magyarization throughout the later nineteenth century.[16]

The Austrian half of the Dual Monarchy had its nationality policy framework set out in Article 19 of the constitution of 1867, but here there was a great deal of

---

[15] For important case studies investigating the late social and geographic spread of linguistic national identity, see A. Moritsch (ed.), *Vom Ethnos zur Nationalität: Der nationale Differenzierungsprozess am Beispiel ausgewählter Orte in Kärnten und im Burgenland* (Munich, 1991), and see generally, E. Hobsbawm, *Nations and Nationalism since 1789: Programme, Myth, Reality* (Cambridge, 1992), 94–100.

[16] A. Sked, *The Decline and Fall of the Habsburg Empire 1815–1918* (London, 1989), 208–12. See also Z. Szász, 'Nationality Policy in the Era of the Dualistic Monarchy: Possibilities and Restrictions', in F. Glatz (ed.), *Études historiques hongroises* (1990), ii. 183–90.

debate among the various national groups over its interpretation. Increasingly on the defensive, German liberals and nationalists construed the language rights guarantees in much the same way as their Frankfurt forebears had, thereby hoping to restrict other groups' public use of their mother tongues to the territories where they were in the majority (or at least a large minority) in order to fend off the perceived encroachment of Slavic-speaking groups. Czechs and others for their part argued that the language equality provisions applied throughout Austria, even for example to Czech speakers in Vienna or Lower Austria, much less in the majority-German Sudetenland of Bohemia itself.[17] The 1880s and 1890s witnessed repeated government attempts at a compromise between Czechs and Germans, but the negotiations always failed and often resulted in the fall of parliamentary coalitions, as in 1897, when the chief minister Count Badeni attempted to gather Czech support for his government by effectively making Bohemia administratively bilingual, a move that ultimately only led to a torrent of German nationalist agitation and to his own resignation. Conflicts over language training in schools between Germans and Slovenes had had much the same effect just a few years previously during the notorious Cilli affair.[18] To the extent that only a small minority within any of the national groups had given up hope for a more liberal and cooperatively federal multi-ethnic empire, the blurring of civic and ethnic categories of national identity observed in the first half of the century still held good—this was not yet secessionist nationalism. Even so, a decided shift towards the notion that political identities must follow cultural ones had taken hold during the second half of that era.

Moreover, such were the dynamics of the period that to some extent it did not matter whether the government was exerting pressure in favour of certain nationalities or in favour of linguistic parity and rights protections (which latter it often did, above all through the courts)—the trend towards linguistic 'Balkanization' continued. The possibility of some kind of multilingualism in state and society shrank, above all at the local level. Even under the conditions of the Moravian compromise of 1905, for example, families were increasingly forced to choose sides and declare a single Czech or German identity rather than maintain a bilingual one as had been possible in the past.[19] Instead, from villages and provinces to the national parliamentary scene, the various national groups increasingly engaged in battles of competitive assimilation over their supposed 'national property', a status contested across the spectrum of symbols of national identity but measured first and foremost in terms of language.

---

[17] Sked, *Habsburg Empire*, 220–1; R. Okey, *The Habsburg Monarchy c.1765–1918: From Enlightenment to Eclipse* (London, 2001), 303–4; and R. A. Kann, *The Multinational Empire: Nationalism and National Reform in the Habsburg Monarchy, 1848–1918* (2 vols., New York, 1950), i. 192–209.

[18] Okey, *Habsburg Monarchy*, 305–8; on the Cilli affair and its populist context, Judson, *Exclusive Revolutionaries*, 249–53.

[19] H. Burger, 'Der Verlust der Mehrsprachigkeit: Aspekte des mährischen Ausgleichs', *Bohemia*, 34 (1993), 77–89; and generally, G. Stourzh, 'Die Gleichberechtigung der Volksstämme als Verfassungsprinzip 1848–1918', in A. Wandruska and P. Urbanitsch (eds.), *Die Habsburgermonarchie 1848–1918* (7 vols., Vienna, 1980), iii. 2, 975–1206.

CONCLUSIONS, COMPARISONS, AND SPECULATIONS

To the extent that it makes sense to think of language-based, ethnocultural forms of nationalism, it was only in the later nineteenth century that they began to take shape in Central and Eastern Europe, in Germany and the Habsburg lands. It was after all from this political environment that the attitudes about minority rights built into the 1919 Versailles Peace Treaty emerged, or for that matter the studies of nationalism by scholars such as Hans Kohn and Friedrich Meinecke that established the civic-ethnic typology in the first place. Without ignoring the increasing emphasis on language and ethnicity seen in nationalist politics and ideology during the decades before the First World War, however, and without denying all utility to the civic-ethnic typology, investigation of language policy and minority rights provisions over the long nineteenth century does on balance suggest the limitations of such a dualistic, even Manichean model of nationalism.

At the level of describing national identity, it may be worthwhile to retain the notions of civic and ethnic brands of nationalism as ideal-types, that is, as catalogues or checklists of important criteria useful to consider in analysing nationalisms. But even here this is only true so long as one recognizes that in many, perhaps most cases, any given nationalism would best be portrayed as a mixture of the two types, in varying proportions and with differing emphases. Rather than thinking of nationalism in bipolar terms, or even as a spectrum in which nationalisms are laid out as points on a line (33 per cent civic and 67 per cent ethnic, for example, or vice versa), it might be more useful to set them out as points or shapes on a plane defined by civic and ethnic axes. Or, choosing a more humanistic rather than scientific image, nationalisms might be even better visualized as tapestries, products of a loom interwoven of civic warp and ethnic woof, but with the specific colours and patterns of the threads proving determinant in the description of any individual case of nationalism. If nothing else, the East–West bifurcation that in most analyses accompanies the cultural-political typology and its attendant modernization theory needs reconsideration. There is simply too much overlap and cross-cutting of categories among the European nationalisms to establish any such geographical pattern. This is even truer when one considers that any East–West divisions according to differing levels of modernity are themselves less clear than previously thought, particularly when definitions of modernization are refined to include more subtle and variegated notions of political culture.

Moreover, at the level of thinking about minority rights and linguistic politics, the civic-ethnic typology has even less to be said for it and is probably only misleading, given that there does not seem to be any correlation between the political or cultural orientation of a nationalist ideology and the actual position of linguistic minorities within the nation. It was not in the black-and-white or the either-or of civic versus ethnic identities that the fortunes of linguistic minorities lay. Rather, attitudes and policies regarding linguistic diversity and minority nationalities depended on the complex interrelationships between cultural and political aspects of nationhood as these developed in distinct political and cultural environments. Toleration, assimilation, forced assimilation, and total exclusion were possibilities that could emerge from almost any type of nationalism in different times and places. Contextual trends at the level of political culture, socioeconomics, religiosity, national identity, and rights discourses were often transnational in scope and could establish commonalities across the East–West or civic-ethnic divides, but within these purported categories positions on nationality rights and linguistic diversity could still vary widely by nation, province, or social milieu. When exploring the historical landscape of European nationalism, to stop thinking in terms of ethnic and civic identities at all would be to lose a potentially useful historiographical compass, but to continue to extrapolate confidently from these categories to the specifics of national identities and nationality policies would be to overlook the opportunities for orienting oneself by stopping to ask the locals for directions.

9

The Habsburg Monarchy

'National Trinity' and the Elasticity of National Allegiance

Mark Cornwall

HARNESSING THE FORCES OF NATIONALISM

It is a truism that the Habsburg Monarchy seriously mismanaged the celebrated 'nationality principle' of the nineteenth century, or, to put it more bluntly, modern nationalism was 'the chief factor in the dissolution of the Habsburg Empire'.[1] As early as 1830, the Austrian dramatist Franz Grillparzer had summed up the various national 'provinces' of the Monarchy as 'horses absurdly harnessed together [. . . who] will scatter in all directions as soon as the advancing spirit of the times will weaken and break the bonds'.[2] Twenty years later a number of Cassandra figures were duly predicting such destruction if the nationality idea was not curbed and channelled effectively by the state. Most notable was the Magyar publicist and liberal statesman, Baron József Eötvös, whose writings can serve as a useful introduction to the dilemmas of the age.

In his exile in Munich from late 1848, Eötvös struggled to make sense of the nationalist ferment that had swept across Hungary and the rest of Central Europe earlier in the year, and to identify the lessons that could be learnt for the future. A key maxim, he argued in his most famous work published in 1851, was that the nationality principle could not be applied in its 'fashionable sense' in East-Central Europe without destroying the existing state structures.[3] By 'fashionable', Eötvös meant a 'revolutionary' and 'linguistic' interpretation of nationality on French lines: namely, that those of a particular nationality should be brought together to express popular sovereignty in a new political organism. In the circumstances of

---

[1] O. Jászi, *The Dissolution of the Habsburg Monarchy* (Chicago, 1929), 250.
[2] Quoted ibid. 11.
[3] József Eötvös, *The Dominant Ideas of the Nineteenth Century and their Impact on the State*, 2 vols., trans. and ed. D. M. Jones (New York, 1996), i. 139.

the Habsburg Monarchy, where historic borders did not coincide with nationality, the imposition of such an absolute and revolutionary principle would be suicidal. But Eötvös also questioned how a concept as nebulous as 'nationality' could be a stable base for territorial restructuring. As he put it, 'the great word "nationality" blares out at us from every direction, but everybody wants to understand it differently'.[4] He himself judged that an individual's national consciousness was primarily an amalgam of two elements, a common language and common memories of the past. To prioritize the former (as had, for instance, the Czech leader František Palacký at the Kremsier Parliament) would usually be at the expense of the latter, violating historic tradition and memory in order to impose a utopian linguistic unity.[5] It would also, as shown in the 1848 revolutions, lead to dominance by one nationality over others, a trend that Eötvös viewed as an integral characteristic anyway of the nationalism which had spread out of France since the 1790s.

The solution, according to Eötvös, was to give priority to historic traditions and the historic element in national consciousness. This meant following not the French but the British or Swiss model of national development, where a sensitivity had been shown to the historic rights of the provinces that had come together to make up a national union.[6] In the same way, the Habsburg authorities needed to balance their own state centralization with a strengthening of the Monarchy's historic territories or crownlands—whether Hungary, Bohemia, or Galicia—in order to serve as focal points for political and 'national' loyalty. Within this framework of self-government, guaranteed constitutionally, it would then be possible to cater for the linguistic and other cultural needs of each nationality. Eötvös was not ignoring the empire's diverse nationalities. He recognized, almost in the parlance of an Anthony Smith or Eric Hobsbawm, the presence of *ethnie* or even of 'proto-nationalism'.[7] But he sought to re-dress the peoples of the Monarchy in their historic 'national' jackets rather than allowing them to shock their immediate neighbours with a linguistic-nationalistic nudity. In each historic territory there would need to be compromise between nationalities calling for 'equal status'. This at least, Eötvös assumed, was one lesson learnt from the horrors of 1848–9. Through this refocusing of the national question, he predicted, 'our grandchildren will see in the debates launched in the name of national rights, which are now exciting our nineteenth century, nothing but drowning men snatching vainly at every object'.[8]

As one of the most erudite Habsburg liberal thinkers on mid-century nationalism, Eötvös provides us with a notable assessment. It cuts across a reductionist notion of East-Central European nationalism as primarily 'ethnic' and West

⁴ József Eötvös, *The Dominant Ideas of the Nineteenth Century and their Impact on the State*, i. 110.
⁵ Ibid., ii. 478.
⁶ P. Bödy, *Joseph Eötvös and the Modernization of Hungary, 1840–1870: A Study of Ideas of Individuality and Social Pluralism in Modern Politics* (New York, 1985), 63–73.
⁷ See A. D. Smith, *The Ethnic Origins of Nations* (Oxford, 1986); E. J. Hobsbawm, *Nations and Nationalism since 1780: Programme, Myth, Reality* (Cambridge, 1997).
⁸ Eötvös, *The Dominant Ideas*, i. 199; ii. 489.

European nationalism as primarily 'civic' or territorial-political.[9] Certainly, Eötvös felt he had experienced ethnic nationalism but viewed it as only one version of the phenomenon of nationhood. He defined ethnic nationalism as something chiefly linguistic which, allegedly, had its roots in revolutionary France and which, optimistically, he hoped a proactive state could ward away from the Habsburg Empire. In its place, he envisaged a network of historically based and constitutionally governed autonomous territories which might follow a specific Western model and grow together into a stable 'civic nation' like Great Britain. What actually happened after 1860, with the collapse of the Habsburg absolutist experiment of the 1850s, was a mixture of these two developments: what Eötvös feared and what he hoped for.

If we are to retain the terminology of 'civic' and 'ethnic' nationalism, we might suggest that the two were increasingly entwined in several regions or developing 'nations' of the Habsburg Empire.[10] This makes the framework of the Monarchy an intriguing one in which to examine the character of nineteenth-century nationalism. It is clear that contemporaries here saw the nation and nation-building from a variety of perspectives, rarely defining the phenomena in exclusively ethnic terms. For example by the end of the century, Rudolf von Herrnritt, a law professor at Vienna University, was proposing that nationalism or national politics in the Empire consisted of three interwoven strands: ethnic, historical, and centralist.[11] If ethnic and historical conjured up the thinking of Eötvös, centralist could imply a wider civic definition of the nation—as an Austrian or even Habsburg patriotic community which was a framework for all of its citizens. We can explore this theory of what might be termed a 'national trinity'—ethnic, historical, and centralist—through examining developments in Hungary and the Bohemian lands. But first some fundamentals about nationalism and its nineteenth-century imperial framework need to be laid out.

DOMINANT AND SUBORDINATE NATIONS

'Habsburg policy is exalted opportunism in the pursuit of an unchanging dynastic idea,' wrote the British journalist Henry Wickham Steed from the perspective of 1913.[12] The priority of Habsburg rulers and their chief ministers in the long

---

[9] This division has coloured much writing on East European nationalism in the later twentieth century, including that of native historians who have usually inclined to a primordial or organic view of their particular nation. See for example the essays in P. F. Sugar and I. J. Lederer (eds.), *Nationalism in Eastern Europe* (Seattle, 1969): notably the essays by Sugar himself and by Joseph F. Zacek on the Czechs. For a recent critique, see M. Todorova, 'The Trap of Backwardness: Modernity, Temporality and the Study of Eastern European Nationalism', *Slavic Review*, 64 (2005), 148 ff.

[10] See the chapters by Brian Vick and Mark Hewitson in this volume.

[11] Rudolf Hermann von Herrnritt, *Nationalität und Recht* (Vienna, 1899), 43–9, 136. He noted that the ethnic-national strand had gained predominance but the others continued to be influential; the historic, for example, was notably present in Galicia.

[12] Henry Wickham Steed, *The Hapsburg Monarchy* (3rd edn., London, 1914), 8.

nineteenth century was simply to preserve the personal power of the dynasty and maintain its 'property'—the empire—in good order both at home and as a great power in Europe. With this purpose Emperor Joseph II in the 1780s had instituted a series of enlightened reforms to make the empire more efficient. For purely practical reasons, he tried to impose German as the common language of administration. Although this caused a backlash in some parts of the Monarchy like Hungary, a German culture and administration remained a lasting legacy of Joseph's reforms across much of the empire. It would be a crucial touchstone against which, in the nineteenth century, developing national groups like Czechs or Slovenes would define themselves. It also meant that German as a perceived 'nationality' in the Monarchy took much longer to emerge, for German-speakers naturally felt greater security within the state culture. From the 1830s at least, German-speakers in the Austrian half of the empire might define their patriotism in civic terms, largely on a non-ethnic basis. Only slowly—by the 1870s—would many tend towards a more ethnic-linguistic definition of their identity to match that of neighbouring peoples.

For the Habsburg dynasty, the nineteenth century was one when the ideas and example of revolutionary France were a constant long-term menace to its power. It reacted at home either with repression, or by making opportunistic political deals with particular national or social groups. The most notorious example of the latter tactic was in 1867. The dynasty made an agreement with the Hungarian 'nation' (in fact with the Magyar gentry), giving it a privileged position and so splitting the empire formally into two halves, 'Austria' and Hungary.[13] This gave the Magyars in Hungary a dominance commensurate with the privileged position already long accorded to German culture in Austria. In other words, it reinforced among the eleven official nationalities (*Volksstämme*) of the empire a system of perceived 'dominant' and 'subordinate' peoples. This, as the different national communities became more educated and cohesive from the 1870s, was a recipe for nationalist struggles that developed at different paces depending on each nationality's social and economic advancement. The dominant German and Magyar elites increasingly moved to shore up their position against 'subordinate' nationalities. They perceived them usually as less cultured or as an ethnic challenge to their own 'nation' which—as we shall see—they often interpreted in an amalgam of civic and ethnic terms.

Earlier in the century, it was rather the tactic of repression that the Metternich regime had used to block subversive ideas from entering its domains. After 1815 the main domestic threat to imperial power was perceived as 'liberalism': those educated men who wished for some form of constitutional government in the Monarchy so that sovereignty no longer lay simply with the sovereign. Besides pressing for political reform, the liberals often had a national agenda as well. They were stimulated to explore national identity, first by the French or British example,

---

[13] The term 'Austria' was not introduced officially until 1915, but is used here to refer to Cisleithania, or the non-Hungarian parts of the Monarchy.

and secondly by reacting after 1815 against the repressive 'Metternich system' of government. In defining their particular 'nation' and carving out a sphere separate from German culture, the early liberal-patriots—whether Czech, Magyar, or Polish—often campaigned with an emancipatory agenda of civic inclusiveness, but still expressed their growing national awareness largely in ethnic, exclusive terms. They were the leaders of communities united by their vernacular and by a common 'mythistory' handed down the generations (and now being reasserted).[14] From the 1780s the Habsburg authorities had unwittingly played their own part in stimulating these 'imagined communities'. Joseph II's reforms had included basic education in non-German languages, something which continued in the decades thereafter and reinforced new notions of common identity based on language or shared memory. Later, Metternich's government after 1815 tolerated and even encouraged a burgeoning national culture for the Monarchy's peoples as a safe 'non-political' outlet for expression. For Metternich himself the state interest was the priority, but he had no problem with the principle of equality for all the empire's nationalities.[15] Their separate cultural-political evolution, however, was then accelerated through mass communication, produced by economic change and the railway revolution of the 1840s. The result was that it proved impossible to immunize the empire from liberal thinking tied to various forms of national consciousness.

In the 1848 revolutions with the fall of Metternich, cultural bonding was suddenly politicized. National-liberal leaders, as part of their struggle for constitutional government in Central Europe, now strove to delimit their own perceived 'historic nation' as well. Often their mission cut straight across the national borders of neighbouring peoples. For example, German national unity faced Czech opposition (and vice versa), while Magyar national unity evoked Croatian or (Transylvanian) Romanian resistance. The Habsburg regime helped in its own way to intensify the ethnic nationalist struggle, not least by acknowledging early in 1848 a commitment to the 'equal status' (*Gleichberechtigung*) of its peoples or nationalities (*Volksstämme*). As Gerald Stourzh has shown, this principle, once laid down, was not forgotten by liberal nationalist leaders.[16] After what was a 'Germanizing' Habsburg regime in the absolutist 1850s, political-nationalist movements immediately re-emerged in 1860 across the Monarchy, equipped again with their mutually contradictory demands from 1848.

---

[14] I am using the term 'mythistory' to illustrate that amalgam of past myths and symbols which early national patriots, like Palacký, constructed for their nation.

[15] See the useful discussion of Metternich's own perception of 'nationality' in H. Rumpler, *Österreichische Geschichte 1804–1914: Eine Chance für Mitteleuropa* (Vienna, 1997), 200–2.

[16] G. Stourzh, 'Die Gleichberechtigung der Volksstämme als Verfassungsprinzip 1848–1918', in A. Wandruszka and P. Urbanitsch (eds.), *Die Habsburgermonarchie 1848–1918*, vol. iii/2: *Die Völker des Reiches* (Vienna, 1980), 1011 ff.

In the subsequent decades, the nationalism on show—the striving on behalf of the 'organic nation'—was expressed very much in ethnic-linguistic terms. Especially this was the case with the so-called 'unhistoric nations', such as the Slovenes, Slovaks, or Romanians, whose claim to nationhood rested largely on their separate language and modern literature and less on 'concrete evidence' of any historic pre-modern existence (however much their nationalists sought for it in the archives). In contrast, liberal leaders from the 'historic nations'—Germans, Magyars, Czechs, Croats, and Poles—had from the mid-century always had an extra arrow in their 'ethnic-linguistic' quiver. Indeed, it can be argued that many of the German elite in Austria continued for decades to view 'the nation' primarily in civic terms. Their privileged status in the Austrian half of the empire (Cisleithania) permitted German-speakers an overarching anational perspective of an 'Austrian nation' whose fortunes were simultaneously tied to the Habsburg dynasty, to German culture, and to a historic territory of which they were the guardians. An ethnic-German dimension was never far below the surface of this identity but for some German-speakers it was certainly subsumed beneath a civic understanding of the German-Austrians' historic role in the Monarchy. In this way, if one is seeking for signs of a 'national trinity', it is best embodied in the outlook of many German-Austrians.

Magyar, Czech, and Croat nationalists also came to define their nationhood in both ethnic and historic-territorial terms, with occasional centralist overtones. In the historic-territorial interpretation, their ancestors had been state creators; their nation—like those in the West—had existed for centuries with its own political elite and traditions on a delimited historic territory. For the Magyar nationalist gentry, whose national perspective was infused with the traditions of the old Magyar nobility, it was especially easy to identify their nation with all historic Hungary—the 'lands of the Holy Crown of St Stephen'—where the Estates since 1526 had secured special privileges from the Habsburg dynasty. The Czech and Croat national leaders were similarly able to construct a theory of historic 'state right' for their nation, basing it on specific territories where they had allegedly exercised their political nationhood from the medieval period onwards. The Bohemian Czech leadership defined this Czech national territory as the historic provinces of Bohemia and Moravia, notwithstanding the number of Germans within these borders or the long resistance of those who held out for a special 'Moravian' nationhood. Croat nationalists made similar claims, some more extreme than others, for the 'reconstitution' of a Croatian historic territory; here, as with the Magyars or Czechs, political symbols such as the Croatian *sabor* or diet were taken as evidence of national continuity.[17] In each of these three nationalist cases, therefore, there was a sense of the nation as something not just linguistically defined, but as having historic-territorial roots on a West European model.

---

[17] C. Jelavich, *South Slav Nationalisms: Textbooks and Yugoslav Union before 1914* (Columbus, Oh., 1990), 3, 12–14. The best study of Croatian historic state right remains M. Gross, *Povijest pravaške ideologije* (Zagreb, 1973).

This defining of 'historic' and 'unhistoric' nations, in the terminology of Friedrich Engels, leads us nearer to a consideration of how far 'civic' elements could be present in these varieties of nationalism. If we take Britain or France as classic civic national models—where on a defined historic state territory civic loyalties had been cultivated to make up for the decline of older socio-political ties and were then forged together in a new state patriotism[18]—then it has always been clear that the Habsburg Monarchy as a whole never managed to achieve this 'patriotic fusion'. A state patriotism of a kind had been consciously cultivated from the time of Maria Theresa, and by the late nineteenth century continued to rest on a number of key centripetal elements, not least the army and (especially in Austria) the bureaucracy. Nor can a certain Habsburg patriotism among many citizens of the empire be denied. But it was always limited in scope because such *Staatsgedanken* never developed far beyond loyalty to the Habsburg dynasty as the embodiment of the empire, and never—even under the constitutional regimes—encompassed any degree of overall popular state consciousness. As Josef Redlich later observed, the dynasty during the crucial decades of Francis II's reign (coinciding with the Metternich years) had singularly failed to focus state patriotism onto a new, non-dynastic concept that would encompass the burgeoning national diversity of the empire.[19] Even Metternich had tentatively sensed the need for this, at least in some form of structural devolution, but his schemes had been blocked by the emperor.[20] The dynasty's attempt—in the 1850s—to forge together a supranational, 'Germanized' and centralized state was a final stab at enforced uniformity. But such an autocracy, which in a different era might have formed the base for some Western-style civic nation, could not for long be pushed forward against nationalist and liberal thinking in Central Europe. To quote Oscar Jászi, dynastic patriotism would remain 'an artificial flower in a time when the idea of the self-determination of nations was growing'.[21]

Into this ideological void, as we have seen, some like József Eötvös hoped that the Monarchy's historic territorial units could, under transformed constitutional regimes, provide new focal points for regional patriotism. The omnipotence of the state would be curbed, but the forces of 'ethnic nationalism' would also melt away. From the 1860s, part of this aspiration began indeed to occur as the dynasty started its constitutional experiments and, specifically, devolved some power to the historic crownlands and kingdoms. In particular, as noted, this meant in 1867 the invention of Dualism: a special deal between the dynasty and the Magyar gentry, giving the latter virtual control of the Hungarian kingdom. Lesser settlements were provided for the Croatian and Polish nobility in Croatia (1868) and Galicia (1873) respectively. Yet this devolution on a historic-territorial basis was unequal and therefore a focus for endless comparison and resentment in the following

---

[18] Hobsbawm, *Nations and Nationalism since 1780*, 85.

[19] Josef Redlich, *Das österreichische Staats- und Reichsproblem*, 2 vols. (Leipzig, 1920–6), i. 86.

[20] See A. Haas, *Metternich, Reorganisation and Nationality 1813–1818: A Story of Foresight and Frustration in the Rebuilding of the Austrian Empire* (Wiesbaden, 1963).

[21] Jászi, *Dissolution of the Habsburg Monarchy*, 447.

decades. In short, the Magyar national claims had been separated and privileged over all others, while in Cisleithania—in order to compensate the German Liberals—the powers given to the provincial assemblies or diets were offset by a firm degree of political centralization based in Vienna.

Moreover, this late constitutional restructuring by the dynasty came at the same time as a resurgence of empire-wide ethnic nationalism. The upshot was exactly what Eötvös had warned against, a clash of 'historic traditions' with 'revolutionary [linguistic] nationalism'. Within the crownland or provincial borders, it usually ended with one nationality striving to dominate. Nowhere was this clearer than in Magyar-dominated Hungary. In the circumstances of 'constitutional' Austria and Hungary after 1867, imperial subjects had also become 'citizens', and nationalism in many regions included civic characteristics. In the various historic territories—Hungary, Bohemia, or the lands of 'German-Austria'—the struggle always had more than a purely ethnic (linguistic-cultural) dimension, even if this was an integral element in each nationalist crusade. Particularly in these regions we can identify a civic nationalism which came principally in two forms. First, there were Magyar and Czech nationalists who used the principle of state-right and historic territory as a basis for their campaigns: in theory at least, this could move beyond a strictly ethnic definition of the nation. Second, there were anational Germans for whom, as we have noted, the nation might continue to mean 'Austria'; they in particular were also most inclined among the nationalities to retain a sense of dynastic patriotism. And, with their emphasis on a centralized Austrian state, they were therefore the principal embodiment of 'national trinity' in the Monarchy.

MAGYAR NATIONALISM AND HUNGARY

Let us now apply these general principles to some case studies from Hungary and Cisleithania. The Magyars, not least because of their semi-independent statehood after 1867, provide one of the best examples of a nationalism that combined ethnic and civic dimensions. Scholars have consistently pointed out the basic contradictions in the Hungarian national model: namely that, in the nineteenth century a Magyar ruling caste strove to impose their notion—their construction—of a common 'Magyar nation' upon historic Hungarian territory.[22] Magyar nationalism, notoriously, had aristocratic roots which persisted well into the twentieth century. The national movement had first erupted in its modern form when at the Pressburg Diet of 1790–1 the Hungarian nobility challenged Joseph II's state-centralizing and Germanizing reforms. This essentially was 'estate nationalism'.

---

[22] In the terminology that follows, I make a distinction in my use of 'Magyar' as opposed to 'Hungarian'. 'Magyar' refers to Magyar-speakers or 'ethnic Magyars' (who ascribed to a Magyar language-based identity). 'Hungarian' refers to the historic territory of Hungary or to all peoples who inhabited this territory. To merge the two terms (as in the Magyar language where there is only one word, *magyar*) goes to the root of the nationalist antagonism prevalent in nineteenth-century Hungary.

The nobility held fast to the feudal privileges extracted from the dynasty and codified in Hungarian law since the sixteenth century, and saw themselves as embodying the 'nation' (*natio Hungarica*) on the basis of historic right and privilege.[23] Since the nobility laid stress on the specific 'Magyar' character of the state and extracted a promise from Leopold II not to introduce a 'foreign language' into Hungary, their feudal protest from the start had taken on a linguistic ingredient. They were defending their privileges with a particular ethnic twist. For on the lines perhaps of Johann Gottfried Herder's famous warning in 1791 that the Magyars were a doomed people, caught between Germans above and Slavs below, the nobility were equally conscious of multi-ethnic Hungary. They knew that it consisted of a large percentage of passive non-Magyars who, in view of the democratic winds blowing across the continent, might soon begin to challenge their 'feudal national' position.

In the following half-century, especially from the 1820s when the Magyar language and literature began to be actively cultivated under the impact of German Romanticism, some of the lesser nobility altered the shape of Hungarian nationalism. They energetically firmed up their own ethnic Magyar identity but also moved towards a more inclusive and less privilege-based view of the 'Hungarian nation'. Under their auspices, the Hungarian Diet pushed through 'modern' language laws against the widespread use of Latin. In 1840 Magyar was declared as the language for all branches of the administration and judiciary; in 1844 it was proclaimed as the 'state language' in governance and education (applicable even in 'autonomous' Croatia). So the notion was solidified among new generations of Magyar-conscious nobles that the Magyar nation and the Hungarian state or territory were identical. It was a short step towards claiming that all those who lived in the country were members of one Hungarian nation.[24]

For while the new nationalists were redefining the nation along ethnic lines with inspiration from native traditions, they were also consciously modelling it on their perceptions of Western nation-states. Just as France had reinvented itself as a nation of French citizens with French as the state language, so it was argued, the people(s) within Hungary's historic borders constituted a Magyar nation that was officially Magyar-speaking. Just as Great Britain was the archetypal stable liberal state with a constitution enshrined in law over the centuries, so this seemed to mirror the Hungarian nation's constitutional and legalistic traditions as well as the Magyar elite's increasing commitment to liberal governance and economic 'progress' for their nation. Whether the French or British model was given precedence, in both cases the Magyar 'reforming generation' aspired to emulate the West or sometimes, particularly by mid-century, came to assume that Hungary was already progressing in tandem with other liberal nations. In other words, they

---

[23] See P. Sugar, 'The More it Changes the More Hungarian Nationalism Remains the Same', *Austrian History Yearbook*, 31 (2000), 131.

[24] Ibid. 134. Sugar points out the difficulty pre-1848 of defining the exact criteria for a member of the 'Hungarian nation'.

imposed their own civic nationalist definition of the nation on Hungary. Or, as one authority has suggested, the Magyar nation state was to be 'an ideological hybrid of estates-national and French republican ideas'.[25]

The shifting of ground in the Magyar case from the 'estate nationalism' of the 1790s to the liberal-ethnic nationalism of the 1840s can be followed in the 'national road' trodden by Count István Széchenyi where liberal and romantic were combined. Born into a multilingual and anational noble society, but with a father who had founded the Hungarian National Museum, the young Széchenyi in his mid-twenties was still only half-conscious of his Hungarian patriotism. It was his experiences of France and Britain at the end of the Napoleonic wars that helped to sharpen a personal national identity. They convinced him, on the one hand, that 'there is no nation in Hungary as yet', and on the other, that his Hungarian fatherland was scandalously backward; after one visit to the West in 1825 he noted in his diary that 'the century is on the march, but unfortunately, I live in a country that is dragging one leg behind'.[26] Significantly, he began his liberal reforming career first by founding a Hungarian Academy of Sciences to cultivate the 'national' Magyar language. It was a noble patriotic gesture, but we might also label it as an early personal act of civic nationalism. Széchenyi was acting on behalf of a more broadly defined Hungarian nation.

By 1848 the conflating of the Magyar (ethnic) nation with the Hungarian (territorial-political) nation had proceeded apace. Partly, it was being imposed on Hungary from above, through the lesser nobility's linguistic laws and a constitutional (anti-Habsburg) mobilization of the population by Lajos Kossuth and others. Partly, it spread across Hungary in tandem with the emergence of a new civil society, centred especially on Buda-Pest where professional people—doctors or clergy—took up the noble example. But mindful of this consistent conflation of 'Magyar' and 'Hungarian', we can usefully disentangle and use these two terms in order to distinguish between ethnic and civic forms of nationalism over the next half-century. On the one hand, there was of course a vigorous ethnic nationalism furthered by the state after 1875: a campaign of Magyarization against non-Magyar nationalities in order to forge together the 'Magyar/Hungarian' nation. This was essentially inward-looking, though it was certainly fuelled by angst over the rise of irredentist national states like Romania and Serbia on Hungary's borders. As elsewhere in the empire, anxieties about the growth of foreign nationalist threats bred in turn a vigilance against nationalist enemies at home.

On the other hand, a civic nationalism on behalf of the broad Hungarian political nation was periodically evident and occasionally took precedence over blunt Magyar chauvinism. This civic nationalism, where citizens of the Hungarian nation state were mobilized or (increasingly) self-mobilized, was especially clear in

---

[25] L. Gogolák, 'Ungarns Nationalitätengesetze und das Problem des magyarischen National- und Zentralstaates', in Wandruszka and Urbanitsch (eds.), *Die Habsburgermonarchie*, iii/2. 1243.

[26] Quoted in George Barany, *Stephen Széchenyi and the Awakening of Hungarian Nationalism, 1791–1841* (Princeton, 1968), 83, 112.

the uneasy relationship between Hungary and the Habsburgs (or the rest of the Monarchy). It was therefore on display during the dynastic crises of 1848–9, the 1860s, and 1903–6. It was dampened down during the classic years of Hungarian liberalism when the ruling elite was self-confident about Hungary's relationship with the dynasty. But it manifested itself also across Hungary on state anniversaries and commemorations, either as part of the nation's mythical past ('St Stephen's Day') or as part of a common memory of the nation's struggle to assert its independence ('15 March'—1848). Hungarian nationalism therefore was essentially Janus-like: displaying its civic face mainly to the outside world while turning its ethnic face inwards in order to Magyarize the nation.

It could be argued that this distinction is a fine one, in that Hungarian nationalism from 1848 was increasingly propagated through an ethnic Magyar filter. The old fluid 'nation' might be glimpsed in Count Batthyany's final words in three languages, issued in 1849 before his execution: 'Allez Jäger, éljen a haza!' But the modern construction had been clear at the start of the revolution when Kossuth had abruptly announced that 'there is only one nation here'.[27] The specifically Magyar dimension to the Hungarian constitutional struggle against the Habsburgs then became more focused as the non-Magyar peoples challenged such a unitary utopia with claims of their own: historic (the Croats), or territorial (Serbs, Romanians) or at least cultural (Slovaks). For the nationalities, these demands made of Hungary in 1848–9 were a historic line in the sand. Similarly, for the Magyar elite, the March Laws extracted in 1848 from the dynasty were something to be held in the common memory and brought up later. A key result of the revolutionary period in Hungary had been Kossuth's mobilization of a broader Magyar national consciousness: the 'nation' had been extended to embrace all those of Magyar tongue.

This nation was then suppressed by the neo-absolutist Habsburg regime. But recent research has shown how in the 1850s and into the following decade, a subdued Magyar-Hungarian nationalism could occasionally be glimpsed when crowds were allowed to assemble. At the funeral processions for patriots like Wesselenyi or Vörösmarty, which spilled over into civic urban space; at annual carnivals in Buda-Pest when Magyar national costumes were to the fore; at the centennial festivities in 1859 for the linguistic pioneer Ferenc Kazinczy—on each communal occasion, Magyar cultural or political memories of the 'national' struggle were stirred and preserved. And when in 1860 the authorities finally permitted St Stephen's Day to be hosted again, the celebration of the mythical Hungarian king's coronation in AD 1000 proved to be a 'nationalist way of rebuking the uncrowned [Habsburg] king in Vienna'.[28]

Through the so-called Compromise of 1867 the Magyar liberal gentry successfully reasserted their theory of one Hungarian political nation and had it

[27] A. Freifeld, *Nationalism and the Crowd in Liberal Hungary, 1848–1914* (Washington, DC, 2000), 65, 95.   [28] Ibid., 185 and see also 105, 126, 143–4, 166 ff.

confirmed by the crown. At the coronation ceremonies in Buda-Pest in June 1867, Franz Joseph's private coronation in Buda in front of the ancient privileged Magyar nobility was followed by a public symbolic act in Pest in front of the urbanized Hungarian citizen-nation. Riding his horse across the Chain Bridge that linked the two halves of the national capital, the king galloped up onto a coronation mound composed of soil sent in from all corners of Hungary. There he raised his sword in four directions to acknowledge the historic boundaries of the Hungarian kingdom. The dualist settlement with the dynasty left Hungary the means to become a nation-state. It was complemented in Hungary itself by the Nationalities Law of 1868. The text worked out by Eötvös and Ferenc Deák emphasized that there was one Hungarian (Magyar) political nation composed of many nationalities. Therein lay a civic-ethnic amalgamated notion of nationhood. All citizens were equal before the law, all were entitled to express their nationality *culturally* while accepting the requirements and integrity of the Hungarian political nation. The Magyar liberals only now recognized Croatia as an equivalent 'political nation', entitled to some territorial (sub-dualist) autonomy. They refused to accept the other non-Magyar leaders' idea of a Hungary of six equal 'state nations', for this could endanger the territorial integrity of the Hungarian nation.[29]

Theoretically, the Nationalities Law, with its magnanimous cultural concessions in education and local government, might have served as a base for fusing together a Hungarian civic nation. Instead, the Magyar ethnic dimension to the liberals' sense of their nationhood (always present as part of their privileged social position over non-Magyars) quickly began to assert itself. From the 1870s a new generation of Magyar politicians under Kálmán Tisza increasingly viewed Magyarization as the leading state idea, the principal way to create a modern 'Western-style' nation-state, centralized and urbanized. The priority was to make good Magyars out of the citizens of Hungary. As one prime minister observed, 'We have only one single categorical imperative, the Magyar state-idea, and we must demand that every citizen should acknowledge it and subject himself uncon-ditionally to it.'[30] Education laws in 1879 and 1907 bypassed the Nationalities Law by enforcing the Magyar language in all state schools. Romanian and Serb confessional schools could escape if they had the private resources, but over twenty years the number of non-Magyar state primary schools in Hungary fell from 47 to 14 per cent. For national activists, the Magyarizing process was inher-ently modernizing and civilizing. One assimilated Magyar, Béla Grünwald, equated it with a 'meat mincer' into which the peasant sons of the nationalities were fed so as to emerge the other end as Magyar gentlemen. Certainly these new generations of assimilated Magyars (notably from the Germans, Jews, and Slovaks) were, in their quest to 'belong', even more committed to shoring up a Magyar nationalist state centred on Budapest. State education in Hungary was

---

[29] Gogolák, 'Ungarns Nationalitätengesetze', 1270 ff.
[30] Kálmán Széll, quoted in Jászi, *Dissolution of the Habsburg Monarchy*, 321.

focused in this direction: ignoring the dynasty, concentrating on the Magyars' glorious past and Hungary's modernizing progress. As a result, by the turn of the century if not earlier, Hungarian patriotism was largely indistinguishable in official policy from Magyar chauvinism. Most notably, it was on display in 1896 in Budapest when in the grandiose Millennium festivities the 'nation' celebrated the arrival of the first Magyar tribes on Hungarian soil in the ninth century.

NATIONALISM IN THE BOHEMIAN LANDS

As in Hungary, in the Bohemian lands Czech or German nationalism came to be expressed largely in ethnic-linguistic terms by the late nineteenth century. But the ethnic struggle was consistently complicated, or perhaps even softened, by additional and overlapping interpretations of the 'nation'. As in Hungary, some Czech and German nationalists by mid-century had adopted a historical-territorial concept of their nation as a community that for centuries had inhabited Bohemia-Moravia-Silesia. In the Czech case, the Bohemian lands were the precise spatial framework for the historic nation. In the German case, the horizons were always broader, with Bohemia-Moravia representing the local homeland but constituting a region that over the centuries had always been part of a wider German cultural nation to the north and the south. If this hazy national vision would persist for many German-Bohemians, the historical-territorial idea for Czechs was embodied in their notorious theory of 'state right' from the mid-1860s onwards. By this time much of the German-Bohemian elite was inclining towards an Austrian interpretation of their nation, partly as a barrier to Czech 'state right' which focused narrowly on the Bohemian lands. Since from the 1860s the Habsburg dynasty was still centralizing political power on Vienna, Germans from the Bohemian lands could ally with German-Austrians to the south and thereby interpret their nation in wider civic 'Austrian' terms.

In Austria from the 1860s the revised constitutional structure of the state allowed more fluid interpretations of the 'nation' than in the Hungarian half of the Monarchy. Signs of a 'national trinity'—ethnic, historical, centralist—were most evident in Austria, particularly in the German-Austrian outlook. But this is not to suggest that some educated Czechs, Poles, or Slovenes, particularly those entering the imperial bureaucracy and army, could not in addition adopt an Austrian, centralist interpretation for their patriotic allegiance. Simply, for many individuals, the ethnic-linguistic interpretation gradually assumed a precedence over all others. Not least this was because in the decades after 1867 it was the nationalities, defined chiefly by linguistic criteria, that secured legal status as the main 'constitutive units of the state'.[31] They did not eclipse but they certainly diminished the significance of Austria's historic crownlands, which earlier in the century some like Eötvös had looked to as the best basis for national conciliation.

---

[31] Stourzh, 'Die Gleichberechtigung der Volksstämme', 1202–4.

Few nationalist struggles in the Habsburg Monarchy had the ferocity of the Czech-German struggle in Bohemia. In essence it was caused by the rise of national consciousness among the majority Czech-speakers (62 per cent of the population), and their populist campaign from mid-century to assert social and political equality within the crownland. This was increasingly resisted by a German social and political elite (37 per cent).[32] The demographic balance in Bohemia (compared to Moravia where Germans were only 28 per cent) was crucial in making the German-Bohemians more obstinate against any compromise. In turn, the vibrant middle-class colour of Czech nationalism made it a more formidable opponent than those largely peasant nationalities challenging Magyar supremacy in Hungary.

From the start in the 1780s, modern Czech identity was principally defined in ethnic-linguistic terms and had a mass popular rather than aristocratic base, for the Czech language was chiefly the preserve of the peasantry. Through state reforms of the 1770s, Czech-speaking communities had been allotted primary schools with Czech as the language of instruction; all further education was in the German language. Joseph II's abolition of serfdom freed a Czech-speaking peasantry to become mobile at a time of revolution in Bohemia's textile industry. Those Czech-speakers who now advanced socially could not but be aware of the German cultural world that dominated Bohemia, reinforced by Joseph II's Germanization of the state administration. Gradually over the next half-century, Czech-speakers would work their way up the education ladder and many would feel the discrimination against their mother-tongue or 'nation'.[33] A notable example—one of the early Czech 'patriots'—was Josef Jungmann who hailed from a poor Czech background, learnt German to advance and finally became a *gymnasium* teacher in Litoměřice (in 1809 the only secondary school where Czech was taught as a voluntary subject). Jungmann himself associated Czech national identity with the Czech language and campaigned for it to be given equal status with German.

This linguistic definition of the Czech nation gained currency after 1815 because of the reality of linguistic inequality. However, for some of those who sponsored Czech culture from the 1790s the nation was initially viewed as 'Bohemian' rather than 'Czech' and the two were not yet conflated. In other words, Czech ethnicity was one small ingredient in a Bohemian provincial patriotism that was resisting the imperial centralization of Joseph II. In contrast to the 'estate nationalism' in Hungary in the 1790s, language demands did not feature at all prominently in the protests of the Bohemian aristocracy. They finally demanded a chair in Czech language and literature to be established in Prague university, and a small group of them began to patronize Czech culture as a distinctive part of their provincial patriotism. Similarly, some of the early Czech

---

[32] The figures are approximate from the 1900 census.
[33] The rise educationally of Czech-speakers is crucial, yet has often been ignored by scholars of nationalism: see for example J. Breuilly, *Nationalism and the State* (2nd edn., Manchester, 1998), 132.

patriots, dabbling in Czech culture only as an 'intellectual game', were not too prescriptive. Miroslav Hroch has noted that they defined themselves as being between an ethnic and a provincial identity: working assiduously to enhance the standing of the Czech language, they did so at first within the framework of a German-speaking noble patriotism.[34] Some observers of a rising Czech identity, such as the Prague academic Bernard Bolzano, warned already in 1810 that the German part of the 'Bohemian nation' seemed to be contemptuous of the Czech-speaking part; as a solution, he proposed to his students a bilingual Bohemian territorial nation.[35] However, this was undoubtedly utopian unless encouraged from above by the imperial authorities through educational reforms, or at least taken up by the Bohemian nobility in the manner of their Magyar 'cousins'. Neither occurred, for German continued to be privileged as the imperial language and Czech-speakers were perceived by most Bohemian nobles as of inferior social standing. Thus after 1815, during the Metternich era, the concept of one Bohemian nation of equal individuals never progressed. Instead an educated Czech public, increasingly conscious of its separate identity, was able to emerge and assume position within an overarching German 'superior' culture.

It is important to stress that, in the Bohemian lands before the 1848 revolutions, the 'nation' was conceived very fluidly and in a variety of ways. It would be anachronistic to impose on the region that Czech-German national polarization which fast seemed to be prevailing by the 1870s. In the turmoil of 1848, according to Jiří Kořalka, varied concepts of the nation converged.[36] To enumerate them helps us understand the limitations of the ethnic-civic model. First, with the Habsburg Monarchy in crisis, there were certainly some in the Bohemian lands who resurrected the idea of a (Habsburg) dynastic state patriotism; they focused their attention on Vienna and the continuation of a centralized state, either with or without a constitution. Second, there were others, often of the Bohemian or Moravian nobility, whose patriotism was centred on the Habsburg Empire's historic territories. In line with József Eötvös's thinking, they sought to uphold a provincial identity and reassert the privileges of regional assemblies against state centralization; they also opposed the 'revolutionary nationalism' emanating from Czech Prague or German Frankfurt. In the words of one speaker to the Moravian Diet in 1848: 'Not language but mentality makes a Moravian; it would be a strange protection if we should be preserved from Germanization only to be Czechified.' Another warned: 'Let us guard against the idea that nationalities are the compass by which one determines the political formation of the Empire.'[37]

[34] M. Hroch, *Na prahu národní existence: touha a skutečnost* (Prague, 1999), 62, 139.
[35] Ibid. 199–200.
[36] For the following see Jiří Kořalka, 'Welche Nationsvorstellungen gab es 1848 in Mitteleuropa?', in R. Jaworski and R. Luft (eds.), *1848/9: Revolutionen in Ostmitteleuropa* (Munich, 1996), 29–45.
[37] Jindřich Dvořák, *Moravské sněmování roku 1848–49* (Telč, 1898), 100, 117: speeches by Leopold Neuwall and Josef Laminet.

Interlinked with these two types of patriotism—dynastic and provincial—were two emerging liberal nationalisms, German and Czech. Both had an ethnic-linguistic base, but if this had been all, their clash might have been quickly resolved. Both also, as we have seen, imagined the 'nation' in historic-territorial terms which had civic implications on a Western European model. Liberals from the German Confederation, meeting in Frankfurt in April 1848 to organize a united German nation-state, envisaged the Bohemian lands simply as part of the broad German historic nation (following the French example where all inhabitants were citizens of the nation-state). This might be generously described as an 'inclusive' civic interpretation of the nation. Alternatively, according to a Czech historian, many Germans simply 'saw in the Czechs an ethnographic adornment on the German national body'.[38] German-Bohemian liberals in particular warmed to the idea of unity with their northern cousins, not least because Austria's fate looked so uncertain, but also because they were suddenly aware that the Czech liberals' vision, if carried out, threatened to drown regional German-speakers in a Czech sea.

In short, the 1848 revolutions seemed to presage as much a pan-Czech as a pan-German solution for the region. Nationalism on both sides was then heightened through fears of where the state borders would run and where power would be centralized. Certainly on the Czech side, the liberal leader František Palacký seemed to define the national struggle chiefly in ethnic-linguistic terms vis-à-vis the German nation. But the clash with German liberalism came particularly because Palacký, as the historian of the Bohemian estates, had long imagined the Czech nation in its own historic-territorial framework. Arguing that the Bohemian lands were the historic homeland of the Czech nation (Czech-speakers of both Bohemia and Moravia), his vision was of territorial autonomy for this nation within a federalized Austrian Empire. Palacký had his own idea here of Czechs as loyal 'Austrians'. He also undoubtedly retained some inclusive sense of all those in the Bohemian lands, including German-speakers, forming part of the same 'historic nation'. However, his broader civic consciousness, his struggle as a liberal for basic civic rights in 1848, could rarely be divorced from his campaign on behalf of an underprivileged Czech nation defined in ethnic-linguistic terms.[39] Palacký's letter to the Frankfurt Parliament in April 1848, refusing to participate in its proceedings, was therefore a watershed like no other. On behalf of the Czech nation, he rejected its incorporation in a German-led national framework. His alternatives, set out at the Kremsier Parliament from late 1848—for a Czech nation flourishing within a federalized Austria—swung between a historic-territorial restructuring and a more radical ethnic-linguistic division seeking to separate Czechs from Germans and unite them with their Slovak 'brothers' to the east.[40]

---

[38] Kořalka, 'Welche Nationsvorstellungen', 38.
[39] On this issue, see Otto Urban, 'Český liberalismus v 19. století', in M. Znoj (ed.), *Český liberalismus: texty a osobnosti* (Prague, 1995), 19–20.
[40] Stanley Z. Pech, *The Czech Revolution of 1848* (Chapel Hill, 1969), 214–16.

Both of course were dead in the water as the Habsburgs restored their authority from 1849 and moved in the direction of a centralized absolutist state.

If the 1850s witnessed a 'détente of the nationalities', it was nevertheless a decade when many Czech communities (for example the Czech minority in the northern town of Reichenberg [Liberec]) first began to explore their national-cultural identity. A recent study has lambasted historians for anachronistically reading ethnicity back into the past, and exaggerating the degree of Czech-German national division in the mid-century Bohemian lands; allegedly, in many communities a local anational allegiance persisted for decades.[41] This may be true of Budweis [České Budějovice] in southern Bohemia, and probably also of Moravia where a Czech identity emerged much more slowly.[42] But there is less evidence that it matched the conditions in urban northern Bohemia. There the local German-speaking elites, with one eye on their northern cousins and another on their southern Austrian brothers, had a peculiar national awareness. They already defined themselves as German, German-Bohemian, or German-Austrian, and added to this was often regional affiliation to a local town or local political landscape. North Bohemia was just one area in the Monarchy where, as Maiken Umbach argues in this volume, regional and national identities could coexist. In regional Bohemian towns like Reichenberg or Eger [Cheb], civic values were trumpeted but an exclusionary ethnic campaign against Czechs was also only too evident.[43]

This is not to deny the continued fluidity of national identity in the 1860s when the Habsburgs restored a constitutional regime. Palacký and others for example stood on an anational ticket in the first elections of the decade. And in a debate of 1861 in the Bohemian diet, his son-in-law František Rieger set out the Czech leadership's view of what actually constituted the 'nation'. Echoing the language of Eötvös, Rieger noted that everybody belonged to a nation but that the word was always defined differently, according to criteria of state, history, or race. Thus the Czechs were a separate 'racial nation', but all the people of the Bohemian lands (Czechs or Germans) were one 'political nation'.[44] This definition matched the Czech leaders' struggle in the 1860s to secure Czech linguistic equality in

[41] J. King, *Budweisers into Czechs and Germans: A Local History of Bohemian Politics, 1848–1948* (Princeton, 2002). King's argument is weakened by insufficient (archival) evidence, and the possible atypicality of Budweis. However, it remains a thought-provoking study, particularly in elucidating the fluidity of national allegiance.

[42] For Moravia, see the excellent short study by M. Řepa, *Moravané nebo Češi? Vývoj českého národního vědomí na Moravě v 19.století* (Brno, 2001); and the essays in J. Malíř and R. Vlček (eds.), *Morava a české národní vědomí od středověku po dnešek* (Brno, 2001).

[43] For a preliminary discussion of this subject, see Mark Cornwall, 'The Construction of National Identities in the Northern Bohemian Borderland 1848–1871', in L. Cole (ed.), *Different Paths to the Nation: National Identity and State-Building in Germany, Italy and the Habsburg Monarchy c.1830–1870* (forthcoming, based on a workshop held at the Centro per gli Studi Storici Italo-germanici, Trento, June 2004).

[44] František Rieger, *Řeči dra: Františka Ladislava Riegra a jeho jednání v zákonodárných sborech*, 2 vols. (Prague, 1883–4), ii. 4–5: diet session of 9 April 1861.

Bohemia-Moravia and at the same time political autonomy for these provinces in a federalized Austria. Rieger perhaps hinted here also at some notion of a 'trinity' for Czech identity, for the Czech leaders still believed in an Austrian state-frame-work. But from the start they were rejecting Habsburg political centralism. In a famous declaration of 1868 they explained that the February Patent of 1861, which had established a centralized parliament in Vienna, had violated the deal made in 1526 between the Habsburgs and the 'Czech nation'.[45]

For sixteen years until 1878 the Bohemian Czechs would boycott the parliament in Vienna, falling back on the claim of Bohemian 'state right', especially after 1867 when the Habsburgs granted political autonomy to Hungary and inaugurated the dualist system.[46] This political boycott certainly helped to foment Czech nationalism at a local level where a new generation of educated Czech-speakers could be increasingly confident about their rights, their improving social status, and their overall demographic dominance over Germans. The populist side of Czech nationalism was most vividly expressed in the mass demonstrations (the *tábor* movement) for linguistic equality held around the Bohemian lands in the late 1860s. At the same time, when in 1870 the Austrian Prime Minister Hohenwart made a bold concession to 'state right' or Bohemian political autonomy, but then withdrew it in the face of German-Bohemian protests, the effect could only be to intensify Czech nationalist grievances.[47] The 1860s and 1870s were therefore critical decades of Czech passive resistance to Habsburg centralism. Politically, the results for the Czech leadership under Palacký were wholly negative, but the campaign in turn helped to further coalesce a sense of Czech national identity—linguistically based, forged increasingly across Bohemia-Moravia, and more precisely delineated from the German Other.

In contrast, many German liberals of the Bohemian lands in the years from 1861 to 1879 cultivated a 'progressive Austrian identity' which in theory had civic, inclusive qualities, but in practice asserted the superiority of German culture in the western half of the Monarchy.[48] Against the Czech claims to 'state right' which might be viewed as a thinly disguised agenda for Czech hegemony in Bohemia, German-Bohemian liberals embraced the February Patent and then the Austrian constitution of 1867, for both asserted centralized government and offered them security in numbers with other German-Austrians to the south.

---

[45] O. Urban, 'Der Böhmische Landtag', in Helmut Rumpler and Peter Urbanitsch (eds.), *Die Habsburgermonarchie 1848–1918*, vol. vii/2: *Verfassung und Parlamentarismus* (Vienna, 2000), 2014–15.

[46] Stepping up their protest, the Bohemian Czech leadership also boycotted the Bohemian diet in Prague from 1867 to 1878. But in a continued assertion of Moravian identity, Moravian Czechs were quicker to return to the Reichsrat and the Moravian diet (in 1873). See M. Řepa, 'Češi, Moravané a spor o pasivní politiku', *Český časopis historický*, 94 (1996), 38–65.

[47] On these crucial developments in accelerating the national divide, see J. Křen, *Die Konfliktgemeinschaft: Tschechen und Deutsche 1780–1918* (Munich, 1996), 144–54.

[48] See the analysis of P. Judson, *Exclusive Revolutionaries: Liberal Politics, Social Experience and National Identity in the Austrian Empire, 1848–1914* (Ann Arbor, 1996), 117–64.

After the Habsburgs' clash with Prussia in 1866 and Austria's exclusion from the new Germany, German-Bohemians could at least gain solace from their leading role in the newly constructed dualist empire. The emperor's chief minister, Baron Beust, who was a Saxon, seemed to provide an extra guarantee that, while this would be a 'German-Austria', it would retain something of its pan-German connections. And despite the temporary scare of the Hohenwart concessions to 'state right', the centralist character of Austria was reasserted in 1873 when deputies to the Vienna parliament were elected directly (rather than indirectly via the provincial diets). The German-Bohemians were thereby overriding the Czech agenda with an Austrian framework of their own. But their own ethnic German credentials were never far beneath the surface. Most notably, in Article 19 of the Austrian constitution (1867), they had been able to ensure that no bilingualism could be enforced in provincial education.[49] It was a ruling specifically designed to combat Czech linguistic expansion in Bohemia. It had the fatal effect of accelerating the Czech-German divide, and burying once and for all any notion of a bilingual 'Bohemian nation'.

In late 1870, on the eve of Germany's unification, the leading German-Bohemian newspaper stressed that 'the German in Austria is very much, indeed exclusively, an Austrian with his whole heart'.[50] However, ten years later the Austrian framework for Germans of the Bohemian lands looked far less secure, for a Czech agenda seemed to be increasingly privileged by the Austrian government in Vienna. In 1879, with the inauguration of Count Taaffe as Austrian Prime Minister, the Czech leaders had finally renounced their boycott and their insistence on 'state right', and moved to participate in the central government as an alternative tactic to secure Czech equality in the Bohemian lands. Here therefore, the Czechs under Rieger began to play the 'centralist' card and continued to do so intermittently until 1914. Through creeping linguistic equality (for example the Stremayr language decrees of 1880), through gradual electoral reform—the real fruits for Czechs of what might be called their 'sham-civic' cooperation with the Austrian centre were to be found in their ethnic gains at the expense of Germans in Bohemia.

In contrast, for German-Bohemians, the loss of power at the centre in 1879 was final and disastrous. It was followed in 1883 by their loss of power in the Bohemian diet, narrowing ever more their sphere of political influence, and pushing them 'back' into the security of their ethnicity. Many of course would retain their Austrian patriotism and seek still to manoeuvre in the Austrian framework through social and economic status. But many of the younger educated generation were pushed in an ethnic nationalist (*völkisch*) direction to defend their national assets (*Nationaler Besitzstand*) against the encroaching Czech. The way was set for a 'small nationalist war' in numerous Czech-German localities. The rhetoric was akin to

---

[49] Stourzh, 'Die Gleichberechtigung', 1012–14.
[50] *Reichenberger Zeitung*, no. 274, 23 Nov. 1870, 1: 'Österreich und Deutschland'.

that employed in actual wars elsewhere in Europe which had sharpened nationalist allegiances. But in the Bohemia lands, the ethnic battle was over language, schools, land, and even human beings (when counted at the decennial census). Both sides—Czech and German—mustered resources and set up propaganda societies from the 1880s to fight their nationalist corner.[51] In reviewing this phenomenon we must remember still that for many individuals or families in rural localities the nationalist battles could still pass them by, rarely precluding mixed marriages, and that nationalist allegiance was not at the forefront of their personal identity.[52] This notwithstanding, by the turn of the century new generations of ethnic nationalists were emerging, shaped in their vigilance by local nationalist societies whose rhetoric mirrored that of the politicians. It was an environment that bred intolerance of all those who were anational or shifting in their national allegiance, demonstrated most clearly by the rise of Czech and German anti-Semitism.[53]

The main German-Bohemian national platform was now to delimit and secure their German ethnic borders vis-à-vis Czech ethnic territory. In contrast, diametrically opposed, part of the Czech leadership continued to stress historic 'state right', and confidently to claim all of the Bohemian lands for the Czech nation. It can be seen therefore that both nationalist protagonists up to 1914 were operating with ethnic, historical, and centralist agendas when it suited their cause. But it was ethnic nationalism, based not just on language but on a perception of ingrained cultural difference, which increasingly undermined any broader Austrian patriotism in the decades before the First World War.

CONCLUSION

By the 1880s the force of ethnic nationalism, with its strong linguistic exclusivity, cannot be denied. However, we have seen that such a simple characterization for political nationalism in the Habsburg Monarchy is inadequate. Exploring the

[51] See Mark Cornwall, 'The Struggle on the Czech-German Language Border 1880–1940', *English Historical Review*, 109/433 (Sept. 1994), 914–51. For a recent overview of these developments see Catherine Albrecht, 'The Bohemian Question', in M. Cornwall (ed.), *The Last Years of Austria-Hungary: A Multi-National Experiment in Early Twentieth Century Europe* (Exeter, 2002), 75–96.

[52] Recently, American historians such as Pieter Judson and Jeremy King have rightly highlighted the danger of simple ethnic labelling by Habsburg historians. Even so, I would argue that by the 1880s a radical nationalist rhetoric was invading communities across the empire, forcing more and more individuals to declare their particular national allegiance according to 'ethnic criteria'. It was a subject which presented itself daily to the public through discussion in their newspapers and their local associations, and was reinforced periodically during elections or census-taking. In other words, ethnic allegiance became a prominent part of everyday public discourse in the Monarchy among educated individuals.

[53] The late nineteenth-century shift of Jewish allegiance from German to Czech is well set-out in Hillel Kieval's essays: *Languages of Community: The Jewish Experience in the Czech Lands* (Berkeley, 2000). For the intriguing notion of Austrian Jews having a 'tripartite identity' (an ethnic-civic amalgam of allegiance, or a variation on our notion of 'national trinity'), see also M. Rozenblit, *Reconstructing a National Identity: The Jews of Habsburg Austria during World War I* (Oxford, 2001), 23.

notion of some 'trinity' of identities—ethnic, historical, and centralist—seems to bring us closer to the real complexity of the nationalist phenomenon in this European space. The trinity was best embodied in the German-Austrians whose nationality, stretching across Central Europe, was often the most hazy. But a combination of ethnic and historic-territorial views of the nation was also to be found among the other 'historic' peoples—particularly the Magyars, Czechs, and Croats. They could construct a historic-territorial framework for their nations on a Western model, a framework that in theory had civic inclusive characteristics but in practice usually had an ethnic nationalist agenda.[54] For 'non-historic' peoples such as the Serbs and Romanians, a historic-territorial model also emerged, but one outside the borders of the Monarchy in the shape of independent Serbian and Romanian states centred on Belgrade and Bucharest. This added an extra, dangerous irredentist element to the nationalism challenging the empire's stability; and irredentism of course was also an ingredient in German, Polish, Italian, and Ruthene (Ukrainian) nationalism.

In the most basic terms, one might still assert that nationalism in the Habsburg Empire was caused by the struggle between dominant and subordinate nationalities, and the drive for internal sovereignty.[55] Yet perhaps its 'ultimate motor', as identified by József Eötvös, was in fact the tension between contradictory ethnic, historic, and centralist concepts of the 'nation' or state within the Habsburg framework. Ironically, despite this tension, and the nationalist rhetoric that often reached fever-pitch as if a military campaign was taking place, the Habsburg framework until 1914 was spacious enough to accommodate some flexibility, not least in the tactics of nationalist leaders who manoeuvred between the centre and periphery. It was during actual hostilities in the war of 1914–18 that this flexibility of allegiance really began to break down. Nationalist causes were reinvigorated when the Habsburg regime, under the banner of patriotic unity, suppressed civic and political freedoms, increasingly stereotyped domestic (national) loyalists and enemies, and alienated many while failing to solve an escalating economic crisis. In turn, by 1918, the nationalist grievances were picked up and deftly exploited in an Allied propaganda campaign which specifically privileged the nationalist agenda in order to undermine the empire's stability.[56] The nationalist mentalities that were bred in Austria-Hungary's last war paved the way for what came afterwards: new 'national states', new state borders, and a narrowing of horizons which produced in the inter-war period a far more virulent strain of ethnic nationalism.

[54] For some alternative ways of categorizing the nationalities, see Robert A. Kann, 'Zur Problematik der Nationalitätenfrage in der Habsburgermonarchie 1848–1918', in Wandruszka and Urbanitsch (eds.), *Die Habsburgermonarchie 1848–1918*, iii/2. 1326–9. Kann for example distinguishes Magyars, Croats, Romanians, Serbs, Slovaks, and Ruthenes as the peoples whose party-politics wholly revolved around the nationalist question in one form or another.

[55] R. Okey, *The Habsburg Monarchy c.1765–1918* (Basingstoke, 2001), 289.

[56] See Mark Cornwall, *The Undermining of Austria-Hungary: The Battle for Hearts and Minds* (Basingstoke, 2000).

10

Denmark, Norway, and Sweden

Pan-Scandinavianism and Nationalism

Mary Hilson

INTRODUCTION

In April 1814, 112 elected delegates assembled at Eidsvoll in Norway. Their task was to draft a constitution for a potentially independent Norwegian state, following the defeat of the Kingdom of Denmark, with which Norway had been united since 1380. The document which they eventually agreed was, for its time, one of the most liberal constitutions in Europe. It established a unicameral parliament (Storting) which possessed both tax-raising powers and a veto over the actions of the crown, elected by a democratic franchise which gave nearly half of adult male Norwegians the vote.[1] Norwegian independence as a sovereign state was, however, to be short-lived. During the summer of 1814, the Swedish Crown Prince sought, and gained, the support of his European allies in upholding the terms of the Treaty of Kiel, which had provided for the transferral of sovereignty over Norway from Denmark to Sweden. Following the resignation of the Norwegian king, the Storting voted to enter into a union with Sweden, and to elect and recognize Karl XIII of Sweden as the king of Norway. In doing so, the Storting was able to negotiate various concessions from Karl XIII's regent, the Crown Prince Karl Johan, with the result that Norway kept its liberal constitution, and its council and Storting actually gained a stronger position than that originally envisaged for these institutions at Eidsvoll. For this reason, the institutions of 1814—above all the *Grunnlov* or constitution—were to remain the central symbols of Norwegian national identity throughout the nineteenth century and even beyond: 17 May,

I would like to thank the editors of this volume, and David Harvey and Hanna Hodacs for their comments on earlier drafts of this chapter.

[1] One estimate suggests that 45.5 per cent of Norwegian men over 25 got the vote. S. Kuhnle, 'Stemmeretten i 1814', *Historisk Tidskrift* (Norway), 51 (1972), 373–90; cited in H. A. Barton, *Scandinavia in the Revolutionary Era, 1760–1815* (Minneapolis, 1986), 344.

when the *Grunnlov* was signed, is still celebrated enthusiastically as Norway's national day.[2]

If the constitutional struggles of 1814 mark the birth of the modern Norwegian sense of nationhood, then these events were paralleled by similar developments in both Sweden and Denmark. The upheavals of the Napoleonic wars resulted in major military defeats for these two states, which had rivalled each other for dominance in the Baltic over several centuries. The financial consequences of Sweden's disastrous war against Russia in 1808–9, which was to result in the loss of Swedish territory in Finland and Pomerania, precipitated a bloodless *coup d'état*, and the arrest and deposition of King Gustav IV Adolf and his heirs during the spring of 1809. The Swedish parliament or Riksdag convened on 1 May to agree a new constitution, which would end absolutism in favour of a balance of power between crown, council, and Riksdag, under the rule of a new dynasty. Meanwhile, although the news of the French Revolution of 1789 had been greeted with enthusiasm in Copenhagen, that enthusiasm produced no great stirring against the absolutism which had prevailed in Denmark since 1660, and was to survive intact until 1848. Even so, the climate of public opinion was becoming an increasingly important influence on the regime, which had since the late eighteenth century embarked on a major era of enlightened reform.[3]

The circumstances surrounding the emergence of the modern Nordic states in the early nineteenth century—the borders established then have, with some minor modifications, survived until the present[4]—point towards the strength of civic nationalism in Scandinavia. Denmark and Sweden had existed as territorial states, with a highly centralized bureaucracy, and a Protestant state church, since the sixteenth century. By the mid-eighteenth century, intellectual and elite groups connected with the bureaucratic class in both states had begun to develop ideas about a distinctive Swedish or Danish national character and national history.[5] Thus the conventional view of nineteenth-century nationalism in Scandinavia suggests that nation-building was a state-driven process inspired by the intellectual traditions of Enlightenment philosophy, which sought to turn the former

---

[2] 17 May was first celebrated on the tenth anniversary of the Eidsvoll meeting, to the dissatisfaction of the Swedish king, who would have much preferred his Norwegian subjects to have celebrated 4 November, the date when the Union was agreed.

[3] For a discussion of this point see Henrik Horstbøll and Uffe Østergård, 'Reform and Revolution: The French Revolution and the Case of Denmark', *Scandinavian Journal of History*, 15 (1990), 156–9.

[4] The borders of Sweden and Norway remain those of 1809 and 1814 respectively, except of course that the union between the two was dissolved in 1905. Denmark's North Atlantic possessions—Iceland, the Faeroe Islands, and Greenland—have gained increasing autonomy, resulting in full independence for Iceland in 1944. Denmark's southern border was not resolved until after the First World War.

[5] For a discussion of Danish national identity before 1789 see Ole Feldbæk, 'Fædrelandet og Indfødsret: 1700-tallets danske identitet', in Feldbæk (ed.), *Dansk identitetshistorie*, vol. i (Copenhagen, 1991). For Swedish eighteenth-century national identity, see Patrik Hall, *Den svenskaste historien: nationalism i Sverige under sex sekler* (Stockholm, 2000).

peasant subjects of multinational dynastic empires into citizens of liberal nation-states: Norwegians, Swedes, and Danes. This process rested on an understanding of the nation that was broad and inclusive. Ethnic nationalism could be perceived as a threat to the *helstatspolitik* of the multinational Danish state, which inspired proposals instead for a citizen's catechism and civic confirmation ceremonies at midsummer to inspire a love of *fædrelandet*.[6] Especially important in this process of civic nation-building was the establishment of some of the earliest national primary education systems in Europe.

Although nineteenth-century Scandinavian nationalism thus contained many 'civic' elements, the distinction between civic and ethnic forms was never a pure one. Romanticism was a significant influence, and was informed, especially after the 1840s, by ideas about the ethnic distinctiveness of the Scandinavian peoples. In recent years, some Nordic historians have argued that the predominance of the Enlightenment tradition in Scandinavia, albeit influenced by Romanticism, was distinctive enough to constitute a Nordic *Sonderweg*.[7] Overall, the phenomenon of Scandinavian nationalism seems to have made little impact on the historical literature on nations and nationalism, and even respected historians can betray a surprising ignorance about developments in northern Europe. Moreover, most accounts of Scandinavian nationalism—and indeed of nineteenth-century Scandinavian history in general—have been written by Scandinavian historians, who are themselves writing within a distinctively nationalist historiographical tradition.[8] This chapter presents an outsider's perspective, and in doing so considers the development of nationalism in all three Scandinavian states, rather than treating them separately.[9] The pan-Scandinavian approach is partly justified by the need to consider the movement for pan-Scandinavian unity as a key element of nineteenth-century Scandinavian nationalism. It is also the case however, that important similarities across the three cases justify a cross-national approach, not least the central and distinctive concept of the *folk*.

CIVIC NATIONALISM IN SCANDINAVIA

The constitutional reforms of the early nineteenth century were to become central to the development of the Scandinavian sense of nationhood, just as the republican tradition formed a key element of French nationalism. As the Norwegian

[6] Laurits Engeltoft, *Tanker om nationalopdragelsen* (1808). Cited in D. Kirby, *The Baltic World 1772–1993: Europe's Northern Periphery in an Age of Change* (London, 1995), 122.

[7] See Øystein Sørensen and Bo Stråth (eds.), *The Cultural Construction of Norden* (Oslo, 1997), Introduction.

[8] See Klas Åmark, 'Att skriva Norges—och Sveriges—historia', *Historisk Tidskrift* (Sweden) (2001), 406–21.

[9] Finland is regrettably omitted for practical reasons, although there seems little reason to doubt that in the development of Finnish nationalism, as in other aspects of nineteenth-century history, 'in all essentials . . . Finland remained much closer to the Scandinavian than to the Slavic-Russian world'. Kirby, *Baltic World*, 135. For this reason, the term 'Scandinavian' is preferred to 'Nordic' for the purposes of this chapter.

historian Øystein Sørensen has suggested, the Norwegian *Grunnlov* of 1814 almost achieved the status of a holy document, which was not under any circumstances to be violated, and which was staunchly defended against the attempted incursions of the Swedish king.[10] Although it bore the clear influences of similar documents of the era—principally those of revolutionary America and France—its authors were also determined to emphasize the Norwegian elements, and to place it within a Norwegian tradition stretching back to the medieval period.[11] Similarly, the new Swedish constitution of 1809 was seen by nationalist historians, such as Erik Gustaf Geijer, Anders Fryxell, and others, as marking the restoration of the traditional partnership between king and people, against the powerful interests of a foreign-influenced nobility.[12] This balance had been undermined by the experiences of the so-called Age of Freedom in the eighteenth century, when the role of the monarchy as the guarantor of the popular interest had been undermined by powerful organized interests in the Riksdag. In Denmark meanwhile, although absolutism survived the revolutionary era intact, the monarchy could nonetheless not afford to ignore the changing currents of public opinion. The presence of the *Frihedsstøtten* or Freedom Monument in Copenhagen, erected in 1797 to commemorate the state-sponsored agrarian reforms, served not merely as a marker of the popularity enjoyed by the absolutist Danish monarchs, in comparison with their less fortunate relatives elsewhere in Europe; it was also a visible and prominent reminder to the crown prince of his obligations as an enlightened ruler and of the role of the monarchy as the defender and protector of the national interest.[13]

Central to the civic concept of the *folk*—or people—in Scandinavia was the free and independent peasant farmer.[14] The so-called *odelsbonde* or *gårdmand* was the main beneficiary of the agrarian reforms of the late eighteenth century.[15] The most far-reaching reforms occurred in Denmark, where the efforts of the crown's Great Land Reform Commission, established in 1786, resulted in the transfer of over half of Denmark's peasant farms into freehold ownership during the twenty years or so after 1790. Thereafter, not only in Denmark, but also in Norway and Sweden, the freeholding peasant farmer achieved a hegemonic status as the ideal embodiment

---

[10] Øystein Sørensen, *Norsk idéhistorie*, vol. iii: *Kampen om Norges sjel* (Oslo, 2001), 81.

[11] Ibid. 66–7.

[12] This narrative has been described by one Swedish historian as 'a political narrative of the nation which has perhaps been stronger than any other in Swedish historical writing.' Hall, *Den svenskaste historien*, 99.

[13] See Horstbøll and Østergård, 'Reform and Revolution', for discussion of this point, in particular their claim that 'The freedom monument expresses the whole programme of the anti-aristocratic, popular absolutist ideology which had reformed the traditional landowner-dominated society from within' (166).

[14] For a discussion of the idealization of the peasantry see also the contributions by Stefan Berger and Vera Tolz in this volume.

[15] The word for a freeholding peasant is in Danish *gårdmand*, in Swedish *odalsbonde*, in Norwegian *odelsbonde*. The term is sometimes translated as 'yeoman'. The generic term *bonde*, in all three languages, is used to denote both 'farmer' and 'peasant'.

of the people or *folk*, to the exclusion of other groups, such as smallholders and landless labourers, within rural society.[16] Perhaps the best-known expression of this ideal in Sweden was to be found in Erik Gustaf Geijer's poem, *Folket var odalbönder* (The People were [freeholding] Peasants), written two years after the Swedish loss of Finland in 1809, and published in the journal of the Götiska Förbundet (Gothic Society).[17] Although agrarian reform in Sweden was not quite as dramatic as in Denmark, nonetheless the second half of the eighteenth century was marked by a great interest in all aspects of agrarian life, and concerted efforts to improve production resulting in a major expansion of the areas under cultivation (including encroachment on traditional Sami areas in the north of the country).[18] The virtues of the free peasant were in part derived from his intimate relationship with the harsh northern climate and landscape in which he and his ancestors had worked, thus cementing the bonds between *folk* and territory.[19]

Although the idealization of the peasant as the true representative of the Scandinavian *folk* clearly carried some romantic elements, it also had a distinctive civic character. As a citizen and a political actor the free peasant was also a political reality. Nowhere was this more clearly the case than in Norway, where *odelsretten*, or the right to freehold, was enshrined in the 1814 constitution. The president of the Eidsvoll assembly, Georg Sverdrup, drew parallels between the new constitution and the rights granted to the peasantry by the medieval Norwegian kings.[20] Even though Norway had not had its own king for over 400 years, it was argued, 'national' continuity was preserved in the institutions and traditions of peasant society. The 1814 constitution, by enfranchising all males over the age of 25 who either owned or leased property, made the participation of the peasantry in national political affairs a reality. Even in Denmark, despite the persistence of absolutism, the *gårdmænd*, as the equivalent group to the Norwegian *odelsbønder*, had increasing opportunities for political participation, through local commissions for the administration of the poor law of 1803 and the school ordinances of 1806 and 1814. In 1831 they gained more influence when, in response to the European revolutions the previous year, the Danish king established four assemblies of the estates (*stænderforsamlinger*) within his territory: one assembly for each of the duchies Slesvig and Holsten, one for Jylland (Jutland), and one for the islands. Although the franchise remained severely restricted—only one in forty of

[16] This idea emerges clearly in the work of liberal historians in the 1830s, who helped to establish agrarian reform and the hegemony of the free peasantry as one of the central narratives in Danish history. T. Kjærgaard, 'The Farmer Interpretation of Danish History', *Scandinavian Journal of History*, 10 (1985), 97–118, 101, n. 11.   [17] See Hall, *Den svenskaste historien*, 118 ff.

[18] The Sami people (or Laplanders) are generally recognized to be descended from the original inhabitants of the Scandinavian peninsula, and were ethnically and linguistically different from the majority population. They lived a largely nomadic existence based on reindeer husbandry, hunting, and fishing in the northern parts of Sweden, Norway, and Finland.

[19] See Hall, *Den svenskaste historien*, 89 ff. for a discussion of this point. For a discussion of this point see also Oliver Zimmer's chapter in this volume.

[20] Sørensen, *Kampen om Norges sjel*, 67.

the inhabitants of the kingdom had the vote—freeholding peasant farmers made up a considerable proportion of those elected to the new assemblies.[21]

Moreover, the peasants were also an important group in the development of the main institutions of civil society in nineteenth-century Scandinavia. The major inspiration here was the Danish clergyman and writer N.F.S. Grundtvig, whose concept of the unity of land, Christianity, and *folk* was one of the main influences on the development of nationalism, not only in Denmark but throughout Scandinavia.[22] His main legacy lay in his success in 'transforming the traditional amorphous peasant feelings of community and solidarity into symbols and words with relevance for a modern industrialized imagined community'.[23] Grundtvigian ideas found practical expression in the associations of peasant society through Denmark and indeed in Norway, especially the revivalist groups of the 1830s and 1840s, and the Folk High School movement of the second half of the nineteenth century. The relationship between religious revival and national awakening is a complex one, but the experience of public life gained through participation in such organizations undoubtedly contributed to the growing political confidence of the peasantry. From the late 1830s, politically active peasants made common cause with bourgeois liberalism, and formed the nucleus of support for the national liberal movement in Denmark during the 1840s.[24]

An important tool in the process of turning peasants into citizens was the relatively early establishment of a national primary education system in the Scandinavian lands. As the Danish historian Ole Feldbæk has noted, there was almost certainly little sense of 'Danishness' among the peasantry in 1789. If this had changed by 1848, when many of these peasants were called upon to fight against Germany, then the national primary schools must be counted as one of the most significant influences.[25] To be sure, the decision of the crown, in 1789, to establish a state commission on popular education was partly driven by the practical wish to educate peasants in new agricultural techniques, but it was also inspired by other concerns: to create patriotic and 'useful' citizens.[26] The final proposals were toned down somewhat, and more emphasis was given to the

---

[21] Kirby, *The Baltic World*, 89; V. Skovgaard-Petersen, *Danmarks historie*, vol. v: *Tiden 1814–1864* (Copenhagen, 1985), 181.

[22] For Grundtvig, see Flemming Lundgreen-Nielsen, 'Grundtvig og danskhed', in Ole Feldbæk (ed.), *Danmarks identitetshistorie*, vol. iii: *Folkets Danmark 1848–1940* (Copenhagen, 1992).

[23] U. Østergård, 'Nation-building Danish Style: State, Nation and National Identity in the Danish Nation-State in the Nineteenth Century', in Ø. Sørensen (ed.), *Nordic Paths to National Identity in the Nineteenth Century* (Oslo, 1994), 50.

[24] See Skovgaard-Petersen, *Tiden 1814–1864*, 185.

[25] O. Feldbæk, 'Skole og identitet 1789–1848: lovgivning og lærebøger', in Feldbæk (ed.), *Dansk identitetshistorie*, vol. ii: *Et yndigt land 1789–1848* (Copenhagen, 1991), 255.

[26] According to the commission, in a proposal submitted to the crown in 1799, the aims of the new schools would be, 'to educate them that be good and upright Persons in Accordance with the Teaching of the Gospels and Common Sense, and to give them such Knowledge and Accomplishments that by the Use of these they can become contented People and *useful Citizens to the State*.' Cited in Feldbæk, 'Skole og identitet', 266. Emphasis added.

practical side when the new system of elementary education was established by edict in 1814. Yet many of the reformers were also concerned that the education system should inculcate a love of the fatherland into the children it was designed to benefit. From the 1820s, partly inspired by Grundtvigian ideas about national and Christian awakening, there was a growing nationalist emphasis to the literary and historical content of school textbooks. C. F. Allen's *Haandbog i Fædrelandets Historie* (1840), which was typical in its emphasis on the centrality of the agrarian reforms, and the *gårdmænd* class which they created, ran to eight editions between 1840 and 1881, and an abridged version appeared as a school textbook.[27] Norway had a fairly comprehensive primary education system even earlier, since the 1730s. As in the Danish—and indeed the Swedish—'folk schools' (*folkskolor*), the curriculum was partly designed to give peasant children the requisite skills for effective agriculture, but also to create good Christians and citizens. In the words of the reformed school law in 1848, 'The aims of the Peasant Schools shall be to support the domestic Upbringing by giving the Young People a healthy Christian Education, so that by this means [they] may acquire the Knowledge and Accomplishments which every member of Society should have.'[28] By the second half of the nineteenth century, schoolteachers had become an important group, supported in their work as 'agents of modernization and nation-builders' by publications such as the journal *Folkevennen* (People's Friend), produced by the Society for the Advancement of Popular Enlightenment (Selskabet for Folkeoplysningens Fremme) to disseminate articles on all aspects of Norwegian history and traditions among schoolteachers.[29] The development of a truly state education system was finally consolidated by reform in 1860, when the Storting voted to support a new national textbook.[30]

Taken as a whole, there is therefore some evidence for the strength of civic nationalism in early nineteenth-century Scandinavia. The monarchies of Denmark and Sweden had been able to establish a degree of territorial integrity and continuity as nation-states in the seventeenth century or even earlier, and from the late eighteenth century made concerted efforts to create and foster bonds of loyalty between state and *folk*. In Norway, the civic institutions of 1814 were to form the central basis of nationalist demands for independence throughout the nineteenth century. As one prominent Norwegian historian has suggested, the pro-independence, pro-democracy Venstre Party of the 1880s was the natural

---

[27] C. F. Allen, *Haandbog i Fædrelandets Historie med stadigt Henblik paa Folkets og Statens indre Udvikling* (Copenhagen, 1840). See Kjærgaard, 'The Farmer Interpretation of Danish History'; Feldbæk, 'Skoler og identitet'.

[28] Lov angaande Almueskolevæsenet i Kjøbstederne, 1848. Cited in D. Thorkildsen, 'En nasjonal og moderne utdanning', in Ø. Sørensen (ed.), *Jakten på det norske: perspektiver på utviklingen av en norsk nasjonal identitet på 1800-tallet* (Oslo, 1998), 266.

[29] A.-L. Seip, 'Det norske «vi»—kulturnasjonalisme i Norge', in Sørensen ibid.; Thorkildsen, 'En nasjonal og moderne utdanning', 267–8.

[30] P. A. Jensen, *Læsebog for folkeskolen og folkehjemmet* (1863). Thorkildsen, 'En nasjonal og moderne utdanning', 269.

inheritor of the traditions of 1814.[31] In all three states, particularly influential was the existence of a strong, centralized, and loyal class of bureaucrats and intellectuals, who played a key role in the development of state nationalism: 'The tradition of the strong Swedish state, combined with an organized education system which was under state control relatively early, worked against the development of an anti-state nationalist movement, driven by intellectuals.'[32] This applied even to Norway. The establishment of a Norwegian university at Christiania in 1813 (previously state bureaucrats had received their higher education in Copenhagen) generated some of the key contributors to the establishment of a civic infrastructure after 1814.[33] Yet this could also provoke competing visions of the nation. After 1837, when peasant representatives gained a degree of control over local government, this was to bring them into more or less open conflict with the urban bureaucracy, at that time pursuing its own national project of modernization and reform. Inspired by the increasingly influential current of national romanticism, a new generation of Norwegian nationalists, most prominently Henrik Wergeland, began to champion the *bønder* as the more authentic representatives of the true national interest, against the Danish influences and outlook of the so-called *intelligenskretsen*, or intellectual elite.[34] The next part of the chapter will examine these and other manifestations of ethnic nationalism in Scandinavia.

ETHNIC NATIONALISM IN SCANDINAVIA

The question of ethnicity had in fact arisen rather earlier than the 1830s. Behind the liberalism of the Norwegian constitution of 1814 lay a heated debate about the relationship between ethnicity and citizenship: were the citizens of the new Norwegian state required to be native-born Norwegians? Several prominent participants in the Eidsvoll debate argued that this should indeed be the case, and that only those born in Norway, or born of Norwegian parents, should be entitled to full Norwegian citizenship, and thus eligible to serve in the state bureaucracy. The problem was eventually resolved by a compromise, which allowed the Storting the right to decide who was and who was not eligible for citizenship, but significantly, Jews—and indeed Jesuits and members of monkish orders—were excluded outright from consideration.[35] The attempted definition, partly at least, of the Norwegian nation and *folk* in ethnic terms reflected the residual fear, among certain groups in Norway, of continued subordination to either Denmark

---

[31] Sørensen, *Kampen om Norges sjel*.

[32] Hall, *Den svenskaste historien*, 305.

[33] S. Langholm, 'The New Nationalism and the New Universities: The Case of Norway in the Early Nineteenth Century', *Scandinavian Journal of History*, 20 (1995), 51–60.

[34] See Sørensen, *Kampen om Norges sjel*; O. J. Falnes, *National Romanticism in Norway* (New York, 1933), 28–33. [35] Sørensen, *Kampen om Norges sjel*, 69 ff.

or Sweden, which was to become a perennial theme of Norwegian nationalism during the nineteenth century.

As far as Sweden was concerned, the loss of Finland in 1809 was significant not only in terms of its constitutional repercussions, but also in that it created a nation-state which was much more ethnically homogeneous.[36] Consequently, after 1809, there was a marked growth of interest in the Swedish people as a distinctive ethnic group. The work of the seventeenth-century scholar Olof Rudbeck on Viking mythology was rediscovered and published by the Götiska Förbundet in its journal *Iduna*. The Götiska Förbundet, founded at Uppsala in 1811, was also active in promoting antiquarian and archaeological research.[37] The popular and influential lecture series on Swedish history, delivered at Uppsala university in the years 1815–19 by the historian Erik Gustaf Geijer, may, like the Götiska Förbundet, be seen as a response to the national crisis caused by the defeat of 1809.[38] Yet even in this context, there was probably a greater emphasis on the historical continuity of civic institutions and virtues, and incidentally on the Protestantism of the Swedish monarchs, than on the existence of a distinctive ethnic spirit or culture.[39]

Unlike Sweden and Norway, and despite the loss of territories after the Napoleonic wars, Denmark remained a conglomerate, multinational state after 1814. Indeed here, expressions of Danish ethnic nationalism could be taken as a sign of opposition to the Crown's *helstatspolitik*, and were to be discouraged. Thus the introduction of *Indfødsretten* in 1776, which restricted the civil service to those born within the territories of the Danish crown was not an expression of ethnic exclusiveness, but rather an attempt 'to create harmony between the Danish, Norwegian and German populations within the conglomerate state (helstat)... [and] to construct a common identity, focused on the absolute monarchy and state patriotism.'[40] Yet it also marked the beginnings of a challenge to the multi-ethnic inclusiveness of the Danish *helstat*, expressed in the emerging sense of difference from, and hostility towards, German influences in Denmark.

The flashpoint in the German-Danish relationship was, of course, the issue of the two southern duchies, Slesvig and Holsten.[41] As in so many crucial border regions, there were no clear-cut lines of linguistic or cultural influence here;

---

[36] S. I. Angell, 'Nasjonale symbol i Skandinavia', in Krister Ståhlberg (ed.), *Norden och Europa: språk, kultur och identitet* (Copenhagen, 1999), 35; B. Stråth, 'The Swedish Path to National Identity in the Nineteenth Century', in Ø. Sørensen (ed.), *Nordic Paths to National Identity in the Nineteenth Century* (Oslo, 1994), 55.

[37] For the Götiska Förbundet, see Torkel Molin, *Den rätta tidens mått: Göthiska Förbundet, fornforskningen och det antikvariska landskapet* (Umeå, 2003).

[38] Hall, *Den svenskaste historien*, 132–40.

[39] Stråth, 'The Swedish Path to National Identity'.

[40] O. Feldbæk and V. Winge, 'Tyskerfejden 1789–1790: den første nationale konfrontation', in Feldbæk (ed.), *Dansk identitetshistorie* ii. 9.

[41] And also the tiny duchy of Lauenburg, which became part of the Danish United Monarchy after 1814. For the sake of consistency, and because the issue is examined here from the Danish perspective, I have opted to use the Danish spellings for the duchies throughout. For discussion of the Slesvig-Holsten question see also Brian Vick's chapter in this volume, 162–3.

instead the population practised an 'everyday bilingualism', while maintaining their loyalty to the Danish crown.[42] The opposition movement which emerged in the duchies during the 1830s was above all liberal, rather than national; it was neither pro-German nor anti-Danish, but sought constitutional reforms and political advance in line with the region's superior economic development.[43] Nor too were demands for the use of Danish over German in certain districts necessarily an expression of nationalism; rather they amounted to an assertion of local rights against the interference of a centralized state and its largely German-speaking officialdom.[44] Nonetheless, there were those who were beginning to argue for a closer bond between Denmark and Slesvig on the basis of a shared language and culture, such as the Kiel professor Christian Paulsen, whose book, *Ueber Volkshümlichkeit und Staatsrecht des Herzogthums Schleswig* (1832) made the case for the 'Danishness' of Slesvig since ancient times.[45] Inspired by Paulsen's arguments, various societies undertook campaigns to promote the use of Danish throughout Slesvig during the 1830s, through the publication and distribution of subsidized books, and the establishment of a Danish-language press.

The Danish king's edict (*sprogreskriptet*) of 1840, which declared that Danish should become the language of justice and administration in those areas of Slesvig where it was used in schools and church, was not so much of an assertion of Danish ethno-linguistic supremacy within the duchy, as an expression of *helstatspolitik*.[46] Yet the edict aroused the hostility of the largely German-speaking estates, to an extent which surprised the regime in Copenhagen, and helped to divide the liberal movements along national lines. Danish liberals appealed to the king to defend the Danish language in Slesvig, and one of their number, Hiort Lorenzen deliberately caused controversy by his insistence on speaking Danish in addressing the Slesvig assembly in November 1842. The situation was further complicated by two external developments. The first was the fear that Holsten, as a member of the German confederation, represented a threat to Danish security policy. The second was the issue of the succession in the duchies. In response to the intervention of the duke of Augustenborg, the king attempted to clarify the situation through an open letter of 1846, which declared that the Danish succession laws (allowing succession through the female line) applied in Slesvig and Lauenburg, but not in Holsten. The liberal movement within the duchies, hitherto concerned with seeking constitutional advances within the Danish *helstat*, now became indivisibly linked with the claims of the Augustenborg dynasty as a means of preserving the unity of the duchies.

---

[42] Kirby, *The Baltic World*, 120; Skovgaard-Petersen, *Tiden 1814–1864*, 192.

[43] Skovgaard-Petersen, *Tiden 1814–1864*, 193–4.   [44] Kirby, *The Baltic World*, 119–20.

[45] Skovgaard-Petersen, *Tiden 1814–1864*, 193.

[46] If anything, the edict was intended as an institutionalization of bilingualism: Danish was to be used alongside German as an official language, but Danish-speaking children were also entitled to instruction in German where their parents wished. Skovgaard-Petersen, *Tiden 1814–1864*, 191.

Meanwhile, the national question had become central to the liberal agenda within Denmark. A leading national liberal, Orla Lehmann, made an influential speech in 1842 declaring the river Eider—the southern border of the duchy of Slesvig—to be the historic southern border of Denmark itself. Denmark need have no claim to Holsten, which after all was a member of the German confederation, but Slesvig, by language, culture, and law, was historically and incontrovertibly part of the kingdom of Denmark. National liberalism was thus a challenge to the multinational *helstatspolitik* of the crown. As yet, it still retained strong civic elements: Slesvig could be considered Danish by virtue of its shared laws and institutions, rather than any sense of shared ethnicity, despite the centrality of the language question. 'Slesvig was an ancient Danish territory, Holsten was German, and the succession laws in Slesvig were the same as in the kingdom. The arguments were overwhelmingly civic, while national self-determination remained somewhat secondary, despite all sympathy for popular Danishness in Slesvig.'[47] Yet the emergence of the notion of a 'Denmark proper' within the United Monarchy, and the schism between Danish and Slesvig-Holsten liberals over the question of the duchies laid the roots for a more assertive sense of Danishness defined by culture and language, and most importantly, differentiated from the culture and language of Denmark's increasingly threatening southern neighbour. It was of course the war of 1864, and defeat by Prussia, which finally cemented such ideas, and by then nationalism had lost many of its liberal elements. But during the 1840s and 1850s there was a further aspect to the notion of a distinctive national community north of the Eider, namely the movement for pan-Scandinavianism.

PAN-SCANDINAVIANISM

The roots of pan-Scandinavianism lay in the 'literary medievalism' which emerged in Scandinavia, as elsewhere, from the late eighteenth century. A new interest in old Icelandic language and literature gave rise to the idea of a linguistic bond between the Scandinavian peoples, which found expression in various projects to enhance the mutual intelligibility of the Scandinavian languages, and to promote the literary connections between them.[48] From the 1820s this was reflected in calls for more cultural cooperation, and in the increased meetings and exchanges between scientists and other scholars across the Scandinavian countries. Despite the emphasis on the shared literary inheritance from the ancient

---

[47] Skovgaard-Petersen, *Tiden 1814–1864*, 197.
[48] There were several attempts to produce dictionaries emphasizing the similarities between the three Scandinavian languages: J. K. Høst, *Svensk haandordbog for Danske* (Copenhagen, 1799); S. Lundblad, *Dansk-norsk och svensk ordbok* (Stockholm, 1819); and the most ambitious, L. K. Daa, *Svensk-norsk haand ordbog* (Christiania, 1838–41). See Åke Holmberg, 'On the Practicability of Scandinavianism: Mid Nineteenth Century Debate and Aspirations', *Scandinavian Journal of History*, 9 (1984), 174–5.

past, early nineteenth-century pan-Scandinavianism was politically a product of the cosmopolitan and universal emphases of enlightenment thinking. The main impulse for the unification of the Nordic peoples lay in the idea that unity was desirable in order to achieve the full potential of northern civilization, which the individual states were too small and uninfluential to realize on their own.[49] It was only later that pan-Scandinavianism became more clearly influenced by the national romantic idea of a nation as a community of descent. The unity of the Scandinavian *folk*, based on 'community in blood and spirit' (*felleskap i blod og ånd*), was a popular theme of the Romantic literature of the 1830s and 1840s, and of the influential journal *Brage og Idun*, founded in 1839, and edited by a disciple of Grundtvig, Frederik Barfod. The strongest support for pan-Scandinavianism was found in Denmark, where it became closely associated with the national liberals' desire for a Danish nation-state, incorporating Slesvig, under a liberal constitution. The national liberal journal *Fædrelandet* became the central focus for both Scandinavianism and the so-called 'Eider policy' proclaimed by Lehmann in 1842. But Scandinavian unity was also attractive to Swedish national liberals, for whom the Norwegian Eidsvoll constitution was held up as a liberal model for a new unified state.

The relationship between liberalism and Scandinavianism became strained however, when the new liberal regime in Copenhagen went to war against Prussia in 1848, and, after an initial hesitation, the Swedish king agreed to send Swedish and Norwegian troops in support of Denmark. Liberals in the Riksdag were initially supportive, but increasingly came to perceive the king's move as a distraction from the constitutional issue. Although liberal newspapers continued after 1848 to propagandize in favour of Swedish assistance to Denmark, there was a marked cooling in enthusiasm for Scandinavianism. The idea of political unity between the Scandinavian states became more closely associated with the dynastic ambitions of the Swedish king, seen by royalists as a vindication of the Swedish-Norwegian union, and marked by unsuccessful proposals to alter the Danish succession and unite the three states under the Swedish king. Swedish liberals, meanwhile, turned their attention briefly to Finland, and following the outbreak of the Crimean war in 1853, the possibility was mooted, briefly, of joining France and Britain to defeat Russia and reconquer Finland to revive a great northern power. These aspirations—which were conclusively laid to rest following the peace of Paris in 1856—represented both a critique of tsarist absolutism, and also of the broadly pro-Russian foreign policy of the Swedish crown.[50] The proposals also suggest the limitations of ethnic pan-Scandinavianism, for there is little to suggest that they were derived from a sense of ethnic, cultural, or linguistic 'brotherhood' between Finns and Swedes, despite the existence of a Swedish-speaking minority in Finland. Rather, the revival

---

[49] J. Sanness, *Patrioter, intelligens og Skandinaver: norske reaksjoner på skandinavismen før 1848* (Oslo, 1959), 3.
[50] N. Elvander, 'Från liberal skandinavism till konservativ nationalism i Sverige', *Scandia*, 27 (1961), 366–86.

of '*storsvensk*' ambitions was driven by more universal concerns: 'The Scandinavian peoples have a great task in the history of humanity, and they will achieve that task more quickly than anyone has imagined if only their strength is boosted through some great thought, some great aim, out of the situation of small-mindedness, peevishness and unreasonableness which we now find ourselves in.'[51] Here, Swedish liberals could find some common ground with those, such as the Norwegian historian P.A. Munch, who distanced themselves from Scandinavianism after 1848, arguing instead for recognition of a broader Germanic fellowship. The Germans and the 'Northerners' were descended from one race, and were united by 'blood and Christianity' against the threat to the east. The crucial frontier for Scandinavia was not the river Eider, but the Torneå, which marked the border between Sweden and the Russian Empire.[52] Later in the nineteenth century these ideas were to become increasingly informed by developing theories of evolution and race, which placed the Nordic/Germanic peoples high up the racial hierarchy.

Various reasons could be put forth for why Scandinavianism failed to result in a unified state similar to Germany or Italy. The suggestion that Scandinavia lacked cultural or linguistic unity is problematic, for, as David Laven shows in his contribution to this volume, there was precious little of this in Italy either. But it is the case that the economic impulse for unification was less strong. An attempt to found an equivalent to the *Zollverein* failed. Most importantly, Scandinavia lacked a Piedmont or a Prussia—a state with sufficient might and ambition to drive through the project of political unity. It was, in fact, Bismarck's aspirations to unite Germany that was to mark the final demise of aspirations for Scandinavian unity. Karl XV of Sweden's promise of 20,000 troops to help Denmark defend the Eider against Prussian aggression came to nothing very much, and proved of little consequence to Bismarck, who crossed the Eider in February 1864, and ignored the Swedish promises of full diplomatic support to Denmark in the ensuing peace conference. So if 1864 marked the 'high tide' of support for pan-Scandinavianism, it also marked the beginnings of a rapid retreat. After 1864 both Danish and Swedish nationalists pursued their own interests, which for Denmark were dominated by the relationship with Germany and the southern border, and for Sweden, as we have seen, were marked by hostility towards Russia. The dream of pan-Scandinavian unity gave way to the markedly less ambitious schemes for intra-Nordic cooperation between sovereign nation-states.

NATIONAL ROMANTICISM

National Romanticism, derived in the first instance from Germany, had a clear impact on Scandinavian culture from the 1840s. As in Germany, the Romantic current found expression above all in a new enthusiasm for the vernacular culture

---

[51] *Göteborgs Handels- och Sjöfarts-Tidning*, 19–21/7 (1854); cited in Elvander, 'Från liberal skandinavism', 371.　　　[52] Sørensen, *Kampen om Norges sjel*, 253.

of the peasantry, as the bearers of an 'authentic' and Scandinavian tradition, and also in the scholarly interest in the language and literature of the old Norse peoples. These ideas undoubtedly had some political influence—in Denmark and Sweden at least—on pan-Scandinavian nationalism from the 1840s, and some pan-Scandinavianists were motivated by ideas of common descent. Yet it would be difficult to categorize pan-Scandinavianism as a pure example of an 'ethnic nationalist' movement. The aspiration for pan-Scandinavian unity before 1848 was essentially a liberal aspiration, linked to demands for constitutional reform, as was the Swedish liberals' attempt to revive interest in Finland at the time of the Crimean war. The vision of a united Scandinavian state was, probably for most Scandinavianists, not the unstoppable destiny of a pre-ordained national group, but instead a practical way to realize demands for constitutional reform, and economic and political modernization. In this way the failed movement for pan-Scandinavianism was clearly analogous to its successful counterpart in Italy. Yet nor was Scandinavianism a pure form of 'civic nationalism': after all, the proclamation of the Eider as the southern border of both Denmark and Scandinavia was clearly premissed on ethnic and linguistic difference, as was the hostility towards Russia.

Support for the Scandinavian ideal in Norway was perhaps most closely associated with the more cosmopolitan outlook of the modernizers, such as Ludvig Kristensen Daa, who saw in the *Zollverein* a model for creating a more democratic, liberal, and industrialized Norway.[53] What Norwegian historians have generally described as the 'breakthrough' of national Romanticism from the 1840s was concerned less with the unity of the Scandinavian *folk* as a whole, more with the special characteristics of the Norwegians. For Norwegian nationalists influenced by these new currents, 'the real Norway' was to be found away from the Danish-influenced towns, in the traditions, dialects, and customs of peasant society, which were enthusiastically studied by folklorists, historians, and philologists. The key influence on these developments was the work of the philosopher Marcus Jacob Monrad, whose understanding of nationality as a primordial and natural category was clearly derived from the German tradition.[54]

National Romanticism in Norway was especially influential in three different ways. The first of these was the interest in folklore as the main expression of the essential character of the Norwegian *folk*, of which perhaps the best-known example was the collection of folktales published by Asbiørnsen and Moe in 1841–4. The second concerns the so-called Norwegian history school, which was associated in particular with Rudolf Keyser and P.A. Munch, and their research in Norwegian medieval history. The aim of these scholars, expressed in the words of another adherent, G.F. Lundh, in 1832, was to show that the Norwegian people were 'one of Europe's oldest historically renowned Peoples, not merely a weak progeny of current Upheavals'.[55] Empirical research suggested that the

---

[53] Ibid. 239 ff.   [54] Ibid. 169.
[55] Cited in O. Dahl, *Norsk historieforskning i 19. og 20. århundre* (Oslo, 1959), 37.

Norwegian people were the original members of the Nordic race, 'north Germans' who immigrated to Scandinavia and settled at Trøndelag, and distinguished themselves from the later mixed groups who settled in Sweden and Denmark.[56] This so-called 'immigration theory' (*innvandringsteorien*) was widely accepted as an objective historical account, but it also provided an ideal myth of origin (*en norsk opprinnelsemyte*) for a Norwegian *folk* distinguished from its neighbours, and it was a myth that was to gain a widespread influence through its dissemination via school textbooks.

The third important element of Norwegian national Romanticism was language. The Norwegian historians drew on contemporary philology to support their work, for, according to Keyser, 'Language is . . . the strongest Expression of the Distinctiveness of a People, and it should be noted . . . that Relationship between Languages, when it is an inner Relationship distinguishable in the roots of the language and its construction . . . always denotes a Relationship between Peoples.'[57] The Norwegians could be shown to be the true inheritors of the language and culture of the Vikings, and thus the purest remnants of the original Norse people.[58] But there was a problem with the Norwegian language. The written language was, to all intents and purposes, very similar to Danish, since it had been principally the language of the state bureaucracy. This had caused some problems at the time of Eidsvoll, and sparked an academic interest in the roots of the Norwegian language, concerned mainly with attempts to establish the difference between 'pure' Norwegian and Danish. The most famous protagonist in the mid-century language debate was Ivar Aasen, whose early researches on the peasant dialects were received with acclaim, as proof that the language of the sagas was still used by the Norwegian peasants. Aasen thereafter devoted himself to attempts to synthesize a purer version of the written language from the peasant dialects— so-called *landsmål* or New Norwegian.

Clearly, therefore, there were strong ethnic elements to Norwegian nationalism, especially as it crystallized into a more concerted movement for independence from the mid-nineteenth century. In this respect, Norwegian nationalism is analogous to East European variants, with its emphasis on a people set apart from the dominant group in the state of which they were a part, defined by common descent, shared cultural inheritance, and language. Nonetheless, Norwegian historians have played down the influence of the national Romantic tradition on Norwegian nationalism. Aasen's work was influenced by the traditions of rural democracy in opposition to the centralizing force of urbanization, as well as by

---

[56] This was presented in Keyser's thesis: *Nordmændenes herkomst og folkeslegtskab* (1839).

[57] Cited in Dahl, *Norsk historieforskning*, 42.

[58] Keyser again: 'There is . . . every Ground to assume that, just as the Norwegian Branch of the Tribe was that which had kept itself most pure from Fusion with foreign Peoples, so too was this same [group] also in Possession of the richest and most uncorrupted Tradition from the Tribe's ancient Past.' Ibid. 46.

national Romanticism.[59] The same ambiguity was found in the Grundtvigian Folk High Schools, which, in their aspirations to awaken the Norwegian national spirit (*folkeånd*) were important promoters of *landsmål*, but were also associated with democratization and the development of civil society.[60] One recent historian of Norwegian nationalism has played down the influence of the Romantic tradition: 'There were clear romantic elements in [the work of] both Munch and Aasen, but only elements. Norwegian national romanticism was not only full of conflicts. It was also not so overwhelmingly romantic as it might perhaps seem.'[61]

What is clear however, is that after mid-century, nationalism in Scandinavia had lost much of its earlier inclusive, civic aspirations, and was instead increasingly based on a sense of ethnic difference, defined by the distinctiveness of Scandinavian language and cultural traditions. This took different forms in each of the three countries. It was perhaps most clearly distinguishable in Norway, where nationalists sought to disentangle their nation from its Danish past and Swedish present. There were strong elements of ethnic nationalism in the attempts to promote *landsmål*, and to distinguish the users of the New Norwegian written language as 'true' Norwegians, against the urban users of the Danish-Norwegian written language (*bokmål*).[62] From the last quarter of the nineteenth century this movement came to be partly associated with the twin struggles for parliamentary democracy and for independence from the union with Sweden, and thus retained a strong emancipatory element; although *landsmål* was also used to assert the separate identity and interests of the rural regions against the centralized power of the state.[63] In Denmark and Sweden late nineteenth-century nationalism was, to a much greater extent than in Norway, part of the official ideology of the state. In Sweden in particular, nationalism was increasingly perceived as a potentially integrating force against threats to the nation that were both internal and external: mass emigration, working-class unrest, and the Russian Empire. In the face of these fears, Swedish peasant culture and traditions were commemorated formally in the open-air museum at Skansen in Stockholm, which was conceived not only as a museum but also as a place of public celebration.[64] The identification of Swedes as ethnic

---

[59] See Oddmund Løkensgard Hoel, 'Ivar Aasen som opposisjonell nasjonalist', in Sørensen (ed.), *Jakten på det norske*.

[60] Thorkildsen, 'En nasjonal og moderne utdanning'.

[61] Sørensen, *Kampen om Norges sjel*, 225.

[62] Ø. Sørensen, 'Hegemonikamp om det norske', in Sørensen (ed.), *Jakten på det norske*, 34–6.

[63] See Maiken Umbach's chapter in this volume. The notion of a centre-periphery divide has been one of the most enduring themes within Norwegian history writing.

[64] S. Sörlin, 'Artur Hazelius och det nationella arvet under 1800-talet', in H. Medelius et al. (eds.), *Nordiska Museet under 125 år* (Stockholm, 1998). For the cult of rural Sweden around the turn of the century, see Nils Edling, *Det fosterländska hemmet: egnahemspolitik, småbruk och hemideologi kring sekelskiftet 1900* (Stockholm, 1996).

Scandinavians, which increasingly drew on theories of race and pan-Germanic brotherhood, also helped to differentiate Sweden from its Slavic neighbours, although that distinction was also cemented by civic elements: the free peasantry in contrast to serfdom, Protestantism, and constitutionalism. Nationalist currents found principal expression in Sweden, as in so many European countries in the late nineteenth century, in calls for increased defence expenditure against a growing threat, in this case from Russia.[65]

CONCLUSION

It is clearly impossible to characterize Scandinavian nationalism—whether in the sense of nationalism in Denmark, Norway, and Sweden respectively, or in the sense of the movement for pan-Scandinavianism—as either purely ethnic, drawing inspiration predominantly from Romantic ideas about ethnic communities of descent in the German tradition, or as purely civic, derived from the French Enlightenment tradition. In Scandinavia, as elsewhere, there were many different ways of imagining the nation. Anthony Smith has attempted to distinguish a 'core doctrine' of nationalism, but points out that in itself this was inadequate as a theory of social change or political action, and thus nationalism accrued many other different meanings and theories in specific contexts.[66] On the surface, at least, Scandinavian nationalism underwent a shift across the nineteenth century. Early nineteenth-century Scandinavian nationalism was broadly liberal in character, and identified the nation as an inclusive community of citizens. From about the 1860s, nationalism in Denmark and Sweden became more anti-liberal and xenophobic, asserting ethnic distinctiveness in the face of perceived military threats from Germany and Russia. In Norway, late nineteenth century nationalism was more clearly liberal, as the movement for national independence developed together with liberal demands for parliamentary democracy directed against the Swedish king. Yet in Norway too, despite the symbolic value of the 1814 tradition, nationalism also drew on ideas about the Norwegians as a separate ethnic community. Bolstered by developing theories of race and eugenics, which ascribed superiority to the Nordic races as an Aryan ideal, ideas of ethnic exclusiveness were carried over into modern definitions of citizenship in twentieth-century Scandinavia. That said, nationalism remained a contentious topic of political debate in Scandinavia, as it did elsewhere. Associated with the popular movements and institutions of civic society, such as the Folk High Schools and

---

[65] There was a marked sympathy for Wilhelmine Germany among some sections of the Swedish right, and certainly among the army, before and during the First World War. See N. Elvander, *Harald Hjärne och konservatismen: konservativ idédebatt i Sverige 1865–1922* (Uppsala, 1961).

[66] A. D. Smith, *Theories of Nationalism* (London, 1971).

the revivalist and temperance movements, nationalism could also be interpreted as a force for radical politics, in opposition to conservative nationalism, even if this too drew largely on notions of ethnic and cultural distinctiveness.[67]

The question might also be posed: what, if anything, was distinctively *Scandinavian* about nationalism in Scandinavia? In other words, what justifies treating the three cases together rather than separately? The idea of Scandinavian/ Nordic exceptionalism in the twentieth century is of course well established, based on the notion of a distinctive 'Nordic model' of politics, social policy, and international relations. Recently, Nordic historians have attempted to extend the idea of Nordic exceptionalism backwards, arguing for the existence of a post-Enlightenment Nordic *Sonderweg*.[68] This *Sonderweg* was characterized by the reconciliation, within Nordic political and constitutional thought, of the two post-Enlightenment traditions: the liberal idea of individual freedom on the one hand; and the Romantic-influenced ideas of community and equality on the other. This blending of traditions, according to Sørensen and Stråth, is above all symbolized in the figure of the Scandinavian peasant, who was simultaneously the embodiment of the Enlightenment tradition as a free and rational political actor, but also the bearer of a genuine Scandinavian culture. Thus the idea of the *folk* in Scandinavia, while carrying some of the associations of concept of the *Volk*, also retained its democratic and liberal elements.[69] The implication here is of a 'middle way' of Scandinavian nationalism, somewhere between the extremes of East and West. Several aspects of nineteenth-century Scandinavian nationalism seem to make the *Sonderweg* argument persuasive. These include the central importance of the peasantry, and the institutions of peasant democracy; the existence of a strong, centralized, but relatively benign state, and the relative non-belligerence of Scandinavian society, which, apart from the conflicts between Denmark and Prussia, remained at peace after 1814. But we should also avoid overplaying the exceptionalist thesis. Although Norden was defined partly against Europe, it was also very much a part of Europe, and ideas and cultural debates were derived from and closely related to wider European currents.[70] As other contributors to this volume demonstrate, the blending of liberalism and community, of the traditions of ethnic and civic nationalism which has been argued to constitute the Nordic *Sonderweg*, was not so very distinctive in a wider European context.

---

[67] For example, see Samuel Edquist, *Nyktra svenskar: godtemplarrörelsen och den nationella identiteten 1879–1918* (Uppsala, 2001).

[68] Ø. Sørensen and B. Stråth (eds.), *The Cultural Construction of Norden* (Oslo, 1997); especially Sørensen and Stråth, 'Introduction', and Uffe Østergård, 'The Geo-politics of Nordic Identity'.

[69] See Lars Trägårdh, 'Varieties of Volkish Identities' in B. Stråth (ed.), *Language and the Construction of Class Identities* (Gothenburg, 1990).

[70] B. Stråth, 'The Swedish Demarcation from Europe', in M. af Malmborg and B. Stråth (eds.), *The Meaning of Europe: Variety and Contention within and among Nations* (Oxford, 2002).

11

Spain

The Iberian Mosaic

Stephen Jacobson

Spanish intellectuals have long ruminated over the so-called 'problem of Spain', the once-mighty world power that poorly confronted the challenges of modernity. Beginning just before the turn of the twentieth century and continuing until a few decades ago, intellectuals retreated into the past with the explicit intention of explaining and perhaps even overcoming the economic, cultural, and political traumas of their presents.[1] In addition to the problem of 'backwardness', one of the principal occurrences that provoked this endeavour was the advent of nationalism in Catalonia and the Basque Country, the two most industrialized regions of the Peninsula. Movements clamouring for self-government appeared in the last decade of the nineteenth century and boldly threw into question Spanish identity and unity. According to nationalists in these places, then and even today, 'Spain' was not a 'nation' but a 'state' in which other 'nations' existed, or as the Catalan nationalist Enric Prat de la Riba once claimed, 'died' or 'agonized'.[2]

For some time now the experience of decadence has been relegated to the past, and scholars have logically adopted a more distant posture. They have examined the 'problem of Spain' as part of history and the historical imagination rather than as an ailment in need of a cure. They have long abandoned the positivistic quest to unearth 'essence', but have instead studied how 'essences' are subjective and have been articulated, transformed, disseminated, and perceived. The problem does not exist as originally posed, since a 'problem' implies a normative judgement, the presence of some unidirectional modernizing process gone wrong. Instead, it is perhaps better described as a 'puzzle'. How should historians make sense of the immense crisis of Spanish identity? Why did nationalist movements appear in

---

[1] This tradition has been studied in Javier Varela, *La novela de España: los intelectuales y el problema español* (Madrid, 1999). For a complete history of Spanish intellectuals and their ideas about Spain, see Santos Juliá, *Historias de las dos Españas* (Madrid, 2004).

[2] Enrique Prat de la Riba, 'Miscelánea jurídica', *Revista jurídica de Cataluña*, 2 (1896), 49 in *Obra completa*, i (Barcelona, 1998), 342.

Catalonia and the Basque Country? Why did they not appear in other places such as Valencia, Navarre, and Andalusia?[3]

Scholars addressing such questions can be grouped into two schools. The first of these has concentrated on the role of the state during the nineteenth century. They have noted that Spanish liberals governed a state void of particularly good natural resources and fertile land, and continually on the verge of bankruptcy. Statesmen lacked the money, will, and vision to 'nationalize' the country around a centralized system of education, a tight network of internal communications, a defined set of holidays, a patriotic history, and even a single language or uniform code of civil laws.[4] These scholars have frequently compared Spain with France, and have argued that where the French state triumphed, the Spanish state proved less than successful or even failed. In many respects, they echo the impressions by José Ortega y Gasset, who in 1921 described Spain as 'invertebrate'. To the eminent philosopher, invertebratism gave rise to 'regionalisms, nationalisms, and separatisms'. Catalan and Basque nationalisms were 'artificial movements, extracted from nothing, without causes or profound motives, that suddenly appeared some few years ago'.[5] In the present-day academy, in which trumpeting the virtues of monolithic and strong national identity does not have much appeal, few serious scholars share Ortega's harsh and hyperbolic value judgements and are doubtlessly sympathetic and sensitive to multicultural conceptions of region and nation. Nonetheless, they do share his characterization: 'invertebrate Spain' has proved to be a useful and durable concept.

A second group of scholars has shifted the emphasis from the state to society. They have emphasized that Spaniards always harboured multiple conceptions of *pueblo, región, patria,* and *nación,* which often intersected and overlapped. During most of the nineteenth century, such 'dual' or 'multiple' patriotisms were compatible with and in fact reinforced the notion of a unified 'nation'.[6] Much like the

---

[3] I have left Galicia out of the analysis. Political nationalism appeared in Galicia but after the time period that concerns this volume. For Galician nationalism, see Justo G. Beramendi and Xosé M. Nuñez Seixas, *O nacionalismo galego* (Vigo, 1995); and Justo G. Beramendi, *El nacionalismo gallego* (Madrid, 1997).

[4] J. J. Linz, 'Early State Building and Late Peripheral Nationalism against the State: The Case of Spain', in S. N. Eisenstadt and S. Rokkan (eds.), *Building States and Nations,* ii (Beverly Hills, Calif., 1973), 32–116; J. P. Fusi, 'Centre and Periphery, 1900–1936: National Integration and Regional Nationalisms Reconsidered', in F. Lannon and P. Preston (eds.), *Elites and Power in Twentieth-Century Spain* (Oxford, 1990), 33–40; B. de Riquer, 'Reflexions entorn de la dèbil nacionalització espanyola del segle XIX', *L'Avenç,* 170 (1993), 8–15; and J. Álvarez Junco, 'El nacionalismo español: las insuficiencias en la acción estatal', *Historia social,* 40 (2001), 29–51. For myths, holidays, and symbols, see Carlos Serrano, *El nacimiento de Carmen: símbolos, mitos y nación* (Madrid, 1999).

[5] I use José Ortega y Gasset, *España invertebrada,* 10th edn. (Madrid, 1957), 39.

[6] X. M. Núñez Seixas, 'The Region as the Essence of the Fatherland: Regional Variants of the Spanish Nationalism (1840–1936)', *European History Quarterly,* 31 (2001), 483–518; J. M. Fradera, 'El proyecto liberal Catalán y los imperativos del doble patriotismo', in A. M. García Rovira (ed.), *España, ¿nación de naciones?* (Madrid, 2002), 87–100; and F. Archilés and M. Martí, 'Ethnicity, Region and Nation: Valencian Identity and the Spanish Nation-State', *Ethnic and Racial Studies,* 24–5 (2002), 245–78.

British nation consisted of English, Scots, and Welsh, the Spanish nation consisted of Basques, Catalans, Aragonese, Valencians, Castilians, Andalusians, and others. These dual identities proved to be more tenable over time in mainland Britain.[7] In Spain, elite groups on the industrialized periphery later shifted allegiances according to interests, and founded nationalist movements that by the early twentieth century convinced increasingly larger percentages of their electorates that dual identities were no longer complementary but antagonistic. By the turn of the century, to be 'Catalan' or 'Basque' was deemed to be more authentic than to be 'Spanish'. Consequently, these regions deserved political structures reflective of this reality. In the case of Catalonia, nationalism was sponsored by professionals, intellectuals, and an ambitious bourgeoisie frustrated with the inability of the state to construct an administrative apparatus able to confront the complex socio-economic problems of a modernizing society. In the case of the Basque Country, nationalism first emerged as a petit bourgeois and a 'petite-intellectual' movement representative of groups antagonized by the brutal and rapid effects of industrialization. However, it later captured much of the industrial bourgeoisie as well.[8] This focus also helps explain why nationalism did not appear in other regions, such as Navarre and Valencia, historic principalities with large numbers of Basque and Catalan-Valencian speakers, where such 'dual patriotisms' were also common. Elites in the traditional capitals of Valencia and Pamplona read their pasts, presents, and futures as being compatible with the unity of Spain. They preferred to defend their interests in Madrid, rather than in, or competing with, industrial cities of Barcelona or Bilbao.

These two historiographical approaches are correct, informative, and arguably compatible, yet both also share one crucial shortcoming. Both treat 'Spain' as an isolated or self-contained entity. Although both make use of comparative methodologies by contrasting the power of the state, the presence of historic or linguistically differentiated communities, and patterns of regional industrialization to occurrences in other countries, particularly France and Britain, both undertake such comparisons as if they were examining independent rather than interrelated entities. Both lack one key ingredient. They pay considerably less attention to the persuasiveness of ideas coming from Europe and the Americas. For nineteenth-century Spain was not the Spain of the Counter-Reformation, a propagator of influential ideas to much of Europe and the world. It was not a country where socio-economic or political phenomena could give rise to original theories, which could then be spread abroad. To be sure, the process worked in reverse. Spain was a country where its literate classes absorbed waves of continental and Atlantic

---

[7] For Britain, see Chris Williams's chapter in this volume; and C. Kidd, *Subverting Scotland's Past: Scottish Whig Historians and the Creation of an Anglo-British Identity, 1689–c.1830* (Cambridge, 1993).

[8] For the relationship between nationalism and class interest, see Jordi Solé-Tura, *Catalanismo y revolución burguesa* (Madrid, 1970); and Juan Díez Medrano, *Divided Nations: Class, Politics, and Nationalism in the Basque Country and Catalonia* (Ithaca, NY, 1995).

influences and modified them in interesting ways dependent on historical circumstances.[9] By concentrating on ideas, the picture comes into increasingly sharper focus.

Conceptions of nationhood can be broadly classified into 'civic' and 'ethnic' traditions. From the eighteenth century onward, Spaniards received most of their political ideas from France, and even those that originated from Britain, Germany, and elsewhere were, until the latter decades of the nineteenth century, usually read in French translation and influenced by French interpretations. For this reason as well as others, Spain followed the path blazed by its more influential, dynamic, original, and powerful neighbour, where the 'civic' tradition initially proved dominant but later became imbued with historicist, ethnic, and racial notions. Outcomes were of course quite different. In France, the ethnic gloss on a strong civic tradition reinforced the image of a united, imperial, and superior nation. In Spain, where the civic tradition was continually intertwined with Catholicism, and where recent history became increasingly spun as a yarn of failure rather than as an epic of success, the rising prestige of ethnic nationalism had the effect of causing a radical rethinking of what and who constituted 'Spain', and helped inspire nationalist movements in Catalonia and the Basque Country.

As a matter of introduction, it is important to avoid possible misinterpretations. The difference between 'civic' and 'ethnic' traditions should not be conflated with the distinction between so-called 'modernist' and 'primordialist' theories. In other words, the presence of 'ethnic nationalism' does not imply the persistence of perennial identities. Rather, both species of nationalism were modern, having their roots in the Enlightenment and reliant on various ethno-symbolic complexes and legal-political traditions—some real and others invented—inherited from the past.[10] Civic nationalism emerged from Rousseau's well-known theory that states consisted of the free union of citizens, who together constituted a sovereign nation able to identify and to pursue aggressively a common good. In contrast, ethnic nationalism had its roots in German historicism and the Herderian doctrine of national self-determination. In its original form, the Herderian vision was more conservative, baroque, historical, and peaceful than the ascriptive, neoclassical, philosophical, and imperial French antipode. However, this changed. In the latter decades of the nineteenth century, renewed European imperial interest in Africa and Asia, paired with the advent of new and convincing scientific theories concerning the superiority and inferiority of races, also endowed ethnic nationalism with bellicose

---

[9] Here I follow Enric Ucelay Da Cal, 'The Outsiders that Count: France and the United States in Spanish Nationalism'. Paper presented to symposium, 'Spanish Nationalism: A Historical Approach', Tufts University, Medford, Mass., 1995. I have been unable to find a published version of this outstanding essay.

[10] This literature is immense, but it is nicely overviewed in Anthony D. Smith, *Nationalism and Modernism* (London, 1998).

potential.[11] It must be noted that the use of the categories—'civic' and 'ethnic'— should not be uniquely associated with the specific country from where these ideas first emerged. Ideas smoothly crossed borders, and became reinterpreted and recycled by different people in various historical contexts in many countries. As used in this chapter, the descriptions 'civic' and 'ethnic' are not sociological 'ideal types' or 'categories of analysis'. They are not bins that different nationalisms can be placed into, nor even 'axes' to be used to determine shapes or proportions.[12] They described distinct idea systems with identifiable origins that through the course of the long nineteenth century became interpreted, misinterpreted, and mixed into a mélange of mutually reinforcing discourses and ideologies concerning the nation.

SPAIN IN 1808 AND 1898: CIVIC AND ETHNIC IDEAS

In February 1808, Napoleonic troops crossed the Pyrenees onto the Iberian Peninsula and inaugurated the era of nationalism in Spain as they had throughout Europe. Outside Spain, the story is well-known and oft-repeated. Johann Wolfgang von Goethe observed the phenomenon at the battle of Valmy in 1792, when a tattered French army made up of conscripts rose up to the battle cry of 'Vive la Nation', and successfully confronted a better-drilled and armed Prussian one. And in 1807, Johann Fichte's famous *Address to the German Nation* made it clear that the spirit of Valmy had penetrated the German states when he urged his fellow Germans to find personal freedom and emotional fulfilment in their collective spirit, and to liberate themselves from the despised Gallican yoke. Spain also followed this script. The country had its versions of Goethe and Fichte, and also received ideas spreading forth from American and French revolutions.

In Spain, Francisco Goya chronicled the horrors of the new credo in his paintings that still hang in the Prado museum today. These chilling portrayals commemorate the heroic but ultimately failed uprising of the people of Madrid on 2 May 1808 and the subsequent execution of the patriotic martyrs in firing squads by French soldiers the following day. Goya, like Goethe, was a critic who understood that the coming of nationalism meant the end of Enlightenment. But there were also many scholars eager to embrace wholeheartedly the spirit of the age. Spain also had its equivalent of a Fichte, Antonio Capmany, an enlightened courtier, a Catalan who had lived in Seville and Madrid, one of Europe's truly great historians turned virulent Francophobe. Like Fichte, his work represented a combination of 'civic' and 'ethnic' ideas then buzzing about Europe and the

---

[11] Here I respectfully disagree with Carl Strikwerda, who, while describing Belgian and Dutch foreign policy, writes that a 'rejection of militarism was one of the clearest signs of the power of civic over ethnic nationalism' (p. 94 above). Both discourses could be peaceful or bellicose depending on historical circumstances. As he in fact shows in the cases of Belgium and Holland, the rejection of militarism was due to practical and not ideological considerations.

[12] In this respect, my approach differs from that of Brian Vick (Chapter 8 in this volume).

Americas. Capmany was a rare talent, but he was also a rather typical patriot, and his pamphlet was reflective of many similar clarion calls to arms then heard across the globe from Buenos Aires to Berlin. His 'ethnic self' was represented in his famous *Sentinel against the French* (1808), a raging diatribe flowing forth from a man with a gifted pen. The title harked back to the well-known opuscule from the Golden Age, entitled *Sentinel against the Jews* (1674).

The *Sentinel against the French* was a modern document. The war was not only to be fought in defence of religion and dynasty, but in the name of concepts only recently endowed with political meaning, such as custom and language. As Capmany wrote, 'We still sing our traditional folk songs, we will dance our dances, and we will dress in our ancient garb. Those who call themselves gentlemen will mount noble horses instead of acting in sentimental dramas and playing a piano reeking of the French. We will return to speak the Castilian language of our ancestors, and disabuse our rich language of ugly French jargon.' Religion was still paramount, and, despite the virtual absence of Jews and Muslims in the territory, the recourse to discursive anti-Semitism remained a true, tried, and tested way to inspire the faithful: 'With this war, we will be better Christians . . . This war is even more holy than that of the Crusades.' The French were 'worse than Jews in their thoughts and more cruel than troglodytes in their works'. Interestingly, the presence of ethnic diversity was what gave Spain its distinctive personality. 'What would become of Spaniards, if there were no Aragonese, Valencians, Murcians, Asturians, Galicians, Extremadurans, Catalans, Castilians, etc. Each one of these names shines bright and looms large. These small nations make up the mass of the Great Nation.'[13]

Spain was not only to be understood in such ethnocultural, linguistic, and religious terms. Capmany was better known for his 'civic self'. He was the premier comparative constitutional scholar of his day and a deputy to Spain's first constitutional convention held from 1810 to 1813 in the Atlantic town of Cádiz, a meeting that constituted the third major experiment of the age following Philadelphia and Versailles. Capmany believed that constitutionalist Spain should adopt Old Regime English or Swiss models, but the younger and more numerous deputies were convinced by the democratic ideas emanating from the French and North American Revolutions.[14] The document was perhaps a blend of both. It followed the British model of constitutional monarchy, but also relied upon

---

[13] Antonio de Capmany, *Centinela contra Franceses* (Valencia, 1808), 10, 18, 24, 94. Interestingly, the pamphlet was picked up and translated in the United States. Antonio Capmany, *The Anti-Gallican Sentinel* (New York, 1809; and Baltimore 1810).

[14] For his constitutional work, see Antonio de Capmany, *Práctica y estilo de celebrar cortes en el reino de Aragón, principado de Cataluña y reino de Valencia y una noticia de las de Castilla y Navarra. Va añadido el reglamento para el consejo representativo de Ginebra, y los reglamentos que se observan en la cámara de los comunes de Inglaterra* (Madrid, 1821). This document was prepared in 1809 for the constitutional convention, although it was not published until later. Much earlier, he had expressed his preference for British and Swiss constitutionalism: Antonio (Capmany) Montpalau, *Descripción de las soberanías de Europa* (Madrid, 1786).

republican revolutionary tenets: the abolition of feudalism, popular sovereignty, the free market, and the extension of judicial rights to all citizens.

The constitution of 1812 reflected the civic nationalism of the French, but the framers encountered problems with how to deal with empire, still the largest in the world. The constitution defined 'citizens' as all 'Spaniards on both sides of the Atlantic who had descended from Spanish families from Spain and the Americas'. With respect to both native-born 'Indians' and black slaves, the framers emulated the United States approach. Indians were citizens, slaves were not. Moreover, in the Spanish document, the pure and mixed-race descendants of one-time slaves were not citizens, even if they were free. This was not because of modern theories of biological superiority, but because they were not descendants of 'free men'. Remaining faithful to liberal principles, and immersed in civic discourse, it never remotely occurred to the deputies to bolster their opinions by appealing to skin colour. Instead, the ancestral stain of slavery—the lack of freedom—was deemed stigmatic and heritable.[15] Such creative hermeneutics were of course more instrumental than ideological. The continentals sought to limit the numbers of Spanish-American representatives in the legislature by decreasing the number of colonials that could be counted as citizens. Not surprisingly, debates in Cádiz helped further provoke colonial movements of independence, led by Creole liberals convinced that civic principles were being contravened in Spain. A decade and a half later, nearly all of Latin America had attained independence and slavery had been abolished in all of the new nations.

Outside its borders, Spain's image remained consistent with past ethnic stereotypes, despite the advent of liberal constitutionalism. If Russia was the nation whose great plains, numerous peasant souls, and endless capacity for sacrifice ultimately exhausted Napoleon, if Britain possessed the technically superior navy and the well-disciplined army backed by public opinion and finances that finally caught up and defeated him, then Spain was the savage land where his tactical plans ran amok and his armies became bogged down. Napoleon himself blamed his defeat on what he termed the 'Spanish thorn', claiming that the incessant guerrilla tactics of the Spanish patriots led him to exhaust his resources in Iberia leaving him undermanned in the East. The reasons for the defeat also echoed similar opinions that foreigners had long held. Known as the 'black legend', Montesquieu famously renewed this myth in his *Persian Letters*. Spain was a country whose internal strength lay in the intransigent Catholicism of the Inquisition, in its rejection of science and belief in superstition, and in the capacity of its population to inflict and tolerate infernal acts of cruelty. The ethnic roots of Spanish decadence stretched to the Middle Ages: to its Semitic (Arab and Jewish) past, or, alternatively, to the warrior and frontier mentality forged during the Reconquest.[16]

---

[15] This crucial point is explicitly and brilliantly made in J. M. Fradera, 'Raza y Ciudadanía: el factor racial en la delimitación de los derechos políticos de los Americanos', in *Gobernar colonias* (Barcelona, 1999), 51–69. See also, T. Herzog, *Defining Nations: Immigrants and Citizens in Early Modern Spain and Spanish-America* (New Haven, 2003), 141–63.

[16] For a detailed history of the the 'black legend', see Ricardo García Cárcel, *La leyenda negra: historia y opinión* (Madrid, 1992).

In the decades following the Napoleonic wars, this image of a people championing virile and even primordial conceptions of patriotism, liberty, and identity remained vivid. Following Waterloo and the Congress of Vienna, most of Europe experienced decades of peace, but Spain remained ravaged by war. From 1808 to 1843, it was perhaps the most violent place in all of Europe, plagued by civil wars between liberals and absolutists in the countryside, revolution in the cities, not to mention devastating and debilitating colonial wars in Latin America. During the second half of the nineteenth century, however, this image became significantly altered. Ferocity gradually gave way to innocuousness. When Europe later devolved into new and intensely nationalist wars in Crimea, and over German and Italian unification, Spanish armies vanished from European theatres. In an era where the capacity to wage war became quickly transformed by industrial technology, Spain could not keep pace. In 1870, a conflict over who would inherit the Spanish throne sparked the Franco-Prussian War, but Spain itself did not participate. Nor did politicians dare enter the First World War, never sure which side to join. From 1837 to 1923, Spain was a liberal and constitutionalist country, but it rarely provoked passions outside its borders.

If absence from continental wars was not enough, the image of powerlessness became definitively welded into the European and Spanish imagination during the next great international armed conflict against a world power. In 1898, Spain went to war against the United States over Cuban independence, in which both populations were buoyed by a jingoistic and chauvinistic press. The Spanish-American War ended in four months. Spain lost its navy and just about all of its remaining colonies: Cuba, Puerto Rico, the Philippines, and Guam. The year 1898—colloquially referred to as the 'disaster'—caused a national crisis of conscience, this time exposing Spain for what it really was: a technologically inferior country with infinitely more bravado than might. It had ceased to become a colonial power just as the rest of the world was amidst the heyday of a new imperial spirit. Contrasts with France and Britain could not be more revealing. The defeat of France in the Franco-Prussian war of 1870, a similar national and arguably racial humiliation, ushered in the Third Republic, a great nation-building project with an aggressive imperial mission. The Boer War had a similar galvanizing effect. In earlier times in Spain, such a national embarrassment could have been followed by the raising of the barricades and the proclamation of a new constitution or even a republic, but in 1898 the streets were quiet and not even the army stirred. In the often-repeated words of one conservative politician, the country was 'without a pulse'.[17]

Spain did not shed this reputation of ineptitude. The decades following the Spanish-American War were not accompanied by increasing national unity, but in fact, by the growing electoral strength of nationalist movements in Catalonia and the Basque Country. To nationalists in these regions, the debacle of 1898 threw

---

[17] For 1898 and its aftermath, see Sebastian Balfour, *The End of the Spanish Empire, 1898–1923* (Oxford, 1997); and A. Smith and E. Dávila Cox (eds.), *The Crisis of 1898: Colonial Redistribution and Nationalist Mobilization* (New York, 1999).

into question the ability of Spanish statesmen to confront the challenges of modernity. Continued colonial skirmishes in the last major colony, the Protectorate of Morocco, did not promote patriotic feeling but swelled popular discontent. In 1921, another embarrassing defeat in Morocco's Anual foreshadowed the end of liberal constitutionalism. Modern history followed a string of devastating losses: Trafalgar (1805), Ayacucho (1824), Santiago de Cuba (1898), and the Anual (1921). The heroes of the most significant victory were largely forgotten. The patriots of the War of Independence were only a memory of yesteryear, not even commemorated in public celebrations or holidays, but confined to history books, which were nonetheless out of the reach of a population whose rates of illiteracy were among the highest in Europe.[18]

SPAIN, 1837–76: LIBERAL NATIONALISM AND THE CIVIC TRADITION

These snapshots of 1808 and 1898 help us appreciate the nature of the historiographical conundrum, but it would be an error to fast forward through the middle decades of the nineteenth century. During this period, the civic idiom continued to dominate discourse concerning the nation, although both religious and ethnic ideas informed notions of what it meant to be Spanish.

Constitutions remained faithful to civic principles but exhibited a notably 'Catholic' gloss. Politicians continued to wrestle with how to address empire. The independence of much of Latin America by 1826 did not mean that colonial questions disappeared, given that Spain retained Cuba, Puerto Rico, and the Philippines. Unable to confront the immensely complicated issue of deciding which rights to extend to Peninsulars, Creoles, Indians, mestizos, mulattos, free blacks, and slaves, constitutional framers in 1837, 1845, 1869, and 1876 denied voting rights and representation to all persons residing in the colonies, regardless of the colour of their skin. As before, if colonials had been counted, their deputies would have substantially diluted the power of their Iberian counterparts. All constitutions after 1812 avoided the word 'citizen', because of its republican connotations, but instead defined who was a 'Spaniard'. All free and non-free residents of the colonies—regardless of race and including the large slave communities of Cuba and Puerto Rico—were nominally classified as 'Spaniards', although they could only enjoy full constitutional rights if they emigrated to Spain.[19]

---

[18] For literacy rates in Spain, see Mercedes Vilanova Ribas and Xavier Moreno Juliá, *Atlas de la evolución en España de 1887 a 1981* (Madrid, 1992). For historiography, see Carolyn P. Boyd, *Historia Patria: Politics, History, and National Identity in Spain, 1875–1975* (Princeton, 1997).

[19] See Josep M. Fradera, 'Why were Spain's Special Overseas Laws Never Enacted?', in R. L. Kagan and G. Parker (eds.), *Spain, Europe and the Atlantic World: Essays in Honour of John H. Elliot* (Cambridge, 1995), 334–9.

The civic spirit was one of the dominant ideological forces within Spain's successful 'liberal' revolution of the 1830s, which succeeded in demolishing the juridical and much of the material basis of the Old Regime and extending legal equality to all Spaniards, who were free to accumulate property and wealth and, if they acquired enough of it, to vote and participate in the political process, however corrupt it eventually became. The percentage of Iberian Spaniards permitted to vote oscillated throughout the century, but remained more or less consistent with the evolution of voting in the United Kingdom, to take one example. In 1890, an electoral law finally instituted universal manhood suffrage, although the persistence of electoral fraud meant that liberal Spain was never even remotely democratic. Moreover, the country remained juridically Catholic. The constitution of 1812 famously stated that 'The religion of the Spanish nation is and will perpetually be Roman Catholic and apostolic', and prohibited the practice of other faiths. Each successive constitution held Spain to be a Catholic country, although none maintained the blanket prohibition. Each extended certain but varying guarantees to the numerous non-believers and the few persons of different religions.[20]

Regional identities initially reinforced an overarching Spanish one. This was clear both in Catalonia and the Basque Country. Catalan liberals, following the example set by Antonio Capmany, interpreted the history of medieval Catalonia and its Corts (the three estates in parliament) as one of the precedents behind the overthrow of absolutism and the arrival of constitutionalism. For their part, the Basques—speakers of perhaps the oldest language in Europe—had long claimed that they represented the pure ethnic stock of the prehistoric Iberians, the tribe from whom all Spaniards supposedly descended. Legend had it that the Basques—or original Iberians—were said to be descendants of Noah who had emigrated to Spain through North Africa after the destruction of the Tower of Babel. The Iberian-Basques comprised the oldest ethnic group in all of Europe, predating the Celts. When read together, Catalans and Basques harked back to their participation in an 'ethnic' and 'civic' prehistory that formed the nucleus of what had become constitutional 'Spain'.[21] Liberalism had returned Spain to its racial and constitutional (ethnic and civic) origins that had been polluted by foreign (Habsburg and Bourbon/Austrian and French) absolutist influences.

As in France, imperialism was altogether compatible with and also reinforced by civic nationalism. The lofty ideal of bringing reason and science to the uneducated in Africa, America, and Asia was rooted in the Enlightenment but was obviously inherited from the missionary pledge to carry faith and salvation to the

---

[20] For reproduced facsimiles of the Spanish constitutions of 1812, 1837, 1845, 1869, 1876, and 1978, see *Constituciones españolas* (Madrid, 1986).

[21] For such dual patriotism, see Juan Madariaga Orbea, 'Crisis, cambios y rupturas (1602–1876)', in I. Bazán (ed.), *De Túbal a Aitor: historia de Vasconia* (Madrid, 2002), 337–484; and J. M. Fradera, *Cultura nacional en una societat dividida* (Barcelona, 1992).

pagan and unconverted. This Christian and liberal 'civilizing mission' became interlaced with explicitly racial overtones. 'New' imperialism began during the late 1850s and early 1860s, during the hegemony of a centrist political party known as the Liberal Union, led by General Leopoldo O'Donnell. An admirer of France's Second Empire, he engaged Spain in northern Morocco (1859–61), Indochina (1858–62), Mexico (1861–2), Santo Domingo (1861–5), and Peru and Chile (1864–5). Morocco was the most important. French liberals began the conquest of Algeria in 1830 and Morocco in 1844, and Spain followed France into the Maghreb. The 'War of Africa', as it was pretentiously called, was met with great fanfare and bravado. The army recruited volunteers by exploiting the same networks that progressive liberals and democrats had previously used to raise militias, and, in the process, invoked the same revolutionary spirit. Volunteerism was most heavy in Catalonia. In a clear demonstration of the compatibility of dual patriotic allegiances, and civic and ethnic ideas, volunteers donned traditional Catalan costume in patriotic defence of the Spanish nation, and vowed to conquer a 'race of slaves'. They were described as 'children of the Almogàvers', harking back to early fourteenth-century crusaders of the medieval principality who ventured to Greece and Constantinople, fought the Turks in defence of Catholicism from Islam, and even supposedly saved the Acropolis from being reduced to dust.[22]

One of the common outcomes of civic nationalism was the rising of a common man to military general and then to national saviour. This phenomenon undoubtedly had ethnic attributes as well. At various points, Spain's left-wing liberal party, known as the Progressives, appeared to have as its leader an equivalent of a Bonaparte, a Bolívar, or a Garibaldi, but its generals baulked when given the chance. The most obvious candidate was Baldomero Espartero, victorious leader of liberal armies during the First Carlist War (1833–9). His dictatorial 'Regency' (1840–3) oversaw some of the most radical conquests of Spain's liberal revolution, including the sale of church lands and the final abolition of feudalism. Yet, following his overthrow in 1843 and exile, he fashioned himself a 'Cincinnatus' rather than a 'Bonaparte'. He retired to the countryside and only re-entered the political arena for a brief spell in the mid-1850s. In 1868, his name surfaced as a plausible candidate for the throne, but the aged general refused. The Catalan Juan Prim— the hero of the War of Africa—was perhaps the next best candidate. The charismatic leader behind Spain's bloodless but democratic 'Glorious Revolution' of 1868, he also shunned the opportunity to lead a movement of masses.[23] In 1870,

---

[22] This is brilliantly described in Albert García Balañà, 'Patria, plebe y política en la España isabelina: la guerra de África en Cataluña', in E. M. Corrales (ed.), *Marruecos y el colonialismo español (1859–1912): de la guerra de África a la 'penetración pacífica'* (Barcelona, 2002), 13–78. For war and Spanish nationalism, see José Álvarez Junco, 'El nacionalismo español como mito movilizador: cuatro guerras', in R. Cruz and M. Pérez Ledesma (eds.), *Cultura y movilización en la España contemporánea* (Madrid, 1997), 35–68.

[23] For Espartero and Prim, see Adrian Shubert, 'Baldomero Espartero (1793–1879): del ídolo al olvido', and Josep M. Fradera, 'Juan Prim y Prats (1814–1870): Prim conspirador o la pedagogía del sable', in I. Burdiel and M. Pérez Ledesma (eds.), *Liberales, agitadores y conspiradores: biografías heterodoxas del siglo XIX* (Madrid, 2000), 183–208, 239–66.

he fell victim to an assassin's bullet of unknown origins. The most likely candidates were Spanish federal republicans disappointed that the coming of democracy had not meant the end of monarchy, or Cuban slave-owners fearful that democracy meant the end of slavery. To Prim and most Spanish Progressives, it had meant the end of neither.[24]

Federal-Republicanism represented the most unadulterated form of civic nationalism in Spain. This ideology occupied the leftist vanguard during the third quarter of the century and provided the inspiration behind the foundation of what was ultimately the short-lived First Republic of 1873. Barcelona was the birthplace of this intensely nationalist, anticlerical, and revolutionary doctrine, which was also popular in various urban centres throughout the Peninsula. Its founder Francisco Pi y Margall admired the organizations of the United States and Switzerland, but he was a radical thinker, not opposed to revolutionary violence, and also fashioned himself a disciple of Proudhon. His magnum opus *Nationalities* (1876) was perhaps the purest version of civic nationalism found anywhere in Europe. He rejected the idea that either race, language, history, or natural frontiers necessarily constituted the essence of a nation, but instead contended that the Spanish nation—and other nations as well—could consist of a multiplicity of races, languages, peoples, and even religions. To Pi y Margall, the nation consisted of a free and voluntary union of citizens with common interests. A federation would 'establish unity without destroying variety'.[25] The idea was of course better on paper than in practice. The short life of the First Republic, undone by the outbreak of civil war and ended by military *pronunciamiento*, meant that this secular and revolutionary message was unacceptable to much of the population. All the same, the federalist vision of a civic nation characterized by the inclusion of various linguistic and ethnic groups remained a durable idea that is still vital and viable today.

THE RESTORATION MONARCHY (1876–1923): THE ADVENT OF 'ETHNIC NATIONALISM' AND 'NATIONAL CATHOLICISM'

Following the Restoration of the Bourbons to the Spanish throne in 1876, nationalism became the subject of explicit discussion in universities, intellectual associations, cafés, meeting places, the streets, and the press. Events taking place outside the borders of Spain were paramount in interpreting events that transpired

---

[24] The Moret Law (1870) prohibited the making of new slaves, and hence meant those born to slaves were free, but maintained the situation of those who were still slaves. Spain adopted a piecemeal approach to abolitionism, and only in 1882 were all legal remnants of slavery abolished once and for all. See Chris Schmidt-Nowara, *Empire and Antislavery: Spain, Cuba, and Puerto Rico, 1833–1874* (Pittsburgh, 1999); and R. J. Scott, *Slave Emancipation in Cuba: The Transition to Free Labor, 1860–1899* (c. 1985; Pittsburgh, 2000).

[25] F. Pi y Margall, *Las nacionalidades* (Buenos Aires, 1945), 25.

within. Following German and Italian unification, attention moved to Alsace-Lorraine. During the scramble for Africa and in the aftermath of the Berlin Conference, social Darwinism added convincing evolutionary notions of superiority and inferiority of nations. As soaring numbers of men and women were incarcerated and sent to madhouses, influential scholarship in the fields of criminal anthropology, psychiatry, neurology, and ethnography popularized biological, genetic, and environmental ideas about behaviour and race. Cuban and Algerian movements of self-government, along with the seemingly eternal problems of Ireland and Poland, were also common topics of discussion. And by the 1890s, decentralist, Catholic, and anti-Semitic ideas of Maurice Barrès, Charles Maurras, and Édouard Drumont flooded across the Pyrenees in the wake of the Dreyfus Affair.[26] In Spain, 'ethnic nationalism' and 'national Catholicism' came to coexist and share political space with the civic tradition.

Basque nationalism has often been regarded as an exemplar of ethno-nationalism in all of Europe.[27] It originated in Bilbao and its environs, the city in Spain which experienced the most radical social and industrial transformation of the last quarter of the century, becoming a thriving centre of heavy, metallurgical industry. Basque nationalists mounted a sustained protest against the massive influx of Castilian-speaking immigrants, pejoratively known as *maketos*, who were forced to shoulder the blame for the destruction of traditional Basque culture and language. In *The Basque Country for its Independence* (1892), its founder Sabino Arana Goiri demanded outright separation. With respect to ethnography, a reinterpretation was in order. Arana and his followers maintained the old myth that the Basques spoke one of the original languages of the Tower of Babel. He even went as far to assert that during prehistoric times Basques had inhabited all of Northern Africa and Western Europe. But he abandoned the traditional interpretation that contended that Basques represented the basic Iberian stock of all Spaniards. Instead, he claimed that the Spanish race essentially comprised 'Latin-Greek-Arabic'. It did not 'conserve any remnants of the primitive race on the Peninsula, which was ours'. Who was Basque was to follow strictly the law of blood (*jus sanguinis*). Arana explained: 'A child of Basques by race would be Basque regardless of whether he had been born in Madagascar, in Dahomey, or if he had been born in Olakueta. In contrast, a descendant of Spaniards born in the Basque country would never be Basque by race.'[28]

---

[26] In general, the reception of such European ideas in Spain has not been explored in detail. One notable exception is Joaquim Coll i Amargós, *El catalanisme conservador davant l'afer Dreyfus, 1894–1906* (Barcelona, 1994).

[27] For this point, in particular, see Willam A. Douglass, 'Sabino's Sin: Racism and Founding of Basque Nationalism' in Daniele Conversi (ed.), *Ethnonationalism in the Contemporary World: Walker Conner and the Study of Nationalism* (London, 2002), 95–113. For the nineteenth-century origins of Basque nationalism, see Jon Juaristi, *El linaje de Aitor: la invención de la tradición vasca* (*c.*1987; Madrid, 1997); A. Elorza, *Un pueblo escogido: génesis, definición y desarrollo del nacionalismo vasco* (Barcelona, 2001); and J. Corcuera Atienza, *La patria de los vascos: orígenes, ideología y organización del nacionalismo vasco* (Madrid, 2001).

[28] S. Arana de Goiri, '¿Somos Españoles?' in *Obras completas* (Buenos Aires, n.d.), 181–6. The original article was found in *Jaun-Goiku eta Laga-Zarra*, 1/4 (17 Dec. 1893).

Catalan nationalism was a more heterogeneous and less radical movement. Its draft constitution, the Manresa Principles (1892) contained 'home rule' rather than 'separation' or 'independence' as its maximalist demand. In the late nineteenth and early twentieth centuries, it was dominated by conservative and Catholic forces, but it always contained a left-wing with roots in the federal-republican movement and a centre respectful of liberal principles.[29] 'Catalanists' remained faithful to the definition of citizenship as articulated in the ancient laws of the medieval principality. These had a rather typical civic and ethnic ring, paralleled those regimes in existence in much of Western Europe, and contained the well-known combination of *jus sanguinis* and *jus soli*. Not only were children and grandchildren of Catalans to be considered Catalan, but so were long-term residents, regardless of the surnames and birthplaces of their parents. In short, the naturalization of immigrants was legally possible and even desirable. Citizenship was not a purely hypothetical issue as it was in much of the Basque Country. Since Catalonia maintained much of its own regime of civil law, these medieval citizenship rules—previously used to determine who was eligible for public employment—were resurrected and reinterpreted in order to distinguish between who was 'Catalan' and hence governed by Catalan civil laws and who was not Catalan and hence governed by the provisions of the Spanish Civil Code.[30]

Catalan nationalism, however, also had a visible ethnic component. In 1887, Pompeu Gener—a member of the Anthropological Society of Paris—published *Heresies* (1887), which went well beyond the comparatively innocuous ideas of Sabino Arana. He not only asserted that racial differences were important, but that some races were superior to others. To Gener, the Catalans comprised 'Celtic, Greek, Roman, Gothic, and, finally Frank. Strong, intelligent, and energetic races.' He conceded that Spaniards also contained Indo-European or Arian ancestry, but these had been hopelessly polluted. The rest of Spain was 'paralysed by a necrosis produced by the blood of inferior races, such as the Semitic, Berber, and Mongoloid'.[31] Using a less erudite language, Narcís Verdaguer, one of the founders of Catalan nationalism, claimed that Spain comprised 'the Catalan race and the Castilian race'. He argued that the latter owed its origins to Africa and that it was characterized by its 'espousal of sublime idiocies, full of words but short on facts, good for the adventurous life of a soldier but inept when it comes to sweat, work, and practical engineering'.[32] The leader of twentieth-century nationalism,

[29] Studies tracing the early components of Catalan nationalism include: J. Pabón, *Cambó* (*c.* 1952; Barcelona, 1999), 71–129; J. Termes, *L'immigració a Catalunya i altres estudis d'historia del nacionalisme català* (Barcelona, 1984); J. Llorens i Vila, *La Unió Catalanista i els orígens del catalanisme polític* (Barcelona, 1992), 23–61; and A. Balcells, *Catalan Nationalism: Past and Present*, trans. J. Hall and G. J. Walker (Basingstoke, 1996).

[30] For the links between law and nationalism in Catalonia, see Stephen Jacobson, 'Law and Nationalism in Nineteenth-Century Europe: The Case of Catalonia in Comparative Perspective', *Law and History Review*, 20 (2002), 307–47.

[31] I use: Pompeyo Gener, *Cosas de España: herejías nacionales. El renacimiento de Cataluña* (Barcelona, 1903), 43, 229.

[32] Narcís Verdaguer i Callís, *La primera victòria del catalanisme* (Barcelona, 1919), 52. This volume consists of a reprint of articles originally published in 1889.

Enric Prat de la Riba, in his *Catalan Nationality* (1906) shared many of these views and added new scientific theories such as social Darwinism, social psychology, and phrenology into the mix. Without a doubt, Catalan nationalism—like all *fin-de-siècle* nationalisms—became characterized by aggressive notions of ethnicity.[33] All the same, it should be noted that both Catalan and Basque nationalisms were dogmatically and doctrinally non-violent, a fact that prevented the outbreak of a 'Second Balkan Front' during the First World War.

The reception of the ethnic tradition in Spain also limited the possibilities of places that could successfully launch nationalist movements. This was the case of Andalusia, which, if ethnic nationalism had remained faithful to historicist theories and immune to medical 'advances' could have been ripe for such an occurrence. Al-Andalus was far and away the most politically and scientifically sophisticated kingdom in Europe of the tenth century, and could have served as a historic basis for the redressing of modern grievances. In fact, it is not difficult to imagine the appearance of a hypothetical regionalist movement that recuperated and renovated the beautiful capital of Córdoba, reclaimed the ancient borders of the Caliphate, and argued that ethnic difference should serve as the springboard for political autonomy. One only has to refer to Bizet's *Carmen* (1875) to appreciate the appeal and power of Andalusian symbols—bullfighters, Flamenco dancers, and popular religion. Although these have been since dismissed as 'external' European 'stereotype', they were popular in Spain as well. All the same, given the inherent presumptions of superiority in pan-European discourse concerning ethnicity and nationalism, such an outcome was impossible. In order to carry this off, intellectuals would have had to seek refuge in an Arab or Semitic past, ethnic categories ironically considered inferior by scientists and anthropologists. In the nineteenth century, it would have been inconceivable for Andalusians to have moved so radically against the grain.

Basque and Catalan nationalism should not be interpreted as 'ethnic responses' to the 'state' or civic nationalism of Spain.[34] This dichotomy is not only simplistic and misleading but simply wrong. There are three fundamental problems with this interpretation. First, as previously mentioned, Catalan nationalism contained many civic elements. The same cannot be asserted for late nineteenth- and early twentieth-century Basque nationalism, as attempting to find civic discourse during this period is bound to be a futile enterprise. All the same, such attributes did emerge during the middle decades of the twentieth century, a result of the deradicalization of the movement that had begun much earlier. In 1903, Sabino Arana died a young man of Addison's disease and thereafter his successors moderated his

---

[33] See Joan-Lluís Marfany, *La cultura del catalanisme: el nacionalisme català en els seus inicis* (Barcelona, 1995); and E. Ucely-Da Cal, *El imperialismo catalán: Prat de la Riba, Cambó, y la conquista moral de España* (Madrid, 2003).

[34] For this contention, see Daniele Conversi, *The Basques, the Catalans, and Spain* (London, 1997), 6–8. Following Winock, he later distinguishes between 'open' Catalan nationalism and 'closed' Basque nationalism.

message. His party, the Basque National Party (PNV) steadily increased their share of the electorate, and incorporated more traditionally conservative and bourgeois sectors of the population, although it must be noted that it always retained its exclusionary core. Moreover, Basque nationalism, like Catalan nationalism, also possessed many influences, which were not as much 'ethnic' as they were 'historical' and 'juridical'. Both Basque and Catalan nationalism harked back to a utopian and constitutionalist past, as contained in their old municipal institutions and laws, the mythical liberties embodied in the so-called *fueros*.

The second problem with counterposing the Spanish 'state' nationalism with Catalan and Basque 'ethnic' nationalism is that the idea of 'Spain' also became imbued with explicitly ethnic conceptions. Following the Spanish-American War, many influential writers associated with the so-called 'Generation of 1898' posited that decadent Spain could only be saved by shedding its artificial and corrupt skin of modernity and returning to the regenerative soul of the *pueblo*—a Spanish *Volksgeist*. Writers searched far and wide for this *pueblo*, but the most influential and exciting theory also had a pronounced regional component.[35] Miguel de Unamuno, a self-professed socialist and a Basque, in his famous *About Casticismo* (1894–5), passionately argued that Spain's salvation lay in mystical, spiritual, eternal, and 'intra-historical' soul and steppe of Castile, which harboured the 'Castilian spirit' and the 'eternal tradition'. As Unamuno noted, '*Castizo* derives from *caste* . . . The word *caste* is ordinarily applied to races or pure varieties of animal species.'[36] Anthropologists also tendered a more empirical and less mystical gloss. In the early decades of the twentieth century, many believed that the strength of the Spanish nation emanated from its 'racial alloy', the mixture of Latin, Germanic, Celtic, Iberian races that characterized all Spaniards, whether they were Castilian, Catalan, Andalusian, or whatever. Racial purity, to which Basque nationalists aspired, simply meant harmful inbreeding, a genetic formula indicative of primitiveness and atavism. Beginning in the 1930s, Spanish fascists would readily embrace and reinterpret these mystical and scientific conceptions of the nation.[37]

The third problem with this misleading division between 'state' and 'ethnic' nationalism is that Spain also contained an influential version of nationalism—later known as 'National Catholicism'—which was neither 'ethnic' nor 'civic'. This became clear in 1882, when the conservative Antonio Cánovas del Castillo, the architect of the Restoration Monarchy and the most influential and dominant

---

[35] This theme is explained in detail in Javier Varela, 'Castilla mística y guerrera', in *La novela de España*, 145–76. For other intellectual articulations of Spanish essentialism, see Inman Fox, *La invención de España: nacionalismo liberal e identidad nacional* (Madrid, 1997).

[36] I use Miguel de Unamuno, *En torno al Casticismo* (Buenos Aires, 1952), 13.

[37] For anthropological theories, see Joshua Seth Goode, 'The Racial Alloy: The Science, Politics, and Culture of Spain, 1875–1923' (Ph.D. diss., UCLA, 1999). For the roots of Spanish fascism in the Generation of 1898 and French and Italian thought, see Ismael Saz Campos, *Los nacionalismos franquistas* (Madrid, 2003).

politician of the day, felt compelled to respond personally to Ernest Renan's famous speech delivered at the Sorbonne, 'What is a Nation?' Pronounced within the context over the acrid conflict concerning Alsace-Lorraine, Renan coined what was to become a famous lemma of civic nationalism by contending that the nation was equivalent to a 'daily plebiscite'. To Spain's oligarchical liberal-conservative politicians, such as Cánovas, intent on avoiding the inevitable advent of mass politics, nothing could have scared them more than a 'daily plebiscite'. Cánovas's *Discourse on the Nation*, however, did not side with those who, by reverting to the importance of language, territory, and race, and ignoring the democratic wishes of the majority of the inhabitants, had contended that Alsace-Lorraine was German. Instead, he sought a middle ground and moved the subject from France and Germany to Spain. He argued that 'nations are the work of God, or, if some of you prefer, nature'.[38] To Cánovas, Spain was a nation because it was historically transcendent, Castilian-speaking, and monarchical. Catholic communion united culturally diverse regions.

Marcelino Menéndez Pelayo, influenced by Charles Maurras, was the person most successful at spreading a grandiose and forceful Catholic vision that was to prove compatible with the coming of mass politics. While liberal nationalism had always relied on rather bland, intellectual, and pan-European theories of nation—ancient constitution, Germanic liberty, Roman virtue—Catholics were able to locate more meaningful symbols intelligible to the largely uneducated, and even much of the educated, populace. By the 1880s, many Catholics who had found themselves in a political desert during the liberal century began to find space on the right of the political spectrum. They celebrated centennials, sponsored national monuments, and wrote histories that found the heart of Spain in the Reconquest, the discovery and colonization of America, and the Counter-Reformation. Spain as the defender of Europe from African and Ottoman Islam, Spain as civilizer of the Americas. St James 'the Moor Slayer', El Cid, the Catholic Kings, Columbus, Hernan Cortés, Philip II, St Theresa, and St Ignatius of Loyola became consecrated as national heroes. National Catholicism ultimately became the dominant ideology in Francisco Franco's Spain, but in the late nineteenth and early twentieth centuries, it was one of many competitors.[39] In any case, this was not limited to 'Spanish nationalism'. Both the Catalan and Basque nationalist right also portrayed their movements as Catholic responses to an oligarchical, liberal, artificial, and secular state, and buttressed their political programmes with homegrown symbols, traditions, local saints, legends, and crusading heroes.

---

[38] Antonio Cánovas del Castillo, *Discurso sobre la nación* (Madrid, 1882), 72. For Cánovas and nationalism, see Carlos Dardé, 'Cánovas y el nacionalismo liberal español' in Guillermo Cortázar (ed.), *Nación y estado en la España liberal* (Madrid, 1994).

[39] The rise and fall of liberal nationalism and the ascendancy of national Catholicism is explained in the monumental José Álvarez Junco, *Mater dolorosa: la idea de España en el siglo XIX* (Madrid, 2001). The seminal work on national Catholicism is Alfonso Botti, *Cielo y dinero: el nacionalcatolicismo en España* (1881–1975) (Madrid, 1992).

CONCLUSION

The categories of 'civic' and 'ethnic' nationalism were not part of any European's nineteenth-century vernacular and have come into academic vogue only recently. Yet, their use does not intend to attribute *mentalités* and discourses to historical actors by retranslating the words of the past into contemporary dictum. Nor are they employed in an underhanded manner to simplify or to judge. While respecting the integrity of the past, these labels effectively and broadly describe two competing, intersecting, overlapping, and, more often than not, mutually reinforcing systems of ideas born in the eighteenth century and brought into specific academic counter-position in 1870 during debates over Alsace-Lorraine. Thereafter, civic nationalism remained more or less faithful to Enlightenment ideals as reinterpreted and updated by Renan, while ethnic nationalism came to be radically transformed, scientificized by powerful *fin-de-siècle* systems of ideas. All of this reverberated and had a tremendous influence in Spain.

The reception of civic and ethnic ideas obviously must be understood within the context of events transpiring within state and society. The backdrop of a 'weak' state, or better yet, a state poorly conceived around French absolutist and then Bonapartist principles, divorced from the socio-economic reality of industrialized and linguistically differentiated historical communities on the periphery, and ultimately incapable of maintaining the harmony between dual patriotisms and multiple conceptions of identity, is absolutely essential to understanding what transpired in the nineteenth century. But this was the stage on which actors performed. It conditioned outcomes, but did not determine them. For neither Basques, Catalans, nor Spaniards were primordial or intra-historical peoples. Nor was Spain either destined to remain unified, condemned to Balkanization, or eternally fated to be caught in purgatory. Rather, powerful and influential ideas about who comprised the nation and how a nation was to be constituted offered a range of possibilities to intellectual and political elites in the centre, periphery, and empire. Upon the Napoleonic invasion, civic and ethnic forms of nationalism served to reinforce the image of a united Spain on the Peninsula, much as they posed fateful challenges to this image in America. In the latter decades of the nineteenth century, the redefinition of ethnic nationalism in all of Europe offered a different range of possibilities to those who sought to provide flesh and blood to the bare-bone political and civic conception of the nation during the advent of mass politics. The disaster of 1898 created political space that converted nascent organizations into mature and durable movements supporting Catalan, Basque, and Spanish nationalism that continue, albeit with different characteristics, to the present day.

PART IV

ÉTAT

12

Nation-States and Wars

European and Transatlantic Perspectives

Jörn Leonhard

INTRODUCTION: TOWARDS CIVIC AND ETHNIC NATIONALISMS

Research on the historical phenomenon of nationalism in Europe has, for a long time, concentrated mainly on single cases of nation-building or on the development of specific typologies, generating ideal types of nation-building processes.[1] One of the most influential typological differentiations was that between political and cultural nations, a model which, based upon Friedrich Meinecke's distinction between *Staatsnation* and *Kulturnation* had an important impact on West German perceptions of nation and nationality after 1945.[2] This distinction was also present in the apparently clear dichotomy between apparently typical Western and Eastern nationalisms.[3] Analyses focusing on this dichotomy operated with

---

[1] See with particular reference to German research literature Dieter Langewiesche, 'Nation, Nationalismus, Nationalstaat: Forschungsstand und Forschungsperspektiven', *Neue Politische Literatur*, 40 (1995), 190–236; id., *Nation, Nationalismus, Nationalstaat in Deutschland und Europa* (Munich, 2000) and id. and Georg Schmidt (eds.), *Föderative Nation: Deutschlandkonzepte von der Reformation bis zum Ersten Weltkrieg* (Munich, 2000); see from an Anglo-American perspective Geoff Eley and Ronald Grigor Suny, 'Introduction: From the Moment of Social History to the Work of Cultural Representation', in eid. (eds.), *Becoming National: A Reader* (Oxford, 1996), and Anthony Smith, *Nationalism and Modernism: A Critical Survey of Recent Theories of Nations and Nationalism* (London, 1998); see for Franco-German comparisons Heinz-Gerhard Haupt, 'Der Nationalismus in der neueren deutschen und französischen Geschichtswissenschaft', in Étienne François, Hannes Siegrist, and Jakob Vogel (eds.), *Nation und Emotion: Deutschland und Frankreich im Vergleich, 19. und 20. Jahrhundert* (Göttingen, 1995), 39–55; for a general European overview see Peter Alter, *Nationalismus* (Frankfurt am Main, 1985); Hagen Schulze, *Staat und Nation in der europäischen Geschichte* (Munich, 1994); John Breuilly, *Nationalism and the State*, 2nd edn. (Manchester, 1993); and Mikulas Teich and Roy Porter (eds.), *The National Question in Europe in Historical Context* (Cambridge, 1993).

[2] Friedrich Meinecke, *Weltbürgertum und Nationalstaat: Studien zur Genesis des deutschen Nationalstaates* (1907), 6th edn. (Munich, 1922), 1–22.

[3] See Heinrich August Winkler (ed.), *Nationalismus*, 2nd edn. (Königstein, 1985).

different historical patterns of apparently successful, handicapped, or failed patterns of modernization. This perspective gained particular attention because of the specific experiences of Fascism, National Socialism, and Stalinism and especially by the developing Cold War confrontation after 1945.

Against this background Hans Kohn and Louis S. Snyder distinguished an essentially political meaning of the nation in West Europe, which according to their definition aimed at establishing a pluralist society, from an East European model of an essentially cultural nationalism, which was characterized by a tendency to focus on cultural and political unity by the systematic exclusion of minorities. The differences between both models—a civic West European concept of nation and nationality, focusing on citizenship and individual rights on the one hand and an ethnic Central and East European one on the other, concentrating on shared myths, culture, and common history—also reflected Popper's paradigm of the 'open society' in the West and its opposite in the East. West European nationalism, as experienced in Britain, France, the Netherlands, and Switzerland, seemed to be based upon existing political realities, thus avoiding mythological constructions. In contrast, different regions in Central and Eastern Europe as well as Asia pointed to the significance of cultural traditions and myths as well as constructs of ethnic unity.[4] The dominating antagonism behind these bipolar typologies was that between a community of equal state citizens, forming a nation on the basis of their political will, and a people's community, generated not by the political will of a sovereign nation but by the definition and communication of certain cultural and mythological bonds. According to this typology, which justified a pioneering and successful 'Western' path of modernization and defined latecomers accordingly, two different social profiles could be applied to these distinct developments. Whereas the Western type of nationalism seemed an essentially bourgeois phenomenon, East European nationalism appeared as the result of the aristocracy's politics or caused by the masses, thus again underlining distinct paths of economic and social modernization.

Another major typology was conceptionalized in the 1960s, integrating elements of Kohn's and Snyder's earlier works.[5] In his influential essay on the typology of the nation-state in Europe, Theodor Schieder presented three different models. First, there was the West European model of nation-states in Britain and France, originating from the successful revolutions in the seventeenth and eighteenth centuries which had constituted these early nation-states as expressions of the political will of its citizens. Secondly, nation-states in Central and Southern Europe were established between 1815 and 1871 through territorial integration, by which hitherto stateless nations were transformed into new nation-states. In

---

[4] See Hans Kohn, *Die Idee des Nationalismus: Ursprung und Geschichte bis zur Französischen Revolution* (Heidelberg, 1950); id., *Nationalismus: Its Meaning and History* (Princeton, 1965), and Louis L. Snyder, *The Meaning of Nationalism* (New Brunswick, 1954).

[5] See Eugen Lemberg, *Nationalismus*, vol. i: *Psychologie und Geschichte*; vol. ii: *Soziologie und politische Pädagogik* (Hamburg, 1964).

contrast to the meaning and representation of the nation's political will in Britain and France, the driving forces behind this process had been, according to Schieder, language, ethnicity, and history. Thirdly, national movements in the East and South-East of Europe represented historical phenomena in multi-ethnic empires. In contrast to nation-building in Central and Southern Europe through integration, Schieder identified a third type of nation-building by means of secession against an existing empire-state, as in the cases of the Russian, the Austrian, and the Ottoman Empires—a long-term process that came to an end only after 1918. According to Schieder, it was not only possible to identify clearly different structural patterns behind these three typologies, but also distinct geographical spaces—Western, Central, and Eastern Europe—as well as distinct periods in which nation-states developed.[6]

During the 1970s and 1980s the discussion about European nationalisms became increasingly dominated by modernization theories.[7] Focusing on the relation between political and socio-economic modernity and nationalism, Ernest Gellner analysed European nationalism with regard to processes of homogenization which according to him were necessitated by the structures of dynamically developing industrial societies.[8] Taking up this approach many historians have concluded that nationalism as a mass phenomenon could not really develop in the socio-economically backward European East before the last third of the nineteenth century. If new typologies were conceptionalized in the 1980s, as for instance in the case of Rainer M. Lepsius's differentiation between *Volksnation, Kulturnation, Staatsnation*, and *Klassennation*, they were usually limited to the study of one particular case, thus avoiding systematic and comparative studies.[9] In contrast, Liah Greenfeld analysed different 'roads to modernity', comparing five cases covering a long period from the early modern era to the twentieth century. Arguing from the English experience in the seventeenth century, Greenfeld identified an 'individualistic civic nationalism' which already encompassed the modern concept of the nation and which, originating from England, was also fundamental for the North American concept of nation and national identity. Confronted with this Anglo-American model, European continental societies seemed to develop their own

[6] See Theodor Schieder, 'Typologie und Erscheinungsformen des Nationalstaats in Europa' (1966), in id., *Nationalismus und Nationalstaat: Studien zum nationalen Problem im modernen Europa*, ed. Otto Dann and Hans-Ulrich Wehler (Göttingen, 1992), 65–86; see also E. Kedourie, *Nationalismus* (Munich, 1971).

[7] See Stein Rokkan, 'Die vergleichende Analyse der Staaten- und Nationenbildung', in Wolfgang Zapf (ed.), *Theorien des sozialen Wandels* (Cologne, 1970) 228–52; Karl W. Deutsch, *Nationenbildung, Nationalstaat, Integration* (Düsseldorf, 1972), and Shmuel N. Eisenstadt and Stein Rokkan (eds.), *Building States and Nations*, 2 vols. (Beverly Hills, Calif., 1973).

[8] See Ernest Gellner, *Nations and Nationalism* (Oxford, 1983); Karl Deutsch, *Nationalism and Social Communication* (Cambridge, Mass, 1962); id., *Der Nationalismus und seine Alternativen* (Munich, 1972); Otto Dann, *Nationalismus und sozialer Wandel* (Hamburg, 1978); and Miroslav Hroch, *Social Preconditions of National Revival in Europe* (Cambridge, 1985).

[9] See M. Rainer Lepsius, 'Nation und Nationalismus heute', in Heinrich August Winkler (ed.), *Nationalismus in der Welt von heute* (Göttingen, 1982), 12–27.

responses, generating nationalisms which were more influenced by indigenous, collective, and xenophobic traditions. According to Greenfeld, despite differences in detail, the European continental societies' opposition to the English individualistic and civic nationalism characterized both Germany and Russia, but had also a profound impact on the French case.[10]

During the 1990s three very different trends have influenced the design of research on nations and nationalisms. First, and in a critical response to Anthony Smith's premiss of an essentially ethnic justification of modern nations, Benedict Anderson introduced the concept of nations as 'imagined communities'. The construct of national self-images concealed the very diversity, heterogeneity, and complexity of social realities.[11] This assumption could easily be combined with Gellner's interpretation describing nationalism as a particular state in the development of industrial societies.[12] The fact that modern industrial societies required at the same time a differentiated and a levelled social basis seemed to explain the success of national myths in a period of accelerated and intensified industrial transformation. Following Gellner's interpretation, the invention of the nation therefore corresponded directly to the need to homogenize societies in a period of dynamic change.[13] Secondly, historians had to respond to the collapse of the Soviet Empire and the subsequent end of the Cold War in 1990–1. This constellation has led to a rediscovery of nation, nation-state, and nationalism as fundamental concepts in the former member states of the Warsaw Pact but also in Russia itself.[14] Thirdly, and against the background of an intensified process of European integration which tends to weaken traditional institutions of the classical nation-state by supranational institutions and at the same time strengthens regions through devolution, research interests have shifted increasingly towards regionalism and federalism in historical perspective.[15] The complex relation between nation and region becomes particularly obvious in the border regions of Central and Eastern Europe.[16]

---

[10] See Liah Greenfeld, *Five Roads to Modernity* (Cambridge, Mass., 1992), on early-modern roots see also Adrian Hastings, *The Construction of Nationhood: Ethnicity, Religion and Nationalism* (Cambridge, 1997).

[11] See Anthony Smith, *The Ethnic Origins of Nation* (Oxford, 1987), and Benedict Anderson, *Imagined Communities: Reflections on the Origin and Spread of Nationalism* (London, 1983).

[12] See Wilfried von Below, 'Nation, Nationalstaat, Nationalismus', in Dieter Hohlen (ed.), *Lexikon der Politik*, vol. i: *Politische Theorien*, ed. Dieter Nohlen and Rainer-Olaf Schulze (Munich, 1995), 357, see Ernest Gellner, *Nationalismus und Moderne* (Berlin, 1991).

[13] See R. Bauböck, 'Nationalismus versus Demokratie', in *Österreichische Zeitschrift für Politikwissenschaft*, 20 (1991), 73–90; Eric J. Hobsbawm and Terence Ranger (eds.), *The Invention of Tradition* (Cambridge, 1983); David Cannadine, *Die Erfindung der britischen Monarchie 1820–1994* (Berlin, 1994); and Geoffrey Cubitt (ed.), *Imagining Nations* (Manchester, 1998).

[14] See Andreas Kappeler, *Rußland als Vielvölkerreich: Entstehung, Geschichte, Zerfall* (Munich, 1992); from an Anglo-American perspective see Geoffrey Hosking and Robert Service (eds.), *Reinterpreting Russia* (London, 1999); and Vera Tolz, *Inventing the Nation: Russia* (London, 2001).

[15] See Heinrich August Winkler (ed.), *Nationalismus, Nationalitäten, Supranationalität* (Stuttgart, 1993); Barry Jones and Michael Keating (eds.), *The European Union and the Region* (Oxford, 1995); and Raimund Krämer (ed.), *Regionen in der Europäischen Union* (Berlin, 1998).

[16] See Langewiesche and Schmidt (eds.), *Föderative Nation*, and Maiken Umbach (ed.), *German Federalism: Past, Present and Future* (London, 2002).

For all the benefits of these typologies and models, none of them has yet systematically concentrated on the meaning of war experiences for nation-building and the development of national self-images, although all approaches show that the history of nation and nationality includes numerous violent conflicts. But how are we to understand the character of nation-states as war machines, and how did the experience of war influence the character of nation-building between the poles of civic and ethnic nationalisms? Did war experiences play a greater role in societies shaped by ethnic nationalism than in those in which civic nationalism dominated? In order to contribute to a fresh look at the relevance of the civic-ethnic model, the following comparison seeks to analyse how concepts of national identity were shaped by war experiences in France, Germany, Britain, and the United States.

WAR AND NATION-BUILDING IN COMPARATIVE PERSPECTIVE

The modern concepts of nation and nation-state were inextricably linked with experiences of war. This is not only true from a German or an Italian perspective, that is to say from the perspective of successful external nation-building through wars, be it between 1859 and 1861 in the Italian case or between 1864 and 1871 in the German case.[17] The long-term process of state-building, by which Europe's political map changed dramatically from the early modern period to the First World War can also be described as a history of warfare and its revolutionary impacts. Most of the numerous territorial states of the early modern period did not survive this violent restructuring of Europe. Between the last third of the eighteenth century and the end of the nineteenth century the number decreased from about 500 units around 1800 to about 20 states around 1900. State-building, much intensified between 1794 and 1815, was directly linked to the experience of wars, and the British war-state of the eighteenth century is a particular illustration.[18] As a part of this complex process, justifications of war changed, pointing to the new meaning of nation and nation-state as dominant paradigms of political and social legitimacy.[19]

---

[17] See the chapters by Ute Frevert, Rudolf Jaun, Hew Strachan, Stig Förster, and Dietrich Beyrau in Ute Frevert (ed.), *Militär und Gesellschaft im 19. und 20. Jahrhundert* (Stuttgart, 1997), 17–142; for the German case see in particular the chapters by Georg Schmidt, Horst Carl, and Nikolaus Buschmann in Langewiesche and Schmidt (eds.), *Föderative Nation* 33–111.

[18] See John Brewer, *The Sinews of Power: War, Money and the English State, 1688–1783* (1988; New York 1989).

[19] See Charles Tilly (ed.), *The Formation of National States in Western Europe* (Princeton, 1975); id., 'Reflections on the History of European State-Making', ibid. 3–83, p. 42; and id., 'States and Nationalism in Europe 1492–1992', in John L. Comaroff and Paul C. Stern (eds.), *Perspectives on Nationalism and War* (Amsterdam, 1995), 187–204.

But war not only accompanied the external processes of state-building. It also represented, at least in contemporary political discourses and in particular from the 1750s onwards, a possible means of political emancipation and participation. War changed its character from a merely dynastic affair and a cabinet war, fought with mercenaries from different countries who did not identify with an abstract notion of nation, to a war fought, in theory at least, in the name of the whole nation and fought by the whole nation in arms. On the one hand, and since the last third of the eighteenth century, new forms of *national wars* or *people's wars*, in particular the American War of Independence and then the French revolutionary wars, meant that more groups of society were now directly affected by war. Warfare based upon mass armies and collective conscription transcended the traditional separation of the civil population from the experience of violent conflict, as had been the aim of traditional cabinet wars since the mid-seventeenth century, fought in the name of monarchical, dynastic, and territorial interests, but excluding the horrors of civil war as they had been experienced in the seventeenth century.[20] On the other hand, national wars strengthened the state's legitimacy as the dominating institution which could provide for the financial and military means of warfare.

A war fought in the name of the entire nation also provoked hitherto unknown expectations of political and social participation. The transformation from the traditional corporatist structures and privileged estates of the European *ancien régime*, from a society of feudal subjects, to a class-based society of citizens was linked to, and partly even caused by, experiences of war. This ambivalence of war—externally as a form of collective aggression and violence and, internally, as a means of participation—is not just the result of the historian's restrospective causality, but stood already behind contemporary war discourses and controversies over the precise meaning and possible justification of war.[21] Thus, the concept of civil war, so dominant in the critical periods of the seventeenth century with its religious conflicts in various European societies, found its way back into justifications of war after 1750. But in contrast to the seventeenth century, it was now no longer a civil war caused by confessional conflicts, but fought in the light of the secular concepts of liberty and equality as derived from the natural right

---

[20] See Herfried Münkler, *Über den Krieg: Stationen der Kriegsgeschichte im Spiegel ihrer theoretischen Reflexion*, 2nd edn. (Weilerswist, 2003), 53–5 and 75–7; see for the German state of research Jörg Echternkamp and Sven Oliver Müller (eds.), *Die Politik der Nation: Deutscher Nationalismus in Krieg und Krisen* (Munich, 2002); Werner Rösener (ed.), *Staat und Krieg: Vom Mittelalter bis zur Moderne* (Göttingen, 2000); and Edgar Wolfrum, *Krieg und Frieden in der Neuzeit: Vom Westfälischen Frieden bis zum Zweiten Weltkrieg* (Darmstadt, 2003), 49–51, 66–8, and 95–7.

[21] See Alan Forrest, 'The Nation in Arms I: The French Wars', in Charles Townshend (ed.), *The Oxford History of Modern War* (Oxford, 2000), 55–73; David French, 'The Nation in Arms II: The Nineteenth Century', ibid. 74–93; and Daniel Moran and Arthur Waldron (ed.), *The People in Arms: Military Myth and National Mobilization since the French Revolution* (Cambridge, 2003); see also Johannnes Kunisch (ed.), *Staatsverfassung und Heeresverfassung in der europäischen Geschichte der frühen Neuzeit* (Berlin, 1986); id., *Fürst—Gesellschaft—Krieg: Studien zur bellizistischen Disposition des absoluten Fürstenstaates* (Cologne, 1992).

philosophy. Already in the 1760s the French philosopher Abbé Mably described the expansionist wars of the eighteenth century as the natural consequence of monarchical despotism. This justified a new and international civil war of all suppressed peoples against their monarchical oppressors, and he regarded such an international civil war as a 'bien', legitimizing in this context the 'nation militaire'.[22] During the French Revolution and the subsequent wars from 1792 to 1815 such ideas assumed a new significance. However, the wars of this period soon demonstrated that the paradigm of an international and revolutionary civil war of all suppressed peoples against their despotic suppressors was soon replaced by national wars between distinct states. Conflicts from the 1790s onwards therefore marked a middle position between traditional cabinet wars that had characterized European history since the end of the Thirty Years War and a new concept of civil war in the name of abstract principles.[23]

The ambivalent complexity of war experiences became more obvious in the course of the nineteenth century: on the one hand, the wars of the nineteenth century were in many ways still fought according to the rules of traditional cabinet wars, although the wars of the 1860s clearly showed signs of transformation from Clausewitz's 'absolute war' into 'total war'.[24] On the other hand, these wars reflected, in theory at least, each individual fighter's identification with a more abstract notion of nationality and nation, and this justification of war was clearly a legacy of the civil war paradigm, as it had become revived through the experiences in America and France since the last third of the eighteenth century. If the contemporary concept of *national war* pointed already to the connection between the citizen's duty to defend the fatherland and his recognition as a politically participating subject, then the *people's war* transcended this connotation even further.[25] Already during the 1760s and 1770s many American writers had referred to the war against the British as a 'people's war', representing a people's ability to organize and mobilize its military in the absence of a monarchical state and at the same time challenging the traditional state's monopoly of arms.[26] In France the prospect of a revolutionary people's war was also seen and perceived as a potential threat by the new revolutionary regimes after 1792. The regimes therefore responded with deliberate attempts to control and channel this development.

In the course of the nineteenth century the people's war generated distinct forms of warfare. Three ideal types can be distinguished. First, guerrilla warfare stood for the ideal type of a people's war. Following the collapse or the paralysis of

---

[22] Gabriel Bonnot, Abbé de Mably, *Des droits et des devoirs du citoyen* (Kell, 1789), 93–4.

[23] See Johannes Kunisch and Herfried Münkler (eds.), *Die Wiedergeburt des Krieges aus dem Geist der Revolution: Studien zum bellizistischen Diskurs des ausgehenden 18. und beginnenden 19. Jahrhunderts* (Berlin, 1999).

[24] Carl von Clausewitz, 'Vom Kriege' (1832/34), in Reinhard Stumpf (ed.), *Kriegstheorie und Kriegsgeschichte: Carl von Clausewitz und Helmuth von Moltke* (Frankfurt am Main, 1993), 318–19.

[25] See Rainer Wohlfeil, 'Der Volkskrieg im Zeitalter Napoleons', in Heinz-Otto Sieburg (ed.), *Napoleon und Europa* (Cologne, 1971), 318–32.

[26] David Ramsay, *The History of the American Revolution: A New Edition*, vol. i (London, 1793), 325.

a state's authority, it was the population which now organized and carried out military actions, not in traditional battles but rather in small, individual actions, exemplified by the Spanish guerrilla war against Napoleonic regular troops in 1808. Secondly, militia armies combined the two principles of voluntary service with that of state control and professional military leadership in order to fight larger battles and to use the mass mobilization of nations in arms. The American War of Independence as well as the early years of the French revolutionary wars after 1792 provide examples of this type. Thirdly, mass conscript armies stood for the attempt to fully control and regulate a people's mobilization for war. It provided the military and fiscal state with enormous new resources of power. The principle of conscription as a means of defending the whole nation also justified the use of force necessary to overcome popular resistance against the rigours of compulsory military service. France during the Napoleonic Empire and Prussia after the early nineteenth century exemplified this type.[27] In all these categories of people's wars particular elements of total warfare were obvious, although *total war* with its new industrial character and hitherto unknown numbers of victims became a collective experience only after 1914. However, already the wars of the second half of the century, the Crimean war, but in particular the American Civil War between 1861 and 1865 and the Wars of German Unification between 1864 and 1871, pointed to a transformation in the meaning of war and a changing character of modern warfare: this was essentially characterized by a new combination of technological progress, based upon increased firepower and railway transport, and mass mobilization in the name of an abstract ideal of nationality and the nation-state. The state's financial, economic, and military means to achieve its aims reached a peak. This new dimension of mobilization also necessitated a new ideological justification of war. War was no longer regarded as a conflict over territory or dynastic interests, but it was fought for the ultimate existence of nations and peoples. This necessitated the stigmatization of the enemy and the overcoming of the traditional separation between a state's armies and its people. The essential distinction between the military and the civic sphere came into question, as both the actions of the North American General Sherman in the southern states of the Confederation during the American Civil War and the popular warfare of the French against the German invaders after September 1870 illustrated.

The intensive interaction between war and nation-building since the eighteenth century is obvious. It included at the same time the new ideal of the politically participating citizen as the natural defender of the fatherland and hence a resurgence of

---

[27] See Stig Förster, 'Vom Volkskrieg zum totalen Krieg? Der Amerikanische Bürgerkrieg 1861–1865, der DeutschFranzösische Krieg 1870/71 und die Anfänge moderner Kriegsführung', in Walther L. Bernecker and Volker Dotterweich (eds.), *Deutschland in den internationalen Beziehungen des 19. und 20. Jahrhunderts: Festschrift für Josef Becker zum 65. Geburtstag* (Munich, 1996), 78–9; see also Ute Frevert, *Die kasernierte Nation: Militärdienst und Zivilgesellschaft in Deutschland* (Munich, 2001).

the civil war paradigm against the idea of cabinet wars, separating the military sphere from that of civil society. From that point of view the perceived national character of conflicts after 1792 provoked civic connotations of citizenship and political expectations, participation through conscription being the most obvious of these. But the nation in arms also marked the beginning of a long-term process towards a radicalization of both national self-images and images of the enemy, thereby integrating many ethnic connotations focusing on belligerent myths and military memories. The following comparison seeks to demonstrate that war experiences in different cases tended to amalgamate civic and ethnic nationalisms, so that any ideal-type separation between the two cannot easily be maintained.

FRANCE: REVOLUTIONARY CITIZENSHIP AND THE NATION IN ARMS

The concept of war nationalism and a nation in arms originated in the years of the French Revolution, but universal and compulsory military service was the consequence of unforeseen events. Many of the French *cahiers de doléances*, which prepared the meeting of the General Estates in Versailles in summer 1789, had demanded the abolition of the royal practice of recruiting provincial militias, and indeed many bourgeois writers had even hoped that a new constitutional regime would mark the beginning of a new era of permanent peace. However, within a few years, conscript soldiers formed the rank and file of the French armies defending the fatherland against the armies of the European counter-revolutionary First Coalition.[28] It was in this context that the idea of a military nation, a nation in arms prepared to defend the revolution's achievements, became prominent. The National Convention decreed that 'the batallion organized in each district shall be united under a banner bearing the inscription: The French people risen against tyranny.' In August 1793 the assembly went even further and laid down the principle of a total mobilization of society in the name of defending the nation: young men were to go forth to battle, married men would forge arms, women were to make tents and clothing, and the aged were 'to preach hatred of kings and the unity of the Republic'.[29]

The old army of the *ancien régime*, in which purchase of commissions had been a privilege of the rich and aristocratic, seemed to be a more than legitimate object of reform. At the same time, there had already been a pre-revolutionary and enlightened concept of conscription. Already in 1772 Rousseau had advised the Poles that only a well-trained militia, recruited from citizens who accepted their duty as the natural defenders of a republic, could assure the defence and existence

---

[28] See Richard Challener, *The French Theory of the Nation in Arms 1866–1939* (New York, 1965), 3–9.

[29] Jean B. Duvergier (ed.), *Collection complète des lois, décrets, ordonnances, réglemens, avis du conseil d'état... de 1788 à 1830*, 30 vols. (Paris, 1834–8), vi. 107–8.

of a free nation.[30] After 1792 it was primarily the harsh military realities which necessitated the formation of armies which were of a far greater size than the professional forces employed in dynastic wars of the earlier eighteenth century. What distinguished the ideological justification which referred to patriotism and egalitarianism as fundamental attributes of the revolutionary agenda was that it generated the expectation that it was the sons of France who had to enrol in the defence of the revolutionary nation. The highest sacrifice for the fatherland had to be shared equally. Equality of all citizen-defenders pointed to emancipation within the political body of the nation. War nationalism thus included an element of political emancipation, of implementing popular sovereignty: if all citizens were called to arms to defend the fatherland, then clearly they could also demand to take part in its political decision-making. The result was the concept of the nation in arms as both an expression of military necessity and political participation. Already in 1789 the French revolutionary and army reformer Dubois-Crancé had underlined the political consequences behind the nation in arms when he had declared before the Constituent Assembly that 'dans une nation qui veut être libre, qui est entourée de voisins puissants, criblée de factions sourdes et ulcérées, tout citoyen doit être soldat et tout soldat citoyen, sinon la France est arrivée au terme de son anéantissement'.[31]

The transformation of the citizen into a soldier, a defender of the revolutionary nation, the idea that the nation had to prove its very existence by war, had a lasting impact on French concepts of national identity throughout the long nineteenth century. Conscript service as both the badge and moral consequence of citizenship became a legacy of the French Revolution, and not only for France, but for the whole of continental Europe. Following the experience of the revolutionary and Napoleonic wars, the concept of a nation in arms and the image of a distinct war nation were regarded as essential elements of the revolutionary legacy and hence suppressed. Thus after 1815, military and political leaders from the Bourbon restoration to the end of the Second Empire had no faith in the conscript soldier whom they regarded as a potential revolutionary. On the other hand, the French people proved more than unwilling to accept the rigours of compulsory military service. Contemporaries after 1870 regarded both aspects as essential causes of the catastrophe experienced in 1870. As a consequence the defeat against Germany resulted in a reform of the French military system, once again focusing on and reviving the concept of a French nation in arms.

---

[30] Jean-Jacques Rousseau, 'Considérations sur le gouvernement de Pologne et sur la réformation projetée' (1772), in id., *Œuvres complètes*, ed. Bernard Gagnebin and Marcel Raymond, vol. iii, (Paris, 1964), 951–1041.

[31] 'In a nation that wants to be free, that is surrounded by powerful neighbours, riddled with deaf and sickening factions, every citizen must be a soldier and every soldier a citizen, otherwise France has arrived at the final stage of its annihilation'; Edmond-Louis-Alexis Dubois-Crancé, Speech, Assemblée nationale, 12 Dec. 1789, in Th. Iung, *L'Armée et la révolution: Edmond-Louis-Alexis Dubois-Crancé, mousquetaire, constituant, conventionnel, général de division, ministre de la guerre 1747–1814*, vol. i (Paris, 1884) 18–19.

Despite the origins of this concept in the French Revolution, it was the military defeat against Prussia/Germany in 1870 which led to the concept of a *nation armée* being put into practice in the form of mass conscription from the 1870s onwards. However, the period between the defeat of 1870 and the outbreak of the First World War in 1914 reflected the diversity of antagonistic interpretations of the idea of a national identity shaped by war and guaranteed only by a nation in arms. Republicans who after 1870 identified positively with the revolutionary legacy turned the concept of the nation in arms into a moral touchstone, a means to measure the moral virtue of republican citizens. In contrast, conservative opponents and critics of the French Revolution regarded the nation in arms as a road towards social anarchy and violent disorder generated by armed mobs. A generation of French military officers who had experienced the humiliating defeat of 1870 primarily saw the necessity to respond to the superiority of the German military model. For them the *nation armée* was a rational instrument to develop mass armies which would be decisive in future mass warfare. This excluded implications of political reform. Such a view was distinct from the political reformers of the Dreyfus era who concentrated on the idea that politically educated citizen-soldiers would form the army of the future, thus weakening the influence of the military hierarchy in French society which, as both the Dreyfus and the Boulanger crises had illustrated, was still very strong. A citizen first, a soldier only as a necessary consequence, the citizen-soldier would become the natural guardian of the French republican nation.[32]

The war of 1870 showed how contemporaries used both civic and ethnic elements to come to terms with the traumatic events. Ernest Renan openly criticized Germany's focus on ethnic homogeneity, arguing that in contrast to the French tradition of national self-determination such a concept would not only lead to a war of extermination, but also stressing the impossibility of separating nation-states on the basis of ethnically defined borders:

> De même qu'une nation légitimiste se fait hacher pour sa dynastie, de même nous sommes obligés de faire les derniers sacrifices pour que ceux qui étaient nés à nous par un pacte de vie et de mort ne souffrent pas violence... Notre politique, c'est la politique du droit des nations; la vôtre, c'est la politique des races...très-peu de pays possèdant une race vraiment pure, ne peut mener qu'à des guerres d'extermination, à des guerres 'zoologiques'... Vous avez levé dans le monde le drapeau de la politique ethnographique et archéologique en place de la politique libérale; cette politique vous sera fatale.[33]

---

[32] See Challener, *Theory*, 46–90.

[33] 'As a legitimist nation is chopped up by its dynasty, so we are obliged to make the final sacrifices so that those who were born to us through a pact of life and death do not suffer any violence...Our politics is the politics of the rights of nation; yours is the politics of races...too few countries with a truly pure race could only lead to wars of extermination, to "zoological" wars...You have raised the flag of ethnographic and archaeological politics in the world in the place of liberal politics; these politics will be fatal for you.' Ernest Renan, Nouvelle lettre à M. Strauss, 15 Sept. 1871, in id., 'La Réforme intellectuelle et morale de la France' (1871), in id., *La Réforme intellectuelle et morale* (1871), 4th edn. (Paris, 1875), 198–9.

But Renan went further; in the context of war, he argued that a nation could not only be a political body defined by the political will, but a community with shared historical memories, and in particular experiences of common suffering.[34] In his Essay *La Guerre entre la France et l'Allemagne* he stressed the importance of wars for any process of national self-realization.[35] Here the civic ideal of the revolutionary nation was overshadowed by a shared history and collective memories:

Une nation ne prend d'ordinaire la complète conscience d'elle-même que sous la pression de l'étranger. La France existait avant Jeanne d'Arc et Charles VII; cependant c'est sous le poids de la domination anglaise que le mot de France prend un accent particulier. Un moi, pour prendre le langage de la philosophie, se crée toujours en opposition avec un autre moi. La France fit de la sorte l'Allemagne comme nation. La plaie avait été trop visible. Une nation dans la pleine floraison de son génie et au plus haut point de sa force morale avait été livrée sans défense à un adversaire moins intelligent et moins moral par les misérables divisions de ses petits princes, et faute d'un drapeau central.[36]

Nations could not only be the consequence of voluntaristic acts, but were the result of long-term processes of shared experiences, and of war experiences in particular.

GERMANY: NATIONAL WARS AND THE DILEMMA OF NATION-BUILDING

Although Germany is usually quoted as one of the most prominent examples of the ethnic model of nation-building, stressing the importance of the *Kulturnation* instead of the West European *Staatsnation*, the focus on war experiences reveals important civic elements as well. Doubtless, the legacy of the anti-Napoleonic wars stood for ethnic connotations of a shared history and common sacrifices, but also for many liberals' hopes to achieve a constitutional state after 1813/15.[37]

[34] Ernest Renan, *La Réforme intellectuelle et morale* (1871), 4th edn. (Paris, 1875), 202.
[35] Ernest Renan, 'La Guerre entre la France et l'Allemagne', in 'Revue des deux Mondes', 15 Sept. 1870, in id., *Réforme*, 123–66.
[36] 'A nation does not normally come to complete self-consciousness except under the pressure of the foreigner. France existed before Joan of Arc and Charles VII; nevertheless it is under the weight of English domination that the word "France" took on a particular accent. A "self" to take the language of philosophy, is always created in opposition to another "self". Thus did France create Germany as a nation. The wound was too visible. A nation in the full flower of its genius and at the highest point of its moral force was delivered defenceless to an adversary, less intelligent and less moral through the miserable divisions of its little princes and for the lack of a central flag.' Ibid. 131–2.
[37] See Karen Hagemann, '*Mannlicher Muth und Teutsche Ehre': Nation, Militär und Geschlecht zur Zeit der Antinapoleonischen Kriege Preußens* (Paderborn, 2002); for contemporary examples see, *inter alia*, *Ideen und Vorschläge zu einer, dem Geist der Zeit gemäßen, künftigen Staats-Verfassung in Teutschland: Von einem teutschen Geschäftsmann* (n.p. 1814); Ernst Moritz Arndt, *Ueber zukünftige Verfassungen in Teutschland* (Frankfurt am Main, 1814); Friedrich Ancillon, *Ueber Souveränität und Staats-Verfassungen: Ein Versuch zur Berichtigung einiger politischen Grundbegriffe* (Berlin, 1815), and Wilhelm Traugott Krug, *Die Fürsten und die Völker in ihren gegenseitigen Forderungen: Eine politische*

After the disillusioning experiences during the revolution of 1848–9, events on the Italian peninsula and the successful national war against Austria in 1859 led again to an intensified public debate about the changing character of war. *National war* as a key concept of these contemporary war discourses, in which especially liberal bourgeois writers played a very prominent role, referred to both hopes for a unified and constitutional nation-state and a radicalized image of the enemy. In a contemporary definition of the early 1860s it was thus pointed out that in any national war every part of the opposing people, that is to say not only the military, was to be regarded as an enemy which had to be defeated in all circumstances. The concept of an international civil war of all the suppressed against their oppressors, which has still been dominant in the enlightened paradigm of war in the later eighteenth century, was replaced by a war fought for the nation, and carried out by a nation in arms. In the words of contemporary German encyclopedias: 'If war shall be fought with the full vigour of the nation, then it has to originate from the will of the nation.' Wars, it seemed, could only be 'fought for great and just, national interests'.[38] Karl Marx, on the other hand, approached the contemporary conflicts from the perspective of ideological criticism. He insisted on international and revolutionary class war as part of the inevitable and historically necessary class struggle. In contrast, national wars only concealed the true character of social conflicts. Consequently, Marx regarded national war as the ultimate instrument by which the old bourgeois society tried to rescue itself. Taking the form of a merely governmental swindle (*Regierungsschwindel*), it only postponed the true character of war which could only be a revolutionary class war.[39]

One of the most telling contemporary analyses on the relation between a new type of national war and popular participation is that of Helmut von Moltke. Undoubtedly one of the most influential makers of modern military strategy in Germany, Moltke had been largely responsible for the successful campaigns of the 1860s and early 1870s.[40] He clearly stood in the tradition of Carl von Clausewitz who at the beginning of the century and against the background of the French revolutionary wars, had distinguished between traditional cabinet wars and the

Parallele der hohen Bundesversammlung in Frankfurt gewidmet von einem Vaterlandsfreunde, inclusive einer Zugabe zu Herrn Ancillon's Schrift über Souveränität und Staatsverfassungen betreffend (Leipzig, 1816).

[38] Berner, 'Krieg, Kriegsrecht (politisch und völkerrechtlich)', in Johann Caspar Bluntschli and Carl Brater (eds.), *Deutsches Staatswörterbuch*, vol. vi (Stuttgart, 1861), 105, and Löbel, 'Krieg', in Johann Samuel Ersch and Johann Gottfried Gruber (eds.), *Allgemeine Encyclopädie der Wissenschaften und Künste* (Leipzig, 1886), 381.

[39] Karl Marx, 'Der Bürgerkrieg in Frankreich', in id. and Friedrich Engels, *Werke*, ed. the Institut für Marxismus-Leninismus beim ZK der SED, 39 vols. (Berlin (Ost), 1956–68), vol. xvii (1962), 361.

[40] See Stig Förster, 'Helmuth von Moltke und das Problem des industrialisierten Volkskriegs im 19. Jahrhundert', in Roland G. Foerster (ed.), *Generalfeldmarschall von Moltke: Bedeutung und Wirkung* (Munich, 1991), 103–15.

new concept of 'absolute wars', which were fought with conscript armies. As the French revolutionary armies demonstrated in the eyes of many contemporaries, mass mobilization gave ideological motives a new relevance. In theory, these new wars would be much more difficult to control by governments. Looking back to the Prussian war against Austria in 1866, Moltke insisted on its character as a cabinet war, thereby defending the primacy of political and military decision-making against the paradigm of an uncontrollable people's war. According to Moltke, the conflict had not been caused by the need to defend Prussia's existence or with regard to public opinion or the 'people's voice', but had been decided in the cabinet as a necessary step in Prussia's interest. It had not been fought for territorial or material gains, but for an abstract ideal, for Prussia's power position in Central Europe against Austrian hopes to retain a hegemony over Germany.[41]

In 1880 Moltke applied this primacy of political and military decision-making to the war of 1870–1. Convinced of the anthropological necessity of wars, he argued in favour of short wars in order to prevent the radicalization of warfare, to achieve a more humane warfare. Yet Moltke was well aware of the necessity to include not only the military to fight a war, but also to mobilize all possible human, social, and economic resources of a nation, of state and society. This reflected Clausewitz's notion of 'absolute war' without already encompassing the notion of a future 'total war'. Moltke concluded that the greatest advantage of a war laid in being a short war. This justified the use of all the enemy's resources, including its finances, railways, food supplies, and even its prestige.[42] From this perspective, Moltke regarded the start of the war of 1870 as a success, because the French armies had been defeated after two months. Only after the new revolutionary regime under Gambetta had started a guerrilla war against the German troops did the war assume a new, more violent character, and directly affected larger parts of the French population.

In stark contrast to his belief in the possible maintenance of political and military control of war, Moltke, in one of his last speeches in the Reichstag in May 1890, pointed out that the traditional concept of cabinet wars had now irrevocably come to an end. He saw them replaced by new peoples' wars as they had developed since 1848. As a fundamental consequence, the governments' and the military elites' ability to direct decision-making was now challenged by new social interests. Wars were no longer fought on the basis of a political and military primacy, but seemed more and more influenced by social interests, social conflicts, and public opinion. Whereas the state had been able to channel and limit the extent of conflicts following the French revolutionary wars, experiences after 1848 demonstrated a possible return of the revolutionary legacy of people's wars. Consequently Moltke argued that the causes which made peace so difficult to maintain were no longer princes and governments, but peoples and classes,

---

[41] Helmuth von Moltke, 'Über den angeblichen Kriegsrat in den Kriegen König Wilhelms I.' (1881), in Stumpf (ed.), *Kriegstheorie*, 600.

[42] Moltke's letter to Johann Kaspar Bluntschli, 11 Dec. 1880, in Stumpf (ed.), *Kriegstheorie*, 488.

pointing in particular to the lower classes' social interests and their will to use revolutionary force in order to improve their socio-economic position. Under these circumstances a short and decisive war seemed no longer possible. Given the enormous armaments of all European powers, a future war was likely to last indefinitely. A decisive reason for this prospect was the fact that mass conscription had transformed the limited size of earlier armies into nations in arms with virtually unlimited human resources. He anticipated that no power could be totally defeated, and that consequently peace treaties would only have a temporary significance. Moltke was convinced that the war of the future would no longer be fought for territorial gains or power positions, but for the very existence of nations and nation-states. The future wars would transform the complete social and political basis of existing nations and of civilization itself.[43]

Moltke's anylysis seems of particular importance: confronted with the wars against revolutionary and Napoleonic France, Prussia at the beginning of the century had introduced universal conscription, and in contrast to the French model exemptions had not been allowed. However, and in contrast to France, Prussia denied any coupling of conscription and citizenship rights. Moltke observed that the new tendency towards national and people's wars, which he saw advancing after the conflicts of the 1860s and 1870s, would ultimately include the right of political and social participation of all classes of society and hence question the foundations of the new German Empire of 1871. The war discourses of the later nineteenth century hence anticipated what would become reality only after 1914: a new concept of national service, based upon the common war sacrifices, by which all classes of society, men as well as women, could demand to participate equally in a democratic society.

BRITAIN: FROM TRADITIONAL ANTI-MILITARISM TO ETHNIC AND RACIAL BELLIGERENCE

In stark contrast to the continental European cases of France, Germany, or Italy, Britain in the second half of the century did not witness a similar debate over national and people's wars. Whenever these concepts were used, they referred to other countries than Britain.[44] This points to particular differences between war experiences and the meaning of the military on the continent and across the Channel. Britain's geographical position, without direct neighbours, allowed her to rely on a relatively small professional army. Even before 1914 the planned size of

---

[43] Helmut von Moltke, Speech in the Reichstag, 14 May 1890, in Stumpf (ed.), *Kriegstheorie*, 504–6; see also Graf Alfred von Schlieffen, 'Über die Millionenheere' (1911), in id., *Cannae: Mit einer Auswahl von Aufsätzen und Reden des Feldmarschalls*, ed. Hugo Freiherr von Freytag-Loringhoven (Berlin, 1925), 286–7.

[44] See Hew Strachan, 'Militär, Empire und Civil Society: Großbritannien im 19. Jahrhundert', in Frevert (ed.), *Militär*, 78–93, and Michael Paris, *Warrior Nation: Images of War in British Popular Culture, 1850–2000* (London, 2000).

the army was less than a quarter that of most continental armies.[45] Furthermore, large standing armies had always been regarded as symbols of absolutist despotism. But in contrast to the continent, where as a consequence of the religious wars of the seventeenth century princes and dynasties had established absolutist rule on the basis of standing armies, the absolutist experiment had failed in Britain with the end of the Stuarts in 1688. The Whig interpretation of these conflicts provided ample room for the identification of standing armies with absolutist and therefore un-English politics. When confronted with increased and intensified armament programmes and the introduction of mass conscription in other European countries, discussions in Britain after 1870 did not focus primarily on a conscript army. Even Lord Roberts, popular president of the National Service League, did not demand a mass conscript army but favoured specific military units capable of defending the British island in case of an invasion.[46] There was no equivalent of continental experiences which, as in the French revolutionary and Napoleonic wars before 1815 and during the conflicts of the 1850s, 1860s, and 1870s, had catalysed discourses over the changing meaning and justification of war.

Furthermore, and distinct from the ideal of a nation in arms according to which all groups of society at least in theory should be trained to defend the fatherland, the British army for a long time was regarded as a microcosm of rural society. According to this view, officers were recruited from the landed aristocracy and gentry, and soldiers represented the uncorrupted virtues of the non-industrial part of British society. Traditional interpretations of the British army in the nineteenth century have highlighted that it was this constellation which prevented any military professionalization by adhering to an amateur ideal of gentleman-officers and peasant-soldiers.[47] But in the light of more recent research this interpretation needs a closer look. In comparison with France, Germany, and Italy, it was not the concept of national war or people's war, such as in 1859–61, 1864, 1866, and 1870–1, that dominated contemporary war discourses in Britain, but the *small wars* which accompanied the expansion of the British Empire. Throughout the long nineteenth century Britain was engaged in more or less constant military actions in her colonies, and these war experiences were certainly distinct from the national wars on the continent between 1848 and 1871. It was also in this context that the army's image as a microcosm of rural Britain was challenged. The military crisis which the British faced in the Boer War seemed, in the eyes of many contemporary observers, to be the result of social degeneration of officers and soldiers, due to urbanization and industrialization in the British motherland.[48] On the other hand, the army

---

[45] See Edward M. Spiers, *The Army and Society* (London, 1980).

[46] See R. J. Q. Adams and Philip P. Poirer, *The Conscription Controversy in Great Britain 1900–1918* (Basingstoke, 1987), 16–18.

[47] Strachan, 'Militär', 79; see also Ian F. W. Beckett, *The Amateur Military Tradition 1558–1945* (Manchester, 1991).

[48] See W. E. Cairnes, *The Absent-Minded War* (London, 1900); L. S. Amery, *The Times History of the War in South Africa 1899–1902*, 7 vols. (London, 1900–9); and H. O. Arnold Forster, *The Army in 1906: A Policy and a Vindication* (London, 1906).

could present itself as one of the most important integrating forces of the Union, as the Curragh mutiny demonstrated. When in March 1914 officers of the 6th Cavalry Brigade in Ireland declared that they were not prepared to march to the north to implement autonomy, Lord Roberts openly supported their position and demanded the resignation of the chief of the General Staff.[49]

As a result of colonial small wars not only the political role of the army changed, but also its social composition, with decreasing numbers of officers recruited from the landed gentry and aristocracy. The army as a whole became more urban and, in contrast to the ideal of Scottish and Welsh soldiers, also more English.[50] Another important change occurred with regard to the liberals' attitude towards army and war. Whereas traditionally historians have pointed to the antagonism between Gladstonian liberalism and its focus on Home Rule for Ireland and the army as a symbol of the Union under English dominance, it seems vital to see that this relation changed fundamentally in the later nineteenth century. With the institutionalization of regular police forces, the army was freed from domestic functions of maintaining law and order. In combination with the heroic and Christian image of the military in colonial conflicts, the army became the very symbol of the British Empire and Britishness.[51] Given the absence of large standing armies in Britain herself, the image of the *true Tommy* as the incarnation of national and Christian values became ever more popular and began to overshadow traditional anti-militarism.[52] That process had started already during the wars against France before 1815 and was revived during the Crimean war and the Indian Mutiny. The civic element of anti-militarism, derived from the conflicts of the seventeenth century and so important for the national self-image, became more and more overshadowed by ethnic and racial connotations of the superior empire-nation. In 1855 Lord Panmure underlined the changing image of the army: 'I trust our present experience will prove to our countrymen that our army must be something more than a mere colonial guard or home police; that it must be the means of maintaining our name abroad and causing it to be respected in peace as well as admired and dreaded in war.'[53] *The Times* in 1856 added that 'any hostility which may have existed in bygone days towards the army has long since passed away. The red coat of the soldier is honoured throughout the country.'[54] The successful repression of the Indian Mutiny provoked numerous reactions pointing to Britain's Christian mission, her pioneering role for civilization and its

---

[49] See Ian F. W. Beckett (ed.), *The Army and the Curragh Incident 1914* (London, 1986).

[50] See Strachan, 'Militär', 86; Gwyn Harries-Jenkins, *The Army in Victorian Society* (London, 1977); Alan Ramsay Skelley, *The Victorian Army at Home* (London, 1977); and H. J. Hanham, 'Religion and Nationality in the Mid-Victorian Army', in M. R. D. Foot (ed.), *War and Society* (London, 1973), 159–81.

[51] See C. E. Callwell, *Small Wars: A Tactical Textbook for Imperial Soldiers* (London, 1896).

[52] See Olive Anderson, 'The Growth of Christian Militarism in Mid-Victorian Britain', *English Historical Review*, 84 (1971), 46–72.

[53] Quoted in C. J. Bartlett, *Defence and Diplomacy: Britain and the Great Powers, 1815–1914* (Manchester, 1993), 126.   [54] *The Times*, 22 Oct. 1856, p. 6.

superiority over barbarism. As the *Baptist Magazine* remarked in 1858: 'The tide of rebellion [has been] turned back by the wisdom and prowess of Christian men, by our Lawrences, Edwardes, Montgomerys, Freres, and Havelocks... God, as it were, especially selecting them for this purpose.'[55]

Whereas continental societies experienced their war ideal in national wars, fought by nations in arms in their collective imagination, the British referred to small wars, in which the army came to represent an imagined empire-nation, which contained many ethnic and racial connotations. In contrast to Europe, the tendency to anticipate a major future war in Europe as a conflict over the existence of the entire nation was a rather late development in Britain. Only after 1890 and in the context of the naval race with Germany, a possible German invasion led to hysterical reactions among the British public, much aggravated by popular novels. These invasion panics had their origins in the sixteenth, seventeenth, and eighteenth centuries when they had focused on Spain and France as the main political and confessional enemies, a perception that was renewed before 1815 and again during the three anti-French panics of 1848, 1852, and 1859.[56] It was only after the 1890s that Germany began to replace France as the anticipated invader of the future. This collective perception increased both the army's and navy's popularity before 1914. But in contrast to continental countries, it was not a cult of a nation in arms that characterized this development, but rather a belated militarization of society, as the numerous paramilitary activities of army and navy leagues, boy brigades, and boy scout movements illustrated.[57]

The case of Britain, usually quoted as an example for the civic model of nation-building, shows that even where there was no cult of a nation in arms, ethnic and racial connotations played an increasingly important role in contemporary war experiences. With the reduced meaning of traditional anti-militarism, the spectrum of colonial small wars offered ample opportunities to stress the superiority of Anglo-Saxon culture, British civilization, and Christianity over barbarity.

THE UNITED STATES: REPUBLIC OF VIRTUES OR COMMUNITY OF SACRIFICE?

In contrast to continental European societies, where the emergence of a bureaucratic and centralized state depended on financing standing armies, the United States had not experienced a similar connection between war and the development of the strong state. The conflict over the North American colonies'

---

[55] *Baptist Magazine*, l (1858), 323.
[56] See Linda Colley, *Britons: Forging the Nation 1707–1837* (London, 1992).
[57] See Strachan, 'Militär', 90; Hugh Cunningham, *The Voluntary Force: A Social and Political History 1859–1908* (London, 1975); Ian F. W. Beckett, *Riflemen Form: A Study of the Rifle Volunteer Movement 1859–1908* (Aldershot, 1982); and Hew Strachan, *History of the Cambridge University Officers Training Corps* (Tunbridge Wells, 1976).

independence was not fought with standing armies but with republican militias. They combined the democratic principle with that of classical republicanism according to which a free citizen was the natural defender of the fatherland.[58] After the Wars of Independence and until the early 1860s the United States did not witness military conflicts on a scale which could have necessitated a more intensified public debate over the alternatives of militias or standing armies. After the British-American war of 1812–15 the threat of a foreign invasion had become highly unlikely. Neither was there an equivalent to the experience of the European wars between 1792 and 1815, nor the national wars in the context of 1848–9 or the *small wars* of the British Empire. This relative lack of belligerent experiences found its expression in the Monroe Doctrine.[59]

More important was the collective memory of the Wars of Independence against the British motherland. Already contemporaries had commented on the surprising fact that the colonists' mainly irregular militias could have defeated an experienced British force, consisting of mercenaries from a whole variety of different European countries. What the contemporary publicist David Ramsay called a 'people's war' was in fact a new kind of war in which the democratic self-organization of an army proved successful.[60] At the same time, this self-organization challenged the traditional separation between the military and the civil sphere, which for the generation of Washington had been so important.[61]

In contrast to France, where the public and enthusiastic mobilization of volunteers in 1792 was soon replaced by the introduction of Carnot's *levée en masse*, justified by references to the ideal of a nation defended by equal state citizens, the United States did not witness the same belligerent nationalism which came to characterize so many European societies, as the examples of France after 1792 and Germany around 1812/13 illustrated. The ideological meaning of war, its significance for the definition of national identity, as a revolutionary mission or in defence against an expansionist enemy, was missing here. The Wars of Independence, though portrayed as a 'people's war', represented only one part of the American Republic's foundation myth, and other elements such as the constitution or the charismatic Founding Fathers seemed to have a much greater significance. The United States experienced the function of war as a catalyst and cause of nation-building not in the form of a national war between states, as Italy did in 1848–9, 1859–61, and 1870–1 or Germany between 1864 and 1871, but in a violent civil war. During four years, more than 620,000 men of the North and the South lost their lives—a figure which was significantly higher than that of all

---

[58] See Stig Förster, 'Ein alternatives Modell? Landstreitkräfte und Gesellschaft in den USA 1775–1865', in Frevert (ed.), *Militär*, 94–118, and Jürgen Heideking, ' "People's War or Standing Army?" Die Debatte über Militärwesen und Krieg in den Vereinigten Staaten von Amerika im Zeitalter der Französischen Revolution', in Kunisch and Münkler (ed.), *Wiedergeburt*, 131–52.

[59] See Reginald C. Stuart, *War and American Thought: From the Revolution to the Monroe Doctrine* (Kent, Oh., 1982). [60] See above, n. 26.

[61] See Förster, 'Modell', 97, and Angus Calder, *Revolutionary Empire: The Rise of the English-Speaking Empires from the Fifteenth Century to the 1780s* (New York, 1981), 804.

American victims of both world wars and the Vietnam war taken together. The new character of the war necessitated not only institutional changes but also a new justification of state action in times of war.

Soon after the beginning of the military conflict, the South replaced the still existing militia system by a regular army of 100,000 men, which were recruited from volunteers. Only after a series of catastrophic defeats did the North respond by a far-reaching reorganization of the military. Against the backdrop of the mass of soldiers killed or wounded in action, the numbers of volunteers soon declined, making the introduction of universal conscription necessary, which the Confederate Congress of the South passed in April 1862, soon followed by similar measures in the North. But contrary to the principle of equality of conscription, a complex system of exemptions made the Civil War, in the words of a contemporary, 'a rich man's war and a poor man's fight'.[62] War provided no opportunity to increase citizens' rights; the suspension of many rights rather stood for the emergence of an authoritarian war state.

The North justified the war by referring to the Southern 'rebellion', underlining the defensive character of a war that was meant to restore and guarantee the Union. In addition, the religious leitmotif of moral cleansing from the South's practice of slavery and national restoration through the purgatory of war played an increasingly important role. Whereas the North relied on the interpretation of the existing constitution and could therefore justify the Union's defence, a distinct concept of a Southern nationality, and not just a particular mentality of the South, did not exist at the beginning of the war. The American South came to develop a war nationalism which had not existed before. It resulted in a Southern culture of defeat, in which religious images of individual and collective sacrifice and victimization dominated.[63] Racial connotations of the white man and his sacrifice dominated.

Finally the American Civil War anticipated many elements of the later *total wars* of the twentieth century: a hitherto unknown degree of mass mobilization, which forced the state to instrumentalize a new concept of nation and nationality in order to justify hitherto unknown numbers of victims; and, at least partly and temporarily, the end of the traditional separation between the military and the civil sphere, between the military and the home front.[64] This radicalization of war in the name of abstract principles became obvious not only in the

---

[62] J. G. Randall and David Herbert Donald, *The Civil War and Reconstruction*, 2nd edn. (Lexington, 1969), 251–2; James M. McPherson, *Battle Cry of Freedom: The Civil War Era* (New York, 1988), 429–31, and Förster, 'Modell', 115.

[63] See Drew Gilpin Faust, *The Creation of Confederate Nationalism: Ideology and Identity in the Civil War South* (Baton Rouge, La., 1988), and Wolfgang Schivelbusch, *Die Kultur der Niederlage: Der Amerikanische Süden 1865, Frankreich 1871, Deutschland 1918* (Berlin, 2001).

[64] See Mark E. Neely, 'Was the Civil War a Total War?', *Civil War History*, 37 (1991), 5–28; Stig Förster and Jörg Nagler (eds.), *On the Road to Total War: The American Civil War and the German Wars of Unification, 1861–1871* (Cambridge, 1997); Manfred F. Boemeke, Roger Chickering, and Stig Förster (eds.), *Anticipating Total War: The German and American Experiences, 1871–1914* (Cambridge, 1999).

guerrilla tactics of the South, but even more so in the actions of the Northern generals Sherman and Sheridan against the Southern population. It was in this context that the concept of 'unconditional surrender' was developed. Despite the United States' return to a standing army of just 25,000 men after the Civil War, it was clear that the traditional militia system had no future in a period of industrialized warfare. In both the North and the South, governments had derived fundamental lessons from this experience, and in both cases this went hand in hand with the emergence of an authoritarian military state and the suspension of habeas corpus rights, contradicting the self-image of a civic republic distinct from the European *anciens régimes*.[65] On the other hand, the period of mass conscription did not last long enough to have a more profound impact on American nation-building. More important was the collective memory of charismatic war leaders, and in the cases of both Lincoln in the North and Lee in the South the aura of martyrdom and sacrifice pointed to dominating religious connotations of national self-images. It was yet another conflict, the Spanish-American War of 1898, which allowed the projection of an American nation unified again by the participation of soldiers of the North and the South against an external enemy.[66]

The Civil War showed that the initial focus on constitutional arguments in the North, the Union's perpetuity as a base for the civic rights of the Republic, was soon replaced by ethnic connotations. Abraham Lincoln stressed the religious dimension, pointing to the war as God's instrument for the nation's moral betterment. After Lincoln's assassination the president changed into a martyr of the nation's republican virtues.[67] However, and as in the case of Renan, Lincoln himself underlined not only the model of democratic self-determination and republican liberty, but also the concept of a national community derived from shared history and common sacrifices in past wars: 'It is for us the living, rather, to be dedicated here to the unfinished work which they who fought here have thus far so nobly advanced. It is rather for us to be here dedicated to the great task remaining before us—that from these honored dead we take increased devotion to

65 See Richard Franklin Bensel, *Yankee Leviathan: The Origins of Central State Authority in America, 1859–1877* (Cambridge, 1990); and Mark E. Neely Jr., *The Fate of Liberty: Abraham Lincoln and Civil Liberties* (New York, 1991).
66 See Kristin L. Hoganson, *Fighting for American Manhood: How Gender Politics Provoked the Spanish-American and Philippine-American Wars* (New Haven, 1998), 107–9.
67 See Erich Angermann, *Abraham Lincoln und die Erneuerung der nationalen Identität der Vereinigten Staaten von Amerika* (Munich, 1984); Gabor Boritt (ed.), *The Lincoln Enigma: The Changing Faces of an American Icon* (Oxford, 2001); for contemporary sources see, *inter alia*, Edwin A. Bulkley, *The Uncrowned Nation: A Discourse commemorative of the Death of Abraham Lincoln, sixteenth President of the United States, preached in the First Presbyterian Church of Plattsburgh, New York (19th April 1865)* (Plattsburgh, 1865), 15; Joseph P. Thompson, 'Abraham Lincoln: His Life and its Lessons. A Sermon, Preached on Sabbath (30th April 1865)', Loyal Publication Society No. 85 (New York, 1865), in Frank Freidel (ed.), *Union Pamphlets of the Civil War 1861–1865*, vol. ii (Cambridge, Mass., 1967), 1149–80, and *The Martyr's Monument: Being the Patriotism and Political Wisdom of Abraham Lincoln, as exhibited in his Speeches, Messages, Orders, and Proclamations* (New York, 1865).

that cause for which they gave the last full measure of devotion—that we here highly resolved that these dead shall not have died in vain—that this nation, under God, shall have a new birth of freedom.'[68]

CONCLUSION: NATION-BUILDING, WAR EXPERIENCES, AND THE LIMITS OF THE CIVIC-ETHNIC MODEL

(1) Typologies and ideal types, as presented above, serve to reduce and to structure complexity. In the case of the historical phenomenon of nationalism, these typologies have also provoked and stimulated comparative approaches. Yet systematic comparisons also reveal the analytical limits and problems of many of these normative dichotomies which too often underline a simple antagonism between West and East European models. Instead, the comparison reveals a fascinating synchronic diversity and diachronic change—a basis from which to challenge many of the typologies' assumptions and periodizations. There was no single European nationalism, but only a pluralism of nationalisms in Europe.

(2) Nineteenth-century European discourses, focusing so much on the concepts of national and people's wars, reflected particular war experiences since the French Revolution. In contrast to pre-revolutionary expectations of a civil war of all suppressed peoples against their monarchical oppressors, the conflicts after 1792 resulted in wars between states, but now fought in the name of nations and on the basis of conscript armies. What the French Revolution generated was a new ideological justification of war, not as a means of dynastic or merely territorial interest, but in the name of a nation of equal citizens. Against this background, the concept of a nation in arms stood for both the military duty of the citizen-soldier and his political right to take an active part in the new nation. But the example of Renan, writing on the 1870–1 war, shows that war experiences always provoked an amalgam of civic and ethnic connotations, going beyond a paradigm of the voluntaristic nation, for which he is still mostly quoted.

(3) Whereas the French concept of a nation in arms was only revived again as a result of the military defeat against Prussia/Germany in 1870, contemporary interpretations of war in Germany revealed a growing scepticism regarding the revolutionary potential of future wars. In 1890 Moltke, the triumphant military leader of 1866 and 1870, had to acknowledge the end of traditional cabinet wars and the advent of a new category of warfare which would challenge the whole architecture of state and society. Mass conscription would not only lead to longer wars but would also necessitate the integration of ever more groups of society,

[68] Abraham Lincoln, 'Address at Gettysburg, Pennsylvania, delivered at the Dedication of the Cemetery at Gettysburg, 19th November 1863', in id., *Speeches and Writings 1859–1865: Speeches, Letters, and Miscellaneous Writings, Presidential Messages and Proclamations* (New York, 1989), 536.

eventually including the working classes, which could then demand political and social participation in return for their military duties. That could eventually challenge the very foundations of the German nation-state as it had been established in 1871.

(4) In comparison, the British case can be described as distinct from the continental war experiences. National wars, shaping the religious and national identity of the British, had rather characterized the conflicts with Spain and France in the early modern period and during the eighteenth and early nineteenth centuries. Instead of the national wars on the continent between 1848 and 1871, Britain witnessed more or less constant military actions in her colonies. The absence of large conscript armies on the British island and colonial *small wars* allowed the development of an imagined empire-nation, symbolized by the army abroad, which came to represent British and Christian values. In contrast to continental cases, belligerent images of the British nation paradoxically developed both earlier and later: earlier in the wars of the sixteenth and eighteenth centuries against Spain and France, and later, in the context of armament races, in the anti-German invasion panics during the decade before 1914. With the disappearance of traditional anti-militarism, ethnic and racial connotations of Anglo-Saxon superiority and British-Christian civilization increasingly dominated contemporary war discourses.

(5) For a long time, the United States lacked both the experience of the European revolutionary wars between the 1790s and 1815 and the colonial *small wars* of the British Empire. The ideological transformation of war in America originated from the myth of a people's war on the basis of militias fighting against the British regular armies in the 1770s. The almost total absence of a military invasion-scenario after 1812/13 delayed the modernization of institutions and justifications of national warfare. American society experienced the new meaning of war only under the particular circumstances of the Civil War. Anticipating elements of the later *total wars* of the twentieth century, the Civil War not only meant the end of the traditional militia system, but marked a new belligerent and religious connotation of the nation, in which ethnic and racial elements eclipsed traditional civic self-images of the virtuous Republic. A more lasting belligerent nationalism, as continental European societies had witnessed it, did not emerge before the Spanish-American war of 1898.

(6) The interaction between war and nation-building since the eighteenth century generated a new ideal of the citizen as the natural defender of the fatherland. Instead of the separation between the military and society, military mobilization in the name of the nation and the expectation of citizens' rights could go hand in hand. The national character of conflicts after 1792, even if rather in imagination than practice, provoked an expectation of participation through conscription, as in France, or constitutionalization as a reward for the wars of liberation against Napoleon. But the nation in arms also marked the

beginning of a long-term process towards a radicalization of both national self-images and images of the enemy, thereby integrating many ethnic and racial connotations focusing on belligerent myths and military memories. That was true not only for Germany, but also, in varying degrees, for France, Britain, and the United States. War experiences in very different contexts and against the background of different traditions tended to amalgamate civic and ethnic nationalisms.

13

Italy

The Idea of the Nation in the Risorgimento and Liberal Eras

David Laven

On 16 May 1896, Francesco Crispi's *La Riforma* remarked:

When the national flag is raised in France, England, Germany, and Russia, people stop talking and every citizen, whatever his party, bows his head in conformity with his national duty. In Italy, on the other hand ... people begin talking precisely when the national flag is raised.[1]

In late nineteenth- and early twentieth-century Italy such disillusionment with the population's widespread indifference, even open hostility, to the newly formed nation-state was by no means confined to Crispi and his supporters. Academics, literary figures, journalists, and politicians repeatedly bewailed Italians' want of patriotism and stressed the need 'to educate the nation' if needs be through 'a baptism of blood'.[2] Although those who expressed such sentiments came from across the whole political spectrum, the overwhelming majority of Italians remained steadfastly unmoved. When Italy finally had the chance for its baptism of blood with the outbreak of the Great War, few Italians were enthused with the prospect of involvement. When Italy renounced its neutral status and finally joined the conflict in the spring of 1915 it was clear that the 'national education' had failed. Gabriele d'Annunzio may have successfully assembled tens of thousands of interventionists around the Capitol as he symbolically kissed the

---

[1] Christopher Duggan, *Francesco Crispi 1818–1901: From Nation to Nationalism* (Oxford, 2002), 432.

[2] Advocates of aggressive militarism as a necessary precondition for forming national consciousness from the so-called left included: the poet, anticlerical, and freemason, Giosuè Carducci; the editor of *Il mattino* and husband of Matilde Serao, Edoardo Scarfoglio; Rocco De Zerbi; Abele Damiani; and the sociologist Pasquale Turiello. Among more conservative supporters of the use of war to form the nation were Alessandro Guiccioli and Antonio Gallenga. Ibid. 412–14. The idea of 'educating the nation' was by no means confined to Italy in this period. See, for example, Stefan Berger's chapter in this volume.

sabre of Nino Bixio and announced the salvation of Italian national honour,[3] but when the prefects were asked to report on public opinion throughout the peninsula, they acknowledged that few people cared about *Italia irredenta* and that the peasantry regarded the conflict with resignation and dread.[4]

The attitude of Italians in 1915 suggests that Massimo D'Azeglio's programme—'Italy's first need is the creation of Italians who know how to fulfil their duty'—had not been realized in the decades after unification.[5] Put in its most simple form, the failure 'to make Italians' (a phrase often attributed to, but apparently never actually uttered by, D'Azeglio) resulted from a lack of will—maybe a simple inability—to bridge the gap between the so-called 'real Italy' and 'legal Italy', between the Italy of the largely illiterate, dialect-speaking, impoverished, and exploited masses, and that of the judiciary and public functionaries, the officer class, and the court.[6] Of course, to describe the failure of the newly united Italian state to turn peasants into Italians would require much more than a short essay. Indeed, it is striking that an equivalent to Eugen Weber's *Peasants into Frenchmen* has still to be written for Italy, although perhaps this simply reflects the size of the task because of the much longer chronological span that would have to be covered by any historian trying to chronicle the Italianization of Italians.[7] Rather than attempting such an ambitious task, my aim in this essay is rather more modest: what I wish to do is simply to highlight the intrinsic problems with the *idea* of the nation in the Italian context.

First, however, I wish to make a preliminary point about the nature of recent writing on Italian nationalism. The historiography of the last decade abounds with works whose titles profess to deal with memories, monuments, images, itineraries, cults, social spaces, kinship, and so on.[8] In examining the different ways in which the nation was conceptualized and imagined, mythologized, and

---

[3] Anthony Rhodes, *The Poet as Superman: A Life of Gabriele D'Annunzio* (London, 1959), 147–9; Philippe Jullian, *D'Annunzio*, trans. Stephen Hardman (London, 1972), 257–8; Christopher Seton-Watson, *Italy from Liberalism to Fascism 1870–1925* (London, 1967), 447–8.

[4] Martin Clark, *Modern Italy 1871–1982* (London, 1984), 183.

[5] Massimo D'Azeglio, *I miei ricordi* (Turin, 1949), 38.

[6] The phrase 'fatta l'Italia bisogna fare gli italiani' was coined by Ferdinando Martini in 1896. See the introduction by Simonetta Soldani and Gabriele Turi in eid. (eds), *Fare gli italiani: scuola e cultura nell'Italia contemporanea* (2 vols., Bologna, 1993), i. 17.

[7] Eugen Weber, *Peasants into Frenchmen: The Modernization of Rural France 1870–1914* (London, 1979). While debate continues over both Weber's periodization and interpretation of the nature of the nationalization of France's peasantry, few would argue with his overall conclusions about the peasantry's sense of Frenchness by the outbreak of the Great War. Any similar study of the emergence of Italian national identity would probably have to continue its narrative up to the 1960s and probably beyond. On the issue of the French conversion of peasants into Frenchmen, see Timothy Baycroft, 'France: Ethnicity and the Revolutionary Tradition' in this volume, 31–2.

[8] See, for example, Bruno Tobia, *Una patria per gli italiani: spazi, itinerari, monumenti nell'Italia unita (1870–1900)* (Rome, 1991); Umberto Leva, *Fare gli italiani: memoria e celebrazione del Risorgimento* (Turin, 1992); Ilaria Porciani, *La festa della nazione: rappresentazione dello stato e spazi sociali nell'Italia unita* (Bologna, 1997); Mario Isnenghi (ed.), *I luoghi della memoria* (3 vols., Rome, 1997–8); Alberto Banti, *La nazione del Risorgimento: parentela, santità e onore alle origini dell'Italia unita* (Turin, 2000). Much of this work has its origins in French historiography, most notably the interest in *lieux de mémoire* stimulated by Pierre Nora. See Baycroft, 'France', p. 28 above.

represented, these studies have undoubtedly done much to deepen our understanding of the uneasy birth of modern Italian identity. It is principally with the
sort of ideas raised by the likes of Banti, Tobia, and Isnenghi that I wish to concern
myself here. Nevertheless, it is important to recognize that the current trend in
historiography is to concentrate on only part of the question of the emergence or
otherwise of national sentiment, tending to emphasize explanations which focus
on culture—albeit in a very broad sense—at the expense of those that look at
socio-economic conditions and practical politics. Alberto Banti, for example,
while recognizing that more prosaic considerations of social, political, and
economic interests could play their part in fostering a sense of nationhood in
pre-unification Italy, argues that ultimately they fail to explain 'the dedication,
even at times the fanaticism, with which many Risorgimento militants fought
their battles'. According to Banti the fact that 'individuals who were often
extremely well-off socially and economically chose to confront grave dangers,
even to the point of risking their own lives' shows that they must have been
inspired by some deeper passion when they opted to challenge the status quo and
to make a new and united Italy. For Banti the origins of their impulse for independence and unification (and on occasion martyrdom) lay in the exposure of
young Italians to a 'canone risorgimentale' of patriotic texts.[9]

Banti's emphasis on the role of the 'canone risorgimentale' begs numerous
questions. Even if one sets aside the issue of the personal (rather than shared)
psychological motivation of many of those who fanatically espoused the national
cause, Banti is wrong to attribute so much significance to the way in which some
of the heroes of the Risorgimento came from comfortable backgrounds. Besides
the obvious point that a great many of those who did risk their lives for the
national cause were *not* especially privileged, there is another basic weakness in
Banti's position: it is simply misleading to suggest that the possession of wealth
and status made an individual immune to political grievances or socio-economic
ambitions. Nationalism would always be used in an opportunist fashion to legitimate self-serving aspirations. For example, it is tempting to ask Banti what he
makes of the conduct of, say, Carlo Alberto, who—under a screen of Italian
nationalism—was prepared to gamble on war with Austria in 1848 and 1849 in
pursuit of his own dynastic ends. Of course, the King of Sardinia-Piedmont was
not acting from socio-economic deprivation, but nor was he inspired by the
'canone risorgimentale'. It is equally important to recognize that, when popular
insurrections broke out in 1848, those on the barricades were not prompted by
reading Foscolo or looking at the canvases of Hayez, or even an artistic engagement with Dante. Revolution came about because of the failure of the Restoration
regimes to address practical problems faced by ordinary Italians.

While the work of Banti and others has cast light on the appeal of the national
idea, it risks underplaying the overwhelming importance of interest: resentment

---

[9] Banti, *La nazione*, 31.

over taxation, lust for office and patronage, desire for representative institutions, the prospect of improved economic conditions and better communications, the promise of anticlerical reforms, or dislike for a ruling dynasty are all more significant than Banti's 'canone' in explaining support for unification. Moreover, if we are to understand the failure of the national idea to win over the overwhelming majority of Italians in the liberal era, it is essential to look principally at the inadequacies of the Italian state, and of the elites who sought to exploit it to defend their own narrow interests. The failure to 'make Italians' in the decades after the seizure of Rome in 1870 must be assessed with regard to education policy and communications, the impact of conscription and policing, the extension of franchise and the role of migration, and so on. Analysing the engagement of a small literate elite with patriotic literature will not explain the Risorgimento, just as examining memorials or museum exhibitions or street names will not ultimately tell us much about why Italy's peasants, in contrast with their German and French counterparts, failed to rally with enthusiasm to 'la patria' in the early stages of the Great War.

ETHNICITY, CITIZENSHIP, AND NATION

As I have already stated, it is not my intention here to examine why so many Italians proved unresponsive to the idea of the nation, so much as to discuss the reasons why that very idea was so flawed and problematic in the first place. One obvious starting point is the difficulty that Italians had in viewing themselves as a clearly defined and homogeneous ethnic group. This is not to suggest that Italian authors of the nineteenth and early twentieth centuries were actively hostile to the notion of an Italian race, but rather that they faced serious problems in defining it, particularly if too strong an emphasis was placed on ethnicity or racial purity. Indeed, it is striking that the terms most commonly used to refer to the Italian people were *schiatta* and *stirpe*. While often used as synonyms of *razza*, neither term is best translated as 'race', implying as they do a sense of family with shared descent and lineage. Indeed, *stirpe* has sometimes been quite deliberately used in the twentieth century in order make a distinction from *razza*, the former suggesting a spiritual dimension that contrasts with the purely physiological sense of the latter.[10]

It was family rather than ethnic blood ties that underpinned united Italy's first law on citizenship. When the debate over qualification for citizenship took place in 1865, some deputies, including Francesco Crispi, urged that citizenship should be based on place of birth—*ius soli*. The formula that was eventually adopted in articles 5–10 of the Civil Code drew instead on the ideas of Pasquale Stanislao

---

[10] Manlio Cortelazzo and Paolo Zolli, *Dizionario etimologico della lingua italiana* (5 vols., Bologna, 1988), v. 1276.

Mancini and Giuseppe Pisanelli. At first glance, they appeared to favour a concept of citizenship based on race. Pisanelli, for example, openly declared that 'race is the principal element of nationality'. When examined more closely, the arguments of Pisanelli and Mancini appear scarcely *völkisch*. Instead, they simply drew on the principle of inherited status embodied in the Piedmontese code of 1837. Citizenship thus depended on being the child of a citizen, or, as Mancini argued '... man is born a member of a family, and the nation is an aggregate of families; he is a citizen of that nation to which his father belonged...' Until the Giolittian reform of 1912, which replaced *ius sanguinis* with *ius soli*, Italian law on citizenship represented little more than the tradition of Piedmontization—rather than nationalization—of the peninsula. This underscored not the existence of an Italian people, but their unity in subjection to the ruling dynasty.[11] Before 1912 to be Italian was no more or less than to be the offspring of a subject of the House of Savoy; after 1912 it was determined by an accident of geography.

For all his talk of 'race' during the 1865 debate, Mancini saw that it was only one element in forming the nation, which was dependent on a cluster of factors: 'la REGIONE, la RAZZA, la LINGUA, le COSTUMANZE, la STORIA, le LEGGI, le RELIGIONI'.[12] Other commentators sometimes appeared happier to adopt a more clearly biological definition of Italians. Thus in the second volume of his long and rambling work, the *Primato* of 1843, in which he called for a federal Italy under papal presidency, Vincenzo Gioberti made it clear that the genius and moral superiority of the Italians could be attributed to the fact that they were the most vigorous descendants of the Pelasgic people, the foremost of the white races. For Gioberti Italians were not only of greater worth than the Celts, Germans, and Slavs, but they were also of more value than their fellow 'Pelasghi', the Greeks.[13] But it is important to remember that Gioberti's vision of a federal future was a result of his acute awareness of the diversity of the Italian peninsula. While seeing this as a product of a variety of historical factors, he attributed it in large part to the original existence of different strains of Pelasgic peoples inhabiting different regions of the country. These different groups had subsequently mixed with one another and with 'swarms of Slavs, Celts, Teutons, Iberians' to create modern Italians, 'tempering without changing the native character of the ancient inhabitants, according

---

[11] Banti, *La nazione*, 168–9. The extension of the Piedmontese citizenship law of 1837 to the rest of Italy took place five years after the transfer of Nice and Savoy to France, supposedly on the basis of the principal of nationality (Savoy at least was French-speaking). In reality, the cession of these territories was no more than payment to Napoleon III for support in the 1859 war of expansion in Lombardy-Venetia. The irony of ceding Garibaldi's birthplace to France should not be overlooked. Nor should the fact that, while French annexation was sanctioned by (rigged) plebiscites, the inhabitants of these formerly 'Italian' lands found that, because they were no longer subjects of the House of Savoy, their nationality had changed.

[12] 'Region, race, language, customs, history, laws, and religions'; ibid. 163; Pasquale Stanislao Mancini, *Saggi sulla nazionalità* (1858), ed. F. Lopez de Oñate (Rome, 1994), 28.

[13] Vincenzo Gioberti, *Del primato morale e civile degli italiani*, ed. Gustavo Balsamo-Crivelli (3 vols., Turin, 1948), ii. 157–64.

to that law of nature, by which races (*le razze*) revive and improve each other physically and morally through reciprocal intermingling'.[14]

If Gioberti's attitude to race—like much of his writing—seems more than a little confused, it is clear that, for all his claims to the superiority of the Pelasgics, he did not believe that the Italians were of pure racial stock. Much the same could be said of Cesare Correnti, a one-time republican who moved subsequently into the pro-Piedmontese camp. In an essay published in 1854 and simply entitled 'Le razze', Correnti stressed the distinctiveness of Latins from the other major European races, the Slavs and Teutons. The Latins themselves he divided into Romanian, Italian, Gallic, and Iberian branches.[15] Yet just as Gioberti did not believe in pure blood lines, Correnti did not see race as principally biological. It was defined by culture, language, and geography rather than purity of blood:

the true frontiers that separate one land from another are debatable, the origins and genealogies of peoples are obscure and mythologized, the oracles of history can be misleading. What alone cannot be denied or put in doubt is the fact that someone is born, and speaks in a particular tongue.[16]

I shall return to the primacy of language in definitions of the Italian nation shortly. What I wish to emphasize here is that—even amongst those who appeared to espouse racist ideologies—few Italians seem to have been really comfortable with racial definitions of their nation. Even a racial anthropologist such as Giuseppe Sergi would write in his *Italia, le origini: antropologia, cultura e civiltà* of 1919: 'Who could distinguish Illyrians, Venetians, Cisalpine Gauls from other groups of Italic peoples?'[17] Meanwhile, others were bluntly outspoken in their objection to any notion of an Italian race: thus the Piedmontese moderate Cesare Balbo described Italy as 'a multiracial community composed of successive waves of immigrants . . . We must have one of the most mixed bloodlines, one of the civilizations with the most eclectic culture there has ever been'.[18]

[14] Vincenzo Gioberti, *Del primato morale e civile degli italiani*, ed. Gustavo Balsamo-Crivelli (3 vols., Turin, 1948), i. 115–16. Gioberti picked up on this theme again elsewhere but with slightly different emphasis. In the second volume of *the primato*, for example, he argued that the consequence of invasion of Italy by Germanic peoples (as in France and England as well) had been merely to 'Germanize' the nobility rather than the population as a whole. The Germans had dominated through strength alone, providing 'il patriziato feudale' and 'le famiglie regnatrici' but relatively little of cultural or moral worth. For Gioberti it was among the non-privileged classes of Pelasgic origin that 'gli uomini colti e grandi in ogni genere' were most likely to be found; ii. 163.
[15] Correnti considered the Turks, Hungarians, Greeks, Basques, Finns, Jews, and Gypsies too few in number to be of any great significance. Banti, *La nazione*, 159.
[16] Cesare Correnti, 'Le razze', in *Il nipote del vesta verde* (1854), cited ibid. 159. On Correnti's position see also Silvana Patriarca, 'Patriottismo, nazione e italianità nella statisticadel Risorgimento', in Alberto Banti and Roberto Bizzochi (eds.), *Immagini della nazione nell'Italia del Risorgimento* (Rome, 2002), 113–32, 121–2.
[17] Giuseppe Sergi, *Italia, le origini: antropologia, cultura e civiltà* (Turin, 1919), 444, cited in Aaron Gillette, *Racial Theories in Fascist Italy* (London, 2002), 28. On Sergi see also G. Boëtsch and J. N. Ferrié, 'Giuseppe Sergi et la "race" méditerranéenne', *Rivista di antropologia*, 71 (1993).
[18] Cited in Banti, *La nazione*, 160. For similar scepticism about the possibility of racial purity given the impact of migration and invasion see the comments of Samuuele Romanin, who published

'THE NATION EXISTS BECAUSE GOD HAS MADE IT'

For most of those who addressed the issue of national identity in the Risorgimento period it was clearly not race that defined Italians, but a mixture of linguistic and geographical features, which, notwithstanding the peninsula's history of foreign invasion, combined with a sense of cultural superiority towards the rest of Europe. As Luigi Pomba's *Dizionario politico nuovamente compilato ad uso della gioventù italiana* stated:

Of all the nations of the world, the Italian is perhaps that which most conspicuously combines all the characteristics of the Nation, except the political. It is thus for its history, on account of its marvellously defined natural frontiers, on account of its language, its origins, its uniformity of conventions and customs, its tastes, and its shared attitude to the practice of the fine arts which are its ancient heritage.[19]

Geography and history, religion, language, and culture, therefore, lay at the root of Italian national identity. But such claims posed as many problems as the idea of a clearly defined Italian race.

There was, of course, nothing remotely new about the view that Italy was geographically and culturally distinct. The notion that Italy's natural frontiers—the Alps and the sea—set Italians apart from other Europeans—'oltremontani' or, less charitably, simply 'barbari'—had been standard amongst fifteenth-century humanists in the habit of citing Cicero's famous tag ('Alpibus Italiam munierat antea natura non sine aliquo divino numine'—'Formerly nature had fortified Italy by means of the Alps, not without any divine intervention'). During the Italian Wars it had become commonplace amongst writers such as the Neapolitan Giovanni Pontano, the Venetian Marin Sanudo, the Florentines Francesco Guicciardini and Niccolò Machiavelli, and even the urbane Lombard Baldesar Castiglione to stress not only that Italians were culturally superior to the foreigners who had overrun the peninsula, but also that it was the Italians' inability to maintain a united front that left them vulnerable to outsiders. In a sense, therefore, it was not foreign strength, but Italy's own failings—or more often those of the peninsula's princes—that left the population vulnerable to outside oppression and tyranny.[20] Such views found echo in the nineteenth century, but the fact that they could be traced back to the Renaissance and earlier did not make it any easier to

his vast multi-volume history of Venice between 1853 and 1861. S. Romanin, *Storia documentata di Venezia* (10 vols., Venice, 1972–5), i. 6.

[19] L. Pomba (ed.), *Dizionario politico nuovamente compilato ad uso della gioventù* italiana (Turin, 1849), 457–8.

[20] Felix Gilbert, *Machiavelli and Guicciardini: Politics and History in Sixteenth-Century Florence* (New York, 1984), 255–70; David Laven, 'Machiavelli, *italianità* and the French Invasion of 1494', in David Abulafia (ed.), *The French Descent into Renaissance Italy 1494–95: Antecedents and Effects* (Aldershot, 1995), 355–69. For specific examples see Machiavelli's condemnation of Italy's princes in the *Arte della guerra* in A. Panella (ed.), *Niccolò Machiavelli: Opere* (2 vols., Milan, 1938–9), ii. 662 and B. Castiglione, *Il libro del cortegiano*, ed. G. Carnazzi (Milan, 1987), 140–1.

deal with the very real problems of internal division and particularism: it was fine for Mazzini to write in the *Doveri dell'uomo* (Naples, 1860) that God had assigned Italians 'the best defined fatherland in Europe … God has established around it sublime, undeniable borders: on one side, the highest mountains in Europe, the Alps; on the other side, the Sea, the immense Sea,'[21] or for the former Mazzinian Crispi to jot laconically, 'The nation exists, because God has made it',[22] but their sentiments were really little different from Metternich's famously dismissive comment that Italy was 'nothing but a geographical expression'. The truth of the situation was that despite its clear physical boundaries, Italy remained hopelessly internally divided: as the commentator André Vieusseux remarked in 1821,

I think the Italians are but imperfectly known, and often unjustly abused and are generally included by foreigners in one common description of character, while in fact the inhabitants of the various states of that much divided country form so many distinct nations. A Tuscan and a Neapolitan, a Lombard and a Genoese, a Venetian and a Roman, are as different from one another, as the Germans are from the English, or the Dutch from the French.[23]

In a sense, the very fact that nature seemed to decree the existence of Italy made its inhabitants' failure to behave as a nation all the worse. The Renaissance humanists had rightly observed the paradoxical situation in which Italy found itself: what made Italians distinctive was their inability to cooperate with one another, leaving the peninsula weak and divided—scarcely a solid foundation on which to construct the nation.

THE LANGUAGE QUESTION

The question that dogged Italian patriots in the nineteenth century was where they could turn if they wanted 'to find' the Italian nation? What gave Italians their unity? One obvious source was the national language. The idea that a national language and literature provided the basis of a national identity was seized upon by nineteenth-century patriots eager to carve an identity in the face of foreign domination and territorial fragmentation.[24] Focus on the 'national' language had the advantage of a long pedigree dating back at least as far as Dante's *De vulgari eloquentia* of 1303, which had called for a common tongue for the entire peninsula.[25] However, there were fundamental disadvantages in seeking to emphasize linguistic unity, given that

---

[21] Giuseppe Mazzini, *Edizione nazionale degli scritti di Giuseppe Mazzini* (Imola, 1935), lxix. 3–145.   [22] Duggan, *Crispi*, 339.

[23] André Vieusseux, *Italy and the Italians in the nineteenth century: or letters on the civil, political and moral state of that country written in 1818 and 1819 with an appendix containing extracts from modern Italian literature by an officer in the British service* (London, 1821), 2.

[24] On comparable debates elsewhere in Europe see, for example, Baycroft, pp. 34–5 above; Mark Cornwall, p. 174 above.

[25] Bruno Migliorini, *Storia della lingua italiana* (Florence, 1995), 168–73.

the issue of language actually served in many ways to highlight divisions within the nation: put simply the dialect-speaking inhabitants of Italy could not understand one another. According to the research of Tulio De Mauro only 2.5 per cent of the population of Italy spoke the national tongue in 1861;[26] Arrigo Casellani puts the figure higher at 9.5 per cent.[27] When it is remembered that many of these 'Italian' speakers were, in fact, Tuscans using their own dialect, which simply happened to be identified with the national language, the diversity of the peninsula becomes still clearer.[28] Moreover, as Banti points out, even if one accepts that perhaps a quarter of the population was able to understand Italian, the number of these who would have been able to appreciate the works of, say, Dante or Machiavelli must have been vastly smaller.[29] This simple fact forcefully undermined the traditional 'cultural' definition of *italianità*: emphasis on a shared literary tradition stood little chance of forming national consciousness in a society where even the literate minority was unlikely to read. Moreover, the appeal to a shared literary tradition could itself prove counterproductive. While Alfieri might archly engage with Machiavelli in his own essay *Del principe e delle lettere*, even to the point of entitling the penultimate chapter 'An exhortation to free Italy from the barbarians', such literary resonance actually highlighted that nothing much had changed between the early sixteenth and the late eighteenth centuries. Meanwhile, the almost obsessive emphasis on Dante as the embodiment of Italian culture in the nineteenth century also emphasized that little had changed in over 500 years.[30]

The problem of Italians not using their national language was not confined to the illiterate masses;[31] Italian was by no means the automatic language of choice

---

[26] Tulio De Mauro, *Storia linguistica dell'Italia unita* (Bari, 1970), 43.

[27] Arrigo Castellani, 'Quanti erano gl'italofoni nel 1861?', *Studi linguistici italiani* (1982).

[28] De Mauro calculates that perhaps 400,000 Tuscans spoke Italian compared with 70,000 Romans and 160,000 from the rest of the peninsula, thus, according to his figures, over half the Italian speakers in the country were in effect just using their local dialect ('. . . in Tuscany and in Rome the local dialects were particularly close to the phonological, morphological and lexical structure of the common tongue; moreover, amid the educational misery of the Papal States, Rome was an island in which popular educational establishments were more efficient and numerous than anywhere else in Italy'). *Storia linguistica*, 43. Or, as Gioberti put it, 'Florence and Rome are today the two metropolises of Italy where the illustrious language, used in written form by the whole nation, issues forth in lively and spontaneous fashion from the mouths of the people.' *Del primato*, iii. 61.

[29] Banti, *La nazione*, 24. Luca Serianni, *Storia della lingua italiana: il Secondo Ottocento: Dall'Unità alla Prima Guerra Mondiale* (Bologna, 1990) has argued that it is important to identify different degrees of ability to use Italian, but this does not get round the fact that for most Italians the language of Dante or Manzoni was essentially alien. For a brief but useful discussion in English of these issues see Derek Beales and Eugenio F. Biagini, *The Risorgimento and the Unification of Italy* (London, 2002), 74–80.

[30] Alfieri himself considered there to have been, if anything, a decline since the days of Machiavelli, describing contemporary Italy as 'at the apex of its baseness and insignificance'. Vittorio Alfieri, *Scritti politici e morali* (Asti, 1951), i. 111–254, 249–52. On the significance of Dante see Bruno Tobia, 'Una cultura per la nuova Italia', in Fulvio Cammarano, Enrico Decleva, Giovanni Montroni, Guido Pescosolido, and Bruno Tobia, *Storia d'Italia*, ii: *Il nuovo stato e la società civile 1861–1887*, ed. Giovanni Sabbatucci and Vittorio Vidotto (Rome, 1995), 427–529, 501–10.

[31] It was not only in Italy that the masses were unfamiliar with their national tongue. Nineteenth-century France, after all, was also characterized by enormous linguistic diversity. The significant

for the elites. It is a commonplace, but one that is nevertheless worth repeating, that both the first prime minister of the new Italian state and its first king spoke better French than Italian; indeed, Vittorio Emanuele II was probably happier using Piedmontese dialect in conversation.[32] Even among Italy's foremost men of letters, Italian did not necessarily come naturally. Just as Vittorio Alfieri, Italy's greatest tragic poet of the eighteenth century, grew up using bad French before mastering cultivated Florentine,[33] so the most significant novelist of pre-unification Italy was also initially uncomfortable with the 'national' language: when Alessandro Manzoni started writing *I promessi sposi* in 1821, his everyday conversation was Milanese, and he wrote French with more fluency and confidence than the so-called national tongue.[34] His trip to Florence in 1827, shortly after the publication of the first edition of the novel, launched him on a process of systematically 'Tuscanizing' his work, which only appeared in its final incarnation in 1840.[35]

Manzoni's attitudes to Italian reveal another problem with using language to define Italian national identity. It was not just that most Italians did not speak Italian, but that they also could not agree what actually constituted the language. Since the early sixteenth-century cultural crisis born of successive invasions by French, Spanish, and Imperial forces, the so-called 'questione della lingua' had never disappeared. At the heart of the question lay a debate about whether 'Italian' should be a composite tongue drawing on a number of different regional variations, whether it should be based on the old Tuscan of the great writers, or whether contemporary Florentine should be the model.[36] In the nineteenth century those, such as Graziadio Isaia Ascoli, who sought to preserve the historical traditions implicit in emulating the language of long dead writers continued to clash with others, like Manzoni, who championed modern Florentine. Both before and after

difference lay in the fact that France's elites spoke the national language. On France's 'wealth of tongues' see Weber, *Peasants*, 67–94.

[32] On Cavour's awkwardness in speaking Italian see Nassau William Senior, *Journals Kept in France and Italy from 1848 to 1852* (London, 1871), i. 291–2, cited in Denis Mack Smith, *The Making of Italy* (Basingstoke, 1988), 73.   [33] Vittorio Alfieri, *La vita* (Florence, 1928), 57.

[34] Barbara Reynolds, *The Linguistic Writings of Alessandro Manzoni* (Cambridge, 1950), 1.

[35] On Manzoni's attitude to Florentine see Maurizio Vitale, *La questione della lingua* (Palermo, 1978), 348–55.

[36] On the so-called *questione della lingua* in the sixteenth century see Bruno Migliorini, *Storia della lingua*, 312–28, and Vitale, *La questione della lingua*, 39–153. For a discussion of the sixteenth-century language question within a political context see Lauro Martines, *Power and Imagination: City-States in Renaissance Italy* (London, 1979), 446–52. The issue of what constituted Italian was to endure until the nineteenth century. It is significant, for example, that the first edition of the *Vocabolario degli Accademici della Crusca* (Venice, 1612) was originally to have been called *Vocabolario della lingua toscana degli Accademici della Crusca*, and then *Vocabolario della lingua toscana cavato dagli scrittori e dall'uso della città di Firenze degli Accademici della Crusca*. The decision to drop the specific references to Tuscan and Florentine usage did not, however, mean that this volume, usually seen as the first Italian dictionary, actually laid claim to being such. The debate did not die out in the eighteenth century either, with figures such as Vittorio Alfieri, Gianfrancesco Galeani Napione, and Carlo Gozzi denouncing the views expressed by the likes of Melchior Cesarotti, who had advocated a less slavish adherence to the Florentine tradition of the Accademia della Crusca. See Migliorini, *Storia della lingua italiana*, 408 and 464–6 and Vitale, *La questione della lingua*, *passim*.

the creation of the Kingdom of Italy, Italian intellectuals agreed that the absence of a national language hindered the development of a shared culture necessary for national unity, but they could not agree what that language should be.[37] As Carlo Tenca observed to Manzoni in 1851, 'We are still groping our way along in search of a language that will unite in a single expression the thoughts and affections of the entire nation,'[38] or as Manzoni himself wrote in an essay of 1868 destined for the Ministry of Education in his capacity as chairman of the commission for the Unification of the Language to which he had been appointed six years previously: 'while we agree that we want this language, what it might be, or could be, or must be has been disputed for five hundred years.'[39] Even among Italy's most esteemed men of letters, the language question continued to divide just as it had in the days of Bembo, Castiglione, and Machiavelli.

ROME

If language raised as many questions as it answered, where else could Italy's patriots look to find symbols of the nation? A potentially seductive idea was to look to Rome for inspiration. After all, the last time that Italy had enjoyed unity was under the Roman Empire. But any notion of continuity between ancient Rome and modern Italy was problematic. While Mazzini was tempted to use the imperial precedent to legitimate proposed Italian expansion in the Mediterranean,[40] many pre-unification thinkers were uneasy about stressing a shared heritage with the ancient empire. In the Restoration era, the close association between Jacobinism and Napoleonic rule on the one hand and classical imagery and ritual on the other made many people uneasy.[41] By the 1820s the rise of Romanticism had also dealt a serious blow to those apologists for classicism who had argued that rather than being a universal European language, Latin was part of an Italian national heritage.[42] Moreover, the models offered by both the ancient Roman republic and the empire could be disturbing. On the one hand, the history of the

---

[37] On the 'questione della lingua' in the nineteenth century see Vitale, *La questione*, 345–611. Problems surrounding the national language, and of the persistence of dialect were, of course, by no means confined to Italy. See, for example, Martin Durrell, 'Political Unity and Linguistic Diversity in Nineteenth-Century Germany', in Maiken Umbach (ed.), *German Federalism: Past, Present, Future* (London, 2002) 91–112. [38] Vitale, *La questione*, 758.

[39] 'Dell'unità della lingua italiana e dei mezzi di diffonderla: relazione al Ministro della Pubblica Istruzione proposta da Alessandro Manzoni agli amici colleghi Bonghi e Carcano ed accettata da loro', in Alessandro Manzoni, *Opere*, ed. Lanfranco Caretti (Milan, 1965), 969–85, 971.

[40] Mazzini's imperialist ideas were exaggerated by the Fascists. Denis Mack Smith, *Mazzini* (New Haven, 1994), 219.

[41] On the use of ancient Roman symbols and history during the revolutionary and Napoleonic era see Andrea Giardina and André Vauchez, *Il mito di Roma da Carlo Magno a Mussolini* (Rome, 2000), 118–59.

[42] Adrian Lyttelton, 'Creating a National Past: History, Myth and Image in the Risorgimento', in Albert Russell Ascoli and Krystyna von Henneberg, *Making and Remaking Italy: The Cultivation of National Identity around the Risorgimento* (Oxford, 2001), 27–74, 32.

republic (and long periods of the empire) was one of internal rivalry and civil war, which scarcely augured well as a model for Italian resurgence. On the other hand, the history of the imperial Rome was one of domination and aggression, which would appeal to unashamed imperialists such as Enrico Corradini after unification,[43] but which was less palatable for most earlier nineteenth-century patriots. Before unification the very glories of ancient Rome simply acted as a foil to set off the ignominy of a disunited Italy, subjected to the whims of the great powers, just as after unification ambitions to turn the Mediterranean into a *Mare nostrum* as it had been under the Romans tended to do little more than highlight Italy's inadequacies within the international arena.[44]

The biggest problem with Rome as a symbol around which Italian nationalists could rally was its close association with the papacy. The one common feature shared by most Italians was their Catholicism.[45] It was not, however, easy to harness this to a national cause since it also created common bonds with non-Italian Catholics within the universal church. The one patriot to exploit Catholicism effectively was Vincenzo Gioberti, who argued that as the centre of a global Catholic culture Italy was ripe for regeneration and a resumption of its moral and civil leadership of the world, and that it was through a redeemer pope that the peninsula would recapture its past glory.[46] Yet, while Gioberti's ideas enjoyed a brief period of popularity in the lustrum after the publication of *Del primato* in 1843, the events of 1848–9 demonstrated conclusively that loyalty to the pope and Italian nationalism were mutually incompatible.[47] Indeed, the fact that the second Rome—the Rome of the popes—was an obstacle to Italian strength and unity was by no means new. The medieval clash between Guelph and Ghibelline was recognized historically as a fundamental cause for Italy's division, and both Dante and Machiavelli—key figures in the pantheon of Italian patriotism—had vilified the papacy for keeping Italy weak.[48] And just as Machiavelli blamed the

[43] For a discussion of Corradini's attitude to *romanità* see Giovanni Belardelli, 'La terza Roma', in Giovanni Belardelli, Luciano Cafagna, Ernesto Galli della Loggia, and Giovanni Sabbatucci, *Miti e storia dell'Italia unita* (Bologna, 1999), 13–20, 15.

[44] On Crispi's ambitions to dominate the Mediterranean see Duggan, *Crispi*, 369.

[45] The relationship between Catholicism and national identity was not an issue solely for Italians in the nineteenth century. See, for example, the Spanish case, discussed by Stephen Jacobson, and that of the Belgians, treated by Carl Strikwerda, in this volume.

[46] For a good brief summary of Gioberti's ideas in *Del primato morale e civile degli italiani* see Bruce Haddock, 'Political Union without Social Revolution: Vincenzo Gioberti's *Primato*', *Historical Journal* (1998), 705–23.

[47] The Papal Allocution of April 1848 symbolized the end of Pius IX's brief flirtation with the patriot cause by withdrawing Roman troops from the struggle against Austria. The pope's subsequent lurch towards conservatism destroyed any hopes that he might fulfil Gioberti's dreams as a 'redeemer pope'. After the 1849 defeat of the so-called Roman Republic he was also held responsible for the French military presence in the city, and, following annexation of most of the Papal States in 1860, he openly and repeatedly condemned Italian nationalism. His position became even more uncompromising after the Italian seizure of Rome in 1870. On Pius IX's conduct during the revolutionary years see Frank J. Coppa, *Pope Pius IX* (1979), 84–111.

[48] Lyttelton, 'Creating', 46. Significantly Machiavelli damned the papacy in all his major works: *The Prince*, *The Discourses*, and *The Florentine Histories*. Perhaps his most forthright statement of the

pope for inviting foreigners into Italy, now patriots denounced the pope for hiding behind a French garrison. It is no surprise, therefore, that the neo-guelphs' peculiar brand of papal *romanità* failed to endure beyond 1849, and that Gioberti himself rejected his earlier position.[49]

The restoration of Pius IX did not mean that Italian patriots forgot Rome as a symbol of nationhood: Mazzini described it as 'the dream of my youth, the mother of all my ideas, the religion of my soul', while Garibaldi would proclaim, 'For me, Rome is Italy'; even Cavour, shortly before his death, remarked that 'Rome alone must be the capital of Italy.'[50] Nor did it mean that no good Catholics supported the cause of unification. However, the implacable opposition of the papacy towards those who dreamed of Rome as an Italian capital certainly encouraged nationalism to be anticlerical in character. The unfortunate consequence of this was that nationalism was incapable of mobilizing 'the one institution that touched the lives of nearly all Italians'.[51] Significantly matters actually deteriorated after the acquisition of Rome in 1870. Pius IX's decision to reject the olive branch offered through the Law of Guarantees in 1871 forestalled any chance of good relations between church and state. Instead Pius IX portrayed himself as 'the prisoner in the Vatican', and called on Catholic states not to recognize the new Italy. Meanwhile, the adoption of the *non expedit* ('it is not expedient') and, in 1877, the more forceful *non licet* ('it is not permitted'), whereby Catholics were effectively forbidden to participate in national politics, helped deepen fissures in Italian society. Although the threat of the left finally led to the 1905 papal encyclical *Il fermo proposito*, permitting electoral activity 'to help the maintenance of social order', the refusal of the Vatican to acknowledge the Italian state helped to sap its legitimacy in the eyes of the population and to create even deeper divisions in Italian society.[52] It was only with Mussolini's Lateran Pacts of 1929 that the Vatican actually recognized the Italian state, paving the way for a reconciliation of

damage done by the church is in the second of these works, where he states: 'The Church ... has neither been able to occupy the whole of Italy, nor has it allowed anyone else to occupy it. Consequently, it has been the cause why Italy has never come under one head, but has been under many princes and *signori*, by whom such disunion and such weakness has been brought about, that it has now become prey, not only of barbarian potentates, but of anyone who attacks it.' Niccolò Machiavelli, *Il principe e altre opere politiche*, ed. Stefano Andretta (Milan, 1976), 143.

49 For Gioberti's perspective after 1849, expressed in his 1851 *Del rinnovamento civile d'Italia* see Giorgio Candeloro, *Storia dell'Italia moderna*, vol. iv: *Dalla rivoluzione nazionale all'unità* (Milan, 1980 edn.), 216–22.

50 Belardelli, 'La terza Roma', 14. It is significant that Mazzini named the newspaper he set up shortly before his death, *La Roma del popolo*, emphasizing as Roland Sarti points out, that the sacred city retained a 'special mission', that Cavour tried in the final months of his life to acquire the city through fair means or foul, and that Garibaldi made two very ill-conceived attempts to seize Rome in 1862 and 1867. On *La Roma del popolo* see Roland Sarti, *Mazzini: A Life for the Religion of Politics* (Westport, Conn., 1997), 212. For Mazzini's comment see his 1864 autobiographical writings: G. Mazzini, *Note autobiografiche* (Milan, 1986), 382.

51 For this characterization of the church see Raymond Grew, 'Culture and Society, 1796–1896', in John A. Davis (ed.), *Italy in the Nineteenth Century* (Oxford, 2000), 206–34, 222.

52 There are numerous accounts of the troubled relations between church and state in post-unification Italy. For a clear assessment in English see Clark, *Modern Italy, passim.*

Catholic and national interests, and a new centrality for *romanità* in the rhetoric of Italian nationhood.[53]

THE USES AND ABUSES OF ITALIAN HISTORY

Rather than turning to the model of ancient Rome or looking to the papacy many nineteenth-century Italian patriots chose instead to follow the romantic passion for the medieval. Central to this was Simonde de Sismondi's vast multi-volume history of Italy's republics which was already well received in liberal Italian circles in the French original even before the publication of its final part in 1818.[54] Sismondi's finished work was almost immediately translated into Italian, and significantly received an ecstatic review from the medievalist Pietro Borsieri in the pages of the liberal Milanese journal *Il conciliatore*. A trend was set that meant for the whole Restoration period the most popular field for historical research, not to mention works of historical fantasy—and the two are sometimes hard to distinguish—was the medieval. Of course, for those who would create a nationalist myth, a focus on medieval history had obvious advantages over looking to the classical past: in terms of religion, language, culture, and political organization there was much greater continuity between the Middle Ages and the modern. Moreover, it was possible to build on Sismondi's emphasis on the role that the Italian city republics had played in the growth of political liberty, and the part that they had played in the cultural revival of the West, to establish the basis of a patriotic historiography.[55] Brave acts of resistance, perhaps most notably the Lombard League (when Italy's northern cities formed an armed coalition in 1167 to resist the German Emperor Frederick Barbarosa), and the Sicilian Vespers (when Palermo rose leading to the massacre of the French in 1282) were seized upon as examples of Italy's readiness to struggle for freedom against foreign domination, often inspiring works of art and literature such as Cesare Balbo's historical novel *La Lega di Lombarda*, Giuseppe Diotti's *Il giuramento di Pontida*, and Francesco Hayez's different versions of *I vespri siciliani*.[56] Meanwhile, Giovanni Berchet called the epoch of the Lombard League 'the most glorious' in Italy's history, and the youthful Mazzini described the period after the foundation of the League as 'worth more than whole centuries of Rome'.[57]

Yet, just as there were difficulties in looking to classical Rome, the Middle Ages carried with them inherent dangers for nationalists and nationalism. While it was just about possible to reconcile an idealized view of the medieval commune with a

---

[53] On the failure of the so-called 'conciliazione' to ensure smooth relations between church and state see John F. Pollard, *The Vatican and Italian Fascism, 1929–32: A Study in Conflict* (Cambridge, 1985).

[54] Jean Charles Léonard Sismonde de Sismondi, *Histoire des républiques italiennes du moyen âge* (16 vols., Paris, 1809–16).

[55] Giorgio Candeloro, *Storia dell'Italia moderna*, vol. ii: *Dalla restaurazione alla rivoluzione nazionale 1815–1846* (Milan, 1978 edn.), 37–9.   [56] Lyttelton, 'Creating', 46–58.

[57] Ibid. 47–8.

desire for a federal Italy, as was the case with Gioberti, romanticizing the Middle Ages posed huge problems for those who wished to found a centralized nation-state: the Italy of the *comuni* was even more fragmented and prone to civil strife than that of the seventeenth to nineteenth centuries. Moreover, it was precisely its internecine rivalry that had made it vulnerable to attack by barbarians from north of the Alps. The even greater glories of the Renaissance—when Italians had undeniably dominated learning and the arts—were also of scant use for patriots: as Machiavelli and many of his contemporaries had repeatedly observed, fifteenth- and sixteenth-century Italy was divided and decadent and easy prey to foreign domination. Put crudely, nineteenth-century Italian patriots were forced to scrape the barrel in pursuit of a national myth. What they did when doing so was to highlight the utter absence either of domestic historical models for nation-building or of genuine national heroes. In 'inventing' their nation Czechs could look back to the once powerful Kingdom of Bohemia or turn to a distinctive Hussite tradition; Hungarians could point proudly to centuries of independence and the glories of Matthias Corvinus; Poles could dream of the seventeenth century when the Polish-Lithuanian Commonwealth stretched from the Baltic to the Black Sea, and glorify John Sobieski who had saved Christendom from the scourge of the Ottomans. In contrast, because of the nature of Italy's political divisions, the peninsula's great soldiers and statesmen had fought and politicked not as Italians but as Venetians or Romans, Florentines or Sienese. Past heroic feats of arms were as likely to have been in battle with fellow nationals as against an outside invader; and there were many examples of Italians acting in alliance with a foreign power when waging war against their co-nationals. The study of history inevitably pushed into the foreground the individual city not the nation as the arena for greatness. Only in literature—written, as we have seen, in a language that was scarcely spoken—did a genuine sense of the *national* exist. And, as we have also seen, in a nation of illiterates, Petrarch, Dante, Alfieri, and Foscolo could do little to kindle national sentiment.[58]

CONCLUSION: 'THE BEAUTIFUL LEGENDS' OF THE RISORGIMENTO

The consequence of the weakness of an Italian national culture and a history that served only to reiterate division and weakness and mutual enmity, was that the Risorgimento rapidly assumed a central importance as a foundation myth in its

---

[58] Antonio Gramsci's well-known attack on the Mazzinians' love for 'the traditional rhetoric of Italian literature' is worth citing here. To Gramsci the so-called Action Party 'confused the cultural unity which existed in the peninsula—confined, however, to a very thin stratum of the population . . . —with the political and territorial unity of the great popular masses, who were foreign to that cultural tradition, and who, even supposing that they knew of its existence, could not care less about it.' Antonio Gramsci, *Notes from Prison Notebooks*, ed. and transl. Quintin Hoare and Geoffrey Nowell Smith (London, 1971), 63.

own right: Confalonieri and Pellico, the Bandiera brothers, Pisacane, Orsini, Mazzini, Carlo Alberto, Garibaldi all became secular saints before the process of unification was completed, and key events—the 1820 revolution in Naples, the 'Cinque Giornate' in Milan, Garibaldi's defence of and retreat from the Roman Republic, the expedition of the Thousand—were all celebrated. Yet even this narrative of sacrifice and heroism was as likely to divide as to unite. The 'Cinque Giornate', for example, the five glorious days in March 1848 when the Milanese had driven the Habsburg forces of Marshal Radetzky from the Lombard capital, offered great potential as a symbol of the bravery of the Italian people in the year of revolutions. Close historical analysis, however, would rapidly reveal the way in which the Milanese revolution's aims as embodied by both the popular rising and the leadership of Carlo Cattaneo had been rapidly betrayed by the Lombard elites: terrified of social unrest, they had sought annexation by Sardinia-Piedmont to guarantee social order. The Piedmontese king, Carlo Alberto, had in turn delayed assistance to the Milanese out of his own distaste for insurrection. Moreover, the two campaigns he subsequently fought against the Austrians were motivated principally by dynastic ambition, and had both ended in ignominious defeats; the second Habsburg victory led to his abdication. It is perhaps no surprise, therefore, that detailed research on Italy's recent past was discouraged in liberal Italy. The archives for the nineteenth century remained closed in order to protect Italy's 'beautiful legends' from being challenged by historical rigour.[59] Yet it is equally significant that when the 'Cinque Giornate' were celebrated those who chose to do so were Milanese. Of thirty-six patriotic pamphlets that were published on the topic between 1860 and 1900—mostly on the fiftieth anniversary of the rising— all but three came out of the Lombard capital itself: municipal rather than national sentiment was once again a driving force when looking back on the past.[60]

Italy's nineteenth-century nationalists of almost all political hues from Mazzinians to moderate apologists for Piedmontese expansion sought to justify unification by presenting it as a kind of panacea that would solve the evident ills of the peninsula.[61] These latter were in turn attributed to the pestilence of foreign, priestly, or despotic rule. The tragedy of unification was that such justifications created unrealistic expectations. For example, the grave economic and social difficulties of the south of Italy had been explained away in terms of the disastrous impact of Bourbon misrule. Unity under the constitutional monarchy of the

[59] The phrase was used by Giovanni Giolitti, the dominant liberal politician of the pre-1914 era, in a parliamentary debate of June 1912. Denis Mack Smith, 'Documentary Falsification and Italian Biography', in T. C. W. Blanning and David Cannadine (eds.), *History and Biography: Essays in Honour of Derek Beales* (Cambridge, 1996), 173–87, 180.

[60] Bruno Tobia, 'Le cinque giornate di Milano', in M. Isenghi (ed.), *I luoghi di memoria: strutture ed eventi dell'Italia unita* (Rome, 1997), 253–72.

[61] See, for example, the views expressed in 'Il credo politico della Società Nazionale' of February 1858 in Denis Mack Smith, *Il Risorgimento italiano: storia e testi* (2 vols., Rome, 1976 edn.), ii. 429–32. On the National Society more generally see Raymond Grew, *A Sterner Plan for Italian Unity: The Italian National Society in the Risorgimento* (Princeton, 1963).

House of Savoy was supposed to bring prosperity and order. Of course, observers as varied as Cesare Cantù and Giacomo Leopardi, Gino Capponi and Giovanni Visconti Venosta had recognized the marked differences between the north and south of the peninsula, and many had warned against the dangers of overly precipitous unification.[62] Few, however, could have predicted the utter contempt and hostility that would characterize the responses of northerners after the annexation of the Kingdom of the Two Sicilies, when they discovered that economic backwardness, lawlessness, disease, and poor communications could not be swept swiftly aside by the broom of the nation-state.[63] Thus Farini, Luogotenente Generale for the southern provinces, wrote to Cavour in November 1860 that the annexation of Naples was 'a gangrene', and exclaimed to the Interior Minister Minghetti; 'It's overwhelming the state of this disgraceful place . . . What an Italy! What liberty!'[64] Faced with the same overwhelming task as the Bourbons had been confronting since the eighteenth century, the new Italian state adopted a strategy of damning and blaming the local population, imposing unsuitable Piedmontese institutions, and, when it encountered resistance to unpopular nation-building, employing massive and brutal repression. The result of such policies was a brutal civil war which raged in the south for much of the 1860s. Unification had revealed that, despite the results of largely rigged plebiscites, Italians not only had a scant sense of national identity but many of them had no desire to be part of an Italian state at all.

The bitter legacy of repression in southern Italy bears testimony to a truth identified by Karl Marx in a biting attack on Mazzini after a failed anti-Austrian rising in Milan in 1853. Ultimately Italian unification could only be imposed from above because it lacked any kind of popular mandate.[65] To attach ordinary Italians to a united state it was necessary to appeal to their material interests, and neither radical romantics like Mazzini nor the pro-Piedmontese moderates were prepared to do this. Those who established the new state were not prepared to introduce the sort of sweeping reforms necessary to attach the population to the new order. However many statues of Vittorio Emanuele II were erected, however many *piazze* were named after Garibaldi or Cavour, the failure of the Italian state to deliver genuine benefits to the masses meant that those masses would remain alienated and indifferent. Crispi's call for a 'cult of great memories' and Giolitti's impassioned defence of the 'beautiful legend' were no substitute for the development of a society and economy that benefited the bulk of the population. In this surely lies the explanation for the tendency of Italians to chat among themselves while the national flag was run up.

[62] Claudia Petraccone, *Le due civiltà: settentrionali e meridionali nella storia d'Italia dal 1860 al 1914* (Rome, 2000), 6–12.

[63] For northern responses to south after unification see Nelson Moe, ' "This is Africa": Ruling and Representing Southern Italy, 1860–61' in Ascoli and von Heneberg (eds.), *Making and Remaking*, 119–53. [64] Petraccone, *Le due civiltà*, 15–16.

[65] 'Kossuth and Mazzini', *New York Daily Tribune*, 4 Apr. 1853.

14

The United Kingdom

British Nationalisms during the Long Nineteenth Century

Chris Williams

Any attempt to investigate the relative purchase of ethnic and civic nationalisms in Britain during the long nineteenth century first has to clarify what is meant by 'Britain'. The United Kingdom of Great Britain and Ireland came into being on 1 January 1801, following the passage of the Act of Union between Great Britain and Ireland during the preceding year. The state of Great Britain was itself of recent origin, having been created in 1707 by the Act of Union between England and Scotland. England had incorporated Wales following earlier Acts of Union in 1536 and 1543. Such 'unions' had been preceded by dynastic mergers: Henry Tudor's victory over Richard III in 1485 allowed the Welsh the comfort of believing that one of their own race sat upon the English throne and the accession of James VI of Scotland as James I of England in 1603 had replaced the 'Welsh' Tudor dynasty with that of the 'Scottish' Stuarts. The subsequent history of the 'British' monarchy was turbulent, as the events of the years 1649, 1688, 1715, and 1745 indicate, but it was stabilized under George III from 1760 and consolidated by Victoria during her reign from 1837. However, the United Kingdom, as created in 1801, lasted just over 120 years: in December 1922 Ireland was partitioned and the Irish Free State launched, leaving the United Kingdom as that of Great Britain and *Northern* Ireland. That eighty-year-old version of unitary state formation appears now to be once more under pressure: referenda in 1997 have led to the establishment of a Scottish Parliament and a Welsh Assembly, whilst there is also an assembly in stuttering existence in Northern Ireland. The possibility of further separatism is no longer beyond contemplation. Particularly in Ireland, and to a considerable extent also in Scotland and in Wales, identification with Britain and with British nationalism has weakened, a weakening accentuated by the shrinking global context afforded to such nationalism by the once mighty British Empire.

The terminology of 'Britain', and thus of 'British nationalisms', may therefore be related to a number of differing states and social formations in the modern period. Strictly speaking, 'Britain' refers to 'mainland Britain'; that is, England, Scotland, and Wales, exclusive of Ireland. The 'British Isles', however, does include the island of Ireland, although the adjective 'British' used in this context is often found offensive by Irish nationalists. Norman Davies and J. G. A. Pocock have suggested alternatives ('The Isles' and the 'Atlantic Archipelago' respectively), although neither has proved popular and it is as simple either to refer to 'Britain and Ireland' or to recognize that the term 'British Isles' was in common and widely accepted usage during the period covered by this chapter.[1] A further dimension is added by the existence and considerable expansion of the British Empire during this same era. In 1792 Britain controlled twenty-six colonies. By 1815 this had expanded to forty-two, and by the First World War 230 million people were under direct British rule in colonies, and a further 50 million lived in British protectorates. A quarter of the world's population and a fifth of the world's land mass was covered by the British Empire, which was 125 times larger than Britain itself.

'Britain' as an entity and 'Britishness' as an identity have therefore to be seen as potentially relevant to a wide range of different peoples: most obviously the English, Scots, and Welsh in mainland Britain, plus the Irish, and quite probably many inhabitants of the colonial empire as well. Nor should one forget either that the populations of Cornwall, the Isle of Man, and the Channel Islands sometimes asserted their own distinctive identities, nor that each of the major national groups was itself divided regionally and culturally, nor that the British Isles was also the home to an even greater range of immigrant populations including Jews, Huguenots, Chinese, Germans, Italians, and blacks. In considering nationalism in Britain during the long nineteenth century one is, therefore, potentially considering at least five critical contexts in which nationalist sentiment might be located, and nationalist mobilization mapped. These are the four major components of the United Kingdom—England, Scotland, Wales, and Ireland—plus Britain as a whole. Furthermore, in each context one might well be investigating more than one form of nationalism. Although it is difficult to distinguish, in England, between English nationalism and British nationalism, it is more straightforward to plot the demarcations in Scotland and Wales between Scottish or Welsh nationalisms on the one hand and British nationalism on the other, and in Ireland one might be thought to be dealing simultaneously with more than one Irish nationalism. The situation is further complicated by the fact that British nationalism meant one thing to the Scots, another to the Welsh, and others again to, for example, both the Irish Catholic and the Ulster Protestant.

---

[1] N. Davies, *The Isles: A History* (London, 1999); J. G. A. Pocock, 'British History: A Plea for a New Subject', *Journal of Modern History*, 47 (1975), 603; id., 'Conclusion: Contingency, Identity, Sovereignty', in A. Grant and K. Stringer (eds.), *Uniting the Kingdom? The Making of British History* (London, 1995), 292–302.

It is important to recognize that these differing nationalisms were not necessarily mutually exclusive. Many nineteenth-century scholars, writing at a time when nation-states were being formed across Europe, regarded the emergence of nations as the natural and logical outcome of centuries of human history. History was written in terms of the evolution and dispositions of 'national character' and nations were seen as fundamentally objective phenomena, based on specific essential criteria (if varying from case to case) such as language, religion, geography, or 'race'. In recent decades modernist and post-modernist works have undermined many of these old certainties. Nations now tend to be seen as 'invented' or 'imagined', as manufacturing historical roots and traditions in the light of contemporary concerns or pressures.[2] What is held to constitute 'the nation' changes over time, as does any sense of a specific 'national identity'. Nations, far from being immanent in history, are historically and socially 'produced' and 'constructed', and are thus open to 'deconstruction' as well. Rather than an individual possessing a single sense of national identity, each of us (and thus individuals in the past too) may have multiple, composite, and overlapping identities. Different identities are deployed in differing 'situational' contexts. For some scholars, identities are relational, generated through binary oppositions: we are defined by what we believe we are not. Gender theorists suggest that discourses of national identity often make ideological and symbolic uses of women, and that women may experience national identity in fundamentally different ways from men.[3] Others go so far as to challenge the notion of a unitary 'self' at all, suggesting that we have fragmented, multiple 'selves'. As Stuart Hall has written: 'If we feel we have a unified identity ... it is only because we construct a comforting story or "narrative of the self" about ourselves ... The fully unified, completed, secure and coherent identity is a fantasy.'[4] Certainly national identities have to interact along multiple axes with other identities, including those of family, class, gender, religion, ethnic group, and locality or region, all of which may have the potential to generate a sense of belonging to a wider collectivity. To a degree any given national identity is built from such identities, although they may well not be fully reconcilable. In this volume the utility of the distinction between 'ethnic' and 'civic' forms of national belonging is investigated: the former generated by possession of certain traits (speaking a particular language, being an adherent of a particular religious faith) and the latter stemming from one's membership of a political community (being a voter, a 'citizen'), irrespective of one's broader qualities or characteristics. Nationalism was thus likely to be highly situational, contingent, and relative: much depended on who you were, in which situation you were placed, and with whom you were interacting.

A final important preliminary qualification is to stress that identifying the logical goal or *terminus ad quem* of any of the above nationalisms may also prove

---

[2] E. Hobsbawm and T. Ranger (eds.), *The Invention of Tradition* (Cambridge, 1983).

[3] N. Yuval-Davis, *Gender and Nation* (London, 1997).

[4] S. Hall, 'The Question of Cultural Identity', in S. Hall, D. Held, and T. McGrew (eds.), *Modernity and its Futures* (Cambridge, 1992), 277.

complex. Nationalism is most easily identifiable in the form of a national liberation movement, aimed at overthrowing some form of colonial rule or imperialist
oppression and, in the wake of such a revolution, establishing an independent
nation-state. That is how much of the recent history of the world may be understood. In the context of the British Isles, however, such an understanding is almost
irrelevant. It is most obviously the case that the Irish republican movement of
the late nineteenth and early twentieth centuries constructed its nationalism in
this mould. However, for virtually all Scottish and Welsh nationalists before
1914, as well as for the vast majority of Irish nationalists, their objectives were
usually more moderate and often less clearly defined: some measure, perhaps,
of 'Home Rule', of administrative devolution, or of legislative recognition of
national particularities. These were nationalisms that often found much scope for
reconciliation with both remaining part of the United Kingdom, and of sharing in
wider British nationalist objectives. An even more intricate dimension is provided
by an assessment of English nationalism and of orthodox British and imperial
nationalisms. If Scottish, and Welsh, and certainly Irish nationalisms aimed at
redressing the balance within the United Kingdom in their favour and away from
England, it was rarely the case that English nationalism was particularly bothered
by whatever benefits their Celtic partners were obtaining from the Union. English
nationalists found their binary opposite(s) elsewhere: in the form of threatening
continental challengers such as France or Germany, or constructed as 'aliens',
potentially capable of undermining the purity and health of the English race. Very
often, when English nationalists spoke or wrote of 'England' and the 'English',
they took such terms to encompass at least the Scots and Welsh as well. Not infrequently the Scots and Welsh followed suit. There was a regular elision between
English nationalism and a British nationalism understood as a centrist, unionist,
and singular phenomenon. As for the British Empire, although that projected
British nationalism onto a much wider stage, it also could lead to tensions
between expansionist imperialists on the one hand, and those who favoured more
limited, 'Little Englander' strategies.

This chapter aims to sketch out the lineaments of the wide variety of nationalisms that could be found in Britain between 1789 and 1914, and to consider how
each might be understood in terms of the common distinction between 'ethnic'
and 'civic' forms of nationalism. The argument will be that it will not do to think
of nineteenth-century Britain as somehow free of nationalism. Nor is it satisfactory to consider Britain as the home only of moderate and liberal forms of civic
nationalism, present though these were. However, ethnic forms of nationalism
in Britain, although clearly in evidence, were rarely 'pure' in their ideology or
objectives. Overall, this chapter suggests that, in the British case, we need to
move away from any crude dichotomy between 'ethnic' and 'civic' ideal types
of nationalism, supposedly with their own points of origin and linear developments, and recognize the frequently highly complex, contextual, and even
contradictory forms taken by real and historic nationalisms.

HISTORIOGRAPHIES

The approach of this chapter is grounded in an appreciation of the multinational character of the United Kingdom, and in an awareness of the plurality of the modern historiography of the multiple nations themselves. In this respect it may be understood as embracing both the rise of separate historiographies in Scotland, Wales, and Ireland, whilst also paying due attention to the wave of scholarship that has engaged self-consciously with the idea and institutions of 'Britishness'. Both areas of development represent deviations from or reactions to the centralizing, homogenizing, and Anglicizing assumptions that governed so much of what has passed for British history.

The first plea for 'British' history was made in the 1970s by the New Zealander Pocock, who argued that no 'true history of Britain' had ever been seriously attempted: '[i]nstead of histories of Britain, we have . . . histories of England, in which Welsh, Scots, Irish . . . appear as peripheral peoples when, and only when, their doings assume power to disturb the tenor of English politics'.[5] Such an 'anglocentric' historiographical tradition had generated its opposite, 'anglophobic' tradition, in Wales, Scotland, and Ireland. Neither was satisfactory: British history had to be understood as interactive, interdependent, multicultural, and constructed on a global stage. Later Pocock claimed that his approach revealed 'the ideological falseness of the claim of any state, nation, or other politically created entity to natural or historical unity', and positioned himself as both 'multinational' and 'antinational'.[6]

Pocock's essays continue to be the most influential statements in favour of 'British' history. Hugh Kearney in the late 1980s preferred to adopt what he termed a 'Britannic' approach, meaning 'the interaction of the various major cultures of the British Isles'.[7] His 'history of four nations' recognized that national units could themselves be dissolved into a number of distinctive cultures, and that such cultures had the capacity to overlap national boundaries. Kearney believed that, conceptually, 'national history' inevitably stressed difference: what marked one nation out from another. His 'Britannic' approach could more easily accommodate change over time and cultural interaction, and was capable of stressing how much the 'Britannic' cultures had in common.

Nevertheless, there remained the suspicion that 'British' history was a Trojan horse of English history writ large, threatening the integrity of Irish, Scottish, and Welsh histories built up over decades through painstaking struggle against being patronized and marginalized. Whatever the future for 'British history', the success of a pluralist approach is reliant on the flourishing of the historiographies

---

    [5] Pocock, 'British History'.
    [6] Pocock, 'The Limits and Divisions of British History: In Search of the Unknown Subject', *American Historical Review*, 87 (1982).
    [7] H. Kearney, *The British Isles: A History of Four Nations* (Cambridge, 1989).

of Scotland, Wales, and Ireland. It is not appropriate here to document the growth of the historical establishments in these countries: suffice it to say that all have well-established journals such as *Irish Historical Studies*, the *Scottish Historical Review*, and the *Welsh History Review*, 'Oxford histories', 'Penguin histories', monograph series, chairs, and universities where such national histories are taught. In each there has been a marked growth of interest since the Second World War, with recent years witnessing the emergence of academically respectable (if not always uncontroversial) texts nevertheless reaching out to a wider reading public.[8] The maturing of distinct historiographies across the British Isles has effectively challenged the claim of Anglocentric histories to speak for all of Britain, as well as facilitating thoughtful contemplation of the interaction of its component parts.

With these many caveats in mind, attention now turns to the historical manifestations of nationalism in the United Kingdom during the period 1789–1914. Initially the focus is on the extent to which a British nationalism was generated, expanded, and sustained, both across England and the British Isles as a whole. There is then consideration of the relationship between the nationalisms of Scotland, Wales, and Ireland on the one hand, and that of Britain on the other.

GREAT BRITAIN

In approaching the power of British nationalisms in this period one cannot avoid the powerful argument advanced by Linda Colley for the history of Britain from the Act of Union between England and Scotland in 1707 through to the coronation of Queen Victoria in 1837.[9] Colley contends that during these decades a powerful sense of British nationalism was forged. This Britishness was not simply English domination imposed from the centre, nor did it replace or suffocate other identities. Rather it was an artifice superimposed onto those older alignments, which retained their own powers of attraction, albeit themselves shot through by regional and local attachments. Although Colley does not altogether discount the importance of internal homogenizing social, economic, and cultural trends (in transport, trade, the press, postal communications, and internal migration) these were secondary to the generation of a sense of unity from without.

Britain was often at war with France in the eighteenth and early nineteenth centuries. These wars were global in their reach and serious in the threats they posed to the British state and empire. Although Britain was never subjected to a full-scale invasion, there were a number of invasion scares. Wolfe, Nelson, Wellington all became national heroes, their images found on everything from woodcuts, fabrics, and ceramics to inn signs. The French Wars of 1793–1815

[8] R. F. Foster, *Modern Ireland 1600–1972* (London, 1988); T. M. Devine, *The Scottish Nation 1707–2000* (Harmondsworth, 1999); J. Davies, *The History of Wales* (London, 1993).
[9] L. Colley, *Britons: Forging the Nation, 1707–1837* (London, 1992).

allowed British women a range of opportunities by which to manifest their patriotism: providing clothing, collecting money, making flags and banners, organizing committees, and lobbying. As for British men, the same conflict witnessed an unprecedented mobilization of the lower orders in regular, militia, and volunteer forces, with close to half a million men in regular and another half a million in territorial forces. Military training may have been a more common working-class experience than factory work, political agitation, or trade unionism. Patriotism was multi-layered but also rational: it offered opportunities for profit and career advancement, for escape and excitement, for the claiming of social status, for the defence of one's homeland and family, and for advancing claims to civic and political participation.

France was not a threat just in terms of its imperial ambitions, was also the world's strongest Roman Catholic power. Since the Protestant Reformation of the sixteenth century the English (and increasingly the Scots and Welsh too) defined themselves by their Protestantism. That Protestantism was at its most united when facing a Catholic challenge from without. Plebeian anti-Catholicism was revealed in almanacs and popular literature, which stressed the providential nature of British Protestantism and encouraged a belief that the British were God's chosen people.

Long-term war with a foreign, Catholic 'Other' was accompanied by the building of a massive overseas empire which also contributed to a sense of British national identity. Not only did the empire provide profits and opportunities in which England's junior partners might share, but ruling over large numbers of non-white, non-Christian subject peoples generated a sense of innate British superiority, mission, and values, reflected through a variety of popular cultural forms. An imperial governing class was formed that was authentically British in scope. The ranks of government and empire were opened to Scots, Welsh, and Anglo-Irish, providing an arena in which national differences could be sunk in a broader imperial culture. Such elites intermarried and blended culturally, converging in wealth and lifestyles. Englishmen established landed estates in Wales and Scotland and the rise of the public schools, recruiting from across Britain, generated a common form of educational experience. Dual identities were more and more common and could be reconciled in an overarching loyalty to 'Britain'. 'British' manners and customs (such as fox hunting) became adopted in contradistinction to continental styles, the elite patronized domestic rather than foreign art, and toured the mountainous districts of Britain rendered attractive by the romantic, picturesque, and the sublime. The monarchy was rehabilitated as a central part of British culture from the late eighteenth century onwards. George III was able to capitalize on the fact that he had been born and bred in Britain, and was reinvented as 'Father of the People' and guarantor of British stability and prosperity.

Wellington's victory over Napoleon at Waterloo in 1815 marks the climax of this interlocking argument. Thereafter Britain was indisputably the greatest power in the world, with the largest empire. That level of security, and the fact that

British Catholics had generally proved to be loyal subjects during the Napoleonic era, facilitated a subtle shift of attitude, especially within the governing class, towards the question of Catholic emancipation. Although when that came, in 1829, it was accompanied by much popular protest from ordinary Britons, toleration was growing and anti-Catholicism was less central to the definition of Britishness than it had been. During the same period there was significant popular involvement in pressing for parliamentary reform and for a moral stance on slavery: the passing of the Reform Act in 1832 and the emancipation of West Indian slaves in 1833 (following the abolition of the slave trade in 1807) facilitated a more enlightened self-image of Britain as the peaceful home of freedom and liberty, superior again in its orderly evolution to its former rival across the Channel. Colley does not view British national identity as fixed by the long period of conflict with Catholic France: rather 'most nations have always been culturally and ethnically diverse, problematic, protean and artificial constructs that take shape very quickly and come apart just as fast'.[10] British nationalism was therefore bound to change. But by 1815 Britain had been first forged as a nation by war, Protestantism, and empire.

This account of the development of British nationalism is not impregnable. It fails to find a place for the Irish, when there is plenty of evidence that many Irish (Catholics as well as Protestants) bought into British nationalism in many different ways. Much of what has been labelled as 'British' nationalism may equally be understood as 'English' nationalism.[11] A focus on wartime patriotism risks confusing rhetoric particular to an exceptional context with a more pervasive if also understated sense of Britishness. Outside the pressures of war, British nationalism was deployed in symbolic but very limited ways and there was no official attempt to make Britishness the 'primary cultural identity' of British subjects: the British state was sufficiently flexible and plastic to allow a plurality of such primary identities to coexist under its auspices.[12] There is also the danger of exaggerating the degree of homogeneity both internally and externally. British Protestantism was by no means united, with particular tensions within the Protestant churches of Wales and Scotland, and to argue that the French were invariably seen as 'Other' underestimates the extent of Francophilia, especially amongst the British governing elite.[13] Yet, notwithstanding such qualifications,

[10] L. Colley, *Britons: Forging the Nation, 1707–1837*, 5.

[11] A. Hastings, *The Construction of Nationhood: Ethnicity, Religion and Nationalism* (Cambridge, 1997), 61–4; G. Newman, *The Rise of English Nationalism: A Cultural History, 1740–1830* (London, 1987).

[12] D. Eastwood, L. Brockliss, and M. John, 'Conclusion: From Dynastic Union to Unitary State. The European Experience', in Brockliss and Eastwood (eds.), *A Union of Multiple Identities: The British Isles, c.1750–c.1850* (Manchester, 1997).

[13] T. Claydon and I. McBride, 'The Trials of the Chosen Peoples: Recent Interpretations of Protestantism and National Identity in Britain and Ireland', in Claydon and McBride (eds.), *Protestantism and National Identity: Britain and Ireland, c.1650–c.1850* (Cambridge, 1998); R. Eagles, *Francophilia in English Society 1748–1815* (Basingstoke, 2000), 2–8.

the argument for British nationalism should not readily be jettisoned. In drawing attention to the importance of the forging of a relatively culturally homogeneous ruling elite, to the enhanced role of the monarchy, to the impressive power of wartime patriotism, and to the externally generated solidarities of conflict with France, Protestantism, and empire, Colley has placed a number of important themes at the heart of the debate. But British nationalism needs to be understood as more diffuse, mutually contradictory, and plastic than Colley allows, particularly once one moves into the mid and late nineteenth century.

For example, in religion one has to distinguish between the continuing uniting power of a militant anti-Catholic Protestantism on the one hand and the religious diversity that existed within the body of the Protestant faith on the other. Anti-Catholic sentiment was actually strengthened in the short term by the controversy over Catholic Emancipation, and gained new impetus from the mid-1840s with the Maynooth agitation and with increasing levels of Irish immigration into Britain.[14] The restoration of the Roman Catholic hierarchy across England and Wales sparked the 'Papal Aggression' crisis of 1850–1 and there were numerous anti-Irish and anti-Catholic riots in the following decade, woven into popular celebrations such as Guy Fawkes' Day, arising out of clashes between evangelical 'missionaries' and the intended targets of their proselytism, sparked by labour market rivalries, or mobilized as a vote-winner by the local Conservative Party. Yet the sense in which Britain was a Protestant nation under serious threat from a foreign Catholic power steadily diminished, and explicit anti-Catholic prejudice became less and less acceptable in respectable circles.

The eventual decline in the salience of anti-Catholicism as a badge of British identity ensured that the fissiparous nature of British Protestantism gained prominence. Neither the Union of 1707 nor that of 1800 had sought to establish religious homogeneity, accepting a Presbyterian religious establishment in Scotland and the de facto popularity of Roman Catholicism in Ireland. In Wales the eighteenth-century Methodist revival and the power of the other Nonconformist churches ensured that the Anglican church's 'establishment' was both precarious and controversial. The 1851 religious census revealed the strength of Nonconformity across much of England as well as the uncomfortable fact that a substantial minority of the population apparently did not attend church at all. Religious diversity was increasingly a 'British' experience, in that most denominations could be found in all parts of the island, but religion remained an important vehicle for the articulation of national identities, especially on the Celtic fringe. The British Isles was 'a religious patchwork quilt of immense complexity', religion an ambivalent force in its impact on British identities.[15]

---

[14] J. Wolffe, *The Protestant Crusade in Great Britain, 1829–60* (Oxford, 1991); D. G. Paz, *Popular Anti-Catholicism in Mid-Victorian England* (Stanford, Calif., 1992).

[15] D. Hempton, *Religion and Political Culture in Britain and Ireland: From the Glorious Revolution to the Decline of Empire* (Cambridge, 1996), 173; J. Wolffe, *God and Greater Britain: Religion and National Life in Britain and Ireland 1843–1945* (London, 1994).

Empire was vital to a sense of Britishness from the late eighteenth century onwards, both in terms of the widespread encounters with the non-white, non-Christian 'Other' and in terms of the opportunities imperial expansion offered to England's junior partners in the United Kingdom. Most work on imperial identities has, however, concentrated on the last three decades of the nineteenth century, the age of the 'new imperialism' and the 'Scramble for Africa', as it was in the late Victorian years that empire was inscribed most forcibly in British culture and politics. Imperialism was found in everything from education and music hall to sport and ideas of the natural world, from popular journalism and juvenile literature to military adventures and missionary activity. Imperial signification was present in advertising imagery and marketing slogans, on cigarette cards and post-cards, in youth organizations and in the vocabulary of popular speech, in museums and school textbooks. The most symbolic imperial occasions were the Golden Jubilee of 1887, the Diamond Jubilee of 1897, Victoria's funeral in 1901, and the subsequent coronation of Edward VII. These spawned imperial paraphernalia including commemorative mugs and plates, toys and games, medals and banners, trinket boxes and scent bottles. One did not have to be a 'jingo' or a rabid imperialist to be affected and impressed by the constant reminders that one was at the centre of a global empire, and one did not have to be English either. Enthusiasm for and participation, real or vicarious, in the adventure of empire was as likely to appeal to the Scots, Welsh, or even Irish as it was to the English. The Scots and Irish were particularly prominent as emigrants, administrators, and soldiers and overseas national differences were more likely to be blurred by a common identification as British. An imperial identity worked to strengthen ties between the constituent nations of the United Kingdom and to generate a sense of British national superiority and pride. No other people could forge its identity on such a worldwide scale, or could believe that its law, its wealth, its military might, its political stability, its particular brand of Christianity, was so worthy of export.[16]

An awareness of the power of popular imperialism in the late nineteenth century is not enough for some postcolonial historians. They have registered unease at the way in which explicitly 'British' history has remade Britain as a 'falsely homogeneous whole', the '*a priori* body upon which empire is inscribed' rather than as a part of the very discourse of empire-making itself. Britain, they allege, may only be understood as part of its own empire.[17] As yet, such assertion has not been sufficiently substantiated by scholarship for this to be taken much further, and one might legitimately prefer to see an imperial nationalism as available to but not always adopted by nineteenth-century Britons. It is not axiomatic that empire constructed British nationalism and one should certainly resist any

---

[16] J. M. MacKenzie, 'Empire and Metropolitan Cultures', in A. Porter (ed.), *The Oxford History of the British Empire*, iii: *The Nineteenth Century* (Oxford, 1999).

[17] A. Burton, 'Who Needs the Nation? Interrogating "British" History', in C. Hall (ed.), *Cultures of Empire: Colonisers in Britain and the Empire in the Nineteenth and Twentieth Centuries: A Reader* (Manchester, 2000), 140–1.

attempt to reduce the diversity of imperial experiences to a single meaning. Postcolonial perspectives tend to prioritize the dependent territories of the non-white empire in discussions of imperial ideology, whereas the primary conception of empire was one which saw it first and foremost as a family of English-speaking 'dominions', largely settled by the British themselves. Such territories not only shared a common language, but many core political and cultural values, extending to forms of religious observance and sporting competition.[18]

ENGLAND

In discussing British nationalism, imperial or not, one is faced with the problem of demarcating it from a sense of English nationalism. Englishness was at the core of Britishness, even if it was not synonymous with it. It is very difficult to think of any 'British' trait that was not also considered to be an English one, very difficult to separate out Britishness from the political, economic, and cultural hegemony of England. Much of what, for contemporaries, constituted the essence of Englishness—representative government, the sovereignty of Parliament, political stability and the avoidance (in recent times at least) of violent revolution, freedoms of speech, religion, and trade, a claim on a historic 'liberty', a confidence in 'progress'—was also at the heart of Britishness.

Work on the evolution of an English 'character' from the late seventeenth century through to the mid-nineteenth century has nevertheless identified certain cultural values that were not necessarily transferable to England's Celtic partners.[19] The English were held to be sincere, honest and decent, candid and frank if reserved, energetic and enterprising if eccentric, self-disciplined and dedicated to honest endeavour and honourable ambitions. The Englishman (it was a masculine concept) was independent, individualistic, proud, and self-reliant. Such characteristics were embodied in the manners and mores of the reformed public schools from the mid-century on, institutions which, along with the universities, inculcated a common code of 'gentlemanly' behaviour. It has been argued that, by the 1860s, as right-wing patriotic and imperial rhetoric gathered momentum, and as the status quo came under threat both from within (reform) and without (economic and imperial rivalry) this 'Englishness' was under stress: that two opposing models—one conservative, ethnocentric, and chauvinistic, based on custom, tradition, and prejudice, the other rational and liberal, based on notions of justice—were threatening to pull it apart.[20] Such a view has been countered by work which stresses the universalist and civilizational (rather than ethnocentric) nature of English self-imagery.[21]

---

[18] A. S. Thompson, *Imperial Britain: The Empire in British Politics c.1880–1932* (Harlow, 2000).

[19] P. Langford, *Englishness Identified: Manners and Character 1650–1850* (Oxford, 2000).

[20] C. Hall, *White, Male and Middle Class: Explorations in Feminism and History* (London, 1992).

[21] P. Mandler, ' "Race" and "Nation" in Mid-Victorian Thought', in S. Collini, R. Whatmore, and B. Young (eds.), *History, Religion, and Culture: British Intellectual History 1750–1950* (Cambridge, 2000).

The significance of cultural definitions of English identity is that they were purely cultural. English 'nationalism' is a misnomer for there was no nationalist movement as such, not even much of an interest in marking St George's Day or in flying his flag. Given the highly variable nature of the historical boundaries of the English state, and the hybridity of the occupants of the English throne, English qualities had always had to survive independent of the state structures of the day. By the late nineteenth century this culture was, however, becoming institutionalized.[22] The English language received an official imprimatur with the establishment of the *New* (later the *Oxford*) *English Dictionary*; English history was codified in the *Dictionary of National Biography*; the idea of an English literary canon bearing English values gathered support, scholars, and students. These developments formed a process of national self-definition enshrining the middle and upper classes as the bearers of national values, and inviting England's Celtic partners to the party only insofar as they learnt the same rules and played the same game, either disposing of their cultural traditions or subsuming them within this refashioned Englishness. And whilst such an Englishness undoubtedly contained the potential to be bold, industrial, commercial, and forward-looking, it appears that, in the late nineteenth century it retreated behind a comforting myth of rural nostalgia.[23] England came to be defined not by the manufacturing powerhouses of the north, nor even by the commercial and financial vigour of the world's greatest city, but rather by the pastoral imagery of the rural south. English architecture, art, literature, and music celebrated a society that was itself vanishing under the pressures of urbanization and agricultural modernization. Such an ideal did not need to confront the problems of American and German economic rivalry, but could take comfort in the organic continuities, harmonies, and tranquillities of a timeless countryside.

How are British or English nationalisms best located in relation to the civic/ethnic model? British nationalism was, by and large, civic in its ambitions and appeal. Early ethnic identifications against Catholicism faded gradually after 1815, as both the British polity and, more slowly, mainland British society came to accept Catholicism as a legitimate religious choice. But ethnic nationalism did not disappear altogether. The 1905 Aliens Act was a reaction to a perceived threat from Eastern European Jews, and was later extended to apply to black and Chinese immigrants. That said, by the end of the nineteenth century there was no clear or unambiguous basis on which to erect a model of ethnic British nationalism. One was, in effect, a citizen of the empire and male residents of the British Isles were progressively enfranchised. One's legal status as a member of civil society was thus largely unaffected by ethnic considerations. With English nationalism one is dealing with a more obviously ethnic set of identifications, but these were also increasingly loose and flexible. Englishness was a set of attitudes, a

---

[22] S. Collini, *Public Moralists: Political Thought and Intellectual Life in Britain 1850–1930* (Oxford, 1991); P. Dodd, 'Englishness and the National Culture', in R. Colls and Dodd (eds.), *Englishness: Politics and Culture 1880–1920* (Beckenham, 1986).

[23] M. J. Wiener, *English Culture and the Decline of the Industrial Spirit* (Harmondsworth, 1981); A. Howkins, 'The Discovery of Rural England', in Colls and Dodd, *Englishness*.

lifestyle, a combination of choices and allegiances, rather than a clearly defined set of racial characteristics. The heterogeneous nature of the ruling classes and the aristocracy, of industrialists and financiers, ensured that no strict ethnic definition could hold water. What then of the other major component parts of the British Isles? To what extent were their diverse nationalisms structured by ethnic or civic imperatives?

SCOTLAND

In the case of Scotland one needs to distinguish between political nationalism on the one hand and cultural nationalism on the other.[24] First, it has been generally argued that political nationalism was weak or absent throughout much of the nineteenth-century in Scotland. The failure of eighteenth-century Jacobitism had tainted Scottish Catholic and Highland culture, and shame and repression inhibited any bold restatement of a nationalist agenda. For some Scots, the response to these traumas had been to endorse the explicitly assimilationist identity of the 'North Briton', embracing modernity and opportunity and distancing themselves from the apparent backwardness of Scottish society.[25] Many intellectuals looked not to Scotland's own history and traditions for guidance as to the future, but instead celebrated the alternative *telos* represented by England's apparent Whiggish progress towards parliamentary government, civil freedoms, and economic prosperity.[26]

Ultimately, 'North Britishness' did not work. The English ignored it, and in the early nineteenth century Scots were offered instead a politically sanitized but culturally attractive reconfigured Highland identity that was rapidly extended across Scottish society. The key moment in the development of Highlandism was a kilted George IV's visit to Scotland in 1822, in an act choreographed by Sir Walter Scott. Royal endorsement was strengthened by Victoria's acquisition of Balmoral Castle in 1848, and full integration into the British establishment followed with army reforms which saw many Scottish regiments, most based in and recruited from amongst Protestant Lowlanders with minimal Highland and usually no Gaelic heritage whatsoever, convert to the wearing of the kilt or of tartan. But this embracing of Highland iconography carried with it no significant political ramifications.

When nationalism did emerge, it was timid and fragile. The National Association for the Vindication of Scottish Rights (NAVSR) (1853–5) championed financial objectives such as protecting the note-issuing powers of Scottish banks and

---

[24] The following discussion owes much to E. W. McFarland, 'Scotland', in C. Williams (ed.), *A Companion to Nineteenth-Century Britain* (Oxford, 2004).

[25] M. Lynch, *Scotland: A New History* (London, 1991), 343.

[26] C. Kidd, *Subverting Scotland's Past: Scottish Whig Historians and the Creation of an Anglo-British Identity, 1689–c.1830* (Cambridge, 1993).

campaigned against the eclipse of Scottish institutions and heraldic symbols. It did not aim to repeal the union between England and Scotland, but wished to see a return to what was believed had been its more even-handed ethos. The NAVSR championed an increase in Scottish parliamentary representation and campaigned for more government expenditure in Scotland, issues which continued to attract attention long after the NAVSR's own demise.

Nationalism in Ireland sparked further interest in a Scottish agenda in the 1880s. A low-key campaign for a Secretary of State for Scotland led to the creation of the office in 1885, conceded by Gladstone in his eagerness to head off any possible link with the land question which had seen independent Crofter MPs returned in place of Whigs in some Highland constituencies.[27] The Scottish Home Rule Association, founded in 1886, appealed to its public not on the basis that the Union was fundamentally unjust, but that Home Rule was one way of ensuring that Scottish interests would not be neglected in the Imperial Parliament. As an all-party association, it reflected the diversity of Scottish politics (less consistently Liberal than Wales) but this also ensured that Scottish demands were easily diluted amongst wider party considerations. 'Scottish home rule bobbed about in the slipstream of the Irish: it did not have their motive power.'[28] Although between 1890 and 1914 measures proposing Scottish Home Rule appeared before the House of Commons on thirteen occasions, and won the support of a majority of Scottish MPs eleven times, none of these bills ever reached the committee stage, as this measure was never considered a priority. Such bills have been viewed as ritual gestures, rather than as serious attempts to engineer constitutional change. The Scottish Liberal Association, although adopting the goal of Home Rule in 1888, never generated a radical nationalist movement comparable with the Welsh Liberals' Cymru Fydd, and the 'nationalist' agenda was frequently reduced to debating the reform of laws dealing with land, licensed premises, fishing, and the shooting of game.

Scottish nationalism was therefore moderate, relatively benign in its attitudes towards England and the English, reconciled to Scotland's membership of the United Kingdom, enthusiastic about the opportunities afforded by empire, and unencumbered by ethnic inhibitions.[29] The vast majority of the Scottish people, after all, spoke English: only about 5 per cent of Scots could speak Scottish Gaelic in 1901, so that language could only be marginal even to a conception of Highland identity. Scotland enjoyed a distinctive civic society, with its own legal and educational systems, and its own religious (if, after 1843, divided) establishment. The Highlandization of Scottish culture offered an attractive but also inclusive ethnic gloss to a civil society that proved capable of accommodating all Scots, be

---

[27] According to Lynch, *Scotland*, 416: 'An ability to stir up apathy was one of the main talents [the office of the Secretary of State] demanded.'

[28] C. Harvie, *Scotland and Nationalism: Scottish Society and Politics 1707–1994* (London, 1994), 17.

[29] R. Finlay, 'The Rise and Fall of Popular Imperialism in Scotland, 1850–1950', *Scottish Geographical Magazine*, 113 (1997).

they Protestant or Catholic, Highland or Lowland, firmly unionist or lukewarmly nationalist.

Qualifying an orthodox stress on nationalist 'weakness' in Scotland, Graeme Morton has advanced the concept of 'unionist-nationalism' to explain how nineteenth-century Scots could feel comfortable with their dual identity as both British and Scottish.[30] Morton suggests that it is anachronistic to examine the strength or weakness of nineteenth-century Scottish nationalism as 'a movement for demanding political citizenship rights', an examination that indeed regularly generates an understanding of such nationalism as weak and fragmented.[31] Rather, in the era of the 'laissez-faire state and the triumph of the bourgeoisie', Scottish nationalism was 'only tangentially parliamentary, was strongly pro-Union, but was nevertheless explicit in its demands for the better government of Scotland'.[32] Local government and voluntary agencies were the means by which such improvements were sought, spheres in which the Scots themselves were in control. At the same time, the Scots celebrated an understanding of their culture as distinctive and valued. Morton's concept of 'unionist-nationalism' has begun to find favour in other contexts, as a study of the Welsh patriot Sir Thomas Phillips indicates.[33]

WALES

Wales had a potentially stronger base for the generation of an ethnic nationalism than did Scotland. The vast majority of the people of Wales spoke Welsh, a primary badge of Welsh nationality, in the late eighteenth century. Industrialization, urbanization, and the major population movements that accompanied those processes gradually led to Anglicization, especially in the south-east and north-east where industry took hold most forcibly. The systematization of education in the late nineteenth century, and the growth of English language print media, also diluted the linguistic purity of the Welsh people, and only 15 per cent of the Welsh people were monoglots by 1901. But Anglicization was highly regionalized, so that there were areas of Wales which remained very strongly Welsh-speaking well into the late twentieth century. Furthermore, in Wales Protestant Nonconformity was very strong: perhaps accounting for up to three-quarters of worshippers. This made Wales culturally distinct from its English neighbour, and highlighted the anomalous position of the established Anglican church in Wales.

The initial fragility of any civic base for Welsh nationalism may be ascribed to the long-term impact of the sixteenth-century Acts of Union. Thereafter, all

[30] Morton, *Unionist Nationalism: Governing Urban Scotland, 1830–60* (East Linton, 2000).
[31] Ibid. 8–9.   [32] Ibid. 10.
[33] C. Williams, 'Wales's "Unionist-Nationalist": Sir Thomas Phillips, 1801–67', *Llafur: Welsh People's History Journal*, 8 (2003).

legislation that applied to England applied also to Wales. Neither the Tudor, nor the Stuart, nor the Hanoverian state was particularly interested in forcing cultural assimilation on Wales and so, notwithstanding certain pejorative attitudes towards the Welsh as a poor, ill-educated, coarse, shifty, garrulous, and untrustworthy people, Wales became a junior partner in the expanding British state. In civic terms Wales was largely indistinguishable from England.

Early nineteenth-century Welsh nationalism thus concerned itself with cultural assertion, with claiming its pre-eminence in a reconfigured sense of the British past. Welsh politics was quiescent, with the exception of the Chartist movement which remained solidly located within the movement's British context. What began to change this was the 1847 report of the education commissioners, the *Brad y Llyfrau Gleision* (Treason of the Blue Books), which attacked the Welsh people for their immorality, ignorance, and Nonconformity, and which identified the Welsh language as a largely malign influence. A furious reaction saw leading Anglicans and Nonconformists vigorously defend Welsh nationality and culture. But this was double-edged, for whilst publicly indignant at the criticisms levelled by the commissioners, many commentators privately conceded the truth of some of their claims. Though the cultural values of Nonconformity were strongly upheld and increasingly asserted, in education and in manners the Welsh moved closer to their English neighbours in the decades that followed.

The Welsh nationalism that gradually clarified in the decades after 1847 was Liberal, increasingly Nonconformist, and moderate. What was most desired was recognition of the cultural and religious identity of Wales. When Irish disestablishment and then later home rule appeared on the political agenda, these causes were taken up in Wales, but more gently. Gradually, the British state responded in kind. What little separatist sentiment there was in Wales in the nineteenth century was killed by kindness.[34] The passage of the Welsh Sunday Closing Act in 1881, the first modern piece of legislation to treat Wales differently from England, recognized Welsh nationalism as legitimate, in an era which saw the creation of key Welsh civic institutions such as a university, national library, and national museum. This was followed by educational provision targeted at specific Welsh needs and, in the twentieth century, by the disestablishment in Wales of the Church of England. The clearest example of a nationalist movement in Wales before 1914 came in the decade 1886–96, when the Cymru Fydd association (literally, 'the Wales to be', but usually rendered as 'Young Wales') attempted to encourage the dominant force in Welsh parliamentary politics, the Welsh Liberal Party, to adopt a more explicitly nationalist agenda. Cymru Fydd advocated Home Rule for Wales and also championed the Welsh language and Welsh language culture. But it collapsed in 1896 at a meeting held in Newport, when many South Walian businessmen and

---

[34] N. Evans, 'Internal Colonialism? Colonization, Economic Development and Political Mobilisation in Wales, Scotland and Ireland', in G. Day and G. Rees (eds.), *Regions, Nations and European Integration: Remaking the Celtic Periphery* (Cardiff, 1991), 253.

labour leaders objected to what they saw as its 'Wales for the Welsh' attitude. As D. A. Thomas MP, a keen critic of Cymru Fydd, responded, he preferred 'the world is our oyster' as his motto, recognizing not only the increasingly multi-ethnic nature of the industrializing society of south-east Wales, but also the opportunities afforded to the Welsh by the expanding British Empire.[35] Ultimately this was a viewpoint that the one-time champion of Cymru Fydd, David Lloyd George, came to share. The Investiture of the prince of Wales at Caernarfon Castle in 1911, a ceremony masterminded by Lloyd George, was a public demonstration of the effective reconciliation of a proud Welshness within a broader British and Imperial context.[36] Welsh nationalism was, in theory, largely ethnic, but as the nineteenth century wore on, the decline of the Welsh language, combined with the increasing integration of the Welsh economy and polity into that of Britain, ensured that ethnic definitions were less persuasive, and Welsh nationalism came to operate in a more relaxed mode, through cultural practices such as Nonconformity and sport (particularly rugby union), which were more receptive towards non-Welsh migrants.

IRELAND

If in Wales, as in Scotland, the British political system was able to show itself capable of accommodating the expression of Scottish and Welsh political, religious, and cultural differences, this was never the case in Ireland, which affords the clearest examples of both strongly framed nationalist objectives (involving a major reframing of the relationship between Ireland and Britain) and, ultimately, of an atavistic embracing of the principles of ethnic nationalism.[37]

The Act of Union of 1800 was a short-term response by the British state to an immediate political and strategic crisis, rather than the culmination of a long-term policy to integrate Ireland more effectively into British culture and nationhood. Prior to the French Revolution, nationalism in Ireland had generally taken the form of Protestant 'gentry' nationalism, expressed by the Anglo-Irish ruling class who wished to flex their muscles vis-à-vis the Westminster government. This 'gentry' nationalism focused on protecting Irish economic interests and on reclaiming greater autonomy in matters of Irish parliamentary business, and had something in common with the earliest manifestations of dissent on the part of the American colonists in the 1770s. It was rapidly

---

[35] C. Williams, 'Democracy and Nationalism in Wales: The Lib-Lab Enigma', in D. Bates, S. Newton, and R. Stradling (eds.), *Conflict and Coexistence: Nationalism and Democracy in Modern Europe* (Cardiff, 1997).

[36] J. S. Ellis, 'The Prince and the Dragon: Welsh National Identity and the 1911 Investiture of the Prince of Wales', *Welsh History Review*, 18 (1996).

[37] The following discussion owes much to C. Kinealy, 'Irish Politics' and Kinealy, 'Economy and Society in Ireland', in Williams, *Companion to Nineteenth-Century Britain.*

overshadowed in the 1790s by a much more radical and challenging nationalism, itself inspired partly by the democratic ideas expressed by the American revolutionaries, and partly by the egalitarian and radical philosophies taking hold in revolutionary France. The outcome was the Irish Rebellion of 1798, led by the Protestant patriot Wolfe Tone, which nonetheless exacerbated existing sectarian tendencies and greatly alarmed both the Protestant ruling class (confronted by the mass mobilization of Catholics) and the British government (anxious about the possible security ramifications of an unstable Ireland open to approaches from revolutionary France, as well as the unsettling example a radicalized Ireland might provide for an already tense domestic situation on the British mainland). Pitt's response was the Act of Union, initially welcomed by many Catholics who believed that a fuller integration into the British state would naturally lead to the granting of full civil and religious liberties, and resented by the Protestant establishment which feared both Catholic emancipation and more intrusive British rule. In retrospect it is possible to see the Act as potentially enlightened: Irish economic growth might have been stimulated, the gap in living standards between Ireland and the mainland narrowed, and the majority Catholic population rewarded with equal citizenship. None of this, however, happened, and by the 1820s the Union had become a focus for Catholic discontent. A distinctly Catholic nationalist movement emerged, led by Daniel O'Connell, which although not fully separatist in intent, was deeply critical of the link between Britain and Ireland, and bitterly demanded a radical recalibration of that relationship.

There is not the space here to document the fortunes of each successive wave of Irish nationalism throughout the nineteenth and early twentieth centuries. It is necessary, therefore, to summarize the different nationalist positions that were adopted by Irish politicians and radicals, both in terms of their attitude towards the Union, and in terms of their definition of the Irish people. Ulster Protestantism was not a nationalist movement but a defensive reaction to the prospect of the creation of a Catholic-dominated semi-autonomous Ireland. It played on British nationalist loyalties, most certainly, but the articulation of a distinctive Ulster Protestant 'nationalism' had to await Partition.

At the more moderate end of the nationalist spectrum one might place both the O'Connellite nationalism of the 1820s and 1830s, and the Irish Home Rule movement which dominated Irish politics from the 1870s onwards. Both were somewhat vague about the precise nature of the relationship envisaged between Ireland and Britain: O'Connell after 1843 demanded repeal of the Union, although this was not seen as equivalent to full-scale independence. Similarly Parnell's objective of Home Rule would, at least initially, have continued to recognize British sovereignty in imperial and military affairs. Neither O'Connell (a Catholic), nor Parnell (a Protestant) conceived of Irish nationality in ethnic terms, but their movements both became largely populated by Catholic supporters. Expressing dispassionate civic nationalism in the abstract, they were viewed by their opponents as effectively mobilizations of sentimental ethnic nationalism in practice. More radical, although similarly constructed in terms of the balance between civic and ethnic nationalist appeals, were movements ranging from Wolfe Tone's United Irishmen to Thomas Davis's Young Ireland. Political independence was their goal, and a civic definition of Irish identity their fundamental and inclusive principle. Both, however, by raising the spectre of radical change, unwittingly inflamed sectarian rivalries and marginalized Protestant support.

Uniting radical objectives and an uncompromising ethnic nationalism were the secular Fenian Brotherhood of the late 1850s and 1860s and the Irish republican movement that gathered pace at the very end of the nineteenth century (Sinn Fein being founded in 1902). Ultimately republican politics were to triumph over more constitutional and moderate nationalisms, but this did not appear to be a likely outcome before 1914. Politically insignificant in comparison with the Home Rulers, republican nationalists nonetheless exercised significant cultural influence, sparking the Gaelic revival, the celebration of a distinctive Catholic peasant cultural heritage, and the 'root and branch' rejection of British sports by Irish cultural nationalists in the form of the Gaelic Athletic Association. This was an Anglophobic and anti-Protestant nationalism that made no attempt to accommodate the non-Catholic Irish.

By 1914 Ireland was in crisis. Attempts to find an effective civic basis for any nationalism (whether aimed at adjusting or at disrupting the relationship between Ireland and the British state) had foundered on the rocks of sectarian mistrust. The contradiction of modern Irish nationalism was that whilst it needed to reach out pluralistically to all Irish people, its popular and emotional appeal derived from a singular Catholic myth, marginalizing the Protestant Irish and forcing them to define themselves as Unionists. But nationalist desire for fundamental change (far in excess of that being contemplated by most Scottish or Welsh nationalists) had not been assuaged. The British state's laissez-faire attitude towards Ireland was fully in character with its attitude towards nationalism generally—it was not interested in nation-building, and such an effort might anyway have proved counter-productive in the Irish context. But the problem with Union was on the one hand that it did not appear to be a long-term solution to Ireland's needs, having proven so fundamentally ineffective at reacting to the crisis of the Great Famine, whilst on the other any modification of the settlement appeared likely to inflame sectarian passions and outrage unionists on both sides of the Irish Sea. Despite Union, 'the integration of Ireland into the British state was to remain an enduring problem of varying virulence'.[38]

---

[38] R. G. Asch, ' "Obscured in Whiskey, Mist and Misery": The Role of Scotland and Ireland in British History', in Asch (ed.), *Three Nations—A Common History? England, Scotland, Ireland and British History, c.1600–1920* (Bochum, 1993), 43.

CONCLUSION

Sometimes it has been considered by Celtic scholars of nationalist leanings that a British identity and nationalism is somehow a manifestation of false consciousness, inherently imperialistic. Britain is, in this sense, of recent manufacture, and quite clearly builds on existing loyalties and identities on the island of Britain and perhaps to a lesser extent across the British Isles as a whole. But consider this statement by Étienne Balibar:

No nation possesses an ethnic base naturally, but as social formations are nationalized, the populations included within them, divided up among them or dominated by them are ethnicized—that is, represented in the past or in the future *as if* they formed a natural community, possessing of itself an identity of origins, culture and interests which transcend individuals and social conditions.[39]

This may well be true of Britain, but although its recent processes of formation may be laid bare for all to see, they are nonetheless no different, qualitatively, from those processes which operated (and continue to operate) in England, Scotland, Wales, and Ireland. All nations, and all ethnic groups, are essentially fictions. It is not difficult to find evidence of identities subsidiary to those of (say) Scotland (a Highland identity, those of the Shetlands and Orkneys), as well as the difficulties engendered by border perspectives (most clearly in the Welsh case). The most commonly identified national component parts of the United Kingdom have never been homogeneous or discrete. Britain is both a multinational state (embracing the peoples of the aforementioned nations) and a nation-state (with that nation being 'Britain'), even if the precise lineaments of that nation-state have varied somewhat depending on where one stood (in Wales, Scotland, England, or Ireland). It has only ever been partially successful as either.

So there was a single civil society inhabited between 1801 and 1914 by the peoples of the British Isles. But the national and ethnic patterns contained within this single civic container were multiple and complex. There was no homogeneous society created, although homogenizing trends were undoubtedly present. Nor was there a clear movement from ethnic to civic nationalism in this period. Ethnic nationalisms attempted to wear civic garb and ideologies of civic nationalism found themselves subverted by ethnic realities. In 1914, residents of England, Scotland, and Wales probably had a stronger sense of a common British identity than had been available to their ancestors a century earlier. This British identity was not uniform, not without its contradictions, and was not necessarily hegemonic. It could accommodate a variety of different meanings and ideological positions, and it could coexist with other, equally valid and potent identities, be those national, regional, local, religious, or ethnic. The fact that elements of this

[39] Balibar, 'The Nation Form: History and Ideology', in Balibar and I. Wallerstein (eds.), *Race, Nation, Class: Ambiguous Identities* (London, 1991), 96.

British nationalism had been in the process of formation from at least early in the eighteenth century had meant that accommodating Irish Catholicism had never been critical to the development of the identity itself, whatever the strategic imperatives of the British state. So the fact that the views of many Irish people appeared irreconcilable with 'Britishness' did not pose a fundamental threat to its maintenance. Scottish and Welsh identities, on the other hand, appeared to be comfortably contained within a flexible structure that rewarded loyalty with opportunity, that allowed Scottish and Welsh nationalisms to 'nest' within a broader, imperial British nationalism.

15

Russia

Empire or a Nation-State-in-the-Making?

Vera Tolz

Questioning the usefulness of the distinction between the 'ethnic' nations of Eastern and East-Central Europe and the 'civic' nations of Western Europe, Rogers Brubaker has offered a more nuanced distinction 'between state-framed and counter-state understanding of nationhood and forms of nationalism'. In the first instance, a nation is territorially and institutionally 'framed' by the state; in the latter it is perceived by nation-builders to be in opposition to some existing state or states.[1]

Brubaker's classification is based on Ernest Gellner's division of Europe into three main time zones in terms of nation-building. The first zone embraced 'the western, Atlantic seaboard of Europe' where a political unit, corresponding, albeit not completely, to a relatively homogeneous cultural area existed before the era of nationalism. The strong dynastic states based on London, Paris, Madrid, and Lisbon 'could transform themselves into homogeneous nation-states'. The task of nation-builders was largely to turn peasants into citizens by integrating them into a new high culture. In the second zone to the immediate east, at the turn of the nineteenth century, the German and Italian elites possessed 'self-conscious' high culture but no single polity. By the end of the century political unification was achieved and followed by the diffusion of high culture through education. The third time zone further to the east embraced the peoples of the land-based empires, Austria-Hungary, the Ottoman and Romanov empires. There a wide range of peasant cultures needed to be 'replaced by normative high cultures *and* endowed with a political cover'.[2] 'It is this [lack of a polity] above all which distinguishes this

---

[1] R. Brubaker, 'Myths and Misconceptions in the Study of Nationalism', in J. A. Hall, *The State of the Nation* (Cambridge, 1998), 300. The validity of Hans Kohn's dichotomy between 'civic' (West European) and 'ethnic' (East European) nationalism has been convincingly questioned in the past few years by other scholars who point to many similarities between nation-building processes in different parts of Europe. For one of the latest examples, see Maria Todorova, 'The Trap of Backwardness: Modernity, Temporality, and the Study of Eastern European Nationalism', *Slavic Review*, 64 (2005), 140–64.

[2] In the case of the Romanov Empire, the model can be applied to major non-Russian nationalities rather than to the Russians.

pattern from "centralization from above." [3] Avoiding the simplification entailed in the ethnic-civic dichotomy, the Gellner–Brubaker typology does not deny differences in nation-building among different peoples and regions.

The Russian case is a good example of where the ethnic-civic dichotomy is not helpful to our understanding of the process of nation-building. It seems to be a mistake to regard Russia as an example of ethnic nationalism, as is often done.[4] Definitions of the Russian nation put forward by intellectuals and implicit in 'nationalizing' government policies in the late imperial period combined cultural (ethnic) and political (civic) elements. Instead, the Russian case underscores the importance of the ambiguous role played by a state. Rejecting the centrality of the ethnic element in Russian nationalism and according significance to the role of the state does not prevent us from identifying the difference between the forms of Russian nation-building and those in the countries of Western Europe. A comparison with those countries, with an emphasis on the similarities, was the perspective adopted by many Russian nation-builders from the late eighteenth century onwards. However, as this chapter will show, this perspective failed to offer a productive framework for analysing Russian developments. It will be argued that in their evolution as a modern nation Russians differed both from those belonging to nations in Western Europe and from the peoples of the three land-based European empires.

Russia can be seen as an example of a peculiar interplay between state-framed (largely promoted by Russian elites) and counter-state (largely, but not exclusively, advocated by representatives of non-Russian minorities) variants of nationhood. It will be argued that three key forces shaped the process of Russian nation-building in the Romanov empire: the peculiarity of Russian state-building, the way this state was perceived by nationally minded elites, and the perception of the relationship between the elites and the 'masses' on the part of those who tried to define the membership of the Russian nation. This study analyses intellectual conceptions of Russian identity in respect of these three main issues as well as government policies in relation to Russian nation-building between the late eighteenth century and the First World War. In conclusion, the article discusses the reasons for the failure of the empire's engagement in nation-building.

RUSSIAN NATIONAL IDENTITY AND RUSSIAN STATE-BUILDING

It seems that from the time the first attempts were made, mostly by Russian intellectuals, to define the Russian nation in modern terms, the Russians differed from both West and East European peoples in two important areas. The first area of

---

[3] E. Gellner, 'The Coming of Nationalism and its Interpretation: The Myth of Nation and Class', in G. Balakrishnan (ed.), *Mapping the Nation* (London, 2000), 98–145.

[4] See, for instance, L. Greenfeld, *Nationalism: Five Roads to Modernity* (Cambridge, Mass., 1992).

difference was related to the peculiarity of Russian state-building and the second to the relationship between the peasantry and the educated elite.

As mentioned earlier, in the 'Atlantic seaboard of Europe' nation-building proceeded within the boundaries of pre-existing centralized polities. In zones two and three, including the non-Russians of the tsarist empire, such polities were absent, when the concept of nation began to spread across Europe, and this absence was seen by nation-builders as a key problem to be addressed. It seems that a crucial difference of the Russians was that, in their case, a state which could have offered a framework for nation-building was also absent, but this absence was not realized by the majority of nation-builders, including those opposed to the existing autocratic regime. Thus the goals of Russian nation-building were not clearly defined.

Several scholars have argued that in the Russian case state-building impeded nation-building.[5] The first set of arguments relates to the timing of the creation of the Russian empire. Moscow's conquest of non-Slavic and non-Christian territories in the mid-sixteenth century occurred at the time when national distinctions were not recognized and it also immediately followed the take-over of other east Slavic principalities, described in the medieval chronicles as 'the gathering of the indigenous Russian lands'. Thus, from the beginning the line was blurred between the absorption into Muscovia of what are now undisputed parts of 'Russia proper' and the territories of people culturally and religiously different from the Russians.[6]

Second, the imperial government suppressed nation-building. The land-based empire perpetuated the existence of the repressive autocratic government, which submerged society and which, in maintaining the privileges of the elite for the purpose of imperial stability, delayed liberal reforms, which could have facilitated nation-building in the nineteenth century.[7]

Third, scholars have contended that Russians failed to grasp the arguments of nationalism. Because of the timing and the way in which the empire had been created, Russians continued to think in pre-national categories in the era of nationalism. Ronald Suny, for instance, concluded that by the time of the First World War, when elsewhere in Europe a nation was imagined as independent from the state and secular, Russia's elites could not imagine the nation separately from the religious community and from the state.[8]

These arguments are in need of some modification. The significance of timing in the creation of empires as opposed to consolidation of national identities

---

[5] H. Rogger, 'Nationalism and the State: A Russian Dilemma', *Comparative Studies in Society and History*, 4 (1961–2), 253–64; R. Szporluk, *Communism and Nationalism: Karl Marx versus Friedrich List* (New York, 1988), 205–40; and G. Hosking, *Russia: People and Empire, 1552–1917* (London, 1997), pp. xix–xxviii.

[6] M. Raeff, 'Patterns of Russian Imperial Policy towards the Nationalities', in E. Allworth (ed.), *Soviet Nationality Problems* (New York, 1971), 30.

[7] R. Suny, 'The Empire Strikes Out: Imperial Russia, "National" Identity, and Theories of Empire', in R. Suny and T. Martin (eds.), *A State of Nations: Empire and Nation-Making in the Age of Lenin and Stalin* (New York, 2001), 23–66. [8] Ibid. 44 and 48.

should not be overestimated. In Western Europe the consolidation of nation-states occurred not before, as Szporluk and other scholars argue, but parallel to the creation of overseas empires.[9] I would argue that *the first problem* with Russia's nation-building was not the undeniable fact that in some way it was impeded by empire-building, but that Russia has never developed into a modern state, which could command broad public loyalties. The roots of such development lie in the pre-imperial period.[10]

Benedict Anderson, John Breuilly, Gellner, and other theorists of nationalism have shown that a certain type of state was in existence in Western Europe prior to the advent of nationalism and modern West European nations emerged within the framework of those states. Particular developments, which took place as far back as in the Middle Ages, laid the foundation in West European societies for subsequent modernization and nation-building.[11]

The development of the Russian polity was different. Before the Moscow principality began to turn into an empire in the second half of the sixteenth century, a century earlier the foundation had been laid for a polity whose political culture was not conducive to modernization and subsequent nation-building. In the fifteenth century, when the Muscovite 'state' began to take shape, the Moscow principality was profoundly different from European societies—it had no major urban centres, few settlements, and a poor level of communication between them. Great Princes' sovereignty in Muscovite Rus included 'the attributes of patrimonial or domainial power, i.e. full ownership of the land and its inhabitants'.[12] In France, for instance, the differentiation of domainial institutions and public ones was completed by the fourteenth century. In Russia it only started in the eighteenth. Even afterwards the distinction between the domainial and public spheres remained vague.[13] While noting the patrimonial origins of the Russian state in the pre-imperial period, historians do not directly relate this feature to an analysis of Russian nation-building.

Whereas Richard Pipes developed the argument about the patrimonial nature of the Russian state, Geoffrey Hosking pointed out that resulting over-centralization was more an aspiration than a reality in Muscovia and in the Russian empire. Hosking convincingly argues that, 'Having to improvise structures often urgently and in adversity, it [the ruling elite] has tended, therefore not to create enduring laws or institutions, but rather to give official backing to existing personal power relationships.'[14] Hosking describes the Russian state

---

[9] See n. 7 on the timing of the creation of the Russian Empire. L. Colley, *Britons: Forging a Nation, 1707–1837* (London, 1992) demonstrates a parallel timing of the empire- and nation-building in Britain.

[10] I am grateful to John LeDonne for helping me think about the Russian case along these lines.

[11] B. Anderson, *Imagined Communities: Reflections on the Origins and Spread of Nationalism* (London, 1991); J. Breuilly, *Nationalism and the State* (Manchester, 1985); E. Gellner, *Nations and Nationalism* (Oxford, 1983).   [12] R. Pipes, *Russia under the Old Regime* (London, 1995), 64.

[13] Ibid. 68.   [14] G. Hosking, *Russia and the Russians: A History* (London, 2001), 5.

throughout the entire period since the fifteenth century as a collection of 'networks of personal dependence'.[15]

Thus the Russians have never had a state which could be a focus of loyalty not just for a narrow group of the ruling elite but for broader segments of society. Therefore, throughout the nineteenth century the majority of the population continued to be bound by a pre-national type of loyalty—that to the tsar personally—while continuing to see the state as an enemy. Only a state capable of throwing bridges across various social, religious, and ethnic divides and reconciling members of society and the ruling elite could offer a framework for enduring nation-building. Such a state might have been able to create a higher loyalty and integrate different social and even ethnic groups. It should be kept in mind that the emergence of the Russian polity as 'networks of personal dependence' had preceded the advent of the empire and its features continue to endure today, when the empire is gone.

The second problem was that Russian nation-builders downplayed the essential differences between the Russian empire and the states with which they compared it. By the turn of the nineteenth century such founding fathers of Russian nationalism as the historians Ivan Boltin and Nikolai Karamzin constructed the argument that Russia possessed everything that the West had and, if it differed, the difference signified Russia's advantage over the 'other', as it indicated the realization of ideals to which the West was only aspiring. Rather than continuing to be affected by pre-national perceptions, these Russian intellectuals understood the arguments of nationalism and were affected by them. Yet the concept of nation did not offer a suitable framework to understand Russian realities, and its application only blurred the ability of intellectuals to analyse the processes in their country.

The comparison with Russia's constituent 'other' ('the West') made Russian intellectuals draw several conclusions. The most significant of them was that the Russians had a state, within whose borders nation-building could proceed, as was the case in Britain and France.

THE RUSSIAN EMPIRE AS A NATION-STATE-IN-THE-MAKING

The First Period: From the Eighteenth Century to the Early Slavophiles

The ideas of nationalism entered Russia from France during the reign of Catherine the Great (1761–96). Under the impact of the Enlightenment, the goals of achieving social and administrative uniformity within the Russian state were proclaimed. The Russians were expected to lead the empire's 'rude peoples

---

[15] Ibid. 203. Hosking does not fully explore the impact of such a polity on Russian nation-building, nor does he mention the significance of the fact that the foundation of this type of policy was laid before the advent of empire-building.

(i.e. non-Slavs and non-Christians) by giant steps toward the common goal of general enlightenment' and to achieve 'a wonderful fusion of all into a single body and soul'.[16]

Catherine promoted what scholars now call missionary nationalism. The key feature of missionary nationalism, which was a source of identity in other modern European empires, 'is the attachment of a dominant core ethnic group to a state entity that conceives itself as dedicated to some larger course or purpose, religious, cultural, or political'.[17] This nationalism is political and any celebration of ethnic exclusivity (but not necessarily diversity) undermines its power. Missionary nationalism, which blurs the distinction between state and nation, is sometimes seen as the main, if not the only, type of Russian nationalism. Yet other ways of defining the Russian nation were also articulated, which focused on the member-ship of a Russian national community rather than on the role and the goals of the existing state. These new definitions started to be put forward from the turn of the nineteenth century by intellectuals, some of whom were in opposition to the state. Their point of comparison was, expectedly, 'the West'. In different periods of Russian history, different countries were seen by Russians as a model to emulate or as an anti-model to reject. However, often they spoke of the non-differentiated 'West' as Russia's 'other'.

In trying to define the Russian nation by comparing Russia with the 'West', educated Russians of the late eighteenth century were confronted with several problems: over 80 per cent of the Russian population were peasants, more than half of whom were serfs without any rights; the government offered fewer liberties even to the upper classes than was the case in Western Europe; the gap between the elites with Western-style education and the common people was perceived as being greater than elsewhere in Europe; Russia was also a country of a greater ethnic and linguistic variety than France or Britain. What could overcome this social, ethnic, and linguistic diversity and unite these disparate elements into one nation?

One way was to equate the Russian nation exclusively with the Slavic com-munity, ignoring non-Slavic subjects of the tsar. In the official discourse, all Eastern Slavs (Great Russians, Little Russians, and Belorussians) were called Russians. Coexisting and competing with this definition was the idea that Russian culture was capable of assimilating and accommodating different nationalities of the empire, including non-Slavs, thus serving as a force capable of creating a single pan-Russian national community on most parts of the territory of the empire. The third idea was that the way the Russian Empire was created made it different from other empires and turned it into a nation-state-in-the-making. It was argued

---

[16] I. G. Georgi, *The Description of People Inhabiting the Russian State*, published in 1776–80. Quoted in Y. Slezkine, 'Naturalists versus Nations: Eighteenth-Century Russian Scholars Confront Ethnic Diversity', in D. R. Brower and E. J. Lazzerini (eds.), *Russia's Orient* (Bloomington, 1997), 39.
[17] K. Kumar, 'Nation and Empire: English and British National Identity in Comparative Perspective', *Theory and Society*, 29 (2000), 575–608 (the quotation is on 580).

that, in contrast to West European empires created by force, Russia came into being through peaceful expansion into sparsely populated areas with the Slavs gradually assimilating non-Slavic or non-Christian tribes. This chapter will argue that in the second half of the nineteenth century, an increasing number of Russian nationalists began to hope for the possibility of the 'nationalization' of most parts of the empire.

The argument about the Russian empire as a Russian nation-state-in-the-making fits the above-mentioned framework of comparing Russia with the 'West' by nationally-minded intellectuals. The Russians could not acknowledge that they did not have a state which could be 'nationalized', as that would amount to an admission that they were not a historical nation as were the British and the French. Any parallel between Russia and land-based empires—the Roman, Ottoman, or Habsburg—had to be rejected. Moreover, the obvious difference between multi-ethnic Russia and the more ethnically homogeneous West European nation-states could be presented as a sign of Russia's uniqueness and advantage.

The historian Ivan Boltin (1735–92) became the first modern Russian historian to create a coherent image of Russia expanding into neighbouring, sparsely populated lands almost peacefully. Boltin contrasted that image with the creation of West European empires by military force. This vision was developed more fully in Nikolai Karamzin's *History of the Russian State* (1819–29). In Karamzin's view, which shaped the approach of Russian-Soviet historiography till the end of the twentieth century, by the twelfth century, the Slavic, Finnish, and Norse people who populated the principalities of Rus were bound by language, religion, civic codes, and customs into a single Russian nationality. This nationality united three main subgroups, the Great Russians (former Muscovites), Little Russians (Ukrainians), and Belorussians. The future of those non-Slavs who were absorbed by the Russian state in later periods was also peaceful, voluntary assimilation into a pan-Russian nationality.[18]

At the same time, Karamzin's *History* focused on the ethnic Russian community, which, in his view, incorporated all East Slavs. Non-assimilated minorities hardly attracted his attention. In the 1830s and the 1840s, the so-called early Slavophiles further developed Karamzin's view of Russian history, state, and nationality. For them, the Russians were Orthodox (Christian) Slavs, whose special positive qualities attracted non-Russians 'into their orbit'.[19] They saw the Russian empire, which they called the Russian state (*russkoe gosudarstvo*), as a Slavic state.[20] The Slavophiles' political goal was to expand the borders of the Russian state to incorporate other Slavs into it. Non-Slavic subjects of the empire were not seen as a challenge.

[18] See Vera Tolz, *Russia: Inventing the Nation* (London, 2001), 161–2.
[19] Orest Miller quoted in N. A. Rubakin, *Sredi knig*, vol. iii, part 1 (Moscow, 1915), 130.
[20] The word *russkii* refers to ethnic Russian, whereas the word *rossiiskii* refers to a civic Russian identity. The official name of the state utilized the civic term *Rossiiskaia Imperiia*.

In the period of early Slavophilism, the goal of ethnic Russian nation-building started to dominate the agenda of the scholarly community. In 1845, the Imperial Geographical Society was set up with the aim of studying the geography and ethnography of the Russian Empire. By 1847, the 'Russian faction' within the Society, led by Nikolai Nadezhdin, won over 'the German faction', led by Karl von Baer, in determining the Society's priorities. The focus on the collection of materials related to the small non-Russian ethnic groups (*inorodtsy*), particularly in Siberia, first pioneered by German scholars in the Academy of Sciences in the eighteenth century and now championed by Baer, was rejected. Instead, on Nadezhdin's initiative, the main focus of the Society became the ethnography of 'the (ethnically defined) Russian nationality' and the geography of 'Russia proper'.[21] By 1851, the work of archaeologists led by the founding father of Russian archaeology Aleksei Uvarov moved from the excavation of ancient Greek colonies on the northern coast of the Black Sea to the discovery of the medieval Slavic burial sites of the Vladimir *guberniia*.[22]

But even in this period of an apparent victory of ethnic Russian (east Slavic) nationalism it was challenged by an inclusive civic definition of the Russian national community. A group of nationally-minded intellectuals of this period who thought about Russia as an inclusive political nation comprised those representatives of the nobility, later to be known as the Decembrists, who in 1825 made a failed attempt to initiate the adoption of a constitution. In his political programme, *The Russian Code of Laws*, a leader of the future Decembrists, Pavel Pestel, articulated the vision of a Russian nation uniting all the people of the empire regardless of their ethnic origin. He applied the French concept of a political nation of equal citizens to the Russian Empire, which he perceived as a Russian nation-state-in-the-making. The second chapter of Pestel's programme discussed methods of creating 'only one people' (*tolko odin narod*) out of the different nationalities of the Russian Empire.[23]

The Decembrists and the early Slavophiles operated in an environment in which their views on the boundaries of the state-framed Russian nation were not seriously challenged by any non-Russian subjects of the empire, except for the Poles. But the Poles were recognized as a separate nation by many Russian intellectuals, including the Decembrists and the Slavophiles. The Decembrists and even some Slavophiles did not oppose granting the Poles political independence.[24]

---

[21] N. Knight, 'Science, Empire, and Nationality: Ethnography in the Russian Geographical Society, 1845–1855', in J. Burbank and D. Ransel (eds.), *Imperial Russia: New Histories for the Empire* (Bloomington, 1998), 116–22. See also, N. Knight, 'Ethnicity, Nationality and the Masses: *Narodnost*' and Modernity in Imperial Russia', in D. Hoffmann and Y. Kotsonis (eds.), *Russian Modernity* (Houndmills, 2000), 41–64.

[22] G. S. Lebedev, *Istoriia otechestvennoi arkheologii* (St Petersburg, 1992), 94–5.

[23] P. Pestel, *Russkaia Pravda* (Moscow, 1993), see ch. 2, 'O plemenakh Rossiiu naseliaiushchikh'.

[24] Rubakin, *Sredi knig*, 154–5.

The Second Period: From the Crimean War to the 1905 Revolution

The first serious challenge to Russian intellectuals' definitions of their nation came in the late 1840s from intellectuals from Malorossia. The historian Mykola Kostomarov (1817–85), among others, challenged the Russian Slavophiles on two key issues. First, he advocated a *federal* pan-Slavic state with cultural and political autonomy for its different peoples. (Russian Slavophiles rejected federalism.) Secondly, Kostomarov disputed the existence of a single pan-Russian nation, suggesting instead that the Little Russians (*malorosy* or Ukrainians) and the Great Russians (*velikorosy*) were two separate Russian nationalities. Starting to develop these arguments in the late 1840s, he fully articulated them in the early 1860s.[25] The concept of a Russian nation uniting all Eastern Slavs was seriously threatened. Within this context, to study and understand the multi-ethnic nature of the Russian state became more important than ever.

One response to this challenge was the recognition in the late 1850s by the first generation of Russian socialist thinkers such as Mikhail Bakunin, Nikolai Chernyshevskii, and Aleksandr Herzen that various peoples of the empire were in fact separate nations with a right to self-determination. Their Russian nation was to be limited to *velikorosy* (Great Russian nationality). Bakunin, for instance, argued: 'We want Poland, Lithuania, Ukraine, Finns and Latvians in the Baltics, as well as the Caucasian region, to receive full freedom and the right to govern themselves according to their own desires, without any direct or indirect interference on our part.'[26] Yet this position had only a very limited number of supporters among Russians. Instead, the challenge of counter-state nationalism strengthened the desire of the Russian elites to further promote state-framed definitions of nationhood.

The reinvigoration in the 1860s and the 1870s of the study by ethnographers of non-Slavic ethnic groups should be understood in this context. The Geographical Society, in particular, refocused its interest and began to organize regular expeditions to study *inorodtsy*. In the 1870s, archaeological and ethnographic centres were set up in the non-Russian borderlands and, in the 1880s, leading specialists in Oriental studies began to insist that Russian scholars should focus on Russia's own 'Orient'—above all the Caucasus and Central Asia.[27] From 1867 onwards, a large number of books were published and public exhibitions were organized to enlighten the broader Russian public about the multi-ethnic nature of the state.[28]

---

[25] For the best analysis of the activities of these Ukrainophiles, see Alexei Miller, *Ukraiinskii vopros v politike vlastei i russkom obshchestvennom mnenii (vtoraiia polovina XIX v.)*, www.empires.ru

[26] Rubakin, *Sredi knig*, 113 and 155.

[27] This view was first formulated by the founder of modern Russian Oriental Studies, V. R. Rozen. (I. Iu. Krachkovskii (ed.), *Pamyati akademika V. R. Rozena* (Moscow-Leningrad, 1947), 120–4.)

[28] N. G. Zalkind, *Moskovskaia shkola antropologov* (Moscow, 1974), 44; Lebedev, *Istoriia otechestvennoi arkheologii*, 176–7.

However, this knowledge of customs and cultures of the non-Russians was not to be acquired, in most cases, in order to recognize Russia's various peoples as separate nations with equal rights. Instead, this knowledge was perceived as necessary to facilitate the integration of all these peoples into one *civic* community within a single state. In fact, among many intellectuals the argument in favour of Russia being a nation-state-in-the-making rather than an empire strengthened in this period.

This is not because Russian nation-builders could not grasp the arguments of modern nationalism about the separation of nation from state or religious community. The problem was that the challenge of the emerging counter-state nationalism failed to alter the premises on which most Russian intellectuals conceived of a modern Russian national identity. They continued to construct Russian identity and analyse Russian state-building by comparing Russia and the 'West'. France, Prussia-Germany, and Great Britain rather than Austria-Hungary or the Ottoman Empire were the countries with which Russia was compared in terms of assimilation and integration.[29] This framework, in which comparison with West European nation-states was the intellectuals' main concern, prevented them from taking the arguments of counter-state nationalists seriously. Moreover, with the emergence of non-Russian nationalism, the Russian intellectual debate over the nature of the Russian state became even more a debate with and against Western Europe than it had been in the time of Boltin and the early Slavophiles. At the time when some non-Russian nationalists began to question the assumptions of the Russians, criticism of Russian imperial policies in the West also stepped up. It was this Western criticism that shaped Russian intellectual discourse about their state from the 1860s onwards. Many intellectuals responded to Western European criticism of Russia's treatment of its non-Russian subjects by sharpening the argument that the Romanov Empire was (at least potentially) a Russian nation-state.

That was particularly true after the 1863 Polish uprising, the suppression of which provoked condemnation of Russia in Europe. The Pan-Slavist Nikolai Danilevskii set the tone for rebutting the arguments of non-Russian nationalists and West European critics of Russian imperialism. His argument in *Russia and Europe* (1869) stemmed from the premiss of modern nationalism that 'a nationality . . . creates the basis of a state, . . . its [the state's] main *raison d'être* is to preserve the nationality.' He asked rhetorically: 'If, indeed, a state consists of a mixture of different nationalities, what national dignity, what national liberty could it maintain and protect?'[30]

Danilevskii's book was aimed at showing that Russia was not a multi-ethnic empire, but a nation-state-in-the-making, where a high degree of unity among the people had already been achieved. In order to prove his point, he took his

[29] Miller, *Ukraiinskii vopros . . .* , 90, 131, 133, 142–3, 195–6, 236.
[30] N. I. Danilevskii, *Rossiia i Evropa* (St Petersburg, 1895), 237.

predecessors' argument about the peaceful nature of the creation of the Russian state to extremes. For Danilevskii, the way the Russians treated the empire's non-Russian subjects could not in any way be compared to how Austria-Hungary and the Ottomans 'suppress and insult' the dignity and liberty of their people.[31] Overall, pan-Slavists of the late nineteenth century were far more concerned than their predecessors with the ability of the Russians to assimilate minorities.

In this period, both conservatives and liberals tended to exaggerate the success of assimilation and to adopt an ever more inclusive definition of Russianness. In particular, intellectuals further developed the idea of 'Russian culture', both as the main unifying force among all the nationalities of the state, and as a combined product of those nationalities. Danilevskii had to claim the existence of a common cultural tradition among all the subjects of the state by greatly exaggerating the extent to which non-Russian peoples had become assimilated into Russian culture, and to which minorities' customs had become incorporated into Russian traditions. Leading liberal historians, Sergei Solovev (1820–79) and Vasilii Kliuchevskii (1841–1911) presented the merging and assimilation of various tribes (*plemena*) into the Russian nation and culture as one of the main themes of Russian history.

This period, especially from the 1880s onwards, was also particularly marked by efforts of intellectuals to incorporate 'Asia' into Russian identity. Emphasizing the 'Eastern roots' of Russian identity, they underscored its uniqueness compared to Europe. The conservatives, such as Danilevskii and Konstantin Leontev (1831–91), argued that Russia was a separate cohesive 'natural-geographical region', combining both European and Asian traditions.[32] In turn, liberals believed that emerging national identities among non-Russians did not threaten Russia's national unity. On the contrary, if support was given to the development of non-Russian languages, cultures, and identities, a unified community was more likely to emerge on the territory of the Russian state. Thus, specialists in Oriental studies argued that emerging national movements in Georgia and Russia's part of Armenia were not a threat but a contribution to the development of a pan-Russian civic national identity.[33]

The Third Period: From the First Revolution to the First World War

The turn of the twentieth century was marked by the growth of national awareness on the part of ethnic minorities resulting in the emergence of doubts about the ability of dominant nationalities in the European states to assimilate them. This

---

[31] Ibid. 37.

[32] Ibid. 72–7. K. Leontev, *Sobranie Sochinenii*, vol. v (Moscow, 1912), 385–8.

[33] N. Ia. Marr, 'K voprosu o zadachakh armianovedeniia', *Zhurnal Ministerstra Narodnogo Prosveshcheniia*, July 2/324 (1899), 243–4; V. V. Bartold, *Sochineniia*, vol. vi (Msocow, 1966), 375. See also Vera Tolz, 'Orientalism, Nationalism, and Ethnic Diversity in Late Imperial Russia', *Historical Journal*, 48 (2005), 127–50.

development led nation-builders among all Europe's dominant nations, even those which are usually classified as civic, to emphasize ethnic components of identity, exclusive of minorities.[34] In Russia, radical nationalist chauvinism with its exclusive ethnic definition of 'Russianness' was further stimulated by the overall crisis of the political regimes, by the reforms aimed at overcoming this crisis through liberalization, and by the high level of representation of ethnic minorities in left-radical revolutionary movements. The wave of reconversion to Islam or return to paganism in Siberia and the middle Volga regions after the April 1905 edict of religious toleration further strengthened pessimism over prospects for assimilation.[35]

Some blamed this state of affairs on the forced nature of government-led Russification and conversion to Orthodoxy.[36] Others called for discriminatory measures against minorities. Although extreme xenophobic nationalism caught the minds of some intellectuals in the last decades of the nineteenth century, right-wing radical organizations were set up only in 1905–6, when political parties were finally legalized. Counting on petty bourgeois town dwellers as their main social base, right-radical organizations also received support from a number of scholars, representatives of the nobility, and government officials. They promoted the idea of 'Russia for the Russians', yet were determined to preserve 'one and united Russia' through the Russification of the minorities. Their attitude towards 'Asian *inorodtsy*' from Siberia, middle-Volga, and Central Asia, among whom nationalist movements did not exist, was far more sympathetic than towards non-Russians in the western borderlands with developed or developing national consciousness. In particular, the Jews were seen as posing the greatest danger for the Russians and their state. Yet the historian David Raskin has argued that among the Russian extreme right in the early twentieth century, religious anti-Semitism still predominated and racial anti-Semitism, already powerful in other parts of Europe, was only starting to emerge.[37] Overall, by 1914 the radical right failed to become a major political force in Russia. It had virtually no support among the peasantry, with the sole exception of the Volyniia region in the western borderlands. Workers were more influenced by socialist propaganda.

Simultaneously, others continued to promote the view of Russia as a nation-state-in-the-making united by common culture as well as political loyalties. Optimism about the success of nation-building within the borders of the Russian

---

[34] Kumar, 'Nation and Empire', 591–2.

[35] R. Geraci, *Window on the East* (Ithaca, NY, 2001), 296–7. Warnings about the weakness of the assimilationist powers of the Russians were heard earlier. For instance, in 1882, Nikolai Iadrintsev emphasized in *Sibir kak koloniia* (St Petersburg, 1882), 16–19, 25–33 that rather than assimilating Siberian *inorodtsy*, Russian settlers often adopted their customs themselves.

[36] S. V. Chicherina, 'Polozhenie prosveshcheniia u privolzhskikh inorodtsev', *Izvestiia imperatorskogo russkogo geograficheskogo obshchestva*, 42: 2–3 (1906), 597–8, 610–1.

[37] D. I. Raskin, 'Ideologiia russkogo pravogo radikalizma v kontse XIX-nachale XX v', in O. T. Vite et al. (eds.), *Natzionalnaia pravaia prezhde i teper*, part I (St Petersburg, 1992), 40–2.

Empire was expressed in this period by Petr Struve and Pavel Miliukov, the leading members of the Constitutional Democratic Party.[38]

ELITES VERSUS THE MASSES IN RUSSIAN NATION-BUILDING

Another peculiarity of the Russian case was connected with the perception of the relationship between the elites and the masses within the nation. In Gellner's first time zone '[p]easant regional idiosyncrasy is an offensive hindrance, and it is to be ironed out . . . by an educational system which holds this to be one of its most important objectives.'[39] In the second zone, despite the German cultivation of the simple *Volk*, 'a sense of national unity is forged against and not in support of regional dialects and lifestyles'.[40] The role of the elites who are the main carriers of the unification process is recognized by their inclusion in the nation. In the third zone, 'a national and state culture is created not in opposition to peasant idiosyncrasy, but on the basis of it.'[41] The elites carrying out nationalization are often educated representatives of the lower classes, who, as in all earlier cases, believe in their own membership of national communities.

The dominant conceptualization of national membership in Russia differed from those described above. Following the reforms of Peter the Great, the gap between the elites and the masses (peasantry) in Russia was greater than in Western Europe. Intellectuals responded to this peculiarity by defining the Russian nation through the exclusion of the elites (in effect, themselves) from it. The first group of intellectuals who offered such a definition of the Russian nation were the early Slavophiles. In the late eighteenth century, liberal Russian journals began to use the word *narod* to mean all the people of the Russian state regardless of their social origin.[42] This made it the closest Russian approximation to the word 'nation', in the inclusive sense, formulated in the course of the French Revolution. But through the efforts of the Slavophiles this definition of the *narod* was challenged.

In line with the German Romantic view, the Slavophiles depicted the peasantry as the preservers of Russian 'national spirit'. Differing from the German tradition, however, the Slavophiles imagined the peasantry to be the *only* group of society entitled to be regarded as the *narod*, as the peasants were not corrupted by Peter's Westernization of Russia. The Westernized elites were to be excluded from the

---

[38] B. Struve, 'Chto takoe Rossiia', *Russkaia mysl*, no. 1 (Jan. 1911), 175–8; on Miliukov, see Terence Emmons, 'On the Problem of Russia's "Separate Path" in Late Imperial Historiography', in Thomas Sanders (ed.), *Historiography of Imperial Russia* (Armonk, 1999), 165.

[39] Gellner, 'The Coming of Nationalism', 137. [40] Ibid. [41] Ibid.

[42] *Beseduiushchii grazhdanin*, October issue (1789), 145. For a detailed discussion of this argument, see Tolz, *Russia*, 85–92.

narod. Instead, they were termed 'the public' (*obshchestvennost*). As Konstantin Aksakov put it: 'The public is a purely Western phenomenon . . . The public speaks French, the *narod* speak Russian. The public follows Paris fashions, the people have their Russian customs . . . The public is only 150 years old; you cannot count the age of the people.'[43]

This view of the peasantry as the main symbol of a Russian nation with qualities distinctively different from Western values, and the resulting exclusion of the 'Westernized' upper classes from membership of the Russian nation had a tremendous impact on Russian public opinion. It was appropriated by some of those Westernizers, who, like the writer Aleksandr Herzen, turned to socialism.[44]

By equating the Russian nation with the peasantry Herzen and his followers, in effect, rejected the definition of a nation articulated by the French Revolution. They stood the argument of the French nation-builders of the time on its head. Indeed, at the time, in the French discourse about the nation, to be fully French was not to be a peasant, while to be a peasant was to be not fully French. The French nation-builders therefore saw it as their task to turn peasants into Frenchmen. In contrast, in Russia in the national discourse of intellectuals, to be fully Russian was to be a peasant.[45]

It is noteworthy that the French concept of nation was a profoundly democratic one. All members of a nation were supposed to be in some sense equal, and any government had to have a popular mandate to rule. These main elements of the modern concept of a nation are 'at the same time the basic tenets of democracy'.[46] In Russia, despite the fact that socialists regularly evoked the tradition of the French Revolution, they rejected the idea of fundamental equality among various strata of society and redefined democracy. From the 1860s onward the word 'democracy' was also interpreted to mean 'the common people—and its opposite was not "dictatorship" but the "bourgeoisie" or indeed the whole of privileged society'.[47] Thus, this socially exclusive definition of nationhood posed another challenge to the inclusive state-framed definition of Russianness.

IMPERIAL POLICIES AND NATION-BUILDING

It was only in the aftermath of Russia's defeat in the Crimean war in 1856 that the imperial government began incorporating elements of modern nation-building in their policies. Aleksandr II's predecessors envisaged Russia as a defender of the

---

[43] Quoted in E. H. Carr, ' "Russia and Europe" as a Theme of Russian History', in R. Pares and A. J. P. Taylor (eds.), *Essays Presented to Sir Lewis Namier* (London, 1956), 374.

[44] A. I. Gerzen, *Byloe i dumy*, parts 4–5 (Moscow, 1983), 161.

[45] E. Weber, *Peasants into Frenchmen: The Modernization of Rural France, 1870–1914* (Stanford, Calif., 1976); J. R. Lehning, *Peasant and French: Cultural Contact in Rural France during the Nineteenth Century* (Cambridge, 1995).   [46] Greenfeld, *Nationalism*, 10.

[47] J. Billington, *The Icon and the Axe* (London, 1966), 378 and O. Figes and B. Kolonitskii, *Interpreting the Russian Revolution* (London, 1999), 122.

Europe of the *ancien régime* from the principles of democracy and nationalism proclaimed by the French Revolution. A brief period when Aleksandr I (1801–25) considered proposals of his government's leading reformer Mikhail Speransky to adopt a constitution, spread education down to the village and introduce legal reforms aimed at the closer integration of *inorodtsy* ended with Speransky's dismissal in 1812. Instead, in his scheme of the Holy Alliance in 1815, the tsar offered his anti-nationalist vision of Europe as 'a single Christian nation'.[48]

The Decembrist uprising and the Polish rebellion of 1830, which confirmed the presence of the ideas of nationalism within the borders of the Russian Empire, forced the ruling elites to come up with their own definition of nationality. It is in this context that the future Minister of Education, Sergei Uvarov, described in 1832 the three pillars of Russia's existence as 'Orthodoxy, Autocracy, Nationality'. In this vision, 'nationality' did not mean a nation as popular sovereignty in a West European sense. Instead, this vague term referred to Russian 'national character', the main feature of which was 'humility' (*smirenie*), best manifested in the people's acceptance of the unlimited powers of the tsar.[49] Thus, the nation was seen as fully subordinate to the dynastic state. In this period, Russification of non-Russians continued to be understood as an administrative, not cultural homogenization. This administrative homogenization had little to do with Russian nation-building, but was aimed at maintaining the stability of the dynastic empire. It advanced or halted depending on what would preserve stability more effectively.[50]

Government policies that could be seen as enhancing nation-building in Russia began with the reforms of the 1860s under Aleksandr II (1855–81). In this period, members of the ruling elite began to demonstrate understanding of the connection between modernizing nation-building policies and economic and military successes. The Russian government should be inspired by the role played by Prussia in achieving German unification or French policies of assimilation, it started to be argued.[51] Aleksandr II and his two successors initiated policies which were aimed at both ethnic and civic homogenization in the empire. The relative weight of each component fluctuated from one period to another. Aleksandr II is best known for his policies of civic homogenization and integration, which included the emancipation of the serfs, introduction of organs of local self-government (*zemstva* and municipal councils), and reforms of the legal system and of the army. The emancipation of the serfs began their slow integration into Russian society, particularly through participation in *zemstva*. Yet this integration was hampered by peasants' continued segregation into village communes. Legal reform was aimed at abolishing socially segregated courts, with the exception of

---

[48] Suny, 'The Empire Strikes Out', 42–3.
[49] N. Riasanovsky, *Nicholas I and Official Nationality in Russia, 1825–1855* (Berkeley, 1959)
[50] In 1849, Nicholas I ordered a short prison detention for a Russian official who, in the name of Russian national homogenization, proposed the abolition of privileges of German barons in the Baltic provinces.   [51] See n. 39.

those dealing with cases involving peasants, and making the justice system public. There was expansion of education, particularly in the countryside. The introduction of a nearly universal male military conscription for a maximum of six years in 1874 also helped to integrate diverse social groups and to spread education. The easing of censorship resulted in the creation of mass-circulation newspapers; the railway boom, which started in the 1860s, also improved communication between different parts of empire and laid the foundation for the development of industries from the 1890s onwards.[52]

In the late 1860s, the government also put forward new initiatives aimed at integrating the people of the non-Russian borderlands, including those below the elite level, into Russian society. The policies, which were described as a spread of civility (*grazhdanstvennost*), were aimed at depriving the kinship-based local aristocracy of their special privileges and included the promotion of local self-government, the establishment of reformed native courts, the abolition of exemptions from military service, and the creation of the 'imperial public sphere', as alphabets were devised for *inorodtsy* without literary culture, books published, and theatres opened in the borderlands. This new policy was aimed at uniting the empire's subjects into one community through imposing on them similar duties and obligations. The introduction of *grazhdanstvennost* in the borderlands had clear parallels with the measures aimed at integrating Russian peasants.[53] Such policies largely replicated policies of civic nation-building in Western Europe, where, during the nineteenth century, peasants were also turned into citizens through state-sponsored education, military service, and exposure to the mass-circulation press.

The policy aimed at creating a unifying civic identity, based on a common set of duties and obligations, and continued under Aleksandr III (1881–94), who is best known, however, for his celebration of ethnic Russian identity. Thus, in 1897, an attempt was made to introduce the policy of *grazhdanstvennost* among the Transbaikal Buriats.[54] But only in 1905, under the pressure of the first Russian revolution, did the tsarist government reluctantly agree to broaden its vision of *grazhdanstvennost* by adding civil and political rights to the concept which hitherto had stressed only duties and obligations. The election of the first Russian parliament, albeit with restricted rights, as well as Prime Minister Petr Stolypin's reforms, were further examples of attempts at nation-state-building along civic lines. In an attempt explicitly defined as the creation of 'loyal citizens' out of Russian peasants, Stolypin's reforms, which were initiated in 1906, facilitated peasants' separation from traditional communes and their transformation into full legal persons.[55] Overall, Stolypin's programme

---

[52] B. Eklof, J. Bushnell, and L. Zakharova (eds.), *Russia's Great Reforms 1855–1881* (Bloomington, 1994).

[53] D. Yaroshevski, 'Empire and Citizenship', in Brower and Lazzerini (eds.), *Russia's Orient*, 58–79. On the expansion of state-sponsored education see B. Eklof, *Russian Peasant Schools* (Berkeley, 1986), 89, 94.   [54] Yaroshevski, 'Empire and Citizenship', 7.

[55] D. Atkinson, *The End of the Russian Land Commune, 1905–1930* (Stanford, Calif., 1983), 57–70.

envisaged the dissolution of estates and ethnic barriers, incompatible with modern nation-state-building.

These civic nation-building tactics went hand in hand with the policies of ethnic homogenization through Russification and conversion to Orthodoxy. Russian language and Orthodox faith were seen by the government as the key markers of Russian identity until the end of the imperial regime. Thus, at the height of Aleksandr II's civic integration policies, the Polish uprising of 1863–4 as well as the promotion of a separate Ukrainian identity by intellectuals from Malorossia triggered the beginning of a more consistent cultural Russification in the Western province and in Malorossia, where the government decrees of 1863 and 1876 prohibited the publication of most books in Ukrainian and the import of Ukrainian-language books from abroad. These measures were justified by the necessity of integrating the Russian nation along ethnic lines, of which Little Russians were seen as an inseparable part, at the time of nation-state-building elsewhere in Europe.[56] Under the last two tsars forced Russification, conversion to Orthodoxy, the abolition of remaining autonomies enjoyed by some nationalities, and the imposition of strict Russian control proceeded more consistently than ever before. After a short respite in the immediate aftermath of the 1905 revolution, Stolypin resumed cultural Russification, thus adding an ethnic dimension to his programme of civic nation-building. At the turn of the twentieth century, the policy of administrative and cultural Russification affected all the empire's non-Russian domains, with Turkestan being the only significant exception.[57]

Russification and other attempts to integrate the empire's diverse subjects into a single imperial Russian nationality were conducted inconsistently, often with the use of crude force, and, in most cases, belatedly as a reaction to real or perceived threat of counter-state nationalism among non-Russian nationalities. Hosking rightly concluded that Russification repelled many members of the Russian elite by its crude chauvinism, while the masses remained indifferent to the government's goals. As for the non-Russians, the impact was often opposite to what the government intended. In Hosking's words, the policy 'stimulated non-Russians, in different ways, to discover or rediscover their ethnic solidarity...and to begin to seek a solution to their problems in national rather than an imperial framework'.[58]

CONCLUSION: THE REASONS FOR THE FAILURE

It seems that intellectual and government elites had to share responsibility for the collapse of their visions of a unified community within the borders of the Russian state. Russian intellectuals could not be criticized for failing to articulate the

---

[56] D. Saunders, 'Russia's Ukrainian Policy (1847–1905): A Demographic Approach', *European History Quarterly*, 25 (1995), 187.

[57] E. C. Thaden, *Russification in the Baltic Provinces and Finland* (Princeton, 1981); R. Suny, *The Making of the Georgian Nation* (London, 1988), chs. 5–7; T. Weeks, *Nation and State in Late Imperial Russia: Nationalism and Russification on the Western Frontier, 1863–1914* (DeKalb, 1996).

[58] Hosking, *Russia: People and Empire*, 397.

concepts of nation, separate from the state and the Orthodox community. As has been shown, they did articulate such concepts. State- and nation-building policies were intertwined elsewhere in Europe. The prior existence of strong states with centralized bureaucracies was essential for the formation of modern (state-framed) national identities in Britain, France, and Spain, where ethnic components did not predominate in the definition of national communities. As Russians often drew parallels between their own country and France and Britain when talking about a Russian national community, it is not surprising that they also underscored the importance of the state. The problem with Russian intellectuals' thinking about nation-building was not so much that they could not separate it from state-building but that they failed to acknowledge that during the 'age of nationalism' the Russians did not have a state within whose borders nation-building could take place. Even those who saw some parts of the empire as not belonging to a 'Russian national homeland', in most cases did not contemplate the creation of a Russian nation-state within 'Russian ethnic boundaries'. This lack of acknowledgement became particularly damaging at the time when the non-Russian elites started to articulate their alternative (counter-state) nation-building projects.[59]

The second important legacy of the Russian intellectual tradition was the concept of a Russian nation which excluded the 'exploiting classes' from national membership. This vision prevented the development of the concept of a nation aimed at eradicating barriers between various estates and social groups, which stimulated democratization in other European societies. Such a socially restrictive definition of nationhood also undermined an inclusive, state-framed concept of a national community.

As for the government, from the time Peter the Great began to modernize Russia, highly inconsistent policies were pursued.[60] Nicholas II (1894–1917) finally conceded the creation of a parliament at the high point of social radicalization, which was opposed to the autocratic state, when it was probably inevitable that state and society would no longer be able to cooperate. Instead, in the wake of and during the First World War, 'the two sides weakened each other', as Struve observed.[61]

Attempts at administrative and cultural homogenization went hand in hand with the retention of privileges and social and class distinctions. The impact of the government's nation-building policies, for instance in the sphere of education or the reconstruction of the army, was undermined by conflicts in views and actions between and even within various government agencies.[62] The above-mentioned policy of *grazhdanstvennost* in the eastern borderlands was undermined not only

---

[59] T. Weeks, 'The National Minorities', in A. Geifman (ed.), *Russia under the Last Tsar: Opposition and Subversion, 1894–1917* (Oxford, 1999), 111–34.

[60] Pipes, *Russia under the Old Regime*, 114.

[61] Quoted in I. A. Sandulov (ed.), *Istoriia Rossii: narod i vlast* (St Petersburg, 1997), 440.

[62] J. Sanborn, 'Family, Fraternity, and Nation-Building in Russia, 1905–1925', in Suny and Martin (eds.), *A State of Nations*, 93–110; and Geraci, *Window on the East*, 223–63.

by the local elites, whose privileges it threatened, but also by the corruption of Russian officials. In a state which was still a collection of 'networks of personal dependence', it was easy for leaders of the Transbaikal Buriats to retain some of their privileges and to ensure the annulment of the Russian proposal for a military conscription in the Buriats through bribing local Russian officials and lobbying the imperial government through patrons in the capital. The Buriat situation was replicated elsewhere in the empire.[63] The size of the country and relative economic backwardness also complicated integration and assimilation.

Last, but certainly not least, the government's modernization policies, which inevitably entailed nation-building elements, came too late to make sufficient progress in bringing non-Russians closer to the state and in integrating Russian peasants into a national community before its cohesion was tested by the First World War.

The 'nationalization' of the peasantry proceeded slowly. Despite a dramatic growth in literacy, by 1913 it still embraced less than a quarter of the rural population.[64] By 1916, 61 per cent of all households still held their land within communal structures (a reduction of 16 per cent compared to 1905).[65] By the second half of the nineteenth century some of the non-Russian elites were already affected by nationalist ideas and began to formulate their own counter-state concepts of nations, based on local cultural traditions. In fact, the tsars' developmental policies of the turn of the twentieth century exacerbated rather than dispelled the centrifugal trends of local nationalisms. The spread of education, industrialization, and the *grazhdanstvennost* policy facilitated the emergence of local intelligentsias ready to embrace the ideas of nationalism, which opposed the state-framed concepts of the Russian elites.

---

[63] Yaroshevski, 'Empire and Citizenship', 72–3.

[64] A. G. Rashin, 'Gramotnost i narodnoe obrazovanie v Rossii v XIX i nachale XX vekov', *Istoricheskie zapiski*, 37 (1951), 45–9. [65] Hosking, *Russia: People and Empire*, 435.

Conclusion

Nationalism and the Nineteenth Century

Mark Hewitson

From whatever side one traces one's way back to the principle, one always reaches the same conclusion: namely, that the social pact establishes among citizens an equality such that all commit themselves under the same conditions and must all enjoy the same rights. Thus by the nature of the pact every act of sovereignty, that is to say every genuine act of the general will, either obligates or favours all citizens equally, so that the Sovereign knows only the body of the nation and does not single out any one of those who make it up.

Jean-Jacques Rousseau, *The Social Contract* (1762), ii. 4.

Nationalism in the West was based upon a nationality which was the product of social and political factors; nationalism in Germany did not find its justification in a rational societal conception, it found it in the 'natural' fact of a community, held together, not by the will of its members nor by any obligations of contract, but by traditional ties of kinship and status. German nationalism substituted for the legal and rational concept of 'citizenship' the infinitely vaguer concept of 'folk', which, first discovered by the German humanists, was later fully developed by Herder and the German romanticists. It lent itself more easily to the embroideries of imagination and the excitations of emotion. Its roots seemed to reach into the dark soil of primitive times....

Hans Kohn, *The Idea of Nationalism* (1945), 329–31.

The history of nationalism in Europe in the long nineteenth century has been distorted by the forward-looking utopianism of the eighteenth century and the backward-looking pessimism of the mid-twentieth century. From the Enlightenment onwards, the idea of the 'nation' was imbued with universal aspirations and expectations of progress. *Philosophes* such as Jean-Jacques Rousseau reasoned that citizens had effectively contracted to join forces in societies—or 'nations'—in return for the benefits which concerted action alone could provide. Contemporaries like Adam Smith, whose *Wealth of Nations* was published in 1776, contended that analogous types of rational decisions had come to typify manufacture and commerce within Europe's national economies. After the experiments of the French Revolution and given the increasingly salient effects of industrialization, European nation-states and nationalisms continued to be associated with the idea of economic and political improvement, which was potentially universal in scope and application.

Such conceptual linkage is arguably still relevant to the different variants of 'modernization theory', which classify and assess forms of nationalism according to their degree of convergence with or divergence from a 'civic' model of political and economic progress.[1] Historians like Hans Kohn, an Austrian emigré, accepted this model. By 1945, however, after the catastrophes wrought by fascism and Nazism, he was struck much more by those nation-states and national movements which had diverged from civic modes of thought and behaviour. With the exception of their counterparts in Western Europe, particularly France and Britain, the majority of nineteenth-century nationalists were now seen to be the forerunners of Italian fascists, German Nazis, and the radical nationalists of authoritarian regimes in Southern and Eastern Europe during the 1920s, 1930s, and 1940s. Kohn's assumption, and that of many of his contemporaries, was that 'ethnic' notions of descent, which appeared to have become so important in the interwar period, had very deep and extensive cultural roots, produced amongst other things by social and political backwardness, the limited impact of the Renaissance and Reformation, and the disparity between state borders and the settlement of ethnic groups.[2] From this pessimistic twentieth-century viewpoint, it seemed much easier to take a wrong turn towards ethnic nationalism than to stay on the original and supposedly correct course towards a civic ideal characterized by liberalism, economic progress, and democracy.

The horrific events of twentieth-century European history have almost inescapably distorted interpretations of nineteenth-century nationalism. The terms of the debate have been further obscured by problems of definition. As the main components of a descriptive typology of nationalism, both terms—civic and ethnic—are ambiguous and potentially misleading.[3] Thus, the word 'civic' does not refer exclusively to citizenship in Rome, with the implicit egalitarianism of the statement 'civis Romanus sum', but also to city-states and cities in general, with their very diverse traditions, ranging from the oligarchy of early-modern Venice to the municipal reformism of late nineteenth-century Birmingham. Likewise, the etymology of the term 'ethnic' encompasses a broad description of heathens, in the Greek root *ethnikos*, and a much narrower definition of a racial group, as has occurred at various times in the chequered history of the academic discipline of ethnology. Certainly, if the word 'ethnicity' is taken in its wider sense of common descent *and* culture, it seems to include the political traditions and practices, or political culture, usually denoted by the word 'civic'. For this reason, some commentators have preferred to treat civic and ethnic definitions of nationhood as two poles, between which lie various combinations of cultural belonging,

---

[1] See the Introduction.   [2] H. Kohn, *The Idea of Nationalism* (New York, 1945), 329–31.
[3] For more on definitions, see the relevant section of Chapter 1.

whether political, economic, social, historical, linguistic, or religious.[4] Other commentators have argued that the distinction needs to be clarified further by introducing terms such as 'voluntary' and 'organic', which serve more effectively to indicate the continuum between contractual or chosen affiliations and commitments, on the one hand, and apparently natural and inescapable identities, on the other.[5] Or to put it another way, since the nineteenth-century meanings of 'organic' (organs of the body, elements of the 'constitution', and executive institutions of the state) and of 'voluntary' (the limits of volition or free will) were also highly contested, it is held to be useful to distinguish analytically and descriptively between conceptions of the nation which seemed to be negotiated or constructed and those which appeared self-evident or unavoidable. Even then, given that the nation was widely believed to be a natural entity and that extreme forms of nationalism were not ruled out by civic participation and liberalism, it makes more sense to describe and assess different types of nationalism by measuring their extent, by gauging proponents' degree of commitment to them, and by determining nationalists' willingness to use violence to achieve their ends.[6]

The dichotomy between civic and ethnic types of nationalism has been understood not only as a descriptive or analytical distinction, but also as an assessment of the significance of different forms of nationalism and as an explanation of their emergence and evolution. Implicitly, civic involvement was evolutionary and ethnic definitions of identity were degenerative, linked respectively to the emergence of voluntary associations, parliamentary politics, freedom of the press, due legal process, protection of minority rights, relative economic prosperity, and complex varieties of social intercourse, all of which were connoted by 'modernization', and to late industrialization and democratization, the existence of a large agricultural sector, a trenchant, feudal nobility, a defensive reaction against the metropolis, the allegedly revolutionary socialism of the urban working classes, and the persistence of long-held superstitions and folk myths, which were frequently overlaid, it is held, by the modern science of Darwinian biology and the modern paranoia of economic anti-Semitism. As a consequence, the civic and ethnic dichotomy was used by authors such as Kohn—and many 'primordialist' and 'modernist' successors—to explain processes of historical change, or different paths of development, rather than merely describing historically specific types of European nationalism in a heuristic fashion. The problem with such historical explanation is twofold: it understates the ramifications of political and psychological collapse in large parts of Europe and in particular sections of continental societies during the period after 1914, which transformed the potential of radical nationalism; and it treats the long nineteenth century, in important respects, anachronistically.

[4] See, for example, M. Hewitson, *National Identity and Political Thought in Germany* (Oxford, 2000), 3.

[5] Oliver Zimmer makes this distinction in Chapter 6 and in id., 'Boundary Mechanisms and Symbolic Resources: Towards a Process-Oriented Approach to National Identity', *Nations and Nationalism*, 9 (2003), 173–93.   [6] See the last section of the Introduction.

The first section of this concluding chapter demonstrates the extent to which such anachronism has been founded on untested assumptions about 'ethnicity'. It argues that a large majority of contemporaries, especially those in the West, accepted the validity of ethnic myths of common descent and racial difference.[7] 'Civic traditions', which are the subject of the second section, rarely served to undermine these ethnic myths. Moreover, the emancipatory, liberal roots of such traditions were often just as prevalent in Eastern and Southern as in Northern and Western Europe.[8] As a result, any attempt to base an explanatory model of nineteenth-century nationalism on a distinction between civic participation, which was supposedly more typical of the West, and ethnic mythology, which is held to have been more pronounced in the East and South, is likely to fail. The third section of the chapter proposes an alternative model, which distinguishes between the extent and the content of various types of nationalism, and which is based on five sources of potential conflict and radicalization: the rapid spread of capitalist production and disputes about distribution; democratization and competition for power within representative polities; the existence of long-tanding cultural differences in an era of changing means of communication; new levels and different kinds of state intervention; and a slow transformation of the European states system and conceptions of inter-state relations and warfare.

THE UBIQUITY OF ETHNICITY

Few nineteenth-century Europeans believed that ethnic and civic traditions of nationhood were opposed to each other. This was even the case in France, where revolutionaries and, later, republicans had self-consciously established voluntary, active, cosmopolitan, and universal types of national affiliation after 1789, at the expense of other historical ties and forms of belonging.[9] Thus, the constitution of 1791, which vowed never to employ French forces 'against the liberty of any people', at once guaranteed foreigners' legal rights and distinguished such aliens linguistically and politically from active French citizens: 'Foreigners who find themselves in France are subjected to the same criminal and police laws as are French citizens... [and] their person, their goods, their industry, their cult are equally protected by law'; yet, as a separate category of persons, foreigners did not enjoy political rights.[10] Most revolutionaries seem to have assumed, despite their unprecedented wish to allow the participation of all citizens in political affairs, that the nation was an easily defined, historically determined entity. Accordingly, in answer to his question 'what is a nation?', Emmanuel Joseph Siéyès, the

---

[7] For instance, see Chapters 2, 10, 11, and 14.   [8] See especially Chapters 1, 3, 7, and 9.
[9] For more on this and further similar points, see Chapter 2.
[10] The constitution was nevertheless radical in allowing naturalization after only five years of residence.

celebrated revolutionary pamphleteer, looked inwards to a 'body of people who join together to live under *common* laws and be represented by the same *legislative assembly*', and who were 'composed of descendants of the Gauls and the Romans'.[11] By 1794, after three years of war, the deliberate exploitation of national differences and popular xenophobia had become an important part of revolutionary Jacobin rhetoric, with foreigners in Paris such as Anarchisis Clootz and Thomas Paine, both of whom had been granted honorary French citizenship in 1792, arrested or executed.[12] For the moment, at least, the attributes, population, and territory of the French nation-state appeared self-evident, distinct from those of its neighbours. Ninety years later, the republican philologist and historian Ernest Renan made a similar set of points in his famous essay *Qu'est-ce qu'une nation?* (1882). As is well-known, he argued that 'nations are not something eternal', but rather 'the existence of a nation (pardon this metaphor!) is an everyday plebiscite; it is, like the very existence of the individual, a perpetual affirmation of life.'[13] However, although asserting that man was not 'enslaved' in his race, language, and religion, he also conceded that a nation was a 'soul', 'the possession in common of a rich legacy of remembrances'. In this context, 'the worship of ancestors is understandably justifiable, since our ancestors have made us who we are'.[14] Throughout these discourses, from the French Revolution to the Third Republic, there was a blurring of the boundaries between civic participation and a sense of cultural or ethnic belonging.

In important respects, nineteenth-century societies—and, therefore, politics—were founded on 'self-evident' assumptions of ethnicity. Partly, such assumptions derived from persisting 'pre-modern' institutions and traditions—agricultural, familial, local, and religious—in most areas of Europe. More importantly, however, they were the corollary of new types of cultural and social transformation, communication, state intervention, and expansion. Thus, the often secular but mystical musings of Romantics and their successors, the rage for classification within post-Enlightenment science, the widening chasm between 'respectable society' and the 'dangerous classes', the new mythologies of a mass press, the advent of military conscription, national demonologies in wartime, and the growth and popularization of imperialism were all visibly 'modern' processes, usually associated with Western Europe, yet they served to consolidate legends of ethnic belonging in countries characterized by civic participation such as France, Britain, Denmark, Norway, Sweden, Belgium, Switzerland, and the Netherlands. Certainly, in these states, as in those of Southern, Central, and Eastern

---

[11] Siéyès, *Qu'est-ce que le tiers état?* (1789), cited in D. Williams (ed.), *The Enlightenment* (Cambridge, 1999), 494–5.

[12] On the development of revolutionary xenophobia, see M. Jeismann, *Das Vaterland der Feinde: Studien zum nationalen Feindbegriff und Selbstverständnis in Deutschland und Frankreich, 1792–1918* (Stuttgart, 1992), 103–58.

[13] Renan, cited in J. Hutchinson and A. D. Smith (eds.), *Nationalism* (Oxford, 1994), 17–18.

[14] Ibid.

Europe, there were few obstacles to hinder the perpetuation and invention of ethnic myths.[15]

Such myths were deeply rooted in traditional societies. They were closely related to religious practice, a sense of place, elementary forms of human organization, and man's relationship to nature. Most societies in nineteenth-century Europe remained predominantly rural and agricultural, allowing an understanding of natural species, animal breeding, and crop cultivation to become analogies of race and ethnicity. In Sweden in the 1880s, 58.5 per cent of the labour force worked within agriculture and fishing; in France, 47 per cent; and in Belgium, 39.5 per cent. Less than 10 per cent of the population in Sweden in 1870 lived in towns of more than 10,000 inhabitants; 21 per cent in France; and 26 per cent in Belgium.[16] Even in Britain, where the agricultural sector accounted for 13.3 per cent of the workforce, only just over half of the population lived in towns. Many of these town dwellers had recently migrated from or retained strong links with the countryside. Furthermore, animals—in particular, horses—were an integral part of city life, providing many of its sounds and smells, and shaping the layout of streets and the construction of housing. Against this background, archaic myths of 'nature' and the 'natural cycle' proved surprisingly tenacious. The language and assumptions of the stock-breeder were widely shared and regularly applied to national and other social groups, with the implication that different human 'breeds' had specific characteristics, as horses had been bred for hunting, dogs for retrieving prey, and cattle for meat. Given that Darwin himself, in *The Variation of Plants and Animals under Domestication* (1868), had confirmed the scientific validity of such animal breeding, there was little to stop urban, educated, modern-minded Europeans, like their distant ancestors and their counterparts in rural areas, from assuming the existence of diverse 'races' with specific attributes and from explaining cultural differences in terms of heredity.[17] Consequently, throughout the long nineteenth century, words for 'race', 'nation', and 'people' were used more or less interchangeably. Despite occasional religious injunctions to respect the commonality of humanity, few challenged the notion that different patterns of heredity or descent had helped to create distinct racial and national 'characters'. It was thus no coincidence that cartoonists throughout Europe portrayed other nationalities and nation-states as animals, distinguishable from each other and from the observer.

The idea that nations were based, at least in part, on descent was given further credence by the centrality of kinship and the family in nineteenth-century societies. Civil society, as the German philosopher Georg Wilhelm Friedrich Hegel pointed out, rested on a dense network of families.[18] In turn, the significance of

---

[15] For obstacles that did exist in the Netherlands and Belgium, which of all the countries of Europe seem to have resisted ethnicization most effectively, see Chapter 5.

[16] Figures from R. Gildea, *Barricades and Borders: Europe, 1800–1914* (London, 1987), 145–7.

[17] N. MacMaster, *Racism in Europe* (London, 2001), 54–5.

[18] J. Keane (ed.), *Civil Society and the State* (London, 1988).

such family structures reinforced concepts of lineage and blood, not only among European aristocracies, but in middle- and lower-class circles, too. Thus, in novels such as Charles Dickens's *Dombey and Son*, Gustav Freytag's *Soll und Haben*, and Émile Zola's Rougon-Macquart series, the question of biological succession within patriarchal bourgeois dynasties played a pivotal role. In real life, clans such as the Koechlin, Geigy, and Sarrasin in Alsace carefully maintained their consanguinity and their inheritances.[19] Heirs of these families were told of their pedigree and familial responsibilities from an early age. 'You know with what heavy costs and with what anxious care we have prepared your present fortune,' wrote Friedrich Daniel Bassermann, from one of the wealthiest bourgeois families of Mannheim, to his son in 1805: 'God has compensated us by allowing us to see you happy— enjoy it, as an upright man should, and do honour to the Bassermann household by your conduct.'[20] Since, in the absence of state welfare and high taxation, most property was still distributed by kinship groups, the family continued to be a common point of comparison for those who were most interested in creating or consolidating nation-states. This was particularly the case within the prosperous, middle-class, and often liberal-minded families of West European cities, as well as within aristocracies throughout the continent. It was also true of sections of the lower middle classes and of large parts of the peasantry, as Émile Guillaumin's account of *La Vie d'un simple* made plain in 1904. In such circumstances, it was tempting for many nineteenth-century Europeans, from both East and West, to see the nation as a community of descent, or as a family writ large.[21]

Extended families often formed the basis of close-knit communities. The enduring significance of locality as the principal locus of political and cultural life helped to reinforce the distinction, intrinsic to ethnic mythology, between neighbours and strangers.[22] This sense of 'here' and 'there' had always been subject to qualification in a densely populated area with considerable migration such as Europe. Furthermore, as Guillaumin noted, the changes of the second half of the nineteenth century, including the expansion of elementary education, the spread of newspapers and improvements in transport, had modified the outlook of peasants and town dwellers about who was foreign and on what grounds. However, in many instances, contemporaries' understanding of national affairs was mediated by their direct experience of local customs. Their suspicion of outsiders remained intact, linked to assumptions about the common descent of insiders, even in multilingual countries such as Switzerland where villages and municipalities (*Gemeinden*) were unusually democratic, powerful, and constitutionally integrated into a nation-state.[23] Accordingly, although liberals such as

[19] E. J. Hobsbawm, *The Age of Capital, 1848–1875* (London, 1975), 282–3.

[20] L. Gall, *Bürgertum in Deutschland* (Berlin, 1989), 96.

[21] Émile Guillaumin, *La Vie d'un simple* (Paris, 1904), was one of the first accounts of rural life by a peasant.   [22] See Chapter 4 on the significance of locality and regionalism.

[23] Oliver Zimmer, although also stressing the voluntary aspects of such localism, examines the historical, geographical, and natural components of national identities in Switzerland in Chapter 6.

Carl Hilty argued that Switzerland was held together by the 'ideal' 'of constituting a nationality which stands head and shoulders above mere affiliations of blood or language', exclusive notions of a Swiss identity or 'character' had been widely adopted by 1848 which were founded on an organic attachment to an unchanging natural environment and a historical rootedness extending back to the late thirteenth and early fourteenth centuries.[24] It was central to such self-understanding that the three valley communities of Uri, Schwyz, and Unterwalden, which were termed 'Urschweiz' or 'primordial Switzerland', had joined together in 'mutual protection of their homeland', as the president of the Swiss Confederation, Emil Welti, put it in 1891.[25] Whether the Charter of 1291, the 'founding document of the Swiss Confederation', or the oath of Rütli and assassination of a Habsburg bailiff by Wilhelm Tell in 1307 was preferred as the official origin of the Swiss nation and state, the idea of a primordial community, rooted in the valleys and forests of the Alps and defending itself against a foreign oppressor, became integral features of a single Swiss character, whose descent could be traced back hundreds of years into the mists of the medieval period.[26] 'The Swiss homeland constitutes such a coherent and richly structured natural whole,' wrote the liberal constitutional lawyer Johann-Kaspar Bluntschli in 1875, 'one that enables the evolution on its soil of a peculiar feeling of a common homeland which unites its inhabitants as sons of the same fatherland, even though they live in different valleys and speak different languages.'[27] Foreigners coming from beyond the fortress of the Alps, which came to symbolize the borders of both the locality and the nation-state in many accounts, were often systematically refused citizenship by the cantons and municipalities themselves, since the latter retained control of naturalization. Despite having fewer powers than their Swiss counterparts, villages, towns, and cities in other countries, many of which remained surprisingly inward-looking throughout much of the nineteenth century, also appear to have functioned as symbols of a national community of common descent, or of the people from 'here'.[28]

Christianity, with its transnational churches and its universal tenets, came into conflict with such local and exclusive ethnic versions of nationalism, especially

[24] See Hilty's essay on 'Die schweizerische Nationalität', cited in O. Zimmer, *A Contested Nation: History, Memory and Nationalism in Switzerland, 1761–1891* (Cambridge, 2003), 200.

[25] Welti speech at the national festival marking the 600th anniversary of the Swiss nation, cited in O. Zimmer, 'Competing Memories of the Nation: Liberal Historians and the Reconstruction of the Swiss Past, 1870–1900', *Past and Present*, 168 (2000), 195.

[26] The liberal historian Wilhelm Oechsli on the Charter of 1891, cited ibid. 194.

[27] J.-K. Bluntschli, *Die schweizerische Nationalität* (1875), cited in O. Zimmer, 'In Search of Natural Identity: Alpine Landscape and the Reconstruction of the Swiss Nation', *Comparative Studies in Society and History*, 40 (1998), 651.

[28] A. Confino, *The Nation as a Local Metaphor: Württemberg, Imperial Germany and National Memory, 1871–1918* (Chapel Hill, NC, 1997); C. Applegate, *A Nation of Provincials: The German Idea of Heimat* (Berkeley, 1990); C. Ford, *Creating the Nation in Provincial France: Religion and Political Identity in Brittany* (Princeton, 1993); J. R. Lehning, *Peasant and French: Cultural Contact in Rural France during the Nineteenth Century* (Cambridge, 1995); S. Gerson, *The Pride of Place: Local Memories and Political Culture in Nineteenth-Century France* (Cornell, 2003).

racial theories of polygenesis, which contradicted biblical conceptions of a single, God-given humanity. Nevertheless, a mystical sense of faith and strong moral beliefs appear at times to have been projected onto the nation, giving believers the impression that they were, indeed, a chosen people.[29] Correspondingly, during wartime, clerics of all the major European churches, with the exception of the Quakers, were prepared to back one nation-state against another. As a pastor from Marburg commented after the defeat of Napoleon I: 'Is this not God's work which we see unfolded before us?'[30] Moreover, instead of undermining such feelings of moral superiority within a chosen, national group, it is possible that secularization led to a further sacralization of the nation by allowing the translation of religious notions of the sacred onto the profane institutions of the state and by creating competition between secular champions of state power and defenders of a 'national' church, both of whom claimed to be the only true representatives of a national community.[31] Critically, in countries such as France and Britain, where secularization was most pronounced, these struggles between opponents and sup-porters of the church took place within societies in which religious observance and belief were still typical of the majority. Even in Paris at the turn of the twentieth century, a supposed 'citadel of religious indifference', between 70 and 80 per cent of marriages and funerals were Catholic, and a similar proportion of children were baptized.[32] At that time, one-third of French children attended Catholic primary schools, despite a thoroughgoing reform of the education system by the anticlerical Jules Ferry from 1878 onwards.[33] Many other militant anticlerical republicans such as Émile Combes, whose ministry carried out the separation of church and state in 1905, had attended Catholic seminaries. Against this religious back-ground, the sacralization of republican versions of a French nation and a concomitant belief in a transcendent, mystical community of descent are more readily comprehensible. As one poet, published in the *Revue des deux mondes* in 1870, put it: 'Since our cause is holy, | Paris, once again a citadel, | Feels the beat in its great walls | Of its resuscitated French heart. | ...If you [Germany] make a tomb of her [France] | Where her race will disappear, | You will not dare to mark this place | With the shaft of your flag.'[34] Almost thirty years later, during the crisis years of the Dreyfus Affair, it is notable that many republicans were not deterred from collabo-rating with conservative, Catholic, and nationalist anti-Dreyfusards by prominent representations of a 'reactionary' and 'real' France of 'la terre et les morts'.[35]

---

[29] See the section on 'Nationalism and Religion' in Chapter 1.

[30] Cited in A. J. Hoover, *The Gospel of Nationalism: German Patriotic Preaching from Napoleon to Versailles* (Stuttgart, 1986), 30.

[31] See G. Krumeich and H. Lehmann (eds.), *'Gott mit uns': Nation, Religion und Gewalt im 19. und frühen 20 Jahrhundert* (Göttingen, 2000), 1–6.

[32] Jean-Marie Mayeur, in J. M. Mayeur and M. Rebérioux, *The Third Republic from its Origins to the Great War, 1871–1914* (Cambridge, 1987), 103–4.

[33] D. Thomson, *Democracy in France since 1870*, 5th edn. (Oxford, 1969), 144.

[34] Jeismann, *Das Vaterland der Feinde*, 201–3.

[35] R. Tombs, 'The Political Trajectory of Nationalism in Nineteenth-Century France', in U. v. Hirschhausen and J. Leonhard (eds.), *Nationalismen in Europa: West- und Osteuropa im Vergleich*

Widespread religiosity and a mystical quest for the soul of the nation appeared, however briefly, to have overcome long-standing antipathies between a clerical and anticlerical camp. Similar types of sacralization—either secular or formally religious—seem to have occurred in other Western European states, including those with strong confessional divisions, such as Switzerland, Belgium, and the Netherlands.[36]

The secular equivalent of religious quests for a national soul could be found within schools of thought such as Romanticism and Historicism, which came to dominate much of the intellectual history of the nineteenth century. Thus, even within the United Kingdom, which lacked a state-sponsored tradition of Romantic national historiography and which was sustained by a specifically imperial form of British nationalism, English, Scottish, Welsh, and Irish identities remained largely unquestioned and continued to imply the existence of communities of different descent.[37] The unification of territories, which had been officially sealed with the dissolution of a separate Irish parliament by the Act of Union in 1800, did little to undermine the perceived integrity of the four national groups which had consti-tuted the United Kingdom, notwithstanding persisting divisions within individual nations—such as that between Lowlanders and Highlanders in Scotland—and broad support for the British monarchy in all areas except Ireland.[38] Romantic writ-ers and historians, in particular, both explored and championed such national dis-tinctiveness, arguing that it demonstrated the efficacy of a liberal constitution and a successful empire, in which diverse groups could not only coexist, but also actively collaborate.[39] Consequently, scholars like Thomas Babington Macaulay, who helped to establish the predominant Whig school of academic history, tended to equate the fates of 'England', 'Britain', and the world, rather than believing that Englishness had been subsumed by a wider British identity or by 'civilization' itself. 'English liberties' and material prosperity were held to have benefited the rest of the United Kingdom, its colonies and, indeed, other states, but not at the expense of national particularity. 'The destinies of the human race were staked on the same cast

(Göttingen, 2001), 137–9. On the diverse culture of right-wing nationalism, see Z. Sternhell, 'The Political Culture of Nationalism', in R. Tombs (ed.), *Nationhood and Nationalism in France: From Boulangism to the Great War, 1889–1918* (London, 1991), 22–38. See also the sections on the 'revolutionary' and 'reactionary' nations in Chapter 2.

[36] O. Zimmer, *A Contested Nation: History, Memory and Nationalism in Switzerland, 1761–1891* (Cambridge, 2003), 124–32, 147–54, 163–95, 226–31; J. C. H. Blom and E. Lamberts (eds.), *History of the Low Countries* (London, 1999), 328–32, 417–19.

[37] On the lack of state-sponsored historical projects, see Mandler, ' "In the Olden Time": Romantic History and English National Identity, 1820–50', in L. Brockliss and D. Eastwood (eds.), *A Union of Multiple Identities: The British Isles, c.1750–c.1850* (Manchester, 1997), 79; on Britishness, see L. Colley, *Britons: Forging the Nation, 1707–1837* (New Haven, 1992); and on imperialism, Englishness, and Britishness, see K. Kumar, *The Making of English National Identity* (Cambridge, 2003). See also Chapter 14.

[38] See L. Colley, 'Britishness and Otherness: An Argument', *Journal of British Studies*, 31 (1992), 314, on conflicts between Lowlanders and Highlanders.

[39] C. Kinealy, *A Disunited Kingdom? England, Ireland, Scotland and Wales, 1800–1949* (Cambridge, 1999), especially 94–118.

with the freedom of the English people,' wrote the Whig historian in the *Edinburgh Review* in 1824, before continuing elsewhere that 'the history of England is emphatically the history of progress'.[40] Even critics of Macaulay and the Whigs, such as the imperialist scholar of state power John Robert Seeley, likewise refused to admit that English expansionism entailed a dilution or transformation of an English 'national character': 'We want land on which to plant English families where they may thrive and multiply without ceasing to be Englishmen.'[41] Popular historians, who harked back to the defiant, insular, 'Merry England' of the sixteenth century, shared similar assumptions, as did Radicals and Romantics, who, respectively, looked to 'Anglo-Saxon' freedoms before the 'Norman yoke' or sought to penetrate the mysteries of national folk tales and landscapes.[42] Of course, national-minded and Romantic writing was arguably more prominent in Wales, Scotland, and Ireland, where authors such as Walter Scott and Samuel Ferguson created heroes and narratives of their respective peoples, yet it could also be detected in the Arthurian poems of Alfred Tennyson and the Anglo-Saxon mythology of Charles Kingsley.[43] Indeed, Englishness had come, by the mid-nineteenth century, to rest on a rich Teutonic or Anglo-Saxon heritage, distinguishing it from the Gaelic or Celtic-influenced cultures in Wales, Scotland, and Ireland, which were explored by Matthew Arnold in his *Lectures on Celtic Literature* in 1867.[44] Some writers—including Lowland Scots such as Robert Knox—understood the distinction between Anglo-Saxons and Celts as an explicitly racial one, with each nationality having a different set of attributes as a subset of a race.[45] Most commentators were less explicit, ignoring the existence of 'Anglo-Saxons' and 'Celts' in all four 'nations' of the United Kingdom. However, they continued to agree with Scott as he asked them to 'let us remain as

[40] Macaulay, cited in B. Stuchtey, 'Literature, Liberty and Life of the Nation: British Historiography from Macaulay to Trevelyan', in S. Berger, M. Donovan, and K. Passmore (eds.), *Writing National Histories: Western Europe since 1800* (London, 1999), 32–3.

[41] Cited ibid. 37.

[42] On popular history-writing, see Mandler, ' "In the Olden Time": Romantic History and English National Identity, 1820–50', in Brockliss and Eastwood (eds.), *A Union of Multiple Identities*, 78–92; on Radical views of English history, see J. A. Epstein, *Radical Expression: Political Language, Ritual and Symbol in England, 1790–1850* (New York, 1994), and A. Goodwin, *The Friends of Liberty* (1979); on Romanticism, K. Robbins, *Nineteenth-Century Britain: Integration and Diversity* (Oxford, 1988), 48–62.

[43] On Wales, see P. Morgan, 'Early Victorian Wales and its Crisis of Identity', in Brockliss and Eastwood (eds.), *A Union of Multiple Identities*, 93–109, and G. A. Williams, 'Romanticism in Wales', in R. Porter and M. Teich (eds.), *Romanticism in National Context* (Cambridge, 1988), 9–36; on Scotland, see C. Kidd, 'Sentiment, Race and Revival: Scottish Identities in the Aftermath of Enlightenment', in Brockliss and Eastwood (eds.), *A Union of Multiple Identities*, 110–26, and C. Harvie, *Scotland and Nationalism: Scottish Society and Politics, 1707 to the Present*, 3rd edn. (London, 1998), 79–101; and on Ireland, R. Foster, 'Storylines: Narratives and Nationality in Nineteenth-Century Ireland', in G. Cubitt, *Imagining Nations* (Manchester, 1998), 38–56, and R. V. Comerford, *Ireland* (London, 2003).

[44] B. Melman, 'Claiming the Nation's Past: The Invention of an Anglo-Saxon Tradition', *Journal of Contemporary History*, 26 (1991), 575–95, and M. Oergel, 'The Redeeming Teuton: Nineteenth-Century Notions of the "Germanic" in England and Germany', in Cubitt, *Imagining Nations*, 75–91.

[45] For more on Knox, see Kidd, 'Sentiment, Race and Revival', in Brockliss and Eastwood (eds.), *A Union of Multiple Identities*, 117.

Nature made us, Englishmen, Irishmen and Scotchmen, with something of the impress of our several countries upon each!'[46] The different 'races' or 'nations' did not seem, in the words of the Scottish prime minister of Britain and rector of Edinburgh University Lord Rosebery, readily to have 'blended'.[47] Age-old cultures and communities of descent appeared to be facts of life.

Science lent respectability to such ethnic legends. Academic disciplines like medicine, biology, zoology, anthropology, and ethnography seemed to have established beyond doubt that 'races' were definable groups with different sets of characteristics, akin to species or sub-species of animals. 'Race', as the British prime minister Benjamin Disraeli put it, 'is all!'[48] Although the words 'people', 'nation', and 'race' were increasingly equated during the course of the nineteenth century, there were still disputes about the origins and mixing of races, and about the coincidence of nationality and race. In Scotland, for instance, the anatomist Knox repeatedly denounced Scottish Highlanders and Irish immigrants in his widely read book on *The Races of Men* (1850) as backward and inferior 'Celts', compared to 'Saxons' from the Lowlands like himself.[49] Conversely, in France, leading anthropologists such as Paul Broca and William Frederick Edwards argued that French territories had been settled by a number of races, with extensive intermarriage between them, often to the benefit of the nations which they had helped to constitute.[50] Nonetheless, most scholars, including Knox and Broca, continued to emphasize the significance of race within national communities, despite disagreeing about the actual and desirable extent of racial mixing in specific countries. Many assumed that a single race had always—or had for a long time—dominated their own national group. Accordingly, a moderate liberal anthropologist like Rudolf Virchow, confronted with the claim of his French counterpart Armand de Quatrefages after the Franco-Prussian war that Germans were largely 'Finnish' rather than 'Aryan', immediately rejected the idea and set up a survey of millions of schoolchildren in order to prove his point.[51] When the results of the survey demonstrated that some Germans were blond, blue-eyed 'long-heads', in the popular terminology of the Swedish phrenologist Anders Retzius, whilst others were dark-haired, brown-eyed 'broad-heads' and the majority were of 'mixed' race, Virchow went on believing in the utility of racial distinctions and maintained that Prussians in northern and eastern Germany—the backbone of the nation—were Aryan.[52] Even before the 'Aryan myth' had been established

[46] Scott, cited ibid. 112.

[47] Rosebery in 1882, cited in Robbins, *Nineteenth-Century Britain*, 5.

[48] Cited in MacMaster, *Racism in Europe*, 14.

[49] Ibid. 13–15. Also, C. Kidd, 'Sentiment, Race and Revival', in Brockliss and Eastwood, *A Union of Multiple Identities*, 117.

[50] G. Mosse, *Die Geschichte des Rassismus in Europa* (Frankfurt am Main, 1990), 111.

[51] Ibid. 112–15; Weindling, *Health, Race and German Politics between National Unification and Nazism, 1870–1945* (Cambridge, 1989), 48–9.

[52] L. Poliakov, *Der arische Mythos: Zu den Quellen von Rassismus und Nationalismus* (Hamburg, 2000), 296–9.

by early nineteenth-century philologists, who postulated that a migration of Aryans from India to Europe explained similarities between Sanskrit, Greek, Romance, and Germanic languages, many European thinkers, including Carl von Linné, Immanuel Kant, and François Marie Arouét Voltaire, had divided human- ity into a hierarchy of superior and inferior races.[53] The work of Charles Darwin, which made biology into the most modern of sciences with the publication of *The Origin of Species* in 1859, added further weight to such racial distinctions, not least by undermining Christians' belief in a godly creation and a common humanity. Darwin himself talked of the attributes of different human races, placing them at the end of a long evolutionary chain, in which 'progress' had depended on the survival of those species best adapted to their environments.[54] Popularizers and followers of the British naturalist such as Francis Galton, Karl Pearson, Georges Vacher de Lapouge, Ernst Haeckel, Alfred Ploetz, and August Weismann ensured that social extrapolations of Darwinism were translated into the 'sciences' of eugenics and racial hygiene, which were designed to improve the genetic stock of the nation. All such projects, whose premisses—contrary to their conclusions— were rarely contested, reinforced contemporaries' certainty that, in Renan's words, 'the inequality of the races is clear'.[55] Few doubted that white Europeans were racially superior, that each nation was composed of an identifiable race or races, and that such racial composition was related to the success, health, or efficiency of the nation-state.

Looking back from the standpoint of 1908, an official in the British Colonial Office was unable to explain the persistence of racism and ethnic legends: 'Contrary to what might have been hoped and expected, and undoubtedly was hoped and expected half a century ago, the growth of democracy and science and education has not diminished but increased antipathies of race and colour.'[56] This racial antagonism derived, especially in Western Europe, from the experience of empire and from a fear of the 'dangerous classes' produced by industrialization. The latter was linked to complex processes of democratization, economic trans- formation, and urban differentiation, as large numbers of middle-class burghers moved to suburbs or to 'respectable' areas of towns and cities. These burghers' liberal understanding of markets and politics undermined many of the old supports of a society of orders, where distinctions seemed natural or divinely sanctioned. In such circumstances, in which Samuel Smiles's injunctions of cleanliness, industry, thrift, and self-improvement had gained new force, the perceived squalor, moral dissipation, laziness, and criminality of the labouring classes suggested to some observers that they were a race apart. 'Beside this civilised society, there are [racial varieties of classes]...which possess neither intelligence, responsibility nor moral sentiment...whose spirit finds no enlightenment nor

---

[53] I. Geiss, *Geschichte des Rassismus* (Frankfurt am Main, 1988), 148–50.
[54] Ibid. 170–1.   [55] Cited in Poliakov, *Der arische Mythos*, 307.
[56] Cited in MacMaster, *Racism in Europe*, 4.

consolation in religion,' wrote the French psychiatrist Bénédict Augustin Morel, whose work during the mid-nineteenth century gave credence to the notion of racial 'degeneration' (*dégénérescence*): 'Some of these varieties have been rightly designated as the *dangerous classes*.'[57] When such anxieties were combined with disillusionment about the declining fortunes of one's own class, as in the case of the spurned and impoverished aristocrat Arthur de Gobineau, they could encourage a rereading of national and European history in racial terms. Throughout the continent, he lamented in his *Essai sur l'inégalité des races humaines* (1853–5), Aryan elites had been corrupted by mixing with indigenous, yellow-skinned 'Finns'. Each nation had squandered its noble, Aryan heritage and had become degenerate: 'If one applies the term "degeneration" to a nation, then it means that this nation no longer has the same inner worth as before, because the same blood no longer flows in its veins.'[58] In many contemporaries' accounts, which—like those of Gobineau—were indicative of the confusion, uncertainty, and social division caused by economic change, this degeneration was not merely the consequence of interbreeding with the 'masses', but also with Jews, who served as a scapegoat for the ills of industrial society and as an archetype of an ethnically exclusive outsider group. In the words of Édouard Drumont, whose *La France juive* (1886) counted more than 200 editions by 1914, French Aryans and Jewish Semites were 'personifications of races that are distinct and irremediably hostile to each other'.[59] Barely challenged, if not always strongly supported, such racial mythologies tended to reinforce the impression, by creating hereditary enemies of the nation, that ethnicity and nationality were identical.

Europe's contact with the wider world had for a long time reinforced assumptions of racial superiority, but they had been countered by awe and fear of the unknown and exotic, and by a Christian belief in a common humanity. From the mid-eighteenth century onwards, as Enlightenment science and philosophy began to undermine important elements of Christian faith, and as imperialism brought Europeans into closer proximity with the Americas, Africa, and the Far East, at the same time as demonstrating the military and economic ascendancy of European states, racism became prevalent, particularly in those countries on the Atlantic seaboard which were most closely involved in colonization and the slave trade.[60] Early nineteenth-century France showed how long-held assumptions, economic self-interest, and state-led imperialism combined to implant the unquestioned 'truths' of racial difference and hierarchy. In 1789, some revolutionaries, such as the playwright and champion of women's rights Marie Gouze, had opposed slavery, which was abolished, and had declared the nobility of black slaves. After a bloody rebellion in Saint-Domingue in 1791, however, Gouze

---

[57] Cited in D. Pick, *Faces of Degeneration: A European Disorder, c.1848–c.1918* (Cambridge, 1989), 52. [58] Gobineau, cited in Mosse, *Die Geschichte des Rassismus in Europa*, 78.

[59] Cited in MacMaster, *Racism in Europe*, 95.

[60] This was true even in the Netherlands and Belgium, where imperialism remained a marginal part of political discourse. See Chapter 5.

quickly reversed her position, writing that 'men were not born for chains, but you prove that they are necessary'.[61] By 1802, with the reimposition of slavery by Napoleon Bonaparte, who was notoriously contemptuous of blacks, the play-wright put forward the argument that slavery had actually civilized those who were subject to it, saving mankind 'from a horrible primitive situation where men not only sold each other but also ate each other'.[62] Debates about race during the first half of the nineteenth century generally pitted similar depictions of blacks, constantly replenished by travellers' tales and planters' polemics, against the more humane arguments of abolitionists. Yet even the opponents of slavery usually assumed the existence of racial differences and inequalities. 'We do not say that the Negroes are geniuses ... but we say that it is false to make them into idiots, and it signifies a lack of brains to build little physiological theories on whether their facial angles are more or less acute, and thus to deny them nearly all intelligence,' wrote one of the principal French abolitionists, Victor Schloecher, in 1840.[63] This sense of white superiority arguably remained widespread for at least a century after the abolition of slavery in France in 1848—a point seized upon by the satirist Honoré Daumier at the time, in a cartoon entitled 'Les Philanthropes du jour', which portrayed an abolitionist kicking the posterior of a black servant with ludicrous vigour. 'I have forbidden you to call me Master,' ran the caption: 'Know that all men are brothers, animal!'[64] With the partition of Africa and the expan-sion of European empires in the late nineteenth century, the commonplaces of racial segregation and categorization, typified by labels such as 'raton', 'bicot', 'wog', and 'nigger', passed back from the colonies to the metropolis and came to characterize both sets of societies, despite the small number of blacks—perhaps 5,000 in France and 20,000 in Britain—in Europe before 1914. Although it is true that a perceived equality of status sometimes overrode such racial barriers, it did not remove a presumption of racial difference, as was apparent when the Prince of Wales insisted at a garden party in 1881 that King Kalakaua of Hawaii should have precedence over the Crown Prince of Germany: 'Either the brute is a king, or he's a common or garden nigger; and if the latter, what's he doing here?'[65] Most contemporaries of the Prince of Wales, who were less interested in court pro-tocol or in the necessity of maintaining fictions of colonial 'self-rule', would have agreed with Edward Wood, who later—as Viceroy of India—insisted on treating Mahatma Gandhi as an equal, that the 'white man' naturally ruled over 'inferior races' of 'black people' around the globe.[66] When the Tory leader Arthur Balfour objected in the same parliamentary debate in 1910—about the administration of Egypt—that it was 'not a question of superiority or inferiority' of races, most MPs

[61] Cited in W. B. Cohen, *The French Encounter with Africans: White Response to Blacks, 1530–1880* (Indiana, 1980), 183.   [62] Ibid.
[63] Ibid. 198.   [64] Ibid. 208.
[65] Cited in D. Cannadine, *Ornamentalism: How the British saw their Empire* (London, 2001), 8. The argument presented here counters Cannadine's own case about status.
[66] Cited ibid. 123.

in the House of Commons gave voice to their disbelief.[67] White Europeans, it was held, were different, by descent, from the rest.

Contemporaries' encounters with colonialism, their experiences of industrialization, and their understanding of science appeared to prove that heredity was an actuating principle of modern societies. Intellectuals and clerics—as well as other less reputable 'mystics'—seemed to provide compelling proofs, in addition to those furnished by age-old local, familial, and peasant traditions, that communities of descent were still relevant. Consequently, as nations became the focus of state activity and communication, the majority of Europeans, from both East and West, appear to have assumed that ethnicity was integral to the nation-state. Such assumptions became especially transparent during the 'national' wars of the nineteenth century, which increasingly relied on the *levée en masse*.[68] They were reinforced, more often than they were challenged, by the advent of a mass press which pitted one 'tribe' against another, as the British Liberal John Atkinson Hobson pointed out in his study of jingoism in 1901.[69] Ethnicity—or descent—was rarely brought into question as one of the foundations of nationhood, even though its precise forms and its significance were sometimes disputed. Rather, ethnic types of belonging coexisted with other kinds of affiliation to, and integration within, the nation-state. In nineteenth-century Europe, voluntary or civic forms of attachment to the nation were not seen to contradict feelings of ethnic belonging, since virtually all citizens accepted that their nation was a natural and primordial entity.

CITIZENSHIP, CIVIC PARTICIPATION, AND LIBERALISM

The French revolutionary model, which has exercised such influence on the historiography of nationalism, seemed to decree that a finite and active citizenry of a clearly defined territory had voluntarily constituted a national, representative system of government, which it elected and controlled, in order to run its affairs, protect its rights, and describe its duties.[70] Such civic involvement is believed to have precluded the more exclusive and virulent forms of ethnic nationalism, which purportedly characterized Central, Eastern, and, even, Southern Europe during the late nineteenth and early twentieth centuries.[71] Western European states, it is held, enacted open citizenship laws on the principle of residence and

---

[67] Ibid.   [68] See, especially, Jeismann, *Das Vaterland der Feinde*.

[69] J. A. Hobson, *The Psychology of Jingoism* (London, 1901).

[70] For more on this, see the section on 'The Revolutionary Nation' in Chapter 2.

[71] The principal recent texts are R. Brubaker, *Citizenship and Nationhood in France and Germany* (Cambridge, Mass., 1992) and L. Greenfeld, *Nationalism: Five Roads to Modernity* (Cambridge, Mass., 1992). In a few cases, for example in the Low Countries, civic involvement does seem to have militated against ethnic forms of nationalism, although not excluding them completely. See Chapter 5.

territory (*jus soli*); they were dominated by self-confident middle classes which succeeded in co-opting other social groups rather than resorting defensively to extreme nationalism, frequently in conjunction with the nobility, in order to safeguard their own position of power; and they retained the emancipatory, liberal, and inclusive origins of nationalism, which extended back to 1789 and beyond. This section challenges the most important components of the case for a distinct 'civic' form of nationhood.

The main elements of the French revolutionary paradigm were not realized before 1914. Citizenship was a case in point. Thus, France's Napoleonic Code Civil gave citizenship automatically to the children of a French father, wherever they were born, but not to children born in France of a foreign father, who had to 'recover' or 'claim' their French citizenship at the age of majority. If they failed to do so, they were treated as foreigners. Later changes to the law in 1848 and 1851 extended the definition of *jus soli* in order to prevent the offspring of foreigners evading military service.[72] When the matter was debated once more in the 1880s, the question of military conscription again proved decisive in applying *jus soli* to those foreigners who had both been born in France and remained there at the age of majority. Yet much of the debate had concentrated on the more 'modern' principle of *jus sanguinis*, as Camille Sée made clear on behalf of the Council of State, which initiated the bill: 'Nationality must depend on blood, on descent, [not on] the accidental fact of birth in our territory.'[73] 'Why revive this feudal principle of nationality based on birth in the territory,' asked Sée, 'when all of Europe, except for England and Portugal, tells us that nationality depends on blood, and when the progress of science permits an individual to move in a few hours from one end of Europe to the other?'[74] In fact, citizenship in the rest of Europe, even more so than in France, was governed largely by practical considerations such as poor relief and was largely ignored by contemporary politicians and citizens alike.[75] In the German lands, citizenship was determined by deportation treaties between individual states until the North German Confederation ruled in its constitution of 1867 that all citizens of a member state were to enjoy equal rights of citizenship in other states of the Bund. The states continued to retain jurisdiction over naturalization—usually still granted on grounds of residency, not descent—until 1913, when the Minister of the Interior of any German state gained the power of veto over naturalizations in another.[76] Prior to the 1890s, when nationalists began to agitate about immigration into the Reich and about the loss of German emigrants' nationality, citizenship laws barely merited discussion in the public sphere. In the absence of widespread immigration and foreign

---

[72] Brubaker, *Citizenship and Nationhood*, 89–94.   [73] Cited ibid. 95.   [74] Ibid.

[75] Exceptions included Switzerland, which had an unusually large number of non-Swiss residents, and, to a lesser extent, parts of the Ottoman Empire, where the definition of citizenship was integral to the definition of new nation-states in the Balkans. See Chapters 6 and 7.

[76] A. Fahrmeir, *Citizens and Aliens: Foreigners and the Law in Britain and the German States, 1789–1870* (Oxford, 2000), 19–43. See also Chapter 3.

travel, citizenship and the laws which regulated it became neither a test nor a symbol of nationality. Foreign immigrants accounted for only 0.6 per cent of the German Empire's population, 0.4 per cent of that of Britain, and less than 1 per cent of those of Austria, Italy, and Sweden. Naturalization, which involved several hundred per annum in most countries, or the purchase of passports for travel abroad concerned only a small number of citizens.[77] Those who were involved repeatedly registered their annoyance at the lack of regularity and order in each state's arrangements. Arguably, the main reason for this disorder was the peripheral nature of citizenship in most states' affairs.

In nineteenth-century Europe, political participation was more significant than citizenship per se. In most states, the two did not coincide. In the German lands, for instance, *Staatsangehörigkeit* or simple citizenship was distinct from *Staatsbürgerschaft* or the enjoyment of political rights. Citizenship in an active, political sense was nearly always exercised within a social or political hierarchy, given the rarity of universal manhood suffrage and the continuing significance of local politics, which usually involved a mixture of notable office-holders, exclusive corporations, and restricted franchises. Until the 1890s, most states' electorates were made up of less than half of the adult male population. Only the Third Republic, the German Empire, the Swiss republic and the monarchies of Serbia, Spain, Greece, and Bulgaria exceeded such a figure at an earlier date. Denmark, Portugal, Hungary, the Netherlands, and Romania remained at or below this threshold as late as 1914.[78] Habitually, many citizens were ignored because of their lack of property or education. In Italy, for example, it was estimated in 1861 that 75 per cent of adults were illiterate, and about 90 per cent in Calabria, Basilicata, and Sardinia. By 1911, the figure had dropped to 38 per cent, but still remained at more than 65 per cent in parts of the south.[79] This lack of *civiltà*, or cultural accomplishment, was routinely used to justify political exclusion.[80] In such circumstances, the political nation was only infrequently portrayed as a sovereign, self-governing people, and civil society was hardly ever seen as a voluntary collective of free and equal individuals, associating on matters of public interest. What is more, where such a politically active and relatively egalitarian civil society did exist, there was no guarantee that civic participation would foster official, inclusive, or benign forms of nationalism. Thus, a comparatively dense network of associations in Catalonia gave rise both to the cultural renaissance of Catalanism (*renaixença*) in the nineteenth century, opposition to judicial 'centralization' in 1888, and the founding of the Lliga Regionalista, which came to dominate Catalan politics, in 1901.[81] Similarly, Bohemia witnessed an unprecedented burgeoning of associations, with 10,547 registered clubs by 1888, yet many of these worked against an official 'Austrian' identity, and a significant number promoted radical, divisive, ethnic nationalism, either German or

---

[77] Ibid. 217.
[78] R. J. Goldstein, *Political Repression in Nineteenth-Century Europe* (London, 1983), 4–5.
[79] N. Doumanis, *Italy* (London, 2001), 101–2.   [80] See Chapter 13.
[81] See S. Payne, 'Catalan and Basque Nationalism', *Journal of Contemporary History*, 6 (1971), 19–27.

Czech.[82] In certain conditions, political participation and civic involvement seemed to have led to a radicalization of nationalist politics. This was a pattern that could be observed in the German Empire, which combined a growing tally of radical right-wing leagues, clubs, and parties, universal manhood suffrage, and the greatest density of associations in Europe, with an estimated one in two German citizens belonging to one by 1870.[83]

The sociology of such 'civic' nationalism yields few clues as to its content. Although middle-class supporters of nationalist causes were often preponderant, they could be found in the ranks of both moderates and extremists. Hermann Bahr, the celebrated Austrian writer, was not alone in noting his father's amazement that his own son could be expelled from Vienna University because of a Pan-German speech at a Wagner commemoration in 1883.[84] In some countries, nationalist movements were composed largely of peasants or nobles. The former was the case in Denmark and Norway, the latter in Russia and, especially, Hungary.[85] In the 'lands of the Crown of St Stephen', the nobility had created and led the 'first reform movement' of 1825–48, and it had been instrumental in establishing the Dual Monarchy in 1867, in which Hungary gained its own government and retained its own diet, with control over everything except foreign and defence policy.[86] Half of the new regime's ministers were noble. In 1861, 61 per cent of deputies were noble, dropping to 41 per cent by 1914.[87] The middle nobility had played a major part in the liberal nationalist opposition to the conservative large landowners during the 1830s and 1840s, calling amongst other things for the abolition of serfdom, equality before the law, the creation of constitutional guarantees against absolutism, the extension of the diet franchise to include all property-owners, and the reform of the county system to include burghers and peasants as well as nobles.[88] These liberals under Ferenc Deák and József Eötvös went on to enact legislation which pledged that, 'in accordance with the fundamental principles of the constitution, all Hungarian citizens [are part of] a nation in the political sense, the one and indivisible Hungarian nation, in which every citizen of the fatherland is a member who enjoys equal rights, regardless of the national group to which he belongs'.[89]

---

[82]   On the number of associations, see D. Sayer, 'The Language of Nationality and the Nationality of Language: Prague, 1780–1920', *Past and Present*, 153 (1996), 202–3; on radical nationalist associations, see M. Cornwall, 'The Struggle on the Czech-German Language Border, 1880–1940', *English Historical Review*, 109 (1994), 914–22. Also, see the section on 'Nationalism in the Bohemian Lands' in Chapter 9.

[83]   D. Blackbourn, *Germany, 1780–1918* (London, 1997), 278. Stefan Berger also makes this point in Chapter 3.

[84]   Cited in R. Okey, *The Habsburg Monarchy, c.1765–1918* (London, 2001), 284.

[85]   See Chapters 9, 10, and 15.

[86]   For more on both reformism and Magyarization, see the section on 'Magyar Nationalism and Hungary' in Chapter 9.   [87]   Okey, op. cit., 315.

[88]   I. Z. Denes, 'The Value Systems of Liberals and Conservatives in Hungary, 1830–1848', *Historical Journal*, 36 (1993), 825–50.

[89]   Law XLIV of 1868, cited in J. K. Hoensch, *A History of Modern Hungary, 1867–1994*, 2nd edn. (London, 1996), 28.

By the 1880s, such nobles had lost much of their reforming zeal, limiting the franchise to 6 per cent of the population and collaborating in rigorous policies of 'Magyarization'. In this respect, the intransigent declaration of Deszó Bánffy, the prime minister between 1890 and 1895, that 'without chauvinism it is impossible to found the unitary state' differed little from that of his moderate liberal successor, Kálmán Széll, who proclaimed that the only 'categorical imperative [was] the Magyar state-idea...which every citizen should acknowledge...and subject himself unconditionally to.... The supremacy and the hegemony of the Magyars is fully justified.'[90] Although the economic position of the middle nobility had altered, with a greater degree of landed indebtedness, many had been incorporated within the expanding Hungarian state bureaucracy. If anything, their status had been enhanced, reflected in the use of the term *dzsentri*, which had been borrowed from the English word 'gentry' to depict middle-ranking nobles as the backbone of the nation. Imitation by other social groups could be detected in the emergence by the 1890s of the expression 'gentlemanly middle-class'. The shifting role of the gentry and nobility within nationalist politics in Hungary— from liberalism to conservatism—seemed to have little to do with their social position. Certainly, the notion of a 'defensive' social alliance between weak middle-class groups and a threatened nobility, which in itself supposedly had the potential to produce radical nationalism, needs to be modified in the Hungarian case, as in many others.

Irrespective of the social background of its 'carriers', or the intermediary role played by intellectuals, nationalism in Central and Eastern Europe, in common with parts of Scandinavia and Western Europe, retained strong traces of its emancipatory origins. It remained, in other words, markedly 'civic'. In spite of its particularity as a result of partition by Prussia, Austria, and Russia in 1795, the case of Poland, which was championed by liberals throughout the continent, illustrates aspects of national liberation that were common to Belgium, Norway, Ireland, Italy, Germany, the Czech lands, Hungary, Slovenia, Croatia, Serbia, Bulgaria, Romania, Montenegro, Albania, and Greece. Polish nationalists, despite being widely seen as eternal romantics yearning for an unattainable goal in quixotic fashion, were not in a position which was conducive to liberal fantasies of emancipation, for they came, like their Hungarian counterparts, from an extensive nobility or *szlachta*, which predisposed them towards conservatism and alliances with their fellow German and Russian aristocrats. Moreover, they were forced to agitate under the repressive conditions of neo-absolutism, a restrictive monarchy or tsarist autocracy, which tended to radicalize political opposition. Nevertheless, throughout the long nineteenth century, Polish nationalists maintained a platform of political, constitutional, and social reform. Consequently, when

---

[90] Cited in Peter Sugar, 'Government and Minorities in Austria-Hungary: Different Policies with the Same Result', in id., *East European Nationalism, Politics and Religion* (Aldershot, 1999), 34–5.

the diet of the Grand Duchy of Poznan met for the first time in 1827, a strong liberal faction demanded a responsible ministry, full control of administration, a separation of functions, and virtual autonomy for Polish lands within Prussia via a personal union with the Hohenzollern crown.[91] The following decades were characterized by a policy of 'organic work' or social reform within the narrow constraints set by the Prussian and Austro-Hungarian authorities. 'Society aims to better each individual,' as one reformer put it: 'That is our task, not revolution.'[92] The history of the Polish lands in the Russian Empire was much less stable, marked by risings in 1830–1 and 1863, but here, too, there was liberalism and, especially after 1863, reform.

Notwithstanding greater radicalism within the National Democratic movement (*Endecja*) from the 1890s onwards, the broad liberal and emancipatory aims of Polish nationalism were maintained until the First World War. 'Nationality is primarily a *psychological* fact and is based on the free and unforced decision of the individual,' wrote one correspondent in the *Przeglad Wszechpolski*: '[It] cannot be based on any external characteristic: place of birth, ethnographic identification or accidental political dominion. Whoever considers himself a Pole, is one'.[93] This sense that an attachment to the Polish cause or mission was sufficient grounds for being defined a Pole was shared by prominent National Democrats such as Jan Ludwik Poplawski and Roman Dmowski, who wrote in his *Thoughts of a Modern Pole* (1903), that 'to be a Pole does not mean just to speak Polish or to feel close to other Poles, but to value the Polish nation above all else'.[94] The imperative remained to create and defend as inclusive a national group as possible, to improve its living conditions, heighten its awareness, and to break free of foreign oppression, not least by favouring constitutional safeguards and parliamentary control of government. 'Our path is the further development of the idea of freedom, equality and brotherhood, the death of absolutism, exploitation and privilege, in whatever forms they appear; it is the continued struggle for independence, the firm, ruthless and inexorable defence of our national rights,' proclaimed Dmowski, at the demonstration in Warsaw to mark the centenary of the Polish constitution of 1791.[95] Even the Polish Socialist Party, founded in 1892, bore the imprint of national liberation, despite criticizing the nobility for overseeing 'stagnation' and prioritizing social reform as a means of emancipation. The first words of its programme reminded members that 'one hundred years have passed since the moment when the Polish Republic, fallen upon by three neighbouring powers, proved incapable of creating

---

[91] W. Hagen, 'National Solidarity and Organic Work in Prussian Poland, 1815–1914', *Journal of Modern History*, 44 (1972), 41.   [92] Karol Marcinkowski cited ibid. 42.

[93] Cited in B. A. Porter, 'Who is a Pole and Where is Poland? Territory and Nation in the Rhetoric of Polish National Democracy before 1905', *Slavic Review*, 51 (1992), 646.   [94] Ibid.

[95] Cited in B. A. Porter, 'Democracy and Discipline in Late Nineteenth-Century Poland', *Journal of Modern History*, 71 (1999), 360. Porter's article, heavily influenced by Foucault, stresses the authoritarian elements of Dmowski's rhetoric, arguably without putting forward convincing evidence and without paying sufficient attention to the imperatives of a society under occupation.

from its bosom enough strength to resist the invaders.'[96] As in Bohemia, the acknowledged necessity of 'national emancipation' pushed socialists in the Polish lands away from the doctrinaire internationalism of Marxists and towards cooperation with liberal nationalists.[97]

The question was, however: to what extent were liberals themselves predisposed towards 'civic' ends such as voluntarism and self-determination? The presence of liberals in government or in a national assembly did not necessarily prevent authoritarianism or preclude an expansionist foreign policy. Many liberals like Alexis de Tocqueville were wary of the 'mob' and continued to advocate property qualifications for voters and a panoply of measures—including organized religion—to control the populace.[98] Other liberals, who came to support the introduction of universal manhood suffrage and more direct forms of government, were frequently pushed into policies that they considered unwise, intolerant, or aggressive. This was true of a great number of liberals across Europe, who felt themselves buffeted by the vacillating demands of 'public opinion' and by the manoeuvring of more populist parties to their left. Even without such public pressure, the civic or political participation of liberals was not automatically to be equated with moderate nationalism, not least because principles such as the rule of the majority, the indivisible nature of sovereignty, the need of a *lingua franca*, belief in progress and civilization, and a commitment to a viable nation-state were all likely to cause conflict in areas of mixed ethnic settlement.

Like many other areas of nineteenth-century Europe, including Ireland, Brittany, and Flanders, Bohemia and Moravia demonstrated how liberalism was, in national terms, double-edged.[99] In the 1840s, liberal nationalists in Germany, encouraged by German-Bohemians like Franz Schuselka, began to contend that 'Bohemia was a German imperial province' in 'its education, its public intercourse, its political and municipal constitutions', which had developed within 'a part of German Austria' under a German king.[100] According to this reading of history, the Czechs, who were still to be found amongst the peasantry but allegedly not among the landed and urban elites, lacked sufficient culture and numbers to become a fully-fledged nation. During the revolution of 1848, Czech leaders such as František Palacký were invited to participate in the

---

[96] Ibid. 368.

[97] On Czech socialists, see T. V. Thomas, 'Bohumil Smeral and the Czech Question, 1904–14', *Journal of Contemporary History*, 11 (1976), 79–98, and J. F. N. Bradley, 'Czech Nationalism and Socialism in 1905', *American Slavic and East European Review*, 19 (1960), 74–84.

[98] L. Siedentop, *Tocqueville* (Oxford, 1994), 1–19, 96–112; A. Jardin, *Tocqueville: A Biography* (New York, 1988), 216–20.

[99] Much of what follows is broadly in line with arguments put forward in Chapter 9.

[100] An article in the Augsburg *Allgemeine Zeitung*, 9 Oct. 1844, possibly by Schuselka, cited in H. LeCaine Agnew, 'Dilemmas of Liberal Nationalism: Czechs and Germans in Bohemia and the Revolution of 1848', in S. Ramet, J. R. Felak, and H. J. Ellison (eds.), *Nations and Nationalisms in East-Central Europe, 1806–1948* (Bloomington, 2002), 57.

Frankfurt Assembly, as inhabitants of an historical territory of the German Bund and the Holy Roman Empire, but not as 'Czechs'. Palacký refused the invitation, because he was 'not a German, at least, I do not feel myself to be one.'[101] From the point of view of Czech liberals, their German counterparts sought to ignore the national character and political rights of the Czech people. 'We Czechs do not have the ambition in the end to be a parasitic growth on the noble trunk of the German oak so that we could thus prevent its growth and healthy and free development', declared František Ladislav Rieger sarcastically at the meeting of the delegation from the Frankfurt Committee of Fifty and the Czech National Committee on 29 March 1848.[102]

Yet the alternative was not obvious, when seen from the standpoint of nineteenth-century political theory and practice, given that Czech liberals continued until 1914 to doubt the viability of an independent Czech nation-state of—at most—six million inhabitants.[103] In the end, conservatives, liberals and socialists alike decided that a federal structure within the Austro-Hungarian Empire was the best solution, preferable to domination by Germans from the West or Russians from the East, as Palacký spelled out in his *Gedenkblätter* of 1874: 'You know that in the South-East of Europe, along the borders of the Russian Empire, there live many nations, markedly different in origin, language, history and habits—Slavs, Romanians, Magyars and Germans, not to mention Greeks, Turks and Albanians—none of whom is strong enough by itself to resist successfully for all time the superior neighbour in the East.' 'They can do so only if a single and firm tie unites them all,' he went on: 'Truly, if the Austrian Empire had not existed for ages, it would be necessary, in the interest of Europe, in the interest of mankind itself, to create it with all speed.'[104] Edvard Beneš, the later premier of Czechoslovakia, made similar points in his doctoral dissertation in 1908.[105] Even within the Habsburg Empire, both old and new Czech liberals found it difficult to accept the rights and interests of Bohemia and Moravia's large German-speaking minority, much less to design constitutional mechanisms to protect those rights and interests in an era of extended franchises.[106] Tellingly, it was not liberals but social democrats like Bohumil Smeral, and his Austrian-German equivalents Karl Renner and Otto Bauer, who devised the most plausible and well-known remedy in the form of 'national', or ethnic, electoral colleges or 'corporations', invested with limited powers of taxation to give them the means to look after the divisive issues of culture and education.[107] Across the

---

[101] Palacký, 6 Apr. 1848, cited ibid. 63.   [102] Ibid. 64.

[103] See Sugar, 'Government and Minorities in Austria-Hungary', 21–52.

[104] Cited in J. Remak, 'The Healthy Invalid: How Doomed the Habsburg Empire', *Journal of Modern History*, 41 (1969), 129.   [105] Ibid. 141.

[106] On the Young Czechs, see S. B. Winters, 'The Young Czech Party, 1874–1914: An Appraisal', *Slavic Review*, 28 (1969), 426–44.

[107] T. V. Thomas, 'Bohumil Smeral and the Czech Question, 1904–1914', *Journal of Contemporary History*, 11 (1976), 79–98.

continent, debates about the nation, even in new states like Serbia, stayed predominantly on liberal ground, but answers to the national question remained elusive.[108]

In most areas of Europe, liberal parties and institutions continued to dictate the main terms of nationalist discourse and politics. New nation-states in the East such as Greece and Serbia witnessed the rapid growth of civil society and the development of a liberal political culture. The 'eclipse' of liberal parties by social democratic, confessional, and peasant parties, which was as much a feature of French, Dutch, and Danish politics as of those of Eastern Europe, certainly implied a revision of liberalism, but not its replacement, since many new politicians adhered to liberal tenets. Constitutional safeguards, a more or less free press, representative government, and parliamentary scrutiny characterized most of the European polities in which nationalism emerged and endured. Yet such liberalism, despite widening political participation and civic involvement, failed to create uniformity or to establish a 'voluntary' conception of national belonging and activity which might have ruled out ethnic or 'organic' myths. Many elements of Europe's liberal traditions that were to prove critical for the development and differentiation of nationalism remained contested or undefined, from disputes about the necessity of assimilation to those concerning the desirability of parliamentary government. The oppression of national minorities and the exacerbation of conflicts between nationalities and nation-states frequently took place in the interstices of such varied liberal principles and frameworks. On some occasions, such oppression and conflicts seemed to be beyond the scope of liberalism altogether, with assumptions about national interests and identity going unchallenged.

Most nineteenth-century liberals, including those in Western Europe, continued to believe in ethnic myths. 'Civic' traditions, which were in some respects more salient in the East and South than in the West, failed to prevent the exploitation of ethnic antipathies. Indeed, they frequently promoted it. Civic involvement and political participation, which appeared to recall the voluntary, egalitarian contractualism of *philosophes* such as Rousseau, in fact were usually predicated on social inequality, marked distinctions between classes, limited franchises and political rights, ethnic forms of citizenship, and widespread assumptions about 'progress', 'civilization', and the superiority of a national mission. *Ipso facto* there was little to stop proponents of such civic traditions espousing extreme forms of nationalism. Certainly, they had not created—and had not intended to create—a politically voluntary type of nation-state, such as had been presaged in the Enlightenment and half carried out during the French Revolution. Voluntaristic or emancipatory liberal principles did continue to exist and to spread, but they were not largely restricted to Western Europe. The idea of a voluntary, civic nation typical of the West, but not of

[108] For the rapid development of civil society and political liberalism in Serbia, which had one of the widest franchises in Europe by the 1900s, see S. K. Pavlowitch, *Serbia: The History behind the Name* (London, 2002), 26–92.

other areas of the continent, arguably reveals more about the historians of the mid-twentieth than of the citizens and institutions of the nineteenth century.

EXPLAINING NINETEENTH-CENTURY NATIONALISM

In much of Europe, nationalism fundamentally altered the conduct, scope, impact, and framework of politics, both domestic and foreign, creating a new and ultimate repositary of power and successfully demanding unprecedented degrees of loyalty and self-sacrifice. It became so significant because it involved not merely the imagining of an extensive, national cultural group, but the formation, maintenance, and modification of nation-states as structures of power, competing with other institutions and interests—multi-ethnic empires, churches, aristocracies, provinces, cities, guilds, international-minded socialist parties and unions—for political ascendancy. The emergence and rise of nationalism to a position of ascendancy was neither inevitable nor uniform. Thus, there were striking differences between radical nationalists such as the French anti-Semite Maurice Barrès or the Pan-German Ernst Hasse, who saw an unchanging *Volk* surrounded by internal and external enemies, and moderate nationalists like the German left liberal Friedrich Naumann or the French socialist Jean Jaurès, who argued that French political traditions and culture placed the Third Republic temporarily in the vanguard of world history, before nation-states were superseded altogether during an age of socialism.[109] Furthermore, there were disparities between areas such as Slovakia, large parts of which had barely been affected by nationalism by 1914, and countries such as France and Germany, whose national histories were long established and widely accepted. Both the extent and content of nationalism differed across Europe and changed markedly during the long nineteenth century. As has been seen, the distinction between civic and ethnic types of nationalism, although not without its uses, is too imprecise and anachronistic to form the basis of an explanatory model.[110] It is necessary, therefore, to put forward an alternative explanation. The following model distinguishes between the scope and the nature of nationalism.

The most important condition determining the extent of nationalism, as a body of ideas and series of actions, was the existence of established means of mass communication. Although nationalist reactions could occur in the absence of mass communication, they were rarely, if ever, sustained for more than a few years. Thus, the Pensinsular war of 1808–14 provoked xenophobic animus against the French and strong sentiments in favour of a Spanish *patria* amongst a significant number of

---

[109] R. Chickering, '*We Men Who Feel Most German': A Cultural Study of the Pan-German League, 1886–1914* (London, 1984), 77.

[110] Some authors in this volume, for example Oliver Zimmer and Carl Strikwerda, find it useful for the analytical purpose of describing nationalism in their respective case studies.

peasant fighters, but such feelings do not appear to have been passed on to subsequent generations or to have created enduring, popular national movements in Spain, except in border areas, where 'Spaniards' remained in close contact with the 'French' and turned a national conflict into a local tradition.[111] 'The evils of Spain', wrote the British liberal John Stuart Mill, 'flow as much from the absence of nationality amongst the Spaniards themselves as from the presence of it in their relations with foreigners.'[112] This lack of popular national consciousness was bemoaned by nationalist intellectuals throughout Europe in the first half of the nineteenth century, including those of long-standing nation-states such as France. In areas like the Balkans, it was commented upon until the eve of the First World War. 'Even forty years ago,' recorded a British observer in 1900, 'the name Bulgarian was almost unknown and every educated person coming from that country called himself Greek as a matter of course.'[113] In Macedonia, he went on, 'race...is merely a political party'.[114] Caught up in the rivalry of powers such as Turkey, Serbia, Greece, and Bulgaria after the turn of the century, Macedonian peasants sought only to avoid strong commitments to any national cause, since such affiliations could entail great danger and, even, death. 'Our fathers were Greeks and none mentioned the Bulgarians,' admitted one villager. 'We became Bulgarians, we won. If we have to be Serbs, no problem. But for now it is better for us to be Bulgarians.'[115] Such fickle allegiances did not mean that Macedonians spoke several languages or that they had adopted new customs and a new 'national' history. Rather, they were from isolated, predominantly local cultures which had been drawn unwillingly into a series of 'national' Balkan wars. For much of the nineteenth century, Montenegro, which became formally independent in 1858, remained so remote that its very inclusion in the Ottoman Empire was open to doubt.[116]

On occasion, the isolation of the majority of the populace could be overcome by integrated and expanding elites. In countries such as Italy, where fewer than 10 per cent of adults could speak Italian at the time of unification in 1861, or in Greece, where merchants and other city-dwellers were the main proponents of nationalism both before and after independence in 1830, a national culture remained the preserve of a small number of large landowners and urban notables.[117] According to the fragmentary statistical evidence available, it appears that such groups were initially preponderant even in countries or regions without

[111] On the weakness of Spanish nationalism after 1814, see J. S. Junco, 'The Nation-Building Process in Nineteenth-Century Spain', in C. Mar-Molinero and A. Smith (eds.), *Nationalism and the Nation in the Iberian Peninsula* (Oxford, 1996), 89–106. On the French-Spanish borderland, see Peter Sahlins, 'The Nation in the Village: State-Building and Communal Struggles in the Catalan Borderland during the Eighteenth and Nineteenth Centuries', *Journal of Modern History*, 60 (1988), 234–63. Also, see Chapter 11 on the weakness of official Spanish nationalism during much of the nineteenth century.

[112] Mill, *System of Logic* (1846), cited in Sahlins, 'The Nation in the Village', 261–2.

[113] Sir Charles Elliot, *Turkey in Europe* (1900), cited in M. Mazower, *The Balkans* (London, 2000), 98.   [114] Ibid. 104.

[115] Ibid. 105.   [116] See, for instance, Pavlowitch, *Serbia*, 59–60.

[117] On Italy, see Chapter 13.

large cities. Approximately two-thirds of patriotic activity in Slovakia, for instance, took place in towns during the first half of the nineteenth century.[118] Likewise, in Norway, 72 per cent of deputies in the national assembly (*Storting*) in 1818 came from circles of officials, merchants, and lawyers.[119] However, this figure quickly dropped, as the number of peasant deputies rose to just under 50 per cent by 1833. In Slovakia, more than 50 per cent of the nationalist intelligentsia came from artisan and peasant backgrounds by the 1840s.[120] Similar patterns of popular participation in nationalist agitation could be witnessed in most European states.

Where such increased participation did not occur, or took place more slowly than elsewhere, nationalists openly voiced their frustration. In unified Italy, the combination of poor elementary education, corruption, banditry, an uncooperative Roman Catholic church, alternation between two broadly 'liberal' political parties (*trasformismo*) and a narrow franchise, which was based on literacy and tax, limiting the electorate to 7 per cent even after reform in 1882, all ensured that the small group of national-minded Italians would have concurred with the philosopher Giovanni Amendola's verdict that 'the Italy of today does not please us'.[121] Most importantly, the south (*Mezzogiorno*), which had previously formed the kernel of the legend of Garibaldi and the Risorgimento, was quickly associated by many nationalists with bribery, crime, and violence and dissociated from the necessary virtues of *italianità*. 'What barbarism! Some Italy! This is Africa: the bedouin are the flower of civilised virtues compared to these peasants', recorded one Piedmontese envoy as early as 1860.[122] Some, such as the Tuscan senator Leopoldo Franchetti, contended that the *Mezzogiorno* was neither European nor Italian; others, even southerners such as Alfredo Niceforo, author of *L'Italia barbara contemporaneo* (1898), postulated that the south was racially distinct, if still part of the Italian nation.[123] Although no such geographical division existed in Greece, nationalists there became similarly disenchanted by their compatriots' lack of national consciousness, in spite of the country's early, 'heroic' struggle for independence in the 1820s. In 1879, two-thirds of settlements lacked a primary school. 'Behold our decline since 1821', wrote the journalist Anastasios Byzantios in the 1870s: 'Where are the Greek dreams of 50 years ago? The descent in our ladder of expectations progresses with the passing years.'[124] Lack of consciousness was widely acknowledged to be the principal cause of national 'failure'.

[118] M. Hroch, *Social Preconditions of National Revival in Europe: A Comparative Analysis of the Social Composition of Patriotic Groups among the Smaller European Nations* (Cambridge, 1985), 106.

[119] Ibid. 36. Also, see the section on 'Civic Nationalism in Scandinavia' in Chapter 10.

[120] Ibid. 103.   [121] Cited in Doumanis, *Italy*, 108. This is very much the tenor of Chapter 13.

[122] Ibid. 96.   [123] Ibid.

[124] Cited in T. Veremis, 'From the National State to the Stateless Nation, 1821–1910', in M. Blinkhorn and T. Veremis (eds.), *Modern Greece: Nationalism and Nationality* (Athens, 1990), 14. See also M. Kitromilides, ' "Imagined Communities" and the Origins of the National Question in the Balkans', 23–66, in the same volume.

Consciousness depended on adequate means of communication and level of education. In the nineteenth century, the former usually consisted of books, journals, and newspapers. To a lesser degree, theatre, art and, after the turn of the century, cinema also played a role in the dissemination of the national idea. Gaps in this network of communication almost invariably stunted the development of nationalism, even in countries such as France, which had a long history of state centralization, Parisian domination, national wars, and revolutions. Official reports from the 1870s revealed that standard French was a foreign language for roughly half the population. Folklorists from the same period counted up to 88 dialects in common use. Until the end of the century, by which time French railways carried 400 million passengers per year and almost universal military conscription had been adopted, movement was relatively rare and restricted in scope. Those who did travel regularly experienced 'a painful feeling of finding oneself a stranger in one's own country', as one Parisian writer put it in the 1880s.[125] In 1825, there were only 65,000 newspaper subscribers in the whole of France. The figure was still low in 1858, with the Paris dailies selling 235,000 copies and the provincial press a smaller number. By 1870, circulation had risen to one million and 350,000 respectively; and, by 1910, five million and four million.[126] In order to read these newspapers, of course, a high level of education— measured in historical terms—was necessary. Learning was not a guarantee of national awareness, as a schools' inspector in the Massif Central found out in 1864, when the children in a village school could not tell him in which country Lozère was situated nor whether they were English, Russian, or French.[127] In certain circumstances, though, education could counteract physical distance and the lack of a mass press, as appears to have been the case in parts of Scandinavia, which had the highest literacy rates in Europe and which saw large-scale popular participation in politics and in national movements from the early nineteenth century onwards.[128] What was important was not collective memory or communication per se, since these were features of oral traditions too, but the ability to communicate regularly and in similar ways with a large group over an extended area. Without this ability, it proved difficult to sustain national cultures and politics.

Although nationalism was produced by other series of events and processes, including wars and conscription, state intervention, and conflicts of interest between contiguous ethnic groups, it was not sustained over a long period without sufficient communication between national and local levels. In Europe, this type of communication sometimes preceded industrialization and, even, urbanization. Thus, predominantly agrarian societies such as Norway and the alpine

---

125 E. Weber, *Peasants into Frenchmen: The Modernisation of Rural France, 1870–1914* (Stanford, Calif., 1976), 82. Also, R. Tombs, *France, 1814–1914* (London, 1996), 302–25.

126 T. Zeldin, *France, 1848–1945: Taste and Corruption* (Oxford, 1977), 192.

127 Zeldin, *France, 1848–1945: Intellect and Pride* (Oxford, 1977), 3.

128 See O. Sorensen, *Nordic Paths to National Identity in the Nineteenth Century* (Oslo, 1994). Also, Chapter 10.

cantons of Switzerland gave rise to broad national movements early in the nineteenth century, as did largely peasant areas such as Galicia, Lithuania, Estonia, Romania, and Serbia during the second half of the century.[129] Yet communication itself remained simply a necessary condition for conceptualizing a nation and propagating national ideas, helping to determine the extent of nationalist agitation. It rarely determined the form which those ideas took, the degree of contemporaries' commitment to national ideals, and the willingness of nationalists to achieve their ends through the use of violence or other extreme methods. In these critical respects, political questions appear to have been uppermost: notably, struggles for economic and coercive power, either within or between states. Such struggles took place in the context of a changing set of ideas and discourses, including new post-Enlightenment hierarchies of 'progress' and 'race', which created enmities between newly defined nationalities and explained novel conflicts over resources and state power in easily understood national terms. However, the effects of imperialism or the impact of the ideas of 1789 were felt, albeit unevenly, throughout much of the continent. Partly as a consequence, it is difficult to discern a direct correlation between the reception of ideas and the strength, commitment, and extremism of nationalist groups at specific junctures in different European countries and regions. Rather, extremism resulted from the conjunction of novel but widely accepted nationalist discourses and particular sorts of economic, political, and international conflict. From a reading of nineteenth-century history, it seems useful to distinguish explanatory types of nationalism on this basis.

The first explanatory type concerns economic conflicts arising from the rapid spread of capitalist forms of production and exchange. Feelings of disorientation and the experience of relative impoverishment, which such economic transformation elicited, were frequently translated into criticism of 'traitorous', 'unpatriotic' workers, and, occasionally, 'corrupt' and 'self-interested' merchants, financiers, and manufacturers.[130] More commonly, they were directed at Jews, who were used as scapegoats to explain the perceived malfunctioning and injustices of a system based on widely accepted principles of property and inequality. Thus, in an early instance of economic anti-Semitism, which resembled that of other disappointed aristocrats like François René de Chateaubriand, the poet Alfred de Vigny lamented in the 1830s and 1840s that 'the bourgeoisie is the mistress of France' and that Jews 'more easily manipulate bourgeois than nobles', effectively seizing control for themselves.[131] Jews were seen by anti-Semites to be parasites on the body of their host nation, destroying livelihoods, companies, and state finances through greed and cunning. The first book of Drumont's best-selling *La France*

    [129] See Chapters 6, 7, and 10.

    [130] For Germany, see Brandt and D. Groh, *Vaterlandslose Gesellen: Sozialdemokratie und Nation, 1860–1990* (Munich, 1992).

    [131] L. Poliakov, *Histoire de l'antisémitisme* (Paris, 1955), ii. 199–200. Also, the section on 'The Other' in Chapter 2.

juive was almost entirely devoted to showing the difference in kind between the 'Semite', who was 'mercantile, greedy, scheming [and] devious', and the true Frenchman or 'Aryan', who was 'enthusiastic, heroic, chivalrous, disinterested, frank [and] trusting to the point of naivety'.[132] To Drumont and other anti-Semites, the Jews and the French were of a different race and nationality. It would be absurd, remarked a reporter of *La Croix*, the country's main Catholic newspaper, to believe that a Jew could become a Frenchman.[133]

Reinforced by a series of financial crises in which Jewish bankers and middlemen were believed to be involved, including the collapse of the Catholic Union Générale in 1882 and the Panama scandal in 1893, the nexus of nationalism, anti-Semitism, and economic change became central to French politics in the late nineteenth and early twentieth centuries. It was no coincidence that the political labels *nationaliste* and *antisémite* passed into common usage at roughly the same time during those years. The same nexus came into existence in most parts of Europe, in the countryside as well as in cities, irrespective of confession.[134] Consequently, the declaration of the Catholic priest and leading activist of the Bavarian Farmers' League, Georg Ratzinger, that 'parasitism can no more be tolerated in commercial life than in nature' was redolent of those of his metropolitan counterparts because both parties felt threatened by the possibility of recession, the incursion of cut-throat competition, and the dominance of big business, whether agrarian, mercantile, or industrial.[135] The fact that such direct economic relations were regularly understood in national terms can be seen in the example of Polish Russia during the mid and late nineteenth century, where reasonably amicable relations between communities of Jews and Poles were undermined by the growth of a money economy, commercial practices, and peasant debt, only to be replaced by violent antipathy towards Jews, despite—in contrast to French anti-Semitic myths—the latter's manifest poverty and detachment from the state.[136]

It is true, of course, that anti-Semitism continued to draw on age-old religious prejudices, which antedated the emergence of modern nationalism by several centuries. In Russia, despite the virtual banishment of Jews from the central territories of the empire, constituting less than 0.1 per cent of the population in Moscow and St Petersburg, such prejudices were widespread and virulent, arguably underpinning the most notorious excesses of anti-Semitism in Europe from the 1880s onwards and swelling the numbers of state-backed anti-Semitic leagues known as the 'Black Hundreds' in the period after the 1905 revolution. The violence of the leagues appeared to be religiously inspired, as one tract, printed at police headquarters in St Petersburg in 1906, made plain: 'Whenever those betrayers of Christ come near you, tear them to pieces, kill them.'[137] Yet

132 Drumont, cited in Poliakov, *The History of Anti-Semitism* (Philadelphia, 2003), 41.
133 *La Croix*, 6 Nov. 1894, cited ibid. 42.
134 See, for example, the section on 'National "Others" ' in Chapter 3.
135 MacMaster, *Racism*, 103.   136 Ibid. 105.   137 Cited ibid. 108.

even amongst tsarist officials and Russian agitators, religious and economic themes were frequently combined. 'The Yids have invaded everything', explained the reactionary Interior Minister, Konstantin Pobedonostsev, to Fyodor Dostoevsky in 1879: 'They are at the root of the Social Democratic movement and tsaricide. They control the press and the stock market. They reduce the masses to financial slavery.'[138] The implication of both government and Slavophile anti-Semitism was that Jews were attacking Russian institutions and people, using the economic weapons which came most readily—and naturally—to hand.

Similar claims were made by right-wing French anti-Semites such as Charles Maurras and Léon Daudet, two of the founders of Action Française, who argued preposterously that Jewish speculation was responsible for natural disasters like the Paris floods of 1910. Some left-wing Radicals such as Georges Clemenceau agreed with the tenor, if not the content, of these conspiracy theories: 'Despised, hated, persecuted because he imposed on us gods of his blood, the Semite tried to come back to fulfil himself by the domination of the earth.' 'It is enough to improve the Christians, still masters of the world, to avoid the need to exterminate the Jews in order to steal from them the throne of opulence coveted until now by people of all places and all times,' he concluded in 1898.[139] In agreeing with *le parti nationaliste*, Clemenceau could look back on a long tradition of economic anti-Semitism on the French left, which included Charles Fourier and Joseph Proudhon.[140] The existence of such a tradition, at a time of declining Catholic anti-Semitism during the middle of the century, suggests that Karl Marx's thesis in *On the Jewish Question* (1843) was perspicacious: Jews had become a scapegoat for the ills of capitalist societies. In turn, the act of scapegoating helped capitalism's victims, who saw themselves as the backbone of the nation, overcome their feeling that the economic system had become anonymous and incomprehensible. The precise effect of perceived victimhood on the strength and content of popular nationalism was determined to a considerable degree by the rapidity and gravity of economic crisis, in conjunction with the size, position, and prominence of Jewish communities, and the rigour of state and church prohibition or sanction.

When economic dislocation coincided with democratization, which constituted a second source of nationalist conflict, radicalization often occurred. According to one line of argument, a sudden extension of the franchise, the creation of representative institutions and formation of new political parties, even without profound economic change, had the potential to fuel xenophobic, intolerant, and extreme forms of nationalism, increasing the likelihood of a diversionary and expansionist foreign policy.[141] In countries such as Serbia, it is held, where the organizations and habits of civil society hardly existed on a national level, the state

---

[138] MacMaster, *Racism*, 106.
[139] Clemenceau, *Au Pied du Sinaï* (1898), cited in Poliakov, *History of Anti-Semitism*, iv. 64.
[140] Poliakov, *Histoire de l'antisémitisme*, ii. 201–11.
[141] See J. Snyder, *From Voting to Violence: Democratisation and Nationalist Conflict* (New York, 2000), 169–80, for most of the following points.

attempted to foster nationalist sentiment amongst a largely peasant population (87 per cent in 1878), instrumentalizing ethnic rivalries and foreign adventures in order to deflect attention away from its own lack of legitimacy and weakness. Both ruling dynasties—the Obrenovics (1815–42 and 1858–1903) and the Karadjordjevics (1842–58 and 1903 onwards)—had come from families of pig farmers in the early nineteenth century. Their willingness to appeal to ethnic solidarity and to stoke up external conflicts was purportedly designed to conceal the precariousness of their own position and the lack of popularity of a corrupt and ineffective state. As the electorate was expanded and new representative institutions introduced through the constitutions of 1869 and 1888, making Serbia one of the most democratic countries in Europe, populist political parties, an ill-informed, uneducated public, and a vestigial, dependent press allegedly pushed successive governments towards an aggressive foreign policy and a series of wars in 1877, 1885, 1912, 1913, and 1914.

However, even in a new state such as Serbia, which gained autonomy within the Ottoman Empire in 1817 and independence in 1878, the impact of democratization was less clear-cut than such an account would suggest, despite the undoubted existence of opportunistic or defensive responses to the advent of mass politics. Through the course of the nineteenth century, a sparsely populated territory, counting only 400,000 inhabitants in 1800 and run by a federation of village communities under the Ottomans, had been consolidated and refashioned into a nation-state, with an Austrian-style Civil Code (1844), a system of primary and secondary education, a bureaucracy whose upper echelons had initially been trained in France, national taxation, a market economy, an army of 150,000 men by the 1870s, strong Constitutional, Liberal, Progressive, and Radical parties, and a National Assembly (1858) which gained limited control over legislation in 1869 and full sanction in 1888. In such circumstances, notwithstanding continuing assassination attempts, government fiat and bureaucratic corruption, nationalism developed within a broadly—and increasingly—constitutional and parliamentary setting. Wars against the old Ottoman oppressor were popular in 1877 and 1912–13, but the campaign against Bulgaria in 1885 was not, leading to a Radical parliament, the liberal constitution of 1888, and the eventual abdication of Milan IV in 1889. The People's Radical party, which the Serbian peasantry returned with a 2 : 1 majority in 1883 and which took office after the demise of the more 'European' Progressives in the late 1880s, maintained constitutional government during the difficult years of court politics around the turn of the century and after the murder of the discredited Alexander I by an army faction in 1903. When the assassination occurred, the parties immediately formed a provisional administration, convened the last regularly elected parliament, restored the constitution, lowered the tax threshold for voters still further, and elected a new king.

Despite the continuing power of the army, which came under attack from the Radical government of Nikola Pasic in the spring of 1914, the decade before the First World War was seen as a golden age of parliamentary politics. Although the Radical party, which gained 90 per cent of the vote in 1904, used the prospect of war and the plight of Serbian diaspora in Austria-Hungary and Turkey to rally its supporters, it was not merely a demagogic nationalist party, but was influenced by the example of the French left and Swiss Radicalism. Its core support amongst the peasantry was not—as far as could be gathered—in favour of war, echoing the view during the 1908–9 Bosnian annexation crisis of one deputy during the earlier crisis of the 1870s: 'If we get Bosnia, that won't make my plot any bigger!'[142] Furthermore, the party spawned the less populist, more moderate and pro-Western Independent Radical Party, which seceded in 1905 in acquiring almost as many seats as its Radical counterpart. Even in Serbia, with its diaspora and its uncertain international position, the consequences of democratization, which had radicalized much of the officer corps, elements of the Radical party, and sections of urban public opinion, were not uniform. Extreme nationalists certainly existed, especially in the army's 'Black Hand', but they were arguably not in the majority.

The mixed effects of democratization were more starkly visible in Germany. Here, too, most parties and voters distanced themselves from radical nationalists, with extra-parliamentary organizations like the Pan-German League being discounted just before the First World War as 'a small, almost comical sect with no significance', in the words of the historian and moderate conservative commentator Hans Delbrück.[143] Indeed, the Wilhelmine electorate had shifted since the 1890s to the left, creating a distinction between a national-minded *Volk*, or citizenry, and a right-wing 'German-national' (*deutsch-national*) public, which numbered between several hundred thousand and three million people in the 1900s. In 1912, 8.25 million out of 12.2 million voters supported the Social Democratic, Centre, left-liberal, and minority-nationality parties, which had few, if any, connections with nationalist associations. Unlike in the 1870s and 1880s, when both the socialists and the Catholic Centre Party had been ostracized and restricted as 'unpatriotic', moderate and left-wing parties successfully resisted attempts after the turn of the century to build a national consensus against them, particularly after the 'Hottentot' election of 1907 orchestrated by Bernhard von Bülow. Throughout the pre-war era, they continued to demonstrate their own patriotic credentials and to contest the terms of national debates. Right-wing nationalists were frequently ridiculed in the press as 'Teutschen' and 'Teutsch-Nationale', or preposterous 'German-nationals', portrayed as bearded, overweight, gullible old men. One cartoon in the Reich's principal satirical journal *Simplicissimus* simply showed them under the banner 'das Volk', as if readers would understand without commentary the ridiculousness of the juxtaposition, recognizing the emancipatory, inclusive, and heroic connotations of the word 'nation' (*Volk*).[144]

---

[142] Cited in Pavlowitch, *Serbia*, 69. The arguments made here are largely derived from this work.
[143] Delbrück, cited in Chickering, '*We Men who feel most German*', 283.
[144] *Simplicissimus* (1897), shown in N. Stargardt, *The German Idea of Militarism: Radical and Socialist Critics, 1866–1914* (Cambridge, 1994), 37.

Within the right itself, such forthright discussion of national affairs, which had been largely beyond debate in the 1870s, 1880s, and 1890s, reinforced a defensive reaction which had been visible since the early nineteenth century. Partly as a corollary of this breaking of a national taboo and partly as a result of the weakening position of the right in an era of mass politics, the posturing and paranoia of radical nationalists became more pronounced in the two decades before the First World War, encompassing more and more areas of domestic and foreign policy-making.[145] There was, intimated one correspondent of the *Alldeutsche Blätter*, 'a broadly based conspiracy ... with the aim of harming Germandom', conducted by Jews, socialists, ultramontanes and Freemasons at home, and by the same groups and other enemy nationalities such as the French, the 'Slavs', and the 'Anglo-Saxons' abroad.[146] 'Enemies all around us: that has always been our position', wrote the leader of the Pan-Germans Ernst Hasse in 1907: 'And that is our good fortune.'[147] Many German Conservatives, whose party had preferred loyalty to the Prussian monarchy—not to the German nation—at its founding in 1876, had subsequently converted to a radical nationalist faith. Consequently, they espoused modern, populist varieties of anti-Semitism, which were included in the Conservative Party's Tivoli programme of 1892, and they backed an increasingly aggressive external policy, which eventually helped to push them into a 'national opposition' to the government of Theobald von Bethmann Hollweg in the 1910s. By this time, it was evident that democratization had at once produced a greater number of more strident extreme nationalists and a more resolute, powerful body of moderate and left-wing opponents. In unified Germany, as in Serbia and elsewhere, the commitment and violence of the former depended to a significant extent on the strength and perceived threat of the latter.

The intersection between the struggle for greater democracy and improvements in communication allowed the expression or 'rebirth' of almost tribal antipathies—a third source of nationalist conflict—between 'ethnic' groups in areas of mixed settlement. Such antipathies, although frequently exacerbated by state intervention, appear in some regions to have been largely independent of changes taking place at the centre. In Austrian Galicia, for instance, it is difficult to detect a specific alteration of state policy which could have initiated the emergence of a Ukrainian—or Ruthenian—national movement. Rather, the Habsburg Empire had continued its traditional policy of non-intervention, allowing the Poles, who still comprised just under 50 per cent of the population in 1910, a considerable degree of autonomy in the province, partly because they provided the area with a more or less self-governing aristocracy, in contrast to the 42 per cent of Ruthenians—or Ukrainians, as they had by then come to be

[145] For more on this, see the section on '*Völkisch* Nationalism' in Chapter 3.
[146] *Alldeutsche Blätter* (1907), cited in Chickering, '*We Men who feel most German*', 79.
[147] Hasse, cited in R. Chickering, 'Die Alldeutschen erwarten den Krieg', in J. Dülffer and K. Holl (eds.), *Bereit zum Krieg: Kriegsmentalität im wilhelminischen Deutschland, 1890–1914* (Göttingen, 1986), 24.

called—who were largely peasants. As communication improved, local struggles for power came to be cast in national terms, based on supposedly objective distinctions of language, culture, and descent. In eastern Galicia, in particular, where the Ukrainians made up 62 per cent of the population and the Poles only 25 per cent, the latter came to be seen as 'foreign' oppressors during the political struggles of the mid-nineteenth century. By the end of the century, both sides had come to admit the existence of two separate nationalities in the province, with many Poles now worried that they would in future be marginalized or banished. 'Our prospects in eastern Galicia are unfavourable,' predicted a Polish scholar in 1908: 'The fate of the English nationality in Ireland, or the German in Czech lands, and the probable future fate of the German nationality in Upper Silesia, serve us as a bad augury.'[148]

The Ruthenians, it appeared to Galician Poles, had used the relative freedom afforded by the non-intervention of the Austro-Hungarian state to define their own identity and interests. 'At that time, Galicia was for us a model in the struggle for our nation's rebirth; it strengthened our faith and hope for a better future,' remarked one eastern Ukrainian leader in his memoirs of his first trip there in 1903: 'Galicia was a true "Piedmont" of the Ukraine because prior to 1906 a Ukrainian press, scholarship and national life could develop only there.'[149] Unlike in Russia, where the Ukrainians were counted as 'Little Russians' and were not allowed sufficient freedom of expression to oppose such a view, Austrian Ruthenians could use their own press and their influence in the provincial diet, which was reformed in 1907, to define a Ukrainian identity in opposition to that of the 'Polish nobility' and, from the 1860s, to that of 'the Muscovite government', as one pamphlet put it in 1867.[150] By the 1890s, the term 'Ukrainian' had been adopted in Galicia to indicate the commonality of the populations on both sides of the border and to distinguish them from Russians. Although not as deep-rooted or primordial as many Ukrainian intellectuals believed, objective cultural differences had played an important role in the demarcation of the region's politics.

Despite the existence of linguistic and cultural differences between Poles, Ukrainians, and Russians, which were based on the existence of a widely used and understood peasant vernacular fashioned by 'national awakeners' into a literary idiom and folk tradition from the early nineteenth century onwards, were such differences any greater than those separating Bavaria and Holstein or the Languedoc and the Île-de-France? Certainly, in the mid-nineteenth century, many Polish observers did not think so, pointing to intermarriage, to confessional similarities between Roman Catholic Poles and Greek Catholic—rather than Orthodox—Ruthenians, and to significant numbers of educated Greek Catholics whose cultural and political affiliations had become Polish (*gente Rutheni, natione*

---

[148] Cited in I. L. Rudnytsky, 'The Ukrainians in Galicia under Austrian Rule', in A. S. Markovits and F. E. Sysyn (eds.), *Nationbuilding and the Politics of Nationalism: Essays on Austrian Galicia* (Cambridge, Mass., 1982).   [149] Ievhen Chykalenko, cited ibid. 51.
    [150] Ibid. 46.

Poloni). 'Before March 1848 a Ruthenian was a person of Greek, and a Pole a person of Catholic religion,' declared the Polish democratic leader Florian Ziemialkowski to the Constitutional Committee of the Austrian Reichstag in 1849: 'There were Ruthenians and Poles in the same family. It is unnecessary to say who has created the split, but this is a difference of religion, and not of nationality.'[151]

Yet, by the end of the century, few Polish nationalists were ready to discount the Ukrainians as 'an artificial nation, invented last year', as Ziemialkowski had done fifty years earlier. In the intervening period, the diffusion of democratic and national ideas appears to have transformed already extant cultural frictions and struggles for power between Poles and Ruthenians into part of a broader set of national conflicts. Czech nationalists, especially, served as a model, not least because they had defended the rights of Ruthenians against the Poles at the Slavic Congress in Prague in 1848, calling on all Slavs to 'respect the national strivings of a people, persecuted by both the Russians and the Poles, and called to an independent existence'.[152] Such national claims were grafted onto older conflicts, which themselves had been linked to cultural and social differences and inequalities. 'The fact that "peasant" and "Ruthenian", on the one hand, and "Pole" and "squire", on the other, have become synonymous, is fatal to us,' wrote one Polish commentator in the 1900s: 'The social element of the national question tremendously facilitates the Ruthenians' work of national education of their people, and makes it difficult for us to defend our position.'[153] In these circumstances, Ukrainian intellectuals, together with recently Polonized Greek Catholic gentry, were willing to readopt the vernacular culture of the majority in eastern Galicia as their own.

Since this culture existed in both Austria-Hungary and Russia, where 22.4 million Ukrainians were to be found according to the census of 1897, Ukrainian nationalists in Galicia were pushed towards accepting the necessity of secession from the Austro-Hungarian Empire. 'The final goal of our striving is the achievement of cultural, economic and political independence of the entire Ukrainian-Ruthenian nation', proclaimed the programme of the National Democratic party, which had come to dominate Ukrainian politics in Galicia after being founded in 1899, winning 17 out of 27 Galician Ukrainian seats in the Reichsrat elections of 1907.[154] Though viewed sympathetically by many Ukrainian nationalists, the Austro-Hungarian Empire promised too few political and economic gains to offset the loss represented by cultural division. Unlike their Russian counterparts, who clamped down much more severely on Ukrainian nationalism in the tsarist empire, Habsburg officials lacked both the means and the will to prevent its emergence in Austria.

It is questionable whether repressive state policies would have prevented the emergence or limited the impact of minority nationalisms over the longer term.

---

[151] Ziemialkowski, cited ibid. 40.   [152] František Ladislav Rieger, 24 Jan. 1849, cited ibid. 32.
[153] Cited ibid. 39.   [154] Ibid. 60.

Many states had failed to impose an official national identity on unwilling minorities, through policies of Frenchification, Germanization, and Russification for example, with the result that state intervention itself came to constitute a fourth source of nationalist conflict in nineteenth-century Europe.[155] Censuses, increased taxation, conscription, elementary education, police, or gendarmerie all bore witness to the extension of state functions, as officials and bureaucracies sought to monitor and restrict the competencies of churches, municipal corporations, aristocracies, and guilds. Local reactions to such unwelcome incursions sometimes took on the form of national protest, either in favour of a larger nation-state, as in areas of Germany and Italy, or in support of greater autonomy or secession, as in Brittany, Ireland, or Bohemia.

With its history of limited intervention and the persistence of predominantly segmental societies on its territory, the Ottoman Empire provided a good illustration of the galvanizing force of state action.[156] Although it had been reformed and undermined, the *millet* system, which divided the empire along religious lines (Muslim, Orthodox, Roman Catholic), remained in place. Each of the Christian *millets* was subdivided into an array of linguistic, historical, and territorial communities, permitting a degree of self-government and perpetuating a patchwork of identities and units of administration, all of which tended to obstruct the emergence of national movements. During the nineteenth century, however, the Ottoman government began to dismantle the old imperial edifice, based on provincial governors, primates, and notables who were directly loyal to the sultan, and to institute a universal form of Ottoman citizenship.[157] Beginning with the *Tanzimat* reforms of 1839 and continuing with the edict of 1856 and the Nationality Law of 1869, Constantinople put forward a policy of 'Ottomanism', in which all were encouraged to consider themselves subjects of the same state. It also altered the way in which *millets* were run, allowing laymen to participate in the election of patriarchs and in administration. The effect of the reforms, which had been designed to appease the great powers and avert further secessions after Serbian autonomy in 1817 and Greek independence in 1830, was to accelerate the nationalization of Ottoman politics, since the core of the new official identity was widely seen to be Muslim and Turkish. At the same time, with the weakening of the religious *millets*, the diverse ethnic and cultural groups of the empire came to perceive themselves as competing nationalities rather than self-governing communities.

As a consequence, the bloodletting and mass migration which had typified the history of the Ottomans in the Balkans—what one British observer in 1803 had described as 'a dreadful picture of anarchy, rebellion and barbarism'—were viewed

---

[155] Brian Vick explores some of the limits of language policies in Chapter 8, for instance.

[156] This paragraph is largely indebted to K. K. Karpat, '*Millets* and Nationality: The Roots of the Incongruity of Nation and State in the Post-Ottoman Era', in B. Braude and B. Lewis (eds.), *Christians and Jews in the Ottoman Empire: The Functioning of a Plural Society* (New York, 1982), i. 141–84.   [157] On the ramifications of this measure, see Chapter 7.

in a new way, with different political results.[158] Thus, nationalists in the Balkans and statesmen throughout Europe reacted with unprecedented shock and vigour to the 'Bulgarian Horrors' of 1876, after Ottoman irregulars had put down a revolt by killing between 12,000 and 15,000 Christians. In 1877, Russia attacked the Ottoman Empire and founded a Bulgarian state via the Treaty of San Stefano, which was subsequently maintained but reduced in scale at the Congress of Berlin in 1878. The atrocities came to be one of Bulgaria's foundation myths. As an ailing empire in the Concert of Europe, the Ottoman state seemed to be trapped: the more it tried to centralize and 'westernize' its structure of government and administration in order to defend itself against the other great powers and to answer its critics in the Christian *millets*, the more it hastened its own disintegration by provoking the increasingly vociferous and effective protests of nationalists. The combination of communal politics, democratization, a weak state, and occasional violent reprisals helped to radicalize some nationalists, easing the transition to the Balkan wars of 1912–13—the second of which pitted the Balkan states against each other—and the spectacle of more than 160,000 dead. 'Men are exterminating "young persons under twelve years of age",' wrote the young reporter Leon Trotsky: 'everyone is being brutalized, losing their human aspect.'[159]

Some nineteenth-century states were more successful in defusing or avoiding expressions of extreme nationalism than others, despite the presence of national minorities on their territories. Partly such success derived from the longevity and legitimacy of the state, the popular appeal of state welfare or education, and the prestige and propinquity of official culture, as judged by the inhabitants of a particular region or by the members of another language group. For these reasons, the Third Republic, notwithstanding its disputed revolutionary origins, was able to turn the various *patois* of France into a single *lingua franca*.[160] Partly the success of assimilation and integration also rested on the scale and popularity of state-sponsored imperialism.[161] Two types of empire are discernible: vast, multi-ethnic polities such as Russia, usually governed by central bureaucracies and absolute monarchs; and maritime empires like that of Britain, which had been acquired from the sixteenth century onwards by Europe's commercial and naval powers.[162] Both Britain and Russia, of course, continued to depend on a core nationality, with the English constituting 69 per cent of the United Kingdom's population in 1871 and Russians 44 per cent of the Russian Empire in 1897. Moreover, it was a widespread assumption in both states that the largest national group had done most to shape the identity and set up the institutions of the empire. Seeley, the

---

[158] Cited in Mazower, *The Balkans*, 88.   [159] Cited ibid. 14.

[160] Chapter 8 shows that language policies were more thoroughgoing in France than in the German lands or Austria-Hungary for much of the nineteenth century.

[161] Vera Tolz makes this point in Chapter 15, arguing that nationalism in Russia was 'state-framed'. On the attractions of empire in Wales and Scotland, see Chapter 14.

[162] D. Lieven, 'Dilemmas of Empire, 1850–1918: Power, Territory, Identity', *Journal of Contemporary History*, 34 (1999), 163–200.

most prominent advocate of 'Greater Britain', was unambiguous on this point: 'When we have accustomed ourselves to contemplate the whole Empire together and call it all England, we shall see that here too is a United States.'[163] Likewise, in Russia, it was widely assumed that the Russians would assimilate the empire's 28.3 million Ukrainians, or 'Little Russians', and Belorussians. 'I am deeply convinced that, alongside all-Russian culture and the all-Russian language, Little Russian, or Ukrainian, culture is a local or regional culture', wrote the liberal Kadet leader Peter Struve in 1912.[164]

Those empires in which the core nationality was numerically small, such as Germans in Austria-Hungary, or in which there were two large cultural groups, such as Muslims and Christians in the Ottoman Empire, found it more difficult to implant a supra-national imperial identity.[165] In Russia and Britain, however, imperial expansion promised Ukrainians and Scots, and many others not belonging to the core nationality, posts, wealth, and glory. Such expansion—or missionary nationalism—was founded on openness towards other cultures. 'Our strength', wrote the geographer and explorer Colonel Mikhail Veniukov, 'lies in the fact that up to the present time we have assimilated subject races, mingling affably with them.'[166] The revolutionary Aleksandr Herzen put forward a similar argument in 1867: 'Why does one assume that we think Europe is Eden and that to be a European is an honourable title? . . . We are part of the world between America and Europe and this is enough for us.'[167] There were debates between Slavophiles like Nikolai Danilevskii and Westernizers such as Boris Chicherin about the degree to which the Russian Empire should become a national entity and about the possibility of reconciling an autocratic state and Russian society, yet few intellectuals were prepared to renounce the empire's civilizing mission or its military and economic potential. Correspondingly, few Russian Ukrainians, in contrast to their counterparts in Austrian Galicia, were prepared to countenance secession, even when confronted by thoroughgoing policies of Russification, rather than institutional autonomy, constitutional legal guarantees, and relative freedom of expression, such as were granted to the Finns and the Scots.[168] Ukrainians, Siberians, and other incipient nationalities in Russia had less opportunity to enjoy what Thomas Carlyle, a Scot, called the 'second grand task' of an imperial English nation; namely, 'the grand Constitutional task of sharing, in some pacific endurable manner, the fruit of said conquest, and showing all people how it might be done.' But they were able to participate in the first task 'of conquering . . . this Terraqueous Planet for the use of man'.[169] In this sense, the

---

[163] Seeley, cited in K. Kumar, *The Making of English National Identity* (Cambridge, 2003), 189.

[164] Struve, cited in V. Tolz, *Inventing the Nation: Russia* (London, 2001), 209.

[165] See Chapters 7 and 9.   [166] Veniukov, cited ibid. 143.   [167] Herzen, ibid.

[168] See S. Velychenko, 'Empire Loyalism and Minority Nationalism in Great Britain and Imperial Russia, 1707 to 1914: Institutions, Law and Nationality in Scotland and Ukraine', *Comparative Studies in Society and History*, 39 (1997), 413–41.

[169] Carlyle, cited in Kumar, *The Making of English National Identity*, 175.

imperial state, although still unsuccessful in the culturally and historically separate areas of Poland and Ireland, did manage to integrate different nationalities and to construct an overarching imperial identity. In the British case, such an identity was already firmly established by the early nineteenth century; in the Russian case, an imperial identity remained quite weak, undermined by illiteracy, the absence of constitutional freedoms, and the gap between state and society.[170]

The British and Russian empires diverged, amongst other things, because of the two states' different external relations and experiences of war. An imperial British identity was forged by a series of successful campaigns from the eighteenth century onwards. By contrast, its Russian counterpart, marked by the country's uncertain position between East and West, was affected by defeat in the Crimean (1856) and Russo-Japanese wars (1905). This external context constituted a fifth and final source of nationalist conflict, serving to create and radicalize national sentiment—in certain circumstances—in a short period of time.[171] The speed and significance of such radicalization depended on the nature of the perceived threat, which in turn related to a country's role in the European states system. In general terms, the functioning of the system hinged throughout the long nineteenth century on the relations of the great powers—France, Britain, Russia, Austria, Prussia, and, later, Italy and Germany—within the Concert of Europe. However, there were fundamental changes which altered the impact of international relations on the genesis of modern nationalism. One concerned the gradual disappearance of established codes of diplomatic conduct, which had been based in part on conservative or monarchical reactions to the French Revolution and in part on aristocratic values and etiquette. Whereas, after 1815, the rules of diplomacy and military engagement were widely shared, couched in religious phraseology and noble codes of honour, they were slowly replaced during the second half of the century by discussions of power (*Realpolitik*), new nation-states, world empires, and the possibility of an international anarchy of powerful states. Thus, by the 1870s, even a commentator such as Walter Bagehot, who had provided one of the most famous accounts of a balance of powers within a liberal state, could contend that 'those nations which are strongest tend to prevail over the others; and in certain marked peculiarities the strongest tend to be the best.'[172] Such Darwinism seemed to make international relations at once more dangerous and less certain, especially since it was accompanied by a shift from cabinet warfare to the *levée en masse*, and from limited public exposure to war and diplomacy to the revelations and interventions of a mass press and organized political parties. Sections of 'public opinion', as it came to be known in these years, found the series of international crises which punctuated the period after 1848 disorientating

---

170 On the former, see Colley, *Britons*; on the latter, H. Rogger, 'Nationalism and the State: A Russian Dilemma', *Comparative Studies in Society and History*, 4 (1962), 253–64.

171 See Chapter 12 and the introductory section to Chapter 1.

172 Bagehot, *Physics and Politics* (1872), cited in T. L. Knutsen, *A History of International Relations Theory* (Manchester, 1992), 182.

and menacing, believing that the security of their own nation-state was at risk.[173] The prominence of 'war scare' literature in Britain, Germany, and France in the two decades before 1914 is indicative of heightened national awareness and anxiety, although it would be wrong to conclude from such evidence that more intensive press coverage inevitably led to more radical forms of nationalism. In many cases, greater familiarity with neighbouring states through a reading of the press appears to have militated against aggressive outbursts of nationalist feeling.[174]

When wars did break out, especially when they involved conscript armies and animated publics, they had the potential to push nationalists towards extremism. Even in revolutionary France, where utopianism had become a political currency, demonization of enemies was commonplace. Thus, opponents were denounced by the most enlightened onlookers such as the *philosophe* Antoine Condorcet as 'barbarians' and 'enemies of humanity'.[175] The revolutionary wars against a coalition of monarchies were depicted as a struggle for freedom and civilization against tyranny, justifying most means of 'self-defence'. As one deputy put it in 1792: 'A quill of fire would hardly suffice to describe in a worthy fashion the energy of courage and heroic dedication of the patriots fighting for liberty and equality against despotism, armed with the torches of barbarism and the bloody dagger of fanaticism.'[176] There are some signs that these manichean assumptions were shared by sections of the populace, at least in Paris and amongst the ranks of revolutionary soldiers, one of whom wrote home that 'we are on one side of the Rhine and the slaves on the other'.[177] There is little indication that such assumptions were perpetuated amongst large numbers of citizens during peacetime after 1815, however, although writers and members of ruling elites sometimes ensured a degree of rhetorical continuity. Certainly, the revolutionary and Napoleonic wars, which witnessed the first instance in Europe of mass conscription, did not give rise to broadly based national movements in the first half of the nineteenth century, even in areas such as Germany, where anti-French feeling was pronounced during wartime and later foundation myths looked back to 'wars of liberation' against France between 1813 and 1815.

During the late nineteenth century, the relationship between war and nationalism in peacetime was more salient, commemorated by public rituals and maintained by active associations of veterans. In the German Empire, there were about three million members of veterans' associations by the early twentieth century and many more millions who had taken part in Sedan Day celebrations, anniversary celebrations of the battle of Leipzig in 1813, and Kaiser Parades.[178] In addition,

---

[173] On 'public opinion' in Germany, see W. J. Mommsen, 'Public Opinion and Foreign Policy in Wilhelmine Germany, 1897–1914', *Imperial Germany, 1867–1918* (London, 1995), 189–204.

[174] For more on this, see M. Hewitson, '*Nation* and *Nationalismus*: Representation and National Identity in Imperial Germany', in M. Fulbrook and M. Swales (eds.), *Representing the German Nation: History and Identity in Twentieth-Century Germany* (Manchester, 2000), 19–62.

[175] Jeismann, *Das Vaterland der Feinde*, 134.   [176] Cited ibid. 138.   [177] Ibid. 140.

[178] 'Gender, Citizenship, the Military and *Heimat* as Integral Elements of the National Discourse', in Chapter 3.

a vast literature of soldiers' memoirs and press articles recalled the wars of unification, learning and relearning the lessons of previous campaigns at most junctures of international crisis. In this atmosphere, despite warnings of future slaughter as a result of improving military technology, the German Peace Association had only managed to recruit 7,000 members by 1907. Similarly, although foreseeing a 'terror without end', with the mobilization of 16–18 million men, socialists like August Bebel were anxious to display their national and military credentials, proclaiming it 'a duty of honour of every man who can bear arms that he has to do so from a given age onwards'.[179] In part because of its place in national mythologies and in part as a consequence of increasing numbers of casualties, war played an integral role during the decades between the Crimean and the First World War in defining a distinctly national pathos and in creating broadly based nationalism.[180] As the experience of both Germany and France after 1870–1 suggests, however, there was no necessary and proportional relationship between either victorious or lost wars and radical nationalism. Accordingly, the 1870s and 1880s in both countries were characterized by the absence of extreme nationalist organizations and by veterans' unease about military conflict. As was the case with economic dislocation, democratization, tensions between nationalities, and state intervention, the willingness of nationalists to countenance the use of violence corresponded to the nature of the conflict—whether the war was popular or just—and to the perceived position of one's own national group—in this case, within the states system.

CONCLUDING REMARKS

Nationalism in the crucible of nineteenth-century Europe was much more complex than theories of modernization allow.[181] The dichotomy between civic or voluntary forms of national affiliation and activity in Western Europe and ethnic or organic forms in Eastern Europe is misleading. Present throughout the continent during the entire century, ethnic myths were at once archaic, involving traditions imported from religions, kinship groups and nature, and modern, resting on Darwinian biology, Romanticism, and the new academic discipline of history. They also derived from novel types of class conflict and imperial expansion, associated with the industrial areas of Northern and Central Europe and with the states of the Atlantic seaboard. By the same token, civic or voluntary types of participation and political liberalism were characteristic of significant

---

[179] Bebel in 1904, cited by J. Vogel, *Nationen im Gleichschritt: Der Kult der 'Nation im Waffen' in Deutschland und Frankreich 1871–1914* (Göttingen, 1997), 223. Also, W. J. Mommsen, 'Der Topos vom unvermeidlichen Krieg vor 1914', in J. Dülffer and K. Holl (eds.), *Bereit zum Krieg: Kriegsmentalität im wilhelminischen Deutschland, 1890–1914* (Göttingen, 1986), 205.

[180] Another example is Spain, as Stephen Jacobson points out in Chapter 11.

[181] See Chapter 1.

parts of Southern and Eastern Europe, as well as the West and North. Moreover, very few nineteenth-century Europeans thought of their nation as a voluntary collective, not even Renan, to whom the idea is usually attributed.[182] Rather, most liberals viewed the nation-state as a natural entity. Consequently, the proponents of liberalism and popular politics often simply accepted the 'natural' parameters of their own nation-state and ignored the cultural differences and national claims of others. Liberals' demands for assimilation, a *lingua franca*, historical rights to territory, progress, and civilization almost always betrayed assumptions about the superiority of their own culture. For this reason alone, ethnic legends—or beliefs about the people from 'here'—rarely contravened or affronted liberal principles of civic participation and improvement.

Given the ubiquity of assumptions about ethnicity and the propinquity of civic and ethnic traditions, it is better to assess and explain nationalism by referring to a different set of criteria. Thus, it is possible to distinguish, on the one hand, between the scope and incidence of nationalism, which was facilitated by new means of communication, and the nature and form of national ideas and nationalists' actions, which can be judged by protagonists' willingness to use violence or other extreme methods to attain their ends. In this last respect, five sources of conflict, which had the potential to radicalize nationalism, were uppermost in nineteenth-century Europe: economic dislocation; democratization; tensions between contiguous, culturally different nationalities; state intervention; and foreign rivalries and wars. It was very unusual, however, for all—or even most—of these sources of conflict to converge, thereby producing a broad and linear radicalization of nationalist activity and a transition from emancipatory, liberal nationalism to right-wing, integral, or conservative nationalism. Instead, different sources of potential antagonism tended to counteract each other, affecting different sections of a particular society in diverse ways. Accordingly, although the second half of the nineteenth century witnessed an acceleration or exacerbation of historical processes—dislocation, intervention, and the demonization of foreign enemies—which were critical to the genesis of modern nationalism, no European country experienced a uniform movement towards extremism, such as occurred during the interwar period.

This absence of a dominant extremism during the long nineteenth century can be explained above all by two paradoxical sets of transformations. The first involved popular mobilization, which was marked by the advent of widening franchises, political parties, and a mass press, and domestic pacification, which saw the emergence of police forces and the abolition of corporal and, in certain cases, capital punishment: here, the greater ability of the disaffected to air their grievances, which could have issued in more extreme forms of economic and reactionary nationalism, was offset by a greater aversion to violence and to radical measures. The second set of transformations concerned industrialization and the

---

[182] For more on this, see the Introduction.

disjunction between internal and external relations, which meant that the types of pacification characteristic of domestic politics and law were not translated into foreign affairs. Improvements in industrial technology in this realm increased states' capacity for destruction without corresponding legal and moral norms to regulate behaviour. Nineteenth-century nationalists were therefore often moderate in respect of their domestic demands and methods, and extreme in their toleration of international violence. The First World War illustrated this discrepancy to a horrifying degree. It also reversed the pacification of domestic politics which had taken place before 1914. In this sense, the radical nationalism of the inter-war years, which has so shaped our understanding of nationalism as a whole, was both a continuation of the nineteenth century abroad and a complete break from it at home. Because of the destruction wrought by radicalized, external forms of nationalism after 1914, historians have tended to overlook internal discontinuities within European nation-states. This volume begins to make up for such a historical oversight.

Select Bibliography

GENERAL

ANDERSON, BENEDICT, *Imagined Communities: Reflections on the Origins and Spread of Nationalism*, 2nd edn. (London, 1991).

APPLEGATE, CELIA, 'A Europe of Regions: Reflections on the Historiography of Sub-National Places in Modern Times', *American Historical Review*, 104 (1999), 1157–82.

ARMSTRONG, JOHN A., *Nations before Nationalism* (Chapel Hill, NC, 1982).

BALAKRISHNAN, GOPAL (ed.), *Mapping the Nation* (London, 1996).

BALIBAR, R., and WALLERSTEIN, I. (eds.), *Race, Nation, Class: Ambiguous Identities* (London, 1991).

BATES, D., NEWTON, S., and STRADLING, R. (eds.), *Conflict and Coexistence: Nationalism and Democracy in Modern Europe* (Cardiff, 1997).

BAYCROFT, TIMOTHY, *Nationalism in Europe, 1789–1945* (Cambridge, 1998).

BERGER, STEFAN, and SMITH, ANGEL (eds.), *Nationalism, Labour and Ethnicity 1870–1939* (Manchester, 1999).

—— DONOVAN, MARK, and PASSMORE KEVIN, (eds.), *Writing National Histories: Western Europe since 1800* (London, 1999).

BHABHA, HOMI K. (ed.), *Nation and Narration* (London, 1990).

BILLIG, MICHAEL, *Banal Nationalism* (London, 1995).

BLOOM, IDA, HAGEMANN, KAREN, and HALL, CATHERINE (eds.), *Gendered Nations: Nationalisms and Gender Order in the Long Nineteenth Century* (Oxford, 2000).

BREUILLY, JOHN, *Nationalism and the State* (Manchester, 1982).

BRUBAKER, ROGERS, *Citizenship and Nationhood in France and Germany* (Cambridge, Mass., 1992).

CUBITT, GEOFFREY (ed.), *Imagining Nations* (Manchester, 1998).

DAY G., and REES, G. (eds.), *Regions, Nations and European Integration: Remaking the Celtic Periphery* (Cardiff, 1991).

ELEY, GEOFF, and SUNY, RONALD GRIGOR (eds.), *Becoming National: A Reader* (New York, 1996).

FORDE, SIMON, JOHNSON, LESLEY, and MURRAY, ALAN V. (eds.), *Concepts of National Identity in the Middle Ages*, Leeds Texts and Monographs New Series 14 (Leeds, 1995).

GELLNER, ERNEST, *Encounters with Nationalism* (Oxford, 1994).

—— *Nations and Nationalism* (Oxford, 1983).

GREENFELD, LIAH, *Nationalism: Five Roads to Modernity* (Cambridge, Mass., 1992).

HALL, JOHN (ed.), *The State of the Nation: Ernest Gellner and the Theory of Nationalism* (Cambridge, 1998).

HASTINGS, ADRIAN, *The Construction of Nationhood: Ethnicity, Religion and Nationalism* (Cambridge, 1997).

HIRSCHHAUSEN, ULRIKE V., and LEONHARD, JÖRN (eds.), *Nationalismen in Europa: West- und Osteuropa im Vergleich* (Göttingen, 2001).

HOBSBAWM, ERIC, *Nations and Nationalism since 1780: Programme, Myth, Reality*, 2nd edn. (Cambridge, 1994).

—— and TERENCE RANGER (eds.), *The Invention of Tradition* (Cambridge, 1983).

HROCH, MIROSLAV, *Social Preconditions of National Revival in Europe*, trans. Ben Fowkes (Cambridge, 1985).

KREJČÍ, JAROSLAV, and VELÍMSKY, VÍTEZSLAV, *Ethnic and Political Nations in Europe* (London, 1981).

LAWRENCE, PAUL, *Nationalism: History and Theory* (Harlow, 2005).

LEHMANN, HARTMUT, and WELLENREUTHER, HERMANN (eds.), *German and American Nationalism: A Comparative Perspective* (Oxford, 1999).

LIJPHART, AREND, *Democracy in Plural Societies: A Comparative Exploration* (New Haven, 1994).

LLOBERA, JOSEP, *The Foundations of National Identity* (Oxford, 2003).

MCCRONE, DAVID, *The Sociology of Nationialism* (London, 1998).

SAHLINS, PETER, *Boundaries: The Making of France and Spain in the Pyrenees* (Berkeley, 1989).

SCALES, LEN, and ZIMMER, OLIVER (eds.), *Power and the Nation in European History* (Cambridge, 2005).

SCHNAPPER, DOMINIQUE, 'Beyond the Opposition: "Civic" Nation versus "Ethnic" Nation', *ASEN Bulletin*, 12 (Autumn/Winter 1996/7), 4–8.

SHREEVES, W. G., *Nationmaking in Nineteenth-Century Europe: The National Unification of Italy and Germany 1815–1914* (Walton-on-Thames, 1984).

SLUGA, GLENDA, 'Identity, Gender, and the History of European Nations and Nationalisms', *Nations and Nationalism*, 4/1 (Jan. 1998), 87–111.

SMITH, ANTHONY D., 'Civic and Ethnic Nationalism Revisited: Analysis and Ideology', *ASEN Bulletin*, 12 (Autumn/Winter 1996/7), 9–11.

—— *The Nation in History: Historiographical Debates about Ethnicity and Nationalism* (Cambridge, 2000).

—— *National Identity* (London, 1991).

—— *Nationalism and Modernism: A Critical Survey of Recent Theories of Nations and Nationalism* (London, 1998).

SNYDER, JACK, *From Voting to Violence: Democratization and Nationalist Conflict* (New York, 2000).

TEICH, MIKULÁS, and PORTER, ROY (eds.), *The National Question in Europe in Historical Context* (Cambridge, 1993).

TRENTMANN, FRANK (ed.), *Paradoxes of Civil Society: New Perspectives on Modern German and British History* (Oxford, 2000).

VIROLI, MAURIZIO, *For Love of Country: An Essay on Patriotism and Nationalism* (Oxford, 1995).

WATKINS, SUSAN COTTS, *From Provinces into Nations: Demographic Integration in Western Europe 1870–1960* (Princeton, 1991).

WOOLF, STUART (ed.), *Nationalism in Europe 1815 to the Present: A Reader* (London, 1996).

ZIMMER, OLIVER, 'Boundary Mechanisms and Symbolic Resources: Towards a Process-Oriented Approach to National Identity', *Nations and Nationalism*, 9/2 (2003), 173–93.

—— *Nationalism in Europe 1890–1940* (Basingstoke, 2003).

FRANCE

BAYCROFT, TIMOTHY, *Culture, Identity and Nationalism: French Flanders in the Nineteenth and Twentieth Centuries*, Royal Historical Society New Studies in History (London, 2004).

BELL, P. M. H., *The Cult of the Nation in France: Inventing Nationalism, 1680–1800* (Cambridge, Mass., 2001).

FORD, CAROLINE, *Creating the Nation in Provincial France: Religion and Political Identity in Brittany* (Princeton, 1993).

GERSON, STÉPHANE, *The Pride of Place: Local Memories and Political Culture in Nineteenth-Century France* (Ithaca, NY, 2003).

GILDEA, ROBERT, *The Past in French History* (New Haven, 1994).

GIRARDET, RAOUL, *Le Nationalisme français: anthologie 1871–1914* (Paris, 1983).

HARP, STEPHEN, *Learning to be Loyal: Primary Schooling as Nation Building in Alsace and Lorraine, 1850–1940* (Dekalb, 1998).

JENKINS, BRIAN, *Nationalism in France: Class and Nation since 1789* (London, 1990).

NORA, PIERRE (ed.), *Realms of Memory: Constructions of the French Past* 3 vols. (Ithaca, NY, 1996–8).

TODOROV, TZVETAN, *On Human Diversity: Nationalism, Racism and Exoticism in French Thought* (Cambridge, Mass., 1993).

TOMBS, ROBERT, *France 1814–1914* (London, 1996).

—— (ed.), *Nationhood and Nationalism in France from Boulangism to the Great War 1889–1918* (London, 1991).

WEBER, EUGEN, *Peasants into Frenchmen: The Modernisation of Rural France 1870–1914* (Stanford, Calif., 1976).

WINOCK, MICHEL, *Nationalism, Antisemitism and Fascism in France*, trans. Jane Marie Todd (Stanford, Calif., 1998).

GERMANY

ANDERSON, MARGARET L., *Practising Democracy: Elections and Political Culture in Imperial Germany* (Princeton, 2000).

APPLEGATE, CELIA, *A Nation of Provincials: The German Idea of Heimat* (Berkeley, 1990).

BERGER, STEFAN, *Germany: Inventing the Nation* (London, 2004).

—— *The Search for Normality: National Identity and Historical Consciousness in Germany since 1800*, 2nd edn. (Oxford, 2003).

BREUILLY, JOHN, *The Formation of the First German Nation State 1800–1871* (Houndmills, 1996).

—— (ed.), *The State of Germany* (London, 1992).

CONFINO, ALON, *The Nation as a Local Metaphor: Württemberg, Imperial Germany and National Memory 1871–1918* (Chapel Hill, NC, 1997).

FAHRMEIR, ANDREAS K., 'Nineteenth-Century German Citizenship: A Reconsideration', *Historical Journal*, 40 (1997), pp. 721–52.

—— *Citizens and Aliens: Foreigners and the Law in Britain and the German States, 1789–1870* (London, 2000).

GIESEN, BERNHARD, *Intellectuals and the German Nation: Collective Identity in an Axial Age* (Cambridge, 1998).

GREEN, ABIGAIL, *Fatherlands: State-Building and Nationhood in Nineteenth-Century Germany* (Cambridge, 2001).

HAGEN, WILLIAM W., *Germans, Poles and Jews: The Nationality Conflict in the Prussian East, 1772–1914* (Chicago, 1980).

HEWITSON, MARK, *National Identity and Political Thought in Germany: Wilhelmine Depictions of the French Third Republic 1890–1914* (Oxford, 2000).

—— '*Nation* and *Nationalismus*: Representation and National Identity in Imperial Germany', in Mary Fulbrook and Martin Swales (eds.), *Representing the German Nation: History and Identity in Twentieth Century Germany* (Manchester, 2000), 19–62.

JAMES, HAROLD, *A German Identity 1770–1990*, rev. edn. (London, 1990).

LANGEWIESCHE, DIETER, *Liberalism in Germany*, trans. Christiane Banerji (Basingstoke, 2000).

LEVINGER, MATTHEW B., *Enlightened Nationalism: The Transformation of Prussian Political Culture, 1806–1848* (Oxford, 2000).

SMITH, HELMUT WALSER, *German Nationalism and Religious Conflict: Culture, Ideology, Politics, 1870–1914* (Princeton, 1995).

UMBACH, MAIKEN (ed.), *German Federalism: Past, Present, Future* (Houndmills, 2002).

VERHEY, JEFFERY, *The Spirit of 1914: Militarism, Myth and Mobilization in Germany,* (Cambridge, 2000).

VICK, BRIAN, *Defining Germany: The 1848 Frankfurt Parliamentarians and the National Question* (Harvard, 2002).

GREAT BRITAIN

ASCH, RONALD G. (ed.), *Three Nations—A Common History? England, Scotland, Ireland and British History, c.1600–1920* (Bochum, 1993).

BROCKLISS, L., and EASTWOOD, D. (eds.), *A Union of Multiple Identities: The British Isles, c.1750–c.1850* (Manchester, 1997).

CLAYDON, T., and MCBRIDE, I. (eds.), *Protestantism and National Identity: Britain and Ireland, c.1650–c.1850* (Cambridge, 1998).

COLLEY, LINDA, *Britons: Forging the Nation, 1707–1837* (New Haven, 1992).

COLLS, R., and DODD, P. (eds.), *Englishness: Politics and Culture 1880–1920* (Beckenham, 1986).

DAVIES, J., *The History of Wales* (London, 1993).

DAVIES, NORMAN, *The Isles: A History* (London, 1999).

DEVINE, T. M., *The Scottish Nation 1707–2000* (Harmondsworth, 1999).

EAGLES, R., *Francophilia in English Society 1748–1815* (Basingstoke, 2000).

GRANT, A. and STRINGER, K. (eds.), *Uniting the Kingdom? The Making of British History* (London, 1995).

HARVIE, C., *Scotland and Nationalism: Scottish Society and Politics 1707–1994* (London, 1994).

HEMPTON, D., *Religion and Political Culture in Britain and Ireland: From the Glorious Revolution to the Decline of Empire* (Cambridge, 1996).

KEARNEY, HUGH, *The British Isles: A History of Four Nations* (Cambridge, 1989).

KIDD, C., *Subverting Scotland's Past: Scottish Whig Historians and the Creation of an Anglo-British Identity, 1689–c.1830* (Cambridge, 1993).

LANGFORD, P., *Englishness Identified: Manners and Character 1650–1850* (Oxford, 2000).

LYNCH, M., *Scotland: A New History* (London, 1991).

MORTON, GRAEME, *Unionist Nationalism: Governing Urban Scotland, 1830–60* (East Linton, 2000).

NEWMAN, G., *The Rise of English Nationalism: A Cultural History, 1740–1830* (London, 1987).

PAZ, D. G., *Popular Anti-Catholicism in Mid-Victorian England* (Stanford, Calif., 1992).

THOMPSON, A. S., *Imperial Britain: The Empire in British Politics c.1880–1932* (Harlow, 2000).

WILLIAMS, C. (ed.), *A Companion to Nineteenth-Century Britain* (Oxford, 2004).

WOLFFE, J., *God and Greater Britain: Religion and National Life in Britain and Ireland 1843–1945* (London, 1994).

—— *The Protestant Crusade in Great Britain, 1829–60* (Oxford, 1991).

THE HABSBURG MONARCHY

BARANY, GEORGE, *Stephen Széchenyi and the Awakening of Hungarian Nationalism, 1791–1841* (Princeton, 1968).

CORNWALL, MARK, *The Undermining of Austria-Hungary: The Battle for Hearts and Minds* (Basingstoke, 2000).

DEÁK, ISTVÁN, *Beyond Nationalism: A Social and Political History of the Habsburg Officer Corps 1848–1918* (Oxford, 1992).

EÖTVÖS, JÓZSEF, *The Dominant Ideas of the Nineteenth Century and their Impact on the State*, 2 vols. (New York, 1996).

FREIFELD, ALICE, *Nationalism and the Crowd in Liberal Hungary, 1848–1914* (Washington, DC, 2000).

JÁSZI, OSCAR, *The Dissolution of the Habsburg Monarchy* (Chicago, 1929).

JELAVICH, CHARLES, *South Slav Nationalisms: Textbooks and Yugoslav Union before 1914* (Columbus, Oh., 1990).

JUDSON, PIETER, *Exclusive Revolutionaries: Liberal Politics, Social Experience and National Identity in the Austrian Empire, 1848–1914* (Ann Arbor, 1996).

KIEVAL, HILLEL, *Languages of Community: The Jewish Experience in the Czech Lands* (Berkeley, 2000).

KING, JEREMY, *Budweisers into Czechs and Germans: A Local History of Bohemian Politics, 1848–1948* (Princeton, 2002).

MARKOVITS, ANDREI, and SYSYN, FRANK (eds.), *Nationbuilding and the Politics of Nationalism: Essays on Austrian Galicia* (Cambridge, Mass., 1982).

OKEY, ROBIN, *The Habsburg Monarchy c.1765–1918* (Basingstoke, 2001).

PECH, STANLEY Z., *The Czech Revolution of 1848* (Chapel Hill, NC, 1969).

STEED, HENRY WICKHAM, *The Hapsburg Monarchy* (London, 1914).

SUGAR, PETER, and LEDERER, IVO J. (eds), *Nationalism in Eastern Europe* (Seattle, 1969).

WHITESIDE, ANDREW, *Austrian National Socialism before 1918* (The Hague, 1962).

ITALY

ASCOLI, ALBERT RUSSELL, and HENNEBERG, KRYSTYNA VON (eds.), *Making and Remaking Italy: The Cultivation of National Identity around the Risorgimento* (Oxford, 2001).

BEALES, DEREK, and EUGENIO F. BIAGINI, *The Risorgimento and the Unification of Italy* (London, 2002).

CLARK, MARTIN, *The Italian Risorgimento* (London, 1998).

—— *Modern Italy 1871–1982* (London, 1984).

DAVIS, JOHN A. (ed.), *Italy in the Nineteenth Century* (Oxford, 2000).

DICKIE, JOHN, *Darkest Italy: The Nation and Stereotypes of the Mezzogiorno, 1860–1900* (London, 1999).

DOUMANIS, NICHOLAS, *Italy: Inventing the Nation* (London, 2000).

DUGGAN, CHRISTOPHER, *Francesco Crispi 1818–1901: From Nation to Nationalism* (Oxford, 2002).

LEVY, CARL (ed.), *Italian Regionalism: History, Identity and Politics* (Oxford, 1996).

SCHNEIDER, JANE (ed.), *Italy's Southern Question: Orientalism in One Country* (Oxford, 1998).

SMITH, DENIS MACK, *The Making of Italy* (Basingstoke, 1988).

THE LOW COUNTRIES

DEPREZ, KAS, and VOS, LOUIS (eds.), *Nationalism in Belgium: Shifting Identities, 1780–1995* (London, 1998).

FISHMAN, J. S., *Diplomacy and Revolution: The London Conference of 1830 and the Belgian Revolt* (Amsterdam, 1988).

GALEMA, A., HENKES B., and TE VELDE, H. (eds.), *Images of the Nation: Different Meanings of Dutchness, 1870–1940* (Amsterdam, 1993).

HERMANS, T., VOS, L., and WILS, L. (eds.), *The Flemish Movement: A Documentary History, 1780–1990* (London, 1992).

KOSSMANN, E. H., *The Low Countries, 1780–1940* (Oxford, 1978).

KUITENBROUWER, MAARTEN, *The Netherlands and the Rise of Modern Imperialism: Colonies and Foreign Policy, 1870–1902* (New York, 1990).

LIJPARDT, AREND (ed.), *Conflict and Coexistence in Belgium, 1830–1980* (Berkeley, 1981).

MALLINSON, VERNON, *Power and Politics in Belgian Education 1815–1961* (London, 1963).

MOKYR, JOEL, *Industrialization in the Low Countries, 1795–1850* (New Haven, 1976).

SCHAMA, SIMON, *Patriots and Liberators: Revolution in the Netherlands, 1780–1813* (New York, 1977).

STRIKWERDA, CARL, *A House Divided: Catholics, Socialists, and Flemish Nationalists in Nineteenth-Century Belgium* (Lanham, Md., 1997).

VAN DAAL, J., and HEERTJE, A. (eds.), *Economic Thought in the Netherlands, 1650–1950* (Aldershot, 1992).

WINTLE, MICHAEL, *Pillars of Piety: Religion in the Netherlands in the Nineteenth Century* (Hull, 1987).

—— 'The Liberal State in the Netherlands: Historical Traditions of Tolerance, Permissiveness, and Liberalism', in S. Groenveld and Michael Wintle (eds.), *Britain and the Netherlands*, vol. xii (Zutphen, 1997).

WITTE, ELS, CRAEYBECKX, JAN, and MEYNEN, ALAIN, *Political History of Belgium from 1830 onwards* (Brussels, 2000).

THE OTTOMAN EMPIRE

ADANR, FIKRET, and FAROQHI, SURAYA (eds.), *The Ottomans and the Balkans: A Discussion of Historiography*, Ottoman Empire and Its Heritage (Leiden, 2002).

AL-QATTAN, NAJWA, 'Dhimmis in the Muslim Court: Legal Autonomy and Religious Discrimination', *International Journal of Middle East Studies*, 31 (Aug. 1999), 429–44.

BIBÓ, ISTVÁN, 'The Distress of East European Small States', in *Democracy, Revolution, Self-Determination, Selected Writings* (New York, 1991), 13–85.

BRAUDE, BENJAMIN, and LEWIS, BERNARD (eds.), *Christians and Jews in the Ottoman Empire: The Functioning of a Plural Society*, 2 vols. (New York, 1982).

BROWN, CARL L. (ed.), *Imperial Legacy: The Ottoman Imprint on the Balkans and the Middle East* (New York, 1996).

CRAMPTON, RICHARD J., *A Concise History of Bulgaria* (Cambridge, 2000).

DERINGIL, SELIM, 'Legitimacy Structure in the Ottoman State: The Reign of Abdulhamid II (1876–1909)', *International Journal of Middle East Studies*, 23 (Aug. 1991), 345–59.

—— 'Some Aspects of Muslim Immigration into the Ottoman Empire in the Late 19th Century', *Al-Abhath*, 38 (1990), 37–41.

—— *The Well-Protected Domains: Ideology and the Legitimization of Power in the Ottoman Empire, 1876–1909* (London, 1998).

DEVEREUX, ROBERT, *The First Ottoman Constitutional Period: A Study of the Midhat Constitution and Parliament* (Baltimore, 1963).

EMINOV, ALI, 'Turks and Tartars in Bulgaria and the Balkans', *Nationalities Papers*, 28 (2000), 129–64.

ERDEM, Y. HAKAN, *Slavery in the Ottoman Empire and its Demise, 1800–1909* (New York, 1996).

FAROQUI, SURAYA, *Approaching Ottoman History: An Introduction to Sources* (Cambridge, 1999).

GONDICAS, DIMITRI, and ISSAWI, CHARLES (eds.), *Ottoman Greeks in the Age of Nationalism: Politics, Economy, and Society in the Nineteenth Century* (Princeton, 1999).

HAYDEN, ROBERT M., 'Constitutional Nationalism in the Formerly Yugoslav Republics', *Slavic Review*, 51 (Winter 1992), 654–73.

HITCHINS, KEITH, *The Romanians, 1774–1866* (Oxford, 1996).

IORDACHI, CONSTANTIN, 'The Unyielding Boundaries of Citizenship: The Emancipation of "Non-Citizens" in Romania, 1866–1918', *European Review of History*, 8 (Aug. 2001), 157–86.

—— 'Citizenship, Nation- and State-Building: The Integration of Northern Dobrogea in Romania, 1878–1913'. Carl Back Papers in Russian and East European Studies, No. 1607, University of Pittsburgh, 2002.

—— 'From the "Right of the Natives" to "Constitutional Nationalism": The Making of the Romanian Citizenship, 1817–1919'. Ph.D. Dissertation, CEU Budapest, 2003.

KARPAT, KEMAL H., 'The Balkan National States and Nationalism: Image and Reality', *Islamic Studies*, 36 (1997), 329–59.

MCCARTHY, JUSTIN, *Death and Exile: The Ethnic Cleansing of Ottoman Muslims, 1821–1922* (Princeton, 1995).

MAXIM, MIHAI. 'The Romanian Principalities and the Ottoman Empire', in Dinu C. Giurescu and Stephen Fischer-Galaţi (eds.), *Romania: A Historic Perspective* (Boulder, Colo., 1998), 105–32.

MAZOWER, MARK, *The Balkans: A Short History* (New York, 2001).

MISHKOVA, DIANA, 'Modernization and Political Elites in the Balkans before the First World War', *East European Politics and Societies*, 9 (1995), 63–89.

NADOLSKI GLIDEWELL, DORA, 'Ottoman and Secular Civil Law', *International Journal of Middle East Studies*, 8 (1977), 517–43.

PANAITE, VIOREL, *The Ottoman Law of War and Peace: The Ottoman Empire and Tribute Payers* (Boulder, Colo., 2000).

PAVLOWITSCH, STEVAN K., *A History of the Balkans, 1804–1945* (London, 1999).

QUATAERT, DONALD, *The Ottoman Empire, 1700–1922* (New York, 2000).

ROTHSCHILD, JOSEPH, *East Central Europe between the Two World Wars* (Seattle, 1974).

SUGAR, PETER F. (ed.), *Eastern European Nationalism in the Twentieth Century* (Washington, DC, 1995).

—— and LEDERER, IVO J. (eds.), *Nationalism in Eastern Europe* (Seattle, 1969).

TODOROVA, MARIA, *Imagining the Balkans* (New York, 1997).

ZE'EVI, DROR, 'Kul and Getting Cooler: The Dissolution of Elite Collective Identity and the Formation of Official Nationalism in the Ottoman Empire', *Mediterranean Historical Review*, 11 (Dec. 1996), 177–95.

RUSSIA

HOSKING, GEOFFREY, *Russia: People and Empire, 1552–1917* (London, 1997).

—— and ROBERT SERVICE (eds.), *Russian Nationalism Past and Present* (London, 1998).

KNIGHT, NATHANIEL, 'Ethnicity, Nationality and the Masses: *Narodnost* and Modernity in Imperial Russia', in David Hoffmann and Yanii Kotsonis (eds.), *Russian Modernity* (Basingstoke, 2000), 41–64.

MILNER-GULLAND, ROBIN, *The Russians* (London, 1999).

ROGGER, HANS, 'Nationalism and the State: A Russian Dilemma', *Comparative Studies in Society and History*, 4 (1961–2), 253–64.

SUNY, RONALD G., 'Empire Strikes Out: Imperial Russia, "National Identity", and Theories of Empire', in Ronald Suny and Terry Martin (eds.), *A State of Nations: Empire and Nation-Making in the Age of Lenin and Stalin* (New York, 2001), 23–66.

SZPORLUK, ROMAN, *Communism and Nationalism: Karl Marx versus Friedrich List* (New York, 1988).

TOLZ, VERA, *Russia: Inventing the Nation* (London, 2001).

WEEKS, THEODORE R., 'Official and Popular Nationalisms: Imperial Russia 1863–1914', in Ulrike V. Hirschhausen and Jörn Leonhard (eds.), *Nationalismen in Europa: West- und Osteuropa im Vergleich* (Göttingen, 2001), 411–32.

SCANDINAVIA

BOLI, JOHN, *New Citizens for a New Society: The Institutional Origins of Mass Schooling in Sweden* (Oxford, 1989).

FELDBÆK, OLE, 'Denmark and the Treaty of Kiel 1814', *Scandinavian Journal of History* (1990).

HILSON, MARY, *Political Change and the Rise of Labour in Comparative Perspective: Britain and Sweden, c.1890–1920* (Lund, forthcoming).

KUHN, HANS, *Defining a Nation in Song: Danish Patriotic Songs in Songbooks of the Period 1832–1870* (Copenhagen, 1990).

KURLANDER, ERIC, 'The Rise of Völkisch Nationalism and the Decline of German Liberalism: A Comparison of Liberal Political Cultures in Schleswig-Holstein and Silesia 1912–1924', *European Review of History*, 9 (2002).

LINDGREN, R., *Norway-Sweden: Union, Disunion and Scandinavian Integration* (1959).

ØSTERGÅRD, UFFE, 'Denationalising National History', *Culture and History*, 9–10 (1991), 9–41.

TRÄGÅRDH, LARS, *The Concept of the People and the Construction of Popular Political Culture in Germany and Sweden, 1848–1933* (Ann Arbor, 1996).

SPAIN

ARCHILÉS, FERRAN, and MARTÍ, MANUEL, 'Ethnicity, Region and Nation: Valencian Identity and the Spanish Nation-State', *Ethnic and Racial Studies*, 24–5 (2002), 245–78.

BALCELLS, ALBERT, *Catalan Nationalism: Past and Present*, trans. Jacqueline Hall and Geoffrey J. Walker (Basingstoke, 1996).

BALFOUR, SEBASTIAN, *The End of the Spanish Empire, 1898–1923* (Oxford, 1997).

BOYD, CAROLYN P., *Historia Patria: Politics, History, and National Identity in Spain, 1875–1975* (Princeton, 1997).

CONVERSI, DANIELE, *The Basques, the Catalans, and Spain* (London, 1997).

DÍEZ MEDRANO, JUAN, *Divided Nations: Class, Politics, and Nationalism in the Basque Country and Catalonia* (Ithaca, NY, 1995).

DOUGLASS, WILLIAM A., 'Sabino's Sin: Racism and the Founding of Basque Nationalism', in Daniele Conversi (ed.), *Ethnonationalism in the Contemporary World: Walker Conner and the Study of Nationalism* (London, 2002), 95–113.

FUSI, JUAN PABLO, 'Centre and Periphery, 1900–1936: National Integration and Regional Nationalisms Reconsidered', in Francis Lannon and Paul Preston (eds.), *Elites and Power in Twentieth-Century Spain* (Oxford, 1990), 33–40.

JACOBSON, STEPHEN, ' "The Head and Heart of Spain": New Perspectives on Nationalism and Nationhood', *Social History*, 29/3 (2004), 393–407.

—— 'Law and Nationalism in Nineteenth-Century Europe: The Case of Catalonia in Comparative Perspective', *Law and History Review*, 20/2 (2002), 307–47.

LINZ, JUAN J. 'Early State Building and Late Peripheral Nationalism against the State: The Case of Spain', in Samuel N. Eisenstadt and Stein Rokkan (eds.), *Building States and Nations*, ii (Beverly Hills, Calif., 1973), 32–116.

MAR-MOLINERO, CLARE, and SMITH, ANGEL (eds.), *Nationalism and the Nation in the Iberian Peninsula: Competing and Conflicting Identities* (Oxford, 1996).

NÚÑEZ SEIXAS, XOSÉ MANOEL, 'The Region as the Essence of the Fatherland: Regional Variants of Spanish Nationalism (1840–1936)', *European History Quarterly*, 31/4 (2001), 483–518.

—— *Historiographical Approaches to Nationalism in Spain* (Frankfurt am Main, 1993).

PAYNE, STANLEY G., 'Catalan and Basque Nationalism', *Journal of Contemporary History*, 6 (1971), 19–27.

—— 'Nationalism, Regionalism, and Micronationalism in Spain', *Journal of Contemporary History*, 26 (1991), 179–91.

—— *Basque Nationalism* (Reno, 1975).

SAHLINS, PETER, 'The Nation in the Village: State-Building and Communal Struggles in the Catalan Borderland during the Eighteenth and Nineteenth Centuries', 60 (1988), 234–63.

SMITH, ANGEL, 'Spaniards, Catalans, and Basques: Labour and the Challenge of Nationalism in Spain', in Stefan Berger and Angel Smith (eds.), *Nationalism, Labour, and Ethnicity: 1870–1939* (Manchester, 1999).

—— and COX, EMMA DÁVILA (eds.), *The Crisis of 1898: Colonial Redistribution and Nationalist Mobilization* (London, 1999).

SWITZERLAND

JOST, HANS-ULRICH, 'Nation, Politics, and Art', in Swiss Institute for Art Research on behalf of the Coordinating Commission for the Presence of Switzerland abroad (ed.), *From Liotard to Corbusier: 200 Years of Swiss Painting* (Zurich, 1998).

KOHN, HANS, *Nationalism and Liberty: The Swiss Example* (London, 1956).

SIEGFRIED, ANDRÉ, *Switzerland* (London: Jonathan Cape, 1950).

STEINBERG, JONATHAN, *Why Switzerland?* (Cambridge, 1996).

ZIMMER, OLIVER, 'In Search of Natural Identity: Alpine Landscape and the Reconstruction of the Swiss Nation', *Comparative Studies in Society and History*, 40/4 (Oct. 1998), 637–65.

—— 'Competing Memories of the Nation: Liberal Historians and the Reconstruction of the Swiss Past', *Past and Present*, 168 (2000), 194–226.

—— *A Contested Nation: History, Memory and Nationalism in Switzerland 1761–1891* (Cambridge, 2003).

Index